. . . so long as the waters shall flow
and the sun shall shine . . .

Also by Wendell H. Oswalt:
Mission of Change in Alaska
Napaskiak: An Alaskan Eskimo Community
Alaskan Eskimos
Understanding Our Culture
Other Peoples, Other Customs
Habitat and Technology
An Anthropological Analysis of Food-Getting Technology
Eskimos and Explorers
Kolmakovskiy Redoubt
Life Cycles and Lifeways: An Introduction to Cultural Anthropology

THIS LAND WAS THEIRS

A Study of North American Indians

FOURTH EDITION

Wendell H. Oswalt
University of California, Los Angeles

Mayfield Publishing Company
Mountain View, California

In memory of
Edward H. Spicer

Copyright © 1988 by
Mayfield Publishing Company

Library of Congress Cataloging-in-Publication Data

Oswalt, Wendell H.
  This land was theirs.

  Includes bibliographies and indexes.
  1. Indians of North America.   I. Title.
E77.08   1988   973'.0497   87-12302
ISBN 0-87484-815-6

Manufactured in the United States of America

10 9 8 7 6 5 4

Mayfield Publishing Company
1240 Villa Street
Mountain View, California 94041

Sponsoring editor, Janet M. Beatty; manuscript editor, Lorraine Anderson; production
manager, Cathy Willkie; art director and designer, Cynthia Bassett; cover photograph,
David Muench. Typeset in Garamond Light by G & S Typesetters; printed and bound
by Maple-Vail.

Acknowledgments   Page 1: Trans. by Knud Rasmussen, *Intellectual Culture of the
Iglulik Eskimos.* Report of the Fifth Thule Expedition 1921–24, vol. 7, no. 1. Copen-
hagen: Gyldendalske Boghandel, 1929. Page 31: Trans. in Frances Densmore, *Nootka
and Quileute Music.* Bureau of American Ethnology Bulletin 124. Washington, 1939.
Page 331: Trans. by. H. R. Voth, p. 53, *Oraibi Natal Customs and Ceremonies.* Field
Columbian Museum, Anthropological Series, vol. 6, no. 2. Chicago, 1905.

Preface

Preparing a fourth edition of *This Land Was Theirs* has been a most satisfying experience. Thanks to the suggestions of students, reviewers, and colleagues, I've made numerous changes: I've reorganized the contents with special attention to the first chapters, weighed some ethnographic reports more judiciously, and deleted text that seemed extraneous or inappropriate. Most importantly, I've updated the information about particular tribes and government policies into the late 1980s. The end result, I hope, is a more useful introduction to North American Indians.

In the present edition the opening chapter answers the most commonly asked questions about Indians, including such matters as Indian identity, prehistory, linguistic divisions, cultural differences, treaties, and administration. Material that was previously found in the final chapter has been moved forward to the second chapter, which focuses attention on the Indian stereotype, urban populations, and current issues, among other subjects. This general information then introduces eleven chapters that offer discussions of particular "tribes." Each of these chapters begins with historical background information and an account of tribal life as reported by early Western observers. Subsequent historical developments are then examined for each people. As each chapter draws to a close, the text emphasizes what has happened to tribal groups in the past sixty years (except for the Natchez, who are extinct), showing that some of them have retained their cultural vitality to the present. The lists of readings and references at the end of each chapter should help students locate additional sources.

The reader will find that no particular theoretical orientation dominates; ecological, ethnohistorical, functional, and other perspectives are used as appropriate. The number of technical terms employed throughout the text is kept to a minimum, and each term is defined with care at its first use. Indian words are italicized and defined when introduced.

I selected the tribes discussed in these chapters to illustrate geographical and cultural adaptations. Probably no two anthropologists would choose to discuss the same tribes in a college course about American Indians. My choices were guided primarily by the availability of reasonably comparable information about peoples I considered representative geographically and culturally. (At the same time, my selection was also affected by my particular interests.)

In order of presentation, the Chipewyan, who live in the interior of northern Canada, represent subarctic hunters. The Kuskowagamiut of southwestern

Alaska are Eskimos whose lives centered on the exploitation of salmon. The Cahuilla, who inhabit an arid area of southern California, are gatherers of plant products, and a portion of the tribe is noteworthy because they are extremely wealthy. The Mesquakie (Fox) were selected because they are one of the few tribes of farmers and hunters in the eastern sector of the Midwest to survive into modern times; unlike most Indians, they purchased all the land they occupy. The Crow of the northern Plains typify foragers who adopted the horse in historic times and emerged as outstanding bison hunters and warriors. Fishers of the Northwest Coast are represented by the Yurok of northern California and the Tlingit of southeastern Alaska. Although the economies of both groups are based largely on salmon, their cultures are quite different. The Hopi of the American Southwest are arid area farmers who in many ways typify Pueblo Indian life. The Iroquois of the Northeast are farmers whose social organization represents an inordinate political complexity and whose history includes an especially important segment during the colonial era in America. The Cherokee of the Southeast are farmers who are reported because they are one of the few tribes in the area who have remained in their homeland and have retained a clear sense of Indian identity. Finally, the Natchez of Mississippi were farmers with one of the most complex ways of life reported among Indians north of Mexico and also were one of the many tribes to be eradicated by foreigners.

In writing about a particular people, I have attempted whenever possible to limit my descriptions to a specific segment of the tribe. The purpose of this technique is to present as nearly as possible an actual culture-carrying unit. For example, in the presentation of the aboriginal Chipewyan, I found it necessary to draw on information about varied segments of the population, and even then the descriptions sometimes were less than satisfactory. Because of more complete data about modern Chipewyan life, however, an adequate description of one community was possible.

Comments about the use of certain words may be appropriate at this point. When generalizations are made about American Indians, this designation is meant to encompass both Indians and Eskimos. The justification for this rests in the observation that the cultural and linguistic differences separating Indians from Eskimos are no greater than those separating many tribes of Indians. Additionally, the United States government has for many years considered Alaskan Eskimos and Indians as one for administrative purposes. The Canadian government, however, recognizes a distinction between Eskimos and Indians. With respect to particular terms of less significance but frequent occurrence, note that *maize* has been used more often than *corn* and *bison* rather than *buffalo;* these usages offer a modicum of exactness.

| Acknowledgments

The ethnohistorical approach of this text is my own, but it has undergone significant modifications since the first edition of *This Land Was Theirs* appeared in 1966. Many of these changes have been based on suggestions by UCLA students, and I am most grateful to them for their help. I likewise have profited from reviews by publishers' anonymous readers; their comments have proved valuable in correcting errors and expanding or condensing particular topics. I'd especially like to thank the reviewers of this edition: Beth Dillingham, University of Cincinnati; Sergei Kan, University of Michigan; William Powers, Rutgers University; Barbara A. Purdy, University of Florida; John Robert White, Youngstown State University; and A. M. Zaharlick, The Ohio State University. In my continued compilation of information about particular tribes, numerous individuals have helped me, and to them my debt is great. The tribes that I restudied for this edition and the specific persons who provided data are as follows:

Chipewyan: Ray Griffith, Larry Hastie, and Judith M. Jacob

Cahuilla: Lowell John Bean, Richard M. Milanovich, and Katherine Siva Saubel

Mesquakie: James Fenlon and Myrtle Keahna

Crow: Richard Real Bird, Janine P. Windy Boy, May Crawford, and Odeltah A. Thomsen

Yurok: Thomas Buckley and Kathy Heffner

Tlingit: Sergei Kan

Iroquois: Michael K. Foster, Annemarie Shimony, and Sally M. Weaver

When the present edition of *This Land Was Theirs* was being contemplated, Janet M. Beatty, a sponsoring editor at Mayfield Publishing Company, provided welcome and much-needed support. Subsequently, as the manuscript was being prepared for publication, her insight, tolerance, and engaging tact smoothed each potential problem before it developed; for this I am most appreciative. During processing of the manuscript at Mayfield, the copyediting of Lorraine Anderson enhanced the presentation in many ways. Once again and as usual, my wife, Helen Louise Taylor Oswalt, made a profound contribution to collecting data and editing the manuscript.

Wendell H. Oswalt

Contents

Chapter 4   The Kuskowagamiut: Riverine Eskimos 106

Chapter 5   The Cahuilla: Gatherers in the Desert 148

Chapter 6   The Mesquakie: Fighters and Farmers of the Woodland Fringe 180

Chapter 7   The Crow: Plains Warriors and Bison Hunters 217

Chapter 8   The Yurok: Salmon Fishermen of California 254

Chapter 9   The Tlingit: Salmon Fishermen of Alaska 290

Chapter 13 The Natchez: Sophisticated Farmers of the Deep South 434

1 Questions about Indians

I arise from rest with
movements swift
As the beat of a raven's wings
I arise
To meet the day
Wa—wa.
My face is turned from the
dark of night
To gaze at the dawn of day
Now whitening in the sky.

Iglulik Eskimo

WE BEGIN our anthropological study of American Indians by focusing on a number of general questions about them. How are we influenced by Indian cultures? Who is an Indian? How many Indians are there today? Where did Indians originate? What do we know of American prehistory north of Mexico? How have Indian cultures been studied? What do we know of Indian languages? How can we group Indian tribes? The answers to these questions will provide a foundation for a more detailed consideration of Indian-white relations and of representative tribes.

| How Are We Influenced by Indian Cultures?

Our thoughts about native North American influences on our lives are commonly of material goods borrowed from them, such as birch-bark canoes, moccasins, parkas, snowshoes, and toboggans. The shortness of this list reflects the vast differences between the life-styles of aboriginal and modern Americans. Our industrial technology is so foreign to Indian culture that they could not be expected to have contributed a great deal to it. Furthermore, we have lost any intimate association with the land, a quality that typified American Indian life. Nevertheless, we should neither minimize nor deny the place of Indians in our cultural heritage.

We tend to forget that we are most indebted to American Indians for our country itself, because this land was theirs. Yet, it is doubtful that the thoughts of most white Americans linger on Indians for very long. We take them for granted, which is a clear indication that they are an intimate part of our lives. We learn about their ways in grade school and something of their history in high school. We may visit Indian reservations and read novels about Indians. These are the ways in which Indians most often intrude on our thinking. Another dimension of their presence is worthy of at least a moment's reflection. Indians are our challenge because our responses to them represent a homegrown experiment in tolerance, understanding, and compassion.

In historical perspective, one enormously important borrowing by white Americans occurred along the eastern seaboard during colonial times. Precariously established early European settlers acquired the knowledge and technology associated with corn (maize) from local Indians. They were taught by Indians how to cultivate and store corn and how to prepare it as food. This Indian technology may not seem significant today, but at that time it was immensely important to European survival, and corn has emerged as one of the most important crops in the modern world.

If we were to cite the discoveries and inventions of Indians in all of the Americas, the earlier list would be much longer because American Indian cultures were most elaborate in Central and South America. To the list would be added beans, chili peppers, chocolate, cocaine, peanuts, potatoes, quinine, sweet potatoes, tobacco, and tomatoes, as well as a few material items such as hammocks, pipes, and the rubber syringe. Again the list is not long, but some of the plants and rubber products are of immense economic importance in the modern world. It may be asked whether from a global perspective North American Indian culture was not comparatively unelaborate, and the answer is yes. This was not from any lack of intelligence among Indians but rather from their environmental setting and its potential for development. The New World was devoid of animals that could be domesticated, such as cows, horses, and pigs, and neither were there grains such as barley and wheat. More important, in the New World the animals and plants with potential as domesticates were not concentrated in one restricted geographical area. A contrary situation existed in the Old World, where the basis for most of Old World civilization emerged in the Near East about 8000 B.C. New World developments, however, are not to be cast aside as failures. One must recognize that in aboriginal Mexico and Peru, complex societies emerged with large populations and elaborate life-styles; in these regions the environmental potential for indigenous cultural developments was far greater than in settings to the north.

American English words and phrases based on a background of Indian contacts persist. Examples such as *Indian summer, happy hunting ground, wild Indian, Indian giver,* and *burying the hatchet* are known widely. When place-names are added, the list becomes staggering; included are the names of not only lakes and rivers but also states and cities. Indian trails were important not only for their names but also as roadbeds for future highways.

Indians played an important role in shaping the belief system of one of the few large and important religions originating in the United States, the Church of Jesus Christ of Latter-day Saints, or Mormons. The Book of Mormon relates that Indians originated from a Jewish population that entered the New World before Christian times. According to Mormon beliefs, Indians descended from the Lamanites; although these were thought to be a degenerate people, the Mormons have been inordinately kind in their dealings with Indians. As noted by A. Irving Hallowell (1958, 461), the inclusion of population theory in a religious dogma "could hardly have occurred anywhere but in early 19th-century America."

In early American literature no subject had greater appeal than the Indians, but their literary image has been far from uniform. The Indian entered into American literature through speeches recorded during treaty deliberations. The oratorical skills of Indians were appreciated, and the texts were printed for general circulation in the eighteenth century. Because Indians were close at hand in the eastern states and were an obstruction when whites coveted more land, they soon were looked on as foes. As the frontier expanded westward in the first half of the nineteenth century, the image of the Indian reverted to that of a non-antagonist, in fact to a romantic figure. Drawing on accounts about Indians, James Fenimore Cooper wrote his great novels and conceived the character of Leatherstocking, a white Indian without literary equal. Henry Wadsworth Longfellow's *Hiawatha* too is a literary monument of this era. One of the most popular nineteenth-century American plays was *Metamora,* and playwrights have continued to build plots around Indians. Included in the first American opera, *Tammany,* performed in 1794, was a Cherokee melody, and the Indian exists in such American folk songs as Charles Cadman's "From the Land of Sky

Blue Waters" and "Red Wing" by Thurland Chattaway and Kerry Mills. Other Indian contributions to the arts are now a part of American history; these include the Wild West show, the Indian medicine show, the cigar store Indian, and the romantic Indian as a subject for painters.

Along the western frontier, Indians came to be regarded as they had been in the East by white Americans who sought land. According to these settlers, the Indian impeded progress and was a form of vermin to be exterminated. After Indians had been defeated in skirmishes and wars and remnant Indian populations were confined to reservations, these people again could be viewed romantically; even before the West was colonized, the Indian was a figure in nearly half of the 320 dime novels originating in the 1860s. The Indian theme never died but was recast with the introduction of motion pictures and radio. Needless to say, American television owes a great debt to the Indian, nor is the Indian forgotten in contemporary novels.

Who Is an Indian?

In the sixteenth century as ever-increasing numbers of European maritime explorers ventured to the Americas, there was no difficulty in establishing who was an Indian. The racial, linguistic, and cultural differences separating Europeans and Indians were apparent to all observers. Indians belonged to the Mongoloid racial stock in obvious contrast with the Caucasian racial background of the intruders. Indians spoke languages that differed widely from one tribe to another, but none could be understood by the explorers. Indians dressed in an unaccustomed manner, and their bodily adornments were unusual, if not bizarre, to a traveler from England, France, or Spain. Then, too, the main crops that Indians raised, maize and beans, were not cultivated in Europe. Thus, the people of the New World stood in striking contrast to Europeans and their ways.

The problem of classifying a person as an Indian became more complex with the arrival of European adventurers, fishermen, missionaries, settlers, traders, and trappers. Three conditions resulting from these contacts were important. First, white men mated with Indian women to produce persons of mixed blood; second, Indians sometimes captured whites and made them "Indians"; and third, some Indians lost their identity by assimilation into white society. To identify an Indian with clarity after the period of early historic contact we must deal primarily with racial and sociocultural factors. Socially, we can imagine that whites who were assimilated into an Indian tribe were considered Indians, in spite of their race. Likewise, Indians who disassociated themselves from other Indians came to be judged as whites. For individuals of mixed Indian and white ancestry, the distinctions were clear when they consistently followed one life-style or the other. Such persons could, however, behave as Indian in one context and white in another, Indian or white exclusively throughout their lives, or Indian at one time in life and white at another. The identification of an Indian has become a matter of definition and is most reasonably considered in a legal sense.

Before considering Indian identity further, one point requires clarification. Euro-Americans classify Aleuts and Eskimos as separate from Indians because of their dissimilar physical appearance and cultures. In racial terms, Aleuts and Eskimos are the most Mongoloid of indigenous New World peoples, and their economic adjustments stand apart from those of other aboriginal Americans. However, the cultural differences separating some Indian tribes from each other are greater than those that separate Aleuts and Eskimos from many Indians. Thus, Aleuts, Eskimos, and Indians all may reasonably be called Indians.

In the history of United States Indian law, a uniform definition of an Indian has not existed. In general, however, if a person is considered an Indian by other individuals in the community, he or she is legally an Indian. The degree of Indian blood in an individual may be important, but under most circumstances this is secondary to sociocultural standing in the community in which he or she lives. Examples will illustrate why there is so much confusion. If an individual is on the roll of a federally recognized Indian group, then he or she is an Indian; the degree of Indian blood is of no real consequence, although usually he or she has at least some Indian blood. *Federal Indian Law* (U.S. Department of the Interior 1958) states that a person may, on some reservations, be considered an Indian even if records show that fifteen of sixteen immediate ancestors were not Indian. However, the real need for defining an Indian is with reference to a specific piece of legislation at a particular time. A person who is on the roll of a tribe and lives on a reservation clearly is an Indian; if that person moves from a reservation but remains on the roll, he or she continues to be an Indian. If he or she receives a clear title to allotted reservation land, he or she may or may not subsequently remain an Indian, depending on the circumstances. Indian status also is lost by voluntary disassociation from other Indians and by identifying with some other social segment of society.

In the United States, all Indians did not become citizens until 1924, when the Citizenship Act was passed by Congress. Previously, about 250,000 Indians had become citizens by other means; the act made citizens of about 125,000 more persons. As early as 1817 individuals were granted citizenship under treaty arrangements if they met certain provisions, such as the acceptance of title to individual lands in contrast to living on tribal lands. For many years the prevailing opinion of the federal government was that Indians who followed tribal customs and were not under the control of the state or territory in which they lived could not be citizens. Becoming a citizen was given a different basis with the passage of the Dawes Act in 1887. This act was designed to break up reservation lands into individual and family holdings. After a man received a clear title to land, he became a citizen, or if he adopted civilized ways and lived apart from any tribe, he also became a citizen. Because he was an Indian he might still retain a special status and receive treaty or other benefits. Thus, he was a citizen with special privileges not granted to other citizens. In 1888 a law was passed making Indian women citizens if they married citizens, the assumption being that these women were following the path of civilization. As noncitizens, Indians were not inducted into the armed services during World War I. However, those who volunteered were made citizens by congressional action. By 1938 seven states still refused to allow Indians to vote, and only in 1948 were voting rights granted to Indians in Arizona and New Mexico. Opposition to Indian suffrage was based on their special relationship to the federal government.

One provision in the Canadian Indian Act of 1876 was that any Indian who had a university education or its equivalent thereby became a citizen. In other instances an individual, or the band by majority vote, initiated enfranchisement proceedings; this method required a probationary period before becoming effective. When a man with a wife and minor unmarried children became enfranchised, his family was granted the same legal status. These provisions were not generally applied to the Indians of British Columbia, Manitoba, or the Northwest Territories. For the next fifty years Canadian Indian policy fluctuated between voluntary and forced enfranchisement. Finally, as a result of the Indian Act of 1951, Canadian Indians became subject to the same general laws that applied to other Canadians. They could vote in national elections and could consume intoxicants legally for the first time.

How Many Indians Exist Today?

In 1980 the United States government recognized 291 tribes in the contiguous states, and 197 native Alaskan populations and villages. The American Indian population for 1980, comprised of Indians, Eskimos, and Aleuts, was largely urban—53 percent—and the overall reported population had increased 72 percent since 1970, to reach a total of 1,366,676. (The difference between the 1970 and 1980 totals is attributable largely to more accurate data collection in 1980 rather than to any dramatic increase in actual population.) This population represented about .6 percent of the total population of the United States. At that time, 24 percent of the Indians lived on reservations, 8 percent in historically occupied areas of Oklahoma, 3 percent in native Alaskan villages, and 2 percent on tribal trust lands. The remaining 63 percent lived elsewhere. The six states with the greatest number of Indians were as follows: California, 198,155; Oklahoma, 169,292; Arizona, 152,498; New Mexico, 105,976; North Carolina, 64,536; and Alaska, 64,047. The six most populous Indian reservations were those occupied by the Navajo in Arizona, New Mexico, and Utah, 104,978; Siouans at Pine Ridge, South Dakota, 11,947; Pima at Gila River, Arizona, 7,067; Papago in Arizona, 6,959; Apache at Fort Apache in Arizona, 6,880; and Hopi in Arizona, 6,591 (U.S. Bureau of the Census 1984).

In 1981 the total Indian population of Canada (excluding Eskimos) was 491,460; 25,390 Eskimos (Inuit) also lived in Canada at that time. The provinces with the greatest numbers of Indians were as follows: Ontario, 110,060; British Columbia, 82,645; Alberta, 72,050; and Manitoba, with 66,280 Indians. Eskimos were concentrated largely in the Northwest Territories (15,910) and in arctic Quebec (4,875). Those Indians who spoke a native language as their mother tongue were predominantly Algonkian speakers (102,905); of this cluster, Cree (67,495) and Ojibwa or Chippewa (19,770) formed the largest groups. Of the total Eskimo population, 18,840 persons spoke the Inuit language as their mother tongue.

About 40,000 Eskimos lived in Greenland in 1980, virtually all of whom spoke Inuit. Only about 20 percent of these people lived in nonurban areas during that year.

| Where Did Indians Originate?

Attempts to determine the region of the world from which American Indians originated are intriguing and have had lasting romantic appeal. Humanists, lay people, and scientists alike have long puzzled over the original home of Indians in the Americas. Surprisingly, each of the major theories advanced to explain the derivation and spread of Indians involves something that is lost to modern times. The Lost Tribes of Israel, the lost continents of Atlantis and Lemuria (Mu), and the sunken land bridge across the Bering Sea—each stands as a candidate for consideration. They share the common characteristic that supporting data must be indirect because fully conclusive evidence remains elusive.

Speculation about Atlantis predates the discovery of the Americas. Once aboriginal Americans were known to Europeans, the idea that Atlantis had been a stepping-stone for early migrants from the Old to the New World seemed logical. Plato reported that Atlantis was a vast island beyond Gibraltar and that it had had a complex civilization before it was destroyed by a cataclysm. The idea lingered among the Romans and was accepted by some persons in medieval Europe, but before the Atlantic Ocean was explored, no one could be certain whether or not the island existed. Christopher Columbus appears to have sailed toward its presumed position, and some thought that the land he discovered was Atlantis. The thesis that native Americans were derived from Atlantis crystallized in sixteenth-century Spain and first emerged with clarity in the writings of Francisco Lopez de Gomara that appeared in 1552. He proposed, for example, that *atl,* which was the word for water among Indians in one sector of Mexico, was a lingering remembrance of their homeland called Atlantis. By the 1880s the island's disappearance still was being attributed to a major cataclysm that had occurred after the people destined to become American Indians had left its shores, and the theory was being advocated by some more staunchly than ever. Each author who supported the theory of this lost island was struck by the cultural similarities between American Indians, usually those in Mexico, and some early Old World civilization, usually Egyptian.

A second lost continent theory involves the postulated prehistoric presence of a great Pacific island called Lemuria or Mu. This thesis has found considerable support among some lay people. Its proponent was James Churchward, and his last book on the subject appeared in 1931. He reportedly traveled in India and met a priest who saw him attempting to decipher some old inscriptions. The priest befriended Churchward and spent two years teaching him what was said to be the original language of people. Later Churchward was shown some secret inscribed tablets that recorded the original creation story, with

Lemuria detailed as the place of human origins. The mystical nature of this theme, the failure of anyone else to be aware of this original language, and Churchward's inability to produce the original or similar inscriptions seriously weaken the entire argument.

Rivaling these lost continent theories is another that contends that Indians are descendants of the Lost Tribes of Israel. Samuel F. Haven (1856) long ago summarized the evidence. Ten tribes of Israelites, defeated by the Assyrians, were removed to the northeastern sector of the Assyrian empire. Here they became lost by wandering into Asia, and they ventured on to a point nearest the Americas, where they crossed the waters to another land. This was the New World, and evidence to support the Hebrew ancestry of the Indians was to be found in certain of their customs, words, and idioms. The theory long has been popular and continues to find particularly active support among members of the Church of Jesus Christ of Latter-day Saints.

A host of other conjectures have been advanced to explain the origins of American Indians. Some speculators have singled out seafaring peoples such as the Carthaginians or Phoenicians as responsible for the original occupation. Others have felt that the Tartars, sometimes viewed as remnants of the Lost Tribes of Israel, were the earliest occupants of the Americas; they were relatively near the New World in geographical terms and were a far-ranging people. The Chinese, Ethiopians, Scandinavians, Polynesians, and Welsh similarly have attracted speculative attention. Cotton Mather in colonial America advanced one of the most unique explanations for Indian origins. He wrote that "probably the *Devil* decoyed those miserable salvages hither, in hopes that the gospel of the Lord Jesus Christ would never come here to destroy or disturb his absolute empire over them" (Drake 1837, 9).

In 1570 the Jesuit missionary Father Joseph de Acosta went to Peru, and about 1580 he began to write his *Historia natural y moral de las Indias*. The book appeared in its first Spanish edition in 1590, three years after he returned to Spain. Acosta reasoned that since Adam was the original ancestor of humanity and since Indians were people, then they must have come from the Old World, which Adam's descendants had peopled. He rejected the ideas of Atlantis or Hebrew origins for Indians, and he did not think there could have been a second ark or that angels accounted for aboriginal New World peoples. He reasoned that the New World and the Old World had been connected, or separated by a narrow strait, because certain land mammals were the same in the respective hemispheres. He felt that people and animals alike had traveled along the same route. The human entry was visualized as having taken place slowly and as having been caused by overpopulation, famines, or the loss of former living areas. Thus, Acosta was the first to advance a land bridge theory and to offer an explanation of why peoples entered the New World. He also theorized that the original occupants were hunters who later developed a more complex way of life. Therefore, any comparisons between New and Old World civilizations could not be very meaningful.

Modern anthropologists support the general thesis of Indian origins first advanced by Acosta. People did not evolve in the New World but migrated to it.

The animals most closely related to humans all are found in the Old World, and no remains that represent early stages of human development have been reported in the Americas. In the Old World, and especially in Africa, bones that are clear markers along humankind's evolutionary trail have been found repeatedly. In the same context, the earliest human remains in the New World date from about 14,000 B.C. and belonged to individuals who were essentially modern in physical appearance. From the fossil record we must conclude that people entered the Western Hemisphere in the relatively recent past.

Geological evidence indicates that former continents did not exist in either the Atlantic or Pacific oceans. Thus, there could not have been continents of Atlantis and Mu to serve as stepping-stones to the New World. Neither does it seem likely that the first people entered the Western Hemisphere by traveling from one known island to another, across either the Atlantic or Pacific oceans. If this were the case we would expect to find their archaeological remains on at least one of the possible islands involved. However, no sites ever have been reported in Iceland, Greenland, the Aleutian Islands, or the islands of Polynesia that would suggest they served as way stations for the first entrants to the New World. Furthermore, at the time people presumably first entered the Americas, they did not possess boats capable of crossing sizable bodies of open water.

In all likelihood the first people to arrive in the New World entered over a land bridge in the Bering Strait area. They probably lingered in Alaska for a considerable length of time and eventually followed western mountains southward into Canada, ventured on into the western United States and Mexico, and finally continued southward into South America. The economic lives of the earliest migrants must have been based on hunting methods adapted to subarctic conditions. The Bering Strait entryway appears to have served as a cultural filter through which only hunters could pass. Their way of life must have been unelaborate, and most of the later complexities in their cultures must have developed in the Americas. In much later times, but long before the arrival of Columbus, new groups of people from the Old World continued to enter the Americas along the Bering Strait route and possibly via a number of other passages.

What Later Influences Came across the Seas?

Although the ancestors of most historic Indians arrived in the New World via the Bering Strait area, in the popular literature about Indians speculations about all-water migration routes have persisted. The idea of pre-Columbian voyages to the New World has almost boundless popular appeal. To think of people setting sail in small boats, headed they knew not where, is spine-tingling. The romance of the idea has led commentators to visualize a wide variety of voyages originating from diverse sectors of the Old World. Even after setting imagination aside, the realities of what may have been are in themselves most inviting.

The only pre-Columbian voyages beyond reasonable dispute must be cited first, and these involved Viking, or more properly Norse, explorers. Iceland was settled in the ninth century by Scandinavians, and within a hundred years Greenland had been discovered. After becoming involved in a series of homicides, Eric the Red was exiled from Iceland for three years. He spent the time, A.D. 982–985, exploring southwestern Greenland, and on his return he organized a colonizing expedition. It left for southwestern Greenland in 986, and additional settlers arrived later. The Greenland colony was occupied by the Norse until about 1540 and had a maximum population of about five thousand persons. Given the turbulent weather in the northern Atlantic Ocean, many ships heading toward Greenland were lost or blown off course. One vessel strayed to the coast of North America but did not land. About the year 1000, the son of Eric the Red, Leif Ericson, purposely sailed for continental North America. In the centuries to follow, a number of planned trips were made to northeastern North America from Greenland, especially to obtain building timber. The Norse appear to have settled briefly in northern Newfoundland at L'Anse aux Meadows, which was discovered and partially excavated by Helge Ingstad. Radiocarbon dates indicate that the site was occupied about A.D. 1000. The presence of a few Norse artifacts and wrought iron at the site leaves little doubt that these were Norse remains. However, no evidence exists to suggest that these Europeans had any influence on the cultures of aboriginal Americans.

If voyagers from the Old World, apart from the Norse, did arrive in the New World during pre-Columbian times, we might expect to find artifacts that they brought with them. Conversely, if travelers ventured in the opposite direction, we would expect to recover objects in the Eastern Hemisphere that were made in the Americas. In spite of the thousands of excavations in which millions of artifacts have been recovered, not one such artifact has been found in clearly valid context. Admittedly, these objects may exist in unexplored sites, and if any are found, our thinking will need to be revised or even reversed. The fact remains that currently there is no reason to think, on the basis of the specific artifact forms discovered, that any pre-Columbian voyagers other than the Norse reached the New World.

If there were substantial Old and New World contacts, we would expect to find evidence in linguistic ties. Relationships between languages cannot be postulated based on a small number of words with the same form and meaning, because such parallels may be accounted for by chance alone. To demonstrate historical connections between languages, clear phonemic and grammatical similarities as well as numerous parallels among words must exist. Is there any evidence of this nature to link pre-Columbian peoples of the two hemispheres? The answer is yes, but it occurs only in the Bering Strait area. The Eskimo-Aleut language family, which spans the American Arctic, and the Chukchi-Kamchatkan family of northeastern Siberia are related closely and belong to the American Arctic-Paleosiberian linguistic phylum. Thus, the New and Old Worlds are joined in linguistic terms but not as speculators might assume.

Expecting to find Old World artifacts in prehistoric New World sites may be unreasonable, if only because few objects probably survived long ocean voyages. Similarly, the speakers of Old World languages could have arrived, but their languages might have passed out of existence when the original migrants died. This raises the question of whether there were *influences* from the Old

World reaching the Americas. As we consider the question we must first make one critical observation. Innumerable examples exist of people in one part of the world inventing artifacts similar to those independently conceived and produced by a distant people. Thus, we must be cautious in deducing that a form had a single place of origin and spread from there. Furthermore, evidence that coherent *groups* of Old and New World artifacts are similar is of greater potential significance than are similarities between isolated artifact types or design motifs.

A persistent but cautious advocate of transpacific contacts has been Gordon F. Ekholm (1964). He has suggested that wheeled toys from Mexico and Asia might have had common origins, and has wondered also whether pottery making in the Americas is not from an Old World source. The iron pyrite mirrors of Mesoamerica and the copper axes used as currency in Mexico during the Aztec period suggest the bronze mirrors and ax money in China. The Olmec people of Mesoamerica exhibited the earliest complex culture in this region, and in its first known stages it was already quite sophisticated but without any local basis. The great Olmec stress on the tiger motif in art recalls a similar stress in the early Bronze Age Shang dynasty of China in the latter part of the second millennium B.C. The cylindrical, tripod pottery vessels found in parts of Mexico and dating from around the time of Christ recall similar shapes in pottery and bronze from the Han period in China. Furthermore, in certain Maya sites of the Late Classic and Postclassic periods are some forms suggestive of Hindu-Buddhist developments in India and Southeast Asia; included are lotus panels, phallic sculptures, tiger thrones, and the "tree of life" motif.

Perhaps of greater importance is the occurrence of certain Asian-like artifact types in sites along the coast of Ecuador, dating from about 200 B.C. As Emilio Estrada and Betty J. Meggers (1961) have noted, this cluster is largely restricted to Ecuador. Included are pottery models of houses with saddle-shaped roofs and columns, figurines with one leg folded above the other, and the coolie yoke. They suggest that a seagoing vessel from Asia arrived and the migrants successfully introduced these and other novelties.

The evidence for pre-Columbian Old–New World culture contacts based on linguistics and artifacts is conclusive only with reference to language ties across the Bering Strait and Norse artifacts in northeastern North America. Hints and suggestions that bonds reached tenuously across the Pacific Ocean exist but are not as yet convincing. Another approach to the problem centers on evidence of a different nature: domestic plants and animals transported by pre-Columbian peoples to the New World. In a symposium organized by Carroll L. Riley, he and his associates considered cultigens. I can do no better than to quote their summary remarks (Riley et al. 1971, 452–53). "The consensus of botanical evidence given in this symposium seems to be that *there is no hard and fast evidence for any pre-Columbian human introduction of any single plant or animal* across the ocean from the Old World to the New World, or vice-versa. This is emphatically *not* to say that it could not have occurred." Thus, the case rests on a largely negative note.

| What Do We Know of American Prehistory North of Mexico?

As we have noted, evidence indicates that the first and most of the subsequent prehistoric human migrants to the New World arrived from the Old World via the Bering Strait region. They gradually filtered south, and by the time Columbus discovered America, Indians had occupied all inhabitable areas. Furthermore, by early historic times vast differences separated the lifeways of Indian groups, depending on their particular settings, contacts with other Indians, and economies. The following overview of prehistory in Canada and the United States is presented as background to the historic life-styles of peoples described in this book.

THE PALEO-INDIANS   A great deal of controversy surrounds the question of when the original migrants first entered the New World from eastern Asia. Intermittently, it has been asserted that the first people arrived twenty thousand years ago or in the more distant past. Yet, in each instance, a careful examination of the evidence has proved these claims false or at least questionable. The weight of current evidence suggests that the earliest immigrants first entered northwestern North America about 14,000 B.C.

In the vicinity of the modern Bering Strait a land bridge existed between about 23,000 and 12,000 B.C. During this cold period, glacial ice covered large areas of the Northern Hemisphere, and worldwide sea levels were lowered by as much as 100 feet. In the sector where eastern Siberia and western Alaska currently exist, there were no major glaciers because conditions were unfavorable for their formation: the amount of annual precipitation was low and the land was relatively flat. When the land bridge called Beringia connected the continents, it served as a pathway for peoples as well as a cultural filter, as mentioned earlier. Only those peoples accustomed to hunting caribou (wild reindeer) and depending secondarily on fish were able to migrate through the region, with its subarctic conditions.

The date of about 14,000 B.C. for human entry is based on the possible amount of time required for people to populate the Americas; sites of this age have not yet been located. The earliest irrefutable evidence of people in North America dates from shortly before the close of the last geological epoch, the Pleistocene, which ended about 8000 B.C. and ushered in the modern geological period, the Holocene. By about 13,000 B.C. the High Plains east of the Rocky Mountains in the United States were populated by vast herds of bison, camels, horses, and mammoth, all potential prey for hunters when they arrived.

A critical year in the discovery of evidence of prehistoric humans in the Americas was 1926. It was then that J. D. Figgins, a paleontologist excavating in northern New Mexico, uncovered the bones of a now-extinct long-horned bison that was much larger than modern species. In dirt from the excavation Figgins found two pieces of a flint projectile point; another point fragment was recovered embedded in clay near the rib of an animal. The next year, after four flint points were found near bison bones, a fifth was observed actually embedded *in* a bone. Work then was stopped, and leading anthropological institutions were asked to send representatives to the site. Those who responded affirmed the validity of the association of fossil bison bones and human artifacts; this evidence never has been challenged seriously. The projectile points were named Folsom after the discovery site, and the bison came to be known as *Bison antiquus figginsi.* The Folsom remains date from about 9000 to 7000 B.C. Artifactual remains were found subsequently in clearly valid association with mammoth bones, again in the western United States. The projectile points usually associated with these sites are called Clovis, and they date from about 13,000 B.C.

The ancestors of the Clovis and Folsom people apparently arrived in the West after leaving Alaska and following an ice-free corridor down through northwestern Canada. The same route presumably was taken by those populations associated with other early forms of projectile points, such as those labeled Eden. All of these people are best known as hunters of extinct herd animals, and most of their sites are in grassy plains sectors of the central and western states. These Paleo-Indians, as they often are called, no doubt lived in small family groups (bands) and probably used some vegetable foods, small game, or fish, depending on the region and their particular background. Their artifacts have been found most often at kill sites and less frequently at camps or more permanent settlements at varied locations in the United States. As the last glacial period drew to a close, the herd animals on which these hunters were so dependent became extinct. Some researchers attribute their extinction to overhunting by Paleo-Indians, but the theory more widely accepted is that they disappeared as a result of climatic changes, especially in the West as it became more arid. Actually, both factors may have been involved. Although the cause of their disappearance has not been resolved fully, the Paleo-Indians' way of life clearly was ending by about 7000 B.C.

THE ARCHAIC TRADITION   As the West and the Southwest became drier, the herds of large animals declined in size, and hunting them decreased in importance. By about 7000 B.C. a way of life adapted to the western deserts already had developed its distinctive character. This new development is sometimes termed the Desert culture. The primary foods used in desert areas were wild plant products and small game such as rabbits and squirrels. Small bands of people occupied open sites or camped in caves and rock shelters on an opportunistic basis as they moved about to exploit varied food resources at different times of the year. Grinding stones became key technological forms as they were used to process seeds, nuts, and other plant products and render them edible. Small animals were stunned with missile sticks or captured in fencelike nets, while spears were used against large game, such as antelope and bison. Basketry became increasingly important for winnowing wild seeds, cooking foods, and storing water. This eminently successful lifeway, termed the Archaic tradition, persisted widely in the West until after the arrival of Spanish and Anglo-American explorers and settlers. The Cahuilla Indians (Chapter 5) represent one form of this life-style as it continued into historic times. In the northwestern Plains the

Archaic tradition also persisted into historic times, but in this area the foragers changed dramatically about 1730, when domestic horses were introduced to them from the south; one such people who came to depend heavily on horses was the Crow (Chapter 7).

Along the Northwest Coast of North America from the Gulf of Alaska to northern California, prehistoric maritime cultures emerged, probably from an Archaic base. Fish and shellfish especially were prominent in these economies, and by at least 1000 B.C. sea mammals were hunted and salmon fished with expanding intensity. Woodworking tools were well established by about 200 B.C., suggesting the manufacture of plank houses and large dugout canoes. These developments provided the general background for the emergence of historic Northwest Coast Indian cultures such as the Yurok (Chapter 8) and Tlingit (Chapter 9).

In the woodlands, along rivers, and in coastal areas of the eastern United States and Canada, Indians lived as hunters and gatherers from about 7000 to 2000 B.C. While these Archaic economies varied widely because local resources differed, most of them depended heavily on wild plant products that they collected. In some areas, however, shellfish, fish, or large game, in varied combinations, dominated as food. The oldest sites usually had relatively brief spans of occupation, but by about 3000 B.C. some sites, especially those along major rivers where food resources were abundant, were being occupied for generations. These people are noted especially for their ground stone woodworking tools such as adzes, axes, and gouges. They also traded widely for raw materials, especially for copper from the Lake Superior region that was processed in the manner of ground stone. The material culture of these people was more developed than that reported among Paleo-Indians, but none of them survived into historic times.

THE NORTHERN HUNTERS   The pioneer migrants into the New World were all hunters, but after expanding into their new environment, those who filtered south eventually developed farming economies, whereas those remaining in the north continued to be hunters. The earliest evidence for northern hunters is associated with inland areas and dates from as long ago as about 9000 B.C. In general, the finds recall Archaic tradition artifact types. The stone tools are similar also to older finds in Siberia and thus demonstrate archaeologically a link between the Old and New Worlds. It is now thought that the Na-Dene Indians, the northern hunters who were ancestors to modern Athapaskan Indians, lived in interior Alaska and northwestern Canada by about 5000 B.C. These distinctly inland people hunted caribou or moose, depending on the locality, and fished; for most of them, their fishing activities increased during times of food stress. The Chipewyan Indians (Chapter 3) are a historic example of Athapaskan Indians who were caribou hunters and fishermen.

The oldest finds associated with coastal hunters are from the Bering Strait region and are identified with the Arctic Small Tool tradition. The sites date from as early as about 3000 B.C. and are associated with the emergence of Eskimo culture. The bearers of this coastal tradition spread into southwestern Alaska and eastward into Greenland. These people primarily were sea mammal hunters, but they harvested caribou on an opportunistic basis or fished for salmon when this was possible. As Eskimo culture developed, the large, open skin boat (umiak) and small, one-person skin boat (kayak) became important aids to hunting; another artifact form that became increasingly dominant and elaborate was the toggle-headed harpoon. Eventually, most Eskimos burned the oil from sea mammals in lamps, which freed them from a dependence on wood for fuel. Their winter mobility increased vastly with the introduction of dog team travel in comparatively recent prehistoric times. The impermanent tents of early Eskimos were replaced by semisubterranean houses built of turf and stone or driftwood, depending on the area. Eskimos are well known for their highly varied adaptations to differing arctic and subarctic conditions. The Kuskowagamiut (Chapter 4) represent one of their major ecological adaptations.

THE FARMERS   In many areas that Indians had moved into, the most radical prehistoric economic change occurred when hunting and gathering was replaced by a primary dependence on domestic plant products. Maize was domesticated in Mexico by about 5000 B.C., and the common bean was domesticated at about the same time in Peru, where squash may have prevailed as a cultigen somewhat earlier. By about 2000 B.C. the cultivation of maize had spread from the south into the American Southwest, and a thousand years later beans and squash also were planted there. These were the primary New World crops raised north of Mexico, and they eventually were planted in most areas where cultural circumstances and ecological conditions favored their growth. Some western Indians not only cultivated maize but developed more productive hybrid strains that enabled them to become increasingly sedentary. This led in the Southwest to the Hohokan cultural tradition that arose in the deserts of Arizona and the Mogollon tradition best associated with highland areas of New Mexico. The Anasazi tradition, which represents the ancestors of modern Pueblo Indians such as the Hopi (Chapter 10), arose primarily from various groups of gatherers identified with the Basketmaker culture. The Pueblo Indian cultures that emerged between A.D. 700 and 1400 are most often associated with pueblo-type dwellings, separate ceremonial chambers or kivas, and elaborate painted pottery.

From an Archaic base some hunters and gatherers in the eastern United States seem to have become farmers as they domesticated the sunflower for its seeds and cultivated other local plants before being introduced to maize, beans, and squash from Mexico. In the Midwest, pottery and burial mounds became prevalent by about 1000 B.C., and the Woodland cultural tradition began to coalesce. The first notable mound builders were the Adena people, who occupied the Ohio River drainage and surrounding areas. At first they lived in small, scattered settlements and probably cultivated plants for food. Flourishing from about 1000 to 300 B.C., the Adena Indians are best known for their elaborate mound burials, long distance trade in raw materials, and skill as crafts-persons. These Indians were better organized than their predecessors. They probably had unilateral descent groups (clans), powerful authority figures such as chiefs, and clear distinctions between high- and low-born persons.

Overlapping in time with the Adena Indians and in the same general area were Indians identified with the Hopewell tradition that emerged about 400 B.C. and prevailed until about A.D. 1100. Hunting and gathering were important in their economy, but they probably also raised maize and other crops. The Hopewell people lived in large, relatively permanent settlements and are noted for their extensive earthworks. Like the Adena people, they paid a great deal of attention to the dead, and they often buried elaborate grave goods with bodies. The Hopewellians had clearly distinguished social classes and probably were organized into clans. They too carried on an extensive trade in raw materials that were used to produce luxury goods. As with the Adena Indians, the fate of the Hopewell primary centers is something of a mystery; their disappearance was rather sudden. One possibility is that after an extended period of dramatic population growth, the environment could not support the number of people and the social structure too became overloaded. Hopewell Indians did survive, however, in other regions. Some had pushed into the Great Lakes area where their descendants made numerous adjustments to the local environment; one of the new groups emerged as the Fox or Mesquakie Indians of historic times (Chapter 6). Other branches of Hopewell culture persisted in New York state, and one group eventually gave rise to the Iroquois Indians (Chapter 11).

Prehistoric Indian culture in the United States climaxed in the Mississippian tradition concentrated in the Mississippi River valley from about A.D. 600 to 1500. With its origin in Mexico, this tradition was based on the cultivation of maize, beans, and squash. The Mississippians were organized into states, each with a clear sense of national identity. Rigid social classes prevailed, with priests and nobles topping the hierarchy. Their ceremonial centers must have required years to plan and construct, with the labor of many people required to build their elaborate terraced temple mounds as well as the house mounds of the elite. Their religious life, with its emphasis on a well-developed calendrical system, sun worship, and a death cult, clearly had its origins in Mexico. In this book the Natchez Indians (Chapter 13) represent a remnant population within the Mississippian tradition. This tradition spread widely in the Southeast, and a more peripheral manifestation led to the emergence of the Cherokee (Chapter 12).

SUMMARY   This brief review of the prehistory of North America north of Mexico should demonstrate that the original American Indian culture developed from that of Asian migrants who were largely hunters. The farming aspects that emerged much later relied on major crops first domesticated by the peoples of Mexico and Peru. The diversity of American Indian life observed by Columbus and his successors represented adjustments of Indian groups to the different ecological settings they reached as they populated the continent. Over some sixteen thousand years this led to the development of hundreds of distinctive cultures. Furthermore, repeated migrations from eastern Asia into North America took place, the most recent being that of Eskimoan peoples (Aleuts and Eskimos) some five thousand years ago. Thus, no mysterious lost continents, lost tribes, or large-scale shipborne migrations in prehistoric times are required to explain the differences among early historic American Indian populations.

How Have Indian Cultures Been Studied?

No matter where Europeans settled in North America, it soon became apparent that Indians had arrived at an earlier time and that a great deal of diversity existed among them. In physical appearance the members of some groups differed greatly from those found elsewhere, and within a community there might be considerable variation. Then, too, some Indians were primarily fishermen as others farmed and still others hunted. They spoke highly diverse languages and organized themselves in ways ranging from small, mobile, autonomous communities to large, stable confederations. To understand this diversity necessitates defining some of the concepts that have proven useful in ordering information about Indians.

Any reasonably systematic account of the lives of a people is called an *ethnography*. Their manufactures, language, social and political organization, art, knowledge, and myths all are ethnographic dimensions. An ethnography is overwhelmingly descriptive and pertains to a brief period of time. In more exacting terms, an ethnography is a descriptive framework for behavioral information about a population for a particular point in time. The peoples considered by ethnographers usually have been aboriginal or are from an aboriginal base, and the time coverage is a typical calendar year. Ethnographic data are collected as systematically as possible and are checked for internal consistency; for these reasons, most accounts by explorers, travelers, or journalists do not qualify. There are two general categories of ethnographies: baseline studies made about life at the time of historic contact and others made for later points in time. A *baseline ethnography* describes a people before they had any significant degree of contact with representatives of literate or civilized societies. Thus, the data represent conditions before the people studied were influenced or disrupted by Europeans, Euro-Americans, or the members of other clearly foreign groups. In a strict sense, a baseline ethnography should be compiled before European trade goods or diseases of European origins prevail. Yet, capable observers seldom were present to record a broad range of information about an Indian population, in a systematic manner, before their customs were altered by agents of Western civilization. The first comprehensive ethnography of an Indian tribe, or of any aboriginal people for that matter, that made a significant impact on anthropology was written in 1851. The author was Lewis H. Morgan, and his study was of the Iroquois Indians in New York state. Thus, ethnography as a distinct intellectual pursuit is comparatively recent in origin.

Trained investigators did not begin making thorough studies of American Indians until the turn of the present century. Usually they attempted to collect verbal information about Indian life at the time of historic contact, or at least for a period as far back in time as an informant could recall. An ethnographer talked with Indians about the past, observed current customs, and consulted written sources. By using these data he or she assembled a *reconstructed baseline ethnography*.

The primary difficulty in such an enterprise was obtaining reliable information about the early historic period. Most ethnographies written by anthropologists about American Indians are reconstructions made long after the first historic contacts of the groups studied. A major difficulty was to validate informants' statements, especially when documentary sources had not been studied thoroughly, a typical failing of early ethnographers. The time factor often could not be held constant for the early historic period, and as a result many descriptions were actually composites of customs at various times. Traditional ethnographies began changing character by the early 1930s, but it was not until much later that most anthropologists realized what had happened. The long-term ideal of reconstructing aboriginal baseline accounts rarely could be realized after about 1940.

Quite obviously, ethnographic information has been recorded by many observers with varied backgrounds and at different times, which leads to a note of caution about their findings. If the biases of an observer are readily apparent, they can be taken into account when evaluating his or her descriptions. In some instances, however, the biases may be so subtle that they escape the attention of someone using the material. In still other cases an ethnographer may be mistaken in what she or he reports. Because a misrepresentation of Indian life may result from these conditions, it is most desirable to check one source against another, if this is possible. Alternatively, the general reliability of the observer must serve as the primary guide to the validity of data. Cultural anthropologists understandably are cautious in their interpretation of field data and seek to use the most valid data base.

As the lives of Indians changed following prolonged firsthand contact with exotic complex societies, the Indians were said to be undergoing the process of acculturation; the end product was either stabilized pluralism or assimilation into the dominant society. Thus, we may consider *acculturative ethnographies* as the second type of ethnography. They present a description of life relating to a brief span of historic time and may be assembled from documents or by observations and interviews.

The first person to focus a field study on contemporary Indian lifeways was Margaret Mead. In 1930 she worked among the Omaha Indians and subsequently published *The Changing Culture of an Indian Tribe* (1932). This was a watershed in North American Indian studies and anticipated hundreds of broadly similar works about Indian acculturation. By 1940 even the most remote Indians had had substantial contacts with Euro-Americans for at least forty years, and indirect contacts had introduced Anglo-American trade goods and exotic diseases long before. Historic changes loomed large in many ethnographic accounts that attempted to reconstruct aboriginal conditions; thus, they were inaccurate as aboriginal baseline studies. Yet, the training of ethnographers continued to stress interviews with informed persons, observant participation, genealogical techniques, reasonable efforts to learn the language of the people studied, and the usually superficial analysis of pertinent historical writings. Because original fieldwork was nearly essential to gain professional status, it remained a dominant training device but with a shift to acculturative field studies of tribes or communities as the aboriginal ideal was replaced by acculturative realities. As ethnographers became methodologically more sophisticated, the emphasis shifted even further. Problem-focused studies began to dominate, with one or more aspects of Indian life singled out for detailed attention. Currently, one trend is toward more intensive studies of Indians in urban environments. This is an attractive field setting for some anthropologists because of their training and because federal research funds are more readily available for studying this highly visible "problem."

Clearly, the data base of old has disappeared, and the study of urban Indians or certain aspects of modern reservation life, such as health or land tenure, has been one response. Another approach, called *ethnohistory* and favored by persons more interested in traditional Indian life, has been the study of pertinent historical documents, often with accompanying field studies for additional information, to plot changes in a people's lifeway. The study of historical records long has been the purview of historians, and some of them, such as William T. Hagan, Roy H. Pearce, Lewis O. Saum, and Wilcomb E. Washburn, have a keen understanding of the Indian in American history. For American anthropologists concentrating on Indians north of Mexico, an appreciation of historical developments has been rather recent. One of the earliest studies was that carried out in 1928–30 by Felix M. Keesing (1939) concerning the Menominee of Wisconsin. The next major work was by Oscar Lewis (1942) and dealt with Blackfoot culture change. Thus, ethnohistory as an anthropological focus is a comparatively new development, and *Ethnohistory,* a journal devoted to the subject, did not originate until 1954.

Ethnohistory has yet to emerge as a significant focus among anthropologists, and possibly it never will. In addition to archival and library research, field studies often are recognized as valuable; some Indians clearly remember certain historical events that have never found their way into written records. The study of historical records has led to major revisions in our understanding about some tribes early in their history. Chipewyan ethnography provides an excellent example. Before the ethnohistorical studies, summarized in Chapter 3, by Beryl C. Gillespie, David M. Smith, and James G. E. Smith, we were not sure which Indians were Chipewyan, where they lived in early historic times, nor how much of an effect the early fur trade had on some bands. All of this new information has appeared since 1970. A doctoral dissertation by Charles A. Heidenreich (1971) about Crow ethnohistory is a fine example of how much new information can be derived from words and illustrations previously recorded about these people. We also are gaining an insightful perspective on modern developments among the Eastern Cherokee with the work of Sharlotte Neely Williams (1978). Yet, we still search in vain for an ethnohistory of such groups as the Cahuilla, Iroquois, or Yurok. The information about the Iroquois in particular is rich but never has been integrated. It probably is true that every tribal ethnography for aboriginal or early historic times could be made far more accurate after a careful study of existing archival and published records. Thus, superior accounts for many tribes are yet to be written.

Two other terms need defining to round out our consideration of how Indian cultures have been studied. *Ethnoarchaeology* is the use of archaeological techniques to acquire ethnographic data about a particular population. The time range represented by the artifacts recovered is of no consequence in a study of this type; the major consideration is that the artifacts must be identified with a particular people. If broad or narrow generalizations are drawn from diverse ethnographies, the study is termed *ethnology,* which is the comparative study of ethnographic data.

Thus far the units for study have been termed peoples or populations, but a clearer distinction is desirable. Different groups of Indians usually are termed tribes, yet no one set of criteria for a tribe accommodates all North American Indians. The difficulties in deriving a concept that encompasses the diversity of social norms and cultural forms may be illustrated by a rather typical definition. Alfred L. Kroeber (1925, 474) stated that a true tribe "has a name, a dialect, and a territory." Yet, among the nearly fifty major Indian groups in California, only the Yokuts of the San Joaquin Valley had all three characteristics. Most California Indians did not have a distinct tribal name; they identified themselves only as members of a particular community. Efforts to define a tribe on the basis of political cohesiveness are equally unrewarding. As John R. Swanton (1953, 1–2) has pointed out, the reported variability seems to defy the use of a single label. The Creek confederation was comprised of dominant and subordinate tribes; the name Powhatan embraced about thirty tribes or subtribes united by conquest; the name Ojibwa (Chippewa) included small groups of people who had little if any sense of political unity; each Pueblo village governed its own affairs and was in a sense a small tribe.

Kroeber (1955, 303–14) attempted to bring some order to the terminological maze. He wrote, "What are generally denominated tribes really are small nationalities, possessing essentially uniform speech and customs and therefore an accompanying sense of likeness and likemindedness, which in turn tended to prevent serious dissensions or internal conflicts." Within such nationalities were smaller sovereign states, usually termed bands or villages, that were in fact economically self-sufficient and had a recognized territory and political independence. Kroeber reasoned that a tribe was rather like a German state before the consolidation in 1871; each state functioned independently although they shared a common language, culture, and ideology. In the United States these Indian units were more properly regarded as nations in the seventeenth and eighteenth centuries. Actually, the concept of a tribe or nation most often was a product of white contact; government officials grouped bands or villages so they could more conveniently negotiate treaties, arrange resettlements, and so on. Aboriginal decision making most often was at the band or village level, although some peoples were consolidated into larger political aggregates. For the chapters to follow, the difficulties in defining a tribe are not overwhelmingly important, but the reader should be aware that the label *tribe* does not always mean the same thing when applied to different peoples. Those interested in pursuing the topic further are referred to a volume on the subject edited by June Helm (1968).

Another aspect of studying Indians that has led to confusion because of its overall inconsistency is any attempt to view the time of historic contact collectively. Historic contact with Indians differed widely in time from one region to another. Many tribes in the eastern United States had been destroyed by disease and homicide or displaced from their lands before others to the north and west ever heard of white people or knew of the diseases that they carried. Historic contact began about A.D. 1000 in northern Newfoundland, while in the Southwest it was 1540, and it was 1885 in one sector of central Alaska. Thus, no single decade or even century represents the contact period. This means that there is a *sliding historical baseline* for the beginnings of Indian history on a regional basis. Swanton (1953, 3–6) has suggested that if A.D. 1650 is taken as a base date, it is possible to establish the indigenous Indian boundaries for the southern and eastern United States as well as for eastern Canada. In the northwestern sector of the continent, no major relocations of peoples appear to have occurred between 1650 and the time of their actual historic contact, making it possible to tentatively include them under this date as well. For the balance of the continent north of Mexico, the date of 1650 is less satisfactory. An adjustment backward in time to around A.D. 1540 might be more accurate to accommodate the peoples of the Southwest. The Plains area would require several dates over a considerable time span. The most important conclusion is that the boundaries and positioning of many tribes on standard ethnographic maps, including those in this volume, are not entirely accurate for any single time period. Instead, they attempt to represent the area of any particular tribe at the moment in history when it was surveyed and located on a map.

What Do We Know of Indian Languages?

By conservative estimates, 1.2 million Indians lived north of Mexico when first contacted, and they spoke about three hundred different languages. In some sectors, such as among Eskimos along the Arctic rim, the same language was spoken over a wide area. In other regions, as in northwestern Canada, a large block of different but closely related languages prevailed. Elsewhere, highly distinct languages might exist in a limited area. In California, for example, far greater linguistic diversity existed than is found in all of modern Europe.

European settlers could ignore Indian customs if they wished since they lived in separate communities, but they could not ignore Indian languages if they hoped to communicate with them. Since typical colonists felt superior to Indians, they seldom attempted to learn an Indian language; most often Indians or persons of mixed blood became bilingual. Yet, for missionaries intent on converting Indians to Christianity it was essential to learn the languages of peoples among whom they worked. The first landmark in American Indian linguistics was the publication in 1663 of a Bible translated into Massachuset, an Algonkian language, by the missionary John Eliot; in 1666 he published an Algonkian grammar.

The first prominent student of Indian linguistics was Thomas Jefferson. He was concerned that these languages were disappearing rapidly, and before he became president in 1801 he had collected considerable linguistic information. Jefferson (1801, 149) reasoned that preserving linguistic data from Indians in the Americas would make it possible to trace the relationships among these peoples. The first comparative linguist of stature in the United States was Peter S. Du Ponceau. French by birth, he served in the Revolutionary War and later practiced law in Philadelphia. Among the notable conclusions drawn by Du Ponceau in his study of languages was that a relationship existed between the Chukchi of Siberia and Eskimos in arctic America. However, no Asian language was identified as spoken in North America, and he suggested tentatively that no South Pacific area languages were spoken along coastal America.

The next linguist of note was Albert Gallatin, the first person to analyze and classify diverse Indian languages of North America. This Swiss-born language teacher became a businessman, later the Secretary of the Treasury, and finally a minister to France and then to England. In 1836 Gallatin published a classification of languages in North America north of Mexico and east of the Rocky Mountains. He also supported Du Ponceau's conclusion about the essential homogeneity of American Indian languages compared with those found elsewhere in the world. When John Wesley Powell published his definitive study of American Indian linguistic families in 1891, he credited Gallatin as the person who previously had contributed the most to the subject. The essence of Powell's classification has withstood the test of time, but he deserves credit primarily for assembling sources rather than for making a highly original contribution. A map was prepared on which fifty-eight language families were identified; it was revised slightly in 1907 and has been reproduced on innumerable occasions. The classification that prevails at present is based on the studies by Gallatin and Powell. Compiled by C. F. and F. M. Voegelin (1966), it appears in simplified form in Figure 1-1.

In conclusion, it should be noted that of the approximately three hundred aboriginal languages spoken during the early historical period, about half are now extinct. Wallace L. Chafe (1967) has estimated that about half of the surviving languages are not spoken by children of the tribes involved, and it seems unlikely that these languages will endure beyond the present century. The languages that seem likely to last longest are Cree, Chippewa, Eskimo, and Navajo; Chafe doubts, however, that they will be spoken 150 years from now.

| How Can We Group Indian Tribes?

Linguists first established relationships among tribes on a sound basis by identifying families of related languages. After the Powell linguistic map was available, the three hundred tribes (defined by language differences) were

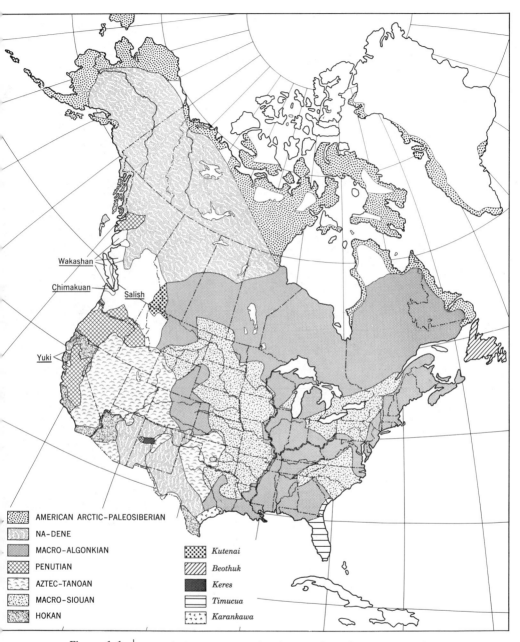

Wakashan

Chimakuan

Salish

Yuki

▨	AMERICAN ARCTIC-PALEOSIBERIAN
▨	NA-DENE
▨	MACRO-ALGONKIAN
▨	PENUTIAN
▨	AZTEC-TANOAN
▨	MACRO-SIOUAN
▨	HOKAN

▨	*Kutenai*
▨	*Beothuk*
▨	*Keres*
▨	*Timucua*
▨	*Karankawa*

Figure 1-1. | Major linguistic groups for aboriginal North America north of Mexico. The widespread phyla are designated in capital letters; the phyla for which there is a single representative language are in italics, and the families for which there are no established phyla are underlined. (After Voegelin and Voegelin 1966; courtesy of the American Anthropological Association.)

Table 1-1. Summary of characteristics of the ten culture areas.

Culture Area	Languages	Subsistence	Descent
Eskimo	Eskimo-Aleut	sea mammals caribou fish	bilateral
Northern Athapaskan	Na-Dene	caribou salmon in west whitefish in east	matrilineal bilateral
Northern Algonkian	Algonkian	caribou moose fish	bilateral patrilineal
Great Basin-Baja	highly varied	acorns pine nuts mesquite beans game	bilateral
Plateau	Salish	salmon hunting collecting	bilateral
Plains	Macro-Siouan	bison in west hunting & maize in east	bilateral patrilineal
Northwest Coast	Na-Dene in north Salishan in middle Wakashan in south	salmon land mammals sea mammals	matrilineal, in north patrilineal, in south

Political Organization	Religion	Housing	Manufactures & Other
charismatic leaders bands	shamans good & evil spirits ceremonies in west	wood, stone, sod in east & west snowhouse in central area	tailored clothing elaborate harpoons umiaks, kayaks, dog sleds sinew-backed bows feuds over women infanticide
charismatic leaders bands	shamans Nakani	double lean-to rectangular log-frame	semitailored clothing spruce root & birch bark baskets toboggans & snowshoes bark canoes deadfalls & snares cannibalism during famines
charismatic leaders bands	shamans shaking tent divination	conical tent	semitailored clothing toboggans, snowshoes bark canoes deadfalls & snares hunting dogs
bands	elaborate female puberty ceremonies shamans diverse supernaturals	impermanent brush, bark, grass	developed basketry seed grinding stones sinew-backed bows nets for land mammals
villages	shamans diverse spirits	semisubterranean winter reed- or mat-covered summer	basketry important bark fiber clothing
bands band alliances military societies warfare important	vision quest guardian spirits emerging ceremonialism	skin tepee	developed bone & skin working dog-drawn travois game surrounds hide shields
villages	potlatch elaborate ceremonial round complex masks	rectangular, plank multifamily	elaborate woodworking dugout canoes social classes, slaves

continued

Table 1-1. (continued)

Culture Area	Languages	Subsistence	Descent
Eastern Woodlands	Macro-Algonkian Macro-Siouan	maize, beans, squash hunting fishing	matrilineal patrilineal
Southwest	Hokan Aztec-Tanoan	maize, beans, squash hunting	matrilineal bilateral
Southeast	Macro-Algonkian Macro-Siouan	maize, beans hunting fishing	matrilineal

grouped into fifty-eight meaningful units, and tribal diversity was reduced to an almost manageable whole. At the World's Columbian Exposition at Chicago in 1893, the Indian collections appear to have been arranged by Otis T. Mason according to the linguistic groups on the Powell map. By 1896 Mason had formulated a means for grouping ethnographic information based on environments or culture areas. The idea of describing Indians in terms of geographical clusters was relatively well accepted at this time, but Mason was the first to detail the characteristics of each area. A *culture area* is a geographical sector of the world whose occupants exhibit more similarities with each other than with peoples in other such areas. Culture areas were in theory determined on the basis of baseline ethnographies and by taking the sliding historical baseline into consideration. The concept was applied to American Indians most systematically by Clark Wissler (1938, 1942), and it has served as the organizational basis for most continentwide discussions of Indians. The system has the advantage of fitting all tribes into a relatively small number of groups. Its major disadvantages are that it refers to a single point in time and tends to stress material culture. We find, too, that one area may include peoples with different ways of life and that tribes along boundaries may share the characteristics of two areas. Finally, no two classifiers agree on the number of areas and their boundaries, which partially reflects the impressionistic basis for the evaluations. But since the culture area approach provides a useful ethnographic overview, I include a table listing the characteristics of the ten areas identified by me and others (Table 1-1), accompanied

Political Organization	Religion	Housing	Manufactures & Other
tribes confederations	developed ceremonial round harvest stress secret societies dogs eaten ceremonially	dome-shaped wigwam multifamily palisades	hide clothing bark canoes
villages	elaborate ceremonial round kiva masked dancers	pueblo-type	developed pottery & basketry cotton garments domestic turkeys irrigated farmland
tribes confederations warfare important	complex ceremonies sun worship priests	rectangular multifamily fortified	feathers over netting for clothing houselike storage facilities "black drink" emetic

by a map of the culture areas (Figure 1-2). Chapters 3 through 13 will explore these characteristics in greater detail as representative tribes for most areas are profiled.

| Additional Readings

Numerous books and many articles designed to present and interpret life among American Indians have appeared in recent years. As a reference guide to varied studies, the reader is reminded that the best bibliographic source by tribe and region is the *Ethnographic Bibliography of North America* (New Haven, 1975) by George P. Murdock and Timothy J. O'Leary. The major limitation of this bibliography is that it does not include works published after 1972. A key data and bibliographic source about all aspects of Indian life from prehistoric to modern times is the *Handbook of North American Indians* (Washington, DC), under the general editorship of William C. Sturtevant. The following volumes have appeared: *Arctic* (vol. 5, 1984), *Subarctic* (vol. 6, 1981), *California* (vol. 8, 1978), *Southwest* (vols. 9, 10; 1979, 1983), *Great Basin* (vol. 11, 1986), and *Northeast* (vol. 15, 1978). *The Columbian Exchange* (Westport, CT, 1972), by Alfred W. Crosby, Jr., is an especially valuable book about the impact of Old World diseases, animals, and plants on American Indian life. Carolyn Niethammer's *Daughters of the Earth: The Lives and Legends of American Indian Women* (New York, 1977), is a chronology of the native American woman's life that rounds out the picture provided by ethnographies of the various tribes.

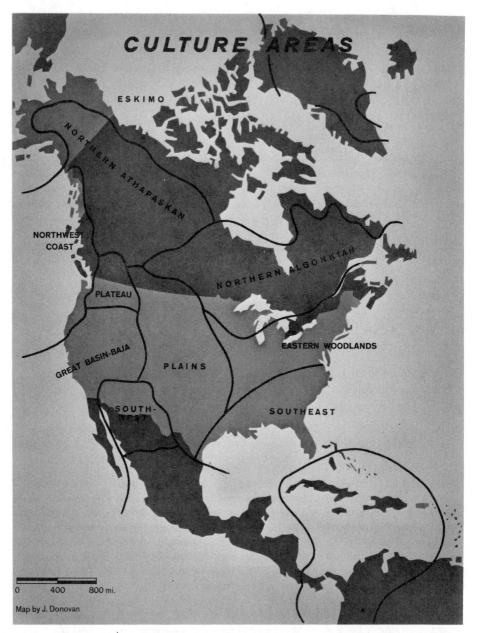

Figure 1-2. | The Indian culture areas for North America north of Mexico. (After Oswalt 1972.)

| Bibliography

Canada Year Book, 1985. 1985. Ottawa.

Chafe, Wallace L. 1967. A challenge for lingusitics today. In *The Philadelphia Anthropological Society,* Jacob W. Gruber, ed., 125–31.

Chard, Chester S. 1975. *Man in prehistory.* New York.

Churchward, James. 1931. *The lost continent of Mu.* New York.

Drake, Samuel G. 1837. *Biography and history of the Indians of North America.* Boston.

Driver, Harold E., and William C. Massey. 1957. *Comparative studies of North American Indians.* Transactions of the American Philosophical Society, n.s. 47, pt. 2. Philadelphia.

Ekholm, Gordon F. 1964. Transpacific contacts. In *Prehistoric man in the New World,* Jesse D. Jennings and Edward Norbeck, eds., 489–510.

Estrada, Emilio, and Betty J. Meggers. 1961. A complex of traits of probable transpacific origin on the coast of Ecuador. *American Anthropologist,* n.s. 63:913–39.

Fagan, Brian M. 1980. *Peoples of the earth.* Boston.

Gallatin, Albert. 1836. A synopsis of the Indians within the United States east of the Rocky Mountains and in the British and Russian possessions in North America. *American Antiquarian Society Transactions and Collections* 2:1–422.

Hagan, William T. 1961. *American Indians.* Chicago.

Hallowell, A. Irving. 1957. The impact of the American Indian on American culture. *American Anthropologist,* n.s. 59:201–17.

———. 1958. The backwash of the frontier: The impact of the Indian on American culture. *Annual Report of the Smithsonian Institution, 1957–58,* 447–72.

———. 1963. American Indians, white and black: The phenomenon of transculturalization. *Current Anthropology* 4:519–31.

Haven, Samuel F. 1856. Archaeology of the United States. *Smithsonian Contributions to Knowledge* 8:1–159.

Heidenreich, Charles A. 1971. *Ethno-documentary of the Crow Indians of Montana, 1824–1862.* PhD dissertation, University of Oregon.

Helm, June, ed. 1968. *Essays on the problem of tribe.* Seattle.

Holmes, William H. 1893. The World's Fair Congress of Anthropology. *American Anthropologist* 6:423–34.

Huddleston, Lee E. 1967. *Origins of the American Indians.* Austin.

Jefferson, Thomas. 1801. *Notes on the state of Virginia.* New York.

Jennings, Jesse D. 1974. *Prehistory of North America,* 2d ed. New York.

Keesing, Felix M. 1939. *The Menomini Indians of Wisconsin.* Memoirs of the American Philosophical Society, vol. 10. Philadelphia.

Kroeber, Alfred L. 1925. *Handbook of the Indians of California.* Bureau of American Ethnology Bulletin no. 78. Washington, DC.

———. 1955. Nature of the land-holding group. *Ethnohistory* 2:303–14.

Lewis, Oscar. 1942. *Effects of white contact upon Blackfoot culture.* Locust Valley, NY.

Oswalt, Wendell H. 1972. *Other peoples, other customs.* New York.

Owen, Roger C. 1984. The Americas. In *The origins of modern humans,* Fred H. Smith and Frank Spencer, eds., 517–63. New York.

Pearce, Roy H. 1965. *The savages of America.* Baltimore.

Powell, John W. 1891. Indian linguistic families of America north of Mexico. *Bureau of American Ethnology, 7th Annual Report,* 1–142.

Riley, Carroll L., J. Charles Kelley, Campbell W. Pennington, and Robert L. Rands, eds. 1971. *Men across the sea.* Austin.

Sanders, William T., and Joseph Marino. 1970. *New World prehistory.* Englewood Cliffs, NJ.

Saum, Lewis O. 1965. *The fur trader and the Indian.* Seattle.

Swanton, John R. 1953. *The Indian tribes of North America.* Bureau of American Ethnology Bulletin no. 145. Washington, DC.

U.S. Bureau of the Census. 1984. 1980 Census of Population. *American Indian areas and Alaska native villages: 1980* (Supplementary Report, PC80-S1-13). Washington, DC.

U.S. Department of the Interior. 1958. *Federal Indian Law.* Washington, DC.

Voegelin, C. F. and F. M. 1966. *Map of North American Indian languages.* American Ethnological Society.

Washburn, Wilcomb E. 1984. A fifty-year perspective on the Indian Reorganization Act. *American Anthropologist,* n.s. 86:279–89.

Wauchope, Robert. 1962. *Lost tribes and sunken continents.* Chicago.

Wax, Murray L. 1971. *American Indians.* Englewood Cliffs, NJ.

Wenke, Robert J. 1980. *Patterns in prehistory.* New York.

Williams, Sharlotte Neely. 1978. Acculturation and persistence among North Carolina's Eastern Band of Cherokee Indians. In *Southeastern Indians since the removal era,* Walter L. Williams, ed., 154–73.

Wissler, Clark. 1938. *The American Indian.* New York.

———. 1942. The American Indian and the American Philosophical Society. *Proceedings of the American Philosophical Society* 86:189–204.

2 Indian-White Relations

*Don't you ever
you up in the sky
don't you ever get tired
of having the clouds
between you and us?*

Nootka

SOON AFTER the discovery of the New World, a great debate raged in Spain about the humanness of Indians. Regardless of the manner in which the conquistadores were received, they argued that Indians were irrational, heretical, and tainted with mortal sin. This attitude served to justify inhumane treatment of Indians and seizure of their land or property. Francisco Vitoria, a professor at Salamanca and the founder of international law, argued against this thesis. He noted that in Europe even heretics were privileged to own property and could not be punished for sins without a trial. Implicit in Vitoria's argument was the acceptance of Indians as human beings. When the exploiters of Indians maintained that the pope of the Roman Catholic church had granted title to all newly discovered lands to the kings of Spain and Portugal, Vitoria countered that the pope had no power over the aborigines and their land, and that title by discovery could apply only to unoccupied lands. In a papal bull of 1537 Pope Paul III proclaimed "that the Indians are truly men and that they are not only capable of understanding the Catholic faith, but according to our information, they desire exceedingly to receive it" (Cohen 1960, 290). Considering Indians as human beings gave the church new millions of immortal souls to be saved. This acknowledgment of Indian humanness, combined with an awareness of Indian ownership of land, served as a guide for colonial governments in all of the Americas. In the years to come, the course of Indian-white relations was to take many twists and turns, as this chapter will show.

Early Indian-White Contacts

Early European maritime explorers found the Indians fascinating because they illustrated what people could be like when stripped of Christian and civilized behavior. (See Figure 2-1.) They were considered savages who lived more like animals than humans; although human in form, they were barely human in their customs. A word often used to describe them was *beasts,* and while their land might be attractive, many settlers felt that the Indians were its blight. A brief review of early contacts in diverse areas conveys an overview of Indian-white relations that leads to a greater understanding of the subsequent course of history.

The Virginia Charter of 1606 provided for bringing God to the savages since adopting Christian ways was equated with being civilized. Land was purchased from the Indians, and settlers were certain that they could live in harmony with these infidels who soon would be Christianized. Before many years had passed about fifty missionaries were sent to the colony to work with Indian children because it was felt that they would learn more readily than adults. The colonists were convinced that their efforts were succeeding since there were no serious hostilities. Actually, the most powerful Indian leader, Powhatan, was waiting and hoping that the colony would fail, but the English grew more firmly entrenched and confident with each year. In 1622 Powhatan's successor decided he had waited long enough, and attacked the colonists. Nearly 350 whites were killed, and the only reason the colony was not destroyed completely was that a

Figure 2-1. | This 1493 woodcut accompanied the Italian printing of the first letter by Christopher Columbus about his New World discoveries. In the background is one of the earliest representations of aboriginal Americans. (From Winsor 1889.)

Christian Indian had warned the English at the last moment. To the colonists the massacre was clear evidence of inborn Indian treachery, and the settlers now felt justified in destroying these savages whom they no longer wanted to understand. The Indians in Virginia were viewed as an impediment to the march of civilization, and within the next fifty years they were systematically destroyed or displaced.

The "Indian experience" of each colony was different because of the settlers' backgrounds and the nature of the Indians encountered. The Anglicans and Roman Catholics who established Maryland in 1634 protected the local Indians against the far more powerful tribes living nearby. Here the Indian lands always were obtained by purchase, the aboriginal population was well treated, and Jesuit missionaries worked to Christianize them. It might be anticipated that the Quaker settlers of Pennsylvania would be the most successful in making Indians into Christians, given their commitment to nonviolence and humanistic tolerance of others. The Quakers stressed the common denominators that unite all people and did not seek to identify differences between themselves and the Indians. They offered the Indians love and peace, but they won few converts. To the Indian, religion meant comparatively little without ritual and ceremony, and the Quaker approach to God was largely devoid of both. The Quakers remained neutral when non-Quakers in and beyond Pennsylvania intrigued and fought with the Indians in their midst and at their frontiers.

The Puritans of New England believed that God would guide their affairs with the Indians, who were to them descendants of Noah through the Tartars who had entered the New World from Asia as fallen people in the grip of Satan. When many Indians died in a "wonderful plague" of smallpox, the Puritans saw it as God's way of furthering the goals of the settlers. The Puritans believed that Indian lands were intended for Christian English use, and purchased these lands only to keep peace. These colonists did not hesitate to raid and war against the Indians or to foster dissension for Puritan purposes. Yet, they also recognized that the savages should be civilized. Missionaries like John Eliot concerned themselves with the Indians, but the number of conversions was small and successes transient. In the missionaries' view, the Indians stood in opposition to civilized persons, and while they might manifest natural virtues, they were not considered noble, as they later were by some writers. Efforts by these colonists to integrate the Indians into transported Western European culture failed for obvious reasons.

The Spanish who first entered the Southwest in 1540 expected to find barbarians or savages and felt a strong obligation to civilize them. Church and civil authorities alike accepted this as their primary goal after realizing that the area was not going to yield great riches. The gross pattern of Spanish life was to be introduced to the Indians, but not as an attempt to replace Indian customs, since they were thought to be without real meaning. The Spanish would decide what was best for the Indians, and the advance agents of their culture usually were Roman Catholic missionaries. They built churches and quarters near established pueblos, instructed certain individuals in Catholic doctrines, and soon recruited others as catechists and helpers. The missionaries usually were responsible for introducing the structure of civil government, new crops, and novel crafts; their goal was to create self-sufficient Roman Catholic communities. The missionaries in New Mexico usually were accompanied by soldiers who reinforced Spanish authority; in general, the priests here treated Indian transgressions far more harshly than did their counterparts farther south. Soon the Eastern Pueblos were paying tribute to the king of Spain, a good indication of the program's effectiveness.

Apart from the mission environment, Spanish frontiersmen impinged on the Indians of New Mexico through the policy of giving land grants to soldiers for services rendered. The great *encomienda* grants in New Mexico did not include any of the large pueblos, but the people who lived in the small communities in the midst of such grants were forced to work these lands for the Spanish, usually with little or no compensation. Before long, Spanish employees of encomenderos were marrying Indians and were acquiring their lands. Abuses in the *encomienda* system engendered a great deal of hostility in some pueblos and eventually led to its abandonment. Smaller land allotments or "village" grants were made from unoccupied lands, or at times from land near an Indian settlement, and once again intermarriage began to bind the settlers and Indians into a single social matrix. Spanish towns, with Santa Fe as the prime example, formed another setting for cultural contact, but since the Indians were drawn to them only for services, their impact was relatively minor.

When the Mexican War for Independence ended in 1821, Indians in the Southwest were granted the full rights of Mexican citizens. All persons born in Mexico became citizens, irrespective of their culture or race, and efforts were made to incorporate Indians into national life. This goal was not achieved in New Mexico, however. Anglo-Americans began to penetrate New Mexico in the 1840s, and their attitudes contrasted rather strikingly with those that previously had prevailed. The mission settlement had no place in their plans. They regarded the pueblo-dwellers as moderately "civilized" but considered most of the less sedentary Indians "wild." The Anglo-American policy was to push Indians aside, either peacefully or by force, to facilitate westward expansion.

Effective Spanish intrusion into California, beginning in 1769, was guided by the same policies that they had brought to the Southwest, but the Indians were quite different. In the Southwest the peaceful Pueblo peoples were sedentary farmers, and the wandering tribes, such as the Apache, were warlike. Most California Indians, except for the farming peoples along the lower Colorado River, were wanderers, moving often in their search for nuts and seeds, but they were far from bellicose. A primary purpose of the Spanish colony in California was to Christianize Indians and have them settle at self-sufficient missions; thus, Indians were very much a part of the economic order. Yet, most of the people who were drawn to the missions, either voluntarily or by force, were unlikely to adapt to a sedentary life in crowded conditions with a rigid work routine. The experiment had clearly failed by the time the missions were secularized, beginning in 1834. Souls had been saved, but the cost in human life had been great.

In the northern portions of the continent, the English, French, and Russian ventures were of a different order. Here the fur trader, not the settler or missionary, usually was the most important advance agent of Western culture. Irrespective of their national origins and time of contact, fur traders viewed Indians very differently from most other white intruders. Indians and traders were joined by economic ties that profited them both. The areas where the fur trade dominated longest were those unsuitable for large settlements of whites, and thus the Indians' way of life was not disrupted by large groups of intruders. Furthermore, the fur trader and the Indian could maintain their relationship only as long as the Indian trapped and retained the essence of an aboriginal way of life.

Many have maintained that French traders dealt with Indians more effectively than did their English counterparts. English traders often have been characterized as intolerant of Indian customs as well as haughty and aloof in business or personal contacts, whereas the French have been depicted as sympathetic and understanding, with an ability to establish good rapport quickly with Indians. In a word, the Indians could be friendly with the French but not the English. Lewis O. Saum (1965) studied primary sources by writers of both nationalities and challenged these stereotypes. The truth appears to be that all parties involved were guided by self-interest that at times made them devious. The French and English vilified each other, and traders of both nations were at times difficult. Regardless of nationality, they could be intolerant or tolerant, cruel or kind, depending on their personalities and experiences with Indians. Another dichotomy often noted between traders does stand as valid: free traders often were unscrupulous compared to licensed traders and those representing large trading companies.

Unlike the white settler on a farm or the land-hungry pioneer pushing westward, whether into Ohio, Manitoba, or California, the trader lived among Indians and became a part of their way of life. A trader was necessarily tolerant of his clientele, if only to further his enterprise; at times his very survival depended on aid from Indians. These were practical men of action, not philosophers; they had the hearts and heads of merchants. In their judgment some Indians and tribes were good while others were bad—it was that simple. They were parsimonious with their praise and often characterized Indians as "scoundrels" and "rascals," on occasion even as "monsters" or "inhuman." Yet, an active and productive Indian was an essential ingredient to a successful trading enterprise, and the Indians as well as the traders appreciated this fact. These generalizations about traders apply to those of English and French origin, who were important over most of the continent. It remains to discuss the Russian fur trade in brief.

When the men who accompanied Vitus Bering on the Russian expedition of 1741 returned to Kamchatka the following year, they brought with them the pelts of sea otter. To obtain more of these valued pelts, a host of small-scale expeditions soon reached the Aleutian Islands, and the Alaskan mainland along the northern Pacific Ocean was discovered. The men who launched these ventures were *promishleniki,* the Russian counterpart of the French *coureurs des bois;* the Russians, however, were bold and cruel. The atrocities that the *promishleniki* committed against the Aleuts and Pacific Eskimos were numerous. Not until the founding of the Russian-American Company in 1799 were the most gross transgressions against aboriginal Americans curbed with a certain degree of effectiveness. Members of the company founded their first station or redoubt along a Bering Sea drainage in 1819, and they built only two other such establishments in this area before the purchase of Alaska by the United States. During the latter part of the Russian era the administrators were naval officers, but it apparently was common for ordinary employees to be criminals from Russia who chose to work for the company in Alaska rather than go to jail in Russia. A number of men

Figure 2-2. | The earliest known illustration of Eskimos, printed in Germany probably in 1567. (From Sixel 1967.)

who held high posts in the company were "creoles," or persons of mixed Russian and aboriginal Siberian or American ancestry; these men appear to have been much more evenhanded in dealing with the fur trade clientele than were their Russian counterparts. One indication of the administration's view of the aboriginal people is the words that the commanders-in-chief used in their official correspondence when referring to them. In the Russian-American Company records for the years centering about 1830 the chief colonial administrator referred to southwestern Alaskans as "savages" more often than by any other term, although the terms "people" or "natives" also were used. By and large, during the latter part of their period of control the Russians assumed a stern but essentially paternalistic attitude toward the native peoples. They always were anxious to expand the fur trade but not at the expense of drastically altering the economic foundations of the Eskimos and Indians with whom they dealt. (See Figure 2-2.)

| Subsequent Destruction and Displacement of Peoples

It seems likely that after initial historic contact far more Indians were killed by diseases introduced by whites than by bullets. It also appears that more Indians were killed by other Indians than by whites, although many such murders unquestionably were abetted by whites. Every tribe probably was subjected to at least one severe epidemic, and there were very few Indians whose way of life was not altered dramatically, or even destroyed outright, soon after contact.

In the following chapters the impact of disease will be documented for specific peoples, and its disruptive force should not be underestimated. Certain diseases that had been prevalent among Europeans so long that they were less virulent could nonetheless be deadly to a virgin population; measles and whooping cough are two examples. Other diseases, such as malaria, raged through Indian and white populations alike. Tuberculosis was a dreaded killer of Indians but was somewhat less lethal for whites.

Records of tribes destroyed by diseases are not difficult to locate; two depressing examples will illustrate the speed of the demise. The Massachuset, whose population was estimated at three thousand in 1600, numbered only five hundred by 1631 as a result of a terrible epidemic, possibly smallpox, and soon thereafter smallpox reduced their numbers even more. By 1663, when John Eliot published a Bible in their language, they were practically extinct. The Mandan of North Dakota possibly numbered about thirty-six hundred early in their history. A population estimate for 1836 was sixteen hundred, but as the result of a smallpox epidemic during 1837 the tribe was reduced to sixty-one. The Massachuset tribe ceased to exist, but the Mandan slowly increased in number from the point of virtual extinction.

Even though an epidemic might not have destroyed a tribe, it might have killed so many people that they could not defend themselves against outsiders or continue their cultural traditions. For example, a malaria epidemic struck in the Central Valley of California and along the Columbia River in the early 1830s. A mortality rate of about 75 percent made it impossible for the survivors to effectively resist subsequent white intrusions or to maintain their ways of old.

The extinction of a population unquestionably is tragic, but another consequence of white dominance was nearly as sad. Because of the intimate associations of Indians with their traditional homelands, their displacement to other areas was often heartrending. One example will suffice. In aboriginal times the Delaware lived in New Jersey and adjacent areas, but in the early 1700s the Iroquois dominated them politically and sanctioned their displacement by white settlers. Before long many Delaware settled in eastern Ohio but only after wandering largely homeless for some time. By 1820 some lived in Arkansas, and others had ventured on to Texas. Some fifteen years later many of them had settled on a reservation in Kansas, from which they were moved to Oklahoma in 1867. Most of them remain there today, but there are Delaware Indians scattered from eastern Canada to Montana, far from each other and from their eastern homeland.

The personal and cultural trauma wrought by purposely displacing a tribe from its home is tragic in itself. But the federal policy of moving all the Indian tribes from one vast area into another violates the very principles on which the United States was founded. Yet, this did happen, and the drama began to unfold with clarity about 1800. One overwhelming argument was advanced to justify assuming control of Indian lands, and it *never* has changed: Indians obstructed the progress of whites who could use land much more effectively, and thus it was the God-given right of the settlers or real estate promoters to obtain such ground. Indian displacement became a blanket policy with the Removal Bill of 1830, and it was supported vigorously by President Andrew Jackson. New England whites could deplore this policy elsewhere because they long ago had resolved their Indian "problem." It was the residents of the southeastern states and settlers venturing into the Midwest who became the wanton, immoral destroyers of Indian property rights and tribal life.

Most surviving tribes with large landholdings east of the Mississippi River were bribed and intimidated into moving westward. By 1831 the states of Alabama, Georgia, and Mississippi had forced the removal of the Choctaw, Chickasaw, and Creek. Mesquakie and Sauk reluctance to forsake their lands led to the Black Hawk War (see Chapter 6), and Cherokee resistance to removal was strong but unsuccessful. The Cherokee had adopted civilized ways and had become successful farmers, which was highly disconcerting to politicians in Georgia who yearned to bring their productive lands under state control. In 1829 the Georgia legislature passed a law incorporating much of the land of the Cherokee Nation as state holdings. Under terms of the act all previous federal legislation and regulations were to be null and void by June of the following year. In addition, Indians were prohibited from testifying in court cases involving whites, and prohibitions were established against interference with removal plans. About this time, gold was discovered on Cherokee holdings, and the governor declared that all gold-bearing lands belonged to the state. The actions of the Georgia legislature led to the famous *Worcester v. Georgia* case, which reached the Supreme Court in 1832. The court judgment, under Chief Justice John Marshall, was that the federal government, not the state of Georgia, was responsible for the Cherokee. This decision led President Jackson to make his famous remark, "John Marshall has made his decision, now let him enforce it." Illegal seizures of land and property by whites, conflicting policies of the Indian leaders, intrigue by unscrupulous whites and Indians, and harassment by state representatives finally led to the 1835 Treaty of Echota and Cherokee removal.

Before the Cherokee treaty leading to their "legal" removal, gross injustices were perpetrated by citizens and representatives of the state of Georgia. Indians were forced from their lands at bayonet point, they were removed in chains without due legal process, they were sold intoxicants in violation of federal regulations, and their movable property often was stolen with impunity. A state law prohibiting a Cherokee from employing a white was used as a pretext for seizing plantations; these then were disposed of to whites by lottery. The Cherokee were allowed by law to transfer land only to the state. When some families finally were forced to leave Georgia, much of the property they carried with them was seized and their money extorted. Food and shelter during the forced migration often were inadequate or nonexistent, and the weakened emigrants were struck by cholera, along with other diseases. Yet, by 1838 when all of these people were supposed to be gone, only two thousand had been deported; the other fifteen thousand still believed that somehow they would not be driven from their homeland. Such was not the case. About seven thousand soldiers under General Winfield Scott moved against the Cherokee, who previously had been disarmed. Scott ordered that within a month's time every Cherokee must be moving westward. Soldiers went from house to house, forcing people to leave at once. Often the Indians were not allowed to take anything with them, and they were impounded in stockades until they could be shipped west. Their journey to Oklahoma is known to the Cherokee as the Trail of Tears; about four thousand people died as a direct result of their forced removal. The Cherokee look back at the Trail of Tears in much the same way citizens of the United States remember the Bataan Death March. But the Cherokee do not see the United States Army as heroic on the Trail of Tears.

Treaties and Indian Lands

Most of the land in North America was being used by Indians when Europeans arrived, but Indians now own and occupy only a very small portion. Most Indian lands were obtained by whites through treaties negotiating the relinquishment of land in one area for that in another, often with monetary compensation as added inducement. The treaty arrangements with a number of tribes have been documented, and it is worthwhile to present here a brief overview of the changing status of Indian lands in historical perspective.

In northeastern North America in the 1700s, the Dutch and English administrators held that Indian tribes were sovereign nations and the legitimate claimants to the lands they occupied. Land acquired from Indians was obtained on a national, not an individual, basis. The pre–Revolutionary War treaties of the British dealt primarily with the questions of boundaries and the acquisition of Indian lands. As early as 1670, during the reign of Charles II, England was concerned that those tribes desiring her protection should receive it; her treaties and agreements with New England tribes date from 1664. By 1755 a bureau had been founded to deal with Indian matters, and formal recognition of Indian title to land was to guide policy in both Canada and the United States.

Between 1778 and 1871 the United States government negotiated formal treaties with Indians in the same manner as with foreign powers. Tribes were classified as dependent nations, and treaties were considered in the same light as other statutes of the U.S. Congress. In some instances early treaties prohibited United States citizens from trespassing on Indian lands without passports, but more often the subordinate position of Indian nations to the United States was made clear by the provisions. It may come as a surprise that in spite of the hostilities between the federal government and various tribes, the United States never drew up a formal declaration of war against any hostile Indians.

Many treaty obligations still are being met by the federal government, though no new treaties have been made with Indians for about a century. Furthermore, treaty arrangements have become the basis for federal Indian law. In treaties the federal government reserved the right to regulate Indian affairs, and seldom was this right relinquished to a state. Once a treaty was negotiated and ratified, it could not be nullified, even if duress, fraud, or improper Indian representation prevailed during the negotiations. Treaties might be renegotiated by mutual government and Indian consent, and a treaty could be superseded by other congressional action. Yet, it was a general policy of the government to interpret ambiguities in treaties in favor of Indians and to consider the circumstances under which a treaty was negotiated. The courts could not interpret a treaty in a manner not intended in the original wording, however.

Treaties with Indians were negotiated by the president of the United States and were binding when approved by the Indians and two-thirds of the U.S. Senate. It is important to note that a treaty could not provide funds for Indians; monetary commitments required separate congressional action. The subjects dealt with in Indian treaties varied widely, and nearly 400 treaties were negotiated. The greatest number, nearly 260, were arranged between 1815 and 1860, during the great westward expansion of white settlers following the War of 1812. The majority of these treaties, 230, involved Indian lands. A block of 76 treaties called for Indian removal from their lands and resettlement on other lands. As early as 1818 a treaty reserved land for a specific tribe, but most reservations were established much later. Nearly 100 treaties dealt primarily with boundaries between Indian and white lands and affirmed the friendly relations between a tribe and the United States. Two tribes, the Potawatomi and Chippewa, negotiated 42 treaties each, which is a record number.

Most early treaties made no attempt to regulate or control the internal affairs of a tribe. But this policy changed as federal power over Indians increased, and treaties began regulating the behavior of tribal members in their own communities. The shift occurred in 1849 in a Navajo treaty stipulating that the federal government could pass and execute in their territory such laws as may be deemed conducive to the prosperity and happiness of said Indians" (U.S. Department of the Interior 1958, 163). By the 1860s the federal government was making treaties that could be amended unilaterally by Congress. This was an anticipation of the end of treaty making. By the mid-1800s it was becoming increasingly apparent that treaties with Indian tribes were unrealistic because of the increased Indian dependence on the federal government. It was not until 1871, however, that the last treaty was negotiated and ratified by the U.S. Congress. The end of treaty making resulted from a dispute between the U.S. Senate and the House of Representatives. The Senate approved treaties, but the House appropriated the money stipulated in them. The failure of the House and Senate to agree on appropriations brought an end to the treaty period.

An interesting sidelight in federal dealings with Indians was the attempt to have Indian representation at the national level. The first treaty of the United States with Indians was with the Delaware in 1778, and it provided that at a future date this tribe might consolidate with others and form a state, with the Delaware as the leaders. The state was to have congressional representation, but nothing ever developed from the possibility. Treaties of 1785 and 1830 proposed that Indians send a representative to Congress, but again this possibility was never realized.

In the United States, Indians have land rights based on aboriginal possession, treaty, congressional act, executive order, purchase, or the action of some colony, state, or foreign nation. Reservations were created by treaty arrangements before 1871, by acts of Congress after that time, and by executive orders of the president. In almost every instance the federal government retained the title to reservation lands. Some treaty reservations were created in recognition of aboriginal title and others in exchange for lands; other treaties arranged for one Indian group to join another on its reservation. Statutory reservations usually consisted of public domain or land purchased by the federal government for use by designated Indians. The legality of reservations established by executive orders was uncertain, but their validity was established in the General Allotment Act (also known as the Dawes Severalty Act or Dawes Act) of 1887. Reservations were created by executive order between 1855 and 1919. This practice met resistance from Congress, however, and was brought to an end except for the addition of some Alaskan reservations. From time to time Indians have purchased lands with their own funds for the group as a whole, and these properties have been supervised by the federal government. Since nearly all of the land that is now the United States was held earlier by European-based powers, the rights of Indians under British, Dutch, French, Mexican, Russian, and Spanish rule have been taken into consideration when a transfer of sovereignty has occurred. In each instance at least some recognition has been given to aboriginal rights of occupancy by the Indians.

As Allan G. Harper (1947) has noted, the Canadian government was not particularly generous in its treaties with Indians, but the promises that were made have been kept rather faithfully. In general, treaties with Canadian Indians were arranged before the arrival of settlers in any area of Indian occupancy; thus, there were no great conflicts between Indians and whites in Canada. The cornerstone of Indian policy was embodied in the Proclamation of 1763, issued at the time British sovereignty was established. This proclamation contained the following guiding principles for Indian-white relations: Indians possessed the rights to all lands not formally surrendered; Indians could not grant to whites any lands that had not been surrendered; land could be surrendered only to the Crown. Between 1781 and 1836, twenty-three treaties were negotiated, and all but one included remunerations to the Indians involved. It was only in the crown colony of British Columbia that the governor had control over Indians, and this special condition ceased to exist after confederation in 1867. In a treaty of 1850 the stipulations of all later treaties were set forth. The major points were that the Crown alone had the right to receive Indian land; reserves were established for Indian use; payment was made for the surrender of land, with perpetual annuities to the Indians involved; and Indian rights to hunt and fish on ceded lands were recognized. Between 1871 and 1921 the final eleven treaties were negotiated.

In Canada the earliest significant grant of lands to Indians was made in 1680 by Louis XIV to a band of Iroquois in Quebec. This land still is occupied by the Iroquois. The next large grant of land was to the Six Nations, who were primarily Iroquois, in 1784. They received nearly 700,000 acres for their loyalty to the British during the American Revolution. Under the Canadian Act of 1870 reserved lands may be held by a particular Indian under an allotment system. This means that the allottees have exclusive rights of use and occupancy. They may pass the land on to heirs or sell it to another Indian of their group, but they do not receive clear title to the holding. Indians with more land than is necessary for their welfare may surrender some and use the money derived from the sale for the benefit of the group. Under certain rare conditions an individual Indian obtained clear title to the land; for example, if he or she requested Canadian citizenship or enfranchisement and it was granted, he or she could obtain title to the land by receiving the consent of his or her group and the dominion government and then paying the band for the land.

As a closing observation about treaties with Indians it must be noted that they seldom were negotiated in any meaningful sense. Representatives of a particular tribe or tribes were assembled, and a treaty was offered for their approval. The signers seldom had any realistic opportunity to modify the terms. Then, too, treaties often were made through chiefs who were sympathetic to the whites, and in certain areas of the United States it was not uncommon for intoxicants to be distributed freely at treaty-making sessions. In addition, the interpreters often could not or did not set forth the details of an agreement in true detail or spell out the implications of what the Indians were losing and what they were gaining. A most important final observation along these lines is that most Indians had no concept of the permanent alienation of land. Since they had never bought and sold land, their concept was that they were granting whites the rights to its use. Thus, many such agreements were not treaties in a strict sense of the word.

Administration of Indian Affairs

In 1775 the Continental Congress of the United States created three agencies, on a geographical basis, to deal with Indians. The commissioners in charge of the northern, middle, and southern areas were instructed to make treaties, to establish friendly relations with Indians, and to prevent them from aiding the British. The general structure of Indian administration was the same as that existing under British control. The persons in charge of the middle area included Benjamin Franklin and Patrick Henry, and their appointment indicates the importance attached to Indians. In 1786 Indian administration was placed under the secretary of war, with north and south departments whose administrators were empowered to grant licenses to trade and live among Indians. With the adoption of the Constitution of the United States, the War Department maintained jurisdiction over Indians. The first Congress of 1789 appropriated funds for negotiating treaties and placed the governors of territories in charge of local Indian affairs. The next year Congress, in an important step toward federal control, began licensing traders among Indians. The Bureau of Indian Affairs (BIA) was created in 1824 within the War Department. Its framework was clarified by a congressional act in 1834, and the only significant alteration occurred in 1849 when the overall control of the bureau passed from military control into the hands of the newly created Home Department of the Interior. Flagrant corruption and mismanagement in the bureau led to the creation of a Board of Indian Commissioners that functioned from 1869 to 1933. It was composed of ten outstanding citizens who were appointed by the president to serve without compensation, and they reported to him. The board oversaw the expenditure of funds for Indians and advised the BIA.

In Canada, Indian affairs were delegated to the commander of the forces in the British North American provinces in 1816. In 1830, their management in upper Canada passed into civil control, but in lower Canada it remained under military jurisdiction. By the Act of Union in 1841, the administration was consolidated into a single Department of Indian Affairs. With the confederation of Canada in 1867, Indian administration passed into the hands of the Dominion of Canada. A separate Department of Indian Affairs was founded in 1880 with a minister who was the superintendent general of Indian affairs. The portfolio of this minister was always held by someone with another ministerial post, usually the minister of the interior. In 1936 the Department of Indian Affairs was changed into a branch and placed under the Department of Mines and Resources. In 1950 it was shifted to the Department of Citizenship and Immigration and then to the Department of Indian Affairs and Northern Development.

The dominion Parliament alone is responsible for legislating for Indians. The general structure for rights and services was framed in the Indian Act of 1876. The administration was to control the management of Indian lands—both the reserves and other lands set aside for use only by Indians—as well as the Indian Trust Fund, an accumulation of money derived mainly from the sale of natural resources on Indian lands. The Indian Act of 1876 also recognized that the dominion government was responsible for relief, education, health services, and Indian-based agriculture and industry. Finally, the Parliament was made responsible for the enfranchisement of Indians to full Canadian citizenship.

Canadian Indians with white blood deserve special comment because of their somewhat different treatment from full-blooded Indians. In general, mixed bloods, or metis, were given all the rights of Indians, and those metis who lived as Indians had the right to be treated as Indians. Efforts by the metis to protect their land rights largely were responsible for the Red River Rebellion of Manitoba in 1869. As a result of this uprising the rights of the metis were more fully acknowledged in Manitoba, but they were not implemented in the intent of subsequent legislation. The metis could obtain either money or land to extinguish their claim, but it appears that some ineligible persons received claims and some allotments may have been duplicated. The success of the metis in Manitoba led those in the Northwest Territories to press their claims. Yet, it took the threat of rebellion in 1885 before the government finally made a settlement offer. In 1899 for northern Manitoba and 1906 for northern Saskatchewan, the claims of metis were recognized in terms of land or money settlements. Those who received money or land had their aboriginal rights extinguished, and any further claims would have to be in terms of inequitable settlements.

The next major revision of Indian policy in Canada, the Indian Act of 1951, is, with its subsequent revisions, the legal basis for current policy. The act sets forth in exact terms the authority and power of the governor in council, the minister, and the minister's field representatives, the superintendents. Robert W. Dunning (1962), in discussing the effects of the act on the Indians, has stressed the power of the superintendent on a reserve and his or her flexibility in formulating and administering local policy. A reserve superintendent determines who may become members of a band, screens enfranchisement applicants, and administers welfare, relief, and education on the reserve. He or she furthermore may accept or veto the nomination of an Indian to a band council.

| Federal Indian Policy

Indian tribes were relatively free and independent nations until the War of 1812 ended. Soon thereafter they became "domestic, dependent nations" and lost any realistic control over their destiny. The Removal Act of 1830 was a clear indication of the change in white-Indian relations. The end of treaty making in the United States in 1871 was another important plateau, but it was the Dawes Act of 1887 that had the strongest effect in changing Indians into white Americans.

THE DAWES ACT Under the terms of the Dawes Act, the president was authorized to allot the lands of most reservations to individual Indians. The Indians were to select their acreage, and the federal government was to hold a trust title for twenty-five years or longer, during which time the land could not be encumbered. Surplus reservation lands then were sold and the funds derived were held in trust for the tribe, subject to use for education and "civilizing" the tribe, when Congress approved this use. Over the next ten years the Dawes Act was modified in some of its aspects to permit the leasing of allotted lands and to validate claims of descendants from marriages that were in keeping with tribal customs. Indian education came to be stressed with particular enactments from 1892 to 1897. These provided for schools and virtually forced the attendance of Indian children, while federal support of church schools was withdrawn. An important supplement was made to the Dawes Act in 1906; it permitted the president to extend the trust period for allotted lands. Again in 1910 the act was revised to resolve problems arising from inheriting allotments, leasing timber lands, and replacing trust patents for reservation lands with others of comparable value. The aim of the Dawes Act and its amendments was to bypass tribal organizations and make land allotments to individual Indians. The act was designed to destroy the tribes by doing away with the land base held in collectivity and at the same time to integrate Indians into the dominant society. Many whites who truly were concerned with Indian welfare felt that the sterile and depressing quality of reservation life should be destroyed and that the means to accomplish this end was to make individual Indians property holders and farmers.

THE INDIAN REORGANIZATION ACT The most basic change in federal Indian policy after the Dawes Act of 1887 was the Indian Reorganization Act (IRA) of 1934. Earlier legislation was designed to force individual Indians to become self-sufficient farmers as full citizens and to break away from tribalism and the stagnation of reservation life, but Indians received their own special New Deal in 1934. The Indian Reorganization Act was intended to end the alienation of Indian lands through the allotment process. In fifty years of allotments, Indians had lost nearly 90 of their 138 million acres of land, and about half of the remaining land was desert. The most effective means to permit retention of the land base was to extend the period of trust holding, which the act did. Furthermore, the act acquired additional land for Indians, declared it exempt from taxation, and placed it under federal control.

The commissioner of Indian affairs from 1934 to 1944 was John Collier, who was deeply committed to the reformulation of American society in a less competitive mold with greater social justice. He hoped in fact that restoring vitality to Indian societies could make them a model for community living for other Americans. Two guiding principles of the IRA were self-government with democratic ideals and parliamentary procedures, and communal enterprises as the best avenue to bettered economic conditions. Tribes were encouraged to form chartered corporations and operate essentially as local governments; revolving credit funds helped those choosing to incorporate. One important condition of the original law was that it would apply only to those tribes that by majority vote decided to come under its provisions. Initially, 181 tribes accepted and 77 rejected the IRA. Fourteen groups came under it because they did not vote, and the act was extended in 1936 to include Alaskan and Oklahoman peoples without their vote of approval. Since Indians in general had come to distrust the federal government, the Indian response to this enlightened legislation was not as positive as had been hoped for by its creators. Some tribes favored allotments and were able to obtain clear title to their land in spite of the IRA. Other tribes, such as those that stressed individual wealth, did not even agree with the principles behind the IRA.

World War II disrupted the implementation of IRA goals, and in the period between the end of this war and the late 1960s the federal government generally pursued policies designed to assimilate Indians into the greater American "melting pot." However, the IRA has remained the legislation with the most critical effect on reservation Indian life thus far in the twentieth century. As Wilcomb E. Washburn (1984) has observed, acceptance of the IRA by reservation Indians in general over the years has led to the revival of tribal life, or its creation among them. The act has contributed significantly to the vitality of tribal political structure. As will become evident in numerous chapters to follow, many tribes probably would have been destroyed by now had it not been for the IRA.

REGULATION OF INTOXICANTS Treaties and laws referring to Indians in both Canada and the United States often made reference to the consumption of intoxicants. In Canada, Indians who were not enfranchised could not buy liquor legally for ordinary consumption until 1951. The Indian Act of 1951 permitted the provinces or territories, with the approval of the governor in council, to allow Indians to consume intoxicants in public places. This condition existed over most of Canada until 1958. Between 1958 and 1963 the restriction was lessened in most provinces and territories to permit Indians to buy alcoholic beverages in the same manner as Canadian citizens in general—that is, either in a public place or from a package store. A band has the option of prohibiting intoxicants on its reserve lands. In the United States the first federal regulation of intoxicants among Indians occurred in 1802. The law was modified periodically to ease enforcement and to cover loopholes. The federal government did not repeal this law until 1953. Prohibition still was possible on any reservation under local option. Before Indians could consume intoxicants in some states, state laws against the sale of liquor to Indians had to be changed.

FEDERAL INTRUSION AND INDIAN IDENTITY Since the 1930s the concept of acculturation has been dear to the hearts of many anthropologists. It has come to mean the steps by which native peoples are gradually absorbed into the dominant sociocultural pattern. With assimilation, acculturation is complete. Yet, few anthropologists are satisfied with the concept because it fails to define the stages leading to assimilation or to explain the persistence of native identity in the face of hundreds of years of pressures to negate it. Quite clearly, the idea of acculturation does not allow for the lasting quality of Indian identity. By far the most bold and innovative approach to the general problem has been conceived and articulated by Joseph G. Jorgensen (1971).

The central idea of Jorgensen's thesis is that tribes were in fact assimilated into national economic and political life as soon as they came to be controlled by the United States. Conversely, it would seem that Indians have maintained their strongest sense of identity in those areas where federal intrusion has been least successful. Jorgensen attributes the deplorable conditions under which most Indians live to the economic order imposed on them. Efforts to gauge relative degrees of acculturation fail to recognize that Indians are enmeshed in a political system that essentially is colonial. He identifies the metropolis as the center where economic and political power are concentrated; the manipulators of this power are able to promote legislation to sustain their goals and insure their growth. Thus, the politically weak rural areas are exploited by the metropolis for its growth, and this applies as well to the rural areas in which Indians live. Indians are subject to the same laws that apply to everyone else, in addition to those imposed by federal control through the BIA.

In developing his approach, Jorgensen notes that most reservations are located in arid and semiarid areas, and it is not possible for the Indians to develop successful large-scale farming enterprises because their small and often scattered plots of ground cannot be cultivated efficiently. Even if all land were farmed at its maximum productivity, the harvest would seldom be sufficient to provide a reasonable standard of living. Since reservations usually are remote from major markets or industrial developments, comparatively few nonfarming jobs are available. The economies of rural areas near reservations have declined as farms in other areas have grown larger and more technologically sophisticated under the management of large corporations. Of great importance in terms of metropolis control, the large-scale farming enterprises have received far more government aid than have the small farmers, a situation detrimental to farming Indians. The BIA has attempted to promote industrial development on and near reservations, but Jorgensen noted in 1971 that the program was mostly talk. This has remained true into the late eighties to a great extent, although some industries were introduced in the 1970s; however, they failed to be viable. With economic conditions so bad on or near reservations, it is understandable that Indians have moved to cities in ever-increasing numbers.

Since Indian migrants to cities have few skills, little confidence, and a foreign cultural tradition, they are not likely to succeed. Often they make a little money and then return to their reservation. If they remain in urban centers, they usually have the poorest-paying jobs and very little job security. In essence, as a result of white political and economic intrusion, Indians are enveloped in a culture of poverty, and the move from a reservation to a city is to substitute an urban ghetto for a rural one.

URBAN INDIANS AND FEDERAL LEGISLATION   By 1980 more than half of all the Indians in the United States lived in urban areas, but until the 1960s urban Indians usually were ignored by anthropologists. Two reasons above all others may account for this neglect. Reservations were the traditional study sites for anthropologists, and equally important, fieldwork in urban areas was the purview of sociologists. Pioneering articles about urban Indians were written in the 1960s by Joan Ablon (1964), Wesley R. Hurt (1961–62), and John R. Price (1968). When "urban anthropology" emerged as a topic of expanding interest in the 1960s, numerous studies were made of Indians in towns or cities, but most of these works are unpublished doctoral dissertations. Published articles about Indians in particular cities are becoming more numerous, yet few persons have attempted to formulate a model to explain why urban populations of Indians exist. In this context I find the approach offered by Karen Tranberg Hansen (1976) as the most insightful.

The essence of Hansen's thesis is that the migration of Indians to urban areas is best analyzed in the context of federal legislation. Hansen points out that while it is difficult to document in detail, the move of Indians to cities and towns is an old and well-established pattern. It appears to have developed as an after-effect of the Dawes Act in 1887 when Indians began receiving individual land allotments and "surplus" land was sold to whites. Land set aside for reservations initially was, in most instances, far less desirable than other land that a tribe had occupied. Then, too, many Indians never accepted farming as a legitimate economic activity for men who had been warriors, and they were ill-prepared for the sudden shift from tribal life to individual responsibility. Furthermore, subsequent legislation did not effectively compensate Indians for their land losses. As a result of this federal policy, significant numbers of Indians began leaving their reservations, where life was not viable for them. The existence of urban Indians first was clearly recognized in a study of the BIA in the 1920s by the Brookings Institution (1928). This analysis noted that the trend toward urban living could be expected to continue and recommended that efforts be made to ease the adjustments for the persons involved; no broad-scale or effective steps were taken in this direction. As noted earlier, the Indian Reorganization Act of 1934 attempted to restore economic vitality to reservations and to increase the land base, but with the beginning of World War II these efforts were discontinued. Off-reservation job opportunities in cities during this war attracted about ninety thousand Indians in 1943 and 1944; about twenty-four thousand others entered the armed forces. When the war ended, most Indians were laid off from their jobs, and large numbers returned to the reservations along with many veterans. How many remained in urban areas is not known, but the number appears to have been great.

With the Indian Claims Commission Act of 1946 the federal government made a move to "get out of the Indian business" by settling old claims. Then in the early 1950s two federal policies had a more profound and immediate influence on American Indian life. One was House Concurrent Resolution 108 in 1953. It was designed to end federal responsibilities to Indians on an established timetable. Menominee and Klamath terminations were an immediate result, and, for some Indians, such federal services as schools, welfare, and law enforcement were placed under state jurisdiction. This was accompanied by a relocation program that encouraged Indians to move to urban areas. It began in 1950 and was soon followed by a vocational training program to teach Indians job skills that were more useful in nonreservation contexts. By the early 1970s about ten thousand Indians were leaving their reservations each year to live in cities either on a temporary or permanent basis. Thus, the purpose of the most important legislation since 1946 has been to force Indian assimilation.

Some Indians, no one knows how many, clearly have become part of the greater society, but often the quality of their lives is dreadful, especially in urban settings. Their high rates of alcoholism, suicide, and unemployment, and their generally low economic status commonly are noted. The BIA maintained that the relocation program was voluntary, which simply is untrue; people were encouraged to leave the reservations and quotas for relocated Indians once existed. Typically, Indians are scattered about poorer areas in cities, and they often return to their reservations to visit or because they cannot find jobs. Yet, despite all the pressures for assimilation, most Indians have resisted successfully, and have retained their identity. They usually associate with other Indians during their leisure time, and some are active in athletic, church, or social groups that are Indian-centered. Thus, it appears that urban Indians have retained much of their cultural heritage. Their adaptation is one of *biculturation*, living in two cultures, rather than acculturation, and although it aids in maintaining their Indian identity, it may also contribute to the negative aspects of their present life-style.

Forces for Indian Identity

Many whites have long felt that their pervasive control of Indians eventually would lead to total Indian assimilation. However, past experience and present trends indicate a great deal more vitality in Indian culture than was recognized by those predicting its doom. By now Indian resistance to white dominance is manifested primarily in religious, political, and legal efforts that have become a part of their cultural heritage.

PAN-INDIANISM   At the time of their first contact with whites, cultural diversity among Indians to the north of Mexico was great. They spoke many very different languages, often gained sustenance by contrasting means, and varied in political structure from unelaborate to highly organized forms. In comparative terms, the European intruders were homogeneous in cultural background, their linguistic diversity was comparatively minor, and their political organization and religious convictions differed only in narrow dimensions. In comparison with the European migrants, the Indians living in the New World were fractured and fragmented along many dimensions, and the agents of Western civilization often exploited these differences to divide them further still. In the face of European threats to their cultural integrity, Indians eventually began to recognize what disparate tribes had in common, and to develop a new sense of identity as Indians that transcended tribal lines.

Pan-Indianism refers to a general sense of Indian cultural identity that unites the members of different tribes. Since the word *Indian* long has been a generic designation for native Americans based on cultural similarities, the prefix *pan* is actually redundant. Nonetheless, *Pan-Indianism* is a term that gained prominence in the 1950s and was applied to a condition that had originated much earlier. A more accurate designation might be *pantribalism* because participation brings together Indians with different tribal backgrounds. Pan-Indianism began in the mid-1700s and eventually emerged as a movement that has become a primary source of Indian identity for many of its members. This has been true especially for those Indians with a weak sense of tribal identity, such as those raised off reservations, and for other persons who consider themselves Indian although they lack the customary biological or cultural heritage.

Over the years varied factors have contributed to the rise of Pan-Indianism. Among the early influences were religious prophets who emerged repeatedly and advocated what Indians must do to free themselves of white control. We know comparatively little about most of these men. One such person was Neolin, better known as the Delaware Prophet. By the 1760s, when he came into prominence, the Delaware and other Algonkians had been displaced from the East by whites and were living in Ohio. They expected a surge of whites into their adopted homeland and were uncertain how to respond. Neolin, like other contemporary Delaware prophets, urged his people to abandon European customs and return to their aboriginal ways. God had revealed to him that if Indians once again lived a simple life, recited certain prayers, and dispelled whites, then game would return and the purity of Indian ways would prevail. Neolin made a map that charted the way to heaven and the obstacles placed along the way by whites. His message was appealing to many Indians, and he won converts not only among his own people but among other tribes in the Ohio Valley. His words had special appeal to the Ottawa chief Pontiac, because this religious revelation served as partial justification for aggressive action. Pontiac planned a sudden attack against British outposts and a general uprising. The Indians took a number of forts and massacred their garrisons, but their attempt to take the outpost of Detroit by siege failed. Indian dominance was of brief duration since the confederation was organized so loosely that the British soon divided the Indians and were able to reconsolidate their position. This is but one example of individual Indians who represented different tribes but attempted to cooperate in furthering a common goal.

Much of the background for Pan-Indianism may be traced to the efforts of men such as Pontiac and the Iroquois prophet Handsome Lake, but there were essential non-Indian elements as well. The most important of these was the formal education process imposed on Indians. In government and mission schools on reservations instruction was in English, and it became the language for communication between members of diverse tribes. It was the boarding schools, however, that had the most profound influence. None was more famous than the Carlisle School in Pennsylvania. It was founded in 1879 by Richard H. Pratt, who was a lieutenant in the army at the time, and was attended by members of far-flung tribes. Pratt's philosophy was remarkably clear. He viewed the boarding school environment as the most useful way station between the reservation and assimilation. His slogan was, "Kill the Indian and save the man!" Carlisle often is thought of as a college because its football team played many university teams, but it was largely a secondary school that stressed vocational training and the fundamentals of English. Indians who attended Carlisle and other boarding schools often had a difficult time readjusting to reservation life. Although some went "back to the blanket," meaning that they reverted to Indian ways, others were assimilated into the white world, and many worked for the federal government in Indian administration.

Christianity also was an especially important influence on Indians in the late 1800s in a number of different ways. Indians from different tribes came to be identified with each other because they were members of the same church denomination. Likewise, white mission advocates helped foster Indian identity by working for their well-being. Missions maintained many schools, and diverse white organizations with Christian backing were concerned with Indian life. These included the Women's National Indian Association (founded in 1879), the Indian Rights Association (1882), and the Lake Monhonk conferences (1883), all of which lobbied for Indian justice. At the same time, members of these organizations sought to assimilate Indians, and most members had little tolerance for Indian customs. These white activists in Indian affairs supported the principles of the Dawes Act but deplored the injustices of its administration. As Hazel W. Hertzberg (1971, 22) has noted in the best study of this era, "All unwittingly the reformers—the Indians' chief friends in court in the white world—thus helped to break down Indian self-respect and Indian attempts at self-help." Many Indian leaders were Christian, but at the same time they often were unwilling to abandon their Indian heritage. They sought accommodation with white customs, and their general approach has endured among many Indians seeking to retain their identity. For many others assimilation into white society was desired and realized.

Indians of many tribes with different historical backgrounds were drawn into Pan-Indianism through the peyote cult. The peyote plant, which grows in central Mexico, is a spineless cactus with "buttons" containing alkaloids that are stimulants or sedatives in varying proportions. When consumed, buttons produce a wide range of reactions. A common response to taking peyote is exhilaration and an inability to sleep for about twelve hours; depression and hallucinations, sometimes including color visions, follow. This non-habit-forming drug was consumed in Mexico in aboriginal times but was not widely used in the United States until more recently. It became popular among Indians of the southern Plains between 1850 and 1900 and spread to other western tribes. Early use in the Plains appears to have been associated with warfare, and it was taken only by men. Indians began using peyote more widely when they were suffering in the dismal aftermath of military defeat, physical displacement, and confinement to reservations. The Bureau of Indian Affairs, Christian missionaries, and white reformers all were actively opposed to the peyote cult, and its adherents were harassed. In spite of the oppression by whites and some Indians there were about twelve thousand members in 1918. Efforts were made in 1916 and again in 1917 to pass a federal law against the use of peyote, but these bills failed. In 1918 as a response to white opposition a group of participants incorporated as a formal religious institution, the Native American church. Although a number of states soon passed laws against the use of peyote (for example, Kansas, 1920; Arizona, 1923), seven states had chartered Native American churches by 1925. As members of a formal religious organization, Indians were afforded far greater protection from persecution than previously.

A typical peyote service among Plains tribes was held in a tepee and lasted all night. Participants sat around a central fire, and peyote buttons were passed for each person to take as many as he chose. A special gourd rattle and a drum were used to produce distinctive music. One person after another chanted his sacred song either in English or in his tribal language. Bibles and crosses might be part of the ceremonial equipment. The goals of the ceremony were to achieve physical and spiritual well-being and to promote harmonious relations with others. Brotherly love, self-reliance, and a disapproval of alcohol all were important values held by participants. The psychedelic experience gained through the use of peyote was never an end in itself.

According to Hertzberg, the peyote religion had appeal because old tribal religions had lost their meaning and Christian teachings seemed remote from reality. Furthermore, this was an Indian religion that united members of different tribes in a common sense of brotherhood. Peyote often was considered a powerful medicine for the diseased, and also the rituals provided an opportunity for social gatherings. Some Indians, such as the Pueblo peoples, Five Civilized Tribes in Oklahoma, and Iroquois, were relatively untouched by the peyote religion, but it had become *the* religion for many Indians by 1934.

The anthropologist James H. Howard (1955) was one of the first to identify the Pan-Indian *movement* and to define the material traits associated with it. He identified the movement's roots as being in Oklahoma, especially among the small tribes originally from the East. Howard felt that racial discrimination against Indians was an important factor fostering solidarity among them. Coupled with poverty, apartheid tended to bind Indians of diverse backgrounds together. Other contributing elements were the peyote religion, intermarriage between members of different tribes, the use of English as the common language, and the schools. Pan-Indianism was identified best with particular traits associated with powwows. The war dance, which possibly began among the Pawnee, originally had religious associations with a men's war society but became a social dance. Men danced as a group, yet each man performed in his own style to the accompaniment of singers and a drum. Thus, no rehearsals were necessary, which made the dance ideal for persons from diverse tribes performing together. A modified Plains Indian scalp dance, the buffalo dance, and stomp dance were likely to be performed; the latter was once a religious dance among tribes in the East. The feather roach headdress, feather shoulder bustle and back bustle of feathers, choker neckband, and hard-soled Plains-type moccasins prevailed among the performers. Indians and whites alike found that the Plains Indian dances were the most exciting and the costuming from this area the most visually appealing.

In addition to the artifacts and dance styles, other characteristics are associated with the Pan-Indian movement. The making of Indian bread is an example. It is a flour-based dough that is fried in fat and is popular at Indian gatherings, but was not an aboriginal food. Behavior patterns typical of Pan-Indian movement members include tolerance of idiosyncratic behavior, consensus-seeking in group decisions, and joking patterns. Many of the qualities associated with pantribalism were strengthened by the civil rights movement. On college campuses, for example, Indians from varied tribes often began at this time to identify closely with one another and to form organizations to further their general goals, a pattern that has endured into the present.

THE INDIAN IMAGE   The Plains Indian has come to symbolize Indians to whites, and we might take a moment to consider how it has happened that Indians in one sector of the country have become representative of all Indians.

Indians of the Great Plains were seen first by Spanish and then by French and English explorers, yet they were nearly unknown until after the Louisiana Purchase of 1803. In 1821 members of Plains tribes visited Washington, D.C., and none was more popular than Petalesharo, the Pawnee who rescued a Comanche girl from being sacrificed to the Morning Star. In three paintings of him by different artists, he wore a flowing feather headdress (see Figure 2-3), and according to John C. Ewers (1965) this probably was the first pictorial record of the feather

Figure 2-3. | Painting of Petalesharo by John Neagle, 1821. (Courtesy of the Historical Society of Pennsylvania.)

"war bonnet." Many other Indians in the same party had their portraits painted, and their exhibit long was a popular attraction in Washington. The earliest picture of a Plains tepee appeared in 1823 (see Figure 2-4), and the first illustration of a Plains Indian on horseback was printed in 1829 (see Figure 2-5). This beginning possibly never would have led to the emergence of the Plains tribes in popular fancy were it not for the efforts of Karl Bodmer and George Catlin, who painted Plains Indians in the 1830s. Catlin especially was important, for he not only painted many pictures of Indians but exhibited his Indian gallery widely in the United States and then in London and Paris. His book *Manners, Customs and Condition of the North American Indians,* first published in 1841, had a wide distribution, and this two-volume work with over three hundred engravings was

Figure 2-4. | The first illustration of a Plains Indian tepee to be published, appearing in 1823. (From Ewers 1965.)

Figure 2-5. | Probably the first published illustration of a Plains Indian warrior on horseback, appearing in 1829. (From Ewers 1965.)

reprinted again and again. To Catlin the noblest Indians clearly were those of the Plains. His paintings and those of Bodmer were copied or modified and also served to inspire other artists to venture west to paint Indians.

The Plains Indian symbol crystallized in Buffalo Bill's Wild West Show that opened in 1883. It was seen by millions of people in Canada, the United States, and Europe during its run of more than thirty years. William F. Cody, or "Buffalo Bill," was a colorful frontier figure who became the hero of innumerable dime novels. The show, a reenactment of episodes in Plains life, was highlighted by an Indian attack on a stagecoach and its dramatic rescue by cowboys led by Buffalo Bill. Other Wild West shows that imitated the original and Indian medicine shows intensified and spread the Plains Indian image. By the turn of the present century Indians all over the country were beginning to dress as Plains Indians for special occasions.

THE NATIVE AMERICAN RIGHTS FUND   Although the federal government has assumed the primary responsibility for American Indians in the United States, missionary and philanthropic organizations long have labored in the cause of Indian rights, especially since the Civil War. These institutions, each with its own particular view of what is "best" for Indians, usually have had a paternalistic attitude and, with rare exception, have failed to make a long-term, positive impact on Indian life. In recent years another institution has developed and already has made its presence felt. It originated with the civil rights movement of the 1960s as American Indians joined blacks and Hispanics in their quest for greater justice. Since Indians were the most deprived group in social, economic, and political contexts, they had the most to gain, but they were in the most disadvantaged position to achieve their goals. Indians seldom had the opportunity to work on behalf of other Indians in nongovernment contexts. This was particularly true in the legal arena, where the most far-reaching decisions were and are being made.

The first public advocates for Indian law emerged in the 1960s as a part of the federal War on Poverty. Following this initial step, the Office of Economic Opportunity sponsored the California Indian Legal Services in 1970 as one means of providing poor Indians with access to lawyers. The success of this program on reservations and in Indian communities was considerable. As a result, the Native American Rights Fund (NARF) emerged from the California Indian Legal Services in 1971. With Ford Foundation support, the NARF incorporated and soon began to operate from headquarters in Boulder, Colorado. This institution is distinct in having only Indians on its steering committee, a largely Indian staff, and lawyers who are Indian.

From the beginning, the NARF set specific priorities that have guided its activities. First among these is the preservation of tribal lands and identity. Accomplishments in this regard include helping to achieve the Passamaquoddy and Penobscot land claims settlement in Maine. The second goal of the NARF is to protect the natural resources of tribes. In this regard they have successfully pursued cases in and out of court to protect Indian hunting, fishing, and water rights, in addition to land claims. The promotion of human rights as the third priority has led to cases involving the religious freedom of Indians in prisons, the voting rights of Indians, and the participation of local Indians in decisions about what is taught in schools. With the accountability of governments as the fourth priority, the NARF has forced the federal government to take action on some long-pending Indian land cases. The NARF likewise has helped native Alaskan villagers resolve problems surrounding their relationship with local and federal governments. Finally, the fifth priority is the development of Indian law. To achieve this goal the NARF has done its utmost to provide legal and research assistance to Indians through library resources and staff efforts.

The NARF is the best example of an American Indian organization established in recent times to work for Indians in thoughtful, humane, and constructive ways.

Recent Attitudes toward Indians

The feelings of white Americans in general toward Indians seem to swing between two extremes, from sympathy to resentment. During the height of the civil rights movement in the 1960s and early 1970s many Americans regarded Indians with sympathy, if not with compassion. Motion-picture stars like Marlon Brando rallied to tribal causes, the depressed economy of Indian groups frequently was the subject of television documentaries, and the Indian folksinger Buffy Sainte-Marie became popular as she recounted old and new injustices. Members of the U.S. Congress less often urged Indian assimilation into the American "melting pot." A "salad bowl" concept, meaning the recognition and approval of ethnic diversity, had come to the fore in America. During this period Indians flexed their political muscles in an unprecedented manner: native Alaskans formed an "ice block" in the statehouse, the Iroquois sought to obtain their wampum back from museums, and Canadian Eskimos attempted to establish their own province in the Arctic. Indian demands received more thoughtful attention from politicians and administrators than ever before.

As the 1970s drew to a close, the civil rights movement had lost its thrust, and social justice was diminishing as a major American concern. With this new climate exacerbated by an accompanying downturn in the economy, Indians and other minorities began to elicit more resentment than sympathy. One particular event in 1977 seems to have led many Americans to develop negative feelings toward Indians. In that year a special White House study group issued a report about the land claims of the Passamaquoddy and Penobscot Indians in Maine. The study group recommended that the four thousand Indians involved be given $30 million in federal funds to settle their claim to 9.2 million acres of land illegally taken from them. The study group likewise recommended that the State of Maine further compensate these Indians with $1.7 million a year for fifteen years. In addition, timberland corporations could be forced to give up as many as 500,000 acres of land under the settlement proposal. State officials in Maine labeled the proposal as "really outrageous" and "crazy." The suggested settlement received widespread and intense media attention, and many non-Indians shared the attitudes expressed by Maine officials. In the final settlement, which was reached in 1980, the Indians received $81.5 million from the federal government; this elicited ill feelings toward Indians in general, particularly among people not familiar with the merits of the Maine Indian case.

Anti-Indian feelings crystallized during this time, especially after other tribes, realizing that the settlement with Maine Indians represented legal precedent, pressed their own claims against illegal land seizures. Constituents urged members of Congress to do something, and there was a serious proposal that the United States abrogate *all* Indian treaties. Other difficulties came to the fore as Indian assertiveness and white hostility were aroused. Because of the attention being focused on energy resources, Indians who controlled gas and coal deposits on reservation lands hoped to exploit these resources in their own way, but corporations controlled by whites stepped in with other ideas. Likewise, intense conflict emerged between whites and Indians, especially in the Pacific Northwest, over state fish and game laws as they were applied to reservations. Whether or not Indians had legal jurisdiction over whites on Indian lands was another concern. The increasingly popular bingo games on some reservations brought growing church opposition, and environmentalists objected to economic development of tribal lands. Certain federal agencies resisted Indian efforts to gain greater administrative control over their own lives, and the matter of tribal sovereignty brought additional conflict. Such sovereignty, which typically has been upheld by federal courts in recent years, creates "nations within a nation," which some whites deplore. These and other contemporary issues are examined in the following section and throughout this book.

| Current Issues

In retrospect, it is surprising that major issues in U.S. Indian-white relations from the 1950s through the 1970s not only have faded but largely have been forgotten. For example, in the early 1950s the federal government began activating a policy to end its responsibilities to Indians. "To get out of the Indian business" within twenty years was a clearly established goal. Among the results of this policy were the relocation of thousands of reservation Indians to urban areas, the Alaska Native Claims Settlement Act of 1971 that was to resolve a major land claim, and the termination of federal responsibilities to two major tribes, the Menominee of Wisconsin and the Klamath of Oregon. By the 1970s, however, official federal policy had changed, and relocation as well as termination had been abandoned. (Federal rights were restored to the Menominee in 1973, and restoration of them for the Klamath was pending in 1986.)

On the Indian side, a commitment to the Pan-Indian movement of the 1930s eventually gave rise to the Red Power movement of the late 1960s. A major contributing factor was the impact of World War II and the Korean War on

Indians who were members of the armed services and afterward refused to fit back into the Indian stereotype. Added to these persons were Indians who were searching for their cultural roots and also college-educated Indians who resented the way the BIA treated Indians. The most radical group to emerge founded the American Indian Movement (AIM) in 1968; its goal was to seek equality for Indians in the civil rights arena. Two dramatic confrontations gained it national attention. First, in 1972 several hundred Indians seized the BIA offices in Washington, D.C., at the end of a march called the Trail of Broken Treaties. They protested federal failure to live up to treaties or seek meaningful solutions to Indian problems. Second, the AIM seized the small town of Wounded Knee on the Pine Ridge Reservation in South Dakota in 1973. (At Wounded Knee Creek, about 300 Sioux men, women, and children were massacred by U.S. Army troops in 1890; this episode and the site have long symbolized white injustice.) In 1973 there was a seventy-one-day standoff of 250 to 400 Indians against 125 Federal Bureau of Investigation agents, 40 BIA police, and 150 U.S. marshals. The siege resulted in hundreds of arrests, and the two major leaders, Dennis Banks and Russell Means, spent years in court trying to vindicate themselves in what Indians and others charged were politically motivated trials. By the end of the 1970s the AIM had few members and no political impact. The Federal Bureau of Investigation files in Washington, D.C., contain 17,725 pages of information bearing on the activities of the AIM, which was said to be revolutionary.

By the late 1970s, the federal government had reconsidered its stance and was reconciled to its continuing moral and legal obligations to Indians, and on the other side, the Red Power movement had failed to achieve its goals by confrontational means. Since that time Indians have continued to seek greater social justice, but other issues have become prominent as well.

INDIAN ALCOHOLISM Between 1802 and 1953, federal laws prohibited U.S. Indians from purchasing intoxicants. After the latter date, and following the revocation of state laws dealing with the matter, the federal restriction no longer applied. To Indians the right to drink has been important symbolically as well as literally. For hundreds of years whites have expressed the opinion that Indians have a tolerance for alcohol lower than their own. Indians have maintained that this is untrue. Some white administrators have gone so far as to use the stereotype of the drunken Indian to rationalize not attempting to resolve depressed social and economic conditions among Indians. The question of Indian tolerance of alcohol has been the subject of many studies, but the one by Lynn J. Bennion and Ting-Kai Li (1976) deserves particular attention. They compared the rate of alcohol metabolism in thirty whites and thirty full-blooded Indians who had had some prior exposure to alcohol. They wrote, "Since our study showed no significant difference between American Indians and whites in rates of alcohol metabolism, the conclusion cannot be drawn that racial variations in proclivity to alcohol abuse can be accounted for by racial variations in alcohol metabolic rates" (1976, 12).

If the conclusion drawn by Bennion and Li is valid, then Indian alcoholism is primarily a product of sociocultural factors. Yet, irrespective of the cause or causes of Indian alcoholism, it is a problem of staggering dimensions. In the recent past *one-third of all Indian deaths* have been associated with the consumption of alcoholic beverages, according to a 1986 Indian Health Service report. Accidents have been responsible for more Indian deaths than any other cause, have been twice the national average, and many have been alcohol-related. Furthermore, 90 percent of Indian homicides and 70 percent of Indian suicides have been alcohol-related.

The high incidence of alcoholism among Indians has been attributed to varied cultural factors. Foremost among these is the relationship between the federal government and Indians who are "wards of the government." These Indians, including all enrollees in federally recognized tribes, have come to rely on federal paternalism, knowing that they always can turn to the BIA for sufficient aid to stay alive. Although they find this dependency relationship useful, Indians feel resentful that it deprives them of full control over their lives. On reservations, where unemployment rates usually are high, Indians feel purposeless and find they are forced to accept a low standard of living with little hope of bettering it. Efforts to turn back to old Indian ways are not meaningful because these ways usually have little place in contemporary contexts. Finally, as the nature of social life has changed, the kinship ties that once bound families together have diminished in importance, casting the individual adrift emotionally more than ever before.

The federal government has recognized the momentous problem of Indian alcoholism and by 1986 had established more than two hundred programs in thirty-four states to combat it. Funded with $24 million, increasing numbers of these programs have been turned over to Indian management and adjusted to local conditions. The best white American solution to alcoholism has been membership in Alcoholics Anonymous, but this program does not seem to work well for most Indians and successful alternatives have remained elusive. It certainly would appear that as long as adverse socioeconomic conditions prevail among Indians, there can be no ready solution to the problem.

U.S. POLICY AND TRIBAL SOVEREIGNTY   In a major 1983 statement about Indian policy, President Reagan stressed that termination of federal responsibilities to Indians was no longer a goal. Instead, the cornerstone of current policy is to remain the Indian Self-Determination and Education Assistance Act of 1975, which was designed primarily to foster tribal self-government. According to President Reagan, federal policies and practices, even after the 1975 act, have inhibited the political and economic development of tribes. He stated that "excessive regulation and self-perpetuating bureaucracy [read Bureau of Indian Affairs] have stifled local decision making, thwarted Indian control of Indian resources, and promoted dependency rather than self-sufficiency."

To break this cycle the president proposed that a higher percentage of federal funds for Indians be earmarked for self-government and for the development of tribal resources. To this end special stress was to be placed on joint ventures between tribes and businesses to develop the economic resources found on reservations. In implementing his policy, President Reagan established a Commission of Indian Reservation Economics to recommend changes in federal laws and regulations affecting reservations. In its 1984 report, this commission was highly critical of the Bureau of Indian Affairs, stating that the BIA aims at "paternalistic control and thrives on the failure of Indian tribes." The report further accused the BIA of incompetent management and excessive regulation of Indian life. The most damning criticism was that *two-thirds of the BIA budget was consumed by the bureau itself,* leaving only a third available as aid for Indians. A primary recommendation was that the BIA be replaced by an agency that would be more competent and less meddlesome in Indian affairs. Another major recommendation was that more money be funneled directly to Indians.

The proposed 1987 budget for Indians, while still administered by the BIA, does reflect a certain emphasis on direct grants to tribes. In this manner the BIA bureaucracy is bypassed partially, and Indian self-government is encouraged. The budget proposal includes $923.7 million and places nearly one-third of these funds under tribal control through contracts, grants, and administrative payments. However, the federal effort for greater fiscal restraint actually reduced the money allotted to Indians by about $40 million from 1986 levels, a factor certain to affect projects planned or under way on reservations.

The current emphasis on Indian self-determination began with a 1970 statement by President Nixon, which was an indirect response to the civil rights movement of the 1960s and reflected the greater national acceptance of ethnic diversity popular at that time. As just indicated, self-determination has continued as a major policy thrust. For Indians to manage their own affairs vis-à-vis the federal government is a *re*introduction of an old concept, Indian sovereignty at the tribal level. The current proposal of government-to-government negotiations is reminiscent of the colonial era, when Indians had complete jurisdiction over their internal affairs. As noted earlier in this chapter, this Indian autonomy was eroded first in an 1849 treaty with the Navajo Indians. Despite repeated government claims that termination of federal responsibilities to Indians is a dead issue, it is reasonable to expect that as tribes assume a greater responsibility in managing their own affairs and develop reasonably sound reservation economies, the federal government will once again seek to end its responsibilities to Indians.

In recent years the case for Indian sovereignty has been strengthened by court decisions concerning Indian jurisdiction over reservation populations as well as over the land, its resources, and the resources of adjacent waters. According to the Native American Rights Fund, between 1959 and 1986 the U.S. Supreme Court rendered about seventy-five opinions on Indian law, and most have favored the Indians involved. The right of tribes to make their own laws has been upheld intermittently by the Supreme Court since 1832, and at present this right clearly is being honored by the courts. The following are among the notable court rulings in recent years. Reservation Indians in the Pacific Northwest have the right to ignore federal and state fishing laws within the boundaries of their reservations; a similar position was upheld for Indians in the upper Great Lakes region. Companies with businesses on reservations can be taxed by the local government without state permission. If bingo is permitted in a state, the courts have ruled that Indians can organize games on their reservations without external control or taxation. Notably for legal purposes, reservation land now owned by whites, which was traditionally under state control, now is under reservation regulation, at least under certain conditions. Thus, when an Indian in South Dakota committed a crime on former reservation land now owned by whites, he was considered at first to be under state jurisdiction. However, the Supreme Court ruled that this was incorrect; the former reservation area remains primarily under tribal and federal jurisdiction. Decisions such as these have strengthened the status of reservation Indians in what amounts to nation-to-nation relations.

BINGO ON RESERVATIONS   While bingo is hardly an ancient American Indian game, it has attracted intense interest among reservation Indians. This is because a 1982 U.S. Supreme Court decision stipulated that Indians can operate bingo games on their reservations if these games are permitted elsewhere in the state. There is no state or federal control over these Indian games, nor are these games subject to any form of taxation except that which might be imposed by the Indians themselves. As a result, Indians can offer jackpots higher than those permitted by state laws. A $1-million jackpot has been offered repeatedly by the Eastern Cherokee, and they commonly have fifty-thousand-dollar jackpots. The precise number of tribes operating bingo games is unavailable, but clearly it is a growth business among them, especially because start-up and operating costs are not great. There were about 80 games on reservations in 1984; the next year, 108 bingo halls were being operated in nineteen states, 30 of them in Oklahoma. Bingo has been termed a "quick fix" for the economic problems faced by reservation residents. This may be especially useful as federal funds available to them decline. In 1986 tribes were earning about $100 million a year from bingo, making Indian gambling the largest legal and unregulated business in this country. Many tribes favor bingo games because money from the games can be used for direct payments to enrolled members and for such varied purposes as road repairs, social programs, and fire-fighting equipment. Bingo games likewise have stimulated reservation economies by providing numerous jobs to Indians, who operate and maintain the facilities. However, some Indians consider bingo games an inappropriate means to earn money, and others object on religious grounds.

As Indian bingo has flourished, opposition by non-Indians has intensified. Church groups object to Indian competition because charity bingo has long been a major source of funds for varied denominations. States object because they cannot tax the games. Law enforcement officials object because they fear that organized crime will infiltrate the games. As a result of outside pressure,

Congress has begun grappling with varied means to control Indian bingo. One major issue is whether states should have any control over bingo on reservations. Although the question had not been resolved as of 1987, it appears that some form of federal regulation of Indian gambling will become law.

CANADIAN INDIAN LAND RIGHTS   The Northwest Territories of Canada, a landmass that is 60 percent as large as all the contiguous states of the United States, is the last major sector of North America in which a modern government has not made a settlement with all the indigenous population. The residents include Eskimos (16,000), Indians (8,500), metis (3,500), and whites (22,000). A first step in extending greater political control to the people of the Northwest Territories was taken in 1967 when the seat of territorial government was moved from Ottawa to Yellowknife. A second step occurred in 1982 when the residents of the territories voted to divide the region into two political units; a target date for the division was set as 1987. The eastern sector is designated as Nunavut (Our Land) by the Eskimos (Inuit) and is dominated by them. The western sector, consisting of a large part of the Mackenzie River drainage, is occupied largely by Indians and metis. A major problem has been to fix the boundary between the two areas; it is to be in the Beaufort Sea sector, which is known to include a large oil reserve that is desired by both groups. The precise boundary is yet to be determined.

Another fascinating development, shepherded in part by Canadian Inuit, has been the emergence of an incipient multinational Eskimo political movement. Eskimo representatives from Alaska, Canada, and Greenland met in 1977 at Point Barrow, Alaska, for the first Inuit Circumpolar Conference. Over one hundred delegates attended, and by the next year they had formulated the Inuit Charter. The major goals of this charter are to preserve the Eskimo homeland for Eskimos and to gain full control over the exploitation of its resources. (In 1986 Soviet Eskimos were scheduled to attend the conference for the first time.) If a Nunavut government is founded in Canada, it could become the nucleus—as some Canadians fear—for an international political confederation of Eskimos.

| Indians and Anthropologists

American anthropologists have had a deep and abiding interest in American Indians for obvious professional and less obvious personal reasons. Since Indians in the United States and Canada have been quite accessible and usually considerate hosts, they have served as the subjects for thousands of ethnographic studies. A well-established tradition in cultural and social anthropology is the study of people in at least one other society as a part of professional training. In this manner the observer not only gains meaningful cross-cultural experience, but assembles a body of information that contributes to a broader understanding of humanity in general. The personal dimension is important because ethnographers often, if not typically, come to feel a great affinity for the people whom they study, and empathize with Indians in a way other whites do not. The field study of an ethnographer has two primary goals: to record the activities of others and to employ this information for the solution of theoretical or practical problems. In recent years a growing number of Indians have become resentful of anthropologists, and we need to ask: What do anthropologists do that displeases Indians?

Describing Indian life would seem to be a relatively neutral activity. This is the main business of ethnographers and is important if only because they describe customs that otherwise would go unrecorded and be lost to history. To record soon-to-be-forgotten information has been a very real concern of many investigators, especially those who have been convinced that they were witnessing the rapid disappearance of aboriginal ways of life. Some ethnographers, especially those around the turn of the century, became secular crusaders who devoted their lives to recording cultural ways before they were gone forever. Surely this is a worthwhile, if not noble, goal.

With aboriginal customs as their focal point, many ethnographers recorded forms of behavior that lived only in the memories of Indians. Counting coup, scalping an enemy, bison hunts, and feather headdresses were given emphasis in descriptive accounts, conveying the impression that these forms and norms typified Indian life in the recent past. Modern Indians sometimes cry "foul" because in their lifetimes, or even during the lives of their grandparents, these customs did not prevail. Such ethnographies did misrepresent Indians because they froze them in time, and this was true of most pre-1930 studies. The false impression conveyed of Indian life became at least an implicit rationalization for administrators and politicians not to make any serious effort to improve the deteriorating quality of Indian life. In retrospect, we can say that anthropologists did not lack compassion, but, unfortunately, they did produce a distorted picture of past practices lasting into modern times.

Directly contributing to this atmosphere of misunderstanding is the fact that aboriginal Indian life often was described in terms of the "ethnographic present." This means that even though an ethnographer was describing extinct customs, the information was reported in the present tense as a literary technique to impart vitality to the behavior described. Indian life of fifty or twenty years ago no longer exists, but many ethnographers continue to describe it in the ethnographic present, which is highly misleading. Criticisms of this technique clearly are valid, especially because so much has happened to Indians historically and in the recent past. It clearly distorts contemporary realities and contributes further to unrealistic views of Indians.

D'Arcy McNickle (1970) has suggested that the use of the ethnographic present, and the failure by ethnographers to present the adaptive changes in Indian lifeways, has led to another unfortunate result, that of abetting the advocates of Indian assimilation. Acculturation studies have been important to ethnographic fieldwork since the early 1930s, and most of them have stressed the negative aspects of reservation life. This hardly has been a criticism of the Indians involved, however, nor has it been intended as a prop for assimilation programs. Instead it often has been an expression of dismay about federal programs as they were administered at the time.

Older Indians often are quite sympathetic when an eager ethnographer arrives to collect information about the past, but younger ones often have neutral or hostile attitudes toward these efforts. The older people see what they regard as the essence of Indian life disappearing, and they are well aware that their children or grandchildren usually have little or no interest in their cultural heritage as Indians. Thus, an old man or woman finds it very satisfying to talk about the past to an ethnographer and have the conversations recorded with care. The attitude of many younger Indians about such information is one of disinterest or of shame about old customs. If or when these younger people decide to learn about their past as Indians, it is probable that they will have to rely on the writings of the very ethnographers that they now resent.

In a discussion of anthropologists and Indians it should be noted that a number of Indians have emerged as outstanding anthropologists with ethnography as their specialization. In fact, white anthropologists long have encouraged—and continue to encourage—Indians to join their ranks. White anthropologists are more keenly aware than anyone else that a perceptive insider is likely to be a far better reporter and interpreter of Indian life than an outsider, even a knowledgeable, understanding one. The names of a number of Indian anthropologists come to mind. Francis La Fleshe (1857–1932), an Omaha, first collaborated with Alice Fletcher and then worked for eighteen years as an ethnographer for the Bureau of American Ethnology. William Jones (1871–1909), of Mesquakie and white ancestry, earned a PhD at Columbia in 1904 and is notable for his research among Algonkian Indians. He was killed by the Ilongots on a field trip in the Philippine Islands. J.N.B. Hewitt (1859–1937), of Tuscarora and white ancestry, was an authority on the Iroquois. Edward P. Dozier (1916–1971), raised in the pueblo of Santa Clara, New Mexico, was noted for his writings on Pueblo Indians.

Possibly a more important question than why Indians object to being studied by anthropologists is: If anthropologists know so much about Indians, why have they not played a greater role as "experts" in guiding cultural change? The basic reason is quite straightforward. The guiding principle behind federal Indian policy in the United States has been assimilation, and the sooner the better. This view runs contrary to the values held by many anthropologists. By training and inclination they find the death of any culture regrettable. At the time the Indian Reorganization Act went into effect, because it was designed to bring vitality back into reservation life, a number of outstanding anthropologists worked for the BIA to further provisions of the act. However, World War II diverted national attention from this program, and the early 1950s ushered in the termination policy, which found little sympathy among anthropologists. In theory the BIA always has been committed to a policy of Indian assimilation, but as most bureaucratic organizations, it has in fact devoted a great deal of energy to its own expansion. Furthermore, bureau personnel often regard anthropologists as "Indian lovers" and neither seek nor welcome their advice. Anthropologists in turn have little sympathy with bureau policies in general and have preferred not to become involved in their programs.

Anthropologists clearly have served Indians in diverse useful and positive ways. Anthropologists have worked for the Department of Health, Education, and Welfare to improve the effectiveness of health programs; they have given evidence before the Indian Claims Commission in order to validate claims; they have testified in vigorous support of the Native American church; they often have served as advisors to Indians in economic development programs. Furthermore, anthropologists have played an important role in interpreting Indian behavior to interested whites, both in the classroom and outside of it.

One chapter of *Custer Died for Your Sins* by Vine Deloria (1969), titled "Anthropologists and Other Friends," is an Indian attack on anthropologists. The text is very clever and often most perceptive. Deloria objects to the use of anthropological data about Indians to build theoretical models. He feels that the models distort what Indians really are. However, models are designed to distill an essence of behavior, not to convey details about reality, and while they may not be beneficial to Indians, neither are they dangerous. Furthermore, he blames anthropologists for many of the ills that beset Indians. The implication is that anthropologists have had a profound influence in plotting the course of federal policies concerning Indians, which is untrue. He also stresses that anthropologists have produced a vast archive of information that is useless to many persons. Yet, these writings are valuable sources for many other persons. Deloria also writes, "Why should we continue to be the private zoos for anthropologists?" The answer is clear. Indians need not accept anthropologists if they are disinclined to do so. If the purpose of a study seems questionable or offensive, the Indians involved have the clear right to refuse their cooperation.

Numerous anthropologists, myself included, are distressed by some of the prevailing criticisms, such as those offered by Deloria. I always have considered anthropologists to be the group of non-Indians most interested in Indian customs and most supportive of Indians. At one time, some, or possibly many, anthropologists hoped that old Indian ways would be preserved, but just as Indians have changed so have anthropologists.

| A Final Note

Indians often have been called the "first Americans," indicating the priority of their residence in North America. Because they were the established occupants when whites arrived, Europeans at first attempted to deal with Indians as if they were nations in the European sense. As whites came to dominate Indians in political and economic terms, they reassessed their position and considered Indians as dependent nations and then simply as tribes.

The administrative paternalism that evolved recognized the unique status of Indians among American minorities. Indians themselves are increasingly aware that their cultural identity is important to them, no matter how different it may be from life when whites first arrived. Many feel that they are *special Americans* to whom national governments have lasting, extraordinary obligations.

Many Indians seek not just tolerance of their ways but meaningful financial and moral support in order that their identity may endure so long as the waters shall flow and the sun shall shine. This is their clear right and our abiding obligation because this land indeed was theirs.

| Additional Readings

One brief but effective history is *American Indians* (Chicago, 1961) by William T. Hagan, and another, which includes pertinent documents, is *A Short History of the Indians of the United States* (New York, 1969) by Edward H. Spicer. For Canada, *The Canadian Indian* (Don Mills, Ontario, 1972) by E. Palmer Patterson II should be studied. *The Indian in America's Past* (Englewood Cliffs, NJ, 1964), edited by Jack D. Forbes, is conceived around quotations by contemporary observers at different stages in Indian history. It provides a good overview in comparatively few pages. *The Indian and the White Man* (Garden City, NY, 1964), edited by Wilcomb E. Washburn, traces the past through documentary sources. For the colonial era the best ethnohistory is *The European and the Indian* (New York, 1981) by James Axtell. The emergence of the Pan-Indian movement is detailed best in *The Search for American Indian Identity* (Syracuse, 1971) by Hazel W. Hertzberg. For historical and modern information about Indian tribes *not* recognized by the federal government, the best general source is the "Report on Terminated and Non-federally Recognized Indians," *Final Report of the American Indian Policy Review Commission* (Washington, DC, 1976).

Superior sources about U.S. government relations with Indians are *American Indians and Federal Aid* (Washington, DC, 1971), by Alan L. Sorkin, and *The States and Their Indian Citizens* (Washington, DC, 1972), by Theodore W. Taylor. A classic study of Indian law by Felix S. Cohen, published originally in 1942, has been updated and republished as *Felix S. Cohen's Handbook of Federal Indian Law* (Charlottesville, VA, 1982), edited by Charles Wilkinson. For the United States other important works are *American Indian Policy in the Formative Years* (Lincoln, 1970), by Francis P. Prucha, and *The Indian, America's Unfinished Business* (Norman, 1966), compiled by William A. Brophy et al. The best study of the General Allotment or Dawes Act is *The Assault on Indian Tribalism* (Philadelphia, 1975), by Wilcomb E. Washburn. *The Reformers and the American Indian* (Columbia, MO, 1971), by Robert W. Mardock, presents the post–Civil War years with insight. A valuable book about research resources pertaining to Indians in the United States is *The Office of Indian Affairs, 1824–1880: Historical Sketches* (New York, 1974), by Edward E. Hill. A more recent and especially valuable policy source is *The Politics of American Indian Policy* (Cambridge, MA, 1982), by Robert L. Bee. *American Indian Policy in the Twentieth Century* (Norman, 1985), edited by Vine Deloria, discusses varied contemporary issues. The sovereignty issue in particular is addressed in *The Indian and American Society* (Berkeley, 1985), by Francis Paul Prucha. Settlement of Passamaquoddy and Penobscot Indian claims against the federal government is vividly presented by Paul Brodeur in *Restitution* (Boston, 1985).

For Canada, *Native Rights in Canada* (Toronto, 1972), edited by Peter A. Cumming and Neil H. Mickenberg, is outstanding. *Indian Claims in Canada* (Ottawa, 1975) was released by the Research Resource Centre, Indian Claims Commission, and is primarily a bibliography, but it includes a very good introductory essay about developments in the recent past. More up-to-date accounts about Canadian Indians are *The Rebirth of Canada's Indians* (Edmonton, 1977), by Harold Cardinal, and *Pathways to Self-Determination* (Toronto, 1983), edited by Leroy Little Bear, Menno Boldt, and J. Anthony Long.

| Bibliography

Ablon, Joan. 1964. Relocated American Indians in the San Francisco Bay Area. *Human Organization* 23:296–304.

Bee, Robert L. 1982. *The politics of American Indian policy.* Cambridge, MA.

Bennion, Lynn, and Ting-Kai Li. 1976. Alcohol metabolism in American Indians and whites. *The New England Journal of Medicine* 294:9–13.

Brookings Institution. 1928. *The problem of Indian administration.* Baltimore.

Cohen, Felix S. 1960. *The legal conscience.* Lucy K. Cohen, ed. New Haven. Reprinted as *Felix S. Cohen's handbook of federal Indian law,* Charles Wilkinson, ed. Charlottesville, VA, 1982.

Cook, S. F. 1955. *The epidemic of 1830–1833 in California and Oregon.* University of California Publications in American Archaeology and Ethnology, vol. 43, no. 3.

Cumming, Peter A., and Neil H. Mickenberg, eds. 1972. *Native rights in Canada.* Toronto.

Deloria, Vine. 1969. *Custer died for your sins.* New York.

Donaldson, Thomas. 1886. The George Catlin Indian Gallery in the U.S. National Museum. *Annual Report of the Board of Regents of the Smithsonian Institution, 1885,* pt. 2 appendix.

Dunning, Robert W. 1962. Some aspects of governmental Indian policy and administration. *Anthropologica,* n.s. 4:209–31.

Ewers, John C. 1965. The emergence of the Plains Indian as the symbol of the North American Indian. *Smithsonian Report for 1964,* 531–44.

Foreman, Grant. 1932. *Indian removal.* Norman.

Francis, David R. 1986, Jan. 16. Eskimos seek their own territory in Canada's icy north country. *Christian Science Monitor.*

Hansen, Karen Tranberg. 1976. Coping with change: Urban migration. Paper presented at the Northwest Coast Studies Conference, Simon Fraser University, Vancouver, British Columbia.

Harper, Allan G. 1947. Canada's Indian administration: The treaty system. *American Indigena* 7:129–48.

Hertzberg, Hazel W. 1971. *The search for American Indian identity.* Syracuse.

Howard, James H. 1955. Pan-Indian culture of Oklahoma. *Scientific Monthly* 81:215–20.

Hurt, Wesley R. 1961–62. The urbanization of the Yankton Indians. *Human Organization* 20:226–31.

Jorgensen, Joseph G. 1971. Indians and the metropolis. In *The American Indian in urban society,* Jack O. Waddell and O. Michael Watson, eds., 66–113. Boston.

La Barre, Weston, 1960. Twenty years of peyote studies. *Current Anthropology* 1:45–60.

Lurie, Nancy O. 1971. The contemporary American Indian scene. In *North American Indians in historical perspective,* Eleanor S. Leacock and Nancy O. Lurie, eds., 418–80. New York.

McNickle, D'Arcy. 1970. American Indians who never were. *The Indian Historian* 3(3):4–7.

Pearce, Roy H. 1965. *The savages of America.* Baltimore.

Peterson, Iver. 1986, Feb. 2. Rights reserved for the reservation. *New York Times.*

Price, John R. 1968. The migration and adaptation of American Indians to Los Angeles. *Human Organization* 27:168–75.

Price, Monroe E. 1983. *Law and the American Indian.* Charlottesville, VA.

Rogers, George W. 1971. Goodbye, Great White Father-figure. *Anthropologica,* n.s. 1–2: 279–306.

Saum, Lewis O. 1965. *The fur trader and the Indian.* Seattle.

Sixel, Friedrich Wilhelm. 1967. Die deutsche Vorstellung vom Indianer in der ersten Hälfte des 16, Jahrhunderts. *Annali del Pontificio Museo Missionario Etnologico già Lateranensi* 30:9–230.

Sorkin, Alan L. 1971. *American Indians and federal aid.* Washington, DC.

Spicer, Edward H. 1962. *Cycles of conquest.* Tucson.

Taylor, Theodore W. 1972. *The states and their Indian citizens.* Washington, DC.

U.S. Department of the Interior. 1958. *Federal Indian law.* Washington, DC.

Washburn, Wilcomb E. 1984. A fifty-year perspective on the Indian Reorganization Act. *American Anthropologist,* n.s. 86:279–89.

Winsor, Justin. 1889. *Narrative and critical history of America,* vol. 2. Boston.

3 The Chipewyan: Subarctic Hunters

Before the flood, caribou were easy to hunt with the bow and arrow, but after it the arrows could not pierce them: it was just as if they were nothing but bone. The hunters had to aim at their heads and hit a vein to make them bleed to death. Then the raven said, "We cannot kill the caribou because they are only bone," and while all others were asleep it stayed up and made magic all through the night. It was the raven that gave the caribou their present form with flesh on their bones, through which the arrows could go. After that they were easy to hunt. This is what we know about the raven.

A myth about caribou and the raven.
(Birket-Smith, 1930, 88)

I HAVE CHOSEN the Chipewyan to represent the Northern Athapaskan culture area for cultural, ecological, historical, and social reasons. They are one of the numerous tribes that controlled interior Alaska and northwestern Canada. Most subarctic peoples depended on caribou and fish for food, and the Chipewyan were reasonably typical in this respect, although caribou were far more important in their diet. We know more about them than about most other Northern Athapaskans, largely because of historical chance. They were reasonably well described by Europeans soon after historic contact, and in 1960 a thorough study was made of a modern community. Furthermore, anthropologists have made comparatively recent ethnohistorical studies and additional field researches among these people. We do not have information of comparable scope for any other Northern Athapaskan tribe. The sociocultural reasons for describing the Chipewyan are equally significant because their lifeway was one of the simplest reported for North American Indians. They illustrate a family-based social type with feelings of solidarity primarily at the band level. The Chipewyan also provide an opportunity to analyze the impact of the fur trade, which changed them from caribou hunters to beaver and marten trappers.

| People, Population, and Language

Chipewyan is a Cree word meaning "pointed skins," a reference to the dangling point at the front and back of the poncholike garment men wore. These people called themselves Dene, meaning "humans," and were unified on the basis of language and life-style. Most, but not all, individuals were related by blood or marriage to other persons who called themselves Chipewyan, and this formed the primary basis for their identity. The major subgroups were territorial and were based on the exploitation of regional caribou herds. By the time of contact with Europeans the Chipewyan numbered about forty-five hundred and had one of the lowest population densities among North American Indians.

The Chipewyan language belongs to the Na-Dene linguistic phylum and the Athapaskan family. The Na-Dene lived from near the Bering Strait to the western shore of Hudson Bay and were scattered southward to the Mexican border. They were primarily inland peoples and were relatively recent migrants to the New World. The major dispersal of the Athapaskan family took place during the Christian era, and it apparently consisted of one closely related group of Indians in northwestern Canada around A.D. 700. Some of these people spread south to form the Pacific group, and another cluster went on to the Southwest. These internal splits were not completed until about 1800. Diversification in the Northern Athapaskans took place between 900 and 1400, with the Chipewyan completing their divergence at the later date. The extremely close cultural and linguistic bonds between the Chipewyan and Yellowknife lead modern ethnologists to consider them as a single people, an interpretation accepted in this book.

Chipewyan Country

The early historic range of the Chipewyan is shown in Figure 3-1. Chipewyan country is a vast expanse of tundra extending as much as five hundred miles from east to west and nearly nine hundred miles from north to south. The climate is continental with long, cold winters and short, hot summers. Everywhere networks of waterways—foaming as well as hesitant streams and rivers, great lakes, and countless smaller lakes—interlace. Barren rocks show obvious signs of glacial wear on their smoothed or striated surfaces. Results of glacial

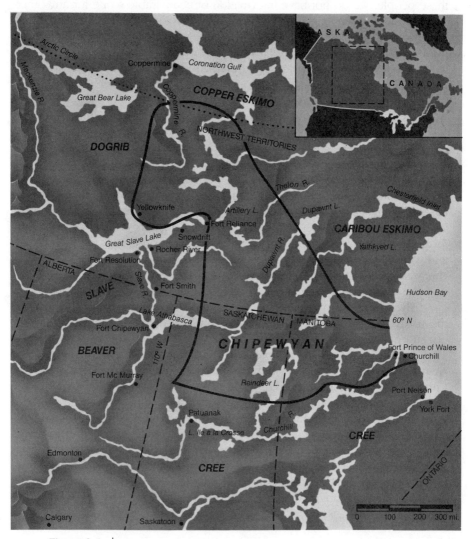

Figure 3-1. | Range of the Chipewyan Indians.

action are especially evident in the north, where rolling masses of bedrock give way to boulder-strewn valleys with adjacent lines of eskers. Lichens alone grow on highlands, but valleys are covered with dwarf birch, mosses, lichens, and willows. This region is known to the Chipewyan as the Barren Grounds, a fitting term now incorporated in geographical writings. Along river bottoms on the southern Barrens stands of spruce appear as outriders of their species; this is the taiga, where the tundra and northern forest meet. Still farther south the spruce are dense, and aspen, birch, and juniper stands are fringed by marshy bogs and upland tundras. The forested area was foreign to the aboriginal Chipewyan, but it became important to them in historic times.

First Contacts with Fur Traders and Missionaries

According to nearly all standard sources, the Chipewyan lived in the northern forests at the beginning of their history and were driven into the Barren Grounds by the Cree after the latter received firearms. However, ethnohistorical studies by Beryl C. Gillespie (1970, 1976) have shown this was not the case. Instead, the Chipewyan lived in the taiga and tundra during early historic times and began to exploit interior forests only under fur traders' influence. The Chipewyan were first encountered by whites in connection with the Hudson's Bay Company efforts to expand the fur trade. Company administrators at York Fort, founded in 1684 along southern Hudson Bay, were anxious to have the Chipewyan trade at the post, but these Indians were afraid to travel through territory occupied by their enemies, the Cree. In 1715 William Stewart went to Chipewyan camps and took with him a Chipewyan woman who induced her people to settle their differences with the Cree and to trade at York Fort. Through the efforts of Stewart, the country to the south of Great Slave Lake soon was open for trade. The next move of the Hudson's Bay Company was to establish a trading center on one margin of Chipewyan country. They selected the former whaling station of Churchill along the western shore of Hudson Bay, and built a post in 1717. The great stone fort named Fort Prince of Wales was erected nearby between 1732 and 1771.

Still the heart of the Chipewyan area had not been brought under realistic European control. As a few "Far Indians" began trading at Churchill, they brought some information about the great area to the north and west. Moses Norton, governor at Fort Prince of Wales, was anxious to open trade relations in the more remote area and to determine the location of a reported copper deposit. The Chipewyan, however, were making tremendous profits as middlemen in the trade with more distant tribes, and as a result they were reluctant to guide Hudson's Bay Company explorers. In 1768 Norton visited England to consult with company officials, and he convinced them that a search for the copper deposits in the northwest would be an important enterprise. When approval for a land expedition was finally given, the name of Samuel Hearne became intimately associated with the Chipewyan, copper, and explorations in northwestern Canada.

Samuel Hearne was born in London in 1745, and after naval service in the

Seven Years' War he joined the Hudson's Bay Company. In 1766 he became a seaman on a small vessel engaged in trading and whaling along the western shore of Hudson Bay and continued this work until 1768, when his fortunes came under the influence of Moses Norton. Hearne was assigned to make the trip into Chipewyan country, and after abortive attempts in 1769 and 1770, he launched a more rewarding third try. The ultimate success of this venture hinged on the Chipewyan guide Matonabbee, who had his own opinions about how to travel. The key to his plan was to take women along to relieve the men of the many burdensome chores, and Matonabbee had six wives at that time. The trip to the Coppermine River and Coronation Gulf was completed successfully in mid-1772 and is one of the most noteworthy feats of individual exploration anywhere at any time. Hearne's maps were not accurate, and for this he has received periodic criticism, but far more important, his book (1795) is a classic in exploration literature and the first balanced account of the Chipewyan. Hearne died a month after his manuscript was accepted by a publisher in October 1792.

The map Hearne prepared and his knowledge of the country facilitated further expansion to the northwest. The first trader to settle in the midst of Chipewyan territory was Peter Pond, who established himself near Athabasca Lake in 1778. The organization of the North West Company in 1783 introduced an era of fierce competition with the Hudson's Bay Company, and not until their amalgamation in 1821 did trading conditions become stabilized. The history of Chipewyan country centered about the quest for mineral wealth, the expanding fur trade, and disappointing searches for a water passage to the Pacific Ocean. Later, missionaries began the search for souls to save. In 1846 Roman Catholic missionaries founded a permanent mission at Lake Ile a la Crosse, and the Anglicans located at Churchill in 1912. Even today, fur and souls attract most outsiders to Chipewyan country.

Aboriginal Life of the Chipewyan

When the Chipewyan were encountered by Europeans, their economy, based on caribou and fish, was well established and probably had been much the same for thousands of years. The baseline ethnographic account to follow examines each major aspect of their sociocultural lives. Although much of the information is based on observations by Hearne, his findings are supplemented by those of later observers as they relate to aboriginal conditions. Introducing the Chipewyan with ethnographic baseline data establishes a point of departure for examining more recent historical developments among these people.

ORIGIN MYTH Most people have at least a passing concern about their beginnings and seek some rationale for their existence. In the absence of a strictly historical perspective, they usually explain their presence in legendary or supernatural terms. Most often a creation myth accounts for their genesis.

The Chipewyan regarded the primordial world as centering about a woman who lived in a cave and subsisted on berries. As the myth goes, in time a doglike creature followed her into the cave and lived with her. She thought that she dreamed this animal turned into a handsome young man who had sexual intercourse with her, but it was no dream, and the woman became pregnant. At this juncture a giant man approached; he was so tall that his head reached nearly to the clouds. With a stick he outlined the bodies of water and caused them to fill. The giant tore the doglike being to shreds and threw its internal organs into the water, creating various fish. He tossed the flesh on the land in bits and it became land animals, and he tore the skin and threw it into the sky to become birds. The giant told the woman that her offspring would be able to kill as many of these creatures as they required and she need not worry about the animals' abundance, since it was his command for them to multiply. The giant returned from whence he had come and was never seen again. In this way, order in the world emerged, and the abundance of game was assured. This tale justified the Chipewyans' indiscriminate killing of game and led to a supernatural association with dogs, since the woman's human offspring were descended from a creature related to the dog. The creation myth was not only taught to children but also guided thoughts about the adult world.

CLOTHING   Chipewyan garments were made from the skins of caribou killed in the early fall when the hides were strong and the hair dense but not long. Eight to ten skins were required to outfit an individual for winter. The upper garment of a man consisted of a loose-fitting, sleeved poncho with the hair side out and the skins cut to a point in front and back. He sometimes wore a fur boa when the temperature was low, and his ears might be protected by a fur band or cap. His ankle-length leggings were of dehaired skins, and moccasins were sewn on at the bottom. In severe weather he draped a caribou skin cape over his shoulders. The garb of a woman included a sleeved dress that reached her knees or ankles; to hold a long dress up from the ground she wore a belt around her waist. Her leggings reached from below the knee to the ankle and may not have had attached moccasins. She also wore a cape, and both sexes used mittens of double thickness. They could slip their hands out of the mittens without the chance of losing them because each was attached to a leather harness that hung about the neck.

SETTLEMENTS AND MANUFACTURES   Habitations ranged from isolated family dwellings to clusters of as many as seventy units, but aggregates of more than a few families usually were of brief duration. The size of a community was above all else a function of the time of year and the local availability of food. People lived in a subarctic variety of the tepee best known from the American Plains. A Chipewyan tent was framed with poles set in a circle and bound together near the top. The cone was covered with as many as seventy caribou skins sewn together, and it measured over twenty feet across at the base. An opening at the apex of the cone permitted smoke from the central fireplace to filter upward. If spruce boughs were available, they were placed around the fire and covered with caribou skins; on these people relaxed, worked, and slept.

Most of their manufactures could be found in and around the tents. A well-supplied camp included tripods of poles from which hung caribou-skin bags filled with meat. Among the possessions of women were cooking and storage containers of birch bark or skin. The women commonly used a basket of folded and sewn bark for cooking by filling it with water, preheated stones, and raw meat. They probably had skin bags in which they kept sewing awls and thread of caribou sinew. The men's tool kits included antler wedges for splitting planks from logs; a crooked knife with a copper blade and antler handle, the most important form of knife; a curved, wooden-handled knife with a beaver incisor for a blade, another highly useful tool for cutting small sections of wood; and a hand drill with a copper bit and an antler handle, the only drill form known. Awls were of copper, and a copper ax head was hafted on a wooden or antler handle. These uses of native copper, and its use in ice-pick points, arrow points, spearheads, and spoons, reflect a reliance on this metal. The copper tools were made by pounding a raw lump of the metal into shape. These people never heated or smelted copper but processed it as they did stone.

CONVEYANCES   The little that is known about aboriginal Chipewyan boats suggests that they had only small skin-covered canoes with wooden frames. These vessels probably served primarily for ferrying people across rivers and for hunting caribou as they crossed lakes. The toboggan for winter transport was up to fourteen feet long and about fourteen inches wide. It was made from thin juniper planks that were steamed and bent upward at the front. The planks were joined to crosspieces, probably with thongs. Chipewyan men, or women if the occasion arose, pulled the toboggans; they presumably did not use dogs as traction animals because of their supernatural associations. If wood was unavailable, the people could make toboggans by using sewn caribou leg skins as a substitute. The cariole, which is a more complex toboggan with sides and a back, was a European invention.

Snowshoes were essential for travel over deep snow. The Chipewyan made them by lacing babiche (thin, dehaired caribou-skin strips) through holes in birch-wood frames. These snowshoes had slightly turned-up tips and were asymmetrical in outline; the outer edge flared, but the inner edge was relatively straight. Men prepared the frames, and women laced the babiche into place with eyed snowshoe needles. When traveling on snowshoes, the men jogged along at a pace that was faster than a walk, and they traveled in this manner for hours at a time.

HOUSEHOLD LIFE   In camp, women prepared meals and cared for children, as did their counterparts throughout most of the world. To these obligations was added one of their most important activities, the task of processing skins, particularly those of caribou. After a caribou had been killed by a man, his wife recovered it, skinned it, and removed bits of flesh and fat with a bone scraper. If the hair was to be removed, the woman propped a wooden beam obliquely in the ground, draped the skin over it with the hair-side up, and removed the hair with a scraper. A dehaired skin often was smoke-cured by hanging it over a pole framework under which decayed wood smoldered. A skin to be used with the hair intact was scraped, softened in water, wrung out and dried, and a paste of partly decayed caribou brains was rubbed on the inner surface. Later the skin was dried once again and finally scraped with a copper-bladed end scraper. The skin probably was rubbed by hand to make it pliable and relatively soft. This process of skin preparation was a key technological complex for the Chipewyan, who relied on caribou skins not only for clothing but also for bedding, dwelling covers, containers, and ropes. It should be added that American Indians did not tan skins in the technical sense of the word.

Favorite foods largely were caribou products: the head and fat from the back, a fetus either raw or cooked, and grubs from beneath the skin. The Chipewyan did not consider steaks and chops luxuries. They ate food, which most often meant caribou meat, or fish if these animals were not to be found, both raw and cooked. In addition to boiling it in a birch-bark container, they roasted flesh over an open fire. The Chipewyan diet rarely included plant products, although a moss soup is reported and moss could season meat soup. Women prepared meals at camp, but men ate first. The women received what the men had not consumed, which might at times amount to nothing. One other food was pemmican, which usually is thought of as characteristic of the Plains Indians. Pemmican, from a Cree word meaning "manufactured grease," was made from lean meat that had been cut into strips and dried by the sun or near a fire. The dry meat was pounded into a powder, mixed with fat, and stuffed into caribou intestines; this highly concentrated food was a favorite of travelers.

SUBSISTENCE ACTIVITIES   When the Chipewyan could not find caribou, they located their summer camps near lakes or rivers, and fish became the staple. The principal fishing device was a gill net, which was made from strips of babiche and strung with wood floats and stone sinkers. The men set these nets across narrow streams, at eddies in rivers, or at spots in lakes favored by lake trout, northern pike (jackfish), and whitefish. Gill nets had the general appearance of modern tennis nets. The dimensions of the openings, or mesh, depended on the size of the species of fish for which a net was set. When these fish attempted to swim through the netting, their heads were held fast by vertical netting strands that caught in their gills.

The Chipewyan felt that each net had its own personality; they did not join one net to another because they believed that jealousy between the nets would prevent fish from being caught. Additional precautions included attaching charms to the corners of a net; without them, the Chipewyan believed, no fish would be taken. Charms often were attached to antler, bone, or wooden fishhooks, and the first fish caught with a new net or hook was boiled, the articulated bones removed intact, and burned. Other fishing implements included dip nets used for fish confined by weirs, which were brush fences across shallow stretches of water. The Chipewyan shot barbed fish arrows from bows and used leisters (fish spears) from canoes.

Fish were an important food in times of stress, but the Barren Ground caribou were the staff of life. The word for meat was derived from that for caribou, and some Chipewyan said that they preyed on caribou herds in the manner of wolves. In the early spring, bands of hunters prepared to range over the Barrens to intercept caribou. At a birch grove on the northern forest edge, a party would cut tent poles and make canoes for crossing deep or swift water. As many as two hundred persons might assemble, including women taken along primarily as bearers. A strong woman carried about 140 pounds of camping equipment, an impressive burden considering the nature of the terrain. While traveling, the men hunted on both sides of the trail taken by the women and young girls as they pulled the heavily loaded toboggans along the most direct route. Dogs, laden with parcels of tent skins, containers, and poles, accompanied the women.

In the fall six hundred persons might gather at well-known caribou crossings and camp in a single locality. Families seeing each other for the first time in months or years followed an established etiquette at their reunion. At first they sat apart from each other and said nothing. Then an older person of one party recounted all of their personal traumas since the last meeting, and women of the other group wailed on hearing of the misfortunes. The fate of the second party next was recounted and responded to. Men then greeted one another, and women exchanged presents as well as good news. When caribou appeared, their number might be truly fantastic. Sometimes so many were killed that only the skins, long bones, fat, and tongues were taken, and the carcasses were left to rot. As the caribou moved the Indians followed, drying as much meat as they could conveniently carry.

When caribou rutted in October, a hunter sometimes attached lengths of caribou antler to his belt so that they rattled as he walked. A bull caribou in the vicinity would think he heard two other bulls fighting over a female and would boldly approach, expecting to lead off the female. A bull could be killed more readily this way than by the usual method of stalking against the wind. At these times hunters used the self bow, a one-piece wooden shaft strung with babiche. Caribou-killing arrows had unbarbed bone or stone points and were vaned with feathers. An alternative and preferable fall hunting method was to drive large herds of caribou into water and kill them from canoes with spears.

In the eastern sector, winter and early spring camps were established on promontories along the forest edge, in localities frequented by caribou and near lakes containing fish. People moved only once or twice during the winter from an ideally situated camp, one accessible to lakes or wide rivers along which caribou normally passed. Here funnel-shaped caribou surrounds were built. Converging lines of brushy poles were erected, with poles at about twenty-yard intervals. When caribou approached the wider end of a funnel, they were unaware of the poles, which sometimes spanned three miles. As animals entered the surround, the women, boys, and some men appeared from behind to herd them. The caribou were driven into a trap, which was a large enclosure of branches at the end of the funnel, with snares set at narrow exits. After the entrance was blocked with trees, snared caribou were speared, and arrows were shot at loose animals.

When the snow was soft and deep, the Chipewyan, on snowshoes, sometimes tracked caribou. This meant following a single animal until it was exhausted from floundering in the snow. In the winter, the men might set gill nets beneath the ice of lakes or jig for fish through holes in the ice with hooks. In the western area of Chipewyan country, fishing was more important than among the eastern bands. Secondary means for taking game included the use of deadfalls for bear, marten, squirrels, and wolverine. The Chipewyan used nets for taking beaver in summer, but in winter, after they had broken open the beaver lodges, they took the animals from retreats beneath the ice along stream or lake edges. They set babiche snares to entangle hares or ptarmigan. Even though these Indians reached Hudson Bay at Churchill, they did not hunt the sea mammals abundant there at certain seasons.

Additional details of Chipewyan hunting and fishing activities could be presented, but it already is obvious that caribou, and fish to a lesser extent, were the primary staples. Relying as they did on very few species, the Chipewyan sometimes found food to be scarce, and people starved. Famine probably was more common among Northern Athapaskans than among any other block of American Indians. At these times the people ate berries, mosses, or other plant products and later consumed items of clothing; under extreme conditions they turned to cannibalism.

SOCIAL DIMENSIONS   These people were described in less than glowing terms by Europeans, no doubt because the Chipewyan firmly believed that they were more intelligent than whites and assumed a haughty attitude toward the outsiders. The men were described as being patient and persevering but morose and covetous. Still, they were peaceful insofar as this meant not shedding the blood of another Chipewyan male. When angry with one another, they wrestled, pulled their opponent's hair or ears, or twisted his neck. As far as honesty went, among the eastern tribes of the Northern Athapaskans, the Chipewyan were ranked as superior to all others; they abhorred a thief. However, they considered whites to be not quite human, and did not really consider taking their property to be theft.

No description of these people would be complete without commenting on the status of women as recorded by Hearne. According to him, females were subordinated in every way, were treated cruelly, and were held in gross contempt by men. Female infants were occasionally permitted to die, a practice viewed by adult women as kindly. In fact, they are said to have wished their mothers had done it for them. Women were beaten frequently, and although it was considered an odious crime to kill a Chipewyan man, it was regarded as no crime for a man to beat his wife to death. We probably will never know whether this was typical behavior toward women, but we may suspect that Hearne exaggerated or that his description was based on the actions of Matonabbee and men associated with him. Matonabbee unquestionably was a very powerful and self-centered person. The treatment of women as recorded by Hearne seems inordinately severe and out of character for Indians north of Mexico. Furthermore, a similar pattern did not prevail among the Chipewyan in more recent historic times.

As was typical for many foragers (collectors, fishermen, and hunters) around the world, the constraints on individual behavior were defined largely on the basis of age and sex. Each household was self-sufficient and could exist in isolation until a member sought a spouse. Group responsibilities or community cohesion hardly existed, and individuals had a great deal of flexibility in their behavior. A man, however, was responsible for his family and typically dominated his wife. Environmental resources were open to exploitation by everyone on an equal basis; family hunting or trapping territories did not exist.

POLITICAL ORGANIZATION   Aggregates of people structured in a formal manner and functioning as cohesive units did not exist among the aboriginal Chipewyan. Instead, as studies by James G. E. Smith (1970, 1976a, 1976b) and others have indicated, local groups were amorphous and highly flexible. In ecological terms it is important to note that regional bands were defined largely on the basis of the separate herds of caribou exploited, and a regional group was divided further into localized bands of one hundred or more people who hunted together. Seasonally, when great numbers of caribou were available, several localized bands might assemble for a hunt. However, when caribou did not follow their normal migration routes, people divided into smaller hunting groups. Conditions influencing the movements of caribou included fires, weather variations such as sudden thaws or blizzards, and, in all likelihood, cyclical variations in their number. The most important observation about the nature of a band is its flexibility in number as a function of local food resources.

Diverse families sometimes united under the aegis of a charismatic leader. Such a man was above all else an outstanding provider with an inordinate ability to take game and fish. Hearne's guide, Matonabbee, is an example. He supported himself, six wives, seven biological children, and two adopted children. Once a man's reputation as a leader was established, fathers of marriageable daughters sought him as a son-in-law. This was to the personal advantage of the father-in-law because the pattern of marriage residence was for a husband to join his wife's natal household (matrilocal residence). Subsequent wives could be sisters of the first, but other women could also be chosen. Such a man had to be physically strong since he was obligated to validate his claim to a wife, especially a younger wife, by wrestling if challenged by another man. Less successful hunters, relatives, and nonrelatives cast their lot with him for greater security. An important characteristic of this form of leadership was that it was very transient. A man could keep his wives and other followers only as long as his powers of persuasion, hunting skills, and physical strength endured. As he began to fail physically, he sometimes could retain his position of authority by craft and intrigue, but this was only a temporary respite before he slipped into obscurity.

The Chipewyan were a tribe, but only in a general sense, and comparatively little political integration existed among the member bands. Conflicts with non-Chipewyan took the form of raids and generally were carried out by the members of a single band. An account by Hearne illustrates this type of hostility. He was accompanying a group of Chipewyan to the Coppermine River mouth when they raided an Eskimo camp. Matonabbee was the undisputed leader, and the raiders were unusually cooperative as they lent equipment to one another. Beforehand each man painted his shield in black and red, adding one or more figures representing supernatural aids. They painted their faces red, black, or with a combination of the two colors, and took off most of their clothing or lightened it so that they could run fast. They launched the attack in the middle of the night and caught the Eskimos asleep. Once alarmed, the twenty or so Eskimos ran naked from their tents only to be speared to death by the attackers. Afterward the Indians plundered the camp and departed. As was typical among northern Indians, the Chipewyan attacked these Eskimos to destroy and plunder from traditional enemies; political advantage and territorial gain were not their goals.

DESCENT, KINSHIP, AND MARRIAGE The Chipewyan calculated their ancestry through both female and male relatives (bilateral descent); the descent group (kindred) was like that which prevails in the United States today. When a man married, he attached himself to the household of his parents-in-law (matrilocal residence), and his ideal mate was his father's sister's daughter (patrilateral cross-cousin). In *recent* times at least some Chipewyan called a father's sister's daughters and mother's brother's daughters (cross-cousins) by the term for sweetheart, a convention that gives strength to the assumption of cross-cousin marriage. As the anthropologist Fred Eggan (1937) has pointed out, a man relied on his son-in-law for support, and the son-in-law in turn was aided by his wife's brother's son. It appears that in the aboriginal system of kinship terminology, the cousin terms were of the Iroquois type. Father's brother's children and mother's sister's children were termed the same as siblings, but different terms were employed for a father's sister's children and mother's brother's children. This terminology would be compatible with cross-cousin marriage. For the generation above an individual, the kinship terms for father and father's brother are alike (bifurcate merging), and mother's brother is distinct. Mother, mother's sister, and father's sister are all termed differently (bifurcate collateral). This terminology indicates that probably siblings and parallel cousins of the same sex (who were terminological siblings), particularly if they were males, extended mutual aid to one another and regarded their cross-cousins as possible mates. With the further presence of wife exchange, we find an integrated network of blood relatives on an individual's generational level. On the parents' generation the same social distance separated aunts and uncles from one another as from parents. The inference is that these individuals were not as important socially or economically as near relatives of one's own generation.

The Chipewyan system of kinship terminology is diagrammed in Figure 3-2. The symbols in this and all subsequent kinship diagrams follow the same patterning. Each diagram represents the kinship terminology that prevailed in early historic times. A circle symbolizes a female, a triangle, a male. Short parallel lines represent marriage. The long horizontal lines and short ver-

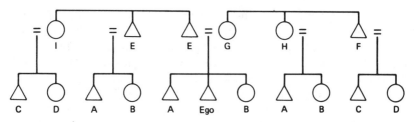

Figure 3-2. | The early historic Chipewyan system of kinship terminology.

tical ones represent descent. The point of departure for examining a diagram is a male "Ego." Each letter represents a kinship term. For example, a male sibling of a Chipewyan Ego is designated as *A* and a female sibling as *B*. These terms are broadly comparable to "brother" and "sister" in English, but note that they are extended to include father's brother's and mother's sister's children; thus, the terms *A* and *B* are applied to some individuals that English speakers would identify as first cousins.

SUPERNATURALISM   External threats to the Chipewyan came from the neighboring Cree and Eskimos. The hostility stemmed in part from the belief that the shamans of these people sent evil by supernatural means to cause illness. The Chipewyan believed that death or disease occurred from natural causes only among the aged. Thus, in theory, each physical disorder of a younger person resulted from the hostile activities of a foreign shaman. Chipewyan shamans attempted to negate the effects of such evil by acting through personal spirits that they controlled. When someone fell sick, a shaman sang and danced to summon his supernatural aids or "shadows," who were animal, bird, or imaginative familiars. He then sucked and tried to blow the intrusive disease substance from the patient. For serious cases a shaman treated an ill person in a special small square tent built with no opening at the top. Death and disease led the Chipewyan to frequent hostilities with non-Athapaskan neighbors, and they made sporadic forays into the lands of their tormentors. In the raid on Eskimos reported earlier, the attackers carried wooden shields on which they had painted designs representing their individual guardian spirits. After the encounter the raiders observed numerous taboos to placate the spirits of those they had killed. A raid of this nature united the participants against a common enemy but did not require elaborate organization. Raids were melees for individual prestige, plunder, potential glory, and tribal security.

In the Chipewyan view of the supernatural world, animistic spirits hovered about constantly, and some were more potent than others. Because the spirits of wolves and wolverine were considered dangerous, these animals usually were not hunted or killed. The bear, too, was considered dangerous; when one was killed, its skin might be burned and the large bones scattered in the four directions. A woman could not touch or step over a bearskin; thus, one placed before a door was a means of keeping women from entering a tent. The spirits of a shaman were powerful, and even the spirit of an ordinary person was sometimes feared. Only a vague notion existed of a future life, a life like that on earth but free from cares, according to one observer. Not all accounts agree, however. One states that the Chipewyan believed that the soul of the deceased crosses a river, and if the individual has been good on earth he reaches an island on which life is free from worry. If he has been evil, he struggles in the river forever.

ENTERTAINMENT   Games and other forms of amusement were few, and the only dancing was a step borrowed from the Dogrib Indians. A popular pastime was the widespread hand game, a guessing game in which two opponents sat opposite each other with ten to twenty counters beside them. One man had an object in one hand and, behind a skin, shifted it. His opponent then guessed the hand that contained the gaming piece. A correct guess gave the winner one counter, and the game was won when one man had all of the counters.

LIFE CYCLE   Tracing the pattern of typical lives from birth to death provides invaluable insight into the forms and norms that produced and sustained the sociocultural system identified as Chipewyan. No ethnography is reasonably complete unless such a sketch is included. While information about aboriginal Chipewyan life histories is not balanced or complete, it does lend itself to presentation in brief.

The Chipewyan, like all other North American Indians, realized that conception resulted from sexual intercourse. As the time of delivery approached, a small tent or brush-covered structure was erected for the pregnant woman away from the main camp. Here she bore her offspring and remained apart from normal camp routine for about a month. Her isolation was enforced whether the group was traveling or at a relatively permanent camp. The mother was cared for by other women, but she had no contact with men. The father did not see his infant until the period of isolation had ended. Similar isolation was the norm for menstruating women and for girls at menarche. The blood associated with women at these times was considered antithetical to fish and game, and men avoided contacts with females in these conditions. Apparently the women were successful in keeping the true nature of the menstrual cycle a secret from men. When a woman sought to avoid her husband, which might be several times in one month, she simply crawled out of the tent beneath a side, to indicate that she was beginning to menstruate, and went to the menstrual hut.

During the first year of life an infant was carried on its mother's back next to her skin; the baby was held in place by a belt that passed from the middle of the mother's back over her breasts. In this secondary "womb" a baby wore only a moss-padded diaper. A female infant was typically named after a form or characteristic of a marten, such as Marten's Heart, Summer Marten, or White Marten. The names for males were taken from the seasons, places, or animals. Unfortunately, little is known about the social environment of children. Males clearly occupied a favored position compared with their sisters, but children in general were treated as adults. Conversations in the presence of children were free and frank.

Childhood betrothals prevailed, and parents were careful to prevent a girl from participating in sexual intercourse before she married. Matches were made by parents or other relatives, and a girl had no choice. The usual marriage was between a pubescent girl and a man who was at least twice her age. Since there was no marriage ceremony, the man simply attached himself to his wife's household. A marriage assumed stability only after an infant was born. Offspring seldom were born during the early years of marriage, and from this it may be presumed that the young bride's adolescent sterility tended to delay conception. A nuclear family (a husband, wife, and children) was neither a stable nor long-lasting unit. The possibility of death by accident, disease, or starvation always existed, and life expectancy was probably less than thirty years for the average person. These factors, plus a growing dislike for a spouse, could rupture a household. Furthermore, wrestling to retain one's wife whenever challenged did not lead to familial stability. Skill in wrestling was developed during youth, and the rule was that the man first thrown to the ground was the loser. An opponent could be downed most readily by grabbing his hair—thus it was cut short—or by seizing his ears—so they were greased. The woman being fought over had no voice in these matters but was expected to follow the winner dutifully.

A wrestling match for a wife did not always end well. In one case the husband killed a potential rival. He and his wife then were forced to live in isolation, and whenever other Chipewyan happened on the couple, they would take everything they owned except their clothing. Women deserted their husbands, but because of the physical isolation of most camps this was a dangerous undertaking. The woman might be caught and beaten by her husband or seized by another man before she found safety with a man she desired. Men guarded their wives jealously, not allowing them out of their sight if the opportunity for adultery existed. Wives generally were faithful to their husbands, even though a particular wife sometimes shared her husband with as many as seven co-wives. The exchange of wives for a night perhaps helped temper any urge to seize a woman for sexual purposes alone. Wife exchanges were made by men and had implications that were more economic than sexual. These established bonds between men resulted in continuing friendship and mutual aid. If one of the men died, his partner assumed the responsibility, at least temporarily, of caring for the widow and her children.

As individuals aged and became less capable of caring for themselves, they were regarded as a burden. Old people had the poorest of tattered clothing, and their food was undesirable. When a camp was moved, they might be left behind in a small shelter, where they would starve alone. The corpse of a person who had died in isolation was not buried when it was found, and the corpse of one who died in camp was simply placed on the ground. In both cases, the bodies were eaten by animals. Property of the deceased was destroyed, and immediate relatives also destroyed their personal property. A widow cut her hair short as a sign of bereavement, and the shorn hair might be placed beside the deceased. She wailed about camp, stripped of her clothing and other possessions, to be aided and soothed by relatives and friends but not to remarry for a year.

In drawing the Chipewyan life cycle discussion to a close it is appropriate to comment on the manner in which these people behaved toward one another, especially on men's treatment of women and the general treatment of the aged. We should realize fully that the area in which these people lived offered either feast or famine. It was one of the most difficult sectors of North America in which to live in aboriginal times because of food uncertainties. The men, as the hunters and primary providers, presumably were often anxiety-ridden about their capacity to feed their families. This at least provides a partial explanation for their harsh treatment of women and the aged. We also must recognize that early writers about the Chipewyan were European males whose own attitudes toward these segments of the population possibly colored their accounts.

| Early Historic Changes in Chipewyan Life

Until a few years ago, Chipewyan history was unknown except in terms of obvious sources such as the work by Samuel Hearne. Recent ethnohistorical studies, however, make it necessary to correct and revise accounts about the Chipewyan, in terms of both baseline and acculturative ethnographies. The thoughtful analyses of historical sources by Beryl C. Gillespie, David M. Smith, James G. E. Smith, and J. C. Yerbury provide a dramatic illustration of what may be learned from existing but previously ignored or underused sources. These works reveal configurations of patterned change that we will consider here.

THE PULL OF CONFLICTING ATTRACTIONS   James G. E. Smith (1976b, 14) aptly characterized the course of Chipewyan life from contact to the present in his statement that "one may view the history of the Chipewyan from the early 18th century to the present as one of conflicting attractions to the caribou of the taiga-tundra ecotone on the one hand and to the fur trade and the fur bearers of the full boreal forest on the other." In early historic times the Chipewyan occupied a major portion of the Barren Grounds and the adjacent taiga; their precise distribution remains disputed. Some bands began moving south and west into the northern spruce forests in the late 1700s, but the change was made slowly and reluctantly by many groups. The Chipewyan wanted European trade goods, however, and by 1721 Hudson's Bay Company agents were encouraging them to trap beaver and marten in the northern forests. The Chipewyan could trap marten without serious disruption of their caribou-based economy, but trapping beaver meant a commitment to life in the forests, where these animals were abundant, which led to an accompanying decline in hunting caribou.

A major technological change aided these people as they sought to participate effectively in the fur trade. It was a shift from walking to the use of a small, one-person canoe and subsequently to the use of large canoes capable of carrying at least two persons, pelts, and supplies. When the Chipewyan first traded at

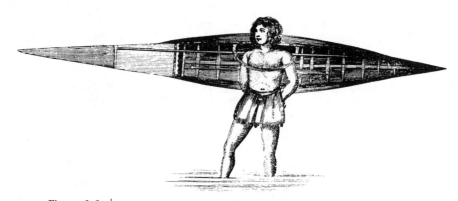

Figure 3-3. | A man carrying a small birch bark canoe in early historic times. (From Hearne 1796.)

Churchill, they arrived on foot. By the 1700s they were building small birch-bark canoes (see Figure 3-3), and by the 1790s they were using much larger canoes to travel in the summer.

EPIDEMICS AND FAMINES Early in their history, the Chipewyan abruptly lost much of their vitality as a result of exposure to new diseases. A severe smallpox epidemic struck in 1781, and an estimated 90 percent of the people died. In 1819, another smallpox epidemic "carried away whole bands" (Simpson 1938, 81). Thus, they had become a remnant people early in their history. Weakened by disease, they were less able to support themselves and more subject to famines. Another momentous change took place as a direct result of the fur trade. When they began to trap intensively, they spent less time hunting caribou and lived within a more tenuous economic system. They desired trade goods and trapped to obtain them but thereby deprived themselves of the opportunity to acquire their basic foods. Thus, if they did not take large numbers of fish and caribou at certain seasons, they faced starvation. Famines made devastating inroads into the vitality of the society; although famines were not new, they now occurred more often. At Fort Resolution in 1833 some "forty of the choicest hunters" died in a famine (Back 1836, 209), and between 1879 and 1881 "many died in hunger and misery."

CHANGES IN LEADERSHIP In aboriginal times the charismatic leader was respected because of his unique abilities, and a number of such individuals, among whom Matonabbee was an outstanding example, are reported. With the advent of the fur trade a different form of leadership developed. Traders preferred dealing with a group representative, not with individuals, and this led to the emergence of trading chiefs (see Figure 3-4). Traders strengthened a trading chief's standing by deferring to him and presenting him with clothing, medals, and a formal reception on his arrival at a post. By the late 1880s, the "chiefs"

Figure 3-4. | A 1913 photograph of Chief Squirrel, a Chipewyan trading chief. (Courtesy of the Canadian Museum of Civilization, neg. no. 26070.)

were distributing the meat of caribou and moose to whomever they chose, irrespective of the wishes of the men who killed the game, although the hunters personally kept the skins or pelts of animals. If this was the norm, we must conclude that a chief possessed authority and some form of power. By 1908 chiefs represented groups in dealings with officials of the federal Indian Affairs Branch, but, as we would expect, they were not very effective.

CHANGING STATUS OF DOGS It is insightful to consider the changing status of dogs among the Chipewyan. Recall that a doglike creature was thought to have fathered these people, and the dog, along with bears, wolves, and wolverine, had strong supernatural associations. In the 1820s the people were convinced by a powerful man that they should not use such closely related animals to do their work, and consequently they destroyed all of their dogs. For this reason, during the early period of contact the people had very few dogs or none at all. Apparently, dogs were not widely used as beasts of burden, nor did they pull toboggans, until sometime in the mid-1800s. Yet, Hearne mentioned that in his time dogs hauled birch poles as hunters moved into the Barrens. Certain taboos still surrounded dogs in the early 1930s. For example, dogs were not shot, and to feed a dog a moose head or bear intestines was thought to bring ill fortune.

CHANGES IN SUPERNATURAL BELIEFS   The unformalized supernatural system of the aboriginal Chipewyan population absorbed Cree concepts, and by the early 1800s they had borrowed the concept of manitou, a supernatural force that pervades the natural world. An evil manitou was blamed for sickness, disease, or bad luck. By 1908, some Chipewyan had learned many of the Cree folktales, including tales that involved a trickster-hero. In these accounts, one animal tricks another, or a supernatural force creates something, and thus becomes a mythological hero.

Dependence on caribou and fish continued, but the prohibitions surrounding the treatment of these species were far from balanced. It was noted that in aboriginal times precautions were necessary in setting fishnets or using fishhooks, yet early references to taboos surrounding caribou hunting are rare. The implication is that this animal could be taken adequately by existing means so that any ritual appeals were unnecessary. By the early 1940s taboos surrounding caribou were being recorded for the Chipewyan living along the eastern sector of Great Slave Lake. For example, if a woman's skirt were to pass over a hunting knife, there was fear that the caribou would not migrate in that direction during that year. A woman was supposed to pierce the caribou's eyeball before she butchered the carcass to prevent the spirit of the deceased animal from reporting its fate to others. The implication might be that these taboos emerged as caribou hunting became less dependable.

| Becoming Modern: Chipewyan at Snowdrift

The character and texture of Chipewyan life began to assume its contemporary form as the people abandoned seasonal camps to settle in villages. The first detailed study of emerging contemporary Chipewyan life was made by James W. VanStone at the community of Snowdrift. VanStone worked there from 1960 to 1962; his findings are presented here along with more recent information about the Snowdrift Chipewyan. Together they indicate the impact on one group of Chipewyan of increasing integration into the fabric of modern Canadian life along with a greater awareness of being Indian.

SNOWDRIFT HISTORY   The settlement of Snowdrift, beyond the margins of aboriginal Chipewyan territory, is in a forest setting along one of the many indentations on the southeastern shore of Great Slave Lake. The people of the area traditionally had traded at Fort Resolution, founded in 1786, but after the Hudson's Bay Company built a post at Snowdrift in 1925, local families began trading there to avoid long trips to distant stores. Yet, it was not until 1954 that most of the current population began to settle at Snowdrift. They did so in response to pressure from the federal Indian Affairs Branch agent at Yellowknife, who stressed the advantages of more sedentary living. In 1960 the village consisted of twenty-six predominantly log houses, Hudson's Bay Company buildings, a Roman Catholic church, and log cabins used seasonally by white sportfishermen and mining entrepreneurs.

The commitment to settled village life was a radical residential shift for these mobile caribou-hunters, and with it came far-reaching changes. The move to Snowdrift radically altered the accepted patterns of social and economic life. Many people now were clustered together, exploiting the same resources, and it became increasingly difficult to maintain their previous standard of living. Furthermore, they were under the control of federal agents, whereas previously these ties had been tenuous or absent. In studying this process of change it is essential to recognize that federal intervention was largely responsible for the new conditions.

THE SETTLEMENT   At Snowdrift, family dwellings had an air of permanence unknown in the recent past. About 1912 the first ridged commercial canvas tent was bought locally, and soon this style replaced the conical tent of old. After 1950 most families began to construct more substantial dwellings. The Indian agent obtained federal support for the construction or renovation of the cabins at Snowdrift. The Indians at first were reluctant to participate in the program since they were hesitant to commit themselves permanently to the village. Most of the dwellings were one-room log cabins with board floors. (See Figure 3-5.) The furnishings included homemade beds, chairs, tables, and shelves. Light was supplied by kerosene lamps, and heat was furnished by wood-burning sheet-iron stoves. A household inventory included trunks or bags for extra clothing and bedding, a battery-powered radio, a hand-operated sewing machine, and utensils. In nearby log storage sheds were frozen or dried fish, dog harnesses, outboard motor parts, traps, snowshoes, fishnets, and rifles. By 1976 nearly all families were living in substantial frame houses. Electric lights and stoves were powered with electricity from a central power plant. The houses had oil furnaces, and oil delivery as well as garbage service was provided. The solid dwellings, services provided, and proliferation of material goods made families increasingly sedentary and committed to Snowdrift. (See Figure 3-6.)

CLOTHING   Most garments were quite unlike aboriginal forms, although a few men wore hooded and sleeved caribou skin ponchos rather than manufactured parkas. From the Hudson's Bay Company store men bought long underwear, shirts, trousers, and sweaters. Women purchased briefs, cotton stockings, dresses, petticoats, shoes, skirts, and sweaters. The most important locally made items of aboriginal derivation were moccasins for men and skin slippers worn

Figure 3-5. | Chipewyan dwellings and a canoe in 1913. (Courtesy of the Canadian Museum of Civilization, neg. no. 26068.)

Figure 3-6. | The community of Snowdrift in 1976. (Photograph by the author.)

by women during the summer. Young girls wore clothing like that of the women, with the addition of slacks and colorful lightweight jackets. Young girls often curled their hair, and young women as well as girls wore lipstick. Young women used commercial perfumes and set off their appearance with brooches, earrings, and finger rings. Young men were particularly fond of wide leather belts with large buckles and short, ornamented, black leather jackets. The implication of the modern clothing styles is at once obvious. The people obtained most items from the store and needed to have something that the outside world valued for their purchase.

CONVEYANCES   In 1960 each Snowdrift family owned a large commercially made canoe, an outboard motor, and a small canvas-covered canoe. Although a form of toboggan existed, it was purchased from the store and was more correctly a cariole, for it had a rear panel and canvas sides. Dogs, not women, pulled the carioles. Each family owned about five dogs, which were chained near the homes. The use of dog teams and outboard motors as sources of power unquestionably had greatly increased the families' mobility. By 1976 the "iron dog" or snowmobile typically was being used for winter travel. This meant a further dependence on cash to buy a snowmobile and keep it in operation, with an accompanying decrease in the need to provide dogs with food. Likewise, the canvas canoes were being replaced by aluminum boats, which required a substantial cash outlay.

SUBSISTENCE ACTIVITIES   Traditional Chipewyan economic life had centered about caribou and fish, and these foci persisted with the addition of trapping furbearers. Even in 1960 most men did not hesitate to abandon their traplines if caribou appeared in the vicinity. The lure of the hunt remained strong, and as recently as 1930 hunting was more important to these Chipewyan than trapping. A trapper was obliged to hunt for food while on a trapline and took primarily hares, ptarmigan, or spruce hens. Likewise, he fished through the ice with a gill net for dog food. It took him one to three days of dog team travel to reach a trapline, and he set commercial steel traps or wire snares for lynx, marten, mink, white fox, and wolverine. Cross, red, or silver fox were not sought since their market value was very low. Trapping was difficult and was surrounded by many uncertainties. A trapper had to obtain enough food for himself and the dog team; wolverine sometimes ate the animals caught in sets or sprung a line of sets and removed the bait; a Canada jay, ermine, or other creature might spring a trap, and in addition, the working conditions on a trapline were difficult. A canvas trapping tent was small and impossible to heat adequately, and the men found it difficult to work alone for weeks on end. Their increasing tendency was to range from the village for only short periods during November and December when the pelts of most fur animals were in their prime.

Trapping was linked to the Hudson's Bay Company, for only at this store could a man exchange his furs for trade items. The account by Hearne of an

Indian's relationship with traders was in many ways similar to the observations by VanStone. The Indians attempted to outwit the trader and resorted to diverse subterfuges to obtain credit. In Indian eyes the only good traders were those concerned with Indian welfare. In spite of their opposing goals, the Indian and the trader were economically dependent on each other. The price of pelts was not very high; in 1959–60 the average take per trapper was worth about $320. Since white fox prices were relatively high, they were trapped conscientiously in the winter. The most important furbearer trapped in the spring was beaver, and there was a federal limit to an individual's take. In theory no man could take more than five animals, and each pelt was tagged before being exchanged at the store. Energetic trappers, however, bought unused tags issued to others and increased their take in this manner. When an Indian agent proposed the registration of traplines, the people opposed the suggestion because they felt it would further restrict their mobility. In the recent past a man had been accompanied by his entire family on a trapline, but often this was no longer possible because school-age children were obligated to attend classes. The income from trapping was not sufficient to meet subsistence needs, and by 1976 the yield from trapping was making no significant contribution to the welfare of the community as a whole. Thus, the one major contribution of these people to the worldwide economic system had ended and had not been replaced by an alternative.

In the early 1960s dependence on caribou was still great, and the late summer hunt was of prime importance. A household head felt that he required about one hundred caribou per year, yet harvests of this magnitude were no longer realized. The people traveled by large canoes to the Fort Reliance area for caribou, and if there were no animals available, they portaged east to the vicinity of Artillery Lake. Burdened by their families, large amounts of equipment, and big canoes, they were unable to reach the best hunting grounds. As a result they were not likely to kill many animals. The meat obtained was smoked and brought back to the village to be stored in the Indian Affairs Branch cold-storage unit. In 1960 nearly half of the households were unrepresented in the fall caribou hunt, although some families shared in the take of others because they had provided a hunting party with equipment.

In the late fall, men set nylon or cotton gill nets in the lake (see Figure 3-7) or along nearby rivers, and fitted them with stone sinkers, wooden floats, and large anchor stones at each end as in aboriginal times. They caught lake trout and whitefish most frequently, hung them out for partial drying, and then stored them as winter food for dogs and people.

Most men began to prefer wage labor jobs to hunting, fishing, and trapping. Few such positions existed, however, and most were temporary. Construction jobs were few after the community physical plant was completed; work on commercial fishing vessels was unpredictable and physically demanding. Fire fighting was sporadic and important but seasonal and recently was abandoned in this region. Serving as guides for tourist fishermen had yet to reach its full potential. Thus, making a living by wage labor was even more uncertain than following subsistence pursuits of old.

Figure 3-7. | A Snowdrift man checking a gill net set beneath lake ice in 1960. (Photograph by James W. VanStone, courtesy of the Field Museum of Natural History, Chicago.)

Aboriginal foods were increasingly replaced by purchased edibles. People preferred fish and meat with each meal, but since these often were unavailable, bannock became an important staple. Bannock ("Indian bread"), the standard fare of poor Eskimos and Indians throughout Alaska and Canada, is made of white flour and baking powder mixed with water into a paste and spread in a greased skillet to be fried. Often this was the only food at a meal; bannock and tea are the bread and water of depressed subarctic living. The dominant method of cooking was by boiling. When families were able, they purchased prepared foods from the store. The imported items most desired were flour, sugar, tea, coffee, crackers, peanut butter, canned meats and fruits, evaporated milk, and seasonings.

DESCENT, KINSHIP, AND MARRIAGE The people of Snowdrift traced their descent along both the female and male lines (bilateral descent), as they had in early historic times. Cousin terminology, however, was of the Eskimo type (similar to the current classification of cousins in the United States). Preferential cousin marriage no longer existed; in fact, people did not recall it as an aboriginal practice. The one hundred years of contact with Roman Catholic missionaries who spoke against cousin marriage probably had produced the change, yet premarital fornication between cousins prevailed.

When a person married, he or she was most likely to select a mate within the community (village endogamy), and immediately after marriage the couple lived with the in-laws who were best able to receive them (temporary bilocal residence). As soon as possible the couple built a separate dwelling and lived alone (neolocal residence). In 1961 most households were nuclear or nuclear core families, the latter being comprised of a nuclear family to which were added a near relative or two of the husband or wife. Plural marriages no longer existed, and capable providers did not attract followers who lived with them. The overall impression is that the nuclear family was still the most important social unit, although it was not as autonomous as before.

SOCIAL DIMENSIONS With subsistence activities and material culture changing so much from aboriginal times, we would expect and do find equally significant differences in other aspects of living. The old attitudes toward women and their harsh treatment as described by Hearne are not reported. Although VanStone was not explicit on the subject, he conveyed the impression that domestic harmony existed. Certain activities, such as food preparation and child raising, remained female obligations, but men performed these tasks when the need arose. Women could profit monetarily from their own labors. A woman who processed a moose or caribou hide or sewed skin garments for someone outside her family was paid directly and retained the profits. The favorable position of women at Snowdrift may have resulted from the fact that they were a distinct minority; for unknown reasons there were fewer young women than men. Since it was difficult to obtain a wife, she was treated with care. (See Figure 3-8.)

Social bonds beyond those based on kinship were new and of expanding importance. Village life produced feelings of unity, and people thought of themselves as economically, morally, and physically superior to persons in adjacent settlements. Other evidence for emerging village cohesion was the widespread sharing of locally available foods. By the time a successful moose hunter beached his boat he had given away most of the meat, and the same applied to a catch of fish. Food had been shared in aboriginal times, but apparently not in as pervasive or egalitarian a manner. Furthermore, an intensive pattern of reciprocal borrowing had developed, and this included major as well as minor items of material culture. These attitudes and their behavioral manifestations clearly were beginning to integrate the community on a social and economic basis.

POLITICAL LIFE The Snowdrift Chipewyan were included in Treaty Number 11, which was signed by the Indians in 1921 and provided them with direct monetary and other benefits. The Indians gave up their aboriginal rights to the land but at the same time were protected in their exploitation of local resources. In exchange, they received tangible benefits such as formal education, health services, and material goods. Each year a band member received a cash payment of five dollars, the band chief received twenty-five dollars, and counselors, fif-

Figure 3-8. | Snowdrift woman sitting in front of a smokehouse in 1976. (Photograph by the author.)

teen dollars each. The Indian Affairs Branch began to provide fishnets, ammunition, and items such as roofing and doors for house construction. Furthermore, families in need, as defined by the Indian agent, received a "ration" from the Indian Affairs Branch through the store. A national program of old-age assistance provided for the welfare of persons sixty-five years of age or older. Even more important was the "baby bonus," or Family Allowance, which was a national program. Every month, each family received six dollars for each child under ten and eight dollars for those ten through sixteen. The program was designed to improve child care, and it probably served this end at Snowdrift.

One result of living in a stable community was intensified contact with the Indian agent. Stationed at Yellowknife, he visited Snowdrift and called meetings on matters of villagewide concern. Attendance usually was poor, and it was difficult to conduct a general meeting because each Indian was inclined to raise issues of personal interest, usually specific requests for aid. Thus, the process of democratic group action failed. Unity, when it was manifested, consisted of a stand against a proposal rather than any positive approach. The Indians preferred to deal with the agent on a private, almost secret basis, concerning specific requests. They felt that an agent was in a position to grant favors, and for him not to do so was regarded as pure stubbornness.

Visits to the village by the Royal Canadian Mounted Police (RCMP) in the 1960s were more a show of power than the result of actual need. Crimes as defined in the Canadian legal system were rare, and the most common cause for arrest was the manufacture of home brew. Since everyone was secretive when making home brew and avoided being seen intoxicated when the police were present, few arrests were made. The Indians felt that it was wrong to appeal to Canadian legal authorities for the settlement of personal disputes, and they rarely did so, although they might threaten such action.

In 1960 the bands were reorganized to make allowance for the physical movements of people from one band to another. Under the reorganization, Snowdrift Indians had their own chief and two counselors or advisors. The Indians had a clear formulation of what they considered to be ideal behavior for a chief: he did not interfere in the affairs of villagers, but he adopted a stern attitude toward Euro-Canadians in general and toward the Indian agent in particular. Whites, by contrast, expected a chief to be cooperative; if he was not, they bypassed him and acted through the trader or teacher. This pattern by whites of accomplishing their purposes undermined Indian authority and contradicted the purpose of having a chief, counselors, and recognized Indian authorities.

For years the Canadian government encouraged the development of local political power at the band level. However, in 1969 federal administrative obligations shifted largely to the government of the Northwest Territories, and this government fostered the democratic process through local settlement councils that were in direct competition with the band. Furthermore, a regional native rights organization became increasingly militant in fostering Indian interests. These competing institutions above all else intensified local factionalism and divided the community in terms of effective political action.

RELIGION AND SUPERNATURALISM   Everyone at Snowdrift was a participating but nominal Roman Catholic. The priest serving the village was stationed at Fort Resolution and visited the settlement frequently throughout the year. He sometimes stayed two months at a time, and he always was present during the Christmas and Easter seasons. Church dogma and belief were understood poorly by the people, but participation in formal ceremonies was high. In general, the Church was regarded as something beyond the context of daily living. The Indians felt that the Church was wealthy and that people should be paid for any labor performed on its behalf. Thus, the feeling of belonging to a church and strengthening its purposes was not understood by the members. Interestingly enough, it was in the supernatural sphere that Indians admitted openly that they were different from whites. The concept of a "bush man" prevailed here as it did among other Northern Athapaskans. In their conceptualization, this creature was a man who wore manufactured shoes and appeared at a distance during the summer. He kidnapped children, but apparently he did not harm adults as long as they remained beyond his reach. The Indians believed that certain supernatural beings could harm them but did not affect whites. They also held beliefs about trapping practices, but these were unknown by whites.

The curing of physical illness had passed out of the hands of shamans, who no longer existed, into the domain of the Indian and Northern Health Services and a lay dispenser, usually the Hudson's Bay Company manager. If a case was considered serious, the nurse at Yellowknife was contacted, and she decided what course of action was to be followed. This nurse, sometimes accompanied by a medical doctor, visited the village at intervals. These Indians were concerned about their health but did not use patent medicines or turn freely to Euro-Canadians for aid. They seemed to enjoy talking about their aches and pains, but they sought treatment only when they were quite ill.

ENTERTAINMENT   Square dancing was a popular pastime, and the steps probably had been learned from commercial fishermen, who often stopped for a few days of relaxation during the summer. Men played guitars or violins and learned dance music by listening to village phonographs or broadcasts from the Yellowknife radio station. The square dances were called expertly by village men, and participation at dances was good. Less formal entertainment included nightly card games, which were extremely popular, particularly blackjack and gin rummy. Men and women often played together, and the stakes ranged from small change and ammunition to three-dollar hands in gin rummy games if men were affluent. While adults were playing cards, children sometimes gambled by pitching coins to a line. The hand game of old was known but seldom played; card games were considered more exciting. (See Figure 3-9.)

The consumption of alcohol was as much a ritual as a form of entertainment, and prescribed drinking patterns rarely were ignored. The only alcoholic beverage regularly consumed was home brew, produced from yeast, raisins, sugar, and water. It was made secretly by two or three men and allowed to age

Figure 3-9. | A summer card game at Snowdrift circa 1960. (Photograph by James W. VanStone, courtesy of the Field Museum of Natural History, Chicago.)

for about twenty-four hours. It was thought better if it aged longer, but anticipation negated the possibility. The men drank the brew in the home of one of the makers or in the brush during the summer, and the object was to become intoxicated. A man would dip a cup into the three-gallon pail, drink the beverage, and pass the cup to the next participant. Normally, some brew was stored in bottles, to be consumed after the brew pail had been drained. When participants became reasonably intoxicated, they visited one house after another, regardless of the time, and drank as they chatted with their reluctant hosts. Sometimes they offered to share their brew, but this was not consistent. The conversations of intoxicated men were about village life, and they became more outgoing during drinking sprees than at any other time of their adult lives. By 1976, home brew had become far less popular than in the recent past. It had largely been replaced by intoxicants imported from the Yellowknife liquor store.

INCREASING DEPENDENCY In a study of folktales, Cohen and VanStone (1963) explored the nature of Chipewyan self-sufficiency and dependency. They analyzed early twentieth-century tales recorded among these people and compared them with original stories written by Chipewyan children in 1961; a sample of Grimm's fairy tales served as control material. As a basis of analysis the authors assumed that "taken broadly, self-sufficiency and dependency refer to a basic and universal quality of all human social experience, namely, action by ego which affects his environment, i.e., self-assertiveness or self-sufficiency, and action directed towards ego over which he has no control, i.e., dependency." Different social systems would be expected to exhibit both qualities in varying proportions. An analysis of Grimm's fairy tales reflected the Protestant ethic and exhibited a high degree of self-sufficiency. The folktales of the Chipewyan exhibited about equal proportions of self-sufficiency and dependency, suggesting that these people had established a balance in their relationship with the environment. An increase in dependency, reflected in the children's stories, suggested two alternative but not mutually exclusive explanations. Either federal welfare programs had made the Chipewyan less capable and less desirous of caring for themselves, or the contact situation had caused them to feel that their efforts to affect the environment were more likely to fail than to succeed.

| Contemporary Developments: Stagnation or New Vitality?

In the early 1960s, VanStone characterized these people as moving toward the stagnation of deculturation. They had lost most of their old design for living and had been unable to replace it with a Euro-Canadian model. This pattern was especially evident in the economic sphere since trapping had only partially replaced the subsistence-based life-style and the existing combination did not provide a satisfactory standard of living. This led VanStone to use such terms as *poor white* and *lower class*. The depressed standard of living at Snowdrift indicated that these people were at the fringe of modern developments in the north. They not only lacked technical skills and formal education, but they had not made the changes in their values that would lead to an improved living standard. Therefore, the more rewarding local jobs went to white Canadians. These Indians might, as Jacob Fried (1963) has suggested, become an increasingly depressed economic class in Canadian society. (See Figure 3-10.)

The effects of changes begun in the late 1950s have become increasingly clear. By the mid-1970s the government had created a comfortable physical environment at Snowdrift when judged by Euro-Canadian standards. The houses were well built, heated with oil, and supplied with electricity. (See Figure 3-11.) Water was delivered and sewage picked up. Nursing station personnel provided local health care, and a community hall had been built. Yet, the Snowdrift Chipewyan had comparatively little confidence in their own abilities and little purpose to guide their lives. One reason was that they felt they lacked an effective voice in decisions about their future. Regional officials of the government of the Northwest Territories at Fort Smith controlled their destiny. The people were accustomed to responding to proposals rather than initiating them. With a commitment to settled village life their previous hunting and trapping economy had nearly disappeared. They had a sense of community identity when dealing with outsiders, but their primary loyalties were to family groups.

Each of the three dominant extended families was represented on the settlement council charged with running local affairs, but they only acted in crisis situations. A major stumbling block was that most council members did not

Figure 3-10. | Girls at Snowdrift in 1976. (Photograph by the author.)

Figure 3-11. | Snowdrift house and tepee in 1976. (Photograph by the author.)

really understand what was expected of them in relation to governmental agencies. When "day trippers," government officials who chartered aircraft to visit for less than a day, visited Snowdrift to explain their programs firsthand, the people listened, but they did not really comprehend. To admit that they did not understand was thought degrading; thus, they agreed without an appreciation of the matter before them.

The Chipewyan of Snowdrift are acutely aware of their economic dilemma, especially after a major source of cash, fire fighting, was discontinued. The council in its most concerted effort tried to have the local area opened for commercial fishing in 1976. They were attempting to break their dependency relationship with the government by initiating a development program of their own, to which government officials were sympathetic. The people did obtain funds for their own commercial fishing operation with boats and other support from the government. However, the enterprise failed, partially because those involved had little business experience and did not follow sound management practices.

By 1982 the Snowdrift population was 257, and community income from varied sources was far less than that of any other settlement in the region. Comparatively small amounts of cash circulated at Snowdrift because few employment opportunities existed locally. Fighting forest fires provided intermittent but unreliable summer employment, and as many as twenty men might work as guides for tourists fishing in the vicinity. One major change in the local economy was the closing of the Hudson's Bay Company store in 1973. The physical plant was bought by a private party from outside the community, but his holdings soon were purchased by the government, which opened a cooperative store. By 1980 the people not only had their own store, but it was beginning to show a profit.

Formal education has emerged as an increasingly visible aspect of village life. A new school was built at Snowdrift in 1985. Parents have taken an expanded interest in the content of the courses offered, and children's attendance has increased. (See Figure 3-12.) However, a high school education can be obtained only by leaving the village and attending boarding school. Some parents are reluctant to permit their children to make this step away from home.

By the mid-1980s the people of Snowdrift and interested outsiders felt that the consumption of alcoholic beverages was the major social problem facing the community. There had been a prohibition on the making of home brew, purchasing, or drinking of alcoholic beverages for about ten years, but alcohol-related incidents remained a problem. During the winter of 1984–85, five persons died returning to the village on snowmobiles after purchasing intoxicants at Yellowknife. These deaths were a severe blow to the community and led to a re-evaluation of alcohol consumption. By the end of the year no home brew was being made, and the importation of intoxicants had ceased. Whether effective prohibition will continue is unknown. One promising sign is that the people have begun to enjoy social dances and other organized community activities without drinking.

One of the most controversial issues of recent years is a federal govern-

Figure 3-12. | Darcy Catholique, a Snowdrift Chipewyan boy, with his toy car. (Photograph by Judith Jacob, 1985.)

ment proposal to create a national park at the eastern end of Great Slave Lake. The people most affected by the park would be the residents of Snowdrift. The federal government has taken the position that the park will not be created if the Snowdrift band members oppose it. In general, the community members do not trust the government and have little faith in the promises it has made in the past. Therefore, their opposition is a foregone conclusion. Fieldworkers have visited Snowdrift to present the government side of the case, but no decision has been made.

| Additional Readings

The information provided by Birket-Smith, Hearne, and VanStone has been emphasized in describing the Chipewyan. A careful examination of the impact of the fur trade on these people is found in the article by J. C. Yerbury (1976). The reader interested in details about early historic Chipewyan material culture and ecological adjustments for the eastern bands should consult the work by Birket-Smith (1930); yet, it is clear that there were, and are, many regional variations in Chipewyan culture. For comparisons with life at Snowdrift, an article by David M. Smith (1976) deals with the Chipewyan at Fort Resolution in ecological contexts, and a monograph by the same author (1973) considers historic changes in religious beliefs at the same settlement. The economic round of the

Chipewyan at Patuanak in northern Saskatchewan is developed fully in articles by Robert Jarvenpa (1976, 1977, 1982). An appreciation of the problems raised by generalizing about Chipewyan kinship terminology is set forth by Henry S. Sharp (1975), and in another publication he examines marriage patterns (1979).

The reader interested in learning more about varied Northern Athapaskan tribes will find the definitive study by VanStone, *Athapaskan Adaptations* (1974), most helpful. The Chipewyan article in the *Subarctic* volume (6) of the *Handbook of North American Indians,* William C. Sturtevant, general editor, (Washington, DC, 1981), provides an overview of these people as well as a comparison between them and neighboring tribes.

For additional ethnographic sources dealing with the Chipewyan and all the other peoples considered in the chapters to follow, the interested reader should consult the ethnographic bibliography by George P. Murdock and Timothy J. O'Leary (1975).

| Bibliography

Back, George. 1836. *Narrative of the Arctic Land Expedition.* London.

Birket-Smith, Kaj. 1930. *Contributions to Chipewyan ethnology.* Report of the Fifth Thule Expedition, vol. 6, no. 3. The bulk of the information in this volume applies only to the Churchill-area Chipewyan as they were in 1923 and as the past was reconstructed with the aid of informants. The descriptive emphasis is on material culture; other aspects of culture and society are incompletely described. In spite of its shortcomings, this study is second only to Hearne's work in importance.

Blanchet, Guy H. 1946. Emporium of the North. *Beaver,* Outfit 276:32–35.

Campbell, Marjorie W. 1957. *The North West Company.* Toronto.

Cohen, Ronald, and James W. VanStone. 1963. Dependency and self-sufficiency in Chipewyan stories. National Museum of Canada Bulletin no. 194, 29–55.

Curtis, E. S. 1928. *The North American Indian,* vol. 18. Norwood.

Eggan, Fred, ed. 1937. *Social anthropology of North American tribes.* Chicago.

Franklin, John. 1823. *Narrative of a journey to the shores of the Polar Sea.* London.

Fried, Jacob. 1963. Settlement types and community organization in northern Canada. *Arctic* 16:93–100.

Gillespie, Beryl C. 1970. Yellowknives: Quo Iverunt? *Proceedings of the 1970 Annual Spring Meeting of the American Ethnological Society,* Robert F. Spencer, ed., 61–71.

———. 1976. Changes in territory and technology of the Chipewyan. *Arctic Anthropology,* 13:6–11.

Hearne, Samuel. 1795. *A journey from Prince of Wales' Fort in Hudson's Bay to the Northern Ocean.* London. (Also published 1796, Dublin. Two more recent, noteworthy editions of this work have appeared. The earlier was edited by Joseph B. Tyrell and published by the Champlain Society in 1911, and the second was edited by Richard Glover and published by the Macmillan Company of Canada in 1958.) Hearne's book is the standard source on the Chipewyan as they lived soon after historic contact. It is indispensable reading for any serious attempt to understand the culture of these Indians.

Jarvenpa, Robert. 1976. Spatial and ecological factors in the annual economic cycle of the English River band of Chipewyan. *Arctic Anthropology* 13:43–69.

————. 1977. Subarctic trappers and band society. *Human Ecology* 5:223–59.

————. 1982. Intergroup behavior and imagery. *Ethnology* 21:283–99.

Jenness, Diamond, ed. 1956. The Chipewyan Indians: An account by an early explorer. *Anthropologica* 3:15–33. This article contains abstracts of the Chipewyan information from a previously unpublished manuscript probably written by John Macdonell in the early 1800s. The descriptions are very good and provide a supplement to Hearne.

King, Richard. 1836. *Narrative of a journey to the shores of the Arctic Ocean.* 2 vols. London.

Lowie, Robert H. 1909. The Chipewyans of Canada. *Southern Workman* 38:278–83.

————. 1909. An ethnological trip to Lake Athabasca. *American Museum Journal* 9:10–15.

————. 1959. *Robert H. Lowie, ethnologist, a personal record.* Berkeley and Los Angeles.

MacNeish, June H. 1956. Leadership among the Northeastern Athabascans. *Anthropologica* 2:131–63. Historical sources are evaluated and the Chipewyan discussed along with other Canadian Athapaskans. The major contribution of this paper is a classification of leadership patterns in aboriginal and historic times.

————. 1960. Kin terms of arctic drainage Dene: Hare, Slavey, Chipewyan. *American Anthropologist* 62:279–95.

Mason, John A. 1946. *Notes on the Indians of the Great Slave Lake area.* Yale University Publications in Anthropology, no. 34. New Haven.

Munsterhjelm, Erik. 1953. *The wind and the caribou.* London.

Murdock, George P., and Timothy J. O'Leary. 1975. *Ethnographic bibliography of North America.* 5 vols. New Haven.

Penard, Jean M. 1929. Land ownership and chieftaincy among the Chippewayan and Caribou-Eaters. *Primitive Man* 2:20–24.

Petitot, Emile. 1884. On the Athabasca district of the Northwest. *Canadian Record of Science* 1:27–53.

Rich, Edwin E. 1960. *Hudson's Bay Company, 1670–1870.* 3 vols. Toronto.

Richardson, Richard. 1854. *Arctic searching expedition.* New York.

Robinson, J. 1944. Among the Caribou-Eaters. *Beaver,* Outfit 275:38–41.

Robson, Joseph. 1752. *An account of six years' residence in Hudson's Bay.* London.

Ross, Bernard. 1867. Notes on the Tinneh or Chepewyan Indians of British and Russian America: The Eastern Tinneh. *Smithsonian Institution Annual Report, 1866,* 304–11.

Russell, Frank. 1898. *Explorations in the Far North.* University of Iowa.

Seton, Ernest T. 1911. *The arctic prairies.* New York.

Sharp, Henry S. 1975. Introducing the sororate to a northern Saskatchewan Chipewyan village. *Ethnology* 14:71–82.

————. 1979. *Chipewyan marriage.* Mercury Series, Canadian Ethnology Service Paper, no. 58. Ottawa.

Simpson, George. 1938. *Journal of occurrences in the Athabasca department, 1820 and 1821.* Publications of the Champlain Society, Hudson's Bay Company Series, no. 1.

Smith, David M. 1973. *INKONZE: Magico-religious beliefs of contact-tradition Chipewyan trading at Fort Resolution, NWT, Canada.* Mercury Series, Ethnology Division Paper, no. 6. National Museum of Man, Ottawa.

————. 1976. Cultural and ecological change: The Chipewyan of Fort Resolution. *Arctic Anthropology* 13:35–42.

Smith, James G. E. 1970. The Chipewyan hunting group in a village context. *Western Canadian Journal of Anthropology* 1:60–66.

————. 1976a. Introduction: The historical and cultural position of the Chipewyan. *Arctic Anthropology* 13:1–5.

————. 1976b. Local band organization of the caribou eater Chipewyan. *Arctic Anthropology* 13:12–24.

Tache, Alexander A. 1870. *Sketch of the North-West of America.* Montreal.

Tyrrell, Joseph B., ed. 1916. *David Thompson's narrative.* Publications of the Champlain Society, vol. 12.

VanStone, James W. 1961. *The economy of a frontier community.* Northern Coordination and Research Centre, Department of Northern Affairs and National Resources.

————. 1963. Changing patterns of Indian trapping in the Canadian subarctic. *Arctic* 16:159–74.

————. 1965. *The changing culture of the Snowdrift Chipewyan.* National Museum of Canada Bulletin no. 209. This report and the preceding one contain most of the reliable information on the modern Chipewyan. Although the data are limited in scope to the community of Snowdrift, the generalizations most probably have wider applicability for other Chipewyan populations.

————. 1974. *Athapaskan adaptations.* Chicago.

Yerbury, J. C. 1976. The post-contact Chipewyan. *Ethnohistory* 23:237–63.

4 The Kuskowagamiut: Riverine Eskimos

When someone has something that is particularly good to eat they take a pinch of it and toss it away, saying "to the dead people who we love the most."

Offerings to the dead according to an old man. (Oswalt field notes)

ESKIMOS* MOST OFTEN are regarded as a happy people who wear skin clothing, hunt seals, live in snowhouses, munch on raw meat, and count wife-sharing among their customs. This characterization is unfair to Eskimos as a whole because the customs of many groups were and are quite different from this stereotype. At the time of first contact with whites, nearly half of all Eskimos lived in southwestern Alaska, where salmon, not seals, were the most important food. They never lived in snowhouses, seldom ate raw meat, and more important, had far more complicated customs than those usually associated with Eskimos. I have chosen to describe the Kuskowagamiut to show that more diversity exists in Eskimo culture than generally is recognized. The Kuskowagamiut depended on salmon for food; not only were these fish predictable in their movements, but also great numbers of them literally swam next to Eskimo settlements. Thus, we have a clear contrast in subsistence base between this group and the one depicted in the accepted stereotype. Further differences between these Eskimos and others will become apparent as we examine the Kuskowagamiut culture in detail.

People, Population, and Language

In the manner of Alaskan Eskimos in general, those living along the Kuskokwim River in the southwestern sector had recognized boundaries (see Figure 4-1) and a group name, the Kuskowagamiut, but their dialect was shared by other Eskimos in the region. No one is certain of their aboriginal population total, but an early Russian explorer estimated their number at seven thousand, which seems reasonable. These people possibly numbered about three thousand in 1880, but the population had declined to about six hundred by 1910, largely as a result of epidemics. Their number has increased steadily since 1920 and approached fifty-five hundred in 1986.

The Kuskowagamiut and all other Alaskan Eskimos southward from the vicinity of Nome spoke a language called Yupik, which had three dialects (Central, Pacific Gulf, and Siberian). Kuskokwim Eskimos were Central Yupik speakers. The early historic Yupik population total may have been about twenty-nine thousand, including two thousand in Siberia. In Alaska north of Nome and extending across Canada to Greenland, the Eskimos were Inupik speakers with relatively minor dialectic differences, and they may have numbered about thirty thousand. In linguistic terms, Inupik and Yupik belong to the Eskimo-Aleut language family and the American Arctic-Paleosiberian linguistic phylum.

---

*Canadian Eskimos and numerous white Canadians are adamant that Eskimos be called Inuit, their name for themselves, and not Eskimo. In this book, *Eskimo* is used as the generic designation of these northern peoples because all Eskimos are *not* Inuit; many who live in Alaska and small numbers in Siberia are Yuit, a designation comparable to Inuit yet distinct from it. Therefore, to use the word *Inuit* for Eskimos in general is incorrect. The Kuskowagamiut call themselves Yuit.

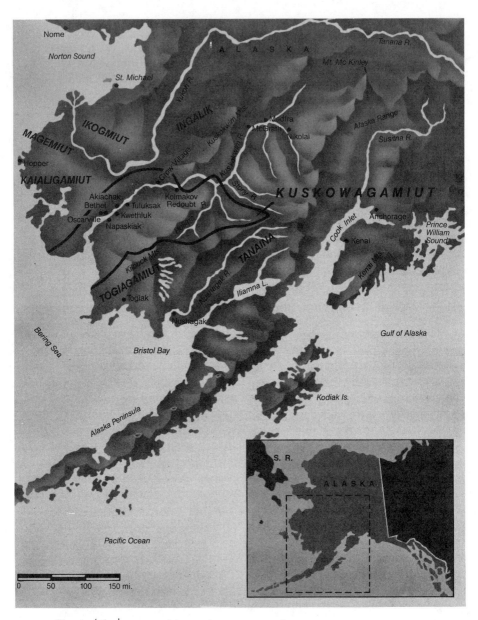

Figure 4-1. | Range of the Kuskowagamiut Eskimos.

Differences among Eskimos

As suggested in Chapter 1, the concept of culture areas often masks, or ignores, significant local and regional differences among the people in a single culture area. This failing of the classification system is well illustrated by the differences among tribes in the Eskimo culture area. They all subsisted on fish and game, had few if any political leaders, and depended on shamans to intercede with supernatural forces. Yet, beyond shared characteristics such as these, many significant contrasts prevailed. For example, diverse kinds of settlements existed in early historic times, and food-getting activities varied widely. In one sector of east Greenland the Eskimos occupied communal houses built of wood, stone, and turf, and there was a single house per settlement. Here the people subsisted primarily by hunting seals from kayaks. Eskimos in central Canada lived on the sea ice in snowhouses most of the year and hunted seals at their breathing holes in the ice. They moved about frequently as small family groups and had no permanent settlements. Eskimos along the northern coast of Alaska maintained permanent villages and built houses of wood and turf; a number of small families lived in each house. They hunted great whales, seals, and walrus; whale hunting in particular required cooperation and coordination of effort. Additional differences in food-getting patterns prevailed among Eskimos, and contrasts in dependability, abundance, and distribution of food resources led to divergences in social life, leadership, and religious behavior from the basic patterns that they shared. Thus, what was typical of some Eskimos was unheard of among others.

First Contacts with Fur Traders

The first direct contacts between Kuskokwim Eskimos and outsiders were with fur traders. In 1819 Russians founded Alexander Redoubt (modern Nushagak), their first settlement along a Bering Sea drainage. From here the Russian-American Company hoped to expand its beaver trade farther north. Eskimos from inland areas north of the redoubt or fort brought many pelts to the Nushagak station. During the summer of 1830, Ivan F. Vasilev, an ensign in the Pilot's Corps, led a small party up a Nushagak River tributary, over a divide to the Holitna River, down the Kuskokwim to its mouth, and back to Alexander Redoubt. Because Vasilev reported favorably on the fur resources of the Kuskokwim, the company built Kolmakov Redoubt as a year-round post along the central Kuskokwim in 1841. The redoubt was operated by the Russians until 1866, when they withdrew in anticipation of the purchase of Alaska by the United States.

Aboriginal Kuskowagamiut Life

Early ethnographic accounts allow us to piece together the following portrait of aboriginal Kuskowagamiut life.

ORIGIN MYTH   No known traditions account for Eskimo movements to the Kuskokwim River system, but one myth does explain the origins of the people, the land, and its configurations. The tale reports that in primeval times the only creature in existence was Raven. He flew about in darkness without a place to land until he grew so weary that he created land in order to rest. He became discontented because his creations could not be seen, and so he went off to find the sun. As he returned to earth with it, some light was detached and formed the Milky Way; the holes burned in the sky by the sun became stars. Once Raven saw the bleakness of his creation he made mountains and valleys, caused plants to grow, and made all the rivers flow into the sea. In order to share the world with others he created animals, birds, and fish. Raven's effort to make people of stone failed, and so he created them from mud. He created spirits to govern all living things, and if people were to prosper, they could not offend these spirits.

APPEARANCE AND CLOTHING   The Kuskowagamiut are relatively short in stature, with long trunks but short legs. The men are lean and muscular, but the women may be plump. Eskimos, the most Mongoloid of New World aboriginal populations, have extremely high cheekbones, distinct epicanthic folds, and shovel-shaped incisor teeth, all reflections of a clear racial affinity with Asian populations. The people are dark-skinned only on their faces and hands where they color deeply from weathering. Many men have rather heavy beards, but in aboriginal times whiskers were removed with tweezers. They wore their hair either long over the shoulders or tonsured with bangs over the face. Women did not cut their hair and might gather it together at the back. They often strung small glass beads, obtained in trade from Siberia before direct contact was made with the Russians, on a sinew and inserted it through a hole in the nasal septum. They usually had pierced ears from which earrings or strings of beads were hung. Likewise, their faces were tattooed from the lower lip to the chin, and they wore one or more labrets, or lip plugs, beneath the lower lip. (See Figure 4-2.) Men wore a medial labret or lateral ones beneath the lower lip, but they were not tattooed.

The winter garment most typical for both sexes was a loose-fitting sleeved parka reaching the calves or ankles, made from ground-squirrel skins with the claws and tails often attached. (See Figure 4-3.) The parkas of women were hooded, frequently trimmed with caribou hair and fur strips, and split up the sides; men's parkas were hoodless and had no slits in the sides. A man protected his neck from the cold with a bearskin collar sewn onto the neck opening of his parka, and he wore a head cover of skin or fur. Men apparently wore short caribou-skin undertrousers in addition to their skin trousers that reached just below the knees. They wore socks of caribou skin or woven grass inside knee-length caribou-skin boots with sealskin soles. Women preferred sealskin boots that reached the hips. Both men and women wore caribou-skin mittens. Garments intended for summer use included rain parkas made from sewn strips of intestine or from fish skins. These parkas were hooded and probably reached below the knees. During rainy weather, people also wore fish-skin boots of varied lengths and fish-skin socks.

Figure 4-2. | An 1884 photograph of a woman with beads suspended from a hole in her nasal septum and a labret beneath her lower lip. (Courtesy of the Moravian Archives, Bethlehem, PA.)

LAND, SETTLEMENTS, AND TECHNOLOGY The Kuskowagamiut lived along the central and lower Kuskokwim River, which is broad and gently flowing in the area that they occupied. The lower river and estuary land is low and laced with diverging waterways, lakes, and ponds. In unprotected areas a tundra vegetation flourishes, but in depressions sheltered from the wind dense willow thickets, rare stands of birch trees, and dwarfed spruce manage to grow. Animal species of economic importance were caribou, muskrat, mink, hare, and river otter. Farther upstream the tundra is less common, and spruce growths become denser. As the central sector is reached, higher hills are encountered, and soon hills and low mountains front the river. Animals along the central river include black bear in addition to the species known along the lower river. Migratory waterfowl pass through the country in the spring and again in the fall, while spruce hens and ptarmigan live in the region throughout the year. Salmon contributed the most

Figure 4-3. | An 1880 illustration of men in long squirrel-skin parkas. The parka of the man on the left is adorned with pieces of cloth and squirrel tails. The other man has his parka bottom held up with a belt around his waist, which was the custom when walking. (From Petroff 1884.)

Figure 4-4. | A settlement photographed in 1884, with houses and caches in the background. In the foreground is a sled for portaging kayaks, with kayaks resting on supports behind it. (Courtesy of the Moravian Archives, Bethlehem, PA.)

to economic welfare, and the most important species were king (chinook), dog (chum), red (sockeye), and silver (coho). In the main river, lakes, and sloughs, blackfish, burbot, northern pike, and whitefish abound at certain seasons. The only other fish of importance are smelt, which ascend the lower river to spawn in the early spring and were taken in dip nets.

Settlements, whether large or small, were built where there was ready access to food resources, especially salmon. Adult women, their daughters, and young sons occupied the houses. These dwellings looked like mounds of dirt because they were built partially beneath the ground and were covered with sod. (See Figure 4-4.) The main room was built in a rectangular excavation extending about fifteen feet in the longer direction. An upright post was placed about six feet away from each corner, and beams were set on top of these posts to join them. A row of wall logs extended from the outer edges of the excavation to the tops of the beams on each side, and the low roof was made with split logs. An opening was left in the center for a skylight, and the removable wood frame fitted there was covered with sewn fish skins or animal intestines. Except for the skylight opening, the entire structure was covered with dry grass and then with sod. Beneath the skylight was a fireplace where meals were cooked, and smoke from the wood fire drifted out through the opening. A house generally included a wood-framed anteroom and a passage that led to the main room; the passage prevented cold air from entering the living area. Around the walls of the main room were low benches covered with grass, grass matting, and animal skins for sleeping; a floor area of dirt surrounded the fireplace.

To a non-Eskimo the odor inside a house would have been its most striking feature. The smells of stale urine, skin clothing that was never cleaned, and dried salmon made a pungent combination. The interior was relatively dark because of the accumulated soot on the walls and ceiling, but some light penetrated the translucent window. This covering was set aside during warm days for still more light from outside. Artificial light came from the fireplace or from bowl-shaped clay lamps. The lamps were placed on stands in front of the rear bench or at the edge of a side bench. Oil, preferably seal oil, burned on a wick of moss. The central floor space was filled with cups, food trays, wooden water buckets, and pottery cooking vessels. Common household items included a woman's sewing equipment in a neatly folded leather container, her semilunar slate-bladed knife or ulu, wooden cutting boards, chipped and ground stone scrapers for processing skins, and awls.

The men's house or *kashgee* was the home of most adult males and older boys. The largest building in a village, this structure served as a bathhouse, ceremonial chamber, and workshop. A large kashgee might measure as much as thirty feet on a side. The walls were made of planks and split logs set vertically, and the roof was cribbed. Access was through a tunnel either at ground level or beneath it, and some men's houses had both varieties of entrance. The floor of a kashgee was covered with planks except for an area some four feet square at the center. Here was a fire pit that could be planked over when not in use, and above the fire pit was a skylight. Kashgee furnishings included two or three tiers of benches around the walls and at least two large bowl-shaped oil-burning lamps to provide artificial light.

Inside a kashgee were all of the tools and equipment used by the men. Conspicuously absent were cooking vessels and eating containers, for these were brought in by females at mealtime and removed after the men and boys had eaten. The most important woodworking tools included the ubiquitous crooked knife, wedges, mauls for driving wedges, slate-bladed adzes, whetstones, and engraving tools. Near each man's assigned position on a bench were his sinew-backed bow and arrows, spears, and other weapons. Hanging from the ceiling on exhibit until a later ceremony were the bladders of animals and the stuffed skins of birds and small animals.

Scattered about a settlement were pits in which stored salmon heads became headcheese and other pits for preserving silver salmon caught so late in the season that they could not be dried. Salmon taken earlier were sun-dried and placed in caches erected on four posts. A wooden platform built on the posts supported a rectangular wooden structure with a gabled plank roof and an oval entrance facing the front. (See Figure 4-5.) Inside a cache were stored dried or frozen fish, herbs, and equipment such as snowshoes and nets. Sleds often were stored on the cache platform beyond the reach of hungry dogs who would eat the lashings.

Figure 4-5. | Women photographed in front of a cache in 1907. Smelt are drying on the pole. (Courtesy of the University Museum, Philadelphia.)

CONVEYANCES From late spring until late fall these people traveled almost exclusively by water, using rivers and sloughs as well as lakes. In the lower river area, each man owned a kayak made by covering a driftwood frame with dehaired sealskins. An extended family unit owned a large, open skin boat or umiak. Along the central river both forms were used in addition to a small type of canoe covered with birch bark and decked a short distance fore and aft. The only other vessel was an improvised umiak made by hunters after animals had been killed. Fresh skins stretched over a rude wooden frame served to carry meat and men from a distant hunting camp to a settlement.

The usual winter conveyance was a wooden sled. The bed was built up on stanchions mortised and bound to the bed and runners with babiche (thin, dehaired caribou-skin strips). Sleds with low flat beds were used to carry umiaks over the snow to spring camps. A small but similar type of sled was carried on the aft section of a kayak or canoe and served to portage the vessel from one lake or slough to the next. Finally, snowshoes were essential for traveling overland when the snow was deep and not crusted, conditions that prevailed in timbered areas. Here snowshoes were long with light birch frames webbed with babiche; elsewhere snowshoes were crude and often improvised.

The lower river families went to their fall camps by umiak before the lakes and flowing waters froze or else waited until after freeze-up and traveled by dogsled. Three or four dogs were harnessed to a sled by attaching individual towlines to stanchions at the sides, a highly inefficient hitching method. In all likelihood, a man pushed at the rear of a sled as women and children pulled in front. Not until about twenty years after the arrival of the Russians were dogs harnessed tandem at the front of a sled as in eastern Siberia.

HOUSEHOLD ACTIVITIES   In a strict sense, household life focused narrowly on females since the only males present were young boys. A man lived with his wife and all their unmarried children only at tundra camps and at summer fish camps maintained away from a village. Ideally, daughters remained with their mothers after they had married and raised the next generation of children in the same house. Only when the number of females overcrowded a dwelling or when a house became uninhabitable did they move. A line of females lived in lifelong intimacy; similarly, males were more closely associated with others of their own sex. The normal obligations of women in these close-knit domestic units included the preparation and processing of food, caring for children, manufacturing and repairing clothing, picking berries and a few other plant products, and collecting firewood. Men were expected to provide their wives with fish, fowl, and land mammals, but their duty did not extend beyond bringing such items to the settlement. Once a harvest was at hand, a man's wife had total responsibility for and control over its preparation and distribution.

DESCENT, KINSHIP, AND MARRIAGE   Aboriginal Kuskowagamiut marriage and residence patterns have been reconstructed from comparatively recent sources, and the accounts may not be entirely correct. These people appear to have attempted to arrange marriages within a community (village endogamy). Since households were comprised of female lines, this meant that a man became associated with his wife's natal unit (matrilocal residence) whether he had been raised in her settlement or elsewhere. Some men, especially shamans, had more than one wife (polygyny), and if so, the women seem to have been sisters (sororal polygyny). Relatives were traced along both the father's and mother's line (bilateral or nonunilineal descent) to a given degree of collaterality; this meant that each person, except for brothers and sisters, was a member of a different bilateral kin group (personal kindred). A mother's sister's child and father's brother's child (parallel cousins) were called by the terms for brother and sister (siblings), but a mother's brother's child and father's sister's child (cross-cousins) were termed cousin (Iroquois cousin terms). For the parental generation the word for mother was different from that for mother's sister, but the latter term was the same as for father's sister; the same pattern applied to father, father's brother, and mother's brother (lineal avuncular terms). We would expect that since parallel cousins were termed brother and sister, their parents would be called mother and father, but such was not the case. Thus, we are led to conclude that this terminology was in the process of change at the time it was described.

SUBSISTENCE ACTIVITIES   After the winter's ice had broken up on the main river and the accompanying high water had subsided, the Kuskowagamiut moved from their hunting camps on the tundra to riverbank settlements in anticipation of the first runs of fish. Gill nets strung with wooden floats and antler sinkers were readied for use. The netting was made from the inner bark of willows or more preferably from rawhide thongs, and a net probably was about thirty feet long and six feet deep. Nets were set in river eddies and tended daily from a canoe or kayak. Whenever possible a man set his net in the same eddy that he had used the previous year; otherwise he lost his claim to it. Since the river channel shifted frequently, no eddy had real permanence. The first species caught was most likely the sheefish, and the few taken were boiled for immediate eating.

A fisherman was most anxious to take king salmon in his set net. After he had caught a number, he took up the net and tied it to all the additional king salmon netting he might have. He placed the net, stored in a wooden container to prevent tangling, in his kayak, and paddled nearby to a straight stretch of river with no obstructions above the depth of the net. He threw out a large wooden float attached to a line leading to the net that he paid out into the water. One end of the net was tied to the kayak, and the fisherman paddled so that the net drifted at right angles to the current. When he saw a float bob violently, he knew a fish had struck the net, and he detached the net rope from his vessel, tied a large wooden float to the end, and threw it overboard. Paddling to the spot where the fish had thrashed, he gently lifted the net from the water and either clubbed the salmon to death or stuck a bone bodkin into the base of its head. He tried to kill the fish as efficiently as possible, for if it thrashed violently it was likely to destroy a section of the net. The fisherman took the dead fish aboard and straightened the net to drift evenly with the current. After a drift of about two miles, he hauled the net in and repeated the process if the take had been small. This fishing technique, called drift netting, was possibly the most important means for taking salmon. King salmon were caught in this manner, and with smaller-meshed gill nets dog, red, and silver salmon were harvested.

When a man finished drift netting for the day, he returned to his base, put the fish in a wooden bin, and covered them with a grass mat to keep flies away. His wife or daughter processed the fish for immediate consumption or for storage. Salmon soon to be used were cut into chunks and boiled in water or were partly dried and later boiled, but most fish were gutted and dried for winter. The heads might be dried for dog food or buried to make headcheese; the roe was eaten after being mashed or mixed with oil, or was dried to serve as preferred food for travelers; the guts were buried or dried as food for dogs. The body of a fish to be dried was cut and hung over a drying rack made from poles, and during wet weather the fish were covered with grass matting to prevent them from molding. Beneath the rack a small fire of alder wood was sometimes built to prevent flies from laying their eggs on the fish and to smoke-cure the salmon. After the fish had dried, they were bundled and stored in caches. Any fish not prepared for drying were placed whole in the ground. Here they decayed slowly and became "stink fish," as later whites termed them. When asked how they could tolerate the smell as they ate these fish, the Eskimos' standard reply was, "We don't eat the smell."

Late nineteenth-century reports indicate that families fished for salmon only until they felt that they had enough to last them the winter. If a man took a large number of king salmon, his fishing for later, smaller species was desultory. Salmon always ascended the river to spawn in the small adjacent streams, but high water made it difficult to net them in certain years. However, starvation from failure of the salmon run apparently did not occur.

Some, or perhaps even most, families did not remain at their villages to fish for salmon but scattered to nearby fish camps along the banks of the river or sloughs. Families camping along stretches of the central river where shallow water ran over a gravel bottom might build weirs across the channel. At intervals in a weir, they set funnel-shaped fish traps of spruce splints facing downstream. In these traps salmon, whitefish, and northern pike were taken. More ambitious individuals maintained similar traps in the narrow streams leading from lakes into sloughs and rivers. At the end of the salmon fishing season, families moved back from their camps, taking with them their winter supply of dried fish.

During early winter the men sledded to tundra camps, where they set fish traps in small streams leading from the lakes. Their primary purpose was to take the small blackfish that left the lakes via these streams during the fall. Blackfish were caught in great quantities and stored frozen in woven grass bags. Later in the winter they served as food for both people and dogs. Another fall activity of the men was to snare hares, marmot, and squirrels; mink and river otter were caught in fish traps or in smaller traps of the same design. Ptarmigan snares were set in clusters around willow thickets, and if beaver were nearby, they were captured in nets set beneath the ice. Whenever possible, men hunted caribou with bows and arrows in the late fall when the animals were fat, their skins prime, and their meat at its best, but caribou were not abundant. By midwinter, people were gathering at their riverbank settlements where caches usually were well stocked with food, and as the weather grew colder they depended almost entirely on stored edibles. This was the ceremonial season, and when supplies were plentiful, few cares disturbed the tranquillity of winter.

With the approach of spring, villagers grew restless and were anxious to return to their tundra camps. They went by dog team before the trails became free of snow and before the sloughs and rivers were covered with melt water. Here, as the last snow disappeared, they harvested ptarmigan and migratory waterfowl with arrows or snares. Women collected berries, especially the high-bush cranberries clinging to the dried bushes from the year before, and men refurbished blackfish traps that they set in small streams leading to lakes.

They set gill nets in larger sloughs for northern pike and whitefish; the surplus fish were dried for later use. Men traveled by kayak once there was open water, hunting and snaring fur animals. When they judged that their take was sufficient or when they simply wearied of the tundra camps, they returned to their river-bank communities. They did so, however, only when reasonably certain that the river ice had broken up and the flood waters had subsided.

SOCIAL DIMENSIONS   Men dominated subsistence activities and lived apart from women, thereby giving rise to social networks focused in the kashgee or men's house. Each male who lived there occupied a specific spot: old men on the bench at the front above the entrance, young men on the opposite bench, middle-aged men on the outer benches, and young boys on the floor. Early in the morning before anyone else was up, someone placed a wand across the exit, indicating that no one was to leave, and old men began to talk to an audience that appeared to be sleeping. In monologues or dialogues they lectured about life from childhood to maturity. They spoke of traditional customs and of new rules as responses to changing conditions. Discussions might be of behavior in public or on trips and of actions necessary in case of accidents or other emergencies. After the presentations were over, those men who planned to travel a considerable distance that day dressed and left the kashgee as others split wood for a sweat bath. Preparations for a bath included removing the planks that covered the fire pit, setting aside the skylight cover, and building a great fire. After the wood had burned to a bed of coals, the gut window was fitted back in place, and men stripped to bathe. In the intense heat their ears might blister before they began to perspire. As the room became hotter, men wailed loudly for the dead who were missing a fine bath. When the heat subsided, they washed in urine and in the winter might sit in the snow to cool off.

After hunting or fishing during the day, men returned to the settlement and went directly to the men's house. A close female relative unloaded the catch and put away the equipment of each man, and after the men had bathed again, women brought in the evening meal and dried the men's clothing. In the early evening men told of what had happened to them during the day, and the old men commented on what was said. As everyone settled down to sleep, an old man began telling a traditional story. The audience at first responded with "e-yee" to encourage the storyteller, but before he had finished, most men and boys were asleep.

POLITICAL LIFE   With villagers living together for at least half of each year, we might expect a degree of political integration, but group decisions that affected the entire community seem to have been rare. This condition is partially a reflection of the fact that subsistence activities were individual, not community, endeavors. A man most likely supervised the hunting and fishing activities of his sons, and an older brother, in the absence of a father, guided the economic life of a younger brother. It is probable, too, that older men informally resolved routine problems, such as disputes over property or hunting and fishing rights. Possibly a wider range of opinion was sought concerning differences with persons in other settlements or the formalities of arranging ceremonies. If any one individual had a prominent voice in the decision making, it probably was the shaman because of his supernatural affiliations. The nonconformity of any individual would lead first to gossip and then to mild ridicule, which was usually sufficient to bring deviant behavior into line with community expectations. If a father was annoyed at the behavior of a son, he would express his dissatisfaction to a close friend during a sweat bath, and this person would make known the father's feelings to the son. Ridicule songs appear to have been sung as a more forceful and face-to-face means of pointing up individual failings.

The most likely secular leader was a highly successful hunter and fisherman who could feed orphans and widows, provide oil for the kashgee lamps, and furnish food for feasts. Such an individual took an active role in all village activities and thereby earned the most worthy title of "a man indeed!"

The most serious rupture of social harmony occurred when a person was murdered by an outsider, but such an occurrence appears to have been rare. If it happened, an influential relative of the deceased assembled the men from his and adjacent communities, entertained them, presented each with a gift, and requested their aid in exacting blood revenge. Balance prevailed after someone in the family of the murderer was killed, and there were no additional murders. Sometimes revenge flared out of hand, and a family feud erupted. This would cease only with the flight or murder of one faction. Formalized war did not exist.

SUPERNATURALISM   When defined as dogma, rules, a ceremonial round, and ritual leadership, religion played a critical role in Kuskokwim Eskimo life. As so often is the case, some aspects of these Eskimos' religious life were integrated with economics and entertainment. Ceremonies and feasts followed a well-developed calendrical cycle, whereas shamanistic activities, the other ritual events, took place primarily at critical and unscheduled times.

Shamans   Shamans were reported to be far more powerful among the Kuskokwim Eskimos than among most others, and male shamans often were members of particular families. Very little is known about female shamans, although some old women clearly did become powerful specialists in supernaturalism. A young male with a predilection to shamanism was apprenticed to a successful practitioner and did not perform independently until he reached adulthood. During his training he acquired supernatural aids, learned to drum and sing, and practiced performing tricks. Shamanistic sessions were held to diagnose, predict, and cure by supernatural means as well as to demonstrate a shaman's power. It also was a shaman's duty to make certain that people observed the necessary behavioral norms, and he became a secular practitioner in performing certain cures that did not require supernatural aids. Other persons, especially elders, also might function as secular curers. When a settlement included more than one shaman, people turned to the one regarded as most capable in times of greatest crisis.

When someone's illness had no obvious cause, a shaman's help was sought. If the patient did not improve or died, the shaman might be accused of witchcraft, in which case he or she could be murdered. A curing session involved apprentices who drummed and sang the shaman's songs while he or she summoned a spiritual helper. When this force had entered the shaman's body, he or she behaved strangely, reflecting the motions and sounds of the helping spirit, which often was an animal. The disease substance was driven from the sick person's body by sucking or brushing it away. It sometimes happened, too, that a shaman, when possessed by a spirit, learned that a villager had caused the illness by breaking a taboo; after the offender confessed, harmony was restored to the universe. Shamans also interpreted unusual events. An eclipse of the moon was thought to anticipate illness and death, an earthquake was an ominous sign, and comets foretold starvation.

Shamans, as interpreters of extraordinary events, played a highly positive role in village life. They sought to understand and explain what seemed to be abnormal behavior in people and unusual happenings in the natural world. Their performances included trickery, such as vanishing acts or sleight of hand, but these possibly are best regarded as mood-setting techniques rather than proof of supernatural powers. Men who were shamans provided for their families in the manner of other men in addition to being well rewarded for the services they performed. Unlike all other married men, male shamans lived in the houses of their wives, which clearly set them apart from other men.

Witchcraft was the ultimate form of antisocial behavior, and shamans who reportedly used their powers against other persons were considered dangerous. The malevolence of a witch in a distant village could be countered by a powerful local shaman, but if he or she were unsuccessful, the victim might die. If a witch exerted power locally, the situation was even more traumatic. Although this form of witchcraft seems to have been rare, if villagers were convinced that one among them was a witch, he or she might be clubbed to death, after which the joints of the body were severed, and the body burned.

Ceremonies The Kuskowagamiut ceremonial round is known incompletely but in enough detail to realize that it was well developed. Ceremonies commonly spanned four days, and people from one or more adjacent villages were guests. The villagers prepared for the celebration by storing large quantities of food, composing songs, and manufacturing dance masks (see Figure 4-6), along with practicing their roles until they were perfected. The general supervision, at least along the lower river, was in the hands of a dance leader who as host made certain that the activities were carried out in a traditional manner. This office tended to pass from father to son. The most important ceremonial event was the Great Ceremony for the Dead, performed every four to ten years, depending on the number of deaths and the time required to assemble

Figure 4-6. | Mask representing a spirit that the Kuskowagamiut believed lives in the ground and leaves no hole when it emerges. According to their belief, this spirit sometimes dislikes men and will jump through them without leaving a mark but killing them in the process. (Photograph courtesy of the Museum of the American Indian, Heye Foundation.)

the assets for holding the event. On alternate years reciprocating villages held a Sending-a-Messenger Ceremony as the climax to yearly ceremonials.

The Great Ceremony for the Dead was designed to free the souls of the dead so that they could rest forever in a world in the sky. The Sending-a-Messenger Ceremony was in honor of the recently deceased and included the institutionalized giving of gifts. The person or persons hosting the celebration were relatives of the deceased and had accumulated food and property in large quantities. Messengers were sent to the guest community with a mnemonic stick on which symbols were carved or appended. An announcement was made formally, and the signs on the stick were to convey the details of the invitation. When the guests arrived, they were greeted ceremonially, and during the evenings of festivities they watched dances and songs commemorating the dead and denoting his or her merits. If the deceased was not a noble person about whom any good could be recounted, the praises of his or her ancestors were sung. The climax of the ceremony came a few days later when gifts were distributed to the guests in honor of the deceased; there was no obligation to make a return gift.

The Bladder Ceremony that was so important at adjacent coastal Eskimo communities also was held by these riverine people. The bladders of all important animals killed were saved because it was thought that an animal's soul was in its bladder. The first birds and small animals killed by boys also were preserved after the meat and intestines were removed. The skins and bladders were hung in the kashgee during the time of the festivities. Included were sporting events, songs, storytelling, gift exchanges, and feasting. On the tenth and final day everyone assembled in the men's house for a feast, and bits of food were thrown on one wall for the dead. The purpose of the ceremony was to renew the game killed, and at the end the bladders probably were submerged in a hole in the river ice. The focus of the event on bladders was not entirely appropriate for Kuskokwim Eskimos since they depended so heavily on salmon, which were not specifically honored. This is an example of a ceremony maintained even though some aspects of its original form were no longer fully pertinent.

LIFE CYCLE A woman gave birth at home, aided by her mother or another female relative. She delivered in a squatting position, and downward pressure was applied to her abdomen if the process was delayed. The birth of a female was a joyous occasion only if the woman desired a daughter. If there were daughters already in the family, or if it was a lean time of the year, female infanticide was likely to be practiced. Infanticide was not restricted to the newborn but might take place at any time during the first two or three years of life. The attitude was that since part of the soul of a deceased individual returned to the body of the next one born, this was no real destruction of life. A baby was named after the person who had died most recently in the local area, and the relatives of the deceased behaved toward the namesake as they had toward the deceased. Parents were known by the name of their firstborn, a custom termed teknonymy. Thus, if the firstborn was named Kamoucha, the mother was called Kamoucha's mother. Names obviously were not sex-linked, and they were changed if their bearers were plagued with misfortune. Growing up in a household dominated by older females, infants and small children were pampered and catered to; this treatment was based as much on supernatural beliefs as on affection. Since an infant was believed to have the soul of a recently deceased individual, he or she mirrored the feelings of the deceased and was appeased in order not to offend the watching spirits. This association decreased in importance as the individual matured and acquired a distinctive personality of her or his own.

A maturing girl soon was integrated into the household routine of the older females. Her toys usually were facsimiles of the artifacts used by her mother, and by the time she was nine years old she was a reasonably capable housekeeper. Indications are that the bonds between a maternal grandmother and granddaughter were extremely close. The granddaughter's activities and world view appear to have been molded largely by this older woman, who occupied the rear platform in a large household. Recognition of the grandmother's importance stems from a study of stories told by contemporary Eskimo girls. These stories, or storyknife tales as they are known, were illustrated with stylized representations of people, boats, houses, and other forms. The drawings were made on a mud or snow surface with an oblong-bladed implement known as a storyknife. Storyknife tales were a vital part of the women's world, and their content suggests that grandmothers originated them and taught them to their granddaughters. No evidence exists of males either telling or listening to storyknife tales. The stories told by a grandmother entertained and also instructed. The main characters most often were a grandmother and her granddaughter; repeated messages in stories were that one should offer food to visitors, that nonrational behavior is expectable from males, and that a granddaughter who disobeys her grandmother brings harm to the grandmother.

By the time boys were ten years old they had left their natal homes and moved into the kashgee. Here they came under the supervision of the older males in their families and under the indirect control of all the older kashgee residents. The boys were no longer regarded as children; more and more was expected of them, even though their activities were supervised casually. Steps toward adulthood were achieved by an adolescent as he increased his hunting skills. The first birds and small animals killed by each boy were skinned and stuffed to be displayed from strings in the kashgee during the Bladder Ceremony, at which the boys danced in places of honor and were feasted. At the completion of the rituals the skins were secreted in a safe location. After a male had killed one of each species of animal, he was considered marriageable. Ceremonial recognition was given a girl when she picked the first of each species of berry, but a more important event was the ceremonial acknowledgment of her menarche. At this time she probably was restricted to one corner of the dwelling, wore old clothing, and observed food as well as behavioral taboos. Possibly at about this time a girl had sexual intercourse with a male shaman; this was essential for a maiden before she could be admitted to kashgee ceremonies.

A female was nubile at about the age of fourteen, but a male was likely to be at least four years older and sometimes as much as twenty years older than his bride. The marriage itself was without ceremony and was arranged by the families of the couple or by an older man directly with the girl's family. Thereafter the man slept with the girl in her mother's house; she was responsible for preparing his meals, caring for his clothing, and processing the subsistence items he obtained. In the event that either member of the couple became dissatisfied with the other, they ceased cooperating and cohabiting. A marriage might also be terminated with a wrestling match. Any man was free to challenge another to wrestle, and the man thrown to the ground was obligated to give up his wife. Women do not appear to have had any voice in these matches. Usually men wrestled only for young women without children. No stigma was attached to divorce, and most individuals had at least two partners during their lifetimes. A marriage tended to stabilize after the woman bore a child, particularly if it was a male.

The activities of adult marriage partners were complementary, and even though marriages may have been brittle, an adult did not willfully remain unmarried for long. In the early years of marriage the partners might remain cool toward one another, but as time passed they were more likely to become congenial partners. The personality of an adult Eskimo manifested a phlegmatic realism, and an even-tempered, jovial person was the ideal. Verbal aggression or physical dominance was abhorred, and to be withdrawn or caustic was considered symptomatic of illness. Aged people were not killed but often came to be respected for their knowledge. Some old men were great storytellers and passed the traditions of their fathers on to the men and boys of the next generation. Old women held forth from the rear platforms of their dwellings with advice and criticism, both of which were offered freely.

A dead person's body was flexed with the knees bound up to the chest. The women wailed, and the men killed the dogs of the deceased. His or her clothing and other property, except those items that were kept as mementos, were destroyed or deposited on the grave. The body was removed through a hole made in the wall of the kashgee or dwelling; according to Kuskowagamiut belief, after the opening was closed, the spirit of the deceased could not find its way back into the structure. The small plank coffin was placed above the ground on four short poles in the cemetery, usually located on a hill or rise near the settlement. At the head of the coffin a board might be placed between two poles; on it were pegged wooden carvings of human faces. (See Figure 4-7).

Figure 4-7. | Grave goods above burials photographed in 1907. (Courtesy of the University Museum, Philadelphia.)

Early Historic Changes in Kuskowagamiut Life

Major changes in aspects of Kuskowagamiut aboriginal life occurred as a result of the first direct Russian contacts and the later impact of Euro-Americans. Traders and missionaries brought economic and religious change, and epidemics sapped the vitality of the people. The epidemics seem also to have accelerated the Eskimos' expansion inland.

RUSSIAN INFLUENCES   Between the beginning of local contacts with Russians in the 1830s and their withdrawal in 1866, two Russian institutions had an important influence on the lives of local Eskimos. These were the Russian-American Company and the Russian Orthodox church. The trading organization was by far the more immediately important, but Orthodox church influence was more enduring. The Russians were searching for new sources of furs, and by the 1820s they had turned to the region north of the Alaska Peninsula. Of the earliest traders we know comparatively little except that two men, Fedor Kolmakov and Semen Lukin, were most instrumental in opening the inland fur trade. Kolmakov was of aboriginal Siberian and Russian ancestry, while Lukin appears to have been of Eskimo or mixed Russian and Eskimo ancestry. Both men traveled widely, exploring the Kuskokwim River drainage and adjacent areas in their quest for furs, especially beaver pelts. Since beaver were concentrated along the central and upper reaches of the river, the lower river held little attraction for them in this early stage of penetration. In 1853, however, trade in white fox pelts began, an indication that the Russians had initiated trading ties with Eskimos along the lower river, since white fox could be obtained only from areas near the coast.

Trading Center   The most permanent inland Russian trading center was at Kolmakov Redoubt along the central river. A stockade surrounded the main settlement, two small cannons were the primary means of defense, and there was a blockhouse with gun ports. The station also included a bathhouse, chapel, living quarters, store, and outbuildings. Lukin was the first manager, and he maintained this position throughout most of the Russian era. He was a religious man authorized by the Orthodox church to baptize converts, and before a chapel was constructed he led weekly church services in the store. He was well regarded by the local Eskimos, and while there were intermittent rumors of pending attacks on the settlement, none ever materialized.

Kolmakov Redoubt was not a bastion in the north. It usually was staffed with about a dozen employees of Russian, Eskimo, or mixed blood, and no military garrison was stationed there. The post never thrived because the worldwide demand for beaver pelts was in decline when the redoubt was founded. Because this was the most remote Russian trading center, the trade goods available usually were small, highly portable, and not readily destructible. Items such as tea, beads, knives, metal containers, needles, and copper ornaments were stocked; even so, the post often was without these imported goods and then dealt only in local products such as oil and dried fish. The overall impression is that the Russians adapated to Eskimo ways and made very few radical changes in the traditional patterns.

Russian Missionaries   The first Orthodox missionary to visit the Kuskokwim was A. Petelin, who arrived from the Nushagak station in the 1840s. We have no knowledge of an Orthodox missionary being stationed along the river until the arrival of Hieromonk Illarion in 1861. He visited Kolmakov Redoubt intermittently until his departure from the area in 1866. By the end of the Russian era, many if not most of the Kuskokwim Eskimos along the central river considered themselves to be Christians. They had been baptized and given Russian names, but certainly did not understand well the core of Christian dogma.

Multiple reasons probably account for the conversion of Eskimos to Orthodox Christianity. In all likelihood, one reason was that the Eskimos had a deep respect for Semen Lukin, the first Russian-American Company trader at Kolmakov Redoubt. A devout member of the Orthodox church, Lukin built a chapel and conducted services at the fort. He baptized heathen Eskimos and possibly rewarded converts with material goods. Another reason is that most leaders of aboriginal religious ceremonies probably perished during the 1838–39 smallpox epidemic (mentioned later). This offered Orthodox workers a greater opportunity to win converts among the survivors. In the same context, shamans who survived lost prestige because of their failure to stop the epidemic. This again lessened resistance to Orthodoxy over the years. On the other hand, Kuskokwim Eskimos initially held the Russians responsible for the epidemic and were bitter against most of them, which no doubt delayed conversions or made the process superficial.

The Russian Steam Bath   Yet another Russian introduction must be mentioned briefly, and this is the Russian steam bath. A bathhouse was constructed by Lukin at Kolmakov Redoubt. The Eskimos trading into these posts were familiar already with bathing in intense heat, but the Russian bath was somewhat different from the sweat bath in the kashgee. It was taken in a small structure, and stones were heated above a stove or in an open fire. When water was poured over the rocks, bathers sat back and enjoyed the hot air moistened by the steam. Initial Eskimo reaction probably was unfavorable, but as time passed the Russian bath was to assume more importance.

Early Epidemic   During the initial period of contact with the Russians, Kuskokwim Eskimos seldom were hostile; in fact, they appear to have welcomed the Russians for the trade goods they brought. However, this harmony was tested severely in 1838–39. During these years, at least half of the riverine Eskimos perished in a local smallpox epidemic. The survivors thought that the Russians had deliberately plagued them with the disease, and some Eskimos from the Kuskokwim massacred the Russians at a post on the Yukon River. The epidemic destroyed the fabric of aboriginal social life, and the distrust engendered probably never completely passed during the Russian period.

AMERICAN INFLUENCES   For nearly twenty years following the 1867 purchase of Alaska by the United States, the only American interest in the Kuskokwim was of a commercial nature. The Russian-American Company, which had held a monopoly on the Alaskan trade since 1799, was bought out by Hutchinson, Kohl & Company, soon to become the Alaska Commercial Company. Kolmakov Redoubt continued as a trading center, but the main post was located nearer the mouth of the river at a village that came to be called Bethel. Neither the Russian nor the early American trading along the Kuskokwim River developed into a major commercial enterprise. The stores were not a great source of profit, and consequently their inventories were quite limited. The change from the Russian to the American period brought no abrupt break in trading patterns; in fact, two of the three traders during the early American period were Russian or of Russian-Eskimo extraction.

Moravian Missionaries   A series of events occurring in Bethlehem, Pennsylvania, in 1883, were to have the next significant influence on Kuskokwim Eskimos. During this year the Presbyterian mission advocate and federal agent for education in Alaska, Sheldon Jackson, spoke to an audience of Moravians at the Moravian College and Theological Seminary in Bethlehem. He convinced church officials that they should take an active interest in the Eskimos of Alaska. Inasmuch as the Moravians had long maintained missions to Eskimos in Greenland and Labrador, it is not surprising that they responded favorably to this request. In 1884 an experienced Moravian missionary from Canada, Henry Hartmann, accompanied by a seminary student, William H. Weinland, set off to find a site for a new mission in Alaska. After traveling as far upriver as Kolmakov Redoubt, they concluded that a small lower river village was best suited for their purpose. The following year Weinland graduated from the seminary, and he, along with another graduate, John H. Kilbuck, and their brides, set off to found a mission center at Bethel. Since that time the line of Moravian missionaries at Bethel has been unbroken. Bethel emerged as the most important town along the Kuskokwim River after the 1908 discovery that a deep channel reached from the estuary as far as the settlement. In terms of regional administration, education, and health services, Bethel has been the focal point through which innovations have been introduced.

A major obstacle faced by the Moravians was that most Eskimos in the vicinity of their mission already were members of the Orthodox church. However, between the time the United States purchased Alaska and 1891, Orthodox church workers virtually had abandoned these converts. The Moravians, with an unbroken sequence of local missionaries from 1885 to the present, substantial support from their home mission, and singular devotion, were able to win over many Orthodox Eskimos in the vicinity. Yet, those in some local villages resisted becoming Moravians; one such village is Napaskiak, soon to be discussed.

Economic Innovations   The feverish search for gold in northwestern North America around the turn of the century brought profound changes to many areas but not to the Kuskokwim River, where major deposits were never found. However, in the 1910s prospectors introduced an important new device for taking fish, the fish wheel. A man who built a wheel was able to harvest vast numbers of salmon with comparatively little effort. The fish wheel is a log raft with a large opening at the center over which is mounted a horizontal axle hung with large baskets and paddles. The river current propels the paddles and baskets, which rotate in the direction of the current. Fish swimming upstream within reach of the baskets are lifted into them from the water and then slide down a chute into a box at the side of the raft. The fish wheel is an extremely effective method for taking fish since it operates in the absence of a fisherman, but it can be used successfully only above tidewater where the water is opaque and flowing rather fast near the bank. In those sectors where fish wheels could be used, the time spent on fishing-related activities was no longer balanced for men and women. Men now had far more free time during the summer months, whereas the work of women intensified since they had to process many more fish at one time.

Another major change in subsistence activities followed the introduction of reindeer among Alaskan Eskimos in 1892. In a program begun by Sheldon Jackson and launched along the Kuskokwim River through Moravian efforts, a small number of reindeer was driven to the lower river in 1901. The Kuskokwim herds increased until about forty thousand head were grazing along the river system in the 1930s. After this rapid increase, however, overgrazing depleted the lichens on which the animals depended for food, and the herds decreased rapidly in the early 1940s. By the end of the decade they were no longer in existence. This, combined with the fact that the local Eskimos had not adapted to the nomadic way of life required of herders, meant that reindeer herding did not replace salmon fishing as the Moravians had anticipated.

Recent Epidemics   Before turning to more recent happenings, we should discuss briefly two events with long-range effects. The first was a severe epidemic that took place in 1900–1901. During these years, miners introduced influenza, whooping cough, and measles that devastated the riverine population. A medical doctor in the area at the time estimated that half the population, including all of the babies, perished. Some villages were abandoned, and the people were seriously demoralized. Continuity with the past was interrupted or perhaps even broken in most settlements. The cultural and social effects must have been great, particularly since this was the gold rush period in which many Anglo-Americans were entering or passing through the area. The Eskimos seem to have reacted by giving up many of their old ways and rapidly adopting American customs.

EXPANSIONS INLAND   The second change, which began after the smallpox epidemic of 1838–39 and accelerated with the epidemic of 1900–1901, involved the movement of Eskimos much farther up the Kuskokwim River. The country that they entered belonged to Athapaskan Indians, and by the early 1840s they had gone far enough inland to share a village across the river from Kolmakov

Redoubt with Indians. The inland migration seems to have followed Eskimo population increases and the greater depletion of the smaller Indian population as a result of the epidemics. Eskimos moved in to fill the partial vacuum. The traditional hostility between most Indians and Eskimos apparently did not exist along the central river. By 1960 Eskimos occupied the banks of the main river as far inland as the Stony River junction, and by 1970 Eskimos had moved to the trading center of McGrath as well as the Indian villages of Nikolai and Medfra. Eskimo genealogies in the recent past suggest a pattern of Indians marrying Eskimos and adopting Eskimo ways. Thus, we see the continuing adaptability of Eskimos in their deep penetration of interior Alaska.

| Modern Kuskowagamiut Life at Napaskiak

The emphasis now shifts to one Kuskowagamiut village, Napaskiak, to plot continuity with the past and historic change. In 1955–56 I lived at Napaskiak and collected information about conditions at that time. The oldest villagers reported that the settlement had been occupied for many generations and that their ancestors previously had lived at nearby villages that were then abandoned. They had no traditions of moving into the area, and the earliest known reference to Napaskiak was on a map dated 1867. Moravian missionaries had visited there repeatedly in the 1880s but had been unable to make a significant number of lasting converts, and by the 1950s nearly all residents were members of the Russian Orthodox faith. Directly across the river from Napaskiak was the settlement of Oscarville, important to Napaskiak because of its trading post. An Orthodox church had been built at Napaskiak in 1931, and a Bureau of Indian Affairs school had opened there in 1939.

THE SETTLEMENT AND MANUFACTURES   Napaskiak stretches along the southeastern bank of the Kuskokwim River, and in 1956 the twenty-seven frame and seven log houses were occupied by 141 persons. The most imposing structures were the Russian Orthodox church and the Bureau of Indian Affairs school with its adjoining residence. Scattered around the houses were caches, fish-drying racks, privies, smokehouses, and bathhouses. (See Figure 4-8).

Closely related nuclear families tended to live in adjacent houses, and the dwellings of larger families usually included two or three rooms, with the second or third rooms serving primarily for sleeping and storage. Each house had an attached anteroom or storage shed that contained a jumble of objects. A gasoline-powered washing machine often was the largest item in the shed; stored there as well were foods soon to be eaten, winter parkas, a chamber pot, and assorted woodworking tools. The rectangular houses usually had at least one curtained window on each side, plank floors, and walls and ceiling usually covered with painted wallboard. Furnishings included a table and chairs, cast-iron woodburning stove with a clothes-drying rack above, a homemade wooden cupboard, and a washstand with an enameled basin. Overhead hung a gasoline

Figure 4-8. | A Napaskiak scene in 1956. In the foreground are racks for drying gill nets and salmon, with a cache and houses behind. (Photograph by the author.)

lantern that supplied the only light in most households; two families owned gasoline-powered generators to furnish their houses and those of near relatives with electricity. Each house contained trunks or suitcases piled somewhere and filled with clothing not then in use. On one wall was always an Orthodox church calendar around which hung prints of icons and a container of holy water. Notably, no household furnishings were of aboriginal form. In most dwellings the only artifact of traditional Eskimo manufacture was a knife or ulu, now made by mounting a blade cut from an old wood-saw blade on an ivory handle.

A search for manufactures in the traditional technology produced few forms. The most obvious examples were canoes and kayaks, but the frames of both styles were lashed together with cords and covered with canvas. The large plank boat made of spruce and powered with an outboard motor had long since replaced the umiak. Raised caches retained their form of old, as did gill nets, although the netting was made from cotton, linen, or nylon twine. Hunting weapons were rifles and shotguns. A few boys used bows and arrows, but they preferred slingshots or air rifles. Most of the equipment necessary for living off the land was purchased ready-made from nearby stores, and even items of local manufacture such as plank boats, sleds, or fish traps were constructed from imported materials.

CLOTHING   Men wore trousers, shirts, underwear, and shoes bought from a local store or a mail-order house. A few men, especially older ones, wore sealskin boots, but they were slowly passing out of style. The most popular outer winter garment was a surplus military parka, but some young men wore tight-fitting, lightweight cloth jackets even in the coldest weather. Conservative women, young or old, wore handmade cotton bloomers and petticoats. More cosmopolitan women and older girls wore ready-made underwear. Most women preferred cotton housedresses, but some wore knit sweaters and slacks. Older women wore sealskin boots, but most of the younger ones wore shoes or short rubber boots. Many women, especially those middle-aged and older, had squirrel-skin parkas adorned elaborately with calfskin trimmings, but skin parkas were being replaced by ready-made jackets. In summer, particularly when cleaning fish, a woman wore a hooded cloth parka over her dress. A male child had the same type of clothing as his father but was more likely to wear skin boots, and a girl's garments were similar to those of conservative women.

SUBSISTENCE ACTIVITIES   Village men took part in varied subsistence pursuits so that their families could thrive. It was essential for the male head of a household to be a salmon fisherman; to vary the diet, he also set traps, nets, or hooks for other fish. He needed to trap furbearers so that he could trade the skins for imported foods and manufactured goods available locally. He worked for wages whenever possible to buy items from local stores or from mail-order houses. Then, too, a man needed to be a capable carpenter and hunter. If he possessed each of these skills, he could compensate for a poor season of trapping, an inadequate harvest of fish, or poor wages by emphasizing an alternative activity. Such flexibility was required since it was almost impossible to fall back on gains from the previous year. Because of this, any decline in a man's subsistence abilities led to a rapid deterioration in his family's living standard.

In the late fall, before the sloughs and lakes froze, some men traveled by boat and outboard motor to tundra camps, where about three men shared a single camp. They shot migratory waterfowl, and after the small streams leading from lakes froze, they set traps for blackfish, which they took by the thousands and cached for dog food. When it was safe to travel by dog team, they returned to the village with their harvests. Most men had remained in the village during this time and had set their blackfish traps nearby.

Fall living in tundra camps was no longer a family practice, and therefore a man was torn in two directions. He had to obtain furs with which to purchase imported goods and foods, but he disliked being away from his family. The women and children remained in the village because children were obligated to attend school and also because most women no longer accepted the primitive living conditions at camp. With the approach of winter, men set hooks for taking burbot through the ice in front of the village, and both men and boys spent a great deal of time cutting firewood at nearby stands of alders. When the mink-trapping season arrived in November, men sledded to their tundra camps. A particular trapping area might have been in a male line for generations. Most were about four hours' travel time from the village, and the farther the man went, the greater his mink harvest would probably be. When he ventured a long distance, he was less likely to make frequent trips to the village and thus had more time to set and check his traps. He set one or two dozen steel traps and needed to check them every few days. In 1956 mink pelts each brought twenty to twenty-five dollars from local traders, and the profit from an average catch for the season was three hundred dollars. Most men stopped trapping shortly before Christmas and returned to the village to participate in the festivities. During the extended Christmas celebrations, families relied on their food surpluses stored earlier in the year. From late December until early spring very few subsistence activities were possible.

Spring brought welcome opportunities to obtain fresh food again. Ptarmigan became plentiful in the willows along sloughs in March, and hares became active and more easily snared. Blackfish again began to ascend small streams and were trapped through the ice. Soon burbot hooks again were set beneath the river ice, and women jigged for northern pike through holes in the ice. As the days lengthened and snow disappeared from southern exposures, preparations were made for the spring move to tundra camps, usually the same ones as those used by men in the fall. By late April most families had settled at camp in tents or small wood-and-sod houses, and everyone was busy. At this time all the villagers craved fresh meat, and the men killed as many ducks and geese as possible. The girls and women collected last year's berries, and men set small-meshed gill nets in sloughs for pike and whitefish. Men and boys then began to concentrate on hunting muskrats, the rationale for going to spring camp. They traveled widely in canvas-covered canoes and kayaks, hunting along the way. In 1956, a relatively poor year for muskrats, the total value of the take per man ranged from twenty to two hundred dollars. When the ice had cleared from the lakes and streams, people returned to the village, using the boats they had hauled to camp on sleds, and arrived just after the breakup of the Kuskokwim River.

By early June large-meshed gill nets were being set in the river eddies, and a few sheefish were being taken. Soon nets were set for catching the season's first king salmon; afterward, these nets were used for drift-netting salmon, the most important subsistence activity of the year. The intensity of netting those species of salmon arriving later depended on how many king salmon were taken. The last salmon of the season, the silvers, were buried whole in oil drums to become dog food during the winter. Because of their Orthodox beliefs, men did not fish on Saturday afternoon or night so that the women would not be obligated to process fish (see Figure 4-9) on Sunday, nor did they normally fish on Sunday.

Salmon fishing was largely village-based because the mobility afforded by plank boats and outboard motors made moving to fish camps unnecessary. Efficient boats and motors also made it possible for men to travel to the mouth of the Johnson River, some nine miles downstream, to gillnet whitefish in the fall or to travel about a hundred miles up the Kuskokwim and its tributaries to hunt moose. Family excursions also were made in the summer to gather berries, par-

Figure 4-9. | A Napaskiak woman filleting salmon in 1956. The fillets were held open with small sticks to assure uniform drying. (Photograph by the author.)

ticularly salmon-berries, which they placed in small barrels and stored for winter use.

The traditional importance of salmon fishing was declining in 1956, for men considered wage labor during the summer essential. As many as twenty men earned about one hundred dollars each unloading supply vessels docked near Bethel. About the same number also were flown to the Bristol Bay salmon canneries, where they earned three hundred to six hundred dollars each for the season, and a few others had summer jobs. Only one man, the general assistant at the Bureau of Indian Affairs school, had a permanent job; he earned about three thousand dollars a year. A form of income unassociated with the immediate environment was the money received from territorial (in 1956) and federal agencies. Thirteen persons received monthly checks from the Alaska Department of Welfare because they were more than sixty-five years of age and without means of support. Two men received Aid to the Blind, and eight families were helped by Aid to Families with Dependent Children. Social security earnings were received by two men over sixty-five and by three heirs of men who qualified. The total community income from these sources was about eighteen thousand dollars a year.

Food habits reflected far greater continuity with the past than did the material inventory. Salmon continued to be the most important staple in nearly all households. The aboriginal processing techniques persisted; that is, fish were dried and smoked or might be buried whole. Smokehouses were used, a possible change from aboriginal times. The principal means for cooking salmon was still by boiling, and dried salmon continued to be stripped from the skin in pieces and dipped into seal oil before eating. However, people considered that a meal of only salmon was plain fare. They ate unleavened bread for breakfast and drank coffee or tea. Coffee was preferred by most, but tea was substituted when a family's resources were low. In the 1950s every family regarded sugar, flour, salt, canned milk, tea, coffee, tobacco, and cooking oils as necessities. They also bought canned meats and fish, crackers, candy, and canned fruits, depending on their resources.

DESCENT, KINSHIP, AND MARRIAGE As of old, descent was traced equally through the male and female lines (bilateral). The kinship terminology included separate terms for father and mother, as well as uncle and aunt terms for the brothers and sisters of one's parents (lineal type). Cross-cousins were called cousins, whereas parallel cousins were grouped with siblings (Iroquois cousin terms). However, some terms for older and younger biological siblings were not normally extended to parallel cousins. The most important set of relationships seems to have been between males who were classificatory or biological siblings, as previously mentioned. By the time a girl was thirteen she usually was courted by older boys, but since marriages still were arranged by older women and parents, courtship did not lead directly to marital ties. If at all possible, parents found mates for their children in the village (community endogamy); alternatively, the girl moved to another village, or, very rarely, to Bethel. A bride was expected to move into the house of her husband's family (temporary patrilocal residence) until the couple could build a house of their own (eventual neolocal residence).

SOCIAL DIMENSIONS Only the persistence and good fortune of a male family head made it possible for a household to prosper, and the relationship between a father and his son was of key importance. A son learned subsistence-directed skills largely through informal instruction from his father. In his father's company a young man was unassuming; although he might covertly disagree with the older man, a son never overtly expressed his dissatisfaction in a face-to-face situation. The pelts that a son trapped and the wages that he earned were at the disposal of his father. The father, too, had first call on the use of the dog team or boat and outboard motor. Ideally, an aged father was cared for by his son, but in all likelihood the old man received Old Age Assistance. With this cash income a father sometimes continued to dominate the economic activities of a household. The relationship between a father and daughter was cooler and more distant. A girl married and moved to her husband's household, offering a father few comforts in his old age.

The bonds between a mother and her daughter were close and overtly warm. After bearing a son, every mother hoped for a daughter to help her with household activities, and a sincere affection bound the pair. A mother sought to find a spouse for her daughter in the community to keep her near, and she vigorously defended the girl against real or imagined abuse from her husband or his family. Mothers also were the most outspoken defenders of their sons but did not express the same warmth toward a son. The relationship between siblings, which extended to parallel cousins, was one of friendship and mutual aid. Married male siblings might live in the same household, draw their food from a common cache, and share equipment. An older male managed the subsistence affairs of the household in the absence of the father. Siblings of the opposite sex were not socially close during their adult lives but could depend on each other in times of crisis. The ties between cross-cousins were looser, and the degree of closeness was largely dependent on the personalities of the individuals involved. These persons joked with one another and, if called on, rendered mutual assistance.

Four or more times a week, nearly all men took steam baths that lasted for hours on end. The small Russian-style bathhouse had an outer dressing room and an inner steam room; each could accommodate about a dozen persons. There were nine such bathhouses in the community, and certain men bathed together frequently. These structures had replaced the kashgee as the place where men bathed and relaxed in each other's company. Unlike the kashgees of old, however, these bathhouses also were used by women. Sometimes a woman bathed with her husband; only in rare instances would one bathe with any other man. In the home the old sexual dichotomy existed still. A woman was primarily responsible for the household's functioning, and her husband was something of an outsider. Thus, a subdued but pervasive individualism dominated home life. It was reflected in the behavior of old people, both men and women, who frequently preferred to live alone in their own houses, a pattern facilitated by Old Age Assistance funds.

The village problem considered most critical by the people and government officials alike was illness, and tuberculosis was the most dangerous disease by far. Among the 180 permanent residents in 1956, 45 had active cases of tuberculosis, and unquestionably there were additional cases. Villagers had vague notions about the germ theory of disease but recognized that no one cure was invariably successful. Therefore, in an effort to increase their chances of recovery, they attempted diverse cures for this or any other serious illness. They tried patent medicines and the traditional pharmacopoeia, then might take steam baths, consult a shaman, drink holy water or pray in church, and finally turn to prescription medicine dispensed by the teacher and the Bethel hospital. A major program of tuberculosis control was being implemented largely through a chemotherapy program at the village level by the U.S. Public Health Service.

The most intensive contacts outside the community were with the urban settlement of Bethel. The five large stores, U.S. Public Health Service hospital, pool halls, restaurants, and theaters were among the greatest attractions in

Bethel for the villagers. Here, too, they met friends and relatives from other settlements and ordered intoxicants flown in from Anchorage. Thus, Bethel was the center of diverse forms of socializing. Contacts with adjacent villages were largely social or religious in nature. A family traveled to visit relatives, attend a funeral, or arrange church business. The only other local trips were taken downriver in the spring to hunt seals and upriver in the fall to hunt moose. A few men went to distant urban centers in Alaska to work briefly; more men went to Anchorage each spring to attend an encampment of their local U.S. National Guard unit. The only other contact with the outside world occurred when a Kuskowagamiut had to stay in a hospital at Anchorage, Seward, or in the state of Washington.

Not all exotic contacts necessitated leaving the community. One could listen to a battery radio, found in most houses, and learn what was happening beyond the local area. "Tundra Topics," broadcast from Fairbanks, was especially popular, for it presented news about isolated settlements. Then, too, people came to the village from urban areas in connection with governmental work. The only outsider to reside in the community was the BIA teacher, but the bureau also sent supervisors and maintenance workers to the settlement on occasion. U.S. Public Health Service field nurses and those working with the special program for the control of tuberculosis made regular visits. Scientists were frequent callers; their work usually had to do with some aspect of public health. An occasional U.S. National Guard officer or enlisted man from the Bethel headquarters came on official business, and the same applied to the U.S. deputy marshal from Bethel. Sometimes even a stray tourist was seen in the village.

POLITICAL LIFE From as long ago as anyone could recall until 1950, Napaskiak had had a kashgee, which served the same functions as in other aboriginal Kuskowagamiut settlements. In the kashgee, two or three older men who were respected for their wisdom constituted an informal council of elders. Their judgment was not likely to be challenged, nor would the opinions of an important shaman be disregarded. In rare instances of irreconcilable differences between families, the weaker family and its allies left the settlement. In 1906 a Russian Orthodox priest visited the village, and his appointed representative became the first "chief." Apparently the head of a large extended family, he soon was replaced by his son, for he was an old man at the time of the appointment. The original duty of a chief was to arrange matters pertaining to church affairs, and this had remained one of his most important functions. In 1947 the first elected chief took office. His duties had come to include secular as well as sacred obligations and were confused in the minds of most villagers. Some said that he was head of the village, but others regarded the Orthodox Church Brotherhood as the collective head of local affairs. The authority of any particular chief seemed to be dependent on his personality. Part of the confusion resulted from the efforts of BIA officials to introduce an elected council into the village. Local bureau personnel were promoting the Indian Reorganization Act, as extended to Alaska in 1936, when the first teacher arrived in 1939. The teacher attempted to induce the people to organize under the terms of the act but never was successful. The villagers did elect a council in 1945 but did not request federal recognition. The council was partially ineffective because its members were reluctant to take any overt action against other persons. The most serious problem was intoxication. The usual course of action was to warn a heavy drinker; on rare occasions, a warrant for an arrest was sworn out with the U.S. deputy marshal at Bethel. Meetings also were called to collect funds for village medical needs, to establish a curfew for school children, or to request that the airline offices in Bethel refuse to accept orders for intoxicants from villagers. However, there usually was little reason for council meetings since little community cohesion existed along secular lines.

Warfare was not a part of village life except as it was imposed through the political control of the United States. Early in World War II the Alaska Territorial Guard was organized as a scouting unit for the U.S. Army at a time when an invasion of the Alaskan mainland seemed likely. In the village unit, older men were appointed as officers, and the younger ones became enlisted men. Very little military discipline prevailed, but large quantities of military equipment were issued. Since men here were permitted to use the clothing and guns daily, real economic advantages were gained by belonging to the Alaska Territorial Guard. After the war ended this organization was replaced by the U.S. National Guard, and the policies changed drastically. The older men were discouraged from re-enlisting, especially if they spoke no English. Promising younger men were sent to special training schools, and regular drills became a routine part of membership. The village unit came to reflect military norms and emerged as a disruptive institution in village life, particularly since it encouraged the overt authority of young aggressive men, an unprecedented village behavior pattern. Younger men regarded the National Guard as romantic and the yearly two-week encampment near Anchorage as a great adventure. The older men who remained in the unit did so because of the monetary rewards.

RELIGION   Christianity was introduced to the Kuskokwim Eskimos in its Russian Orthodox form, and in the 1950s all of the people at Napaskiak, including a practicing shaman, considered themselves Christians. (See Figure 4-10.) Since there had never been a resident missionary, Orthodox dogma was not well understood. Most villagers agreed that helping other people when in need was one of the most important Christian ideals. The people also believed that after an individual died, the soul automatically went to hell if he or she had not been baptized or if death was from suicide; otherwise, God evaluated a person's deeds, and on this basis admitted the spirit to heaven or hell. At times the ghost of a dead person was thought to have returned to the community; to decrease the likelihood of a visitation the windows of the deceased's former abode were opened after death and closed after burial. An icon was hung on the door to prevent the spirit from returning through the doorway.

The ceremonial cycle duplicated the Orthodox church calendar elsewhere in the world. Along with regular church services, special observances were held

Figure 4-10. | Napaskiakers and the Russian Orthodox bishop of Alaska in 1956. (Photograph by the author.)

at Russian Christmas and New Year's, the Epiphany, the Easter season, and during the annual church conference. Russian Christmas was of far greater importance than any other ceremonial event, and preparations were elaborate. The choir practiced Russian Christmas songs in both Russian and Eskimo, the men hauled and chopped enough wood to heat their houses during the holiday season, ordered wine through an airline, and made ready the ceremonial equipment, and the women prepared special foods. Finally, visitors arrived from surrounding communities. During three days of processions, the choir announced the birth of Christ in each household by singing Christmas songs while carrying a guiding star made of metal. Since the singers and their followers were fed at each house, most of the three nights were taken up with eating vast quantities of food. The Russian New Year was celebrated by putting lighted kerosene lanterns on the graves of the dead, as was done also at Russian Christmas. At about midnight, fireworks and guns were shot off while the Christmas trees that had decorated the houses for the season were burned in front of the village. The climax of the event was a short service in church about the ideals of behavior for the coming year.

One reason for the ineffectiveness of the village council was that the Orthodox Church Brotherhood long had cared for the crisis needs of the community and held monthly meetings to deal with ongoing problems. The general purpose of this organization was to coordinate church activities and to provide welfare aid for members. Because all of the families participated in at least some Orthodox church functions, with only one man claiming membership in another church, the welfare provision embraced everyone. The brotherhood had elected officers with established duties. The specific obligations of its members were to prepare coffins and bury the dead, to arrange for the annual trip of the bishop to the area, to aid the aged, to maintain the church structure, and to perform certain ceremonial obligations. From the time of its organization in 1931, the brotherhood provided food and funds to families without means of support until this function was assumed by the Alaska Department of Welfare and the BIA shortly after World War II.

Recent Developments in Eskimo Village Life

At Napaskiak and other riverine Eskimo villages, changes have been more rapid and dramatic since the mid-1960s than in any other comparable span of historic time. We focus briefly here on some of these changes.

IMPACT OF GOVERNMENT PROGRAMS   The Great Society program launched by President Johnson in 1965 had a profound impact on life in these small communities. The federal government found living conditions in western Alaskan settlements to be the poorest in the nation, and this led to a proliferation of federal programs for directed culture change. First and foremost, many substandard houses were replaced by new dwellings (see Figure 4-11), wells were drilled for safe water, and generators were installed to provide electricity. It became apparent, however, that not all of these projects would lead to lasting benefits. Many of the new houses were poorly built, costly to heat, and difficult to maintain. The wells and electrical plants often were unreliable, and the same was true of the sewage systems that had been installed. Neither the federal government nor the local people had the capacity to maintain the infrastructure, and the result by the 1980s was not as positive as the federal planners had expected.

Villages that at first began to take on the appearance of suburban American communities have suffered from maintenance problems in more recent years. Nonetheless, new construction has continued, particularly of churches, community halls, post offices, and schools. Although the old-style bathhouses and caches remain, most other evidence of the long-established material culture has disappeared. Some canvas-covered canoes and kayaks exist, but many others are falling to pieces from obvious disuse. Within the houses, notable changes involve the quality of imported furnishings, including the addition of oil-burning space heaters and television sets. Household inventories are much larger than ever before, reflecting a considerable capital investment. More money has been

Figure 4-11. | By 1970, new houses at Napaskiak were heated with oil stored in drums. Caches were at ground level, and outhouses were built behind dwellings. A house had few windows and multiple doors with substantial locks as protection from roving drunks. (Photograph by the author.)

spent as well on aluminum boats with large outboard motors and on the snow-mobiles that largely have replaced dog team travel.

By the mid-1980s the riverine Eskimo population had increased dramatically, due in part to a decline in the infant mortality rates and better health maintenance. The younger adults, who came from large families, have begun to raise large families of their own. No longer is the population seriously affected by tuberculosis, the primary killer and crippler in the comparatively recent past. Through U.S. Public Health Service efforts, the death rate from tuberculosis, which among native Alaskans in 1950 was 653 per 100,000 (compared to 22.5 for all races in the United States at that time), was reduced to 3.7 in 1969 and became nonexistent in 1970.

The dramatic population increase of the 1960s to the mid-1980s was accompanied by a growth in affluence. Family incomes typically increased despite a decline in the amount of trapping brought about by comparatively low fur prices and disaffection with the rigorous physical activity required. In large measure, family incomes grew because of the many village construction projects for which local people were hired. In addition, commercial salmon fishing in the Kuskokwim River began in 1959; this was a major source of new income, especially along the lower river, where the harvest quota was greatest. However, in 1972 the state introduced "limited entry permits," which restricted the number of fishermen and thus reduced the number of families profiting from the endeavor. By 1982 the commercial salmon harvest was worth about $4.2 million to fishermen in the region, with the average income ranging between $3,000 and $5,000. While this is a significant amount of cash, commercial fishing, now that it has stabilized, benefits comparatively few Kuskowagamiut.

INTOXICANT CONSUMPTION   Another major change centers around the consumption of intoxicants: the scope and intensity of drinking has mushroomed. The people have had more money to spend on alcoholic beverages, and alcohol became easier to obtain when a liquor store opened at Bethel in 1963. The store closed in 1973, and liquor no longer can be sold legally at Bethel. However, the community now has become a thriving center for bootleggers. In the 1950s intoxicant consumption was not prevalent enough to be the disruptive force in the community life that it had become by the early 1980s. Deaths by drowning attributable to drunkenness have become commonplace, and murders and cases of spouse and child abuse are numerous. In the 1950s doors to houses had simple interior locks or just a piece of cord wrapped around a pair of nails on either side of the jamb. By 1970 the outer door of each house had a substantial lock, and sometimes the door from the covered porch to the house interior was locked to protect family members from being disturbed by drunks entering their home. The local option law introduced by the state in 1981 has changed the drunkenness pattern in some villages. Residents can now vote to prohibit the importation and sale of alcoholic beverages, except for sacramental wine, in their individual villages. Numerous Kuskokwim Eskimo communities, including Napaskiak, have voted to become dry. However, the rigor with which the law is enforced varies widely from one village to the next, and alcohol-related incidents remain commonplace. (See Figure 4-12.)

Figure 4-12. | By 1970, Napaskiak and other Kuskowagamiut villages often had a local person appointed by the state as a public safety officer. (Photograph by the author.)

CHANGES IN BETHEL   When the Moravians founded their mission head-quarters at Bethel in 1885, they anticipated that this settlement would become a house of God. Such it was until the gold rushes began in 1900 and local Eskimo life began to slip from Moravian control. In the gold-rush era, Bethel became the major regional transportation center because seagoing vessels could dock there and transfer their freight to boats for transshipment up the river. The gold seekers and other outsiders began to expose local Eskimos to an alternative American life-style, one far less rigid than that of the Moravians. At this time Eskimos in the region who were dissatisfied with village life, for whatever reason, began moving to Bethel. Here they found greater individual freedom and intermittent opportunities to work for whites, an alternative to living off the country.

As a result of its location, Bethel gradually became the major trading center for Eskimos in the region and the administrative center for federal and state agencies. Beginning with the War on Poverty in the mid-1960s, growing numbers of government offices opened in the community; within ten years they numbered forty-three. Bethel was no longer an Eskimo settlement, a change well reflected in the composition of the population. In 1960, 1,132 native Alaskans and 126 nonnatives lived in Bethel, but by 1982 the numbers of natives and non-natives were nearly equal, about 1,750 each. As the major contact community along the Kuskokwim River, Bethel has attracted hundreds of Kuskowagamiut who lived in villages before the 1960s. For some it is a new home; for others it serves as a way station until they move to another Alaskan town or city, especially Anchorage, or to another state.

Many villagers consider Bethel an exciting place to visit or live because there is so much more activity than in a village. Furthermore, work opportunities are more plentiful in Bethel than in the villages. Although many residents find Bethel an attractive place to live, the transient rate is high, and the town has retained an unsettled, frontier atmosphere. In recent years Bethel has had the highest per capita homicide rate in the United States, the gonorrhea rate has been twenty-five times the national average, and the number of rapes has been astronomical. Intoxicants have been at least partially responsible for many of these problems. Villagers often go to Bethel to drink and "let off steam," but for permanent residents there is more involved. Most of these people have found that it is impossible for them to pursue their traditional life-style in this setting, and yet they are unable to fit comfortably into the way of life of the whites nor can they compete successfully with whites for most jobs. Some find comfort in a Christian religion, but others turn to alcohol as a means of escaping from the problems of their new lifeway.

| Alaskan Native Land Claims

Because the Eskimo land base is so important to their livelihood and sense of identity, a brief review of Alaskan Eskimo land claims is appropriate here. When Alaska was purchased from Russia by the United States in 1867, the treaty provided that "the uncivilized tribes will be subject to such laws and regulations as the United States may, from time to time, adopt in regard to aboriginal tribes in that country." No formal effort was made by the federal government to consider aboriginal land claims until 1906. At that time individuals could gain "restricted" title to 160- acre plots, but few selections were made because the grants were inappropriate in terms of their Eskimo needs.

The first effort by aboriginal Alaskans to organize for their rights as citizens was in 1912 when the Alaska Native Brotherhood was founded, but this effort, discussed in Chapter 9, was restricted largely to the Tlingit of southeastern Alaska. The Indian Reorganization Act of 1934 encouraged the establishment of reservations, but few Eskimos or Indians claimed lands under its provisions, and no large blocks of land were set aside along the Kuskokwim. The greatest threat to local Eskimo control and use of land came when Alaska became a state in 1959. The new state was granted the right to select 103 million acres of land from the public domain. In 1961 Guy Okakok, an Eskimo from Point Barrow, was instrumental in organizing the group Inupiat Paitot (the People's Heritage); Howard Rock, a Point Hope Eskimo, founded the newspaper *Tundra Times* in 1962; and in 1966 the Alaska Federation of Natives was organized. All of these efforts were directed primarily at achieving a settlement of native claims throughout the state. The first important victory was the imposition by Secretary of the Interior Stewart Udall of a "land freeze" on state selections. Finally, after years of proposals and counterproposals, the Alaska Native Claims Settlement Act was passed by Congress and became law in 1971. The major provisions were that Alaskan natives were to receive fee simple title to 40 million acres of land and that $962.5 million was to be paid to the Alaska Native Fund over a period of years as compensation for extinguished claims. The money was to come from congressional appropriations and 2 percent of the mineral revenues from certain federal and state lands in Alaska. U.S. citizens in or from Alaska having one-fourth or more Aleut, Eskimo, or Indian blood were enrolled and became stockholders in regional corporations and usually village corporations as well. In general, the regional corporations held mineral rights to village lands. Payments were from the Alaska Native Fund to regional corporations on a per capita basis; the regional corporations retained part of the money and turned the balance over to village corporations and to individuals.

By 1985, Calista, the local regional corporation established under the settlement act, had lost nearly $43 million from total assets of about $70 million because of incompetent management. Dividend payments to shareholders have been negligible, and the typical Kuskokwim Eskimo has not benefited from the act monetarily. Since one provision of the act is that stock shares, which represent land as well as money, can be sold to the public after 1991, the possibility exists that outsiders will purchase shares and thereby reduce the land base of the Eskimos. In 1986, efforts were made to convince Congress to change a provision of the settlement act to extend the grace period for stock alienation or to permit only native corporation members to buy any shares for sale, but these efforts failed. In brief, the Alaska Native Claims Settlement Act as it stands today provides the Kuskowagamiut with neither the secure land base nor the sound economic future visualized by its planners.

The failures of Calista Corporation managers have produced frustration in some villages, and in some cases villagers have begun to react. The people of Akiachak have responded in the most innovative manner. In 1948 they voted to organize a tribal (really village) government under provisions of the Indian Reorganization Act, and they elected a village council as their local government. They likewise voted to become a second-class Alaskan city in 1974, and at that time they formed a city council government. By 1983 the Akiachak population was 438, of whom 40 were non-Eskimo. The Eskimos feared that the growing number of local whites might come to control the city through its council, and therefore they voted to withdraw from being a second-class city. This led to full Eskimo control of local government because the tribal council was restricted to members of the native community. The decision to revert to this council as the exclusive form of government also was fueled by the fear that the village would lose control over its lands in 1991 if outsiders purchased its stock. By transferring stock ownership to the tribal government, they hoped to insure control of the land after 1991. In another move along the same lines, in 1984 the Akiachak Eskimos and those in the nearby village of Tuluksak formed the Yupiit Nation, whose goal is self-government in cooperation with state and federal authorities. Since its founding, the Yupiit Nation has been joined by other villages. This is an *Eskimo* effort to form a quasi-reservation so that they can gain control over their own affairs, including village schools, law enforcement, and community services in general. The Calista Corporation has fought the grassroots "Akiachak Revolt," considering it a threat to the corporation, but its efforts have been unsuccessful. The Yupiit Nation seems to be emerging as a viable new institution, and since it is of Eskimo inspiration, not artificially imposed by the federal government, it has a reasonable chance of maintaining the support necessary for success.

One positive contribution of Calista as well as of some federal and state agencies has been attempts to revive or sustain the traditional Eskimo culture through varied programs. Prominent have been bilingual education programs in the schools, Yupik language courses at the Bethel community college, and attempts to emphasize the local Eskimo cultural heritage in other, varied ways. For the most part, these efforts have failed or met with only moderate success. One important reason is that the younger generation often views Americanization as the most reasonable means to insure a secure future.

All of the attempts to strengthen Eskimo identity, whether directed by themselves or by others, are meaningful but will be nonproductive if the land base is eroded. The most critical factor in sustaining a sense of being Eskimo on a long-term basis is the continuing identity with the land, and this will be in jeopardy after 1991 unless the settlement act is changed before that date.

Comparisons between the Kuskowagamiut and the Chipewyan

Although both the Kuskowagamiut and the Chipewyan were hunters, fishers, and trappers in aboriginal times, significant contrasts are reflected in their cultures. The Chipewyan were far more mobile than the Kuskokwim Eskimos and lived in smaller, less stable communities. The Kuskokwim Eskimos had relatively permanent settlements, larger aggregates of people, a well-developed ceremonial life, and more material goods than the Chipewyan. These differences are in part explained by the more reliable food resources available in southwestern Alaska. The reader may care to consider why Kuskokwim Eskimo culture was not more elaborate in aboriginal times, why leadership was not more fully developed among them, and why their traditional lifeway was not more durable in the face of Russian and American contacts. Comparisons among these peoples in terms of their responses to contacts with Euro-Americans are also worthy of consideration.

This chapter and the previous one, about the Chipewyan, have included reasonably full information about life at particular villages in the 1950s and 1960s. Studies of northern communities have been appealing to anthropologists because of the continuity they exhibit from aboriginal times to the present. Acculturative ethnographies of comparable scope are far less frequent for peoples presented in later chapters. Thus, the Chipewyan and Eskimo data provide a better opportunity to plot recent historical changes at the village level, and comparisons are invited along these dimensions.

Additional Readings

Alaskan Eskimos in the Bering Sea region are known for the complexity of their technology; the best descriptions of their material culture are in the monograph by Edward W. Nelson (1899). Unfortunately, comparatively few recent studies have been made about Kuskokwim Eskimos. An ethnoarchaeological monograph by Wendell H. Oswalt and James VanStone (1967) gives some insight into the material changes introduced to the region by the Russians and early Americans. In his book about Alaskan Eskimo education, John Collier (1973) devoted a major portion to the Kuskowagamiut; more than any others, this study analyzes the methods and results of the BIA school system. *Alaskan Eskimos* (San Francisco, 1967), by Wendell Oswalt, is a comprehensive study of aboriginal conditions for the Eskimo population in all of Alaska, with considerable stress on the southwestern populations. The *Arctic* volume (5) of the *Handbook of North American Indians,* William C. Sturtevant, general editor (Washington, DC, 1984), is the best single source for descriptions and comparisons of the Eskimos of southwestern Alaska with those living elsewhere.

Bibliography

Anderson, Eva G. 1940. *Dog-team doctor.* Caldwell.

Arnold, Robert D., et al. 1976. *Alaska native land claims.* Anchorage.

Collier, John. 1973. *Alaskan Eskimo education*. New York.

Johnson, M. Walter. 1971. Tuberculosis in Alaska. Paper presented at the Second International Symposium on Circumpolar Health, Oulu, Finland.

Kilbuck, John H. N.d. Something about the Innuit of the Kuskokwim River, Alaska. Manuscript in the Archives of the Moravian Church, Bethlehem, PA.

Mason, Lynn D. 1972. *Disabled fishermen*. PhD dissertation, University of California, Los Angeles.

Nelson, Edward W. 1899. *The Eskimo about Bering Strait*. Bureau of American Ethnology, 18th Annual Report, pt. 1.

Oswalt, Wendell H. 1963a. *Napaskiak: An Alaskan Eskimo community*. Tucson. This 1955–56 study of one Kuskokwim Eskimo community supplies virtually all that we know of contemporary riverine Eskimo life in southwestern Alaska.

———. 1963b. *Mission of change in Alaska*. San Marino. A historical reconstruction, supplemented by the author's field notes, of Kuskokwim Eskimo life, with concentration on the period from 1884 to 1925. Additional summary information is provided on the Russian era and events subsequent to 1925.

———. 1964. Traditional storyknife tales of Yuk girls. *Proceedings of the American Philosophical Society* 108:310–36.

Oswalt, Wendell H., and James W. VanStone. 1967. *The ethnoarcheology of Crow Village, Alaska*. Bureau of American Ethnology Bulletin no. 199. Washington, DC.

Petroff, Ivan. 1884. *Report on the population, industries, and resources of Alaska*. United States Department of the Interior, Census Office.

Weinland Collection. The William Henry Weinland collection of manuscripts, letters, and diaries. Henry E. Huntington Library, San Marino, CA.

Wrangell, Ferdinand von. 1839 (German edition). *Statistical and ethnographic data concerning the Russian possessions on the Northwest Coast of America*. St. Petersburg.

Zagoskin, Lavrentiy A. 1967. *Lieutenant Zagoskin's travels in Russian America, 1842–1844,* Henry N. Michael, ed. Anthropology of the North: Translations from Russian Sources, no. 7. Arctic Institute of North America, Toronto. This early historic Russian traveler's account is the primary source of information about aboriginal Eskimo life along the Kuskokwim River.

5 The Cahuilla: Gatherers in the Desert

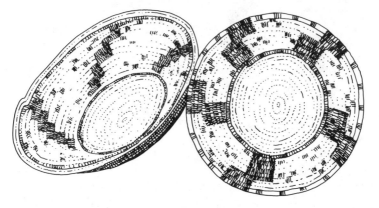

His food gave out, his water gave out,
Leave him now, go away from him:
Isilwelnet. [enemy name]
[repeated as many times as desired]

Bury him now, plant him now:
And then they buried him, and then they planted
him:
Pehuetematewilwish.

There stands the whirlwind, there stands the
whirlwind
Where they burned him, where they burned him:
Puchueulchalmalmia.

Three "enemy songs" among the Desert Cahuilla
collected by Lucile Hooper. (1920, 345)

THIS CHAPTER EXAMINES the lives of the Cahuilla Indians, representatives of the Great Basin-Baja culture area. A major reason for selecting the Cahuilla, as for selecting the other peoples described in this book, is that the ethnographic and historical data about them are more comprehensive than is typical for most tribes. We have a fine Cahuilla ethnobotany by David P. Barrows (1900), a comprehensive account compiled around the turn of the century by Alfred L. Kroeber (1908), and a somewhat later report by Lucile Hooper (1920). In 1959 Lowell J. Bean began reconstructing an aboriginal baseline ethnography, and he has emerged as the ranking authority on the Cahuilla.

Anthropologists have not been the only persons with a vested interest in the Cahuilla. They have attracted attention from BIA employees, land speculators, lawyers, and especially municipal officials in the resort city of Palm Springs. For the most part, the concern of these persons has been neither humanistic nor philanthropic but monetary. Certain reservation lands are of fantastic value, and very few Indians occupy them. A look at the Desert Cahuilla affords an excellent opportunity to analyze the relationship between a now-prosperous Indian group and their Anglo-American neighbors. Although we tend to think that the era of grabbing Indian land is not only past but best forgotten, the Cahuilla example illustrates that Anglo-Americans have not changed their goals, simply their methods. All of this is especially interesting when we realize that among the Cahuilla, it was the women who resolved their serious land problem. Until recently the Palm Springs Cahuilla had the only Indian council comprised of women. In a historical context, the Cahuilla have been endowed with romantic appeal through the novel *Ramona*. Once fabulously popular, it depicts the life of a Cahuilla woman, and its writer, Helen Hunt Jackson, played a significant role in the lives of southern California Indians just before the turn of the century.

In the following discussion of the Cahuilla, the stress is on the Desert group and the Palm Springs (Agua Caliente) subgroup. However, it was not always possible to determine from a souce whether a specific trait prevailed in both the general desert region and at Palm Springs. As is true of most ethnographic reconstructions, the text to follow does not apply in every detail to a single community, but it does represent a composite for the desert region.

| Population and Language

The Cahuilla lived in the interior of southern California (see Figure 5-1) and numbered thirty-six hundred, or possibly many more, in early historic times. By 1885 their population had declined to about eight hundred, and it remained at this level for some sixty years. In 1986 about seventeen hundred retained their identity as Cahuilla by being on the tribal roll, but most did not live on reservations. In early historic times and more recently, they identified themselves as members of the Desert, Mountain, or Pass groups, but a sense of tribal solidarity probably originated in response to Mexican and Anglo-American contacts.

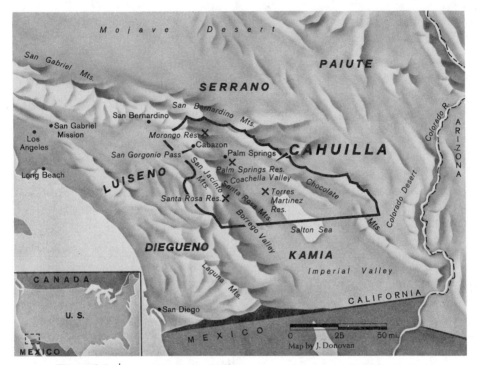

Figure 5-1. | The Cahuilla area with major reservations indicated.

The Aztec-Tanoan linguistic phylum, which is represented widely in the western United States and Mexico, includes Cahuilla. These Indians belong to the Uto-Aztecan language family. The emergence of the Cahuilla as a separate people is revealed through linguistic rather than archaeological researches. Unfortunately, no archaeological sites excavated and reported on in published sources provide clues to their past. Linguists, however, do offer some insight into the past affinities of these people. Kenneth Hale (1958), after analyzing the vocabularies of certain Aztec-Tanoan languages, concluded on lexicostatistical grounds that the Cahuilla became a separate linguistic group about 1000 B.C.

| Early Historic Contact with Whites

The Cahuilla often are classed as Mission Indians, but this is not an accurate label. They were not subject to the mission environment in the manner of coastal Indians in southern California, and most Cahuilla had only indirect contact with Roman Catholic missionaries. The first Europeans to travel into Cahuilla country were Pedro Fages in 1772 and Juan Bautista de Anza in 1774, but neither made any known impact on these Indians. De Anza attempted without success to establish an overland route from Mexico to Alta California. Following the War for Independence in Mexico, attention again turned to the interior of southern California. At the request of Indians in the San Bernardino area for a mission, an outpost or rancho was established among them in 1819. Jose Romero was charged with opening an overland route, and a small party set out from Tucson in 1823. An expedition member's diary makes apparent that the Desert Cahuilla, at least those as far south and west as Palm Springs, were in close contact with the San Bernardino mission rancho. Some of the people in the Coachella Valley were raising maize and pumpkins, crops that they probably acquired from Colorado River area Indians, and the Cahuilla of the desert were growing watermelon, an Old World domestic plant introduced by Europeans to the New World.

Before 1834 the California missions were under the control of Franciscans, who introduced most European ideas and technology to the region. After this date some missions, including the one founded at San Gabriel in 1771, became secularized, and the missionaries lost control. In 1834, the San Bernardino rancho was sacked and burned by Indians. With secularization the rancho passed into private ownership, and marauding Indians raided the herds of live-stock. A Mountain Cahuilla leader, "Captain" Juan Antonio, and his small band were recruited to end the raids, which they did with great success. In 1846 the United States acquired California, and a few years later, in 1852, the San Bernar-dino rancho was purchased by Mormon settlers. During the late Mexican and early American periods, raids by Mohave, Paiute, and Yuma for livestock, espe-cially horses, contributed to the hostile attitude of whites toward most Indians in southern California. The Cahuilla were not combative by nature and apparently played an insignificant part in these raids. Since they did not intrude on the activ-ities of whites, the Cahuilla were left very much to themselves.

In 1850 the U.S. Congress sent a special commission to California to nego-tiate treaties with Indians and assign lands to them. A Cahuilla treaty arranged in 1852 set aside land from San Gorgonio to Warner's ranch, an area about forty miles long and thirty miles wide. The U.S. Senate, however, refused to ratify any of the eighteen treaties with California Indians. Congressional resistance stemmed from a number of facts: the commissioners had committed the govern-ment to spend a great deal of money, white citizens of California were vig-orously opposed to the treaties, and it was thought that some of these lands might contain gold.

In 1852 Edward F. Beale was appointed superintendent of Indian affairs in California, and he selected Benjamin D. Wilson as the subagent for the southern part of the state. Wilson, a former mayor of Los Angeles, was a landowner and merchant married to a Spanish American. In a report that may have been written by Wilson's friend Benjamin Hays, we have contemporary comments about the Cahuilla and a good account of conditions among southern California Indians. The Wilson Report noted that the last ties with missionaries had been severed in 1834 and that old ethnic groups had been disrupted by 1852. Living among the Desert Cahuilla were Diegueno and Luiseno Indians; one of the Cahuilla leaders was a Yuma. The elders and many others spoke Spanish by this time. The Indians worked as underpaid laborers and domestics on the ranchos of whites and were frequently intoxicated. The report pointed out that under Spanish law the Indians had rights to their settlements and pasture lands, and in theory the State of California recognized Indian land rights. The report characterized state laws as "*All* punishment. *No* reform!" But the positive recommendations of the Wilson Report made no recognized impact on early American policy, probably in part because of the recent rejection of California Indian treaties by the U.S. Senate.

In late 1852 Beale recommended that lands be set aside for Indian occupation; this was the beginning of the modern reservation system in the United States. The lands would be military reservations as well as places where Indians could be instructed in farming and other skills. Soldiers were to be stationed there to maintain order, and the military would be supported from surplus Indian harvests. The first reserve opened at Tejon in 1853, and after initial success Beale's political enemies charged that he was making a personal profit from the reservation. Although he finally was vindicated fully, the reservation system had lost its impetus and did not become important in California.

In the mid-1850s, Cahuilla males reportedly numbered about thirty-five hundred. These figures unquestionably included many non-Cahuilla, but in any event Indians far outnumbered the local white settlers. The Indians were discontented after the federal government failed to set land aside for their exclusive use; they complained that they had not received farm equipment as promised and that whites were trespassing and squatting on traditional Indian lands, as well as taking water and wood. In 1862 a smallpox epidemic spread from Los Angeles, and although the number of people who perished was not recorded, the epidemic probably was a significant factor in eroding the people and their way of life. Throughout the latter part of the nineteenth century, some Cahuilla worked on the ranches of whites, the men as laborers and the women as domestics. The men also tended orchards and vineyards, cut mesquite wood, and labored at salt works. When the Southern Pacific railroad was being built through the area in the 1870s, they were employed as laborers. They continued to collect products of the desert, and farmed some of the better-watered localities.

| Aboriginal Life of the Cahuilla

Cahuilla tradition states that these people originally lived in the desert but were forced to flee to adjacent mountains by a great flood, a probable reference to the emergence of the inland sea that once covered much of the present lowland and subsided about five hundred years ago. The San Jacinto and Santa Rosa mountains where they sought refuge consist of steep granite ridges and barren tablelands at medium elevations, but higher up are streams, open meadows, and forests of oak and pine. After the flood subsided, the Desert Cahuilla moved into the Coachella Valley, a desert environment in which cacti, mesquite, and screw beans were economically important plants. The region has very little precipitation, and summer temperatures may reach 120° F. Precipitation, when it does come, is often torrential and causes widespread erosion. Furthermore, severe dust storms may whip across the valley. Some sectors, particularly in the eastern part of the Desert Cahuilla range, are devoid of vegetation. The Pass Cahuilla occupied the country surrounding San Gorgonio Pass; here were open grassland and some oak groves as well as desert areas.

ORIGIN MYTH   In the Cahuilla culture, ties with the mythological past were very important. Their well-developed origin myth goes as follows. In the beginning, there was no earth or sky or anything or anybody; only a dense darkness in space. This darkness seemed alive. Something like lightning bolts seemed to pass through it and meet each other once in a while. Two substances that looked like the white of an egg came from the lightning bolts. They lay side by side in the stomach of the darkness, which resembled a spider web. These substances disappeared. They were produced again, and again they disappeared. This was called the miscarriage of the darkness. The third time they appeared, they remained, hanging there in this web in the darkness. The substances began to grow and soon were two very large eggs. When they began to hatch, they broke at the top first. Two heads came out, then shoulders, hips, knees, ankles, toes; then the shell was all gone. Two men had emerged: Mukat and Tamaioit. They were grown men from the first, and could talk right away. As they lay there, both at the same time heard a noise like a bee buzzing. It was the song of their mother, Darkness (Hooper 1920, 317).

With this great event the natural world began to emerge as an orderly system; at least this was said to be so by the Iviatim, the descendants of Mukat and Tamaioit, who have come to be known in the ethnographic literature as the Cahuilla (Coahuillas, Kawia), a word that may have meant "masters."

Once the twin creators existed, Mukat reached into his mouth and then into his heart to remove a cricket, another insect, a lizard, and a person. These creatures were charged with driving away the darkness, but they failed. From their hearts the creators removed tobacco, pipes, and a coal to light one pipe. Mukat and Tamaioit argued over which one was born first and which was the more intelligent. Mukat became associated with making things black, and Tamaioit made forms that were white. Together they created the earth, ocean, sun, moon, people, and some plants and animals. Finally Mukat and Tamaioit disagreed so violently that Tamaioit disappeared beneath the ground, taking with him many of his creations. It was then that mountains emerged, the earth quaked, and water from the ocean overflowed, forming streams and rivers. After this Mukat lived in a big house with people and animals who had human qualities. The moon was there as a lovely female who instructed women about marriage, child rearing, and both menstrual and pregnancy taboos. Mukat, who had created her, desired to make the moon his wife. She knew this but said nothing. Since she could not marry him because he was her father, she traveled to her present home in the sky. When she was asked to return, she said nothing; she only smiled. One day, while in a humorous mood, Mukat caused the people to speak different languages. As the sun grew hot, some of these people sought shelter and were transformed into different plants and animals. Those who stayed with Mukat remained human. He told the people how to make bows and arrows and how to shoot at each other, which led to the first deaths. It was about this time, too, that the sun turned people different colors. Those people who were nearest the sun's rays became Negroes, those who were far away stayed white, and the Indians turned brown because they were in between.

The people became angry with Mukat after he had caused a rattlesnake to bite a friendly little man, the moon woman to leave, and people to kill one another. They decided to kill Mukat but did not know how to do it. Mukat lived in the middle of the big house and only went outside to defecate when everyone was asleep; this a white lizard discovered. One night a frog caught the feces of Mukat in his mouth, and Mukat grew ill. The shamans pretended to try to cure him, but Mukat became sicker. As he was dying, he sang songs and told the people how to conduct a mourning ceremony in memory of the dead each year. After his death, Mukat was cremated, the big house was burned, and the essence of the world was established.

SETTLEMENTS AND MANUFACTURES   Desert Cahuilla settlements usually were clustered around hand-dug wells and water holes, but the Palm Springs people lived near streams flowing from canyons at the base of the San Jacinto Mountains. Communities were permanent as long as the water supply lasted. Their dwellings were substantial rectangular structures with forked mesquite posts at each corner; in the post crotches rested roof beams. Along the sides and on the beam tops were arranged lengths of brush held in place with horizontal poles. (See Figure 5-2.) On some houses the brush was smeared with a coat of mud, and a layer of dirt was added to the roof. At the front of a house was a

Figure 5-2. | Palm Springs Cahuilla homestead, ca. 1900. (Courtesy of the Southwest Museum, Los Angeles, CA.)

Figure 5-3. | A 1907 Desert Cahuilla granary. (Photograph by Alfred L. Kroeber, courtesy of the Lowie Museum of Anthropology, University of California, Berkeley.)

ramada or porch constructed like a house but walled only on the windward side. A settlement included a bathhouse framed with posts and poles; built in a shallow pit, it probably was covered with brush and then a layer of earth. A fire was built in the fireplace, and smoke was allowed to drift out the doorway until the people were ready to bathe. Cahuilla caches were of a distinctive form and were found in every settlement. They usually were raised above the ground on a pole platform and were made by intertwining small branches; they looked very much like birds' nests some two to four feet high, and were used to store plant products. (See Figure 5-3.) The only other structures were a brush enclosure used for certain ceremonies and a large enclosure walled on three sides and attached to the house of a male leader. Among the Palm Springs Cahuilla in 1925, the social and ceremonial leader occupied the dance house, which was about forty feet in diameter with walls of fitted boards and a palm-thatched roof. At the back was a room where the sacred bundle was kept; in front of the structure was a fenced enclosure.

An aboriginal house stayed relatively cool even in the hottest weather. The inside was dark from the soot on the walls, and natural light filtered in only through the doorway. On one side of the entrance were a woman's food-grinding stones. People the world over who collect seeds as food usually use a set of stones to crush the shells. The Cahuilla spread seeds on a flat or slightly concave stone called a milling stone, quern, or metate, and pulverized them using a smaller stone called a hand stone or mano. On the other side of the doorway was a pottery vessel used for water and filled each morning. Toward the center of the room, fire-blackened cooking pots encircled the fireplace; at the back of the house, blankets and animal skins served as mattresses. Attached to the roof beams or in the thatch were bundles of plants or dried meat for future use. Near every house a section of log set vertically into the ground served as a mortar: the top was flat except that the center was hollowed out a foot or more in depth. A smooth pole some two feet long served as the pestle. The combination was designed to pulverize mesquite beans, which were an important item in the diet.

Most artifacts around a settlement were made from plant fibers. Baskets, usually fashioned by coiling and often having black geometric designs woven on the sides, were the most varied cluster of forms. Among the more common styles were globular baskets used as utensils or containers for small objects, and round forms for food or seed storage. (See Figure 5-4.) Mescal fiber nets used as carrying baskets looked like small hammocks and had loops at each end for cinching cords. A woman carrying a basket passed the cord over her forehead and rested it against the front of a flat-topped cap made of basketry that she wore.

The only domestic animal, the dog, served as a pet and watchdog rather than as an aid in hunting. The dog was not an ordinary pet because it was believed to possess certain supernatural powers. According to Cahuilla belief, dogs could understand human conversation but could not speak, and like people, they had souls. In the origin myth, at the time of Mukat's death, the people had only one dog, and among the twentieth-century Desert Cahuilla, some dogs still were named after the first dog. Other dog names referred to their appearance or to some behavioral characteristic.

CLOTHING   In aboriginal times, clothing seems to have been nonexistent, although it is possible that women wore short skirts of plant fiber and men wore breechclouts. A more certain item of apparel was footwear, which consisted of sandals made from mescal fiber pads. Women sometimes wore the basketry hats mentioned earlier. They were tattooed on the chin, and certain men, most likely

Figure 5-4. | A Cahuilla woman, Louisa Costa Rice, making baskets for the tourist trade in 1938 at the Soboba reservation. (Photograph by Maxine Smith, courtesy of the San Bernardino County Museum.)

leaders, had their nasal septums pierced and a deer bone inserted in the opening. Both males and females wore strings of beads in their pierced earlobes. The beads were thin curved and circular pieces of shell received in trade from the coastal regions of southern California.

SUBSISTENCE ACTIVITIES   The Cahuilla identified three primary seasons: the budding of trees, hot days, and cold days. Some persons divided the year into eight more specific seasons, each associated with the development of mesquite beans. The beginning of a season arrived when a particular star appeared;

this was a moment for rejoicing and a time to make preparations for an appropriate collecting activity. Star watching was especially important in the spring when food supplies might be low and edible plants were ripening.

The most important Desert Cahuilla food plant was the mesquite tree, which grew in groves from the desert floor to heights of thirty-five hundred feet in better-watered areas. Stands were particularly numerous near springs or streams and in washes. In the early summer the Indians picked the blossoms, roasted them in a pit of heated stones, formed them into balls, and stored them in pottery containers; later they boiled the balls in water and ate them. Mesquite beans ripened from June through August, depending on the locality. At this time, or even earlier if pods were to be artificially ripened in the sun, entire families picked them. Children helped by climbing the trees to dislodge pods from high branches. The pods were not gathered indiscriminately, for the beans of some trees were regarded as more palatable than those from others. The pods could be stored from one year to the next, which may have been necessary on occasion, since the trees of a particular grove were not equally productive every year. The Cahuilla crushed the ripened pods in an upright wooden mortar with a stone or wooden pestle, and made the juice into a beverage. The pods might be ripened artificially, picked ripe, or gathered after they had fallen from the trees. The dried pods, either complete or broken into small sections, were stored in raised caches. Further processing included grinding the pods in a mortar or on a milling stone. The meal then could be placed in pottery or basketry containers and moistened; when it had dried, the cake of meal was removed and stored in the rafters of a house. Sections of the cakes were broken off and eaten as a snack or carried by travelers as food. The meal could also be made into a gruel or soaked in water to make the mesquite juice beverage. Loose ground meal was stored in pottery or basketry containers to be made into gruel later.

The mesquite bean was the most important staple, but the people of the desert areas also ate screw beans. The screw bean or tornillo grew under the same general conditions as the mesquite and was processed in the same manner. In ethnographic studies of California Indians, acorns often are specified as an important staple. This clearly was the case over much of the state, but the acorn was not as important among the Cahuilla as elsewhere. Of the six varieties available, the acorn from the Kellogg oak was preferred for its taste and consistency. As was true with mesquite beans, when the first acorns were collected, they were eaten ceremonially in the homes of male leaders. If an individual collected acorns prior to this ceremony, she or he was expected to become ill or die. In the groves controlled by patriclans, or groups of families related through males, each family owned particular trees, and in October and November the men climbed their trees to knock ripe acorns to the ground. Women cracked the acorns between two stones, spread the kernels out to dry for several weeks, and then pulverized them with pestles in stone mortars. To remove the bitter tannic acid the meal was spread out on a loosely woven basket or in a depression made in sand. In either case grass or leaves were placed in the leaching basin to prevent the meal from washing away. Then water, either cold or warm, was poured over the meal several times; during this process the mixture was stirred. The capabilities of a woman were measured by her skill in leaching and grinding acorn meal. Finely ground meal was made into cakes and baked in hot coals, while coarse meal was made into a gruel. Acorns that were not ground at gathering time were stored in platform caches.

Mesquite and screw beans were the most important foods, but over sixty different plants played a part in the diet. Growing in well-watered localities was a species of *Chenopodium* locally called careless weed. The seeds were collected, ground, and baked in cakes. One of the most important seed-producing grasses was chia, a member of the sage family. A seed beater dislodged the seeds from the whorls onto a flat basket. They were parched and ground to be baked into cakes or mixed with water to make a nourishing drink. When the century plants or agave of the canyons produced stalks, the stalks and "cabbages" were roasted in sand pits heated with stones. To this list of foods could be added many others, but the examples cited suggest the broad range of plants collected and the varied means of food preparation.

Contrary to expectations, the overwhelming emphasis on plant foods did not mean that hunting was neglected nor that the inventory of weapons and traps was impoverished. Adult males trapped animals and also stalked, chased, and intercepted them. The principal weapon was a shaft (self) bow with a plant fiber bowstring. The arrowshafts were vaned with split feathers, and shafts simply sharpened at the point probably were meant for birds and small game. Arrows with cane shafts and wooden arrow points probably were used against large game and enemies; some arrows apparently were tipped with poisons made from rattlesnake venom and other toxic substances. Another weapon was the nonreturning boomerang, commonly called a throwing stick when reported in western North America. It was a flat, curved piece of wood thrown at birds and small game. Hunters also used calls and decoys to lure game near enough to kill with arrows. Additional facilities for taking game included nets set along trails, deadfalls, and snares. Hunting was surrounded by numerous restrictions. For example, the Desert Cahuilla regarded mountain lions and grizzly bears as shamans and avoided killing them. When a mule deer was killed, people gathered to sing all night and eat the deer the following morning. In general, a man or boy did not consume any of the animals that he killed. Rabbits, squirrels, and other small game taken by a young boy in a communal hunt usually were given to his mother's family. The kills of an adult male were given alternately to his own family and to his wife's family.

DESCENT, KINSHIP, AND MARRIAGE All the peoples described previously traced their descent through their father's *and* mother's hereditary lines; this is the bilateral (nonunilineal) descent system familiar to us since it currently prevails in the United States. (Our descent system should not be confused with our pattern of typically taking our father's surname. This practice may give some added stress to the father's line, but a mother's line may be equally or more important in the lives of some individuals.) Many people around the world give special stress to the male *or* female lines. The Cahuilla emphasized one line and thus had a unilineal descent system. Since they considered the male line far more important, their descent system was patrilineal, and a married couple resided with or near the husband's family (patrilocal residence). A typical Cahuilla settlement was formed around a group of males who traced their descent to a *known* common ancestor (patrilineage). Closely related patrilineages with a *presumed* common ancestor comprised a larger unit (patriclan), which was the most important social and ceremonial group.

In the kinship terminology, a male individual distinguished among his older and younger male and female siblings and made similar distinctions between his father's brothers and mother's sisters. He employed still other terms for his father's sisters and mother's brothers; these did not take relative age into consideration. A male individual referred to his father's older brother's and his mother's older sister's son and daughter by the same term as for his older brothers and sisters. Similarly, he referred to the son and daughter of his father's younger brother and mother's younger sister by the same terms as for his younger brothers and sisters. In essence, parallel cousins (children of father's brother and mother's sister) were termed the same as siblings, with the same age distinction as for siblings. For cross-cousins (father's sister's and mother's brother's children), the male-female kin terms were the same but different from those for siblings or parallel cousins. This cousin terminology is of the Iroquois type, while the terms on the first ascending generation are bifurcate collateral. The Iroquois cousin terms make particular sense since moiety exogamy (marriage outside each of the two basic tribal subdivisions) existed. Thus, certain near relatives, such as father's brother's children and mother's sister's children, were of one's own moiety and reasonably called brother and sister. Cross-cousins, on the other hand, were of a different moiety and termed differently, but in spite of the terminological difference one could not marry a cross-cousin. (See Figure 5-5.)

SOCIAL DIMENSIONS   In the Cahuilla origin myth, Mukat and Tamaioit were associated with the wildcat and coyote respectively, and all Cahuilla identified with one or the other of these groups (moieties). Among the Desert Cahuilla, the Wildcat moiety included eight clans, and the Coyote moiety con-

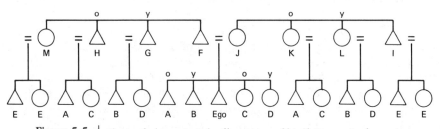

Figure 5-5. | The early historic Cahuilla system of kinship terminology.

sisted of ten clans. In aboriginal times the members of each clan theoretically occupied a single settlement, but in actual fact, persons from a number of clans might live in one settlement. We may presume that at one time all the members of a patriclan lived in a single village. As their number increased and they could not support themselves at the village site, the surplus, most likely members of a junior patrilineage, formed a new village or joined another clan at its settlement. A clan section or patrilineage founding a new village might eventually become so expanded that it qualified as a clan, with its own name and leader, or clan "chief," called a *net*. The office of net usually passed from father to eldest son (primogeniture), and it included extremely important obligations. Nets lived in dwellings with dance houses attached and were the trustees of sacred clan bundles. A net directed subsistence activities, settled conflicts between members, represented the clan before other clans, and was responsible for the correct performance of ceremonies.

In sum, small family groups lived in a village and were related through males to a known common ancestor (patrilineage). In the same settlement were members of other patrilineages, but all the people residing in a community assumed that they had a common male ancestor (patriclan). Among the Desert group there were about eighteen clans, and their members were divided into two groups, the Wildcats or Coyotes (moieties). Moiety exogamy prevailed, which meant that a Wildcat was obligated to marry a Coyote and vice versa. Persons in opposite moieties maintained a joking relationship and friendly rivalry.

POLITICAL LIFE   Hereditary leaders did not exist above the clan level, and in instances where the activities of one clan impinged on those of another, the differences were resolved by the nets in council. Decisions of a clan as a collectivity were made by the net, who ideally was a man of exceptional abilities. A net was required to know the boundaries of all clan lands, all clan traditions, and a broad range of esoteric facts important to the clan's viability; he also was expected to be a good orator and fair-minded. He did not possess more material property than anyone else, but families presented him with the first fruit of any plant harvest, which was partial compensation for the time he devoted to clan activities. At the rear of the net's house was a small room where sacred objects, termed the "heart" of the clan, were kept. Eagle feathers were a vital part of each sacred bundle. Clearly, the net, as conveyer of clan knowledge and guardian of the most sacred clan objects, was the paramount leader.

A second important political and religious functionary was the *paha*. His role existed only in certain localities, and his exact duties have not been reported in detail. Apparently, where the office existed the paha was primarily responsible for ceremonial preparations and the maintenance of order on such occasions. In addition, he was a leader of hunting parties and a spokesman and messenger for a net. Upon his death he was replaced by a son or another close male relative.

Formalized warfare or even feuds with neighboring ethnic groups were rare. To the east the desert area had no permanent occupants as far as the Colorado River; here the aggressive Yuma lived. The Cahuilla feared the Yuma, but the intervening desert was an effective barrier to intensive contacts. The Chemehuevi, who lived to the east along the Colorado River and into the deserts of California, were friendly with the Desert Cahuilla. The southern neighbors of the Desert Cahuilla were the Yuman-speaking Kamia, but contacts with these people have not been described in any detail and are assumed to have been infrequent.

RELIGIOUS ACTIVITIES   Shamans were responsible for dealing with intermittent disaster and personal trauma, while the net and paha guided ceremonies focusing on the life cycle and belief system. The Eagle-Killing Ceremony belongs to the latter category and was a highlight in religious life.

The Eagle-Killing Ceremony symbolized the continuity of a lineage. According to Cahuilla belief, the eagle was one of the species originally created by Mukat. It was said that the eagle lived forever and by permitting itself to be "killed" by people it assured them of life after death. Thus, although lineage members died, the lineage would continue as had the eagle as a species. Furthermore, the flight of the eagle symbolized the magical course of shamans when they led human souls to the land of the dead. The ceremony also provided a means of obtaining eagle feathers, essential for replacing ceremonial artifacts that had worn out, been destroyed, or exchanged in previous rituals.

In the mountain lands of some clans were eagle nests that were closely watched. A guard was posted to observe the nest from a vantage point, and when the eggs were laid, the clan was notified and a feast was held. When the eaglets were well feathered, the clan net, regarded as their owner, sent men to retrieve one or more of the nestlings. A captured eaglet was caged in the net's house and fed by his family. When it attained full plumage, the neighboring clan or clans were notified and the ceremony planned. After everyone had assembled, the members of a guest clan sang special songs throughout the night about the death of eagles. They were joined in song and the accompanying dances by the audience. Next, the eagle was removed from its cage and rolled into the clan's ceremonial mat, and it was held by the net's nuclear family members as they danced in a circle. As dawn broke the eagle screeched and died, probably from being squeezed gradually. Its body was placed by the fire, and people wailed over its death. After the sun had risen, the eagle was skinned. The net kept the feathered skin; the body most likely was burned. The skin was rubbed soft and placed in the sacred bundle. Some feathers might be made into a ceremonial skirt, and others were set aside for adorning images in the Mourning Ceremony.

Among the Desert group the status of a shaman was not hereditary, and a number of practitioners might belong to a single clan. A shaman often had been ill frequently as a child, and the healer who treated him had become aware of the child's potential as a curer, magician, and seer. As a young man the novice dreamed of a song that became a tangible manifestation of his inordinate powers. Mukat was responsible, in Cahuilla belief, for implanting the dreams and guardian spirits identified with shamans. A novice danced before the people of his clan for three nights and afterward was qualified to pursue his calling. In his dreams he eventually learned other songs, dances, feats of magic, and bewitching methods. In his dreams, too, a shaman learned of herbal cures for particular ailments or at other times of harmful or curative spells. When not drawing from his pharmacopoeia, he attempted to cure by sucking on the afflicted part of a patient's body. Reputedly, he removed the disease object without breaking the skin. Sometimes he applied plant products externally; golderino weed was put on a snake bite, and an unspecified plant product was used on the bite of a poisonous spider. Only a few plants were used in curing, however, which contrasts with the extensive botanical knowledge and the many uses of plants as food. Certain creatures, such as the coyote, fox, hummingbird, and owl were considered messengers for shamans who brought warnings of impending illness. As a youth a shaman did not accept material rewards for his services, but as he grew older and became established, he charged a fee.

If a shaman became malevolent in the use of his special powers, he posed a threat to the security of a community. In the latter part of the nineteenth century, one old man was considered the world's most powerful shaman. When shamans exhibited their skills, he always performed last and challenged the others to kill him. None was able to do so because he was protected by spirits on all sides. Finally, the old shaman was told by a man of a different clan to stop killing people. The man who gave the warning was soon struck by a "pain" that no shaman could remove, and he died. Everyone knew that the old shaman was responsible. A man from the shaman's clan and men from other clans met and decided that he must be killed. The executioner was to be the net of another clan because he was strong and brave. This man and another visited the sorcerer and were invited to spend the night. After everyone else was asleep, the net crushed the old man's skull with a stone pestle. At the head of the victim's bed were found a variety of small feathers and the skin of a gopher snake, objects used by the old man to make pains. As they were trampled into the ground, a thunderlike sound was heard. In the morning people came to view the body, and later the same morning the body and the house were burned. This is one of the rare recorded instances in which collective action was taken for the good of all the people.

ENTERTAINMENT Of all the forms of recreation for the Cahuilla, the most important was *peon,* a hand game that was played at secular gatherings and during ceremonies. A team from one village played against one from another settlement. Shamans aided their respective sides, while women sat behind the men of their team and sang at certain times during the game. One person was the mediator, and it was his duty to keep a fire burning by which the game was played, to hold the stakes, settle disputes, and take charge of the tally sticks. The game was played by eight men, four to a side, who knelt or sat cross-legged with a blanket between them. Lots were drawn to determine which side would first have the peons. A peon was a small bone tied to a string about two feet long; at the opposite end of the string was a small piece of wood. Each man on the starting team held the wood in one hand and the peon in the other and crossed his arms with his fists beneath his armpits. These men then took a blanket in their teeth to hide the manipulation of their hands. They swayed from side to side in time with the singing of the women on their side, switched the peons back and forth, and then suddenly dropped the blanket, revealing their arms still crossed and fists beneath their armpits. They continued swaying, and their opposites attempted to guess which hand held the peon. For every correct guess the second team took the peon, but with each incorrect guess the first team received one of the fifteen tallies. A particular game ended when one side had lost all four peons or had won all of the tallies. Then a new game was started and new stakes put up. Peon was played frequently throughout the night, and as one player tired he was replaced by another.

Other games included races between two groups of men. Each group kicked a wooden ball for several miles and then back again to the starting point. The men on each team took turns kicking the ball, and the team that finished first was the winner. Another race took place on the night of a new moon. The first boy to see the moon would call the others, and they would race to a spot where they could swim. After swimming they raced home, and by so doing they supposedly brought good luck in the coming month. Cat's cradles were made by persons of both sexes. This skill had supernatural implications since the people believed that before a person's spirit could pass into the world of other spirits, it was required to make string figures.

LIFE CYCLE At critical times during an individual's life, he or she followed numerous rules, and one of these periods was pregnancy. A potential mother refrained from eating any more than necessary; she drank only warm water, ate very little meat, and consumed no salt. In Cahuilla belief, if a pregnant woman ate fruit pecked by a bird, her infant would have sores; if she ate meat from the legs of game, a breech presentation would result; but if she was industrious when pregnant, her offspring would be energetic. These were but three of the rules to insure a safe delivery and a normal offspring. As soon as a woman gave birth and expelled the placenta, she lay in a specially prepared trough dug in the floor of a house. The depression was lined with hot sand, and after the woman stretched out, more hot sand was piled over her body. Here she remained for about ten days, leaving the trough only to urinate and defecate, to have the sand reheated, and to be bathed with hot water each morning. During the month following parturition, the mother remained subject to food taboos, and the father could eat no foods containing salt. A nursing mother did not have sexual intercourse with her husband, for to do so was thought to spoil her milk. She was the object of teasing if she weaned her infant early.

An offspring was not named formally until several children had been born into the clan and each child's parents had accumulated food and wealth for a feast. This meant that children were between the ages of four and twelve before being named; if they had not been formally named by thirteen, they would be known by nicknames throughout their lives. The naming ceremony was held in the clan dance house, with the members of the fathers' and mothers' clans invited. The participating children received traditional names of deceased ancestors selected by the clan net. The names for males tended to be of animals, birds, or insects, and those for females were most often from plants or household artifacts. The ceremony climaxed with singing and dancing as the net held each child up and shouted her or his name three times; afterward the name was repeated by the audience. Sometimes a net would not state the real name for fear an "enemy" clan would learn of it and incorporate it into their songs. In this case the correct name was revealed in secret. A father also might acquire a new name at this ceremony and thereby gain additional standing. Following the naming ritual, presents such as food, baskets, deerskins, and even ceremonial equipment were distributed to the guests. With the presentation of gifts the ceremony concluded.

When a Desert girl approached adolescence, she was tattooed by her mother's sister as guests from the operator's clan watched. The tattoos were made with cactus thorns pricked in straight or angled lines from the lower lip to the chin, and black paint was rubbed into the wounds. At this time the earlobes of a girl were pierced. When a girl menstruated for the first time, the net summoned the clan of the girl's mother to a ceremony that began in the evening. A fire was built before the net's house to heat the ground, and afterward a trough was dug. The girl was placed in the depression, and her body was covered with hot sand. Throughout the night the members of the girl's clan danced and sang around the pit. In the morning the girl was removed, bathed in warm water, and her head covered with a white paint. For the next three weeks she was subject to food taboos very much like those surrounding pregnancy. The girl stayed in or near the house, and she scratched her head with a special implement rather than her fingernails to prevent her hair from dropping out. Subsequent menstrual periods were surrounded by the same taboos, and in addition, a married woman was forbidden to touch her husband when she was menstruating. The good health of a couple supposedly depended on how well the woman obeyed these rules.

Some Desert Cahuilla do not appear to have initiated adolescent males, but an appropriate ceremony prevailed at Palm Springs. Boys between the ages of ten and eighteen were selected by elders for initiation and taken to a brush enclosure outside the dance house. The boys were secluded there for five days and saw only those persons who brought them special foods. During three nights the old people danced until morning. The climax came on the fourth night when the initiates were brought out and given a drink of cooked jimsonweed, or *toloache* as it is known in Spanish. After taking it, the boys danced briefly, but they became dizzy and were placed in a corner while the older people continued to dance. The following evening the effects of the jimsonweed had worn off, and for the next five nights the boys were taught how to dance, sing particular songs, and behave correctly as adults. This ceremony seems to have symbolized the initiates' death as children and their rebirth as knowledgeable adults. The only forms of body mutilation among males were piercing the ears and the nasal septum. The latter operation was not common and was performed only on young boys with promise as leaders. In the opening at the base of the nose pieces of deer bone were inserted.

When members of different clans assembled, especially for the tattooing of a girl or the piercing of a boy's nasal septum, songs known as enemy songs might be sung. Between clans, especially those geographically removed from one another, a rivalry of unknown origins existed. Members of competing clans composed derisive songs in which they incorporated the personal names of individuals in rival clans. These names had been bestowed by a net in secret, and the fact that they were known to the members of other clans was shameful. First one clan performed and then the other, with victory going to the side mentioning the most names of rivals and heaping the greatest abuse, or to the clan whose members were physically able to sing longer. Enemy songs were an obvious means for giving vent to aggressive behavior in a socially approved manner. (These were not comparable to the dueling songs sung by two hostile Eskimos in some sectors of the Arctic.) The joking relationship between moiety members served the same purpose in a friendlier atmosphere.

The Desert Cahuilla marriage pattern included not only moiety exogamy but a prohibition against seeking a spouse from known relatives on either side of the family. Since genealogies were not rememberd over many generations, one could marry a distant cousin in the opposite moiety. A thirteen-year-old girl was most likely to wed a male of eighteen from a nearby community. The match was arranged by parents, and after the formalities had been settled, the bride was led into the groom's house (patrilocal residence). She sat facing a corner with her back to the assembled relatives of the groom. The groom then sat next to the girl, and the couple was given food as the boy's relatives ate. When the feasting was over, the couple was considered married, and that night the newlyweds were given a single blanket with the theory that if affection did not bring them together the cold desert night would. A girl who was unhappy in the home of her in-laws might return to her mother's home, but if she did this repeatedly, the presents that had been given were returned and the marriage considered dissolved. The groom and his parents had the right to expect the bride to bear an infant within two or three years. Failure to do so might annul the marriage and again mean a return of the wedding presents. A man could, if the woman's parents agreed, receive a younger sister of his wife if the latter died (sororate). It was less common for a woman to marry her deceased husband's brother (levirate). Among these people monogamy was the prevailing form of marriage, and familial relationships appear to have been quite stable.

In the routine of adult life, a woman was the outsider in the extended family household of her husband. The husband and wife were expected to be reserved in the presence of others, and the wife generally was retiring when with her in-laws or around men. Ideally, younger persons were thoughtful and unselfish in their dealings with older persons; these values were instilled in children when they were small. Young boys who hunted or collected the first plant products of the season were expected to take them to the aged. (See Figure 5-6.) The most respected adults were those men who hunted best and those women who could work most efficiently.

In early times, death brought immediate destruction of a Cahuilla household: on the morning following the death of a person, the body of the deceased

Figure 5-6. | Pasqual, a Cahuilla man said to be ninety years old, circa 1890. (Courtesy of the San Bernardino County Museum.)

and the house in which the death had occurred were burned. In later aboriginal times, however, this pattern was modified. When an individual died, the members of his or her and other clans assembled, bringing presents. The body was washed, dressed, and taken to the clan dance house of the deceased. Here the assembled mourners sang over the body throughout the night. If a man had died, the creation narrative was sung; for a woman, a song about the moon was sung, since it was the moon who had originally instructed women. The body was burned the morning following death, and within a week the person's house and possessions were burned.

Each fall or winter a seven-day Mourning Ceremony was held for clan

Figure 5-7. | Cahuilla shaman with a live coal from a wood fire in his mouth, photographed in 1963, possibly during a Mourning Ceremony. (Courtesy of the Lowie Museum of Anthropology, University of California, Berkeley.)

members who had died during the previous year. This was the most complex Cahuilla ceremony, and an essential feature was a narration of the origin myth, in which Mukat had described the proper death rituals, which had been performed for the first time at his death. The clan net, paha, and others began preparations months in advance for the yearly ceremony. Guests were persons from other clans who were related to the deceased by marriage and those individuals who had brought gifts following the death. Members of each clan arrived on a specific night so that the assembled group was not overwhelming. The first three nights, shamans of the host clan or other clans performed tricks, danced, and attempted to communicate with the spirits of the dead. At one Mourning Ceremony a shaman tied a band about his head and inserted clusters of owl feathers in it. He attached another cluster of owl feathers to a stick about eight inches long that he held in his hand. As he sang and shuffled around the fire, he began trembling violently and then pushed the stick down his throat three times. The third time he brought up a small black object said to have been a lizard. After the "lizard" was removed from his heart, he stopped shaking. A more common performance upon such an occasion was for the shaman to place live coals in his mouth and swallow them. (See Figure 5-7.)

Throughout the following three nights, different clans sang all night long. Those individuals singing the last night aided the relatives of the deceased in making images of each person who had died and for whom the ceremony was being held. The images were nearly life-size and were constructed from reed matting and clothed with deerskins. The male images had bows and arrows and eagle-feather headdresses; the female images had baskets decorated with eagle feathers. At sunrise on the final day, guests were presented with food and gifts. The host net led a procession in which he was followed by women, each carrying the image of a near relative. Then came the throng of participants and attendants. The people gathered in a circle in front of the dance house, and the images were placed in the center of the circle as the people danced, sang, and wailed. Objects of wealth were thrown over the images to show respect for the dead. These items could be retrieved but not by members of the clan hosting the ceremony. Next, the images were carried to a designated place and burned. People who had been invited to the ceremony were presented with strings of beads made of small round shell disks, and then they departed. The souls of the dead were now believed to be released, further mourning was thought unnecessary, and their names were no longer mentioned.

The presence of a soul in a living person was thought to be manifest when people fainted or dreamed; on those occasions their spiritual essence was thought to wander. The Cahuilla also believed that spirits left the bodies of persons months before they died. A spirit's wandering might be unknown to its possessor, or the individual might become ill and a shaman be summoned to retrieve her or his soul. When the soul of a person was beyond recall, it supposedly went to a place created in the east by Mukat. Here stood two mountains that clapped together and then separated. As the story went, souls found their way to these mountains, and once there a deathless guardian spirit questioned and tested them. After passing the tests, which included making cat's cradles and answering questions, the soul attempted to go between the clapping mountains. Only those who had lived according to the rules of Mukat were able to pass untouched. Otherwise they were crushed by the mountains and became butterflies, bats, trees, or rocks nearby.

Historic Changes in Cahuilla Life

Ethnohistorians have yet to plot the changes in Cahuilla life from early historic to modern times, and we are limited to the observations of diverse reporters. We know that by 1925 farmlands were owned by clans, as probably had been the case for about a hundred years, but the amount of arable land was small because water was scarce. Changes in dwelling forms were notable at this time since frame houses had replaced the aboriginal type; a frame house was not burned until three members of the household had died. In the desert, a clan dance house still was occupied by a net and his family, but it looked different because the roof now was pitched like that of a shed. By the late 1950s few aboriginal traits remained. Although acorns still were processed, they were consumed only on special social and ceremonial occasions.

Social life moved in new directions as the present century began. The rule of moiety exogamy fell into decline, and money was substituted for the gifts formerly presented to a bride's family. The girl's family received thirty dollars around the turn of the century, but twenty-five years later a female infant was termed scornfully "a paper," meaning a marriage license that no longer brought a gift. The pattern of leadership long had been impinged on by diverse outside influences. Supraclan leaders did not exist in aboriginal times, although one outstanding charismatic leader, Juan Antonio, emerged in the mid-1800s. In order to exercise effective control over the Cahuilla, whites appointed chiefs or captains through whom they dealt. Informants said that one such person was appointed as the Desert Cahuilla leader and was given papers and a horse by the Mexicans as symbols of his authority. When he died, the office passed to his son. These leaders, even as late as the 1920s, were not effective spokesmen for their groups.

Ceremonial life reflected reintegration and disintegration during the same period. The major shift was toward combining unrelated ceremonies with the Mourning Ceremony into a fiesta week. For example, among the Pass Cahuilla in the late 1880s, the Eagle-Killing Ceremony was joined with the Mourning Ceremony; the eagle feathers were used to decorate the images, which were burned two days later. In aboriginal times the people had cremated their dead; under Spanish, Mexican, and Anglo-American influence, they began to bury the dead. Interment sometimes included placing food, clothing, and bedding with the body in the hope that these things would be useful to the spirit if it did not soon find a permanent resting place. Changes in the Mourning Ceremony included dressing the images in manufactured clothing, even hats and veils. Coins and buttons replaced shells for the eyes of the images, while noses and ears were represented with appliqued pieces of cloth. Coins were thrown on these images near the end of the ceremony. Indian-owned lunch counters sold food and coffee to participants and observers. By 1931 the Mourning Ceremony at Palm Springs had become biennial and was held by alternating clans for the dead of the two previous years. Among the Desert Cahuilla, one of the last nets died in 1958. He had directed local ceremonial life, but when he died, the ceremonial structure, his house, and all of the ceremonial equipment were burned, an end not only to his life but also to the net ceremonials.

As the 1980s unfold, land holdings best symbolize the identity of the Cahuilla as a people as well as their Indianness in general. In a broader cultural context, some Cahuilla, possibly most youth, are largely uninterested in their Indian background. Those elders who have such an interest find it difficult to convey to the younger generation. Most Cahuilla no longer speak their language, their distinctive craft skills have died out, and they have not had a ceremonial house since 1958. The last shaman died in 1984, but there is one woman who learned the ceremonial songs and is able to carry on this part of the religious tradition.

Palm Springs Cahuilla Land Rights

In the course of Desert Cahuilla history, especially for the Palm Springs group, a dominant theme from the late 1860s onward has been Indian rights to land. In 1869 the superintendent of Indian affairs for California hoped to set aside lands for Indians before whites encroached further, and he succeeded in

Figure 5-8. | The Cahuilla woman Ramona Lubo at her home, probably photographed around 1900. Her life was fictionalized in the novel *Ramona* by Helen Hunt Jackson. (Courtesy of the Southwest Museum, Los Angeles, CA.)

establishing small reservations in San Diego County the following year. Then in 1875 President Ulysses S. Grant authorized the founding of the Agua Caliente (Palm Springs) and Cahuilla reservations. A Mission Indian agency began to function out of San Bernardino in 1879. For the first time slight but realistic efforts were being made to recognize the needs of Indians in southern California. In 1881 Helen Hunt Jackson published a book entitled *A Century of Dishonor,* a scathing indictment of the treatment of American Indians. Because of her crusading interest in Indians, she was retained to report to the commissioner of Indian affairs about the Indians of southern California. Her study was conducted with Abbott Kinney, and their report, in part a chronicle of wrongs against Indians and partly a series of recommendations, was submitted in 1883. This study did not make the impact on Indian policy that Jackson felt was essential, and so she decided to write a novel about the plight of these people. As a novel, *Ramona* was highly successful, but it failed to bring about the reforms advocated by Jackson. (See Figure 5-8.)

EARLY LAND DISPUTES   The problem of Palm Springs Indian land rights is complex, but the diverse legal maneuvers must at least be presented in brief. The modern reservation, created in 1896 under the conditions of the Mission

Indian Relief Act of 1891, set aside thirty-two thousand acres in essentially a checkerboard pattern around the town of Palm Springs in Riverside County. The Mission Indian Relief Act was based on the Dawes Act of 1887, and the keystone of this act was allotment of reservation lands to family heads. After a period of twenty-five years an allottee could, with approval of the secretary of the interior, receive a fee patent title to the land, making him the legal owner and entitling him to do whatever he might choose with the land. Allotments were first issued in 1923, and the land per family was limited to 160 acres. A federal agent went to Pair Springs to assign allotments to the band members, regardless of whether or not they accepted the division of land into individual parcels. Many persons were so dissatisfied with the comparability of the assigned lands that in 1927 the agent made allotments only to Indians who requested them; nearly half of the members made requests. These allotments consisted not of 160-acre parcels but of packages of a five-acre parcel of irrigable land, a 40-acre parcel of dry land, and a 2-acre lot in the town of Palm Springs. None of the 1927 allotments were approved by the federal government, and the Indians took legal action in the late 1930s to force approval. Meanwhile, the Indian Reorganization Act of 1934 was passed, bringing a basic change in Indian policy, which was to oppose further allotments. As this policy applied to the Palm Springs land dispute, further allotments were prohibited unless the Indian group voted against coming under this act. The Palm Springs band voted against it, and thus allotments were still possible. BIA officials were very much against allotments, however, and they obstructed allotted land grants at Palm Springs as elsewhere. The courts held that the secretary of the interior could not be forced to make allotments, which brought the litigation down to 1940. New action was taken the following year to have the allotments approved. The U.S. Supreme Court required a review of the litigation; the result was a 1946 verdict that the allotments were valid. Some allotments were approved in 1949; the ones that were unapproved involved conflicting claims, but finally selections were approved for the entire band.

One of the suits involving allotment selections resulted in a 1950 court decision that allotted lands should be of approximately equal value for each individual since this was the original intent of the law. In actuality, the allotment values, based on 1949 estimates, ranged from approximately $17,000 to $165,000, with a total value of lands allotted and pending allotment being about $7.4 million. To equalize the allotments, the BIA proposed that the secretary of the interior organize a tribal corporation and convey to it all of the tribal assets. This organization would be empowered to issue equalization stock redeemable from the sale of or income from the lands managed by the tribal organization. Persons who held equalized allotments would receive only membership stock until the equalization process was complete. Then all members would receive dividends equally.

A U.S. Senate bill proposed in 1957 was to provide equalization of allotments along these general lines, but the Indians objected and sent tribal representatives to Washington, D.C., to seek modifications. BIA representatives refused to make any changes and stated that if this legislation were not passed, the tribal reserves would be used to equalize the allotments. These reserves, the cemeteries, hot springs, and particularly the canyons, were the prime centers of tribal identity; to allot them would be to destroy the tribe as a social and political unit. During a hearing in 1957, it became evident that the bill was not in the best interests of the Indians, nor could it be considered just. Probably the most dangerous provision was that a tribal corporation was to be established and given title to all unallotted land. It would issue equalization stock to bring each individual's allotment to the value of the most valuable allotment and would redeem the stock from income or from disposal of the land. This was in fact a liquidation corporation, and the BIA could not really offer either legal or moral justification in its defense.

In 1959 two new bills were introduced in Congress, and these became law. The major provisions of one of them, the equalization bill, Public Law 86-339, were that (1) allotments would be made to all band members who had not received them, but no future-born members would receive allotments, (2) equalizations would be made on the basis of 1957–58 appraised land values, and the cemeteries, Roman Catholic church, hot springs, and certain canyons were to remain tribal reserves not subject to allotment, but all other lands were to be allotted regardless of prior acreage limitations and in proportion to the highest monetary value of the prior allotments. The second bill, Public Law 86-326, provided that reservation lands could be leased for a period not exceeding ninety-nine years except for grazing land, which could be leased for not more than ten years. The 1957–58 allotment appraisals ranged from approximately $75,000 to $630,000, in contrast with the 1949 appraisal range of $17,000 to $165,000. Obviously, the land was rapidly becoming fantastically valuable. Even with the passage of the first bill, it was impossible to equalize the allotments fully. Some 80 percent of the band obtained allotments valued at not less than $335,000; the remaining 20 percent of the allotments had values in excess of $335,000. Most of the land was still in trust status by 1962 and thus was not producing income. However, changes in leasing laws made it likely that over the next ten years individuals would derive considerable profit from it. The first large leasing enterprise was the Palm Springs Spa complex at the hot springs. (See Figure 5-9.) The spa was completed in 1960 at a cost of $1.8 million, and an adjacent hotel, also on Indian land, was completed in 1963. In 1961 the City of Palm Springs purchased lands allotted to eight Cahuilla adults and twenty-two Cahuilla children for $2,979,000, which was shared by the allottees.

WOMEN'S LEADERSHIP ROLE   The most notable aspect of all the Palm Springs land disputes is the leadership role assumed successfully by women. When the issues were coming to a climax in 1957, the band included only thirty-two adults and sixty-four minors. At that time there were ten adult males and twenty-two females; of the males two were in the U.S. Navy, two were over seventy years of age, and two were incapable of handling their own affairs. At this point only two courses of action were possible: either the band could trust the BIA and its lawyer to handle its business affairs completely, or the women could assume the role of leaders. The Cahuilla decided to pursue the latter alternative.

Figure 5-9. | The Palm Springs Spa, built on lands leased from the Agua Caliente Band and photographed in 1986. (Photograph by the author.)

Figure 5-10. | The Palm Springs Tribal Council in 1959. From left to right are Elizabeth Monk, Le Vern Saubel, Eileen Miguel, Doro Joyce Prieto, and Priscilla Gonzales. (Courtesy of the *Palm Springs Desert Sun.*)

Aboriginal sociopolitical life had set no precedent for female leadership, except that a woman did occasionally hold an office in trust for a son and old women sometimes were very active in clan ceremonies. The net was always a man, and in the early historic period whites appointed Indian men to act as intermediaries and later as reservation leaders. These persons seem to have been clan leaders. In the Cahuilla acculturation process a differential rate of adaptation for females and males appears to have developed. The men continued to follow a "collecting" pattern in their economic activities; they worked only sporadically as grape pickers, ranch hands, woodcutters, or railroad laborers. In their jobs they interacted most often with other Indians, not whites. Women, by contrast, often worked as domestics in the homes of whites and therefore became much more familiar with the new ways. This was possibly an important reason why women could become the stable core around which the society was reorganized. In 1935 a woman became secretary to the band business committee, and by 1954 an all-woman tribal council had been elected, with Vyola Olinger as chairperson. Mrs. Olinger, who was an active member of the band, was an apt choice, for she was not only intelligent and articulate but willing to work constructively with the BIA officials. The men had by this time come to distrust virtually all proposals by the bureau. Under the tribal council of women the major land disputes were resolved. In 1961 a young male was elected to the council, and this brought an end to the era of all-female political dominance, but it was the women who had handled the vital issue. (See Figure 5-10.)

LAND ISSUES IN THE 1960s By the early 1960s a small group of determined Indians had gained a settlement, and seemingly the avarice of whites had become just another episode in our blemished past; justice had prevailed. Alas, it was not to endure. In 1967, George Ringwald, a reporter for the *Daily Enterprise* of Riverside, California, wrote a series of articles about the administration of Palm Springs Cahuilla lands and funds. He demonstrated beyond any doubt that greedy whites still were taking grossly unfair advantage of Indians. Among the individuals involved in the immoral and often illegal handling of Palm Springs Cahuilla affairs were BIA personnel, a Superior Court judge, a municipal judge, a former mayor of Palm Springs, a Palm Springs real estate broker, and a host of attorneys-at-law. As a result of Ringwald's journalism the BIA was forced to conduct an investigation into the system of court-appointed guardians and conservators. It was demonstrated, for example, that a municipal judge and one attorney had, over a seven-year period, collected $485,000 in fees. From 1956 to 1967, approximately 40 percent of the $10.8 million received by eighty-four estates had gone to conservators, guardians, or their attorneys under the supervision of the Riverside County Superior Court. Congressional action in 1968 put an end to the conservator and guardian management of these valuable lands.

A fair-minded person would hope that Palm Springs Indian problems with the BIA, some local developers, and city officials would have ended by the 1960s, but such was not the case. When Palm Springs incorporated as a city in 1938, its governing body included Indian land as part of the city without consulting the Indian owners. Over the years the city passed zoning ordinances and in 1965 adopted a master plan that included presumed control over the Indian lands in the city. The Palm Springs Indians in turn formed a zoning commission and prepared zoning ordinances of their own. Theirs did not agree with those of the city planners. In 1966 the Indians won a judgment against the city with reference to zoning procedures, but the city still had not made the required modifications by 1972. The Indians initiated further zoning litigation in which they accused the city of preventing the development of Indian lands and thereby decreasing its value. For example, at one street intersection where white and Indian land met, shopping centers and other businesses filled the corners belonging to whites, but the Indian land had not been developed because the city had not granted the necessary permits for development. Among the issues brought before the courts in the early 1970s were whether Indian land could legally be included in a city without consent of its owners and whether city zoning ordinances applied to such land represented an infringement on the governing rights of the tribe.

THE MODERN SCENE   In the late 1970s, a court decision elsewhere found that Indians have control over the zoning of their lands within a city. As a result, the City of Palm Springs and local Indian planning commissions began to work together closely and effectively for their mutual benefit. However, the comparatively adverse economic climate by the mid-1980s led to a total lack of new construction. Furthermore, the development of Indian land involves another problem common to reservations where allotments were made generations ago. By the 1980s the original allotments had been subdivided among heirs so often that the plots tended to be small and scattered. Since developers prefer large units, numerous owners of small adjacent allotments must agree to the joint lease or sale of their holdings, and negotiating this is not always possible.

The total assets of the Palm Springs or Agua Caliente Band of Cahuilla were estimated at $200 million in 1975, making its members the wealthiest Indians in the United States on a per capita basis. This wealth is not distributed evenly, however. About 115 of the 269 enrolled members had allotments in 1986. The annual income from these allotments ranged from about $10,000 per individual to more than $200,000 in 1986. Yet, those persons who do not have allotments are sometimes poor. In keeping with traditional Cahuilla values, wealthy persons often share their riches with their less-affluent relatives, perhaps buying them new cars each year, providing money for vacations, or paying medical expenses.

Now that the Agua Caliente Band has a more equitable relationship with the City of Palm Springs and their joint efforts for the sound economic development of city land are going smoothly, the Indians have turned increasingly toward an emphasis on their heritage. One result of this concern is the active participation of the current band chairman, Richard M. Milanovich, in state and national organizations centering on Indian affairs. In addition, the preservation of archaeological sites has become an important goal, and plans are under way to launch a museum and a publication series. Perhaps the Cahuilla Indians' sense of roots is best expressed in a conscious effort to not just preserve but to revitalize their heritage as Cahuilla.

Comparisons with Other Indians

Although a small number of Cahuilla appear to have farmed in early historic times, they were principally foragers like the Kuskokwim Eskimos and the Chipewyan. The Cahuilla, of course, were primarily collectors of plant products, while the others were almost exclusively hunters and fishers. The resource base of the Cahuilla obviously was far richer and more diverse than that of the Chipewyan, which makes an inviting point to explore in terms of accompanying social and political adaptations. The Kuskokwim Eskimos, like the Cahuilla, had a dependable food supply, but these Eskimos did not develop social and political institutions like those of the Cahuilla. The reason, at least in part, turns on the nature of environmental differences; it might be a useful exercise to compare all of these peoples in terms of their environments, especially the diversity of species harvested, species mobility, and the seasonality of food resources, and to try to explain social and political differences in these terms. Note, too, that the Cahuilla, far more than any of the others, emphasized ties with the mythological past, physiological changes during adolescence, formal marital arrangements, and death. The reasons for this contrast invite further study, hypothesis formulation, and thoughtful speculation.

A Note about Clan

The word *clan* was defined in this chapter as a unilineal descent group with a presumed common ancestor, and it will be used in this manner throughout the book. A clan may be traced along either the male line (patriclan) or female line (matriclan); in this book a prefix is used when the rule of descent of a particular people is first identified and thereafter if required for clarity. Originally the word *clan* was restricted to people who traced descent through females, and the word *gens* was used when these ties were traced through males. The word *gens* is no longer employed, and *clan* now applied to both cases.

George P. Murdock, in *Social Structure* (1949, 68), proposed that *clan* be more rigidly defined. In his terms a genuine clan has a unilineal rule of descent uniting a core of members; residential unity, meaning that residence and descent are consistent (for example, matrilineal descent and matrilocal residence), and social integration, especially in the acceptance of in-marrying spouses. Murdock proposed that *sib* be used to refer to a unilineal descent group through males (patrisib) or females (matrisib) if the other qualifications for a clan were not met, and there is good precedent for this usage. Following Murdock's definition the Cahuilla did not have clans since in-marrying spouses were not integrated into membership; instead they had patrisibs. The differentiation by Murdock has not been widely accepted, however, and in terms of the more standard pre-1949 definition of a clan the Cahuilla had clans.

Additional Readings

Early historic Cahuilla material culture is best presented in the monographs by Lucile Hooper (1920) and Alfred L. Kroeber (1908). Again, and as usual, comparatively little has been written about recent developments among the Cahuilla, and as noted previously no one has attempted to plot their ethnohistory. Fortunately, however, studies by Lowell J. Bean and Katherine S. Saubel (Sauvel) supplement and in part supplant the pioneering work of David P. Barrows (1900) about plant use and should be consulted for thorough understanding of subsistence patterns. Lowell Bean has written a brief account about the Cahuilla in the *California* volume (8) of the *Handbook of North American Indians,* William C. Sturtevant, general editor (Washington, DC, 1978). This volume provides a wealth of information about the neighbors of the Cahuilla as well.

Bibliography

Bancroft, Hubert H. 1890. *History of California.* 7 vols. San Francisco.

Barrows, David P. 1900. *The ethno-botany of the Coahuilla Indians of southern California.* Chicago. Reprinted by Malki Museum Press, Banning, CA, 1967. A general history of the Cahuilla precedes a description of the local geography. These sections are followed by a discussion of houses, baskets, and plant use. The botanical information in particular is quite comprehensive and serves as a standard source.

Bean, Lowell J. 1963. Cahuilla ethnobotanical notes: The aboriginal uses of the mesquite and screwbean. *Archaeological Survey, Annual Report 1962–1963,* Department of Anthropology and Sociology, University of California, Los Angeles, 55–76.

———. 1972. *Mukat's people.* Berkeley. This work demonstrates that insightful ethnographic reconstructions occasionally can be made long after the era of early historic contact. Bean explains the relationship of the Cahuilla to their food resources and the accompanying influences on other aspects of their lives. His study is especially perceptive on subjects such as world view and values that have been neglected by most other students of the Cahuilla.

Bean, Lowell J., and William M. Mason. 1962. *Diaries and accounts of the Romero expeditions in Arizona and California.* Los Angeles. The publication of these records offers a previously unknown historical dimension to the Cahuilla. Their primary value is in conveying certain details of Cahuilla acculturation by Spanish Americans.

Bean, Lowell J., and Katherine S. Saubel. 1961. Cahuilla ethnobotanical notes: The aboriginal uses of the oak. *Archaeological Survey, Annual Report 1960–1961,* Department of Anthropology and Sociology, University of California, Los Angeles, 237–49.

———. 1972. *Temalpakh: Cahuilla Indian knowledge and usage of plants.* Malki Museum Press, Riverside.

Beattie, George W., and Helen P. Beattie. 1951. *Heritage of the valley.* Oakland.

Bolton, Herbert E. 1931. In the south San Joaquin ahead of Garces. *Quarterly of the California Historical Society* 10:211–19.

Bourne, A. R. N.d. *Some major aspects of the historical development of Palm Springs between 1880 and 1938.* MA thesis, Occidental College.

Caughey, John W. 1940. *California.* New York. (See also Wilson, Benjamin D.)

Ellison, William H. 1922–23. The federal Indian policy in California, 1846–1860. *Mississippi Valley Historical Review* 9:37–67.

Gifford, Edward W. 1922. *California kinship terminologies.* University of California Publications in American Archaeology and Ethnology, vol. 18.

Hale, Kenneth. 1958. Internal diversity in Uto-Aztecan: 1. *International Journal of American Linguistics* 24:101–07.

Hooper, Lucile. 1920. *The Cahuilla Indians.* University of California Publications in American Archaeology and Ethnology, vol. 16, no. 6. Most of what is known about the aboriginal Cahuilla is found in this ethnographic reconstruction, a similar reconstruction by Alfred L. Kroeber, or the analysis of social life and settlement patterns by William D. Strong.

Jackson, Helen H. 1881. *A century of dishonor.* New York. (An 1890 edition contains the *Report on the conditions and needs of the Mission Indians of California.*)

James, Harry C. 1960. *The Cahuilla Indians.* Los Angeles.

Kroeber, Alfred L. 1908. *Ethnography of the Cahuilla Indians.* University of California Publications in American Archaeology and Ethnology, vol. 8, no. 2. This brief but valuable ethnography, which concentrates on material culture, supplements the reconstructions by Lucile Hooper and William D. Strong.

Land allotments on Agua Caliente reservation, Calif. 1958. Hearing before a Special Subcommittee of the Committee on Interior and Insular Affairs, House of Representatives, 85th Congress, 1st session. Serial no. 17.

Murdock, George P. 1949. *Social structure.* New York.

Phillips, George Harwood. 1975. *Chiefs and challengers.* Berkeley.

Ringwald, George. 1967. *Riverside Press-Enterprise* and *Riverside Daily Press* articles.

Rush, Emmy M. 1932. The Indians of the Coachella Valley celebrate. *El Palacio* 32:1–19.

Shinn, George H. 1941. *Shoshonean days.* Glendale.

Strong, William D. 1929. *Aboriginal society in southern California.* University of California Publications in American Archaeology and Ethnology, vol. 26. The best information about aboriginal social structure, the movements of people, and settlement patterns.

Transmitting report by Subcommittee on Indian Affairs. State of California, Senate Committee on Rules, Resolution No. 8. Sacramento.

Wilson, Benjamin D. 1952. *The Indians of southern California in 1852.* John W. Caughey, ed. San Marino.

6 The Mesquakie: Fighters and Farmers of the Woodland Fringe

When I was perhaps seven years old I began to practice sewing for my dolls. But I sewed poorly. I used to cry because I did not know how to sew. Nor could I persuade my mother to [do it] when I said to her "Make it for me." "You will know how to sew later on; that is why I shall not make them for you. That is how one learns to sew, by practicing sewing for one's dolls." . . . And so I would always practice sewing for my dolls!

An anonymous Mesquakie woman describes her childhood. (Michelson, 1925, 295)

MOST INDIAN POPULATIONS in the east-central United States disappeared long ago, but a small group known as the Mesquakie or Fox have survived despite a history of wanderings and sufferings. In colonial times the French set out to destroy them and were nearly successful. Later the Mesquakie resisted the settlement of their lands by whites, and the turmoil climaxed in an Indian war. The survivors were displaced, causing their number to become depleted even further. The Mesquakie were haughty, independent, and had an exceptional nobility of purpose. A striking instance of their resilience began in 1846. After being defeated and relocated by whites a generation earlier, some Mesquakie left their reservation in Kansas and returned to an area of Iowa where they once had lived. They bought small parcels of land from whites and settled down to follow their old way of life. Although their aboriginal customs were rapidly disappearing by the turn of the twentieth century, the Mesquakie have managed to retain both their identity and their Iowa lands to the present.

The ability of the Mesquakie to endure in the Midwest and to retain their identity is a compelling reason for reporting their lifeway. In addition, conveying the diversity of Indian life requires that all significant economic adaptations be considered. Hunters, fishers, and plant collectors have been presented, and it is time to consider Indians who farmed. The Mesquakie not only cultivated domestic plants but also depended on foraging activities and therefore represent another economic focus.

Two difficulties emerged in preparing an account of past life among the Mesquakie. First, most pertinent information does not date from the period of early historic contact. Thus, an aboriginal baseline account, one describing the Mesquakie before their customs were altered by fur traders, cannot be presented. However, the Mesquakie are regarded as highly conservative, and except for superficial changes, we can assume that accounts about their recent past are more representative of aboriginal patterns than would be the case for many American Indians. A second difficulty in dealing with the Mesquakie is their close association with the Sauk (Sac). Separating the historical Mesquakie and Sauk is impossible in some instances. Although my descriptions are confined to the Mesquakie insofar as possible, frequent reference to the Sauk is required.

| Origin Myth, Population, and Language

The name Mesquakie, by which these Indians know themselves and which translates as "Red-earth People," stems from the red earth of their creation as recorded in their origin myth, which goes as follows. At a place that is not on earth and is so far away that no one is able to travel there, a place where it is always winter, lives Wisaka. In the remote past he lived on earth with his younger brother, but the manitous (supernatural forces) met in council and plotted to kill the brothers. They killed the younger brother, but Wisaka survived. First they tried to kill him with fire. Then they created a great flood, but Wisaka climbed a tall tree on a mountaintop, a canoe appeared at the top of the tree, and he paddled about on the water. A turtledove brought him twigs, and a muskrat

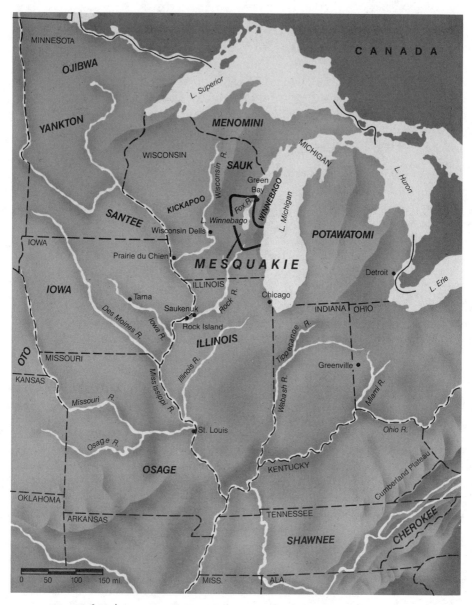

Figure 6-1. | Aboriginal range of the Mesquakie Indians.

brought mud from which he made a ball. He threw it into the water, and it grew into the earth as we know it. Wisaka created all the things on earth, including people. The Mesquakie, according to their traditions, have such great antiquity that they do not know when they first arrived on earth. They were the first people to dwell on the land made by Wisaka, and they lived by the sea. From the sea came a great fish with the head of a man. As this fish walked on the land, he became fully human, and he was followed by other fish who made the same transformation. These individuals established a community near the Mesquakie, and every aspect of Mesquakie life was copied by the fish-turned-to-men. These were the manitous of the world. When Wisaka formed the Mesquakie, they were red, the same color as blood. As time passed, people grew more distant from the manitous, and the world in which they lived changed. In recent times animals and birds have begun to disappear, and the manitous who control the universe are unhappy about this new state of affairs. Sometime in the future the manitous will destroy the earth, the Mesquakie will revert to their original red condition, and the world will begin again.

The Mesquakie appear to have received the name Fox when members of the Fox clan of the Mesquakie tribe told a party of French that they were Fox. The Mesquakie and the Sauk, with whom they are closely identified, numbered about 6,500 persons at the time of historic contact; possibly 2,000 were Mesquakie. In the 1950s nearly 1,000 Mesquakie lived in Oklahoma, 500 in Iowa, and 125 in Nebraska. By 1970 about 500 lived in the vicinity of Tama, Iowa. In 1976 there were 902 persons on the tribal roll; by 1986 the number had grown to 1,010.

The Mesquakie, Sauk, and Kickapoo were neighbors and spoke closely related languages in the Algonkian linguistic family, one of the nine families comprising the Macro-Algonkian phylum. Algonkian speakers occupied a vast sector of eastern Canada and a smaller area in the eastern United States. Remarkably, the other groups with whom they are affiliated linguistically include two small northern California tribes, the Yurok and Wiyot. The earliest historical records locate the Mesquakie along the Fox River of eastern Wisconsin. (See Figure 6-1.) In our classification, the Mesquakie represent the Eastern Woodlands culture area.

Early Contacts and Conflicts with Whites

The first 160 years of Mesquakie contact with whites were characterized by unsettled relations and sporadic hostilities. Pressure from white settlers threatened to drive the Mesquakie off their lands, but they rallied behind Indian leaders to resist. The era of open hostilities finally ended with Mesquakie settlement on a reservation in Iowa.

HOSTILITIES WITH FRENCH AND AMERICAN SETTLERS   The first direct contact between the Mesquakie and Europeans was in 1665 as the French entered the western Great Lakes region. In 1670 the famous Father Claude Jean

Allouez founded a mission among them, but he could convert only the ill and dying. As the French pushed west, they armed the Ojibwa (Chippewa) and the Siouan-speaking enemies of the Mesquakie. This led to French and Mesquakie conflict, which tipped in favor of the French after they founded Detroit in 1699 and made peace with the powerful Iroquois a year later. Because the French continued to arm their enemies, the Mesquakie sought aid from the British and from friendly tribes. The Iroquois assured the Mesquakie of a home among them if they were defeated by the French.

Hostilities with the French began to peak in 1728 when nearly five hundred whites and twelve hundred allied Indians moved against the Mesquakie. The destruction of Mesquakie settlements was a severe blow, and by 1730 the French and their Indian allies had killed nearly twelve hundred Mesquakie. The Mesquakie survived only because surrounding Indians released their Mesquakie prisoners and because the Sauk sheltered and protected them against the French; soon both the Mesquakie and Sauk were forced to flee south. Peace was made with the French in 1737. Subsequently the Mesquakie began returning to Wisconsin, but they did not feel secure until the British assumed control of the Great Lakes region and replaced the French at the Green Bay post in 1761. Before long the Ojibwa drove the Mesquakie from Wisconsin to Illinois, where they came into increasing conflict with white Americans around 1800. By then the Mesquakie were dependent on the fur trade to obtain goods, and they often were in debt to traders. Still, the relationship between the Mesquakie and Sauk and traders, especially the British, seems to have been very good. The Mesquakie expected certain privileges, such as being entertained when they were at the trading post, receiving gifts from the traders, and being cared for in times of stress. At the same time, they relied on trusted traders to help guide tribal and village affairs. The influx of additional white settlers to the Northwest Territory increased pressure on the government to move all Indians from the Midwest. The position of the Mesquakie and Sauk was not favorable since they had sided with the British during the American Revolution.

In 1804 a small party of Mesquakie and Sauk went to St. Louis and signed a treaty with the United States releasing their lands along the Mississippi River. Trade goods worth two thousand dollars were distributed to the Indians plus an annuity of six hundred dollars to the Sauk and four hundred dollars to the Mesquakie. The treaty authorized further settlement of Illinois lands by white settlers. The Treaty of 1804 was the cause of great anger against white Americans. Not only had the Indians at St. Louis not been authorized to negotiate, but the tribe as a whole did not know that a treaty was under consideration until after the chiefs returned from St. Louis. The Mesquakie felt that they had been deceived and that these lands had been seized illegally. This treaty was the one document to which white Americans referred constantly in asserting their claims to Mesquakie and Sauk lands. The treaty was made, the damage was done, but the bitterness always lingered in the minds of the Indians.

The most serious difficulty whites had in dealing with Indians stemmed from the conflicts between tribes. These not only disrupted trade but made white settlement of the country difficult. To end the fighting, in 1805 the government invited the major tribes in the upper Mississippi River drainage to a council held at St. Louis with Governor William Henry Harrison of the Northwest Territory. To impress the Indians with the power of the United States, select Indians were taken to visit Washington, D.C. About a third of the group were Mesquakie and Sauk. Even as some chiefs were in Washington, however, others were on the warpath against the Chickasaw and Osage. Thus, this effort to bring a peaceful settlement of Indian differences failed. In 1805–1806 Mesquakie and Sauk war parties roved along the Missouri River raiding Osage camps and killing whites. Settlers brought increased pressure on the government of the Northwest Territory to arrange a more effective settlement of Indian differences. To compound the governor's problems, additional settlers entered the Northwest Territory between 1806 and 1812. They were particularly active in clearing the land and establishing farms between the Ohio and the Mississippi rivers, precisely the region with the greatest Indian unrest.

INDIAN LEADERS AND RESISTANCE TO WHITES   By this time Indians in the Midwest were desperate, and they rallied around a Shawnee Indian leader best known as the Shawnee Prophet. He reportedly had died and been reborn; while dead he had visited the land of the spirits and been given a view of the future. This messiah saw contentment only for those who gave up white ways and returned to the old Indian way of life. With Greenville, Ohio, as the center of his activities he received tribal representatives from the surrounding region. The movement coalesced into an effort to rid the country of the Long Knives, or white Americans. With the Treaty of 1804 as the rallying point for their grievances against white Americans, the Mesquakie and Sauk were ready and willing to follow this confederation organized by the Shawnee and actively fostered by the British. In the Battle of Tippecanoe Creek of 1811, the Shawnee Prophet's prestige was destroyed by Harrison's stand against the Indians. Although the battle was not decisive, it was unlikely that an Indian confederation could emerge afterwards. In early 1812 an Indian delegation that included Mesquakie and Sauk went to Washington, D.C., and this time they were well received because the War of 1812 had erupted into open conflict. The most white Americans could hope to do was to keep the Indians from joining in the conflict on the side of the British. To prevent Mesquakie and Sauk participation, white Americans decided to move these Indians to Missouri, where they would be beyond effective contact with the British. They succeeded in moving approximately fifteen hundred members of the combined tribes to these new lands.

The fortunes of the Mesquakie and Sauk soon were guided by two Sauk leaders, the pro-British Black Hawk and Keokuk, who emerged as pro-American. Black Hawk (see Figure 6-2) had distinguished himself as a warrior at the age of fifteen, and by nineteen he had led a party of two hundred warriors against an equal number of Osage. In this conflict nearly half the Osage had been killed; Black Hawk alone had killed six persons. By 1812 he had become the most respected leader of the combined tribes. Early in the War of 1812 he journeyed to

Figure 6-2. | Black Hawk, the Sauk warrior who allied himself with the British and led his people to resist white American control for twenty years. (After McKenney and Hall 1934.)

Green Bay, Wisconsin, with two hundred warriors, and was well received by the British. They convinced him that the first effort should be to secure the Great Lakes region.

While Black Hawk was away, American troops threatened to destroy the principal Sauk village of Saukenuk near the mouth of the Rock River in Illinois. The people had decided in council to flee, but an unimportant Sauk, Keokuk, asked to be heard. He was a fine orator and maintained that they should resist the white Americans. His persuasive speech convinced the people, and when the American force failed to arrive, Keokuk became a hero. By his abilities as an orator and determined stand against the Americans he established himself as a rival of Black Hawk.

Black Hawk's effort to contain the Americans was moderately successful, but by the fall of 1814 the course of the War of 1812 had changed in the Northwest Territory. The Indian war was not well managed by the British, and the American forces were consolidating. The Treaty of Ghent brought an end to the conflict, but the Mesquakie and Sauk were deeply divided since those who had settled in Missouri had been largely neutral and most of the others had fought the Americans. Despite the American victory, many Indians in the Northwest Territory still looked to the British for help in their struggle against the Long Knives. Unsettled conditions among the Mesquakie and Sauk led to sporadic raids against frontier settlements and clashes with those Indians on whose lands they encroached. To end these killings, white Americans called a meeting in 1820 of Indians along the upper Mississippi. By now Keokuk had emerged as a powerful instrument of white appeasement in the central prairies. He was willing to abide by American decisions as long as they furthered his own interests, and the effective influence of Black Hawk declined.

Finally, in 1825, the Treaty of Prairie du Chien was signed by the Mesquakie, Sauk, and Siouans. Boundaries were established, and Indians were to give up their ties with the British. Although the Mesquakie ceded lands that subsequently were occupied by whites, the Indians did not leave, causing further conflict. Five years and another treaty later found Black Hawk still determined to resist. His followers did not have enough food for the winter of 1830–31 because they had sold most of their equipment to obtain intoxicants. To complicate conditions further, heavy snowfalls made it impossible for the Indians to hunt efficiently. By this time Black Hawk was desperate and appealed to other tribes to form a confederation to resist the whites, but to no avail. In the spring of 1831 Black Hawk and his "British Band" returned to Saukenuk, and the women began planting corn. The three hundred warriors in the party maintained an uneasy peace with white settlers. To remove the Indians, militiamen were dispatched to put down what was termed an Indian uprising. Saukenuk was bombarded even though the Indians had left, and the village was destroyed. Black Hawk was forced to agree not to return to Saukenuk and to submit to Keokuk as the leader of the combined tribes. At this point it would seem that resistance against white Americans was no longer feasible, but Black Hawk's determination was renewed by a false report from one of his subordinates that other tribes and the British had promised support.

In the spring of 1832 the British Band, including two thousand persons of whom more than five hundred were warriors, crossed the Mississippi River and moved toward Rock Island. By this time the frontier was in turmoil, volunteer militiamen were called out, and troops were moved into the area to prevent Black Hawk from reoccupying his traditional country. The American military effort was hopelessly confused; at the same time, Black Hawk was unaware that he had been deceived by his lieutenant. As Black Hawk traveled up the Rock River, he came in contact with the Potawatomi. They told him they could not give his people the corn they needed, and they also warned that no British were going to aid the Indians. Under these circumstances, Black Hawk felt that he must surrender, and he sent a party of warriors back to the camp of the whites beneath a flag of truce. The whites, however, who were not under any realistic military command, misunderstood the purpose of the warriors and killed one of the three Indians carrying the flag. The other two and the Indian scouts who had followed them raced back to their encampment. Black Hawk now was forced to fight. He rallied around himself forty warriors to hold off the whites. The Indians ambushed the oncoming whites, and soon the militiamen were fleeing in panic. The rest of the troops were routed, and all were swept along in the retreat. These disorganized volunteers fled to relate exaggerated stories of the Indian numbers and of the defeat they had suffered. After the skirmish, Black Hawk and his followers returned to the American camp, looting and mutilating the bodies of the slain whites, and then they withdrew to the headwaters of the Rock River. When a regular military contingent reached the battleground, they found that only eleven individuals had been killed by the Indians. As the Indians retreated, they massacred a group of whites on a farm and sent scalping parties into the settlements along their path. This caused settlers and the government to demand decisive action. American forces were reinforced, and by the end of June the United States military operation included about thirty-six hundred men, had cost about $300,000, and still had not defeated the Indians.

The Americans moved on the Indians from two directions, and Black Hawk made a desperate effort to rejoin Keokuk or to find refuge in the prairies. Black Hawk reached the banks of the Wisconsin River before the Americans were near enough to attack the entire band; they drove the Indians they could reach into the river bottom, and killed nearly seventy warriors. In spite of earlier deaths from exposure and starvation, abandonment by their few allies, and casualties in battle, the British Band numbered 150 as it crossed the river bottom and reached the eastern bank of the Mississippi River. Black Hawk advocated retreating farther north, but the majority felt that their best chance for survival was to cross the Mississippi. Fifty moved northward with Black Hawk, and 100 escaped across the Mississippi River. Black Hawk eluded capture until he reached the vicinity of the Wisconsin Dells; here he was made a prisoner, and the Black Hawk War was ended.

REMOVAL TO IOWA   The ensuing treaty required that the Mesquakie and Sauk forfeit about six million acres of land along the western bank of the Mississippi River in the state of Iowa. They agreed to keep some of their land as a small reservation. As immediate compensation for the ceded lands they received the services of a blacksmith, a gunsmith shop, and an annual allotment of tobacco and salt. They also were given winter provisions and $40,000 for paying debts to traders. Over the next thirty years they were to receive further payment of $660,000 for the cession. The treaty stipulated that Black Hawk and other chiefs were to be taken to Fort Monroe on Chesapeake Bay as prisoners to prevent further violence along the frontier. Black Hawk arrived in Washington, D.C., in late April of 1832 but was a prisoner at Fort Monroe only briefly. He was released in the custody of Keokuk and was given a tour of the major cities in the eastern United States to impress him with American power. He was overwhelmed by the seventy-four gun warship *Delaware,* amazed by the mobs of people that surrounded him, and awed by the arsenals that the Americans maintained. According to the historian William T. Hagan, if Black Hawk had accompanied one of the earlier Indian parties to Washington, D.C., and had realized at that time the power of white Americans, the Black Hawk War probably would never have been fought.

| Early Historic Life of the Mesquakie

Information about the Mesquakie before 1730, when they lived in their Wisconsin homeland, is negligible, and much the same is true for the next hundred years. Thus, to reconstruct an aboriginal baseline ethnography for these people is impossible. Alternatively, there are acceptable descriptions of the way they lived during the latter part of the nineteenth century after they had had prolonged contact with Europeans and Euro-Americans. The account to follow is not as full as might be hoped because it is drawn from diverse sources, few of which considered the Mesquakie at length.

APPEARANCE AND CLOTHING   The appearance of Mesquakie men was striking, largely because of their roached hair style (as worn by Black Hawk; see Figure 6-2). A man shaved all the hair from his head except for a palm-sized tuft at the crown. Most of the tuft was about two inches long, but at the center grew a scalp lock that never was cut and usually was braided. From this braid hung an eagle quill, and along the middle of the tuft were attached lengths of deer hair that very frequently were painted red. The typical clothing of a male included a skin cape for cold weather, a buckskin breechclout, leggings, and high-topped moccasins. Women dressed their hair by parting it in the middle and drawing it to the back of the neck. Most probably, the women wore long buckskin dresses and short leather moccasins. Young children usually wore only a long, loose shirt, and older children followed adult clothing styles.

SETTLEMENTS   Summer villages were in lowlands along rivers and streams where the ground could be cleared and crops planted. The dwellings were oblong, bark-covered structures with pole frames up to forty feet long and twenty feet wide. Along each interior sidewall was a raised bark- and skin-covered platform that served as seats and beds. In the open space at the center of the house were fires for cooking and heating. Clusters of lodges were occupied from April through much of September, but in the winter small family groups dispersed to follow a wandering life. The winter dwellings were oval structures framed by placing the ends of poles in the ground, bending the poles, and tying them together at the top. Over the framework were placed reeds or mats, and at the doorway hung a bearskin.

SUBSISTENCE ACTIVITIES   The economic cycle around 1820, and most likely before, was divided into two phases. In the spring and summer the Mesquakie tilled lands adjacent to their lodges. Here the women planted and maintained the gardens while the men hunted. The principal hunting weapon was the bow and arrow; the bow was sinew-backed, and arrows were placed in a buckskin quiver. The most important game animal was deer, valued not only for its meat but for its skin and fat. Birds and small game were hunted, as was the bear, which the Mesquakie considered a choice meat. The staples, however, were the maize, beans, and squash cultivated by the women and the wild plant foods that they collected. These foods were dried and stored in cache pits, in bark baskets, or in the rafters of a bark house. In mid-September when families left their summer settlement they took a small quantity of corn and their other possessions to a winter hunting area. The scattered families lived in dome-shaped structures until the number of game animal kills declined in late winter. They then assembled in large camps and were inactive until they began to trap beaver in the spring. Following the beaver-trapping season they traveled back to their villages, planning the trip so that they would arrive simultaneously. They did this to minimize the exposure of small groups to hostile peoples and to prevent anyone from taking provisions from another's cache.

By the time records about food habits are reasonably complete, we find that an iron kettle hung from a hook above the fire was the usual cooking utensil. The Mesquakies' primary staple was maize, and they prepared it in many ways. They boiled or processed it as hominy by leaching the shells with wood ash and washing away the lye. They also parched it in a fire but most often ground it into meal and boiled it as gruel. They processed squash fruit for storage by cutting it into rings that were dried in the sun. Among the wild plants they collected were broad-leafed arrowhead corms, either gathered from the plant rootlets or robbed from muskrat caches. These "potatoes" were boiled, sliced, and strung on cords hung from the rafters of a bark house. A potatolike growth was the groundnut, which grew along the plant roots and was as much as three inches in diameter; it was peeled, boiled, sliced, and dried to be cooked with meat in the winter. Additionally, the Mesquakie collected sugar-maple sap, which was an important seasoning in cooking, and used a few plants specifically for seasoning. They ate hickory nuts, butternuts, and walnuts, and consumed wild fruits either at the time of collection or after they had been dried.

DESCENT, KINSHIP, AND MARRIAGE   The most important Mesquakie kinship ties were traced through males (patrilineal descent); persons with a presumed but unknown common ancestor comprised a patriclan, the most important descent group. The members of any clan were obligated to seek spouses from another clan (clan exogamy). The leading clans were named Bear, Fox, Wolf, Thunder, Swan, Eagle, Sturgeon, and Bear Potato; the largest ones and possibly the oldest were the first four. The succession of paramount chiefs was from particular clans. The Fox, Thunder, and Bear clans contributed most chiefs, the leaders of war parties, and council members; the other clans normally provided only councilmen. The clans appear to have formed two groups (moieties) that rendered reciprocal services in ceremonial activities; the Bear and Wolf recipro-cated with the Eagle, Fox, and Thunder clans. It must be added, however, that the exact nature of these mutual obligations is not known.

A second type of moiety division has been recorded. In this arrangement each person was assigned to one of two groups, the To'kana or Kicko, depending on birth order and the father's affiliation. A firstborn was usually assigned to the division to which his or her father did not belong, and the second to the group of his or her father's affiliation. The third belonged to the moiety of the first and so on. Assignment was irrespective of the sex of the person and had nothing to do with marital arrangements. Between the members of the moieties, a friendly rivalry existed. They competed in games, and the division was important in cer-tain festivities, hunting arrangements, and the assignment of camp police.

In the Mesquakie kinship terminology collected in the 1930s we find that on a male individual's generational level specific terms existed for older brother and older sister, whereas younger brothers and sisters were grouped as younger siblings. These terms were extended to father's brother's children and to moth-er's sister's children. There were additionally distinct and separate terms for father's sister's son and daughter as well as for mother's brother's son and daughter. The terms for father's sister's son and daughter were the same as for sister's son and daughter (Omaha cousin terminology). On the generational level above the individual, we find that the word for father was extended to fa-ther's brother, but there was a different term for mother's brother, extended to all males in the direct line from mother's brother—for example, mother's brother's son, mother's brother's son's son. The terminology for males on the first ascending generation above the individual is bifurcate merging. (See Figure 6-3.) The most important observation to be made about the terminology is that there was the inclination to group individuals on both sides of one's family into a small number of categories and to ignore generations.

In kinship behavior, egalitarian relationships tended to exist between sets of individuals. For example, the behavior between a father and his son tended to be as between two brothers in the ideals of modern American society. Among

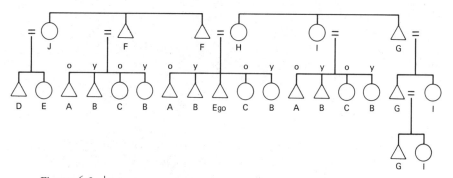

Figure 6-3. | The historic Mesquakie system of kinship terminology.

the Mesquakie, the mother-son relationship was more like that between sister and brother. Again, between a father and his daughter, the brother-and-sister attitude prevailed, while the mother-daughter relationship paralleled that of a father and son.

SOCIAL OVERVIEW According to the able analysis of early historic Mesquakie life by Natalie F. Joffe (1940), the most important social and economic unit was the small extended family. It might include about forty individuals since a man sometimes had two to five wives, and their children sometimes brought spouses into the household. In addition, there might be household members from other tribes who had been adopted or were considered captives. Female prisoners might marry Mesquakie men, and their offspring were regarded as Mesquakie. A family group also might include individuals adopted to take the place of deceased persons; these individuals did not take up residence in the household but were regarded as members of it.

POLITICAL LIFE Political control was organized around the village and the tribe, but little is recorded about the tribal level of action. The paramount chief was from a particular lineage in the Bear clan, and other clans contributed lesser chiefs. In the event that the elder son of a chief could not or would not succeed his father (primogeniture), the title and position were passed to a younger son, a brother, or a nephew of the chief. The chief organized village subsistence activities and raiding or war parties. He was in office for an extended period of time, and his influence was great even though he had little power. He was expected to be nonaggressive, and he served as an arbitrator in collective discussions. The council, which made communitywide decisions, had a required membership from different patrilineages but also included other men with outstanding qualities. The village chief listened to discussions and attempted to reconcile conflicting views. The chief and council were quite powerful, but their actions most often were guided by tradition. The Mesquakie, as Walter B. Miller (1955) has stressed, were rugged individualists who knew what was expected of them, and in normal activities they strongly resented any attempt to direct their behavior. As the Jesuit missionary Father Allouez (Miller 1955, 286) wrote long ago, "These people are self-willed beyond anything that can be imagined!"

To illustrate how the political system operated, it is instructive to follow what took place when a man killed his wife. She was, of course, a member of a different clan, and her male relatives summoned the murderer to appear at their main lodge. He did as he was directed and squatted on the floor while the men of the woman's clan seated themselves on the platforms. One man held an ax that would be used to smash the murderer's skull if he were to be executed. When the jury was assembled, a man at one end of the line silently nudged the person next to him; this was a vote to kill the murderer. This man nudged the one sitting on his far side and so on until one man failed to nudge his partner; this indicated that he did not approve of the death penalty. Since a unanimous verdict of guilt was required, the murderer was not doomed to die, and his relatives were permitted to offer gifts as compensation. This example demonstrates that the crime of murder was not judged on the tribal or village level but was considered an offense against the kin group of the deceased individual. The example also illustrates that alternatives of action—death or compensation—were possible.

WARFARE   One activity at which the Mesquakie excelled was physical combat with enemies, but this was war only in a loose sense of the word. Aggression against other Indians or against whites was organized by the tribe or by individual raiding parties. A national war such as those fought against the French, white Americans, or the Osage met with overall approval, but even these actions rarely involved large numbers of warriors and large-scale battles. Raids organized by individuals against a particular enemy to accomplish a specific purpose were most common. Warriors ventured forth to secure hunting areas against intrusion by others, to acquire new lands on which to hunt, to avenge the death of a Mesquakie, or to gain prestige and honor. A war leader was able to organize a raid if he had had prior success and possessed supernatural power. He supervised the strategy, but his authority was limited since any warrior could return home at any time without a loss of honor. Even though a warrior might submit to the temporary control of a war leader and follow instructions, he was obliged to bend to the war chief's modicum of authority only during the period of the raid. The important point is that the Mesquakie war leader had more authority and power than any other individual at any other time, and yet his prerogatives were very few indeed. As if to emphasize the temporary nature of his position, after returning from a raid he was not allowed to enter his settlement until he had been purified ceremonially.

Mesquakie society heaped a great deal of honor upon the successful warrior. To be a great warrior was a value instilled in boys from early childhood. A male child was given portions of the eyebrow or heart of a brave but slain enemy so that he might eat them and acquire the qualities of the deceased. A boy attempted to join a war party as soon as possible so that he might boast of his exploits according to the custom for all warriors. Anyone could attempt to lead a war party; if he dreamed and his dreams were judged propitious by other warriors, they pledged themselves to join the raid. Before departure, the people sang war songs, and men abstained from the company of women. Although a woman might join her husband on a war party, she would not have sexual intercourse with him during the trip. A raiding party advanced slowly, hunting along the route and caching dried meat for the return trip. If the party numbered twenty or more persons, they took along a sacred bundle for supernatural protection; a smaller party relied on the party leader's medicine bundle to secure supernatural aid. Some men served as scouts, and one was designated as the cook. The party always planned an attack to surprise the enemy. If the party was successful, the return was led by the man who made the first kill; in defeat, each warrior returned home as best he could. If the party took captives, they often killed the aged ones on the way home. A successful raid ended with a scalp dance and feasting at the village of the warriors. A woman could gain important status and rights among men if a male relative permitted her to club the head of an enemy he had killed. For a Mesquakie man to steal horses was considered honorable; however, horses were relatively unimportant and such theft did not have the social value reported among most Plains Indians. A warrior could and usually did take new names repeatedly if he excelled in warfare. Warfare among the Mesquakie was not nearly as elaborate as among many Plains Indians, but it did manifest most of the important features found farther west.

RELIGION The most distinctive characteristics of Mesquakie religious life were the importance of personal rapport with supernatural forces and the secondary role of group ceremonies. Supernatural matters centered in the concept of manitou, a fickle, mysterious, and pervasive quality in nature that persons communicated with for power. Manitou was approached with humility and apprehension, and it could impart to the seeker a sense of strength. The usual way to contact a manitou was by fasting for a prolonged period, but this force might be seen or heard at critical or even ordinary moments. It might manifest itself through a song, an object, or a ritual. The central religious concept of manitou was as an abstract, impersonal, and pervasive supernatural force. Yet, it was received by an individual, and a personalized manitou was drawn into the experiences of an individual. The blessing and cooperation of a manitou had no built-in permanence. It could be lost at any time, and therefore an individual receiving such power always sought to reinforce it. The varieties of manitou were endless. The force could be animal, human, organic, inorganic, material, nonmaterial, natural, or supernatural.

To gain the cooperation of a manitou an adolescent boy darkened his face with ashes and fasted alone in the forest for four days and nights or perhaps longer. Near the end of his isolation he dreamed of a manitou or received a vision that included instructions. The receipt of power was contingent on following rules set down by the supernatural. These usually included the avoidance of menstruating women and a periodic offering of tobacco to the manitou. In addition, other instructions might be given, such as wearing a certain item of clothing, singing a particular song, or obtaining an object that would become the basis for a medicine bundle. The Mesquakie thought that if a boy behaved properly in his relationship with a manitou, the association was lasting, but if the boy failed in his duties, the manitou withdrew support. If this happened, a youth fasted and isolated himself again to obtain an affiliation with another manitou. A faithful manitou was believed to remain with a man not only during his life but also after death. Whether women had relationships with the manitou is not known.

The most important personification of a supernatural force was the *Gitche Manitou,* the Great Manitou. Another was the creator and culture hero Wisaka, addressed as "my nephew." Other creatures associated with mythology might be helpful; bears, deer, and snakes were thought to make one swift of foot. An individual's contact with these animals served as a basis for the emergence of a sacred bundle, the essence of Mesquakie ceremonialism. The founder learned essential rituals from a supernatural, and a cult developed around each bundle. Affiliation with a sacred bundle and its ceremonies was along a clan line, but an outsider could be incorporated into a group by learning the rituals and by being invited to participate.

The most important annual ceremonies were held by clans during the spring, summer, and winter. The spring and summer rituals were held in the bark house of a clan. Here singers and drummers consistently sat on the south side of the structure. Hoof or ground rattles were used by certain clans, and rasps were used by others. Participants performed four dances and ate three times, with the main feast following the third dance. In all the ceremonies an emphasis was placed on dogs as ceremonial food, seating position according to moiety, and the sacrifice of tobacco. A ceremonial leader committed ritual speeches to memory and punctuated his delivery of them with accounts of other episodes. Such an individual followed established tradition in his performances, and his authority was limited to these specific times.

The most important supernaturals, apart from manitous, probably were witches envisaged as either human males or females. Witches reportedly were often from the Bear clan, and they learned their skills from other witches. The nearness of a witch at night was supposedly indicated by flashes of light or a hissing sound made as it passed. Witches' evil power took diverse forms: swelling of part of a person's body or death from no apparent cause was believed to be a witch's doing. If a person was bewitched, certain techniques could be used to turn the malevolent power back against the witch.

The Mesquakie considered most phenomena as supernatural. Thus, the sun was seen as a man, a manitou, and the grandfather of the Mesquakie; he was not always considerate of the people. The moon, as their grandmother; he was thought to have a gentle quality and could be looked upon at any time. The months were named and associated with the arrival of each new moon. The Milky Way was considered a river of stars, and other stars in the sky were thought to be either persons who had died and had gone to live in the sky, or else great manitous. The four stars forming the body of the Big Dipper were thought of as a bear, followed by three stars who were hunters. According to myth, they killed the bear in the fall, and its blood fell to earth, turning the leaves of some trees red and fading the color of others. Then the bear came back to life, and the hunters pursued it for another year. The color red symbolized the fall of the year; it also signified hostility and was used for decoration. Black was the color for winter, for fasting, and for mourning. Green was for spring and peace; it was the special color of the chief's clan. Yellow symbolized summer.

Curers among the Mesquakie used plant products and to a far lesser extent animal substances to heal patients. Whoever collected a plant had to follow certain rules. Songs were sung before removing roots, and an offering was placed in the ground where a root had been to appease Grandmother Earth, because plants were seen as the hairs on her head. The earth was considered the grandmother of Wisaka and the Mesquakie as well; her name was Mother-of-all-Things-

Everywhere. Plants' conversation with one another supposedly was heard as the wind blowing through trees. The Mesquakie believed that plants could be happy or sad and that they mated in the spring and bore fruit in the fall. Wisaka was appeased so that plants would be potent cures. There were proper methods and a proper season for collecting medicinal plants, and only stipulated amounts were harvested.

LIFE CYCLE   For a woman to conceive, the Mesquakie believed that repeated copulations with one man were essential, and during pregnancy many restrictions surrounded her behavior. For example, to ensure a normal birth the woman abstained from eating nuts so that the embryo would not break through the membrane; she could not touch a corpse for fear her baby would die or stare at a corpse for fear it would make the baby cross-eyed. In childbearing a woman knelt and leaned forward, supported by a rawhide strap. She did not cry out no matter how severe the pain. If the delivery was long and difficult, a shaman or woman sang around the outside of the hut but usually offered no other assistance. Parturition took place in a small hut away from the family dwelling, and here the mother was cared for by an old woman for ten days after the birth. For the next twenty days she slept in the main house apart from the other occupants.

A baby was placed on a cradleboard and carried by its mother for nearly a year. As children grew older, the parents did not favor one child over another unless a boy became an outstanding hunter. Children were told not to visit other families often, for if they did people would think that they always were in search of something good to eat. They were expected to be retiring and honest, and when someone died, to fast and be quiet. These fastings prepared boys for the fasts in later years that were an important part of becoming a man. Abstaining from food also was emphasized for girls, especially as their menarche approached; the goal was for them to have a long and good life. These ideals may not have been followed exactly, but they did constitute the normal expectations for children. A role assumed for two years by young males of high social standing was that of a "slave" in the service of a chief. After this period the volunteer was freed from the drudgery of menial tasks such as cooking and camp chores throughout his life.

As mentioned earlier, the relationship between a father and his son was somewhat comparable to the behavior between brothers in our society. Hunting instruction began when a boy was about seven, and by the time he was twelve he had been given a gun and was expected to obtain small game. He was taught not only objective hunting skills but associated magical practices. When a boy killed his first game, a feast was held in his honor, a widespread practice among North American Indians. A son who disobeyed was not punished physically but was instructed by his father to fast. To fast and seek solitude were not new to the child, but the requirement intensified as he grew. While the boy was still young, he was expected to seek out a manitou. When he went alone into the forest on his quest, his parents mourned the loss of their son; after establishing this supernatural relationship, he would no longer be a child. Fasting and painting one's face with ashes made a young man able to approach a manitou and encouraged it to grant the young man success in the hunt and in war, and give him longevity as well.

At about the same age that a boy began to receive hunting instructions, a girl was taught domestic skills by her mother. She learned to sew, to cook, and to care for the garden. About the age of twelve, she began to acquire the more complex skills necessary in making moccasins and house mats. At her first menstruation she was isolated from the settlement in a small hut where she lived for ten days with a blanket over her head. Her companion during this isolation was an old woman who instructed the girl about adult behavior. At the end of this initial isolation the girl bathed in a stream, and her skin was pierced, especially about the back and sides, until she bled freely. The bloodletting was to ensure that the girl would not menstruate excessively. She then moved within sight of the settlement, living there for twenty days. After this time she took a second bath and finally was permitted in the family dwelling once again. During subsequent menstrual periods, a woman was isolated in a hut. She was believed to be not only potentially dangerous to herself but to men and supernaturals. Supposedly, if she were to touch her hair, it might fall out; if she ate sweet or sour food, she might lose her teeth; and she could kill a tree with her touch or cause a crop to fail if she ran through a garden. Most important manitous supposedly abhorred menstruating women, and such women were avoided by men so that they would not jeopardize their special powers.

A girl did not marry until she was skilled in making fine beadwork and ribbon applique. Her behavior was supervised carefully by her mother and her mother's brother, who was a joking relative. He not only joked with her but made certain that she behaved properly since he would be shamed if she misbehaved. She was taught not to be promiscuous nor to giggle, for giggly girls were open to sexual overtures. As a boy became a young man, he was expected to be respectful toward girls and to have sexual intercourse only with the girl he planned to marry. A young man sometimes courted a girl by playing a flute near her home, which was an attempt to lure the girl outside. The melody of the flute conveyed his desire, but for a girl to accept the lure invited seduction. The parents of a courting couple preferred to have the man visit their home openly to win their daughter in marriage.

The principal means for obtaining a wife was by bride service, but less commonly a couple might elope. A suitor usually established a friendship with the girl's brother and broached the subject to him. The girl of course was from a different clan than the man, and after the girl's family declared the match acceptable, they usually required the services of the groom until the first offspring was born. Alternatively, a man's family presented the girl's family with gifts in lieu of bride service by their son. This was attempted especially when the boy's parents did not want to lose him as a hunter. If gifts were accepted in place of bride service or when the service was completed, the couple was free to establish an

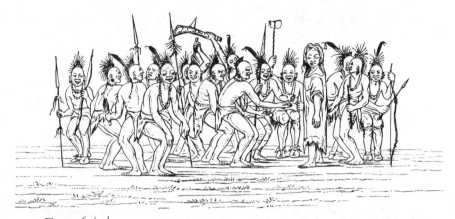

Figure 6-4. | Mesquakie and Sauk dance to the berdache, after an 1836 painting by Catlin. (From Donaldson 1886.)

independent household or to join either set of in-laws. An elopement occurred when a man persuaded a girl to join him on a summer hunt; on their return he presented the parents of the girl with gifts. Another less common arrangement was for a girl to be offered to a warrior by her father. This happened when a man had rendered extraordinary service to the family of the girl. For example, if a warrior prevented the scalping of a man's dead son, gave the son a warrior's interment, or rescued the son from an enemy, he might be offered the sister as a wife.

At least a few Mesquakie men remained unmarried and lived as transvestites. A dance held annually centered about and emphasized the position of such a person. The *berdache,* as he was termed by the French, was danced around by men who had had a sexual relationship with him. (See Figure 6-4.) A transvestite dressed like a woman, and because of his unusual role he was regarded as sacred.

The dissolution of a marriage usually resulted from sterility or from an inability of a couple to tolerate one another. Some personality characteristics such as extreme jealousy or ill temper led to divorce. When a marriage was dissolved, any presents that had been exchanged during the marital arrangements were returned, but personal property was retained by each partner. Sometimes a husband left his wife after a few days of marriage; this was said to have occurred when the bride was not a maiden. In extreme cases of a wife's infidelity the offended husband might kill the couple; a milder alternative was for the husband to cut off his wife's ears or bite off her nose. A wife had no recourse in the case of a husband's infidelity.

A conspicuous characteristic of Mesquakie adult life was that it was dictated by tradition. Each individual knew what was expected of him or her and was resentful of being directed by another person in any manner. He or she was responsible for all personal decisions and met institutional obligations without supervision. Communication with the supernaturals was done by the individual, with no one standing between the person and the manitou. Because individualism was the norm, it is not surprising that the Mesquakie resented being told to do anything.

When an adult died, three forms of interment were possible. The body might be placed on a scaffold or in a tree; an honorable interment for a warrior was to place him in a sitting position above the body of a slain enemy. Most common perhaps was to dig a shallow pit and arrange the body in a seated position with the head above the ground and covered with rocks or a small shed. Food and water were placed with the body, but weapons were not, since spirits might use them against the living. At the foot of a grave a stake was erected after the bark was peeled from it. Among the final acts were sprinkling tobacco on the body and killing a dog on the site of the burial. The dog's spirit supposedly protected and guided the dead to the next world. Just before the body of a warrior was abandoned, an old warrior recounted the number of persons the deceased had killed, which meant that their souls would serve as his slaves in the land of spirits. The ritual leader distributed the property of the deceased, along with items contributed by relatives of the dead person, to his helpers.

After disposing of the body, the clan to which the deceased belonged held a mourning ceremony. A second dog was killed and its hair singed by four firebrands taken from the hearth of the deceased. The dog was cooked, and the clan's mourning songs were sung until about midnight when the participants ate the dog. The principal mourners dressed in tattered clothing and blackened their faces. They remained in this state up to four years, which was the maximum time limit before an adoption ceremony and an end to mourning. The adoption ceremony was performed by the relatives of the deceased and served to release the soul of the dead permanently. According to Mesquakie belief, the soul had left the earth after four days but returned at intervals until the adoption rituals were completed. If this did not happen within four years, the soul became an owl. The adoption was of an unrelated friend of the deceased who was of the same sex and approximate age. This individual assumed the kinship position of the deceased but also retained her or his own prior kinship ties. If the deceased was a warrior killed by an enemy, the adopted warrior was obligated to kill an enemy in order to release the widow from mourning.

Each individual was believed to have two souls that served different purposes. A small soul came from a particular manitou and was equated with the individual's life; it left the body at the time of death and through subsequent adoption ceremonies was reborn three times. The larger soul, from Wisaka, had entered the neonate's body at birth and was never reborn. The world of spirits was believed to be divided into two sections: in one section lived persons who had been good on earth, and in the other, persons who were evil. Some of these concepts may have been inspired by Christian missionaries.

| Recent Historic Changes in Mesquakie Life

Recent historic changes in Mesquakie life centered on these people's tribulations in finding a homeland. As was the case for all other Indians, their land was important to them primarily because of the subsistence base it offered, and relocation necessitated changes in their subsistence activities and other aspects of their traditional way of life.

DISPLACEMENT AND RELOCATION Following the end of the Black Hawk War in 1832, the Mesquakie and Sauk lived on such a small, inadequate reservation in Iowa that they could not possibly follow their traditional way of life for very long. They hunted and planted crops until the land was depleted of game, and then they turned to the west to hunt bison. Soon this was an unprofitable subsistence base, and they spent more and more time wintering among whites. They dealt with unscrupulous traders, dishonest Indian agents, and generally hostile whites. They were plagued with disease, and consuming intoxicants became almost a way of life. As if these troubles were not enough, internal dissension between the Keokuk faction and another brought serious conflict. Furthermore, the Mesquakie and Sauk were thrown into close contact with their Siouan enemies, and the resultant raids led to an embittered attitude on both sides. To cap all of this, an increase in the number of local white settlers forced the Mesquakie and Sauk to move again. White Americans concerned about them attempted to introduce modern farming methods, but the Indians would have no part of the program. Neither would they permit schools to be established, and they rejected the efforts of missionaries to convert them to Christianity. Their crystallized pattern of hostility against white customs was based on two hundred years of bitter experience. In 1842 these Indians were forced to sell all of their land in Iowa and to relocate at the headwaters of the Osage River in Kansas.

The Mesquakie obtained nearly 400,000 acres of land in Kansas as a grant from the federal government, but it was prairie country, and their farming and hunting economy was ill-adapted to it. They hunted bison and other game but depended largely on annuities from the government. Hunting on the prairies brought them into conflict with the Arapaho, Comanche, and Kiowa, who resented Mesquakie and Sauk intrusion. The number of warriors among the Mesquakie and Sauk always was small, but they were brave and had superior firearms, received from traders when they had lived farther to the east.

The Mesquakie never were reconciled to their Kansas reservation, and between 1846 and 1852 some of them returned to Iowa, where others had remained. They bought and settled eighty acres of land in Tama County. Legal recognition of these Mesquakie was extended by the state government, and the land was held in trust by the governor. In 1858 and 1862 other Mesquakie from Kansas moved to Iowa. Amazing as it may seem, the Indians were welcomed by whites. Altruism was the motive of some, and interest in the annuity payments received by the Indians was the motive of others. When the Mesquakie and Sauk in Kansas were forced by white settlers and the federal government to give up their reservation and move to Oklahoma in 1869, still more Mesquakie returned to Iowa. By about 1870 some three hundred Mesquakie Indians lived in Iowa, and they began to settle down to a new way of life in the Tama area.

As the modern Mesquakie are quick to point out, their land near Tama is not a reservation in the sense that it was set aside for them by the federal government. The holdings, which officially are termed the Sac and Fox Settlement, consist of land purchased by the Indians themselves. It likewise should be noted, as stressed by Michael D. Green (1983), that the Sauk and Mesquakie are separate tribes that were "joined" by the federal government solely for administrative convenience. Each of the tribes has maintained its distinct identity.

LIFE AT THE IOWA SETTLEMENT   The Indians who remained in Iowa or returned to the area in the mid-1800s were miserably poor. Their economy was based on hunting and trapping, gardening, begging, and selling curios. Whenever they obtained surplus money, they purchased additional lands. They remained extremely distrustful of outsiders; for example, their children did not

Figure 6-5. | Mesquakie men on horses with summer sun shade and reed-covered dwellings in the background, circa 1904, Tama, Iowa. (Courtesy of the State Historical Society of Iowa.)

attend the public school built in 1876. Family units continued to frequent hunting and trapping areas in the winter. In the late 1880s the Mesquakie still refused to allow their children to attend school, and the men would not learn the skills necessary to become farmers. In 1894, after the sale of land allotments that had been held for them in Oklahoma, they were able to expand their holdings in Iowa to twenty-eight hundred acres. Apparently at about this time they began to rent to whites farmlands that did not belong to the core of their holdings, and they used the rent money to pay taxes.

A visitor to the Mesquakie lands in Iowa in 1897 and 1898 reported that the population was about four hundred and the winter dwellings were oblong, pole-framed structures with mat coverings, just as in aboriginal times. (See Figure 6-5.) The ground inside a house was covered with old blankets, and a fire in a central fireplace provided warmth, light, and heat for cooking. The only items seen in one such dwelling were containers and food. The standard fare seems to have been flour, lard, and maize. The flour was fried in lard to make a bannock, which was eaten with dried sweet corn. Dogs remained an important source of meat for festive occasions. A few families, particularly those of younger men, lived in frame dwellings with adjacent outbuildings. In the summer the people lived along the bottomland near the Iowa River in dwellings covered with boards and bark topped with mats. Inside, a platform extended along the length of the room on both sides. An additional structure was a hut nearby for menstruating women.

CHANGING STYLES By the end of the last century most Mesquakie had abandoned their old hair and clothing styles. A few men still kept the traditional hair style, but most of them had long hair braided into a small pigtail from which silver ornaments and beadwork hung. A man's most important ornament was made from silver and protected his scalp lock. Men dressed in store-bought shirts and trousers except at home, where they wore a breechclout and blanket. Moccasins had changed from buckskin to cloth, and the skin cape was replaced by a blanket or shawl. The shirts and skirts of women were made from calico; women wore at least two shirts, which were loose at the waist and buttoned at the front. They wore two or more skirts, which hung loosely from the hips to just below the ankles for younger women and girls and reached just above the ankles for older women. (See Figure 6-6.) Women wore short woolen leggings that reached their knees. They preferred beaded shawls, but those who could not afford shawls wore blankets. Men and women alike were partial to silver jewelry, which was considered "good medicine."

Modern Mesquakie Life

The Mesquakie of Iowa are one of the few contemporary Indian groups to survive in the central Midwest, and as a small Indian enclave among whites, they have fought hard to retain their distinct cultural identity. A factor contributing to

Figure 6-6. | A Mesquakie woman with her child, circa 1900. Although the dress is typical, the furniture is not, and thus the photo was probably taken in a photographer's studio. (Courtesy of the State Historical Society of Iowa.)

their success has been that they occupy land obtained by purchase and have an especially close identity with it. It is fortunate, from an ethnographic perspective, that anthropologists at the University of Chicago became especially interested in these Indians as early as 1932. Under the direction of Sol Tax, systematic studies of Mesquakie life were initiated, and these provide most of the information to follow.

SETTLEMENT AND SUBSISTENCE By 1937, Mesquakie lands near Tama, Iowa, consisted of one large 3,800-acre parcel where the people lived, and another 520 acres that were tilled by white farmers on leases. The population of 450 supported themselves either by farming or by wage labor. If a family did not farm, its plot could be leased to another Mesquakie. A family dwelling consisted of a frame house with usually one or two rooms, and adjacent outbuildings included a barn, corncrib, chicken coop, roofless privy, and canvas menstrual hut. During their monthly periods or at childbirth the women ate in the menstrual huts but slept in the houses. Another important structure was made of canvas or mats covering a frame of poles and used as sleeping quarters; it was rectangular, resembling the summer house of old, and was often attached to an arbor. On the arbor platform men sat and children played, and much of the cooking was done by women over an outdoor fire nearby.

The average family income in 1937 was about five hundred dollars per year, including money from all sources. About half of the ninety-one families farmed, and the others supported themselves by wage labor. In the farming activities, women cultivated garden plots after the land had been prepared by the men, and the men raised the field crops, which were important sources of cash income. Men who did not till the soil labored in nearby towns.

Food habits reflected a certain degree of continuity with the past, since maize was shelled and dried or made into hominy as of old, and squash was sectioned, dried, grated, and stored for future use. The people still collected local plant products and took small game. New crops included oats, alfalfa, potatoes, beets, and onions. They obtained wheat flour and most meat and dairy products from a store, and their maize was ground at a commercial mill. Innumerable dogs were kept, and young ones remained an important ceremonial food. About half of the families owned horses for hauling buggies and wagons or for plowing and riding, but it was primarily younger persons who rode horses. The material culture in the late 1930s seemed typical of rural Iowa. About half of the families owned automobiles, and families did most shopping in Tama, where the storekeepers made some effort to stock goods with an appeal to Indians, including shawls, silk neckerchiefs, and beads. Special items for use on festive or ceremonial occasions, such as seed beads, were purchased from mail-order houses; deerskins were obtained from other Indians.

By the mid-1950s the Mesquakie were supporting themselves as skilled and unskilled laborers and artisans in communities surrounding the reservation. Most often they commuted each day, but in some instances they returned to the reservation only on weekends. The Mesquakie had all the obligations of other United States citizens; they paid all the diverse forms of taxes and had the same rights to vote or to receive relief if they were without economic means. At that time about eight families received relief, paid for by state and federal governments. The Indians also received from the federal government some services not offered to non-Indians, such as health care.

SOCIAL DIMENSIONS   In the 1930s and continuing to the present, a typical residence unit included a husband, wife, their biological children, unmarried relatives, and perhaps children by a former marriage. These nuclear-core households were the economic and social units, although all residents might not contribute equally to the family's support and the near relatives of the couple often were transient. In general, a new household was established near the home of relatives and tended to be more closely linked to the wife's family than to the husband's. Yet, relatives on both sides of the family (kindred) offered the typical individual a widespread network of kin, numbering between fifty and one hundred persons, distributed among about a dozen households. It is significant that although the Mesquakie were patrilineal, the important social ties in their daily lives were with both sides of the family. Family ties were expanded through adoption, which was of the same nature as in aboriginal times, a deceased relative being replaced by an adopted individual of approximately the same age and sex. Although adult life centered about the family, many forms of entertainment existed outside the family. Tama pool halls were frequented by men and boys; a men's baseball team and a girls' softball team were active, and during the winter gambling was an important form of diversion for men and women.

THE ANNUAL POW-WOW   One of the most pleasurable and lasting of all new Mesquakie institutions has been the Pow-Wow held each August. From the time the Mesquakie returned to Iowa, whites probably had been invited to attend certain of the ceremonies. In later years nonreligious attractions were added, although the religious core of the celebration remained. In 1913, as a response to white enthusiasm, the Pow-Wow was organized formally as a four-day affair, primarily intended as entertainment for whites. The committee controlling the Pow-Wow was structured as a tribal council, with representatives selected from the fifteen major family lines. In 1922 the group was reformulated as a corporate body in a legal sense, with a constitution, officers, and committee members. By 1951 committee membership had been expanded, and even though the positions were elective, the idea of representation by major family groups was preserved. By the early 1950s the rather elaborate Pow-Wow arrangements were guided largely by the committee secretary, a person familiar with whites; since such matters as publicity and the various forms of local arrangements had to be managed through whites, she or he served as a link between the Indian and white communities. There was no real authority to guide the event;

Figure 6-7. | Young dancers at the Tama Pow-Wow, circa 1959. (Courtesy of Joan Liffring Zug.)

the participants followed traditionally established norms for the celebration, which resembled a county fair but had a strong Indian emphasis. By 1951 there were twenty-four family souvenir and food concessions; the old dances and songs were performed (see Figure 6-7), and a guitar group sang cowboy songs. In good weather it has not been unusual for ten thousand persons to attend the event, with most families camping at the Pow-Wow grounds. All normal routine ceases when the time approaches, and this is the one time of year that the people all work together as Mesquakie.

ATTITUDES: MESQUAKIE AND WHITE The attitudes of local whites and Mesquakie toward one another are of continuing importance since the groups frequently interact. In the 1950s whites considered the Mesquakie lazy, which they were by white standards, and as living off federal dole, which largely was untrue. They thought the Indians were sexually promiscuous and physically dirty. These attitudes probably were reasonable in light of observed Mesquakie behavior; nevertheless, Indians clearly were not as lawless as the whites thought. Furthermore, the whites regarded the Mesquakie settlement as temporary and expected them to be assimilated into the American melting pot. By contrast, the Mesquakie thought that the whites were greedy and aggressive, which they were by Indian standards, and that their behavior was artificial. The Indians also believed that they were discriminated against. Both groups agreed that the Mesquakie had been maltreated in the past; this made the whites feel guilty and led to hostility from the Mesquakie.

POLITICAL LIFE Mesquakie political institutions understandably had changed a great deal by the 1930s. Divisive factionalism existed and appears to have originated in a controversy over recording individual names for a tribal roll in 1876. The members of a conservative faction refused to tell the Indian agent their names, but the progressives did so, which led to inequities in the annuity payments. In addition, a chief was appointed in 1881 who was not a member of the Bear clan. No issue was made of the fact at the time, but when the chief later led the progressives, the conservatives questioned his right to the leadership. This division continued to be important in the 1930s. Families, but not clans, tended to act as units in the factionalism, but these differences did not affect ceremonial activities in which clans were important. Marriages tended to be within a faction, but when they did cut across factional lines, it was most often the woman who joined the side of her husband.

In 1916 the last chief appointed a council that functioned until 1929, when a council was elected. The elected members of the contending factions could not agree, however, and they never met. Although elections continued to be held, the council remained inactive, owing to internal differences. Then in 1937 the tribe organized under the Indian Reorganization Act, and the seven elected council members began to work together. However, the details of council operations were not recorded. Mesquakie lands continued to be held in trust by the

federal government but were subject to taxation, eminent domain, and other judicial procedures that applied to any individually owned land in the state. Personal differences usually were settled verbally, although women sometimes
fought and one man might strike another on the head. The most common
offenses prosecuted were drunkenness and differences over property rights.
These legal actions often were brought by Indians, but they did not seek intervention from whites for problems such as theft.

The status of warrior once again became important in Mesquakie life during World War II. Forty-seven Mesquakie veterans of the armed services emerged
from the war, and of these, twenty-two became members of a local American
Legion post organized in 1949. Initially, the Mesquakie veterans had joined the
Tama post, but when they were refused intoxicants, they resigned. The federal
restriction against selling intoxicants to Indians was still in force although it had
been suspended when Indians were in the armed services. The Mesquakie post
was founded through the efforts of a white legionnaire from a nearby community, and the post served primarily as a means for veterans to find greater recognition in white society. The large public meetings, involving both Mesquakie and
whites, were attended well by both members and nonmember veterans. The
Mesquakie community turned to the veterans for leadership, but this was not
forthcoming since veterans were no better able to cope with local problems
than any other segment of the population. Initially, the leader preserved the Mesquakie ideal of behavior and assumed authority only with reluctance. While the
next leader was more assertive, the group would have foundered except that a
white veteran assumed the organizational responsibilities. When he left, the organization passed out of existence, partially because federal officials learned that
beer was kept in the government building and withdrew permission for the
Indians to meet there.

RELIGION   The concept of manitou persisted, and still does, and formal
religious activities coalesced around the sacred bundles of the clans or voluntary
religious associations. Christianity, the use of peyote, and the nonaboriginal
Drum Society all offered limited opportunities for religious participation. The
peyote cult, mentioned in Chapter 2, was small in 1937, although ceremonial use
of the cactus had been known since around the turn of the present century.
Peyote was valued mainly for its reportedly curative properties; a person who
had tried other cures and then turned to peyote often continued to take it after
he had recovered. The Drum Society was a religious group organized in 1932
and probably was derived from the Potawatomi. The members were from the
progressive faction even though they believed the power of the ceremony to be
derived from a manitou. The ritual involved the use of four drums, and the ceremonies were held four times a year. The drums were associated with particular
leaders, each having specific functions.

Religion still focused on the sacred bundles, which were hereditary either
in a patriclan line or across clan affiliations. Forty sacred bundle groups in
eleven major categories existed, and within each category were major and
minor bundle groups. Membership in a sacred bundle group could be acquired

through an invitation, which most often was extended to an individual who was a good singer and knew the songs associated with the particular bundle group. Certain reciprocal functions linked the groups into various activities. The bundle affiliations did not regulate marriage, although this was apparently once an ideal. The ceremonies were held in summer longhouses and extended from morning until sunset of a single day. Food was prepared by the hosts, and the most important dish was stewed puppies that had been ceremonially killed with clubs. The stew was served by members of another sacred bundle group, and after the meal the bones carefully were collected and burned. The dances were in sets of four, and the sacred bundle was opened and various items used in the ceremony. Both men and women participated in the summer rituals, but only men were active in the winter festivities.

Witchcraft and sorcery were still very much a part of Mesquakie life in the 1930s. Malevolent power was obtained in a vision quest, and a sorcerer might take the form of a bear or snake. If a potential victim could shoot a gun at the spot where a witch was thought to be, the sorcerer supposedly would die within four days. One important use of sorcery was as love magic, and if properly employed, it was believed to lead to the irresistible attractiveness of the user. A nonresponding victim would be driven to insanity and eventual suicide. The ability to cure, which came from a vision, was limited to shamans, who employed a variety of techniques. A shaman visited the patient, and if he was compensated enough he accepted the case. The curing procedure entailed singing, administering herbs, and sucking out the disease. Because a bear or snake supposedly had given supernatural power to the medicine man, a claw or bone formed the core of his medicine bundle and might be used to suck out the substance causing the illness.

In the 1950s the supernatural system continued to be organized around the traditional ceremonials. Apart from the yearly Pow-Wow, clan-affiliated religious activities most often brought people together. The clan organization, which was weak and somewhat vaguely defined, served primarily as the structure around which the traditional religious ceremonies were organized. According to Charles Callender (1978), clans probably had served the same general function in the past. Community elders provided the greatest support for the old religious system, and some middle-aged persons followed their lead. Younger Mesquakie tended to be nonreligious, but some seemed ready to adopt Christianity if they were not restrained by elders. The forty Drum Society members still tended to be progressive. In the late 1940s about a dozen persons participated in the peyote rituals. About thirty Mesquakie were members of two Christian denominations, the United Presbyterian and Open Bible Gospel churches; both were maintained and encouraged by whites, although some meaningful Mesquakie leadership was beginning to emerge.

MESQUAKIE IDENTITY Because the Mesquakie are surrounded and greatly outnumbered by whites, interested outsiders repeatedly have wondered whether the tribe can survive and retain its distinct identity. A partial answer was provided by Steven Polgar (1960) in his study of three Mesquakie boys' "gangs" in 1952 and 1953. One group of boys who interacted habitually with one another was a gang as this term is used in American society, but other groups of boys were not gangs in the same context. The members of the first group had a high rate of absenteeism in school, and they were suspected of theft and property damage. The clothing they wore was Indian in its type; they preferred bright-colored clothing and Navajo jewelry. Most of them were from nonnuclear families, and their relatives were not active in local politics. The members were cold to both white and Indian worlds and were delinquent in both worlds. The second group of boys was oriented toward white society as well as their own in a positive manner. This was especially true of its leader. These boys did not wear flashy clothing, and they were participants in the traditional clan ceremonies. They did not habitually participate in the Pow-Wow or other less traditionally oriented activities, as did the first group. It was from the second gang that Polgar expected the traditionally oriented leaders of the next generation to emerge. The third gang was much more oriented toward the attitudes held by the dominant white society. All the members had spent at least a few years away from the settlement, and they were able to compete successfully for jobs in white society. In addition, three of the eight members entered college. Six of the eight still danced in the Pow-Wow, however, and most attended the clan ceremonies.

Figure 6-8. | Adrian Pushetonequa, a Mesquakie artist, in 1972. (Courtesy of John M. Zielinski.)

These boys had begun to find acceptance in white society and were able to move away from Mesquakie traditions although they did not wish to sever their ties with Mesquakie culture.

From this analysis of Mesquakie boys' gangs, it is apparent that one gang was composed of boys whose behavior was antisocial in the eyes of both the whites and the Mesquakie. The members of the third gang were moving rapidly and successfully toward assimilation into the dominant white society. It was the members of the second gang who seemed most likely to carry forward a continuity in Mesquakie life. They appeared to be adapting to both social settings successfully through the process of biculturation. At the time I made superficial observations in the early 1980s, Polgar's predictions appeared to be proving correct. The greatest proponents of Mesquakie culture among adults at that time were those who had been members of the second type of gang. (See Figure 6-8.)

Settlement of Land Claims

In 1969 the federal government partially rectified injustices of old. In that year the U.S. Indian Claims Commission awarded the Mesquakie and Sauk of Iowa nearly a million dollars for lands ceded in 1830 for which they had not received just compensation. Each adult received $500, with a like amount held in trust for each person under eighteen years of age. Sixty percent of the settlement money was held by the Mesquakie Tribal Council for planning and development. Of the nearly 800 persons on the tribal roll, only about 500 lived in or near their lands in Iowa at that time. With an inadequate land base, economic conditions had forced some persons to leave. A further settlement in 1976 ended a twenty-eight-year court battle over seventeen million acres of land taken by the federal government for which the Mesquakie had not been compensated. Of the $6.6 million payment, each adult received nearly $6,000, and this amount was held in trust for each of the 329 minors to receive when they reached the age of eighteen. About $1.3 million was held in trust by the federal government for tribal projects. It does not appear that the cash received by the 573 adults will have any long-range impact on their lives.

Life in the 1970s and 1980s

By 1986, the total enrolled Mesquakie-Sauk population was 1,010. Of this number, 467 lived at the Mesquakie Settlement, along with 137 nonenrolled individuals. Employment at the settlement depended largely on temporary construction projects, such as building the new tribal headquarters. (See Figure 6-9.) As a result of the sporadic nature of jobs at the settlement and in surrounding areas, the unemployment rate in 1986 averaged about 67 percent. Another problem for job-seeking Mesquakie has been their limited educational background, which means that they can compete only for unskilled and semi-skilled jobs. In addition, the depressed economic conditions in rural Iowa in the mid-1980s created a further disadvantage for all residents, the Mesquakie among them.

Figure 6-9. | The Mesquakie had a new building as their tribal headquarters by 1981; it was managed by tribal members such as Don Wanatee. (Photograph by the author.)

A good indicator of the poor economic climate is that in 1985 the vast majority of Mesquakie families received some form of direct welfare assistance; Aid to Families with Dependent Children and Indian Relief funds have been dominant in this respect. With an average monthly household income of about five hundred dollars in 1978, most families lived beneath the poverty line. Furthermore, the housing of many families is and long has been woefully inadequate. (See Figure 6-10.) About a quarter of the homes flood in the spring, and about half of them do not have central heating, indoor plumbing, or an indoor water supply. Under the Housing Improvement Program the BIA has been building new houses, as many as five a year, yet compared with the needs the replacement rate is slow. One recent and highly successful housing development is a center for the aged. It was completed in 1982 and is now the home of forty persons.

The despair of many Mesquakie about their life situation probably is best reflected in the scope of alcohol and drug abuse. By 1981 about seventy adults and youths were enrolled in counseling programs; they represented only a small proportion of those identified as potential participants. In recent years most arrests, nearly all cases of child neglect, numerous deaths, and suicide attempts have been attributed to overconsumption of alcoholic beverages. Although Mesquakie administrators have developed comprehensive programs to cope with the problem, their success rate has not been great because of the conditions under which most of the people live.

Figure 6-10. | Curtis Youngbear at his home in 1972. (Courtesy of John M. Zielinski.)

Figure 6-11. | By 1981 the Headstart program at the Sac and Fox tribal complex near Tama was enjoying success. (Photograph by the author.)

The prognosis for the future of the Mesquakie is not the best, but this has been true ever since they began to return to Iowa nearly 140 years ago. Yet, despite adversity they have retained their distinct identity, bought more land, and nurtured their sense of cultural pride. Their continuing individualism, coupled with their secure land base, seems likely to sustain them in the foreseeable future. (See Figure 6-11.)

Comparisons with Other Indians

Many contrasts separate the Mesquakie from the other peoples thus far presented. For example, no aboriginal baseline study of the Mesquakie was ever done, they have been battered by history far more than any of the others, and we have no contemporary study of them. Yet, comparisons are feasible and worthwhile along certain dimensions, especially in religious life. Note that the individual supernatural experience was stressed among the Chipewyan, Eskimos, and Mesquakie, but among the Mesquakie it was far more pervasive. The Mesquakie emphasized supernatural power through personal rapport with a manitou. Their ritual calendar was not well developed, although the emphasis on clan ceremonials has clear parallels with the Cahuilla and is worthy of further consideration. The egalitarian nature of Mesquakie social structure is an important characteristic, and one might seek also to explain why a superior deity was addressed as a nephew or why a mother treated her daughter as she did her sister. Can an explanation be based on Mesquakie personality type, history, economic adaptations, or perhaps a combination of these factors?

Additional Readings

As a background to modern Mesquakie and Sauk history, the book by William T. Hagan (1958) and the listed article by Michael D. Green (1983) are required reading. For accounts of more traditional aspects of Mesquakie life, the writings of William Jones and Truman Michelson are best. Chapter-length studies by Natalie F. Joffee (1940) and Sol Tax (1937) provide a wealth of information about conditions in the 1930s. *The Face of the Fox* by Frederick O. Gearing (1970) is the best account for the period from 1948 to 1959. For a brief discussion of traditional Mesquakie life, the listed article by Charles Callender (1978), in the *Northeast* volume (15) of the *Handbook of North American Indians*, William C. Sturtevant, general editor (Washington, DC, 1978), is best. This volume also provides the best comparative overview of other Indians in the region. John M. Zielinski (1976) has published a pictorial history of the Mesquakie of Iowa that includes recent pictures and text in an attractive format for the general reader.

Bibliography

Bicknell, A. D. 1901. The Tama County Indians. *Annals of Iowa* (3rd series) 4:196–208.

Buffalo, Milo, 1981. *Community housing status report*. Sac and Fox of the Mississippi in Iowa.

Caldwell, Joseph R. 1958. *Trend and tradition in the prehistory of the eastern United States*. American Anthropological Association, memoir no. 88.

Callender, Charles C. 1978. Fox. In the *Handbook of North American Indians,* William C. Sturtevant, gen. ed., vol. 15, *Northeast,* 636–47. Washington, DC.

Catlin, George. 1844. *North American Indians,* vol. 2, 207–17. London.

Donaldson, Thomas. 1886. The George Catlin Indian Gallery in the U.S. National Museum. *Annual Report of the Board of Regents of the Smithsonian Institution, 1885,* pt. 2 appendix.

English, Emory H. 1951. A Mesquakie chief's burial. *Annals of Iowa* (3rd series) 30: 545–50.

Gearing, Frederick O. 1970. *The face of the Fox.* Chicago.

Gearing, Frederick O., Robert McC. Netting, and Lisa R. Peattie. 1960. *Documentary history of the Fox Project 1948–1959.* Chicago. The Fox Project of the University of Chicago Department of Anthropology was designed to compile information about these Indians and to apply anthropological knowledge in the solution of Mesquakie problems. The volume includes documents relative to the project as well as selections of various published and manuscript studies. The information provided is basic to any realistic understanding of the development of modern conditions among the Mesquakie of Iowa.

Green, Michael D. 1983. We dance in opposite directions. *Ethnohistory* 30:129–40.

Green, Orville J. 1912. The Mesquakie Indians, or Sac and Fox in Iowa. *Red Man* 5:47–52, 104–109.

Hagan, William T. 1958. *The Sac and Fox Indians.* Norman. Hagan's definitive history of the Sauk and Mesquakie begins with the early historic period and is carried through in detail to the reservation period in Kansas. There is very little information for the time after 1860.

Hoyt, Elizabeth E. 1963. The children of Tama. *Journal of American Indian Education* 3 (1):15–21.

Jenks, Albert E. 1900. The wild rice gatherers of the Upper Lakes. *Bureau of American Ethnology, 19th Annual Report,* pt. 2, 1013–1137.

Joffe, Natalie F. 1940. The Fox of Iowa. In *Acculturation in seven American Indian tribes,* Ralph Linton, ed., 259–331. New York. The 1937 field study of the Mesquakie near Tama, Iowa, by Joffe, when consulted in conjunction with the 1932 and 1934 field data of Sol Tax for the same people, provides an excellent view of the historical background and emerging modern conditions for the group.

Jones, William. 1905. The Algonkin manitou. *Journal of American Folk-Lore* 18:183–90.

———. 1911. Notes on the Fox Indians. *Journal of American Folk-Lore* 24:209–37.

———. 1939. *Ethnography of the Fox Indians.* Bureau of American Ethnology Bulletin no. 125, Margaret Welpley Fisher, ed. Jones, who was of mixed Mesquakie and white descent and an anthropologist, was killed in the Philippine Islands in 1909. Some of his field data on the Mesquakie were edited and published by Truman Michelson and Franz Boas a few years after his death. About twenty years later his notes were presented to the Smithsonian Institution and were edited for publication by Margaret W. Fisher. This volume is ably annotated and is an essential source on the Mesquakie. It provides a rounded view of Mesquakie life for the period just before 1900.

McKenney, Thomas L., and James Hall. 1934. *The Indian tribes of North America,* vol. 2. Edinburgh.

Michelson, Truman. 1913. Review of *Folk-lore of the Musquakie Indians of North America* by Mary A. Owen. *Current Anthropological Literature* 2:233–37.

———. 1922. How Meskwakie children should be brought up. In *American Indian Life,* Elsie C. Parsons, ed., 81–86. New York.

———. 1925. The autobiography of a Fox Indian woman. *Bureau of American Ethnology, 40th Annual Report,* 291–349. The Mesquakie woman recounting the story of her life supplies a wide range of ethnographic details concerning her people for what must have been late in nineteenth century. It is only to be regretted that the autobiography is not longer and more detailed.

———. 1925b. Notes on Fox mortuary customs and beliefs. *Bureau of American Ethnology, 40th Annual Report,* 351–496.

———. 1930. Notes on Fox gens festivals. *Proceedings of the Twenty-Third International Congress of Americanists,* 545–46. New York.

———. 1936. Miss Owen's "Folk-lore of the Musquakie Indians." *American Anthropologist* 38:143–45.

Miller, Walter B. 1955. Two concepts of authority. *American Anthropologist* 57:271–89.

Owen, Mary Alicia. 1904. *Folk-lore of the Musquakie Indians of North America.* London. It is difficult to know how much of this volume is reliable in view of the criticisms by Truman Michelson (1913, 1936). In compiling the material on the Mesquakie for this text, I used only Owen's information on material culture. This section of the book does not come under fire from Michelson and, in fact, is almost praised.

Polgar, Steven. 1960. Biculturation of Mesquakie teenage boys. *American Anthropologist* 62:217–35. Polgar made a field study of teenage boys during the summers of 1952 and 1953, and established that although some of the boys seemed on their way toward assimilation into white culture, others were delinquent in both Mesquakie and white cultures, and still others were able to participate successfully in both white and Indian cultures. This is a very insightful paper and probably reflects an acculturation pattern for many Indians other than the Mesquakie.

Quimby, George Irving. 1966. *Indian culture and European trade goods.* Madison.

Rideout, Henry M. 1912. *William Jones.* New York.

Smith, Huron H. 1928. *Ethnobotany of the Meskwaki Indians.* Bulletin of the Public Museum of the City of Milwaukee, vol. 4, 175–326.

Stucki, Larry R. 1967. Anthropologists and Indians: A new look at the Fox Project. *Plains Anthropologist* 12 (37):300–317.

Tax, Sol. 1937. The social organization of the Fox Indians. In *Social Anthropology of North American Tribes,* Fred Eggan, ed., 243–82. Chicago. The core of this article is devoted to Mesquakie kinship terms and social units, but additional information is provided about conditions among the Tama area Mesquakie as they lived when Tax visited them in 1932 and 1934. The emphasis of the chapter, however, is on a reconstruction of the social system of the past.

White, Leslie, ed. 1959. *Lewis Henry Morgan, the Indian journals, 1859–62.* Ann Arbor.

Zielinski, John M. 1976. *Mesquakie and proud of it.* Kalona, IA.

7 The Crow: Plains Warriors and Bison Hunters

I wonder how my grandchildren will turn out. . . . They have only me, an old woman, to guide them, and plenty of others to lead them into bad ways. The young do not listen to the old ones now, as they used to when I was young. I worry about this, sometimes.

Observations by Pretty-shield, an elderly woman in the early 1930s. (Linderman, 1932, 23)

PLAINS INDIAN LIFE long has captivated the interest of white Americans and Europeans, sometimes to the point that they ignore all other Indians. The image of warriors astride horses recklessly chasing herds of bison or enemies across the plains conveys a sense of daring and freedom. The Crow typify this life-style shared by other Siouans* and Algonkians such as the Blackfoot, Cheyenne, and Gros Ventre. The Crow are presented here because any book about American Indians would be incomplete without including a people of the northern Plains. Their lifeway, based on hunting herd animals from horseback, and their emphasis on warfare represent a major regional configuration in North American Indian culture, that of the Plains culture area. The Crow also illustrate the flexibility of some Indians in making ecological adaptations. About seventy-five years before their first contact with whites, the Crow began receiving domestic horses, and they molded their economy around this animal in a remarkably brief period.

Origin Myth, Population, and Language

These people called themselves Abarokee (Absaroka), which means "Children of a Large-Beaked Bird" in Hidatsa. The reference may be to either a raven or an extinct bird. Or it may be to the waterfowl that figure prominently in the Crow origin myth, which goes as follows. Once there was only water, and waterfowl alone lived on it. The only supernatural was the sun, called Old Man or Old Man Coyote. He went to the waterfowl and told a large mallard that it was not good to be alone. He told the mallard to dive and try to retrieve some earth, but it failed. Two other species of duck also failed, and finally on the fourth try a grebe was able to bring up a little mud between its webbed feet. By starting in the east and traveling west Old Man Coyote spead the mud to make the earth. A wolf appeared on earth and then a coyote, and a person at a distance became transformed into tobacco, the only then-living plant. Old Man Coyote made people from mud and then created the mountains, trees, and hills.

Before whites made lasting contacts with the Crow, the tribe suffered a series of terrible smallpox epidemics. The early French trader François A. Larocque (1910) estimated that they occupied three hundred tepees in 1805, but he reported that two thousand tepees had existed just before the first smallpox epidemic. In 1833 the Crow had eight hundred tepees with an estimated population of sixty-four hundred. By the early 1930s their number had declined to about sixteen hundred, but in 1985 there were about seventy-three hundred Crow. Their language belongs to the Macro-Siouan linguistic phylum and to the Siouan family. Their closest linguistic relatives are the Hidatsa, and in the comparatively recent past the Crow and Hidatsa probably were one people.

---

*The Crow are Siouan in the sense that they are linguistically related to the Sioux, the popular name for the Dakota Indians. The Siouan linguistic family includes the Crow and Dakota plus the Assiniboine, Hidatsa, Mandan, and Omaha.

Crow Life before Historic Contact

Diverse opinions prevail about Crow origins and their movements in pre-historic times, but none is entirely acceptable. Traditional Crow history, refer-ring to the not-so-distant past, states that they came from a place with many lakes, which is thought by some to have been the Lake Winnipeg area in Manitoba, Canada. They settled briefly in earth lodge communities along the Missouri River as farmers and hunters who came to be called the Hidatsa. Differences between two chiefs led one of them to separate with about five hundred followers; this new group emerged as the Crow. Perhaps the split occurred in the 1700s since

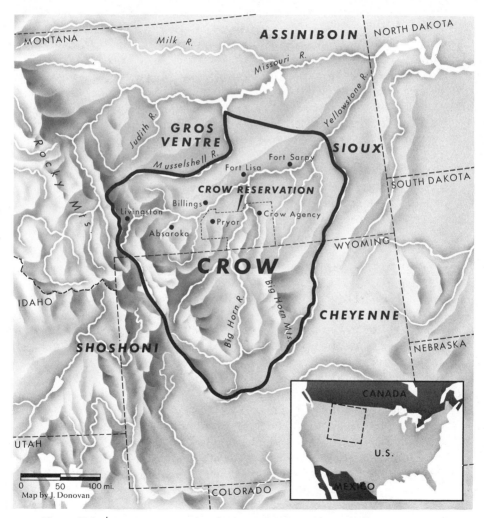

Figure 7-1. | Historic homeland of the Crow Indians.

some Crow remained closely identified with the Hidatsa as late as the 1830s. We can assert with reasonable confidence that the Crow began moving south and west about 1700 and began living in their historic homeland about 1750. (See Figure 7-1.)

As domestic horses introduced into the New World by Europeans began to reach the Crow soon after 1730, Crow life began to assume its historic focus. In aboriginal times they were a hunting people with dogs to bear packs and pull travois. The Crow were accustomed to a mobile way of life, and the horse vastly increased their movements. A host of Plains tribes raided for horses or exchanged horses for firearms and other imported manufactures. The availability of horses at the eve of white contact heralded a virtual cultural revolution. As wandering hunters the Crow had a distinct advantage over sedentary Indians who farmed at earth lodge communities and were stationary targets—for example, the Pawnee, who were semipermanent farmers. With horses, Crow economic and combative activities expanded. They could strike a distant enemy suddenly or travel far to hunt. By the same token, they were subject to raids by other equally wide-ranging equestrian hunters, and these widespread contacts facilitated the rapid spread of deadly new diseases. With horses as pack animals the Crow could transport large quantities of dried meat, accumulate more property than before, and build larger tepees. The aged were no longer a burden; they could be transported easily by horses. With old people living longer, the basis for cultural learning broadened. The horse, as a unit of wealth and an object of prestige, resulted in social distinctions between those who had many horses and others with only a few animals.

Early Contacts with Whites

Initial contacts with whites apparently were in the 1740s, and the Crow soon earned a reputation as clever thieves and shrewd traders. Early in their history they also had the distinction of disdaining alcohol, which they called "white man's fool water." The 1804–1806 expedition of Meriwether Lewis and William Clark traveled through Crow country on its return from the Pacific coast in 1806, but it is not clear whether the explorers met any of these people. In the early 1800s the heart of Crow country reportedly was in the Big Horn Mountains, where they lived as a loosely integrated tribe. About 1825 two rival chiefs, Arapooish and Long Hair, disagreed and split the people into two groups. The Mountain Crow, as the followers of Long Hair, ranged south of the Yellowstone River in southern Montana. The followers of Arapooish, the River Crow, lived farther north along the Musselshell and Judith tributaries of the Missouri River.

In the early decades of the nineteenth century, fur traders and mountain men were attracted to Crow country in their quest for beaver, and these Indians became involved in the competing interests of trading companies, free traders, and white trappers. The impact of the fur trade was not as great as might have been expected because of the difficulty in obtaining access to the region, the presence of hostile Indians, and the declining market for beaver pelts. The first trading station in Crow country was Fort Lisa, built in 1807 at the mouth of the Big Horn River, but it and numerous other forts of the period failed. The first Fort Sarpy, for example, at the junction of the Rosebud and Yellowstone rivers, was founded in 1850. Previously, the Crow had traded bison hides and beaver pelts at forts among the Arikara and Mandan along the Missouri River. With the founding of Fort Sarpy, the Crow camped in the vicinity during the fall and winter to harvest bison skins that they exchanged for trade goods. Crow at these camps were easy prey for Assiniboin, Blackfoot, and Sioux raiders. During the summers the Crow attacked their enemies to avenge their losses, but they declined in number because they faced so many hostile tribes. Fort Sarpy was abandoned and burned by the resident trader in 1855. It had proved very difficult to bring in trade goods and take out pelts along the dangerous rivers. Furthermore, persons stationed there often were the virtual prisoners of surrounding Indians.

A terrible smallpox epidemic in the early 1830s was described by the fur trader Edwin T. Denig (1961), but by no other observer; the same disease struck in 1837 and again in 1848 but not as destructively. Yet, in 1849 an influenza epidemic was said by one observer to have killed 150 persons and 600 by another reporter. In addition, the Crow were outnumbered by their Blackfoot and Sioux enemies. For example, there probably were at least two and a half times as many Blackfoot as Crow.

As the United States began to assert control over the region in 1825, the government sent an agent up the Missouri River to the Mandan villages where the Crow were visiting. A treaty of friendship was signed by Long Hair, but Arapooish refused to sign. Among the treaty conditions was Crow recognition that the United States controlled Crow country and had the right to regulate trade and intercourse. The Crow further agreed not to harm white Americans locally or to trade with aliens. By and large the Crow were faithful subjects, and the eventual protection provided by the U.S. Army probably saved them from extinction at the hands of the Sioux.

Father Pierre-Jean DeSmet was the first Christian missionary to seek out the Crow. He visited them in 1840 and in 1842, being well received on both occasions. They were friendly and admired him, but he had no impact on their lifestyle. After hearing the tenets of Catholicism, one man responded that only two Crow men would not go to hell for killing, stealing, and other non-Christian behavior.

In 1851 the first Treaty of Laramie was negotiated; in it, land in northern Wyoming, southern Montana, and western South Dakota was set aside for the Crow. By agreeing to the conditions of this treaty, the Crow and other tribes involved were granted annuities, while the federal government obtained the right to build forts and roads in the region. The treaty was amended in 1852, limiting the annuities to ten years, but the Crow refused to sign the revision. They gradually abandoned the Big Horn Mountains under pressure from the Sioux, because game animals were disappearing and because whites were moving into the area on their way to a gold strike in western Montana. The second Treaty of Laramie in 1868 confined the Crow to a reservation south of the Yellowstone River in southern Montana; they have continued to live on a small portion of this area to the present.

Early Historic Crow Life

By the time Euro-Americans became familiar with the northern Plains in the early 1800s, the lifeways of local Indians already had begun to change as a result of indirect contacts with whites. Pressures brought about by other Indians who were forced westward by whites were beginning to build, and the fur trade was making an impact. Most of all, however, the domestic horses received earlier from the south had altered Crow cultural ways dramatically. The ethnographic account to follow attempts to describe Crow life before the direct impact of white influences became intense.

APPEARANCE AND CLOTHING   To the Crow, a handsome man was tall and had a straight nose and a face free from blemishes or scars. The noble appearance and bearing of Crow men attracted favorable comment from most early travelers. Men greased their long hair and sometimes made it even longer by gluing on additional human or horse hair. One great chief, Long Hair, was inordinately concerned about the length of his hair for supernatural reasons and grew it to about ten feet in length. Men plucked their whiskers, and both sexes apparently removed axillary hair. Strings of ornaments hung from the hair on each side of a man's head, and his ears were adorned with abalone-shell earrings cut into angular designs. Men painted their faces red and highlighted their eyelids with yellow paint. Bear-claw and bone-disk necklaces, as well as bone pendants, were popular. Men in general, and young men in particular, were fastidious about their appearance. Men wore hair-trimmed leggings held up by tucking the top ends into a belt. Other items of male clothing included a shirt, moccasins, and a bison robe.

Crow women were not pleasingly portrayed and were often reported as wearing dirty, greasy clothing. When they mourned the loss of a relative, which was often, their hair was cut short, and their faces were spotted with clay and dried blood from self-inflicted wounds. Dresses of deerskins or mountain sheep skins reached from the neck to mid-calf. The most distinctive characteristic of their dresses was that the fronts and backs were decorated with rows of elk teeth; openings on each side of a woman's dress were for nursing an infant. Women wore moccasins and leggings from their thighs to their knees. Young boys went naked until they were about nine and then wore the clothing of men; girls dressed in the manner of women.

SETTLEMENTS   The Crow had no permanent villages but moved from one campsite to the next in search of game. After so many people died from smallpox, most of the tribe camped together for protection against enemies. Camps

Figure 7-2. | A Crow tepee, after a painting by Catlin. (From Donaldson 1886.)

were dominated by tepees framed with about twenty poles, each some twenty-five feet long, set in the form of a cone and covered with bison skins. An opening was left at the top as a smoke hole, and two external poles were attached to flaps at the top of the cover to open or close the smoke hole. (See Figure 7-2.) Before the Crow had horses to carry tepee poles and covers, it appears that their dwellings were much smaller. There was a fireplace at the center of a tepee, and along the sides toward the back were hide mattresses beneath sleeping robes; the seat of honor was at the back and center. Other structures of importance were circular arbors with conical roofs made from boughs and used as sun shades, and small dome-shaped sweat lodges where men bathed in a ritual context by pouring water over heated stones.

When a band moved, the caravan might be miles in length. Scouts kept a lookout for enemies, and hunters scattered in search of game. Men wore their best buckskin garments and carried their weapons in case of a sudden attack. Women rode astride horses as did men, and from the saddle of a wife's horse hung her husband's shield and sword if he owned one. Small children were tied to saddles, but five year olds rode alone. Meat, tools, utensils, and other property were packed in skin containers tied to horses. One horse carried a tepee cover and another dragged the poles. Some horses pulled pairs of tent poles with a frame attached to carry wounded or ill persons; this conveyance, a travois, was in earlier times pulled by dogs. The most important purpose of dogs appears to have been to warn of the approach of enemies or strangers.

USE OF HORSES Wild horses lived on the North American Plains during the Pleistocene era, but they disappeared about 8000 B.C., or perhaps in more recent times, possibly hunted to extinction by Indians. The domestic horses used by Indians in North and South America all were descendants of those introduced by Europeans in historic times. The Spanish took domestic horses to Mexico in A.D. 1519, and by the end of the century large herds of domestic and feral animals ranged over northern Mexico. Thus, North American Indians did not begin to use domestic horses until the early 1500s. Horses possibly began to filter into the historic Crow area by 1730, and therefore these people had only had access to horses for about seventy-five years before they began to be described in reasonable detail by whites.

Crow men, women, and children always were described as excellent riders who depended on horses so much that they were poor walkers. (See Figure 7-3.) Their saddles were high in the front and back but were not used for hunts or during war. Most horses could be guided without a bridle. A rider leaned in the direction in which she or he wanted to turn, and a horse turned in that direction until the rider sat upright.

Around 1850 a horse was worth from sixty to one hundred dollars and was

Figure 7-3. | A Crow woman on horseback. (Courtesy of the Field Museum of Natural History, Chicago.)

the major form of wealth as well as the standard medium of exchange. In a proper marriage, a groom presented horses to the brothers of the bride. In later times, ten good arrows equaled a horse in value, and a woman skilled at preparing hides for a tepee cover might receive a horse for her labor. Personal conflicts in a camp, which usually involved women, might be settled with horses. If a man eloped with the wife of another, the offended husband took all his rival's horses; in doing so he not only had the support of his clan members but the backing of most persons in the camp. The offender kept the woman, and his clansmen gave the former husband horses to compensate for his loss, although eventual repayment was expected. The same pattern prevailed if all a man's horses were stolen.

By the mid-1800s the Crow had more horses than any other tribe east of the Rocky Mountains. A poor person owned at least twenty animals, and a middle-aged man had up to sixty. The Crow received horses in trade from the Flathead and Nez Perce, but they more often obtained them during raids. Raids for Crow horses by the Blackfoot and other tribes, especially the Sioux, meant that younger men spent a great deal of time guarding the horses. When an enemy raid was expected, the best horses were tethered at the entrance of their owners' tepees so that riders could pursue horse thieves quickly at any time. Once it was realized that horses had been stolen, Crow warriors gave pursuit, each riding his fastest horse and leading another. They rode day and night, and when the first horse was exhausted they rode the other; when it gave out they might continue on foot. If they caught up with the thieves, they first attempted to recover their horses and then killed and scalped an enemy if it was possible to do so without the threat of losing one of their number.

SUBSISTENCE ACTIVITIES   Part of the Crow habitat in the 1840s was described by Denig (1961, 139) as "perhaps the best game country in the world." He reported immense herds of bison from the Rocky Mountains to the mouth of the Yellowstone River and herds of hundreds of elk along the river as well as many black-tailed and white-tailed deer. Antelope covered the prairies and badlands near the mountains, while in the mountains were many bighorn sheep and grizzly bears. The truly majestic Rocky Mountains, high valleys, fast-flowing streams and rivers, meadows, hot springs, and great forests characterized this idyllic land.

The Crow economy was based on hunting large game, especially bison, deer, elk, and antelope; in fact, they did not eat fish or berries. Except for the maize that they traded from the Hidatsa for a change in diet, the most important use of plant products was as seasoning for meat dishes. Cooperative hunts were the norm, and the purpose was to kill or maim herd animals by driving them over cliffs or riverbanks. Alternatively, animals were driven into a valley with a single narrow exit, and a fence was erected after the animals were confined. The planning and coordination required for large-scale hunts was supervised by the camp police, and to further insure success, hunting rituals were performed.

The bow and arrow was the primary weapon for the hunt or for war. The wood-shafted arrows were tipped with points of bone or stone. Bows were fashioned from bison or mountain sheep horn or elk antler; pieces were cut, smoothed, spliced, glued, bound together, and then backed with sinew (composite, sinew-backed bow). Arrows were carried in skin quivers that were ornamented with porcupine quills.

A woman's life was physically demanding. She supplied the household with firewood and water, cooked the food, cared for children, collected plant products, and made and repaired all the clothing, skin containers, and tepee covers. Women were also responsible for erecting and taking down tepees. A woman groomed her husband, saddled his horse, and took off his leggings and moccasins in the evening. Women usually followed men on bison hunts and skinned the animals killed. One of women's most highly developed skills was working skins. Depending on the skin involved and the purpose served, hides or skins were dehaired, prepared on one or both sides, smoked or not smoked. To break down its texture and make it supple, a skin was spread with a preparation made from bison brains and liver. In addition to processing bison hides for tepee covers and skins for clothing, women made small skin pouches for pipes and sacred objects. The best known rawhide container, termed a parfleche, was folded, often painted with designs, and was used primarily for storing and transporting dried meat or pemmican. Although other American Indians were skilled in basketry, pottery, weaving, and elaborate wood carving, the Crow did not practice these crafts.

For men, camp life was as leisurely as it was busy for women. They made tools and equipment, but these were not time-demanding activities. Some men were part-time specialists in making bows or arrows. The major pursuits of men, hunting and fighting, usually took place at a distance from a campsite.

DESCENT, KINSHIP, AND MARRIAGE   Descent was traced through women (matrilineal system) since each person was identified with the mother's clan (matriclan). Thus, an individual was a member of the same clan as his or her mother, mother's sisters and brothers, mother's mother, mother's mother's brothers and sisters, and so on. The thirteen named Crow clans reported for both the Mountain and River Crow included Thick Lodge, Sore-Lip Lodge, Tied-in-a-Knot, and Bad War Honors. Clan members usually were dispersed over a broad area, as was typical; in other words, Crow clans were not localized. The number of clan members interacting intently with one another depended to a great extent on the time of the year and the availability of food. When bison herds were large and accessible, many clan members could live near one another. As the large bison herds declined, clans became less integrated.

Clans were grouped into two, or in one case, three units (phratries) that were not named; one of the two-clan clusters may have been a single clan. It appears that in most instances a spouse was from any other clan (clan exogamy). Yet, the bonds between some paired clans seem to have been so close that members could not marry each other (phratry exogamy). The residence pattern after

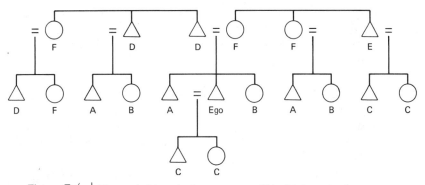

Figure 7-4. | The early historic Crow system of kinship terminology.

marriage appears to have been temporarily matrilocal, and following the birth of a child the husband was free to set up an independent household.

The Crow kinship terminology is the type designated by their name, Crow. The Crow termed father and father's brother alike and used a different word for mother's brother. Likewise, father's sister was termed differently from mother and mother's sister, who were termed alike (bifurcate merging). Furthermore, father's sisters' daughters and their daughters' daughters were termed as father's sister; the term really designated women of the father's clan from his generation downward. The same logic applied when father's sister's husband was termed father, as was his son. The ignoring of generational distinctions in these contexts made clansmen equivalents. In a like manner, the term mother was extended to her clan sisters. (See Figure 7-4.) The most rigid behavioral taboo prohibited a man from talking with or having any contact with his wife's mother or her grandmothers. Likewise, a woman did not interact with her daughter's husband or her daughter's daughter's husband.

SOCIAL DIMENSIONS   The worst possible insult was for one Crow to say to another, "You are without relatives," meaning that the accused had no merit. Supportive relatives protected one from slander, came to one's defense in times of conflict with others, and provided material aid in times of stress. A matriclan was the largest integrated social unit, and one's obligations to it were great. Although members of the same clan do not appear to have camped adjacent to one another, they often ate together.

The bonds within a clan were most severely tested when a person from one clan killed someone from another clan. In these rare instances, the members of the murdered person's clan were obligated to kill either the offender or one of his clansmen. The matrilineal focus in Crow society should not be interpreted to mean that a father did not feel strong bonds of blood with his sons. In fact, as Robert H. Lowie (1935, 18) recorded, when someone asked a special favor a common phrase was "By the love you bear your children, I beg you."

Nearly every man belonged to a voluntary association (sodality) that played a major part in his social life. Young male relatives of recently deceased members or persons with outstanding achievements were actively recruited. Since intense rivalry prevailed among sodalities, a man usually belonged to only one. Among the Crow the best-known of these fraternal organizations were the Lumpwoods and Foxes. Each such tribewide organization had its own distinctive styles of adornment, dance, and behavioral characteristics, but the core activities were much the same.

Formerly the Lumpwoods had been called the Half-shaved Heads. They had received their prevailing name when a member had counted coup, meaning touched an enemy, with a knobbed club; thus, Knobbed Sticks is a more proper designation for them than Lumpwoods. In the fall after the first snow, Lumpwood men met and ate in the tepees of one member and then another. The membership was distinguished partially on the basis of age grades, and officers served for one year. The four pairs of officers were called elders, straight-staff bearers, hooked-staff bearers, and rear men. Being offered a pipe and smoking it were symbolic of selection and acceptance of an office. Men often were reluctant to become staff bearers because after a straight shaft was planted in the ground by its bearer during a battle he could not retreat from the spot unless another Lumpwood rode between him and the enemy. After a hooked staff had been placed in the ground, it could not be moved, and the bearer defended it until he was killed. The bearers of these staffs counted a double coup if they struck an enemy because of the danger involved.

Sodality members extended mutual aid to fellow members in stressful times; they sometimes fought together, and they honored by excessive mourning a member killed in battle. One Lumpwood behavioral peculiarity was that when a member mourned the loss of certain relatives the other Lumpwoods had the right to make jokes about the loss to his face. This behavior would have been very insulting to anyone else, irrespective of the circumstances.

The Foxes were organized much the same as the Lumpwoods, and competition between the two sodalities was keen. This was most dramatically expressed in the abduction of wives. In the spring either group could initiate the proceedings, and any man was free to abduct the wife of a member in the other fraternity if he had been her lover. Sometimes a woman was kidnapped without cause, and women sometimes hid to avoid abduction. A wife might also successfully plead with a potential abductor and not be taken away. Men who suspected that their wives would be abducted often made a point of being away during these times. Yet, if they were present custom dictated that they should make no effective effort to prevent their wife's capture. These women were paraded about and were received as brides by their abductors' families. A stolen wife could not return to her husband; a man caught sleeping with such a woman was tied up and smeared with feces. This period of license lasted about two weeks, and then the Lumpwoods and Foxes went on the warpath, each attempting to count coup first so that they could ridicule their opposites. After the first snows fell the rivalry abated, only to surge again the next spring.

WARFARE   The Plains Indian stereotype is that of a bloodthirsty killer for whom war was by choice a dominant cultural focus. Yet, economic factors best account for the intensity of warfare on the plains and prairies. We find that the Crow rarely killed whites although they often had ample opportunity and just cause, especially to kill white trappers (mountain men) in their midst. This situation contrasted with the animosity between white trappers and the members of surrounding tribes. Furthermore, when the Crow were at peace with another people they appear never to have initiated a new conflict. Their primary reason for launching a raid was to avenge the death of a Crow killed by the members of another tribe. Unlike most Plains Indians, the Crow killed men but usually captured women and children; the children were adopted and captive women worked beside Crow wives. An adopted boy who was raised as a Crow did not hesitate to kill men from the tribe of his birth. In rational terms, by not initiating a war and by assimilating captives the Crow compensated for their relatively small number and their losses in war. They went to war most often for a combination of three purposes: revenge, glory, and horses.

The word translated as "chief" really meant "good, valiant," and to achieve this title a man had to perform four feats: lead a successful raid, capture tethered horses from an enemy camp, be the first to touch an enemy (count coup), and take a bow or gun from a live enemy. Warriors who performed each of these deeds at least once were chiefs, but this did not mean that they were political leaders. The greatest living chief in 1910 was Bell-rock; he had led at least eleven war parties, taken at least two tethered horses, counted coup six times, and seized five guns. Such a man boasted of his achievements at public gatherings, depicted his brave deeds on a robe that he wore, and had distinctive adornments on his clothing. To take a scalp was important but was not ranked as a major achievement, and when a man listed his war honors he did not mention scalps.

The foremost weapon of war was the bow and arrow, but it soon was replaced by the gun. Spears sometimes were used, but they apparently were not very important. (See Figure 7-5.) For close combat a war club with a stone head bound at one end of a wooden shaft prevailed. The shields men carried had a purpose more supernatural than practical, except in defensive circumstances. These circular pieces of bison hide might have bird skins, feathers, or animal tails hanging from them. Either a shield or its leather case was painted with symbols or scenes revealed to its owner in a vision. (See Figure 7-6.) Men also went forth with ornamental sticks used to count coup. These were tied together at intervals with skin strings ornamented with quills.

Ideally, each youthful male longed to achieve personal honor in battle and believed that the greatest glory was achieved by dying young in warfare. Yet, every effort was made to prevent the death of a Crow in combat, and a war party was never considered successful if it lost a single member. The fearless in battle were persons convinced of their invincibility on supernatural grounds or else reckless by nature. Still, the positive value placed on an early death was a recurrent theme in Crow child-rearing. Typically, a young man eagerly sought his first

Figure 7-5. | George Catlin (1926, vol. 1, 216) wrote of this painting of a Crow warrior, "I have painted him as he sat for me, balanced on his leaping wild horse with his shield and quiver slung on his back, and his long lance decorated with the eagle's quills, trailed in his right hand." (From Ewers 1965.)

opportunity to join a party of raiders. As a novice he performed menial tasks such as carrying the meat supply and hauling water. He likewise was the butt of jokes as a part of his informal initiation into the life of warriors.

An attack was organized by a raid planner, who usually achieved his position from a dream or vision that detailed the tribe to attack and the booty to be gained. An ambitious warrior not blessed with a personal vision could turn to a shaman and, by following the shaman's instructions, succeed. Some warriors might doubt an announced leader's abilities and decline to follow him, but re-

Figure 7-6. | This is one of the finest Crow shields, and it was famous for its power. It belonged to the chief Arapooish and is said to represent the moon. Attached to the left side of the cover are the head and body of a crane. At the top right is an eagle feather and below it is a deer's tail. (Courtesy of the Museum of the American Indian, Heye Foundation.)

cruiting a war party does not appear to have been difficult, especially for previously successful war leaders. Raiders typically set off on foot with a supply of moccasins often carried by dogs. As they approached enemy territory, the scouts were especially watchful. Once an enemy camp was sighted the war leader performed sacred bundle rituals. To further insure success, each participant attached sacred objects to his body and painted himself in an appropriate manner. One or two warriors were chosen to enter the enemy camp, usually late at night, and to drive off as many horses as possible without being discovered. The party made its escape by riding the remainder of the night, all the next day, and the following night before relaxing. As the warriors approached their home camp, they shot guns into the air and paraded the captured horses. The booty belonged to the raid leader, but he freely gave horses to the participants. These raids often were dangerous ventures. If a horse was not captured for each raider, some warriors were forced to return on foot and risked being overtaken by the pursuing enemy. Raiders sometimes went for days without food and rode so long and hard when attempting to escape that their "buttocks were worn out."

As warriors the Crow were daring and merciless enemies. In open battles, especially if a number of Crow were killed, they slaughtered every man and then tortured the wounded to death. Hands and feet were cut off, eyes gouged out, and intestines exposed to be pierced with sharp sticks. The brains and hearts of the dead were hurled in the faces of the living while the victors scorned their victims. It should be added that in defeat Crow warriors suffered a similar fate.

A newly taken scalp was the focus of a three-day celebration. Warriors carrying their weapons, their faces painted black, and wearing their finest clothing danced in a partial circle to the accompaniment of drums and rattles. The scalp was carried on a pole, and the warrior who had made the kill mounted a horse and was led by a chief in the midst of the dancers. That night young men walked around the camp, and at each chief's tepee they sang songs about his particular accomplishments. During the next day the scalp was tied to the bridle of a horse on which a young man rode while beating a drum and singing. When many scalps were taken in a battle, the celebration was far more elaborate and sometimes included a reenactment of the conflict.

Denig (1961) reported that a Gros Ventre girl was captured by the Crow at about the age of ten and became a great chief. As a child she preferred the activities of boys, and her adopted father encouraged this behavior. She soon was playing with bows and arrows, riding fearlessly, and as a youth she was trusted to guard horses. As an adult she always wore women's clothing, and when her adopted father was killed she became the head of his household. Later in a raid against the Blackfoot she killed and scalped one enemy and counted coup over another. She came to be known as Woman Chief after she consistently distinguished herself in other raids. Before long she sat as an equal in the council of chiefs. Woman Chief deplored the idea of doing woman's work and obtained first one woman as a "wife" and then three more. Thus, she lived as an honored person for twenty years until she tested a peace with the Gros Ventre and was killed by them after they discovered her origins.

When a man was killed by an enemy, everyone in the camp mourned as the body rested in state outdoors. The face of the corpse was painted, he was clothed in his best garments, and was especially honored by members of his military society. They cried and sang over the body as drums were beat. They pierced their limbs and bodies with arrows or cut themselves with knives. These men also distributed the dead man's property. Relatives took the body to a tree or scaffold for interment and wept. Their period of mourning did not end until a member of the enemy tribe that had killed him was murdered. Thus, it was near relatives who most encouraged warriors to avenge deaths.

POLITICAL LIFE Control of the day-to-day Crow social unit or band was in the hands of a man who had performed each of the four honored deeds in war and had demonstrated the qualities of a leader. His authority expanded further if he was generous with booty, a shaman of note, and an able narrator of tales. Thus, individual achievement, open to nearly all, was the avenue to honor and prestige in a political context. Tacit agreement determined who was to be band chief, and no formal installation ceremony existed. A band chief decided when a campsite was to be abandoned, where to move, and the placement of tepees. Yet, he had little control over people since he neither judged nor punished in a manner often associated with chiefly powers. It appears that as long as the people who camped together enjoyed good fortune, their chief retained his office. When he failed he was replaced quietly and informally. One of his most important duties was to appoint the members of a particular military society to take charge of the spring bison hunt. At larger camps the chief appointed an outstanding man as a crier; his duty was to ride among the tepees repeatedly making announcements about matters of public interest and making the chief's opinions known about matters of current concern.

Within a camp or band of the Mountain or River Crow, members of the thirteen clans formed the largest political entities. They dealt with each other as equals, and they recognized no superior authority to which they all were responsible. Feuds between clans were the greatest threat, but intermediaries attempted to settle conflicts as quickly as possible before they became emotionally charged and out of hand. Language, culture, and common social norms unified clans. Crow survival was partially contingent on cooperation among clans for common good. If a segment of a clan separated from the main body, it could muster comparatively few warriors and would be destroyed by enemies. The tranquillity of camp life in tribal tradition was upset the most when an aggressive person with a small number of related followers dominated. This especially was true of a person who was regarded as having powerful supernatural guardians. Such individuals might seize the horses or wives of others, but, as Lowie (1935) pointed out, such a man was a de facto but never a de jure leader.

The members of the military society policing a bison hunt could and did severely punish nonconformity. The worst offense was for men to hunt bison alone or in small groups, because this scattered the herds and made it difficult for others to kill bison on the legitimate communal hunts. Likewise, on a group hunt, if a man broke and charged a herd prematurely, he might scatter the animals and ruin the opportunities of others. These nonconformists might be whipped, their weapons destroyed, and the kill seized. The warrior society in charge also had the right to prevent raiding parties from setting forth at inopportune times, and they attempted to settle differences between the people in camp peacefully, especially when a feud threatened to erupt between clans. Disagreements between members of different clans may have been reasonably common, but for one Crow to kill another was almost unknown. Any crime, except murder, could be compensated for with an exchange of property.

When the Crow split into two major bands, the River and the Mountain, it was Arapooish (Arapoosh, Sore-belly, Rotten-belly) who led the River Crow. A brief sketch of his life illustrates the qualities of leadership that he possessed. Arapooish was a retiring and even surly person who said little but spoke in an authoritarian manner. As a relatively retiring shaman he controlled powerful supernatural forces, and he apparently had many wealthy clansmen. He was fearless in battle. Time and again he successfully raided horses from enemies without any loss of Crow life. He saw to it that the Crow always were on the alert for enemies and that raiders who approached were killed. Arapooish was a confident aggressor and able tactician in the large battles that he planned. In a battle against the Cheyenne, more than 1,000 horses were captured, 200 Cheyenne men killed, and 270 women and children captured; the Crow lost 5 men. But Arapooish was a man possessed, and he courted certain death when he charged a Blackfoot fortification in 1834 shouting "One last stroke for the Crow Nation" (Denig 1961, 183) and was killed. Arapooish came to be known as *the* Chief.

RELIGION   The individual basis for Crow supernaturalism centered about a highly personal rapport with a guardian spirit. An unsought spirit aid might reveal itself, but far more often it was gained in a vision quest. All personal glory, power, and wealth ultimately were attributed to valid visions. Thus, religion among the Crow was not a tightly integrated system of beliefs with accompanying dogma. In Crow linguistic expression, a vision or a dream of supernatural portent were the same. A youthful male sought a personal spirit aid as he began to emerge into the world of adults. If he was fully successful, he might seek no other vision later in life. Were he to do so it usually was to cure a sick child or in an extraordinary quest for vengeance.

The Vision Quest   A vision seeker sometimes, or perhaps most often, first purified himself by taking a sweat bath. Stones were heated in a fire near a small dome-shaped and skin-covered bathhouse. The stones were taken inside where water was sprinkled on them to produce steam that was an offering to the sun. In ideal circumstances the seeker next went to a mountaintop where he fasted, drank no water, and wailed. Lightly clad and covered only with a robe at night he slept until the sun began to rise. The seeker then chopped off the final joint of his left forefinger, placed it on a buffalo chip, and held it up as an offering to the rising sun with an accompanying prayer for glory and success in life. As the blood flowed he fainted and was unconscious until evening, but he could not sleep in the cold of night. Three nights passed, and on the fourth one he could not sleep until late because of the cold. With sleep came a vision.

Alternative ways prevailed for obtaining a vision. One man might have another cut slits in his chest or back through which one end of a thong was passed, the opposite end being tied to a pole. The aspirant ran around the pole until he tired; he rested, only to run again and again. He might or might not tear the thong free in his quest. Another means to the same end was to have one's back pierced with two holes and a thong tied from them to a bison skull that was dragged about in the first stage of the search for power.

A supernatural visitant might assume the form of an animal such as a bear or bison, a bird, an insect, the earth, moon, or stars. A person could be blessed by association with more than one such power, and literally anything might be revered by an individual. The sun was the supernatural to whom a direct appeal was made, but it rarely was the actual source of power received; thus, it was not a god worshipped in the usual sense. The supplicant might be taught a sacred song, learn of a symbol that could be represented graphically, or be instructed to follow certain taboos. A feather, a stone with a strange shape, a braided rope, or a weasel skin, among other forms, symbolized the receiver's power and formed the core of a sacred (medicine) bundle. A bundle and its power could be transferred to a near relative after proper instruction and even purchased by a non-relative; thus, the control of supernatural forces could pass from one generation to the next. The degree to which any particular bundle was revered depended directly on the fortunes of its possessors.

Tobacco Ceremonialism In Crow as in other ceremonial societies, purification in a sweat bath was a prelude to rituals, smoking tobacco was important, incense was burned, and songs were repeated four times. Tobacco was considered to have great supernatural power and symbolized Crow tribal identity. The seeds of sacred tobacco reportedly were from the originally cultivated strain, and it was thought that the Crow would endure only as long as they continued to plant these seeds. Furthermore, tobacco ceremonialism supposedly contributed directly to year-to-year prosperity because the planters had the power to influence events in the natural world, such as warding off disease and renewing the supply of game. The role of tobacco planter was hereditary although a person could purchase the right and be adopted into the Tobacco Society. The ritual included fasting and abstaining from water for days and then having one's arms and chest cut and burned to produce wounds that healed slowly and left deep scars. In exchange for the honor of receiving sacred tobacco seeds, a tobacco planter gave up all his worldly goods.

The Tobacco Ceremony began with the ritual sowing of tobacco near the end of April. As soon as this was done, the participants put up a huge tepee that would accommodate as many as three hundred people and decorated the interior with cloth streamers adorned with beads and other ornaments. Here people ate and danced for three days to the music of bells, drums, rattles, and whistles in a deafening combination. When these ceremonies were completed, the people moved off a short distance each day, indicating their reluctance to leave their sacred tobacco plants. To encourage the seeds to germinate, a Tobacco Society member was placed in charge of rainmaking and was given as much as three thousand dollars' worth of property to sacrifice to the rain clouds. With the gifts hanging from nearby bushes the rainmaker smoked and prayed for rain. If he was successful, all the gifts became his property, and he gained great fame. If he failed, he blamed people for not fulfilling their vows. In late August the people returned to the tobacco plot, harvested the crop, and collected seeds.

Tobacco was smoked only by men. The most important times were when

Figure 7-7. | A Crow man in ceremonial costume smoking a pipe. (Courtesy of the Field Museum of Natural History, Chicago.)

making peace with other tribes, during rituals, or by shamans in curing severe illness. Even when tobacco was smoked on less ceremonious occasions, the first puffs were dedicated to the earth, heavens, spirits, and the sun. Each man present took only four puffs and then passed the pipe on to the person on ·his left, because this was the direction in which the sun moved. Furthermore, each man had personal smoking habits. One man would not smoke if a pipe had touched grass, another would not smoke if women were present, and another would insist on emptying his pipe on bison dung. These details were dictated by individual relationships with guardian spirits. (See Figure 7-7.)

Subgroups of the Tobacco Society emerged from time to time on the basis of individual revelations, but they did not compete overtly with one another. Apart from planting sacred tobacco seeds, the most important ceremony was the initiation of new members, which was regarded as a form of adoption. Before initiation a novice was instructed in the rites and rituals of the group and then formally presented to it. A married couple usually was inducted together, and membership normally was for life. Another means of induction was for a man with a sick child to pledge him or her to membership, or himself to become a member, if the child recovered.

The Sun Dance   The sun as a powerful if remote supernatural was the focal point of the most sacred Crow ceremony. A man pledged that he would hold a Sun Dance in return for obtaining a special vision that revealed how to avenge the killing of a relative. The commitment was so great that an elderly person might have witnessed only about six performances. The person making the pledge was called a whistler, and he sought out a shaman who owned at least one sacred doll. These small wooden or skin-covered figures had painted features, Morning Star designs, and feathers attached to them; they also were used to bring war parties success. A doll served as the vehicle through which the whistler obtained his vision. The shaman and whistler were the central actors in a great ceremony that attracted all the tribe. As the preparations began, the whistler fasted and became haggard in appearance. Bison tongues were collected as special food for each noonday meal during the ceremony. A special kilt was made for the whistler, and after many preliminaries involving incense and smoking, a special lodge was built a few miles away. The whistler, painted with cross-shaped designs symbolizing the Morning Star, blew a whistle and danced slowly toward the lodge while holding a wooden hoop with the doll figure representing the sun attached at the center. He tied the doll to a lodge pole at eye level. At the same time, other men who sought visions had their bodies daubed with white clay and slits cut in their chest or back to receive skewers tied to lines attached to lodge poles. Each man pulled against his skewer until it ripped free. The whistler neither ate nor drank water after entering the lodge; here he gazed at the doll and danced before it as one chief and then another described his deeds of valor and acted out his moments of glory. The whistler, who was not skewered, slept at the lodge, and a sham battle was fought the next day as the whistler danced on. His performances might extend over days until he finally received a vision that he usually did not reveal. At this point the ceremony ended, and the whistler sought out the enemy.

Shamans Physical disabilities and death usually were attributed to supernatural causes such as ghosts or breaking taboos. One category of health-care practitioners depended primarily on secular knowledge. They used plant products, lanced a swollen part of the body, or applied a poultice as ordinary treatments. A particular root that was considered a cure-all was rubbed on sores, placed on an aching tooth, or chewed and swallowed to cure a cold. The botanical pharmacopoeia was extensive and most often appears to have been applied in a secular context. Other curers, more properly shamans, had the ability to treat specific traumas because of revelations in visions. Included were cures for snake or spider bites, wounds, or disease caused by a foreign object in a patient's body. Shamans were very adept at sleight of hand; they appeared to transform bark into meat or mud balls into beads in either public or private performances. Competitive exhibits of their skills often were dramatic contests. These were men who had the most powerful guardian spirits, and it was primarily in this respect that shamans stood apart from persons who had less potent spirit aids.

Sorcery sometimes was practiced by ordinary persons to settle grudges against other Crow by supernatural means, but it appears to have been relatively uncommon. One technique was to draw the figure of an antagonist along a riverbank near the water's edge, burn incense, and blow smoke toward the figure. As the water washed the drawing away, the victim was expected to die. Other magical practices supposedly could cause lifelong disabilities in the target person. The only sure safeguard against sorcery was considered to be for the victim to have more powerful supernaturals working in her or his behalf.

LIFE CYCLE As the time for a birth approached, the husband, other men, and boys were excluded from a tepee, and the woman was aided by a male or female specialist who was well paid. The woman knelt over padding and grasped two sticks. To hasten delivery she might be given potions or her back might be rubbed with a special preparation. The particular aid used depended on the techniques that the birth specialist had learned in a vision or had obtained by purchase from someone else. A woman present at the delivery cut the umbilical cord, and part of it was encased in a container that hung from the cradleboard of a baby girl and later from the back of her dress. The new mother observed food and behavioral taboos for a brief period, but the father's activities were not restricted. Within a few days and without ceremony, a neonate's ears were pierced with a hot awl; the holes were held open with small greased sticks until earrings could be inserted. Offspring were placed in cradleboards and rocked to sleep with lullabies. Water was poured into the nose of a small child who cried often, and such a child soon learned to stop crying when someone said, "Bring the water!"

A few days following his or her birth an infant was named, but names were neither sex nor clan specific. The father asked a noted warrior to select a name, based on one of the warrior's personal achievements and gave the warrior a horse in return. Names often were descriptive phrases; for example, a new-born girl might be named Captures-the-Medicine-Pipe or a boy His-Coups-Are-Dangerous. As a name was given, the infant was tossed into the air four times (four was a sacred number among the Crow), each time higher than the last. Women changed their names when someone with a like name died, and men assumed new names to commemorate brave deeds or to improve their fortunes. Nicknames, often based on unusual behavior, might be more commonly used than formal names. For example, a man who took an old dog with him to carry his moccasins on the war path came to be called Old Dog as a result.

Adults placed few constraints on the behavior of children. Children might interrupt adult conversations at any time and typically were both forward and self-confident. The freedom of boys was especially boundless. Denig (1961, 154) wrote, "The greatest nuisance in creation is Crow children, boys from the ages of 9 to 14 years. These are left to do just as they please. They torment their parents and everyone else, do all kinds of mischief without either correction or repri-mand." Boys swam and played water games, hurled sticks at each other with the ends covered with mud or mud and live coals. Individually or in teams they shot at targets with arrows, and the arrows were stakes for the winner. In the winter boys coasted down hills on toboggans made by covering bison rib frames with rawhide. Every youthful male ate part of a raw grizzly bear heart to bring him strength and a clear head in times of trouble. Thus, he could say "I have the heart of a grizzly" in the face of adversity. When meat was plentiful in a camp, boys might cover themselves with mud so that they could not be identified and run into camp where meat was hanging to steal as much as possible before they were chased by old women. The thieves cooked the meat away from camp, and the boy who had stolen the best piece ate the choice parts first. Boys hunted small game, and after a bison hunt they might ride out to kill the calves, bringing home the meat and giving the skins to girls for tepee covers. A pair of boys some-times became close friends, and the bond could extend into adult life when they fought together and shared the same woman, either as a wife or mistress; these men referred to each other as "Little Father" and were closer than with any other persons.

At about the age of ten, boys and girls began imitating the camp life of adults, an activity called "calfskin tepee." Girls from affluent families had small tepees that they set up at a distance from the camps of their parents. Boys pre-tended to be their husbands and took food from their families for their "wives." The boys organized themselves in the manner of men, even to the point of kid-napping girls belonging to another group. When the boys killed a coyote or wolf, they returned in triumph with a piece of the pelt as a "scalp," and the girls danced with it in imitation of women dancing with scalps obtained by warriors.

Puberty went unacknowledged for males and females alike, although when a girl or woman menstruated she was prohibited from approaching sacred objects and avoided a wounded man or men preparing for a war party; most persons denied that women were isolated physically during menstruation. Girls appear often to have married before they reached puberty, and while marriage to a person in one's own clan was forbidden (clan exogamy), it also was considered in bad taste, at least in the eyes of some persons, to seek a spouse from the clan of one's father. To marry someone from a father's clan with whom no blood ties could be traced was acceptable although not desirable.

Marital arrangements varied, although the parents of a girl often seem to have had some influence, if only because a daughter was so young when she married. A man might meet a girl while she was alone and propose that they elope, offering her a horse for going off with him. A couple could summarily announce that they were going to live together or a man might seek the aid of a go-between to make the arrangements. Young men seldom hunted before they married. They slept late and spent most of the day grooming themselves to show off on their horses. They courted girls with flute music and sometimes did not return home until daylight.

The most proper marriage proposal, especially for a woman of virtue, was for a man to offer horses to the girl's brother and meat to her mother; these arrangements produced the most lasting marriages. A man who had offered wealth for his bride had the right to claim her younger sister in marriage (sororal polygyny), and the girls' parents were likely to agree when the first daughter was well cared for. In the early 1800s perhaps half of the men had more than one wife, and apparently a few men had as many as twelve. They did not all live together, and some might simply have been betrothed to him. A woman could marry her deceased husband's brother (levirate), but she would not be forced into the union.

Crow sex life was free and open, especially for men, but women were far from pawns. Men and women alike might have many love affairs and made little or no effort to conceal their feelings and sexual activities; their philandering ways often were noted. When a married woman took offense at the affairs of her husband, she might hold him up to ridicule in songs about his behavior. Men and women alike hurled "a fine variety of beautiful epithets" at each other, according to Denig (1961, 151) and other observers. A woman could leave her husband and take her children as well as her property, including horses, skins, and the tepee, with her; boys not fully dependent on their mother joined their father. Yet, after a couple had separated, irrespective of the reason, they could not live together again without bringing disgrace on them both. As noted previously, during a particular time each year, a Fox or Lumpwood could abduct and marry another man's wife if she previously had slept with him. If he did seize her, the woman could not return to her husband. Divorce was common except for virtuous women and could be initiated by either partner. Just as a marriage was without ceremony, so was a divorce. Men were expected to be unfaithful to their wives; in fact, for a man to keep the same wife for many years was considered unmanly and a source of ridicule. Yet, some men were jealous of their wives to the point of always taking a favorite wife along on a hunt and strongly resenting it when she committed adultery.

Male transvestites, or berdaches, were reasonably common among the Crow and were not regarded as abnormal, but as a third sex. According to Denig (1961) some boys preferred the company of girls in their preadolescence and eventually were dressed as girls by their parents. They then embarked on a lifetime of female activities and might "marry" a man. It also should be noted that there were sacred aspects of being a berdache. For example, in the Sun Dance certain rituals could be performed only by a berdache.

The hand game was a very popular form of entertainment, with garments and beadwork commonly bet on the outcome. To the accompaniment of beating drums and songs, a pair of male or female players participated. One person held an elk tooth or bone gaming piece in one hand and gestured wildly while switching the piece from hand to hand. If the guesser failed to identify the hand that held the piece, he or she lost a tally stick; the person who obtained all the tally sticks, three or ten in number, was the winner. Women also played dice games for stakes. One game involved placing six dice that were marked on one side and plain on the opposite face in a wooden bowl and shaking them. The game was scored with tally sticks according to the combination of plain or marked dice facing up. A popular game called shinny or stickball was played by women in the spring. The object was for the members of two teams to drive a ball to opposite goals by using curve-ended sticks. Another widespread game played by men was hoop-throwing, and they bet on the outcome. The object was to throw a dart through a rolling hoop that might have webbing in the middle. The man whose dart entered the hoop or passed nearest to it won a tally stick.

When someone died, the body was painted, clothed in fine garments, and shrouded in part of a tepee cover. The spirit was told not to turn back and the body removed under a side of the tepee to prevent further deaths in the household. Interment was either in the crotch of a tree or in a scaffold above four support poles. After the body had decayed, the bones sometimes were removed and placed in a crevice of rocks. Mourners from the immediate family pulled out their hair or cut it short, slashed themselves with knives, and often cut off finger joints. The practice of removing a finger was so common that scarcely a person had complete hands. However, men usually did not mutilate their thumbs or the fingers used to draw a bow or shoot a gun. The soul of a person was believed to first linger near the corpse, perhaps giving an owl-like cry, but to later go to the camp of the dead. The Crow had little interest in the fate of souls; although they believed that ghosts might return to harm the living, they also considered ghosts to be a source of helpful visions.

The expectation in this matrilineal society was for material property to be passed down along the female line, going to brothers, sisters, and their heirs rather than to a man's sons. But a dying man's request to pass his property to nonclan members was honored. A man could bequeath horses to his wife or sacred objects to an eldest son. Even when bequests were not made along the maternal line, they usually were made to an immediate family member.

| Later Historic Changes in Crow Life

Effective federal control over the Crow began with the second Treaty of Laramie in 1868. This treaty established a clearly defined reservation, and the first Crow agency was built at Mission Creek near the modern town of Livingston, Montana. It was moved to Absaroka in 1875 and then to the town now called Crow Agency in 1884. From the beginning of the reservation period, the federal goal was to destroy the traditional basis for Crow life. Christian church services were to replace heathen ceremonies, the people were to wear "civilized" clothing and live in log cabins, the men were to become farmers, and the children were forced to attend school. (See Figure 7-8.) Furthermore, Indian agents were always powerful, and they often were corrupt.

Diverse circumstances combined to the detriment of Crow prosperity. Foremost was the abrupt decline of the bison population in the Yellowstone Valley. From 1879 to 1882 some 250,000 bison hides were obtained there; in 1882–83 the harvest was 45,000 skins, but after 1883 bison had virtually disappeared. Most animals were killed by white hunters, who took the hides, tongues, and only a little meat. For many whites, the slaughter was worthwhile to make way for cattle. Thus, the economic basis for Crow life disappeared almost overnight. The most immediate result was to make the people dependent on Indian agents to obtain food and goods promised by treaty and badly needed for sur-

Figure 7-8. | Crow schoolchildren. From left to right: ?, ?, Russell White Bear, Henry Shin Bone, Annie Wesley, Addie Bear-in-the-Middle, Fanny Butterfly, Kitty Deer Nose. (Courtesy of the Montana Historical Society.)

vival. But these agents often cheated the people and provided most food to those Indians willing to accept federal policies, which was in direct defiance of treaty arrangements. Frequent Sioux raids contributed to Crow desperation until 1876, when these conflicts had nearly ceased. Whiskey traders operated just outside the reservation border and were a further cause of trial and trauma. The impact of the Homestead Act of 1862 began to be felt in the 1870s as whites surged into Montana Territory. These newcomers resented the fact that eight million acres of land was reserved for the Crow, and pressured the federal government to reduce the size of the reservation; they were successful in 1882, 1891, and again in 1904. Efforts from 1910 to 1919 to have Congress withdraw even more Crow land from the reservation failed. Whites insisted that the Indians did not use the land effectively—a dominant theme in frontier history—and Congress responded by liberalizing the lease laws. With grants of land to railroads and for a dam, the Crow holdings had declined to about two million acres by 1968.

After the disappearance of bison in the early 1880s, life lost much of its meaning for the Crow. Perhaps the greatest trauma was psychological. With the reason for moving about gone and enemies no longer a major threat, the people had very little to occupy their time; boredom and idleness dominated reservation life. Farming was proposed as a new economic base, but the first politically appointed agents usually knew little about either Indians or farming. The monetary rewards offered people to farm went begging, and during the early reservation years only agency employees planted crops. The most appealing work for men was to serve as scouts for the U.S. Army. In time, however, some Indians turned to agriculture, and one of the first to do so was the great chief Plenty Coups. His example encouraged others because he faced the white world in a painfully realistic manner. Indian agents made great efforts to have the Crow abandon their tepees and live in log cabins. Even when houses were built for them many people preferred to camp in nearby tepees. (See Figure 7-9.) The cultural geographer John W. Stafford (1972, 132) summarized the prevailing white attitudes in terms of "good" and "bad" Indians. "The idea of a good Indian was nurtured. To the 'good' Indian who cooperated by cutting his hair, sent his children to school, and took up farming were given special monetary rewards, wagons, and cattle. Other 'good' Indians were given jobs in the agency. Leaders who cooperated were flattered with trips to Washington. On the other hand 'bad' Indians were threatened with loss of rations."

The Dawes Act of 1887 attempted to make the Crow, as well as other Indians, farmers and to destroy tribal life by treating each family individually. The head of a Crow household was forced to accept a 160-acre land allotment, but most people still did not recognize farming as a legitimate occupation. As soon as they could, many persons leased or sold their allotments to whites. A revised Allotment Act of 1920 increased the size of the Crow holdings to about 1,000 acres per person, of which 320 acres could not be alienated for twenty-five years. Crow declared competent could sell their remaining 680 acres, and many did as soon as it was legally possible. As a result, white and Indian lands form a check-

Figure 7-9. | A Crow camp. (Courtesy of the Field Museum of Natural History, Chicago.)

erboard on the reservation. Over the years, even those Crow who have attempted to keep their land have been faced with one problem above all others: as land has been inherited, the plots have been divided time and again.

| Modern Crow Life

Surprisingly little has been published by anthropologists about the Crow of recent decades. The impression gained is that significant aspects of traditional life continued to flourish in the middle decades of the twentieth century. (See Figure 7-10.) Sacred bundles continued to be regarded as sources of power, but a traditional Sun Dance had not been held since about 1875, and sweat baths were more often taken for pleasure than for purity. The military societies apparently had disappeared and men could not recall the names of some sodalities. The Tobacco Society and its daughter chapters continued to function; plots of sacred tobacco were planted with accompanying ceremonies, and new members were adopted.

THE NEW SUN DANCE   Fred Voget (1952) has documented well tradition, change, and reintegration in the early 1940s in an account about the introduction of the Wind River Shoshoni Sun Dance to the Crow. A biographical sketch of

Figure 7-10. | Crow women chatting while working on hides in 1941. The woman on the left is Woman-on-Top-the-Ground, and the one on the right is Well-Known-Writing. (Courtesy of Fred W. Voget.)

one of the principals, William Big-Day, born in 1891, is revealing. He lived in the Pryor area, the most isolated sector of the Crow Reservation with the most conservative population. As a youth he frequently was ill and seldom attended school or had meaningful contacts with whites. He was baptized a Roman Catholic but was forced to leave the church as he began participating in peyote rituals when he was about thirty-five. Like many other Crow he felt that Christianity imposed unreasonable restrictions on a person's life. When he was about nineteen, he began to dream that he should fast and seek a vision in the mountains to gain success and wealth. He did not do so until he was about forty, when he sought power to cure illness in himself and others. His first attempt failed, and the second time, some four years later, he was only partially successful. Big-Day subsequently dreamed of hearing songs that made people happy. A short time later he attended a Shoshoni Sun Dance, where he heard the songs of his dreams and was flabbergasted. The next year he participated in the dance and was also cured of a chest pain by John Truhujo, the man of Shoshoni and Mexican ancestry who led the dance. This convinced Big-Day of the power of the Shoshoni Sun Dance. When his adopted son was desperately ill during the winter of 1939, Big-Day held the boy up to the sun and pledged to participate in a Sun Dance if the child recovered. When this came to pass he kept his pledge. The next year his brother's child was ill, and Big-Day vowed to hold a Sun Dance among the Crow if the child recovered. When this child was well, a dance was held in 1941 with the assistance of John Truhujo. In 1943 another Crow held a Sun Dance to help insure the safe return of his warrior sons fighting in World War II, and still others held additional dances.

William Big-Day and others who were key personalities in the introduction of this form of Sun Dance among the Crow shared a number of critical characteristics. Each had either rejected or abandoned the economic life of whites and subsisted on income from land leases and odd jobs. In the modified and yet traditional economic system the only way to increase one's wealth was through shamanism, but the practitioners of old had all died. Big-Day and another Sun Dance leader had little faith in Western medicine, which was no small consideration, and they were discriminated against by whites, which made it very difficult to succeed in white terms. Then, too, these leaders had been expelled from Christian churches. Each rejected the white American value system, and Big-Day sought to develop a new religion that would "bring a new life to the Indian" (Voget 1948, 646). Thus, this was an embryonic nativistic movement.

POPULATION, LAND, AND ECONOMY   Much of the information about the early reservation era was drawn from a study by the geographer John W. Stafford (1972). His work is also an important source for what happened from 1934 to the early 1970s. Perhaps the most striking recent trend noted by Stafford has been the rapid growth in Crow population. Crow numbers reached an all-time low of about 1,625 in the early 1930s, but with improved health care beginning around this time, increased rapidly and soon were doubling each generation. By 1942 the reservation population was about 2,100, and in 1969 the figure was 3,500, a 66 percent increase. This growth rate of 2 percent a year was nearly double that of the United States in general. Furthermore, in 1942 about 250 people worked and lived off the reservation, and this number had increased to about 1,500 by 1968. Some of these Crow were well established elsewhere, but others came and went with the job opportunities. Thus, the expectation is that in difficult economic times the reservation population will expand significantly, leading to increased stress in finding local employment.

Equally notable has been the most recent decrease in the reservation land base. By 1961 nearly a third of the reservation land had been sold to whites, and much of the remaining land had little water for grazing stock or for farming. The federal government then initiated the policy of prohibiting the sale of reservation land to whites, and between 1961 and 1968 the Crow tribe bought about fifty-five thousand acres that previously would have been purchased by whites.

The lease of reservation lands to whites for grazing cattle and later for farming has been a significant source of income as well as a serious problem. The first lease was to the U.S. Army in 1882 for grazing cattle, and to increase food production during World War I thousands of acres were leased to whites for raising wheat. The Crow Allotment Act of 1920 permitted "competent" Indians to lease or sell their lands. Those who leased often were persuaded by whites to sign leases at very low rates, and some of these whites became wealthy. Revisions in the leasing laws consistently have favored whites, and the only condition beneficial to the Indians is that most leases are short-term. Few Crow have ever been willing to become farmers, and since they have not usually had the resources to raise stock on a large scale, lease arrangements have been appealing. By 1962 most land allotments, about 90 percent, had been leased to whites for grazing cattle or for farming. The Crow know full well that leases are profitable to whites at Indian expense, but they can do little about the situation. For example, when a white owns land along a stream and a Crow owns adjacent land without water, the Indian's holdings are of little value because there is no access to water. However, for the white who has water, leasing the Indian land at a low rate can be very profitable. The same applies to small, scattered parcels of Indian-owned land. They cannot be used effectively by the Indians and again may be leased at very low rates. A significant reason for continuing leases as a major source of income is that the pattern is well established.

The allotment process was a gross intrusion on the integrity of the Crow tribe—as it was meant to be—but the problems it created for later generations were and are nearly overwhelming. A serious difficulty stems from the failure of the federal government to make reasonable allowance for births, deaths, and population growth. No land was set aside, as in some Canadian treaties, for future generations. An extreme case will illustrate the magnitude of the problem. One 160-acre allotment made in 1887 had passed to 245 heirs before 1967, when it was consolidated into 86 claims. Of these, the largest was for about 11 acres, and the smallest was for 0.0014 acre! The land was not physically divided, but all the heirs held an interest in it and shared any income derived from it. Most land with many owners is leased by the BIA, and annual payments are made to the heirs. The yearly profit for the person owning the 0.0014 acre just mentioned would be less than a cent if the rent rate were fifty cents per acre. The same conditions prevail for leasing dry farmland or the small parcels of irrigated land.

Money received from land claims against the federal government has become important developmental capital. The Crow began their first suit in 1904, and in 1961 they finally received a settlement of $9.2 million. Then in 1963 they received an additional $2 million for land sold to the federal government for construction of the Yellowtail Dam and Reservoir. Apart from small dividends paid to enrolled members, these monies have been concentrated in three programs: land purchase, industrial development, and a loan program to help individuals become more self-sufficient.

It might seem as though cattle ranching could serve as a sound economic base for many Crow, but this is not the case. Over the years diverse efforts have been made to encourage ranching, but in 1968 only 9 percent of the reservation families raised cattle and the herds usually were small. A successful rancher requires not only a block of grazing land but also a large capital investment and knowledge about raising and marketing cattle. Again, farming has had little potential because in 1968 only about 13 percent of the trust land was suitable for dry farming and less than 2 percent could be irrigated. This is one good reason why the Crow have been reluctant to become farmers. The sale of land to whites,

Crow biases against farming, and their acceptance of leasing arrangements or wage labor employment are additional factors. It appears that since 1953 fewer than fifty Crow have farmed or ranched. Stafford (1972) compared Crow land use with that on the nearby Blackfoot, Cheyenne, and Sioux-Assiniboin reservations and found that these tribes were more successful farmers. He concluded that the major difference was the far less rigid control by the BIA of Crow leases than of those of the other tribes.

Most local opportunities for wage labor have been in farming or ranching for whites. The BIA and the U.S. Public Health Service employed about 130 people in 1969, and about 100 persons found seasonal work in commercial sugar beet operations. Local jobs in construction have also been important, but the seasonal unemployment rate has been as much as 45 percent or more. In 1966 an industrial park was built at Crow Agency with federal funds and money received in land settlements with the federal government. Among the firms established there was a carpet mill that employed seventy-five people in 1967, but it closed in the late 1970s. In 1986 there were no factories or businesses operating at the industrial park.

GOVERNMENT   The Crow adopted a formal written constitution in 1948 and amended it in 1961. They chose a somewhat distinctive town council type of government in which each adult member of the tribe is entitled to vote at any general council meeting. Meetings usually are held quarterly and deal with any issue of tribal interest. Tribal officers are elected every two years, and special committees represent each of the six districts of the reservation. Furthermore, committees are elected to deal with specific issues, such as enrollments, land purchases, and industrial development.

The Contemporary Scene

Not following the typical pattern of Indian tribes, most Crow, 5,600 of them, still lived on their reservation in 1986. About 360 others lived nearby, and approximately 1,350 made their homes at more distant localities. A traveler along reservation backroads would find that Indian homes have the same general appearance as those of whites who live in their midst and own about 40 percent of the original reservation. The most obvious signs of a Crow home are a distinctive Indian name on the mailbox, and tepee poles, used for special occasions, leaning against a house or tree. Younger Crow dress in contemporary American styles, but many older women still wear long braids, long and full dresses, moccasins, and leggings. Most men dress in modern clothing, although some wear long braids and many favor high hats. (See Figure 7-11.) Since numerous Crow have married whites, some residents are not obviously Indian in appearance.

Select aspects of traditional culture have persisted, and among the most important of these is the Crow language. The vast majority of adult Crow speak

Figure 7-11. | Kevin (Crow Boy) Old Horn in 1985. (Photograph by the author.)

their language at home, and as a result about 80 percent of the children entering school speak Crow. At the Pryor Public School on the reservation, for example, children are instructed in Crow and in English from kindergarten to the eighth grade. Many concepts, such as those in mathematics, are taught in Crow and later are reinforced in English quite successfully. Few tribes in the United States are using their indigenous Indian language with comparable vitality.

It is by now a well-established Crow tradition to seek accommodation with whites while striving to retain their Indian identity. As long as they lived apart from whites and seldom intermarried, this identity was not difficult to maintain. Yet, these conditions have changed. Furthermore, innumerable tourists travel through the reservation each year, especially in the summer. The greatest local attraction is the Custer Battlefield National Monument, administered by the U.S. Park Service. In 1985 the Custer monument, on land purchased from the Crow, was visited by about 264,000 people, all of whom traveled through the reservation. In response to the popularity of this site, the tribe built the Sun Lodge Motel and a Crow Indian Heritage Center near the battlefield. Their fairground likewise is nearby, and here the annual Crow Fair first was held in 1904. After World War II the fair became an increasingly popular tourist attraction, and it has come to include not only a rodeo, horse races, and Indian dances, but Indian foods as well. The fairground is billed as the "Tepee Capital of the World" because of the many tepees erected during the fair. (See Figure 7-12.) In a real sense the Crow are exploiting the American Indian stereotype of tepee dwellings and horse-

Figure 7-12. | Tepees erected by campers at the 1986 Crow Fair. (Courtesy of Odelta A. Thomsen.)

riding bison hunters. Yet, for them this characterization is appropriate, and in one sense tourism helps the Crow reaffirm their sense of identity.

In 1986 many residents of rural America faced economic uncertainty, and this situation was compounded on the Crow Reservation. During the winter of 1985–86 the unemployment rate was 95 percent. In the summer as some jobs became available in construction, farming, mining, and ranching, the unemployment rate dropped to 75 percent. Most Crow residents lived on their allotments and often leased the ground to white farmers and ranchers. However, with depressed wheat and cattle prices, the lease holdings have been far less profitable than in the recent past. In 1985 economic conditions had become so poor that nearly forty non-Indian farmers in the reservation area were attempting, unsuccessfully, to sell their holdings. Likewise, those Crow who farmed and sought money from the tribal loan fund for expenses were being denied loans because of the adverse economic climate.

During the energy shortage in the 1970s it appeared that the billions of tons of low sulfur coal on Crow Reservation lands would soon produce a secure future for the tribe. Yet, as the strip mines initially were developed, most Crow profited little because of collusion among some Indians, the BIA, and private mining companies. Furthermore, the State of Montana enacted a heavy severance tax on coal mining operations in 1977. This meant that mining costs became much higher than in adjacent states, which led to declining production in the Crow mines. In the recent past the yearly tribal income from coal mining operations was about $2.3 million a year, but it had declined to $1.3 million by 1985; money received from coal has been the major local source of tribal income.

In some ways the future of the Crow is bright because they remain closely identified with each other and they have retained an appreciable land base. They have exploitable economic resources and an increasing capacity to manage their own affairs. In 1986 they had plans to develop their own power plant, begin a hog-raising operation, and launch a trout farm as well as expand local tourism. The most difficult problem they face is the precipitous decline in those funds from the federal government on which they have come to depend. In 1981, for example, they received about $11 million in federal assistance; in 1985 this figure had dropped to $1.3 million. With this austerity at the federal level, the Crow face a serious need to become more self-sufficient, but economic conditions in general make this difficult at the present time.

| Comparisons with Other Indians

Crow subsistence pursuits invite comparison with those of the Chipewyan. Both depended primarily on large herd animals for food and hunted these animals both seasonally and cooperatively. Obvious differences prevailed that can be explained by environmental contrasts, but what specific traits could be considered a direct result of their common economic foci and what sociopolitical correlates can be isolated?

Three peoples with clan organizations now have been described. The Cahuilla and Mesquakie had patriclans while the Crow had matriclans. In each instance, individuals felt a primary allegiance to the clan of their birth. What are the traits common to the clans of all three peoples, and what are those found among tribes with either matriclans or patriclans? One might also seek to identify examples where the prevailing clan system seems incompatible with the lifestyle, and to explain why this is so.

Voluntary associations or sodalities existed among most of the peoples described, and we can seek to identify their common attributes. We also can compare their aboriginal forms on the basis of purpose, recruitment or durability, and then note changes in historic times. The next step would be to explain why some sodalities endured and others became extinct.

Sacred bundles were a central focus for religious behavior among the Cahuilla, Mesquakie, and Crow. Comparisons might be made on the basis of their acquisition, purpose, integration into ceremonies, warfare, and social life. If we assume that personal association with sacred bundles was a basic configuration, can we also identify the logical steps by which they might emerge as clan or tribal symbols of unity?

Enough different tribes have been described at this point to identify distinct stages in Indian-white contacts. Most peoples received Euro-American trade goods before they met explorers. What were the contact stages that followed, why did they vary, and what general processes can be identified?

| Additional Readings

Robert H. Lowie's book *The Crow Indians* (1935) is the standard general source. This work, and Lowie's technical monographs about the Crow, cited in the following bibliography, contain much information about these people in the late 1800s. One of the best accounts by a fur trapper is the book by Zenas Leonard (1959), and Edwin T. Denig's report (1961) is the best record by a fur trader. The autobiography of the Crow chief Plenty Coups collected by Frank B. Linderman (1930) is a sensitive and highly informative report of Crow life spanning a period from the hunting and fighting days to the reservation era. Thomas D. Bonner's (1972) account of the life of James P. Beckwourth, a black man living among the Crow, is a colorful and usually reliable report for the early fur trade era. The unpublished doctoral dissertation by John W. Stafford (1972) contains a wealth of information about the reservation era down to 1971.

The massacre of Lieutenant-Colonel George Custer and his command at Little Big Horn in 1876 is of some interest in Crow history because Custer's scouts were Crow. A great deal has been written about the Battle of Little Big Horn; the events leading up to the massacre are well described in the journal of Lieutenant James H. Bradley edited by Edgar I. Stewart as *The March of the Montana Column* (Norman, 1961).

The best regional overview is *Indians of the Plains* (New York, 1954, 1956) by Lowie. The best regional ethnohistory is *Indian Life on the Upper Missouri* (Norman, 1968) by John C. Ewers; everything that Ewers has edited or written about Plains Indians is worthwhile. The best ethnohistorical study dealing exclusively with the Crow is the doctoral dissertation by Charles A. Heidenreich (1971).

| Bibliography

Bonner, Thomas D. 1972. *The life and adventures of James P. Beckwourth*. Delmont R. Oswald, ed. Lincoln.

Catlin, George. 1841. *North American Indians*. 2 vols. London. (Later editions in 1880, 1903, 1913, and 1926.)

Daniels, Robert E. 1970. Cultural identities among the Oglala Sioux. In *The modern Sioux,* Ethel Nurge, ed., 198–245. Lincoln.

Denig, Edwin T. 1961. *Five Indian tribes of the upper Missouri.* John C. Ewers, ed. Norman. From 1833 to 1854 Denig was a fur trader in the upper Missouri country. His description of the Crow is outstanding for its breadth and clarity.

DeSmet, Pierre-Jean. 1905. *Life, letters and travels of Father Pierre-Jean DeSmet, S. J., 1801–1873,* vol. 1. Hiram M. Chittenden and Alfred T. Richardson, eds. New York.

Donaldson, Thomas. 1886. The George Catlin Indian Gallery in the U.S. National Museum. *Annual Report of the Board of Regents of the Smithsonian Institution, 1885,* pt. 2 appendix.

Ewers, John C. 1965. The emergence of the Plains Indian as the symbol of the North American Indian. *Smithsonian Report for 1964,* 531–44.

Hanson, Marshall R. 1960. *Plains Indians and urbanization.* PhD dissertation, Stanford University.

Heidenreich, Charles A. 1971. *Ethno-documentary of the Crow Indians of Montana, 1824–1862.* PhD dissertation, University of Oregon. Verbal and pictorial accounts of the Crow by fur traders and travelers are examined for insight into the changes in Crow life produced by the fur trade.

Hilger, M. Inez. 1970. Notes on Crow culture. *Baessler-Archiv,* n.s. 18:253–94.

Kurz, Rudolph F. 1937. *Journal of Rudolph Friederich Kurz.* Bureau of American Ethnology Bulletin no. 115, J. N. B. Hewitt, ed. Washington, DC.

Larocque, François A. 1910. *Journal of Larocque.* Publications of the Canadian Archives, no. 3, L. J. Burpee, ed.

Leonard, Zenas. 1959. *Adventures of Zenas Leonard, fur trader.* John C. Ewers, ed. Norman. Leonard was a mountain man who was among the Crow in the 1830s. His is one of the rare accounts about the Rocky Mountain fur trade by a participant. The information provided about the Crow is superior.

Linderman, Frank B. 1930. *Plenty-Coups.* London.

———. 1932. *Red Mother.* New York.

Lowie, Robert H. 1912. *Social life of the Crow Indians.* Anthropological Papers of the American Museum of Natural History (APAMNH), vol. 9, pt. 2. New York.

———. 1917. *Notes on the social organization and customs of the Mandan, Hidatsa, and Crow Indians.* APAMNH, vol. 21, pt. 1. New York.

———. 1918. *Myths and traditions of the Crow Indians.* APAMNH, vol. 25, pt. 1. New York.

———. 1919. *The Tobacco Society of the Crow Indians.* APAMNH, vol. 21, pt. 2. New York.

———. 1922a. *The religion of the Crow Indians.* APAMNH, vol. 25, pt. 2. New York.

———. 1922b. *The material culture of the Crow Indians.* APAMNH, vol. 21, pt. 3. New York.

———. 1922c. *Crow Indian art.* APAMNH, vol. 21, pt. 4. New York.

———. 1924. *Minor ceremonies of the Crow Indians.* APAMNH, vol. 21, pt. 5. New York.

———. 1935. *The Crow Indians.* New York. (Revised, 1956.) The major work about the Crow under one cover. For details about diverse topics see Lowie's monographs just cited.

Maximilian, Alexander P. 1906. *Travels in the interior of North America.* In *Early western travels, 1748–1846,* Reuben G. Thwaites, ed., vol. 22–24. Cleveland.

Russell, Osborne. 1955. *Journal of a trapper.* Aubrey L. Haines, ed. Portland.

Stafford, John W. 1972. *Crow culture change.* PhD dissertation, Michigan State University. Stafford is a cultural geographer and the only person to systematically analyze contemporary Crow life in detail. In addition to abundant information about modern Crow economic life he provides a great deal of background information about the development of the Crow Reservation in historic terms.

Thwaites, Reuben G., ed. 1905. *Original journals of the Lewis and Clark Expedition, 1804–1806,* vol. 5. New York.

Voget, Fred. 1948. Individual motivation in the diffusion of the Wind River Shoshone Sundance to the Crow Indians. *American Anthropologist,* n.s. 50:634–46. An excellent study of cultural change and its stimulus among the Crow.

———. 1952. Crow socio-cultural groups. In *Acculturation in the Americas,* Sol Tax, ed., 88–93. Chicago.

———. 1984. *The Shoshoni-Crow Sun Dance.* Norman.

Wildschut, William. 1960. *Crow Indian medicine bundles.* Contributions from the Museum of the American Indian, Heye Foundation, vol. 17.

8 The Yurok: Salmon Fishermen of California

*To make deer-hunting medicine, first you learn to see
the bush that's in front of you, then the bush behind that bush, then
the deer behind the bush behind the bush that's in front of you, then
the spirit of that deer. Now you can call the deer, his spirit, and he'
walk up to you. The people with the strongest medicine learn to fly
out, their spirits, and find the deer that way.
A well-educated person learns to see two sides to everything while at the same time seeing the whole.*

(Buckley, 1979, 37

INDIANS ALONG the Northwest Coast had far more abundant and dependable sources of food than did other peoples north of Mexico who hunted, fished, and collected. Salmon contributed the most to their plenitude, but other fishes and sea mammals frequently were important edibles. The Northwest Coast culture area as a whole is best known for its massive totem poles and giveaway feasts or potlatches, yet a great deal of local variability prevailed and requires recognition. Near the northern range of the Pacific salmon lived the previously described group of Eskimos, the Kuskowagamiut, who depended heavily on salmon for food but did not develop a highly complex life-style because of other constraints. The Yurok, who lived near the southern limit of salmon in present-day northwestern California, represent an amalgamation of Northwest Coast Indian emphasis on wealth and prestige with a simpler material culture typical of northern California Indians. The comparatively unelaborate nature of Yurok technology and social norms attracts attention. Perhaps the most interesting facet of Yurok life was the great stress placed on personal wealth. The individualistic nature of Yurok society also was reflected in the absence of any villagewide or tribal power structure.

| People, Population, and Language

The name Yurok means "downstream" in the language of the Karok, their neighbors to the interior. The aboriginal Yurok may have numbered about three thousand persons, who lived on some seven hundred square miles of land dominated by Douglas fir and redwood forests. By 1910 they numbered seven hundred, and their land base had been reduced drastically. In 1986 they numbered about two thousand, but most of them did not live on reservation lands, and many had been marrying whites for generations. In early historic times most Yurok lived along the Klamath River, and these are the ones stressed in the pages to follow, although Yurok settlements also were maintained along the adjacent coast. (See Figure 8-1.) Comparatively little contact was maintained between the coastal and riverine Yurok during the late aboriginal period, and this produced dialectic and cultural differences. Their language was most closely related to that of the Wiyot to the south. The Yurok and Wiyot are members of the Macro-Algonkian linguistic phylum but are a long distance from their linguistic relatives in the eastern United States such as the Mesquakie.

| First Contact with Outsiders

The Portuguese explorer Sebastian Cermeno probably discovered Trinidad Bay in 1595. The area was revisited in 1775 by Spanish explorers and by the English navigator George Vancouver in 1793. From 1800 to 1817 the Yurok were involved in the fur trade. Like most other Indians along the north Pacific coast, they hunted sea otter and exchanged their pelts for trade goods. Between 1818 and 1848, little known contact with whites took place, but in 1849 the mining of placer gold on the Trinity River made Trinidad Bay the most important trans-

Figure 8-1. | Aboriginal range of the Yurok Indians.

shipment point for goods and equipment destined for the mines. The Yurok as a whole had little contact with outsiders prior to 1849, but from that time forward exotic influences expanded greatly, both in scope and intensity.

Aboriginal Yurok Life

For the aboriginal Yurok, the center of the world was near the Klamath and Trinity river junction, and from there the earth was thought to extend in a seventy-five mile radius. Surrounding this mountain and forest country was supposedly an ocean of water and then a sea of pitch. Westward beyond the water lived a culture hero, the Widower across the Ocean, and north of his home lived the salmon, then dentalium shells, and finally another supernatural to the northwest. At the edge of the land to the south was the country of geese, and on their migration north they were believed to fly through a hole in the sky and disappear. Thus was the world conceived by these stay-at-home Indians.

ORIGIN MYTH   According to the Yurok origin myth, the Widower across the Ocean made soil that he kept in a deerskin container, and by spilling it he created the firm earth of the world. Since he could not see his creation, he caused the sun to give light in the daytime and made the moon to give light at night. The earth was without life, and to replace the desolation he created the varied landscape, with streams flowing to rivers and these emptying into the ocean. He made the forest and the animals. The first animal he created was a white deer, and then a red eagle to command the skies. After creating other animals and plants the Widower formed the first real man of soil and then created a woman to keep him company. This couple wandered from their home in the north and finally came to settle in the Klamath River valley.

GEOGRAPHIC CONCEPTS   The Yurok view of the world was exact: the land was a flat, circular expanse that rested on water and was surrounded by it. As breakers rolled in from the sea, people observed the gentle rise and fall of the land. Instead of designating regions, the Yurok concentrated on naming particular localities or spots on the landscape. Thus, they did not name the Klamath River but conceived of it in terms of particular locations along it or on adjacent streams. According to the Yurok, to traverse the land by canoe from one side to the other, a distance of approximately 150 miles, required twelve days. As would be expected, the Yurok were not great travelers; they had contact with their neighbors but apparently did not journey deep into the territory of other peoples. Not only did they refuse to go abroad, but they regarded strangers as a threat, thinking that normal people stayed close to home with relatives and friends. Directions were not conceived as cardinal points on a compass but in terms of water flow: there was an upstream and there was a downstream, and it did not matter to the Yurok if a river meandered in different directions. Calculating direction in terms of water flow was applied to the coast also, north being regarded as downstream. People usually traveled by boat, but they also maintained overland paths. These trails were thought of "like people" and had designated rest stops along them; to pause at a spot that was not a traditional resting place supposedly invited ill fortune.

APPEARANCE AND CLOTHING   Yurok women wore basketry hats over their braided hair adorned with flowers. As children they were tattooed with three parallel bands from the lower lip to the chin; their tattoos were said to have been made so that older women would not look like men. Women pierced their ears for wearing ornaments and had necklaces of bone, shell, or small pieces of fruit.

Figure 8-2. | A Yurok woman dressed in her finest garments. (Courtesy of the Lowie Museum of Anthropology, University of California, Berkeley.)

They wore a short apron of skin with shells, nuts, or pieces of obsidian attached to the fringe. A longer skin apron was placed over the first and partly obscured the inner garment. On ceremonial occasions women wore elaborate shell-covered aprons and many strings of shell beads. (See Figure 8-2.) Little girls wore aprons after they were about two years of age, but boys went without clothing, except for furs worn during the winter, until they reached puberty.

Men wore their hair long and loose over the shoulders or else tied it in a knot on top of the head; in his hair a man might wear a garland of flowers or feathers. Facial hair was plucked with hinged mussel-shell tweezers. A man's ear-lobes were pierced to hold ornamental pins of bone or shell. Men painted their faces with line and circle designs, using white pigment to signify mourning, red for joy, and black for war. Several lines were tattooed on a man's arm to serve as gauges for measuring lengths of dentalium shells that were used as money. Most young men folded skins around their hips, but older males as well as some younger ones wore no clothing. When traveling overland a man wore skin moc-casins, and when hunting in deep snow he wore knee-length leggings and used snowshoes. During cold weather both men and women wore skin capes.

SETTLEMENTS   Yurok villages were built along the banks of the Klamath River, on the borders of coastal lagoons, or where streams and rivers flowed into the sea. Most settlements were composed of three to seven houses, sweat houses, and menstrual huts. (See Figure 8-3.) Each dwelling was named and identified with a specific male line (patrilineage). Villages appear to have been abandoned often as the result of floods, disease, family quarrels, or simply from boredom with the setting.

The rectangular houses, about twenty feet across, were built in deep ex-cavations. The thick adzed planks, set vertically to form the walls, were as much as ten feet high at the center of the house front and back. At the peaks were ridge plates, and at right angles to these, overlapping roof boards extended from the ridge to beyond the sidewalls; poles were tied over the roof to hold the boards in place. A rectangular opening was left near the center of the roof to permit smoke from the interior fire to escape and sunlight to enter. A house was en-tered through a round hole in a front wall plank, and the area in front of the doorway was paved with flat stones. Inside a house, some four feet from the door was a partition; the room was piled with driftwood, trash, and assorted equipment such as large, cone-shaped carrying baskets, seed beaters, and trays for collecting seeds. A large door in the center of the partition opened onto the main living area. Dominating the room was a central pit up to five feet deep and ten feet square, reached by climbing down a notched log. Earth at the sides was retained by a series of logs, and in the center of the pit was a small stone-lined fire pit. Overhead a pole framework was suspended from the ceiling, and from it fish were hung to dry. All the members of a family ate around the fireplace; women and children usually slept there. Scattered about were wooden serving trays for meat, twined cooking baskets for preparing acorn meal, and similar but smaller baskets in which food was served. Spoons were made from antler, a mussel shell, or the top of a deer skull. Wooden bowls nearby were used for washing one's fingers after eating, and small redwood stools served as seats for men. At the side of a house sometimes was a lean-to of planks that served as a menstrual hut; in other cases, the menstrual hut was a separate structure built a short distance from a dwelling.

A bathhouse served from one to three dwellings, and it was here that adult males lounged and men and boys bathed as well as slept. (See Figure 8-4.) No prohibition prevented women from being in bathhouses, and they sometimes

Figure 8-3. | A group of Yurok houses. (Courtesy of the Lowie Museum of Anthropology, University of California, Berkeley.)

slept there on cold nights. However, men did not relish having women in a bathhouse, saying that they had too many fleas. The women in turn maintained that the men talked too much in the bathhouses and they would just as soon not be there. A bathhouse was built in a pit that measured about ten by fourteen feet. The vertical sidewall planks, about four feet in length, reached just to ground level, while the vertical end wall planks were cut to form a gabled roof, which was spanned with a ridgepole and roof planks. On the top of the gable an old canoe was placed facing downward to prevent water from seeping in along the ridge. The area around the entrance in a sidewall was paved with stones. The floor of a bathhouse was paved with stones or planked and was reached by descending a notched log; a stone-lined fire pit was near the center of the room. In one of the end wall planks was a small, round exit hole. The only furnishings

Figure 8-4. | Bathhouse in the foreground and dwellings in the background, Yurok area, circa 1910. (From Thompson 1916.)

were pillows made from blocks of redwood. The wood for a bath was collected by men, and as they returned to the bathhouse, they sang songs to bring good fortune. A fire was built, and the wood was allowed to burn down to a bed of coals, after which the men undressed and entered. They placed covers over the entrance and exit and sat in the intense heat for about half an hour. After crawl- ing out the exit, they lounged on the stone paving in front of the entrance and repeated the songs they had sung while gathering the firewood. Once they had cooled off, they swam in a stream or river and returned home to their evening meal.

CONVEYANCES   The craft item requiring the most time to produce was the dugout canoe, made from a driftwood log of redwood. The log was split in half by pounding antler wedges into it with stone mauls, and a fire was built along the center of one section of the split log. The charred wood was cut away with a shell- or stone-bladed adz and the process repeated until the vessel was hollowed out. A typical canoe was eighteen feet long and fifteen inches wide, with a rounded bottom and sides some forty-five inches high. At the front of the canoe on the inside, a small knob of wood was left, with a shallow hole in its center. This was the "heart" of the canoe, and without it a vessel was thought to be "dead." Pitch from conifers was used to caulk cracks in the wood, while cross-pieces fore and aft prevented the sides from warping. These vessels were propelled by poles or long-bladed paddles used by men standing in the front; a shorter paddle was used as a rudder by a man seated in the stern. Neither paddle form included a crutch handle. These canoes were designed for river travel and drew as much as six inches of water when fully loaded. Given the rounded bottoms of these boats, a man sitting in the stern could quickly change course to avoid obstructions in the rushing water. When they traveled in the ocean, men sang songs and recited formulas to prevent their boats from capsizing and to keep the water smooth. Considering how ill-adapted such a vessel was to ocean travel, these precautions seem quite reasonable.

The only other manufactured form for travel was the snowshoe. Used by men hunting in deep snow, snowshoes were small with grapevine outer frames and wooden crosspieces.

SUBSISTENCE ACTIVITIES   The most important food was salmon, termed "that which is eaten" (Waterman 1920, 185), followed by acorns and then by the far less important game and plant products. Success in getting food depended to a large extent on access to sites with exploitative potential. These usually were owned by an individual, family, or community and included fishing spots along the river, oak groves, seed collecting areas, places for snares along game trails, and stretches of riverbank extending about a mile inland. The most important riverine localities were sites where salmon could be dip-netted easily. Pools with an eddy where salmon rested while ascending the river to spawn were particularly important spots to own. A platform was erected over the pool, and it was fished with a long-handled dip net lowered into the water. (See Figure 8-5.) As soon as a fish was caught, the net was jerked from the water and the salmon clubbed over the head. In a single night a fisherman might take as many as a hundred salmon this way. The right to use an eddy was owned by an individual or a group of individuals and could be sold for money, inherited, or bartered away. Its worth was determined by the number of fish that could be taken. As many as ten men might jointly own an excellent dip net site, but these pools were not everlasting, for a shift in the river channel could change the productivity of an eddy. Gill nets were used, and these as well as the netting for dip nets were made from iris leaf fibers. The nets were weighted with stones, and floats most likely were made from short sections of wood. Salmon also were taken with seines and with toggle-headed harpoons. The harpoon shafts were as much as twenty feet long, and at the forward end were two slightly diverging foreshafts. To each foreshaft was attached a toggle harpoon head with a line leading from the head to the shaft. When a salmon was struck, the harpoon head detached, and it was drawn in with the hand line. Salmon were split with a flint-bladed knife, dried, smoked on a rack over the fireplace in a house, and then packed in baskets.

Kroeber (1925, 87) wrote with economy and precision, "Acorns were gathered, dried, stored, cracked, pulverized, sifted, leached, and usually boiled with hot stones in a basket." Unshelled acorns were stored in large baskets inside the house and were later processed by removing the nuts from their shells and pounding the meal on a stone slab with a pestle. The bitter acid was leached by placing the ground meal in a sand basin and pouring hot water over it. Acorn meal was cooked by placing hot stones in a basket containing the meal and

Figure 8-5. | A man on a fishing platform raising a dip net. (Courtesy of the Lowie Museum of Anthropology, University of California, Berkeley.)

water. The mixture was stirred with a spatula to prevent the stones from burning the woven container.

Land animals were hunted with a bow and arrows, but the practice does not appear to have been important. The hunting bow was strung with a sinew cord and backed with strips of sinew (sinew-backed bow). A feather-vaned arrow had a separate wooden foreshaft with a stone arrow point attached. Arrows were carried in a quiver made by turning the skin of a small animal, such as a fox, inside out. (See Figure 8-6.) Deer and elk were chased with dogs but probably were more often taken in snares. Dogs were never eaten since their meat, like that of reptiles, was considered poisonous.

A fish or mammal killed for food was not, in Yurok thinking, really destroyed. The spirit continued to exist, leaving only its physical form behind for the hunter or fisherman. A number of restrictions on the taking of salmon will be cited later, but here it is appropriate to mention some of the observances

Figure 8-6. | A young Yurok man with bow and arrows for hunting land animals. The swordlike object in his right hand probably is an obsidian blade. (Drawn by Seth Eastman from a sketch by George Gibbs in 1851. Courtesy of the Smithsonian Institution, National Anthropological Archives, neg. no. 2854-F-27.)

surrounding deer. This animal was thought to have many likes and dislikes that had to be accommodated to kill it successfully. Deer supposedly did not like a house that seemed unoccupied; they were attracted to hunters from dwellings where there was smoke. The reason for washing one's hands in flowing water after eating deer meat was to avoid drowning the deer. Deer meat was eaten from wooden platters, and care was taken during a meal so that none of the meat dropped to the floor. It was thought that only by observing these and other taboos could deer be taken successfully.

The Yurok were not farmers, but they planted tobacco. The plants were cultivated and the crop harvested for use by the grower or for sale to others. The mature leaves were dried in the sun or by a fire, pulverized, and placed in baskets. The cultivated species apparently was the same as the local wild tobacco, but the latter was not smoked for fear that it might have grown on a grave. Tobacco was smoked in tubular pipes that most often were made from wood, and the smoke was inhaled. Most men smoked just before bedtime, but some old men were addicted to tobacco and smoked more often. Old female shamans appear to have been the heaviest smokers; other women did not smoke.

MONEY AND WEALTH   In the broadest sense, money is a divisible and portable class of objects having a standardized value and acceptable in exchange for goods or services. In terms of this definition, money clearly was important among the Yurok, and dentalium shells were the most widely circulated form. These small mollusks had tusk-shaped shells that ranged up to about three inches in length. They were most abundant in the coastal waters off British Columbia and were collected there with a rakelike device that was thrust into the sandy ocean bottom to stab as many dentalia as possible. In western North America the shells were traded from the subarctic to southern California. Among the Yurok, as with most Indians, the shells were named and graded according to size, with the largest shells having the greatest value. An eleven-shell string, with each shell 2½ inches long, was valued at about $50 during the early American period; a string of the same length with fifteen 1⅞-inch shells was worth only about $2.50. Other monetary units included redheaded woodpecker scalps ranging in value from 10¢ to $1.50 each. Ordinary deerskins, after being prepared for ceremonial use, were worth from $50 to $100; skins of albino deer were valued at from $250 to $500, although they were never sold. Blades flaked from black obsidian were worth $1 for every inch in length until they reached a foot; blades longer than this were worth a great deal more.

Many, if not most, items of material culture were scaled in value against dentalium shells. Around the turn of the present century, a small dugout canoe was worth a thirteen-shell string or three large redheaded woodpecker scalps; a house was valued at from three to five strings of shells; an oak grove from one to five strings; a fishing spot from one to three strings; a shaman's fee from one to two strings; a slave one string; and a woman's basketry cap filled with tobacco one small shell. A few items were so valuable that they normally could not be exchanged but were passed along a patrilineage. These were most important as exhibits during ceremonial occasions. Included were fine albino deerskins with transparent hoofs and huge obsidian blades nearly a yard in length.

The preceding account of money is a traditional one that is not incorrect, but it fails, as John and Donna Bushnell (1977) have noted, to take into account the overwhelming symbolic importance of wealth among the Yurok. The ownership of wealth not only indicated social worth but symbolized the presence of those spiritual qualities needed to acquire it. Furthermore, the land of dentalium shells, called Dentalium Home and supposedly located across the ocean, was a supernatural figure sometimes regarded as a creator. Therefore, the shells and other highly valued objects, according to the Bushnells (1977, 128), "are intimately linked to the world of immortals and characteristically emit supernatural power that redounds to the good fortune and wealth of those who possess them."

LEGAL SYSTEM   Yurok customary law was based on the idea that wrongs were committed against individuals, and claims were calculated in terms of material goods rather than physical punishment. All claims were settled with the exchange of specific forms of material property. Marital arrangements, which led to the exchange of money, will be considered later, but it is fitting to mention other legal situations in which wealth changed hands. Any deviation from a behavioral norm necessitated a compensatory settlement, and extenuating circumstances rarely were considered. The age, sex, and previous behavior of an offender were unimportant, but his or her wealth was relevant. Finally, once a dispute had been settled, no further recourse was possible. The major grounds for claims were murder, seduction, adultery, saying the name of a deceased person, trespassing, or a shaman's refusal to treat a person who was ill. Failure to ferry someone, even an enemy, across a river led to a claim. If someone injured himself while on the land of another, the owner was responsible for compensation. This was true even of a trespasser, but the landowner would likely press a counterclaim for trespassing. If a shaman refused to accept the responsibility for treating a patient and the person died, the shaman was liable. To pass before a village by boat when a family in the village was mourning a death from natural causes was grounds for a claim. If a person became hopelessly in debt because of some drastically antisocial act, he could, in lieu of payment, become the slave of the one he had offended. For example, if a poor person struck the son of a rich man, he could settle his debt through "debt-slavery" of himself or one of his female relatives. "Slaves" were never killed or abused but performed the more difficult subsistence tasks. A slave owner was free to integrate the individual into his household or to maintain his or her status as a slave. Foreigners or prisoners from raids were never made slaves. The former always were killed if they arrived unannounced, and prisoners were held for ransom.

DESCENT, KINSHIP, AND MARRIAGE   In the Yurok social system the most important ties were those along a line of males. It is tempting to regard the descent system as strictly patrilineal, and unquestionably a man was most concerned with his relatives along a male line. Still, there was recognition of a wife and her relatives in calculating social ties. Perhaps it would be best to characterize these people as patrilineal with a distinct and recognized tendency to consider relatives on both sides of a family as important (bilateral descent).

In the kinship terminology, a man referred to his father by one term; for his father's brother and his mother's brother, he used another term. For the mother's side of the family, the terminology was comparable to that on the father's side (lineal terms). Thus, the Yurok employed terms for the parental generation that are of the same type as those used in the United States today. On an individual's generation, the term for sister extended to all female first cousins, and the word for brother extended to all male first cousins (Hawaiian cousin terms). It would seem that if cousins were called brother or sister, the parents of these individuals would be referred to as mother and father, but such was not the case. (See Figure 8-7.)

The only bar to marriage was the prohibition against taking a spouse from among near relatives. An individual in a small settlement was obligated to seek a mate from elsewhere since all the occupants were near relatives, but a partner could be found easily in another village or another tribe. At the same time the tendency in large settlements was to find a mate in one's home community (village endogamy). It has been reported also that men tended to seek their wives

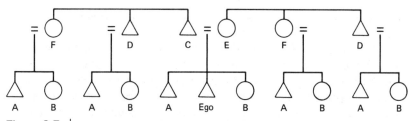

Figure 8-7. | The early historic Yurok system of kinship terminology.

from downstream settlements. Ideally, the couple lived in the settlement and house of the groom (patrilocal residence), but alternative arrangements were not unusual. Were a man's wife to die before she bore three or four offspring, the woman's family was obliged to offer one of her sisters or female relatives to replace her (sororate). Conversely, when a married man died, his brother was expected to marry the widow (levirate).

SOCIAL DIMENSIONS   Personal ambition and extreme individualism dominated Yurok social life. The core members of each community were persons who traced their descent along the male line to a known common ancestor (patrilineage); within this unit were lines of familial authority, with a wealthy old man most likely to have jurisdiction over other members of the unit. A hamlet contained one or more patrilineages, each structured as the other, but no organized system of villagewide authority existed. An individual also was bound in a network of kinship ties with persons in other settlements through bonds of blood and marriage. There were also riverine and coastal dialect groups, but this dichotomy did not have known political ramifications. Then there were the adjacent Karok, Hupa, and Wiyot, from whom one might acquire a wife. Relations with these people were structured as with in-laws. Finally, there were strangers, equated with enemies. Thus, any alliances not based on kinship or marriage seem to have been absent.

Within a patrilineage and beyond it, worth was based on ownership of material property, and families were either rich, well-to-do, or poor. It was difficult to move up in social standing since everyone coveted wealth and was reluctant to part with it, but the possibility of a poor boy acquiring riches through persistence and supernatural aid did exist. The Yurok believed that constant thoughts about money led to its acquisition. Meditating about wealth when preparing for, taking, or resting after a bath was thought to be most propitious. An ambitious young man was urged to fast and work hard for ten days while concentrating on dentalium shells. When he gathered wood for the bathhouse, he collected it from the upper branches of trees where he visualized the dentalia to be hanging. As he bathed, he thought of shells, and when peering intently into the river, he imagined that he saw huge dentalium shells. Such a person would say to himself, "I want to be rich," and he would make a tearful invocation for wealth, but not to any particular spirit or supernatural power. In Yurok belief, the primary earthly force that counteracted the quest for money was women. A young man seeking wealth was warned not to have anything to do with women, and an adult man was not to copulate with his wife in the house where his wealth was kept.

The nature and texture of life varied widely from one Yurok family to another. An almost insurmountable social barrier separated very rich, aristocratic families from the poor, and poverty was thought to have a genetic basis. A person supposedly was poor, lazy, and ill—except for instances of sorcery—because these conditions prevailed in his or her family line. The economic distinction was apparent in various dimensions of life. The speech of aristocrats was different from that of commoners, and the rich were wary and guarded in what they said. Rich people were "high class" and lived "clean" lives. An aristocrat knew the law and adhered carefully to its letter, while poor persons were far less familiar with it and also were careless, unclean, and lacked social graces. To prevent an ambitious commoner from reaching a position of power, wealthy men practiced sorcery to dissipate the commoner's wealth or lead to deaths in his family. Thus, social distinctions ran deep throughout a Yurok's life, and to improve one's condition was quite difficult.

As would be expected, formal warfare could not exist in this society where political ties were absent. Conflicts that did erupt were between families, and they might develop into small or great feuds, depending on the size of the families involved, their wealth, and how quickly a settlement could be arranged. Fighting was with bows and arrows except for using short stone clubs in hand-to-hand combat. Protective armor was made either from elk hide or vertical wooden rods bound together, and it seems to have been worn only during prearranged battles. Serious feuds apparently were caused by murders committed either in the heat of anger or by witchcraft. In either instance, the near relatives of the dead person sought revenge. They might approach their enemy's village secretly and attack before the defenders could rally, or they might ambush the offending family on the trail. Following a successful raid or ambush the contending parties might negotiate a meeting to settle their differences. The two sides armed themselves, painted their faces, and formed lines separated by the distance an arrow could be shot. They sang songs and performed a dance of settlement; at this point fighting might resume if the arrangements broke down. Otherwise, negotiations continued uninterrupted. The contesting parties carried with them the full amount of property necessary for a settlement. The side that had killed the most people and destroyed or seized the greatest amount of property was the "winner" but was at the same time required to relinquish the most property. The items to be distributed were placed in baskets and held over a fire as songs were sung and a dance performed. This ritual was to cast away any feelings of hostility and to make any lasting feelings of vengeance the responsibility of the other party. If all went well, the settlement was made, and neither side could make further claims nor hold a grudge.

RELIGION AND SUPERNATURALISM   The only time that diverse Yurok families cooperated fully was in fulfilling ceremonial obligations. Collective rituals were held to renew and perpetuate the natural world with its resources as an orderly system. The principal ceremonies were performed to prevent disease, famine, and cataclysms such as earthquakes and floods. The ceremonial procedures supposedly were based on precedents set by immortals before the present race of people occupied the country, and the formulas recited concerned these immortals. Ceremonies were fixed calendrically and usually were held at the spots where they reportedly had been enacted for the first time. During certain ceremonies men displayed their wealth and greatest treasures, and Deerskin and Jumping Dances might be held. Curing and sorcery were also a part of Yurok belief.

Ceremonies An abbreviated account of the most elaborate ceremonial performance, the Kepel fish-weir ceremony, illustrates the integration of subsistence activities and religious rituals. The community of Kepel was on the south side of the Klamath River, and at the nearby village of Sa'a were the sacred house and bathhouse associated with the Kepel ceremonies. At Kepel the river is wide but shallow, and it was easy to drive stakes into the gravel bottom to support a weir. Before the weir at Kepel could be built, the people had to perform a ceremony at the Klamath River mouth to remove the prohibition against eating salmon caught that year. A ritual formulist dominated the Kepel rituals, assisted by a man and a woman. The formulist or weir chief achieved his position by memorizing all the recitations required to build the weir; this knowledge was passed from a father to one of his sons. The rituals began in the late summer when persons in a village near Kepel presented to the weir chief a deerskin robe that he wore throughout the ceremonies. During the next ten days, one or more of these principals became deeply involved in ritual duties. These included visiting sacred spots, burning incense, fasting, dancing, singing, bathing in a special manner, and reciting formulas. After a ritual visit to the places where the weir poles were to be cut and where the weir was to be anchored, the male assistant went to adjacent communities to announce the date for beginning construction of the weir. On that day each man who responded was assigned to a work crew, probably of ten men; each crew was responsible for a named section of the weir.

The following morning and for the next five days the crews cut and limbed small pine trees, peeled the bark off, and split the poles lengthwise. They also collected hazel shoots for binding the poles into mats that were carried to the weir site. On the fifth day the weir chief cut a pole for each end and the center of the weir. After he split the center pole, the workers split other poles and then joked for the remainder of the day. At this time no offense could be taken against jokes at one's expense, no matter how abusive they might be. Actual construction of the weir was begun the next day, with the first pole driven by the weir chief, who used a special maul weighing about fifty pounds. As he drove the pole into the river bottom, he prayed for salmon. Others drove the remaining poles into the gravel at different angles so that the current would not dislodge them. The formulist and his male assistant arranged the first stringer along the tops of the poles, and after the other stringers were arranged, all were bound into place. On the downstream side of the weir the workers constructed ten traps, each about twelve feet long and fourteen feet wide, with movable openings at each end; the woven mats were placed in the pole frames to complete the weir-trap. Near the south bank an opening was left in the stringers so that boats could pass through and some salmon could escape.

At noon on the tenth day, boys made ribbons of bark, imitations of pipes, and other carvings that they attached to a pole raised near one end of the weir. The female assistant ran from Sa'a to the site with a basket of acorn dough and placed it on a pile of sand. Girls began dancing and later stopped to cover the female assistant with their bodies as a boy threw a basket of water high in the air, attempting to shower the girls. As he did this, other boys climbed on the pile to protect the female assistant from the spray and from the poles the workers let fall simultaneously on the throng. Afterwards, the people in the pile rapidly dispersed on all fours. The three principals then returned to the weir, and the male assistant removed the first salmon caught. Part of it was taken by the female assistant for her evening meal, but no one else could eat salmon until the following day. The nearby dance ground was cleared for the Deerskin Dance. One was held here and another at a spot ten miles downstream. The ordinary participants attended one dance or the other and then returned home, but the weir chief and his male assistant remained at the site until the weir was destroyed two to three months later.

A Deerskin Dance was a colorful event, with each male dancer wearing the skin of a civet cat or deer around his waist. The dancers were not clothed above the waist, but around each man's neck hung massive strings of dentalium shells. Each man's head was adorned with a brow band of wolf fur and a stick on which eagle or condor feathers were arranged to appear as one very long feather. Each dancer carried a pole with a stuffed deer head at the top and the deerskin hanging loose to sway back and forth as the pole was moved. (See Figure 8-8.) In the center of a line of dancers were a singer and two assistants dressed similarly to the others. The line of dancers stamped one foot and then the other, the standard dance step. While they performed, as many as four other men paraded before the dancers, blowing whistles and holding obsidian blades encased in deerskins. These men wore a double layer of deerskins wrapped around their bodies, wolf-fur brow bands, and another band of leather around their heads with the canine teeth of sea lions attached. From their heads hung netting painted with designs and fringed with feathers. During the Deerskin Dance, as at ceremonies in general, members of the host community danced and were followed by performers from each represented village. Morning and evening dances were given by each group for a twelve-day period. On the final day, men danced with their finest white deerskins, and others displayed their most beautiful obsidian blades.

Formal ceremonies at the Kepel fish weir ended with the performance of a two-day Jumping Dance held a few miles above Kepel. Dancing males wore a double layer of deerskin about their hips and many necklaces of dentalium shells. Each man wore a deerskin headband covered with woodpecker scalps and trimmed with a white band of deerskin; a white plume extended above his head on a stick. From the sides of his headpiece hung long skin flaps that swung rapidly as he performed. In one hand a dancer carried a cylindrical basket with

Figure 8-8. | Deerskin dancers ready to perform, circa 1900. Note the obsidian blades held by the men in the foreground. (Courtesy of the A. W. Ericson Collection, Humboldt State University Library.)

an opening along one side. (See Figure 8-9.) Two steps were performed in the Jumping Dance; both involved hopping or jumping as the baskets were lowered.

After the Kepel weir was readied for use, three traps were reserved for the principal participants in the ceremony, and the others were designated for particular individuals and their relatives. Salmon were removed from traps with dip nets in the mornings; afterward the weir chief opened the upper ends of the traps for great numbers of salmon to escape upriver. Many of the fish caught were processed for future consumption. The people fished for two to three months, always with the weir chief and his assistants nearby. The weir finally was destroyed by the rushing water, and the ceremonialists as well as the fishermen returned to their homes.

While the Kepel fish-weir ceremonies were the most elaborate, portions of the Yurok population participated in other ceremonies as well. At the junction of the Trinity and Klamath rivers in a community called Weitspus a ceremony was held to renew the world each September. It was designed specifically to avert natural disasters and disease. At two coastal villages, a village at the Klamath

Figure 8-9. | Jumping Dance performers, circa 1900. (Courtesy of the A. W. Ericson Collection, Humboldt State University Library.)

River mouth and another a little less than halfway between the Trinity junction and the sea, four other world-renewal ceremonies were held. Yurok participation in these and other ceremonies produced a form of integration along sacred, not secular, lines.

Another popular celebration, called the Brush Dance by Anglo-Americans, was held to treat an ill child, but it also served as entertainment for most participants. The event was held in a dwelling from which the roof and part of the sidewalls had been removed. On the first night a formula was recited for the ill child, and men danced about the fire holding boughs. Nothing took place the second night, but on the third and fourth nights the Brush Dance continued until dawn. On each night a series of three dances were performed by competing sets of dancers. The sick child was integrated into the performances with the recitation of formulas and the waving of torches above him or her.

Formulas were very important in the Brush Dance as well as in calendrical ceremonies, and they also served individual needs under other circumstances. Some formulas involved the recitation of a list of sacred spots that someone long ago had visited to accomplish a particular purpose. Others were recitations or prayers, including the spirit responses. Offerings of tobacco and the use of plant products were associated with the formulas.

Curing   Women were the healers among the Yurok, and they usually acquired their power in a dream, either unanticipated or sought-after, about a dead shaman. From this deceased curing specialist the potential shaman obtained a "pain," considered a tangible object that entered her body and became the nexus of her power. Once she had acquired power, the next step was to bring it under control by fasting and dancing in a bathhouse for ten days under the supervision of other shamans. The goal was for the novice to be able to vomit forth her pain and to swallow it again. As a further step the aspirant and a male relative visited a supernatural spot on a mountain for one night during the summer. On the mountain the woman recited a formula, smoked, and danced near a fire. Another ten days in the bathhouse, performing as before, was followed by a dance around a large hot fire to bring the pain fully under the woman's control. This dance was the final step in becoming a shaman.

When a woman was asked to heal a patient, she negotiated the amount of payment with the relatives of the sick person before she attempted a cure. A female curer's equipment consisted of a pipe, two strings of feathers in her hair, and an ankle-length skirt. She effected a cure by chanting over the patient, smoking, and dancing for as much as six hours. A long session sometimes was necessary to see into the body of the patient and to locate the pains that caused the disease. The pain, or pains, were then removed by sucking. If the shaman was unable to remove the pains, she referred the patient to another curer. If a patient died, the shaman returned her fee.

In a second category of curers were males who probably did not acquire their power from supernatural sources but intensified it by supernatural means. They visited mountaintops, recited formulas, bathed ritually, and smoked in order to reinforce their power. These men relied on a pharmacopoeia consisting of plant and mineral products. This knowledge and the position was passed from father to son or to another close male relative. Like a female shaman, the male was paid before he attempted a cure and returned the payment if he was unsuccessful. Among the illnesses treated were wounds, snakebites, and chronic diseases, as well as other forms of unidentified sickness. One source states that male curers served as a check on the ambitions of female shamans. Apparently, the duties of female and male shamans were distinct, females handling cases of psychological ailments with supernatural cures and males treating physical disabilities from natural causes.

Sorcery   Some female shamans had the reputation of using their powers for antisocial purposes, the motivation being material profit. These shamans allegedly made a person ill and then collected a fee to cure her or him. Another technique was to leave one of multiple pains in the body of a person who was treated in order to be called back when this pain became troublesome. Other persons were more truly witches; they reportedly acquired a malignant object by purchase or special knowledge and used it to kill individuals. If the possessor of such a power went out at night, the power was thought to appear as sparks or as a bluish light. It could be placed on the end of a miniature arrow and shot from a small bow at the home of the victim. It was thought that the victim would die if not treated by a shaman. A person also could be harmed by a poison made of crushed meat from a dog, frog, rattlesnake, or salamander. After the poison was added to a victim's food, the individual would supposedly remain healthy for a year but then become ill and die if not cared for by a very powerful shaman.

When a person's rights were violated and just compensation could not be obtained by legal means, the only alternative was to turn to a sorcerer. These usually were men, and they customarily charged as much as a bride price, which meant that their services could be commanded only by aristocrats. A sorcerer was either of high social standing or was attempting to achieve higher status. He owned two to twelve "poisons" that ranged in effectiveness from very mild to lethal; each strength was represented by a different miniature arrow. The mildest form was said to produce a headache or cold and the middle level to cause chest pains that led to the victim's confinement. From the eighth level upward, all were lethal and were associated with behavior while sleeping. Once the fee and the degree of illness to be induced were agreed upon, the sorcerer went outside the victim's house disguised as a dog. He shot the mildest arrow from a miniature bow and returned at specified intervals to shoot arrows until he reached the level of illness desired. When the victim showed symptoms of illness, a shaman was hired to extract the "pains," but very few shamans had the power to remove lethal arrows. If a shaman could suck the pain from a victim, she spit it out of her mouth, and the arrow supposedly rose into the air and flew back to its maker, with only the shaman seeing the return. It was essential for a sorcerer to handle the objects of his power with great care. When not in use, they were buried in a cache of stones, but it was necessary for the owner to use the force of the poison at least once a month. If he did not, it was thought that the power would harm his children, or himself if he was childless. This form of sorcery possibly developed during the early historic period when the economic position of aristocratic families was threatened by white intruders who began to control key economic resources.

LIFE CYCLE   The first time a woman conceived, her offspring was born after ten months, according to tradition, but later births followed nine-month pregnancies. Most births were in the spring, but not because a mating season existed, as once was suggested. The reason is that a man stored his material wealth in his house, and riches were believed to be diametrically opposed to sexual activity. To have sexual intercourse in the house was to invite poverty, and thus couples were most likely to copulate in the summer when sleeping outdoors. A pregnant woman worked hard, ate little, and was concerned about how her physical actions might affect the fetus. For example, she worried that she might bear a large neonate if she ate too much and slept excessively.

In giving birth a woman rested on her back with her feet braced against a midwife and her arms bound with leather straps suspended from the ceiling. During labor she was told by the midwife when to lift herself with the thongs. The newborn was steamed over wild ginger, and a preparation made from

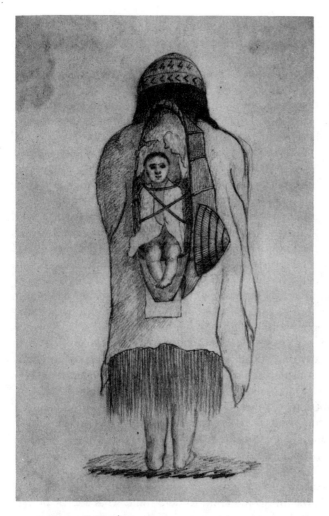

Figure 8-10. | A woman with her child in a cradleboard. (Drawn by George Gibbs in 1851. Courtesy of the Smithsonian Institution, National Anthropological Archives, neg. no. 2854-F-21.)

ground land snail was applied to the navel. The severed cord was put inside a pine tree branch that had been split to receive it. Because these people thought that the colostrum from the mother's breast was harmful to ingest, an infant was fed hazelnut soup for the first ten days and then was nursed. After twenty days a grandmother, probably most often the paternal grandmother, began to massage the infant's leg muscles to encourage it to crawl. Between the time of birth and the healing of the navel, parents observed food taboos, and they were prohibited from having sexual intercourse until the baby crawled. Cradleboards were made in such a manner that the infant sat, with its legs hanging free. (See Figure 8-10.)

The baby could move its legs at any time, which was in keeping with the desire to have it crawl at a tender age. Many, if not most, aspects of rearing an offspring were designed to encourage self-reliance. This attitude clearly was reflected by the practice of weaning at one year, which was earlier than among most American Indians.

A child was named when he or she had clearly demonstrated a systematic recall capacity, probably at about eight years of age. The names for males were selected by fathers, and for females by mothers; each family seems to have had its own set of personal names. Nicknames of girls often contained some reference to their marriage, such as Married a Rabbit. Personal names were used in referring to or addressing individuals, but they were dropped when someone married.

The Yurok believed that each child had a unique personal spirit derived from the energy of the Universe, which acted against itself and sent its waves through everything. According to Thomas Buckley (1979), an ethnographer of the Yurok, this infusion of energy was thought to occur ten weeks after conception. At an early age a child was not considered capable of learning systematically. His or her readiness to learn was based on a capacity to remember, not on chronological age; the process of learning began as she or he matured. At this time each child was taught on an individual basis since each one was viewed as different from the others. The information taught primarily involved ways to think and behave in particular situations. It was uncles and aunts who taught children; parents were considered too close to them, while grandparents were too emotionally involved with grandchildren to be routine teachers.

A child was taught comparatively little in a formal way; the Yurok felt quite strongly that an individual could learn only by experience. For example, aristocratic families placed an inordinate emphasis on table manners, and a child was expected to learn the proper etiquette by observing others. If a maturing offspring seized food greedily, ate greedily, ate rapidly, and did not chew thoroughly, his or her meal basket was turned upside down as an indication of parental disapproval. It was up to the child to determine what she or he had done wrong and to correct this behavior. Some instruction was formal, however. A child might be shown rocks shaped like figures and told they formerly were persons who did not follow social norms. One rock in particular was pointed out as once having been an errant child. Animals and birds, too, were the subjects of stories about proper behavior. One particularly vivid tale concerned the greedy buzzard who put his entire head in his soup while it was still hot. He scalded the top of his head and henceforth could eat only old, rotten food. Another dominant concern of parents was to insure that a child learned not to offend the dead. Any direct statement about the dead or reference to items associated with death was considered a form of swearing. A rude gesture used as a means of swearing was to hold out one's hands with the fingers outstretched and the thumbs together, since this was thought to be how the dead swore. The probable reason for disapproving of such behavior was that it led to claims by the relatives of a deceased person. To discourage words or gestures of this nature, a mentor placed nettles against a child's lips or hands, a very effective punishment.

A child sooner or later came to understand what the people conceived of as the law; everything was subject to this law. The essence of the law, which was above all else an expression of the Universe, was *truth,* because it was correct and proper at all times. As Buckley (1979, 30) has noted, "All education and training must move in respect of each unique person's individuality while, at the same time, insuring the success of the results as far as this is possible. That is, the interface between individual and society is specified by culturally defined truth expressed in a legal idiom." An individual who learned a great deal of the law was called a "well-educated one," which was an exalted achieved status. The key to education was to learn to perceive "facts" in perspective. In this context, objects as well as behaviors, thoughts, and feelings were objectified as *things* to be seen and understood. A child first learned to comprehend the nature of material things as an essential step toward understanding things that were nonmaterial. To draw distinctions between the two, such as between a tree in a physical sense and a spiritual one, a child was encouraged to be reflective and was given clues, not answers, by instructors. Youths were encouraged to be contemplative, to do their own thinking, and especially to be true to themselves. This was how they not only became upright adults but acquired the spiritual power that brought them both wealth and inner contentment.

The most important skill to be acquired by a young girl was basket weaving, since a great deal of prestige accrued from making excellent baskets. After watching older women make baskets for years, a girl attempted to weave her first one when she was about six years old. She tried a simple form, and often after the first few rows were completed, her mother ripped out the poor weave and gave the basket back to the girl to do again. The learner received little credit for "trying" because a basket either served its purpose or it did not. If a girl's interest and abilities were sustained, a skilled basket weaver instructed her informally. Only one set of weaving techniques existed, and therefore all baskets were similar, differing only in quality and to a lesser degree in design elements. Not all girls became good basket weavers.

When a girl first menstruated, she spent most of ten days sitting silently in a corner of the house, facing away from the fire. Whenever she needed to scratch, she used a special stick, and she wore a skirt of inner bark like that of a female shaman. The girl moved about as little as possible but brought in a load of firewood each day. For at least the first four days she ate no food, under the assumption that the longer she fasted the more wealth she would accumulate later in life. When she did eat, it was at the bank of a roaring river where she would hear no sound but the water. Each night she bathed the number of times equal to the days of her confinement, except that on the ninth night she bathed ten times. At dusk of the tenth day each small child living nearby washed her back. Finally, her mother or another woman told her she would have ten boys and ten girls.

The preceding account is based on traditionally accepted writings about the initial menstruation of Yurok females, which imply that during their first and subsequent menses women were isolated because of their capacity to contaminate anything with which they had contact. For a menstruating woman to seduce an unknowing man was considered odious; thus, the impact of menstruation on women and men alike was interpreted largely negatively. However, a field study among the Yurok by Buckley in 1978, coupled with his examination of unpublished field notes collected by A. L. Kroeber in 1902, leads to a reevaluation of published accounts about menstruation and sheds new light on Yurok social and religious life. Buckley emphasizes that the data are not the best and his reconstruction of the menstrual complex is tentative, but his nonetheless is an important interpretation to consider.

On her "moontime," as the Yurok called menstruation, a woman was isolated from males for ten days and ate separate meals prepared in particular containers. Furthermore, men were expected to refrain from hunting or participating in ceremonial activities when their wives or daughters were menstruating. One rationale for isolating women at this time was negative: menstruating women were considered highly polluting. Yet, a positive reason existed as well: a menstruating woman was thought to be at the height of her power because the flow of blood purified her. This was why she refrained from ordinary tasks and concentrated instead on the purpose and meaning of her life. The Yurok drew a clear analogy between the purification men sought in their sweat baths and that sought by women in menstrual isolation. Men seeking wealth secluded themselves in a bathhouse, avoided contact with fertile women, and ate special foods for ten days. In a similar fashion, Yurok women during their menses attained purification and supposedly had the greatest capacity to attract wealth.

From these data it becomes obvious that if the women of a household menstruated at different times, the normal household routine frequently would be disrupted. Buckley suggests that this may not have been the case because of a menstrual synchrony among the fertile women in a household group. (Menstrual synchrony is widely recognized as occurring among women who interact frequently, such as in college dormitories. In 1986 a major newspaper reported that a female pheromone can diffuse through a large room with sufficient strength to synchronize the menstrual cycles of women who customarily occupy the room.) Presumably, the women in a Yurok household, or in clusters of closely related households, interacted often. Furthermore, it may be, as Buckley cautiously suggests, that Yurok women synchronized their menses by being exposed to the full moon. (It has been demonstrated that the exposure of a woman to light while she is asleep may affect the onset of menstruation.) The lunar cycle was known to be highly significant among the Yurok in calculating time, and this awareness of lunar change may have led them to use photic stimulation to influence the onset of menstruation as required for synchrony. In any case, the menstrual synchrony that apparently existed meant the absence of all fertile adult females from the household at one time, which may have been more advantageous than constant disruptions of routine.

A maturing girl of good breeding was watched carefully by her parents to make certain that she did not fornicate. The prohibition was not so much a matter of morality as to prevent the girl from becoming pregnant and thereby decreasing the amount of bridewealth she would bring. A girl who conceived before marriage attempted to abort by placing heated stones on her abdomen; if successful, she threw the fetus in the river. A young man was exhorted to work hard at adult skills, to carry wood for the bathhouse frequently, and to concentrate on money.

Property exchanges at marriage were critical because a person's social standing depended on the amount of bridewealth offered at the time of his mother's marriage. At the bottom of the scale was a nonlegitimate offspring who had no formal standing. Next was a poor person, whose father had offered little for his wife; he in turn could provide his son with very little bridewealth. A third level of prestige was achieved by persons whose fathers had offered substantial wealth. Finally, some persons' rich fathers provided far more wealth than was necessary to consummate a marriage. Marital arrangements were not a simple offering of a given amount of wealth to the bride's family; instead there often were manipulations and compromises. According to the ideal, a man with wealth suggested a suitable amount of material goods to the girl's relatives, had it accepted, and took the girl to reside in his settlement (patrilocal residence). Such was a "full marriage." Any particular groom was unlikely to possess enough wealth of his own to satisfy the girl's relatives, but his father or father's brothers ideally gave the young man the necessary balance. The bride of a wealthy man brought with her a considerable amount of property, which partially offset the outlay of the groom and his relatives. A girl of high social standing might bring ten baskets of dentalia, otter skins, a canoe, deerskins, and other small assorted valuables. It was possible also for a man with a small daughter to be deeply in debt to a man with a young son and to offer the girl in marriage when she was quite young. In this case, the girl would grow up in the household of her prospective in-laws and would marry the boy after puberty. Sometimes a father was so covetous of his wealth that he refused to give his son a sufficient amount for a full marriage. If the son worked hard, sweated often in the bathhouse, cried for wealth, and fasted, after about four years the girl's relatives might feel sorry for him and permit a full marriage.

Another form of marriage was "half marriage," which meant usually that the groom could not accumulate the necessary wealth to make a full-marriage payment and was forced to be content with lower social standing. He offered his potential father-in-law all the wealth he possessed and went to live in the girl's village, either in the same house or in a nearby house (matrilocal residence). In a typical marriage of this sort, the children of the couple were affiliated with the wife's family, and the bridewealth given at the marriage of their daughter went to the wife's kinsmen. Furthermore, the woman in a half marriage could correct her husband openly and supervise his subsistence activities, while the children were under her direct control even concerning their marital arrangements. A half marriage sometimes was negotiated quickly if a girl was pregnant, to prevent the social stigma of bearing a bastard. Finally, a greedy father of a girl who was a successful shaman might force a half marriage upon her to continue his claim on her earnings. In a record of 356 marriages, 25 percent were half marriages, indicating that either the number of persons with little wealth was small or that extenuating circumstances often were involved in a marriage. At the same time, full marriages were not all equal, for very rich men would offer far more than the minimum amount of wealth necessary in order to acquire increased prestige for themselves and their children.

Possibly the most common grounds for divorce was failure of the wife to conceive, and if she could not be replaced by a kinswoman, the bridewealth was refunded. If a man abused his wife in a full marriage so much that she returned home, the husband was obligated to pay the woman's family an additional amount before he could receive her back. If he did not do so, the girl's family probably would return part of the bridewealth, and the couple was considered divorced.

Following a death, the corpse was washed, but it was touched as little as possible. The deceased was painted, clothed, wrapped in a skin, and placed on a plank for twenty-four hours. Mourners wailed before the body, and then it was removed from the house through an opening made in a wall. After additional rituals the body was carried to a cemetery maintained in the midst of the settlement to prevent wild animals from disturbing the dead. A grave was excavated and lined with planks; the plank on which the corpse had rested in state served as the coffin lid. During burial the mourners wept, sang appropriate songs, and said good-bye as they stated their relationship to the deceased. One stone marked the head of a grave and another the foot; a wide plank was placed across the grave and staked in place. A fence was built around the grave, with posts at the head and the foot; on the posts were fastened crosspieces from which hung deerskins, with the heads and bodies stuffed with grass. Items such as baskets and plates were placed on top of the grave.

The spirit of a good person was believed to travel a narrow, winding trail north until it climbed a ladder into the sky to a peaceful afterlife. The soul of an unworthy individual supposedly traveled a broad trail to a river where an old woman and a dog lived. Sometimes the dog drove the soul back into the dead person's body, and he or she came to life again. This was rare, and if it did happen, the person was not happy and would meet a sudden death. When the old woman had control of the soul, she sent it across the river in a waiting canoe of the Yurok type but without a "heart" near the bow. A young man propelled the canoe and landed the soul in a damp, depressing land where food, although plentiful, was unpalatable. As described, these beliefs about the fate of souls sound as if they might be of Christian derivation.

Early Historic Influences on Yurok Life

Just as for other peoples, early historic influences on Yurok life were brought to bear by contact with whites and other Indians. Some of these contacts resulted in friction, some in sharing of religious ideas, and some in federal government definition of land rights.

FRICTION WITH FOREIGNERS When gold miners moved into the Trinity River country in 1849, the most dramatic effect on the Yurok was the realization that foreigners, equated with enemies, were permanently in their midst. Their primary contacts were with traders, who offered not only useful material goods but intoxicants as well. These Indians not infrequently fought whites when either or both were intoxicated. Another serious problem was that of compensation in Indian terms. In one instance a trader hired Indians to transport supplies for his store from the coast, and when the canoemen drowned, the trader was held responsible. When he would not compensate the relatives of the deceased, they laid siege to his store. He summoned U.S. Army soldiers as protection, and finally the Indians retaliated by killing a white who had nothing to do with the affair. Problems such as these during the early period of intensive contact appear to have been relatively common.

THE 1870 GHOST DANCE   Within a generation of the first intensive contacts with whites, the Yurok were exposed to a form of Ghost Dance. It was originated in 1869 by Wodziwob, a Paviotso Indian (Northern Paiute) who was said to have died about three years after having his most important visions. He and a disciple were said to have returned from the place of the dead with the report that the dead would come back to earth. The Ghost Dance was performed at Paviotso meetings, but they did not consider it important. As the doctrine spread in Oregon and California, it changed from its original form. Yurok reaction to the basic tenets is revealing. The dogma spoke of an end to the present world when nonbelievers, including whites, would turn to stone; believers would survive and be joined by the dead. Some Yurok, however, thought that all people would die, and others that everyone would survive the world's end. All Yurok thought that if individual wealth were not exposed during the Ghost Dance performances, it would be worthless in the new world. To facilitate the return of the dead, the Yurok removed fences from graves in some localities. The message appears to have won support for a short time, with the strongest adherents being the young and the poor, but the Ghost Dance of 1870 made no lasting imprint on Yurok life, possibly because the doctrine had no precedent in their mythology and was without the traditional formulas that formed the core of Yurok supernaturalism.

ESTABLISHMENT OF THE RESERVATION   In 1864 the Hoopa Valley Reservation was established by the U.S. Congress in an area occupied aboriginally by the Hupa (Hoopa) and Yurok. The Hoopa Extension was created by an executive order of the president in 1876 in an area that was exclusively Yurok. These reservations adjoined one another, and the separate rights of the Hupa and Yurok were not explicitly defined. By 1898 most of the thirty thousand acres of the Hoopa Extension had been allotted to individual Indians, and the balance of the land was sold to whites, with the proceeds earmarked for Indian welfare. Those persons with allotments were encouraged to sell their valuable timberland to whites, and by 1971 only about thirty-four hundred acres remained in the hands of individual Yurok. By contrast, most of the Hoopa Reservation land was not allotted. Thus, the Yurok, who are identified primarily with the extension rather than the Hoopa Reservation, now are virtually landless. This has led to a great deal of bitterness with the Hupa, who emerged as exclusively identified with the Hoopa Reservation, where most of the land is still held by the tribe and is quite valuable.

| Modern Yurok Life

Published anthropological information about the Yurok in the recent past is nearly nonexistent. Fortunately, however, two anthropology students at the University of California, Los Angeles, Cynthia Burski and Dorothy Hosler Runge, visited the Yurok in 1965 and graciously made their field notes available to me. Most of the information that follows is from their work.

RELIGION AND SUPERNATURALISM   In 1927 the Indian Shaker church gained converts among the Yurok, and by the 1930s it had enough adherents to become influential in local life. One result was that sorcery by professionals almost disappeared, although knowledge about it remained widespread. It apparently was not uncommon for a person to whistle near an "enemy's" house at night as a means of frightening the occupants, but this "deviling" was more often mischievous than harmful. Among the Yurok in the late 1960s persons still were suspected of practicing sorcery if they had threatened somebody who became ill months or even years later. Individuals also were suspect if they behaved in a suspicious manner—for example, if they wandered alone late at night. Suspected sorcerers, who most often were old, poor, and lived alone, were avoided.

Attendance at Christian church services seemed to be the most important form of organized religious activity. The world-renewal ceremonies had died out long ago, but the Deerskin Dance still was held sporadically. One was given in 1955, and the next was held during seven days of August 1964. Reportedly, in 1955 most of the boats were lost in a flood, and their destruction made traveling to a dance difficult. The same year, much of the ceremonial equipment was destroyed by fire; this caused the long delay between Deerskin Dances. The secular Brush Dance continued to be held on the Fourth of July and lasted for three days.

During December of 1964 a severe flood occurred along the Klamath River. The amount of Yurok property swept away or damaged by the flood was great, and the region was designated as a national disaster area. Some thirty-five Yurok houses along the Klamath were completely destroyed. The people were appalled by their material losses but were able to receive temporary supplies and clothing through the disaster program. Some Yurok had predicted that disaster would follow the cutting of a road through a sacred mountain by the Division of Highways two years before. Other Yurok offered a host of other possible causes for the disaster. They noted, for example, that a Deerskin Dance held at Hoopa had not lasted the traditional number of days. Furthermore, in the fires built during a recent Deerskin Dance, driftwood, not the traditional timber from the mountainsides, had been burned. Another mistake connected with this dance was that water had been sprinkled on the dance area by a truck before the event. Then, too, one man had refused to display his wealth at the dance, which again had invited disaster. The people were distressed also because cemeteries were washed away by the flood and the bones of the dead exposed. The tradition-oriented Yurok explained the continuing rains of January 1965 as being caused by the exposure of bones of the dead; they thought the rains would continue until the bones once again were covered.

ATTITUDES: YUROK AND WHITE   The views of many local whites about these Indians were stereotypic and fell into an expectable pattern. The Indians were considered drunkards with little or no respect for the law; dirty, irresponsible employees; and generally unreliable. Unquestionably, the opinions of the whites had a certain amount of truth to them, for the consumption of intoxicants did seem to be important to many Yurok, and the attitudes of many of them toward wage labor were not shared by whites. The Yurok considered whites to be greedy and felt that they looked down upon Indians. More important to the Yurok were their specific complaints against the Hupa, who they felt were unjustly favored by the BIA, and against BIA officials for both real and imagined injustices.

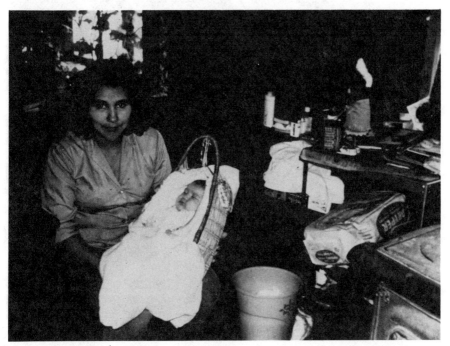

Figure 8-11. | A mother with her infant in a traditional cradleboard in 1965. (Courtesy of Dorothy Hosler Runge.)

Figure 8-12. | The heirlooms of a Yurok man in 1965. (Courtesy of Dorothy Hosler Runge.)

SOCIAL LIFE AND SUBSISTENCE   Modern Yurok social life still was built on the nuclear family residence unit, but Yurok of both sexes showed a striking tendency to marry whites. Yurok clothing did not differ from the garments of whites in the area since both men and women wore store-bought clothing exclusively. Yurok homes were large, rectangular frame dwellings with four or more rooms. One characteristic of households was their cluttered appearance, the result of a great accumulation of material goods. Household furnishings included both expected items such as refrigerators, stoves, tables, and chairs, and many seemingly useless items. The clutter apparently was compatible with older housekeeping norms. Houses contained collections of baskets, an overt sign of their Indian heritage. (See Figures 8-11, 8-12.) Production of baskets was limited since few women retained the skill to make them, and they were sold primarily to Yurok. The bathhouses, which once were so extremely important, had ceased to function. Stools, which were one of the few items of aboriginal furniture, were occasionally seen in the dwellings, but they were regarded more as heirlooms than as furnishings. The traditional forms of Yurok wealth, such as elaborate ceremonial costumes, dentalium shells, and white deerskins existed as treasures.

Subsistence fishing for salmon had become less important, although certain family fishing spots were owned and trespassers prosecuted. The timber industry was the primary source of employment, followed by road construction. During the summer months, numerous men served as hunting and fishing guides for tourists. Loggers earned $3.50 an hour, and in a nine-month season an individual might accumulate as much as $7,000. This was the most lucrative type of employment, especially when wages were supplemented by unemployment insurance payments for the balance of the year.

| Recent Developments

Recent developments in Yurok life have had to do with Indian rights and traditions coming into conflict with governmental control. In particular, the issues of the Gasquet-Orleans Road, fishing rights, and land claims have been prominent. Each of these issues has landed in the courts for settlement.

THE GASQUET-ORLEANS ROAD   Since 1974 a single issue has united the Yurok and their Indian neighbors against the whites having an interest in land once owned by the Yurok, meaning the U.S. Forest Service. Debate has centered on the completion of a road to link the town of Gasquet near the Oregon border and Orleans along the Klamath River. The road would cover a distance of about fifty-five miles within the Six Rivers National Forest. Begun in the mid-1930s, the project had been completed except for seven miles by 1974. This stretch became the center of the controversy. The purpose of the road was to open up a previously inaccessible area for logging, thereby minimizing timber hauling costs; in addition, it was expected to provide a popular scenic drive for tourists. The Hupa, Karok, Tolowa, and Yurok Indians objected to the road's completion because the last segment would cross lands sacred to them. It was to this area that individual Indians went when they were "called." Apprentice female shamans went there to acquire power, and individual men visited its sacred spots to experience the "power, beauty, and essence" the Yurok refer to as essential to their religion past and present.

In their suit to halt completion of the Gasquet-Orleans Road the Indians have been joined by varied environmental groups who are concerned with the wilderness aspect of the area. In 1983 a federal district court judge ruled in favor of the plaintiffs. His judgment was based on the Free Exercise Clause of the First Amendment of the U.S. Constitution. However, by late 1986 the judgment was being challenged in court by the U.S. Forest Service, and the eventual outcome of the case is unpredictable at present.

FISHING RIGHTS   With a clear basis in subsistence patterns among aboriginal riverine Yurok, salmon fishing has once again become an important source of food. However, since most of the land along the Hoopa Extension now belongs to whites, the State of California has claimed jurisdiction over fishing rights. Yurok dissatisfaction with this arrangement peaked in 1969, when a Yurok was cited by the California Fish and Game Department for gill-netting salmon along the lower river. By 1975 the courts had ruled in favor of the Yurok, upholding their aboriginal fishing rights. In 1979 the BIA issued regulations that permitted the gill-netting of salmon by Indians for subsistence and ceremonial purposes; commercial fishing by Indians using gill nets was prohibited, however. By that time also, non-Indians were prohibited from taking salmon from the Klamath River in keeping with state law because the spawning population was dangerously low. The salmon fishing controversy was resolved by 1986. Federal authorities established fishing regulations for subsistence and ceremonial use of salmon, and these were administered by the BIA. From time to time a few Yurok push for a commercial catch limit, but the vast majority of the Yurok oppose commercial salmon fishing along the Klamath River.

LAND CLAIMS   Many Yurok difficulties have been building over the years and are without ready solutions. The sale of most allotments on the Hoopa Extension have effectively destroyed their traditional land base. Their distinct tendency to marry whites attenuates their identity as Indians, and alcohol consumption has for some persons reached alarming proportions. Furthermore, they have been unable to organize a tribal council, making collective action difficult. But there is a brighter side.

By the late 1940s the timber on the Hoopa Reservation had increased so much in value that lumber companies were seeking permission to harvest it. In leading the negotiations, the BIA compiled a roll of persons eligible to make the decision and to reap the profits. The roll was limited to Hupa on the reservation, and they voted to approve the exploitation of their timber by lumber companies. By 1972–73 each of the nearly fourteen hundred Hupa had received about three thousand dollars as their share of the forestry operation, a record high payment.

They had also used timber money to build a community and shopping center complex and improve reservation housing. However, lawyers representing about thirty-three hundred Yurok went to court seeking a retroactive share and future shares in Hoopa Reservation resources in what came to be known as the Jessie Short case. The Yurok contended that the Hoopa Reservation and the Hoopa Extension were a single unit conceived to benefit all of the Indians involved. The U.S. Court of Claims ruled in favor of the Yurok, and the U.S. Supreme Court refused to review the case. With their far greater number, it appeared that the Yurok might come to control the Hoopa Reservation. The Hupa understandably contested the role of the Yurok.

By 1986 a settlement was near and yet remained elusive. In 1985 the U.S. Court of Claims ruled that the Yurok would receive nearly $24 million as their share of payment for timber harvested on the Hoopa Reservation, but it was unclear how the $55 million in a timber escrow account was to be divided. The ruling judge urged the Yurok and Hupa to resolve their differences and reach a compromise settlement. However, since the Yurok do not have a tribal council or any other form of tribal government, it has been difficult for them to respond to this ruling. As a result, the BIA has assumed a negotiating role for them. It appeared by late 1986 that the former Yurok land base, the Hoopa Extension, might be reconstituted. The federal government has proposed that the Yurok use the claims settlement money they received from their timber suit to purchase land along the Klamath River for the Yurok as a tribe, not for individuals. This would give the tribe a land base and might encourage an incipient effort toward organizing its own form of government.

| Comparisons with Other Indians

Yurok values invite comparison with the contemporary American ethos as influenced by capitalism and the Protestant ethic. Walter Goldschmidt has presented a systematic comparison of the values of northwest California tribes, drawn primarily from Yurok sources, with the Protestant ethic. Goldschmidt (1951, 513) summarized the Indian pattern as "a system in which the individual was placed chiefly by personal acquisition of wealth which in theory was freely attainable by all, with both status and power resting upon the ownership of property." A basic value was attached to hard work, obtaining wealth, self-denial, and the full responsibility of the individual for his or her own behavior, which was consistently aggressive.

The ways in which people coordinate and combine their diverse activities as a harmonious unit may be termed sociocultural integration. To explore the aspects of integration it is helpful to identify three primary networks: the interactions of people in social and political terms, human relations with the supernatural, and the relations of people with the environment. Integration is broadly expressed in the articulations of these three dimensions, according to Mischa Titiev (1963, 598–99). Note, for example, how loosely integrated Chipewyan caribou hunting was with supernaturalism, but the comparatively high degree of integration between Yurok rituals and construction of the Kepel fish weir. Further comparisons between peoples presented in this book serve to point up differences in integrative networks among them and from our own life-style.

Additional Readings

The best discussion of Yurok material culture is by Alfred L. Kroeber (1925), and the best account of their personality is by Erik H. Erikson (1943). Lila M. O'Neale (1932) has written a very insightful analysis of Yurok basket making in terms of individual weavers. The best ethnographic accounts are by Kroeber and his collaborator Robert Spott (1942). The book by Lucy Thompson (1916), a Yurok woman, is a fine account of an Indian about her own people. The Yurok article in the *California* volume (8) of the *Handbook of North American Indians,* William C. Sturtevant, general editor (Washington, DC, 1978), provides an overview of these Indians and neighboring tribes.

Bibliography

Buckley, Thomas. 1979. Doing your thinking. *Parabola* 4(4):29–37.

———. 1982. Menstruation and the power of Yurok women. *American Ethnologist* 9:47–60.

Burski, Cynthia, and Dorothy H. Runge. 1965, January. Field notes.

Bushnell, John, and Donna Bushnell. 1977. Wealth, work, and world view in native northwest California. In *Flowers of the wind,* Thomas C. Blackburn, ed., 120–82. Socorro, NM.

Cooke, Sherburne F. 1956. *The aboriginal population of the north coast of California.* Anthropological Records, vol. 16, no. 3.

DuBois, Cora. 1939. *The 1870 Ghost Dance.* Anthropological Records, vol. 3, no. 1.

Erikson, Erik H. 1943. *Observations on the Yurok: Childhood and world image.* University of California Publications in American Archaeology and Ethnology, vol. 35, no. 10. Erikson, a psychoanalyst, visited the Yurok in the 1930s and collected information primarily about children. His field observations and the ethnographic data collected by others are interpreted in terms of psychoanalytic theory to provide a rare dimension in the analysis of ethnographic sources.

Gifford, Edward W. 1922. *California kinship terminologies.* University of California Publications in American Archaeology and Ethnology, vol. 18.

Goldschmidt, Walter. 1951. Ethics and the structure of society: An ethnological contribution to the sociology of knowledge. *American Anthropologist* 53:506–24.

Heizer, Robert F., and John E. Mills. 1952. *The four ages of Tsurai.* Berkeley. The only systematic Yurok archaeology is reported in this history of one coastal settlement. The travelers' accounts are an invaluable source on Yurok history.

Hoopa Area News. 1964. Vol. 9, no. 3. Mimeo.

Klamath River Indian People. N.d. *A final, desperate appeal for justice to the president and the congress of the United States by the Klamath River Indian people of the Hoopa Valley Indian Reservation, Humboldt County, California.* Mimeo.

Kroeber, Alfred L. 1925. *Handbook of the Indians of California.* Bureau of American

Ethnology Bulletin no. 78. Washington, DC. (Reprinted 1953, Berkeley.) The first ninety-seven pages of this volume contain a well-balanced ethnographic description of the Yurok.

———. 1976. *Yurok myths*. Berkeley.

Kroeber, Alfred L., and Edward W. Gifford. 1949. *World renewal, a cult system of native northwest California*. Anthropological Records, vol. 13, no. 1.

Lake, Robert G., Jr. 1982, Sept.–Oct. The sacred high country and the G-O Road controversy. *Wassaja*.

McDonell, Terry. 1975, May. Bury my heart in the Hoopa Valley. *San Francisco*.

O'Neale, Lila M. 1932. *Yurok-Karok basket weavers*. University of California Publications in American Archaeology and Ethnology, vol. 32, no. 1.

Spott, Robert, and Alfred L. Kroeber. 1942. *Yurok narratives*. University of California Publications in American Archaeology and Ethnology, vol. 35, no. 9. Robert Spott was an old and well-informed Yurok who related to the recorder, Kroeber, historical accounts, tales of the more distant past, and myths. The historical accounts are particularly enlightening since they provide insight into the functioning of the sociocultural system.

Stearns, Robert E. 1889. A study of primitive money. *Report of the U.S. National Museum, 1887*, 297–334. Washington, DC.

Thompson, Lucy. 1916. *To the American Indian*. Eureka. Written by a Yurok woman, this book is one of the key ethnographic sources and ranks with the studies by Alfred L. Kroeber.

Titiev, Mischa. 1963. *The science of man*. New York.

Valory, Dale K. 1970. *Yurok doctors and devils*. PhD dissertation, University of California, Berkeley.

Waterman, Thomas T. 1920. *Yurok geography*. University of California Publications in American Archaeology and Ethnology, vol. 16, no. 5. This monograph is one of the most fascinating specialized studies about the Yurok. The detailed analysis of Yurok geographical concepts and the ways in which the Yurok conceived of the world offer a dimension of culture rarely considered systematically.

———. 1922. All is trouble along the Klamath. In *American Indian Life*, Elsie C. Parsons, ed., 289–96. New York.

———. 1938. *The Kepel fish dam*. University of California Publications in American Archaeology and Ethnology, vol. 35, no. 6.

Waterman, Thomas T., and Alfred L. Kroeber. 1934. *Yurok marriages*. University of California Publications in American Archaeology and Ethnology, vol. 35, no. 1.

9 The Tlingit: Salmon Fishermen of Alaska

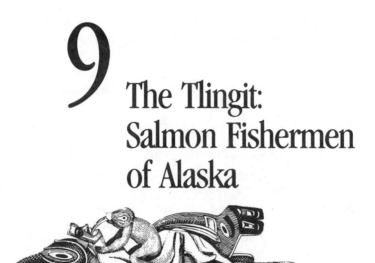

The world is rolling around for all the young people; therefore let us not love our life too much, hold ourselves back from dying.

A song about the earth composed by Dry Bay George. (de Laguna, 1972, 792)

WE PROBABLY HAVE more information about the Tlingit from early historic to modern times than about any other Northwest Coast salmon fishermen. The Tlingit serve as an excellent example of a people who lived in a land where food resources usually were abundant. They stressed wealth as well as social achievements within family lines. They did not organize politically at the tribal level; instead, narrowly defined bonds of kinship focused their economic, political, and social lives. Totem poles and potlatches, characteristic of Northwest Coast Indians in general, prevailed among the Tlingit. Totem poles usually are assumed to have been an aboriginal characteristic of Northwest Coast Indians, but this chapter will show that they are a relatively recent development, quite possibly stimulated by the fur trade. The Tlingits' complex social networks and ceremonial life invite comparison with other salmon fishermen represented in this book—the Kuskowagamiut and Yurok. In addition, the Tlingits' long-term success in coping with Western society contrasts with the less-successful adaptation of peoples described previously.

People, Population, and Language

Tlingit, which means "people," is the term by which these Indians call themselves. Their language belongs to the Na-Dene phylum and is a single language at the family level. They possibly numbered ten thousand at the time of historic contact; by 1986 about seventeen thousand Indians in southeastern Alaska identified themselves as Tlingit. (See Figure 9-1.)

Early Contacts with Explorers and Fur Traders

As early as 1582 a Spanish explorer sailed along the Tlingit coast, but he apparently made no contact with the people. An expedition led by Vitus Bering sailed from Kamchatka in 1741 to determine whether the Asian and North American landmasses were continuous. The ship that Bering commanded anchored off Kayak Island, at the northern fringe of Tlingit country, and although the sailors saw no people, they found a camp with a burning fire. The commander of the other vessel, Alexei Chirikov, anchored off the southern shores of Tlingit country. He sent two boats to investigate the coast, but neither boat returned. Indians later paddled two canoes toward Chirikov's ship but withdrew before making contact. On the return voyage Bering and his crew were forced to winter on what came to be known as Bering Island off the coast of Kamchatka. Here Bering died, but his men returned to Kamchatka the next year with valuable pelts of sea mammals. Russian adventurers hastily formed trading and hunting expeditions and sailed to the Aleutian Islands in a quest for furs, especially for sea otter pelts because of their extremely high value in China. Before many years passed, Russian fur hunters and traders had reached the Alaskan mainland. In the late 1700s competition from European and American trading vessels seeking sea otters increased.

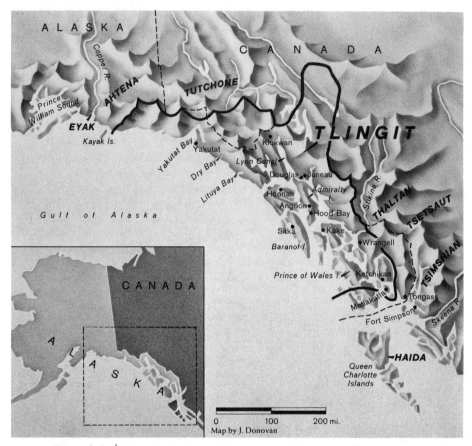

Figure 9-1. | Range of the Tlingit Indians.

The following account by the northern Tlingit recalls the visit to Lituya Bay by Captain Jean de La Perouse of the *Astrolabe* and Paul-Antoine de Langle on the *Boussole,* the first Europeans to visit the locality. One day during the summer of 1786 a Tlingit hunter looked seaward from Lituya Bay on the Gulf of Alaska and was startled by what he thought he saw. Imitating the call of a wolf to signal important news, he ran to a nearby village. As people gathered, he called, "Raven is coming." He told them that Raven was white and could be seen on the horizon to the west. Everyone knew that Raven had been white before he was turned black, and thus his reappearance as white was not surprising. This was a great moment because Raven, their creator and culture hero, had said he would return to reward people who obeyed his teaching and to turn the others into stone. Some persons looking seaward peered at the white object through hollow stalks of kelp so that they would not be blinded by Raven's brightness. As Raven came into the bay, he folded his wings. Those individuals who expected to be turned into stone stood erect and cut their chests with stone knives; others who felt no guilt began painting their faces to receive this great and honored visitor. One wise old man decided to go out to Raven and ask to be turned into stone so that others might be spared. He paddled a canoe to Raven and was lifted, canoe and all, from the water onto Raven's body. Here the old Tlingit saw men with white faces, brown hair, and blue eyes; their clothing was strange to him. The old man began to wonder whether he truly was in Raven's midst. A man far better clothed than the others appeared, and the old man assumed him to be Raven. The old man asked for mercy, but the man in fine clothing sent for food. One of the foods seemed to be a section of a human skull, and something else looked like maggots. Finally he was offered a red liquid that looked like blood; he declined to eat any of these things. The well-dressed man then crossed his hands in the air twice, and the old Indian knew that this was not Raven after all since the sign he made was the one used for trading. The old man exchanged his hat and garments of sea otter skin for a piece of iron and a small bell. Then, without clothing, he got into his canoe, was lowered into the water, and paddled back to the village. He carried his prizes ashore and told the people of his great experience.

As competition increased, Russian merchants moved to gain firm control over the north Pacific trade. In 1799 the Russian-American Company was granted a monopoly by Czar Paul I. The Russian-American Company was dominated by one man above all others, Alexander Baranov, who had established a permanent base on Kodiak Island in 1791. Baranov's first contacts with the Tlingit were in Prince William Sound, where he and his party were mistaken by Yakutat Tlingit for Chugach Eskimos and attacked in the middle of the night. The Russians and the Aleuts who were with them fought off the Indians, but each side suffered casualties. This encounter with the Tlingit, like all earlier contacts by traders and explorers, was hostile. Early European explorers and traders often described these Indians as haughty, aggressive, thieving, and bellicose, especially when they outnumbered intruders. A fort and trading post were established at Sitka in 1799, and as long as Baranov was there the Indians did not attack, since they respected his bravery. After he left in 1801, the Indians destroyed the fort and killed the members of the small garrison. In 1804 Baranov, hoping to establish a fortress on a steep hill formerly occupied by the Indians, returned with almost nine hundred men. The Tlingit withdrew to a nearby fort, and the Russians founded their hilltop settlement, New Archangel (Sitka). Anchored before Sitka was the *Neva,* which under the command of Urey Lisiansky was the first vessel to sail to Russian America from European Russia. The Indians were determined to drive the Russians away if possible, but they could not withstand the bombardment from the *Neva* and withdrew from the fort.

After Baranov's retirement in 1818 a succession of administrators controlled the fortunes of the Russian-American Company, and relations with the Tlingit fluctuated with the abilities of the chief administrator. Throughout the latter part of the Russian period, Sitka was the primary trading center for the Tlingit, but American trading vessels and traders of the Hudson's Bay Company competed successfully for Tlingit pelts. The destructive Indian and Russian hunting techniques led to a rapid decline in the fur trade. When the Russian flag at Sitka was lowered on October 18, 1867, and the flag of the United States was raised, one era came to an end as another began.

| Aboriginal Life of the Tlingit

Among all the aboriginal peoples of the world who lived as hunters, fishers, and collectors, those of the Northwest Coast of North America achieved the highest level of cultural complexity. Their lifeways were in many respects more complex than those reported among numerous aboriginal farming groups. The Tlingit are reasonably typical of these Indians; as was true of other Northwest Coast populations, the richness of their culture was based on the abundance of salmon and the reliability of this major food source.

ORIGIN MYTH   According to the Tlingit, the first people simply existed, and no explanation was sought for their ultimate origin. From these people, according to one tale, arose a woman whose sons were killed by her brother. She decided to commit suicide, but an old man told her to swallow a heated beach pebble. The woman followed his instructions and became pregnant. She bore an offspring, who was Raven in human form. When Raven was older, he visited his uncle despite his mother's warnings that this man had killed his ten older brothers. The uncle attempted to kill Raven, but because of his supernatural powers Raven saved himself. Finally, Raven caused a flood, and all the people perished except for Raven and his mother, who donned bird skins and flew into the air. Raven stuck his beak in the sky and hung there for ten days. After the water subsided, he fell to earth and landed on a heap of seaweed. Raven went to the house of Petrel, a man who had always existed. In a small locked box on which he sat, Petrel kept water, and when Raven was thirsty, Petrel gave him only a little. Raven tricked Petrel into thinking that he, Petrel, had excreted in his bed. While Petrel was outside cleaning his blanket, Raven drank more than his fill of water and then flew to a tree with pitch in it. Petrel built a fire beneath the tree, and the smoke turned Raven from white to black. Later the trickery of Raven released the stars, the moon, and finally the sun into the sky. Raven was a creator or releaser of forces in the world, a culture hero, and above all else an inordinate trickster.

APPEARANCE AND CLOTHING   The Tlingit people were lean, medium to tall in stature, and had skins no darker than those of many persons in southern Europe. Women wore their hair loose and had striking adornments. From a woman's pierced earlobes hung ornaments of shell, stone, or teeth, and her nasal septum was pierced to receive a bone pin. Each woman also wore a large medial labret inserted through a hole beneath the lower lip. (See Figure 9-2.) The initial opening was made about the time of puberty and was fitted with increasingly larger labrets until the hole was as much as four inches across; as one

Figure 9-2. | A girl in the Yakutat area with earrings, a nose pin, and labret. (Sketched by Don Tomás de Suría in 1791. Courtesy of the Western Americana Collection, Yale University Library.)

observer noted, these women could not kiss. Men wore their hair loose and rubbed it with grease; while their whiskers were not numerous, they were nonetheless plucked. When a male was young, his nasal septum was pierced, and through the opening a small ring was suspended. Men wore ear ornaments like those of the women, and a man of great achievements might have bits of wool or small feathers stuck in several small holes around the outer edge of his ear. Facial paints were worn by men and women on special occasions and as protection from temperature extremes and insects.

Adults of both sexes dressed in long-sleeved shirts of dehaired skin, over which they wore sea otter skin capes with the fur facing outward. The processed skin undergarments of women reached from the neck to the ankles. During severe weather they wore moccasins made by interior Indians or styled after their footwear. Tlingit hats, worn for hunting and ceremonies, were woven from roots or grass and were shaped like a truncated cone with a flat top. Their clothing hardly seems adequate to an outsider, but these people conditioned themselves to accept temperature extremes. They not only bathed in cold or icy waters but lived in scorching houses.

LAND AND SETTLEMENTS   Tlingit country is a mass of mountains that reach a sea marked by islands, deep bays, and glaciers. This verdant land with its tranquil and turbulent waters had rich exploitative potential. Along the northern third, impressive mountains abruptly meet the sea, and sheltering bays are rare. In the balance of Tlingit country innumerable large and small islands front a fractured coastline. The mild temperatures and heavy precipitation produce a lush and varied vegetation, including stands of red cedar and Sitka spruce. Considering the geographical configuration, it is understandable that travel by boat was far more important than walking, although paths to the interior existed along certain rivers and over low divides and were negotiated for trading or raiding ventures.

Winter villages were built along bays, inlets, or the lower courses of rivers, near good fishing grounds and where canoes could be landed safely. The square plank-covered houses had gabled roofs. At small villages, houses were built in a line facing the water, but the houses in larger settlements were arranged in rows. The plank-covered floor of small dwellings was at ground level, but the central area of larger houses was dug down about three feet. Along the sides at ground level were board or mat enclosed compartments to be used for sleeping, bathing, or storage. Around the fire pit were stones to be heated in the fire and placed in containers for cooking food. Overhead along the beams were stored hunting and fishing devices, and fish might be hung from the roof beams to dry. Among the northern Tlingit, in particular, the house of a leading lineage was likely to have decorated wall partitions or panels called heraldic screens. It appears that behind these screens were the apartments of the house chief. Around the entry to a house, or even around an entire village, were palisades to protect the occupants. A bough-covered structure might be leaned against the outer wall of a house or built close to it for women to use during menstrual periods or childbirth. Scattered about a settlement were pole racks were drying fish, and a short distance away, either toward the forest or sea, were clusters of graves. At summer camps, where the winter supply of fish was obtained, families lived in flimsy plank structures, some of which were walled only on the windward side.

The people were divided into named geographical groups called *kons,* and each had a principal village. From north to south the first kon was Yakutat, with its most important settlement along Yakutat Bay. The most powerful kon was that of the Chilkat, with four major villages along the shores of the upper Lynn Canal. One of these, Klukwan, had sixty-five houses and about six hundred residents. The only interior group, the Inland Tlingit, lived around a series of lakes and occupied the largest area. The other kons, each of which had at least one large village, were the Auk, Taku, Huna, Killisnoo, Sitka, Kake, Kuju, Stikine, Henya, Tongass, and Sanya. Tlingit tradition relates that the kons arrived in their present area from the south, somewhere around the Skeena River, except for the Kake, who came from the interior.

Within a village the land was owned by groups of persons who traced their descent to a presumed common female ancestor (matriclan), and land was subdivided among house groups. Plots of ground near houses were owned by the adjacent households, but village paths were common property. Trails were cleared by community members as a group, and the beach was open to use by everyone. Each kon had its geographical boundaries, and each village controlled the sector it exploited. Within the domain of a village, each represented clan had particular localities defined as its own. Unclaimed sectors could be exploited by anyone. A clan, or portion thereof, owned fishing streams, land of a stream's drainage used for hunting, sealing islands, mountains inhabited by mountain goats, ocean banks, berry patches, and house sites. They conceived of ownership in terms of specific spots used rather than as geographical areas exploited.

MANUFACTURES AND HOUSEHOLD LIFE Tlingit craft skills rank high among tribal peoples anywhere in the world. Their manufactures in bone, stone, and wood are justly famous. In a typical aboriginal household were a wide variety of wooden containers. One style was made from a thin plank of cedar that was steamed and bent into a rectangular form, then overlapped and sewn with root. A wooden bottom was fitted into place and a top sometimes added. Some of these boxes had bulging sides that were painted or carved. The largest and most elaborately decorated boxes were used for the storage of valuables, and others were used for cooking or food storage. Another common wooden form was made from a single piece of wood and ranged from round to oval to rectangular in outline. To these basic forms were adapted various animal shapes, such as a beaver lying on its back, with its head at one end, legs on the sides, and tail opposite the head. Other household items included dishes, spoons, and ladles of mountain sheep or goat horn. Oval lamps of pecked and polished stone furnished light as fish oil burned on a moss wick.

Family members gathered around the fire pit to rest, eat, or work during the day. At the fireplace meals were prepared at irregular times of the day for as many as thirty house occupants. Boiled foods were cooked in wooden or woven containers. Water was placed in them, and hot stones were dropped in to simmer the meat or fish before the lid was put on. Fish were boiled, roasted, or dried, and served as the principal food, supplemented by flesh from land and sea mammals. Also eaten were shellfish, vegetable products, and fruit, particularly a wide variety of berries, but these foods were relatively unimportant; however, shellfish were important in times of food stress. Boiled foods were dipped from their cooking containers in large spoons, which served as plates, and large quantities of water were consumed at every meal.

ART Northwest Coast Indian art long has attracted the attention of Westerners because of the monumental aspects of its totem poles produced by men and the fine workmanship evident in the robes and woven baskets manufactured by women. The dominant materials worked by women were flexibles such as wool and the root fibers of spruce or cedar. Their most famous woven products were Chilkat robes, which were made from mountain goat wool with symbolic patterns produced by using wool dyed black and yellow. Six months or more

Figure 9-3. | Chilkat woman weaving a dance robe. (From Krause 1885, vol. 1.)

were required to make a single robe. (See Figure 9-3.) Women also wove baskets, making named patterns of geometric design. Men usually worked with predominantly hard materials such as red cedar, copper that was pounded and incised, horn, and ivory. They often included symbolic patterns, especially clan crests, as decorative elements on their totem and house poles, canoe parts, and ladles.

The crest of a clan was carved on any object by a member of the opposite moiety who held a rank equal to that of the individual requesting the carving. By preference this would be a wife's brother; if such an individual was not a capable carver, he could hire someone else of either moiety to make the object. The man who was first asked to do the work paid the craftsman and in turn was paid by his brother-in-law. Carvings produced in this manner fulfilled ritual obligations, and the labor involved was ceremonial.

Among the common elements in symbolic art were symmetrical, stylized figures. Animals most often were the subject matter, but human figures also appeared. Sometimes these seem to have been portraits of individuals. Tlingit art was not as complex as that of those Indians to the south; neither was it so monumental, possibly because of the scarcity or absence of great cedar trees in most of the Tlingit area. The Tlingit did excel in producing a wide variety of imaginative masks used by performing shamans. The human faces might be supplemented with animal figures, which were the familiars of shamans. The carvings on utilitarian objects served to enhance their beauty and bring prestige to their owners. Distortion was an important consideration in Tlingit creations, since traditional forms were adapted to diverse surfaces. Carving a bear on a totem pole was very different from fitting the bear motif on a rectangular vessel, the handle of a horn spoon, or a flat screen painting. Another characteristic of artistic symbolism was that it emphasized features of an animal as a key to its identification. The beaver was characterized by its incisor teeth and tail, while the killer whale was keyed to its prominent dorsal fin. So it was with other totemic representations. Prominent and recurring characteristics included the skeletal motif, the use of joint markers, and the prominence of stylized eyes. Tlingit craftsmen employing these motifs produced outstanding works of art.

CONVEYANCES The most important Tlingit manufacture for subsistence activities was the canoe, normally built in the winter when unhurried production led to attractive and sound vessels. The best wood was from a straight-grained red cedar blown over by the wind or felled by building a fire at the base. With a stone-bladed adz the log was hewn and scraped. To spread the sides of the hollowed log the cavity was filled with water, and hot stones were dropped into it. As the log expanded, pieces of wood were wedged across the gunwales to give the sides the desired degree of flare. The outer sides might be painted with designs and the bow carved. A small canoe carried two or three persons, whereas larger ones held sixty persons and were forty-five feet long. Canoes were propelled with paddles, and an extra-long paddle was used for steering. When not in use, a canoe was covered with mats or blankets to protect it from the sun, and water was sprinkled over the sides. A small canoe made from a cottonwood log was used for fishing and river travel.

Snowshoes were essential for overland mobility during the winter, especially among the Chilkat, who went inland to trade at this time of year. The light maple or birch snowshoe frames were heated over a fire and shaped; the netting was made from rawhide thongs. The shoes were about four feet long and ten inches wide at their broadest point, with rounded toes that turned up at the front and pointed heels.

SUBSISTENCE ACTIVITIES   Terrestrial fauna included both black and grizzly bears, fox, wolves, wolverine, lynx, and deer on some islands. Scattered caribou herds occupied mainland plateaus, and mountain goats as well as mountain sheep frequented the coastal ranges. Smaller species included hare, squirrel, ermine, porcupine, muskrat, and a few beaver. Among the marine mammals were whales, hair and fur seals, sea lions, and sea otter. Of all the fish the most important were the salmon and candlefish (eulachon); halibut, haddock, trout, and herring also were caught. Along the edges of the sea were edible algae, crabs, sea urchins, mussels, and cockles. Avifauna included the bald eagle, raven, owl, and migratory waterfowl that summered in the area.

The subsistence cycle ebbed during the winter, and even March did not offer reliable weather for fishing. Nonetheless, it was during March that the subsistence year began anew. Canoes were repaired, fishing gear was readied, and men waited anxiously. In calm weather they fished for halibut along the coast fronting the Pacific Ocean. Two men fished from a canoe, maintaining about fifteen lines with baited V-shaped hooks and a wooden floater for each. When a fish was hooked, they paddled to the bobbing float, raised the line, and clubbed the fish to death as it was boated. Trout fishing with baited hooks also was important at this time. Following the ice breakup in March women fished for trout with gill nets of rawhide with inflated bladder floats and stone sinkers. One woman usually paddled a canoe as a second handled the drifting net. Clams and mussels were collected in large quantities and were either dried and smoked for future use or were steamed in a pit by pouring water over hot stones and a leaf covering. The pelts of fur animals were prime in March; fox, mink, wolf, and river (land) and sea otter all were sought. Some of these animals were trapped in deadfalls, but sea otter were hunted with harpoon darts.

Candlefish were a rich source of the oil that was drunk during feasts but more commonly served as a dip for dried salmon. These small fish were taken in traps or dip nets in the spring as they ascended rivers. Their processing began by placing the fish and water in a canoe half-buried in the sand. Heated stones repeatedly were dropped into the mass, and as the oil from the cooked fish came to the surface it was ladled into wooden containers. In mid-April herring spawned in shallow bays and were so numerous that they could be impaled on sharp tines set in the side of a pole. The tine-studded pole was drawn back and forth in the water, and the pierced herring were shaken off into the canoe. They either were eaten soon after being caught or were strung on ropes and dried.

Chilkat men traveled inland trading fish oil to Athapaskan Indians in exchange for caribou skins, moccasins, sinew, and lichens to be used for a particular form of dye. During the summer great canoes were paddled south to Haida and Tsimshian country, and in early historic times trading canoes ventured as far as Puget Sound. They carried copper from the Copper River and other local products to exchange for dentalia, haliotis, shark teeth, and slaves.

Sea mammals usually were hunted with harpoon darts that had a line running from the detachable dart head to the shaft. When an animal was struck, the barbed dart head held beneath its skin, and the shaft was dragged through the water as the animal sounded. When it surfaced, the captive was harpooned again or killed with a spear or club. The most important species hunted were dolphin, seals, sea lions, and especially sea otter in early historic times. Only the Yakutat Tlingit hunted great whales, and they seem to have done so under stimulus from their Eskimo neighbors. From the ethnographic accounts it would seem that sea mammal hunting was not very important; neither does it appear that inland hunting was important at most settlements. If bears or mountain goats were pursued, they were cornered with the aid of dogs and killed with bone-pointed spears.

In the late summer berries were collected and stored with candlefish oil in airtight boxes. Salmon eggs, oil, and berries were similarly mixed and preserved. If large land mammals were killed, their flesh usually was cut into strips and sun-dried or else boiled and stored in oil. Some foods were stored for winter at this time of the year, but it was not until September that the winter food supply became a major concern. Diverse species of salmon were taken during the summer, but no great effort was made to catch and dry quantities of them until September. The species available included dog (chum), humpback (pink), king (chinook), silver (coho), and sockeye (red), and these were taken from July through December. The principal salmon-fishing device was a funnel-shaped trap set with the mouth opening downstream. The stream was blocked with a weir, which opened only at the trap. Fish caught in September were cleaned and hung on racks to dry or were smoke-cured in the house. After being dried or smoked, they were bundled and stored. As soon as a house group had obtained enough salmon for the winter, the members left their fishing camp and settled down in their village until April. Very little food was gathered during the winter months, for this was the season of feasting, storytelling, and recreation.

In subsistence activities men dominated as the procurers of edibles, and women played the key role in households. The principal wife of the Keeper of the House was responsible for allocating domestic female tasks. The capacity of these women to process food, especially salmon, was a critical factor in the prosperity of a household. As Frederica de Laguna (1983, 81) has noted, "The whole Tlingit economy of subsistence and luxury wealth rests ultimately on the stores of dried salmon prepared by the women."

DESCENT, KINSHIP, AND MARRIAGE   The people of each kon were divided into two groups (moieties) that were represented in each of the geographical areas. The moieties were named Raven and Wolf, with the Wolf moiety called Eagle in the north; these were in turn divided into named descent groups traced through females (matriclans). The Tlingit considered that certain personality characteristics were associated with the moieties. Raven people were expected to be wise and cautious, and the Wolves quick-tempered and warlike. According to Aurel Krause (1885), the clans of the Raven moiety included the Frog, Goose, Owl, Raven, Salmon, and Sea Lion. Clans of the Wolf moiety included the Auk, Bear, Eagle, Shark, Whale, and Wolf. These lists, although far from complete, identify the important clans in early historic times. Someone who was not a member of any clan was thought of as a stranger and was addressed as uncle or son-in-law, reflecting his in-marrying status. At Klukwan the most important clans were the Wolf and Eagle; these were divided into named subgroups that probably were lineages. Within each clan the lineage with the greatest wealth was most influential. Ideally, the leadership of a lineage was passed from a man to his sister's son, but apparently this practice could be bypassed by appointing a new chief while the old one was still alive. Each settlement with a number of clans represented had more than one chief, but one dominated because of his wealth and personality. A person in one moiety was obligated to seek as a mate someone in the opposite moiety (moiety exogamy); further ramifications of marital arrangements are presented in the section about the life cycle.

Each clan recognized a particular settlement as the place of its ultimate origin. Although a clan was identified initially with a specific site, by the time of historic contact a number of different clans usually were represented in most villages. If a clan was large in a particular settlement, it was divided into lineages represented by house groups. In theory, the clans of each moiety possessed distinctive titles and associated design motifs that only members could use. These might be lent temporarily or even usurped by a more powerful clan. Again in theory, only members of the Raven moiety had the right to the raven design, and only those of the Wolf moiety, the wolf design. House names usually were derived from a clan myth, from the clan's name, or by assuming the name of another clan's house for legendary or historical reasons. Moieties were each divided into a number of matriclans that in turn were divided into house groups composed of nuclear families, again related through females.

Nuclear family unity did not exist among the Tlingit because the parents were of different clans and moieties. Since various clans were represented in most areas, geographical groupings acted as a unit only in those rare instances when a feud affected all sections of the clan. A clan had no common leader or unified territory, and even crests often were identified with localized lineages rather than with the clan as a whole. Finally, each clan included persons ranked as nobles, commoners, or slaves, depending on the social standing of particular lineages.

In the kinship system we find that a single term embraced all the people of the grandparent generation. To these persons the individual was attentive and respectful. The ties between a mother and her son were close even though the son might leave home to live with his mother's elder brother, who was for him the most powerful individual in Tlingit society and his authority figure. Fathers were considered too lenient to discipline their sons effectively, and of course a father did not belong to his son's clan or moiety. Parents especially were concerned about the welfare of a daughter, who would command a large bride price only if she were well-mannered and a maiden; thus, she always was watched by someone. A mother's sister was called by a term for diminutive mother and was treated as one's mother. The "little mother" term was extended to all the other women of her moiety in her generation. A mother was aided and advised in raising children by her sister. A father's sister was termed differently from mother and mother's sister, with the father's sister word extended to all women of her moiety in both her generation and the next descending generation. The father term was unique, but a diminutive word for father was employed for father's brother and extended to the other men of his moiety of his generation as well as the next lower one. A man treated his father's brother with respect, and a girl on rare occasion married her father's brother.

A man ideally married his father's sister, and because she was a potential mate, their relationship was always warm. At one's generational level a man distinguished between older and younger brothers, and these terms were extended to the other men of one's generation and moiety. Older and younger male sibling distinctions were highly important because an older brother had the first rights of inheritance, greater authority, and more ceremonial responsibilities. A woman made the same distinction among sisters. There also was a particular term for a man's sister and one for a woman's brother; these were extended to all the members of that sex of the individual's generation and moiety. Brothers were socially and physically close since they were of the same clan and lived in the same house; with a sister a man was supposed to be distant and withdrawn, although he was concerned for her welfare. A mother's sister's children were termed brother and sister, and the boys were raised in the same household as the mother's children. The terminology for the first ascending generation was essentially bifurcate merging, and the cousin terminology was of the Crow type. One overriding principle governed the kinship terminology of the Tlingit: to separate blood relatives in one's own moiety from those in the opposite moiety. The average adult avoided using relationship terms in direct address in everyday conversation for fear of offending someone, since a great deal of emphasis was placed on an exact ranking of individuals. Thus, nicknames and given names were in common use. Relationship terms were employed primarily on ceremonial occasions. (See Figure 9-4.)

SOCIAL DIMENSIONS The most important social and economic unit was the household, and it had a significant place in the ceremonial life of the clan and moiety. A house group ideally was composed of a male and his brothers, as

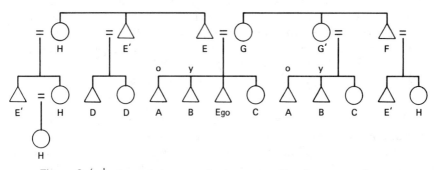

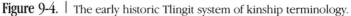

Figure 9-4. | The early historic Tlingit system of kinship terminology.

well as his mother's sister's sons who were classificatory brothers, and the sons of the sisters of these individuals, plus the sons of the daughters of these sisters. All were members of one matrilineage, and there were additionally the in-marrying spouses. A household of this nature functioned as an economic unit, with members working for their common welfare. In particular it was brothers, led by the eldest, the Keeper of the House, who aided one another in feuds, potlatches, and other matters of house group concern. The importance of the Keeper of the House in directing house group life cannot be overestimated. He directed the economic activities of household members and was deferred to by the other men in his residence unit. The house group leader allotted items obtained in trade, was given choice foods, and was freed from any humble form of household labor. It was this man, the eldest brother, who represented the household in ceremonial activities as well as in clan councils. Furthermore, when he died the rights to his position fell to the next oldest person called brother. In addition to the position of Keeper of the House, the wealthiest of the local household heads in any clan, and thus the ranking Keeper of the House, was designated Rich Man. These men more than any others were responsible for the fortunes of their clan units.

Within a household the Keeper of the House and his principal wife outranked all other members. Older brothers and sisters outranked younger ones, while bastards and slaves ranked lowest. The same system prevailed between the members of a leading lineage and of the secondary ones within a clan. The highest-ranking persons were aristocrats, chiefs, and the wealthy. Their status was based on birth, personal character, accomplishments, age, and either inherited or acquired wealth. Commoners as such did not exist; instead, most persons within lineages were junior members who could be ranked against other persons in broadly similar positions. Furthermore, just as households and lineages were ranked against one another within a clan, so it was among the clans of a moiety. The members of lowly clans were poor, whereas those of lofty clans were rich, hosted elaborate potlatches, and had splendid artifacts as clan heirlooms. The leading members of some aristocratic clans reportedly could not sleep at night because they thought so intently about their greatness.

In this social setting, based as it was on rank, classes did not exist. Instead, wealthy and prestigious households competed with one another within a clan and beyond it for high status that changed with the fortunes of these units. In the absence of social classes, the rank of a household, a clan segment, or a whole clan relative to another such unit constantly was being reassessed. The comparative wealth and prestige of these units was tested in numerous ways, such as in potlatches, and, to a lesser extent, in the erection of totem poles.

TOTEM POLES   Of all the fascinating subjects connected with the Northwest Coast Indians, none has received more attention than totem poles. Their size and romantic appeal have long invited description and comparison. The first account of a Tlingit totem pole was the report of Alexandro Malaspina in 1791 about a Yakutat area mortuary pole. The most detailed discussion of Tlingit totem poles is by Edward L. Keithahn (1963), who reports that carved posts in house interiors and mortuary posts existed among the Tlingit in prehistoric times. He also observes that it was not until between 1840 and 1880 that the pole standing apart from a house became common along the Northwest Coast. Even during this era, totem poles were not widespread among the Tlingit, and Keithahn questions whether any great totem poles could have been carved before the general availability of iron-bladed tools; however, a well-developed woodworking technology predates the use of iron tools on the Northwest Coast. The erection of great totem poles became a means for house groups who became wealthy through the fur trade to record their increased prestige. Some aspiring persons did not have the right to carve the heraldic crests, and so they originated new symbols such as the bull and ship, basing their right to use these forms on the claim that they were the first to see them. When the Krause brothers were among the Tlingit in 1881–82, Aurel noted that one totem pole was found among the Chilkat, none among the Sitka and Killisnoo groups, but many at the Stikine settlement near Wrangell.

Tlingit totem poles were erected for varied purposes. The four main posts inside houses normally were not carved, but they were faced with carved pillars or panels, some of which still stood inside modern Tlingit houses at Klukwan in the early 1960s. The pillar faces were carved with clan crests. Often included were abalone shell inlays, and sometimes human hair or ermine fur was attached. A second form was the mortuary pole with a box at the top for the burnt bones and ashes of the dead. In historic times a crest figure was placed on the top of this form, and the ashes were placed in a recess at the back of the pole. A later style of mortuary pole had story figures carved on it. (See Figure 9-5.) A third type was the memorial pole, which most often was raised by a maternal

Figure 9-5. | The earliest illustration of a Tlingit mortuary pole and graves, 1791, for the Yakutat area. (From Malaspina and de Bustamante y Guerra 1885.)

Figure 9-6. | Chief's house with painted front and totem poles in 1899. (Courtesy of the Smithsonian Institution, National Anthropological Archives, neg. no. 43, 548-H.)

nephew or a younger brother in memory of a house group leader who had died. These poles were erected within a year of the commemorated person's death and were not habitually raised at the site of interment. Memorial poles not only honored the dead but validated the succession of the new house group leader. Modern forms of memorial and mortuary poles are tombstones made of granite or marble, with crests carved on them by the monument companies. The heraldic pole, the fourth form, was erected at the front and center of a house, with an oval opening near the base that served as the house entrance. Carved and painted on a pole of this form was a tale associated with the house group. (See Figure 9-6.) The fifth type, the potlatch pole, was the most recent form to develop. These were raised to enhance the prestige of the family group who had accumulated and distributed wealth earned by trading furs or working directly for whites. Such poles recorded the holding of an elaborate potlatch. The sixth and final form was the ridicule pole, which usually was raised to force a house group to recognize and compensate for a debt. For example, one ridicule pole is said to have been carved and erected to shame a white trader for not repaying a potlatch given in his honor.

For the Tlingit, the erection of a totem pole was an end in itself. A pole carved and raised for a particular purpose was unimportant afterward as a physical object. As a pole tilted with age or threatened to fall, it was not supported in any manner. Restoration necessitated ceremonial involvements and an outlay of wealth equal to that expended when the original pole was raised, and therefore it was more sensible to erect another pole and bring even greater honor to the house group. Since poles deteriorated rapidly in this damp area and comparatively few new poles were raised after the turn of the present century, most have rotted away.

The totemic symbols exhibited on poles were associated with one or the other of the moieties, with clans, or with house groups. All of the Raven moiety members employed the Raven design as their primary symbol. The Wolf moiety had the Wolf as its chief totem in the south and the Eagle in the north. Not only the actual crests but the names of animals associated with a clan were important, and their uses were validated through the potlatch system. These honorific names often drawn from the clan or moiety totems tended to pass from great-grandfather to great-grandson. The animals associated with a moiety could be killed and eaten by moiety members, however, and the uniform eating habits of all the tribe indicate no taboo on eating one's totemic species.

ENTERTAINMENT Gambling was an important pastime among adult Tlingit males, and some men were so addicted that they sometimes lost prized possessions and even a wife. The most important form of gambling was a hand game in which one man guessed which hand of an opponent held a uniquely marked stick. The game was played by teams, but only one man of each team handled the sticks at any one time. Other adult diversions included dice games and a ball game in which the purpose was to drive a ball along the tidal flats to the opponent's goal. Boys played a game that involved throwing a stick at a rolling wad of grass. They also wrestled, hunted, and swam for entertainment. A favorite diversion among little girls was to arrange beach pebbles in the form of figures.

POLITICAL LIFE   Conflicts between Tlingit moieties were common, and modern Tlingit liken their disputes to relations between European nations. For real or imagined injuries, either material goods were exchanged or a life was taken. The nature of a settlement depended on the ability of the guilty to pay and the power of the offended to collect. Minor conflicts eventually were settled at feasts that included property settlements. When a person was grievously offended, the only acceptable retribution was the offender's murder, but this was bound to lead to a retaliatory killing. When the persons murdered were of unequal rank, there was the further problem of establishing a value for each death. Sometimes when an individual felt badly wronged and had no means to retaliate, he committed suicide, and his relatives then pressed for compensation. On occasion, clan disputes were settled by a duel between warriors who represented each group. Murders were from ambush, as were raids against other clans or tribes. The only crimes occurring within a clan were incest and witchcraft, each punishable by death. It should be stressed that overall political unity did not exist within a moiety, and some of the bloodiest feuds were between clans of the same moiety.

Raids were conducted to avenge deaths and to obtain slaves. Preparations for impending conflict involved abstaining from all contact with women, and fasting. In addition, a warrior conditioned himself for combat by bathing in the sea, even at the coldest time of the year, and by being whipped by an older man. As a raiding party traveled, it seized property from camps along the way irrespective of whether the residents were friendly or not. A shaman always accompanied the party and predicted events of the near future. Plans for an attack on an enemy community were kept secret, and the foray was launched at dawn. Rod or skin armor protected a man's body; his face was covered with a mask, and his head with a wooden helmet. All the enemy men who did not escape were killed with daggers; women and children were taken as prisoners. A reprisal attack would be expected to avenge the murders. Copper-bladed daggers, spears, and war clubs appear to have been the most important weapons. Scalps were taken at times, and the scalped person's head sometimes was impaled on a stick and exhibited. The men in a war party sang of victory as they returned to their village, and the paddle of each warrior killed was propped up at the spot he had occupied in the boat. To bind peace, hostages might be exchanged and kept for a year or longer. Peacemaking followed a pattern of ceremonialism, which climaxed with the exchange of hostages, termed deer since they were to behave as timidly as these animals.

Most slaves were captured in raids or purchased from peoples to the north or south. Others were the children of indebted men who could find no way out of their dilemma except to offer themselves and as many of their children as necessary to cancel the debt. These slaves, unlike the captives, might be redeemed. Slaves usually were well cared for by their masters since they were a valuable form of property. Yet, some reports picture the lot of slaves as extremely difficult since they performed all odious tasks and might at any time be killed at their owner's fancy. Sometimes slaves were killed to emphasize the importance of their owner—for instance, when he built a new house. To gain prestige one man might kill a number of slaves; his rival would be obligated to kill a greater number, and so it went until one contestant had no more slaves. The ownership of slaves apparently provided prestige more than economic gain. The proportion of slaves to free persons is not known, but ten slaves in a house was a large number.

RELIGION AND SUPERNATURALISM   The Tlingit crystallized their knowledge about the natural world and integrated it into a loosely ordered system. They thought of the world as a flat expanse with the sky as a dome above the earth. They believed that everything that existed in all this space was alive: spirits lived on the sun and moon; stars were the lights of distant towns or houses. They sometimes named clusters of stars, and they identified Venus. A rainbow was thought to be the path of dead souls to the upper world, and the northern lights, human spirits playing. For the Tlingit, everything on earth was possessed by a spirit quality, which had subordinates or helpers; each trait, every fire, and everything that one did had its main spirit and helpers.

Tlingit shamans reputedly were the most powerful on the north Pacific coast, and their effectiveness came from the spirits they controlled. The usual manner in which a clan acquired a new shaman was for the spirit of the clan's shaman to leave his body at death and enter the body of an upstanding clan youth. Nephews who aspired to the position went into trances around the dead man's body, and the one who remained in a trance the longest was most likely to be named the successor. After this supernatural visitation the novice and certain near relatives went into the forest, ate little, and searched for a sign. The most propitious was to see a bird or an animal drop dead; the spirit of this creature henceforth aided the novice. After the young man demonstrated that he had his uncle's power, he inherited the ceremonial equipment.

Shamans controlled the spirits represented on their masks (see Figure 9-7), and while most spirits served specific clans, some could be controlled by any shaman. The latter category included a spirit associated with the souls of persons who were lost at sea or died alone in the forest. The primary protecting spirit was represented as the main figure on a mask, and helping spirits also might appear. A secondary spirit might be posed around the eyes of a mask, thereby increasing the vision of the primary spirit. A shaman neither cut nor combed his hair, and about his neck he wore a bone necklace and a small whetstone, the latter used for scratching his head. A shaman owned rattles that had spirit associations and were used in his performances. The split tongues of animals, especially the river otter, and the claws of eagles were sources of power; both appear to have been placed in bundles of cedar bark, grass, and devil's club. After a shaman bathed, he rubbed himself with the bundle, and he

Figure 9-7. | Shaman's mask of painted wood. (Courtesy of the Field Museum of Natural History, Chicago.)

used it in all his rituals. Among the spirit helpers were those of the sun, the sea, and the crest animals of the shaman's clan. After summoning his spirit helpers, a shaman cured an afflicted individual by blowing, sucking, or passing an object over the locus of the disease, which drew out the cause. Other services of a shaman included locating food sources and predicting the future. A shaman and his family usually lived in a separate residence, and in the forest near the house was his shrine. From time to time shamans retreated for extended periods to intensify their spirit relationships.

A number of charms appear to have been employed by ordinary persons. Made from parts of plants, they were used in such diverse activities as foreseeing the future, attracting a woman, making one wealthy, or improving hunting abilities. A few additional items seem to have served as secular cures, but these were rare and apparently unimportant. In general, it would appear that curing and supernaturalism were shamanistic matters. It is interesting that salmon, which were the all-important subsistence item, were not dealt with in a sacred manner. They simply were accepted as present and were caught and eaten. Even in Tlingit mythology, salmon play a relatively unimportant role; they seem to have been regarded as a constant part of the environment.

Witchcraft most often was performed by obtaining an item intimately associated with the victim and using it in a representation of the victim in the form desired. If a person became ill, the cause was attributed to sorcery, and the offender was named by the curing shaman. Persons accused of being witches usually were women, children, or slaves. They were tortured to extract a confession or even killed if a confession was not forthcoming. An accused witch was bound by clan members and given no food or water for eight days or even longer. If the person was a witch and did not confess, death was expected at this point; if the accused confessed, the bewitching substance was scattered in the sea, and the individual presumably resumed an ordinary status.

LIFE CYCLE   Childbearing was prohibited within the mother's home because it supposedly would bring ill fortune to the men of the house. Thus, a birth took place in a shelter never visited by men. During the birth, slaves and a midwife, always a member of the opposite moiety and preferably the woman's husband's sister, aided the woman. Inside the structure a pit was dug and lined with moss, and a stake was driven into the center of the hole. While giving birth, the woman squatted in the pit, holding the stake. After the birth the umbilical cord was cut and placed in a bag hung around the neonate's neck for eight days; the umbilical cord of a boy later was placed under a tree where an eagle had nested to make the boy a brave adult. To prevent a baby from crying repeatedly, the first cry was caught in a container and buried where many people walked so that it would be smothered as the baby grew. The baby was wrapped in skins, with moss for a diaper, and was tied to a board. The mother carried the cradleboard with her or hung it from a roof beam when she was in the house. She placed woodworm burrowings on her nipples so that as the baby nursed she or he would swallow the burrowings and would be neat in later life. A child was nursed for three or four years and was given its first solids after about a year. An infant born to a woman without a husband normally was suffocated. A baby was named after a maternal ancestor; the name itself was taken from an animal associated with the clan. With the birth of a son the parents referred to themselves by the son's name, as the father or the mother of the son (teknonymy).

Children were encouraged to behave in a manner appropriate to adults of the same sex. They were taught to restrain any sign of emotion, to be dignified and aloof. They were physically punished only if they refused to bathe in cold water during the winter; they were expected to take cold baths daily from the time they learned to walk. When boys moved to the household of their mother's brother, they were switched by this man after bathing and were forced to run up and down the beach. After this physical exertion, they were instructed by older men in the customs and history of the clan and learned certain skills by watching the men perform routine tasks. As a boy grew, he came increasingly under the influence of his maternal uncle and performed tasks for this older man rather than for his father. A boy tended to gravitate toward a particular uncle whom he wished to emulate in his exceptional skills relating to carving, hunting, or the supernatural. The uncle gave honorific names to his young charges and taught them clan lore, but no secret initiations took place. The most important nephew was the oldest, for he would inherit from his maternal uncle not only material property and wives but titles as well. Even while young, boys were free to use a maternal uncle's tools with permission. If a mother died, the father was obliged to place the offspring in the custody of the mother's siblings.

When a girl first menstruated, she was confined to a brush-covered shelter or to a separate compartment in the house behind the heraldic screen. Her face was covered with charcoal, and she was attended by female relatives and a slave if her parents were wealthy. A high-born girl was isolated for a year, and one of lower birth was confined for at least three months. She drank water through a bird-bone tube and went outside only at night, even then wearing a broad-brimmed hat so that she would not taint the stars with her gaze. During isolation her mother instructed her about proper female behavior and taught her clan myths and songs. At the beginning of her confinement, her lip, nasal septum, and possibly her earlobes were pierced by a woman of the opposite moiety. When she came out of seclusion, she wore new clothing, and her slave attendant, if she had one, was freed. The girl would marry soon, and to insure that she remained chaste she slept on a shelf above her parents' bed. The rank of a person was reckoned through both sides of the family and depended largely on the amount of bride price paid by one's father for one's mother; thus, parents attempted to provide a daughter with all the advantages of careful rearing and wealth.

Moiety exogamy was strictly observed, and a match was initiated by the suitor, who used a go-between to approach the girl and her family. If favorably received, he sent presents to his future father-in-law. The most desirable marriage partners, in decreasing order, were a father's sister, brother's daughter, father's sister's daughter, and finally, mother's brother's daughter. In the ideal form of marriage with father's sister, the groom assumed the role of his mother's brother. However, the most common marriage was with a father's sister's daughter, and this was preferred by a young man. Marriage to near relatives served two important functions: to keep wealth concentrated and to provide spouses of nearly equal rank.

A wedding ceremony was held in the bride's house. Here relatives of the groom assembled as he sat in the middle of the floor wearing his most elaborate ceremonial garb. The bride was concealed in a corner of the house and was lured to sit beside the groom by the singing and dancing of the assembled group. The guests were feasted, but this was not a formal potlatch event. A month after the ceremony the couple was considered married. Marriage residence was with the family of either spouse (bilocal), depending on the wealth and standing of the principals. If the couple moved into the man's household, the bride's relatives presented him with property equal to or exceeding the value of that presented by his relatives. A man of wealth might have multiple wives (polygyny), with the first wife holding a rank superior to that of any subsequent spouses; five wives appear to have been the maximum. A woman sometimes had more than one husband (polyandry) but only if the second husband was a brother (fraternal polyandry) or near relative of the first. A widow customarily married her late husband's brother (levirate), and if the deceased husband did not have a brother, his sister's son married the widow. If neither category of individual was available, a widow could marry any man of her former husband's clan. If his mother's brother died, a man was obligated to marry the widow even though he might already have a wife, and he inherited his uncle's wealth. In spite of the ideal that a man should live in the house of his mother's brother, inherit his wealth, and marry his daughter or another person in this line, his father's clan attempted to lure him into its domain. This especially seems to have been true for a boy who had married into the community. When a married woman was seduced, blood revenge might be exacted by her husband, or the seducer might make a property settlement. If the seduction was by a near relative of the husband, the offender was expected to become the woman's second husband.

To outsiders, the Tlingit were not likable. Physicians for the Russian-American Company at Sitka in 1843–44 described the people as follows (Romanowsky and Frankenhauser 1962, 35): "The Kolosches are proud, egoistic, revengeful, spiteful, false, intriguing, avaricious, love above all independence and do not submit to force, except the ruling of their elders." Still, adults were patient and persistent; they never seem to have hurried; and they angered only with provocation. During the fishing season they worked long hours, but winter was a time for leisure. During the winter women made their famous robes and baskets; in general, women appear to have had less free time than men. The social position and respect that a woman commanded depended on her personality and standing within her clan; a woman with abilities was listened to by men. Women had well-defined rights, and relatives who were willing to come to their defense in case of any injustice from the husband's side of the family. An individual, whether male or female, was expected to behave in accord with his or her rank. Persons were of higher rank if their clan was large, wealthy, and powerful.

Still, not all such persons were noble in their behavior, in which case they were treated as though they belonged to a lesser clan. Were a person from a high-ranking clan to behave coarsely as judged by fellow clan members, he or she might be killed by them.

DEATH AND THE MEMORIAL POTLATCH   Death, as a major aspect of the Tlingit life cycle, received dramatic focus in funeral ceremonies, memorial feasts, and especially in memorial potlatches. In combination, these involvements provide great insight into the substance and symbolism of Tlingit culture and merit separate attention. The conventions surrounding the Tlingit dead in the nineteenth century have been reconstructed by Sergei Kan (1983, 1986), who emphasizes the meaning behind the rituals and ceremonies.

Shortly after a death, funeral preparations were begun by members of the deceased person's immediate lineage, who washed the body and dressed it in ceremonial garments; at this point the ghost of the corpse was thought to remain in the dwelling. The wake to follow spanned as many as eight days for an aristocrat or four days for a commoner. The body rested in state at the back of the house, where it was surrounded by items of personal wealth and by lineage or clan possessions. (See Figure 9-8.) Throughout the wake, the principal mourners, who were the lineage members most closely related to the deceased, painted their faces black, fasted, and observed other taboos as they wailed, sang "crying songs," and spoke both to the deceased and about him or her. It was during a wake that close relatives within a matrilineage exhibited their greatest solidarity, concentrating on their obligations to the deceased and to their lineage

Figure 9-8. | A man lying in state amidst his wealth, circa 1890. (From Porter 1893.)

ancestors. One of their more important activities was to burn food and tobacco in the fireplace as offerings to their matrilineal ancestors. At this critical time, paternal and affinal relatives (members of the opposite moiety) performed the necessary household activities, freeing the mourners of routine, and thus polluting, concerns. Members of the opposite moiety also visited the mourners each evening to comfort them and received token gifts for their efforts.

Following the wake, the body was removed through either a temporary opening made in the back of the house or through the smokehole above the fireplace. Males of the opposite moiety cremated the corpse, and some of the person's possessions were consumed in the flames. It was the duty of females of the opposite moiety to collect the ashes and bones, which were put in a box and temporarily placed in a grave house. Afterward, the primary mourners bathed, dressed normally, and hosted the first of a series of small feasts for those of the opposite moiety who had helped them. At these events, food and tobacco again were offered to the matrilineal ancestors of the deceased. This series of small celebrations ended when the spirit of the deceased was believed to have entered the "village of the bones' people," the Tlingit term for the cemetery behind each village. The dead usually were buried behind the house of their clan, although the ashes and bones of aristocrats might be placed in mortuary poles. In their afterlife, the dead were believed to follow the life-style of their immediate descendants. Obligations to the recently deceased did not end until a new box, a repaired grave house, or a mortuary pole was provided for the remains. This was taken care of by the same group from the opposite moiety that had aided the bereaved relatives throughout the wake.

A corpse was considered dangerous to lineage members, and certain distinctions were drawn about it. The flesh, for example, was considered soft and wet, in contrast to the bones, which were thought of as solid and dry. The bones were thought to be intermediate between the flesh and the spirit; by cremation the bones, which were pure, were released from the polluted flesh. A ghost supposedly dwelled with the bones, and through cremation it was made warm in the afterlife. Because the fireplace in a house served as the medium through which to communicate with the deceased of a lineage, the burning of food and gifts was a means by which the living provided for the dead.

The memorial potlatch, held following extended preparations, was to compensate moiety opposites for their help at the time of a death. A second purpose was to end the period of mourning, and a third one was to transfer the names and certain items of property of the deceased to a successor. Kan emphasizes that the Tlingit potlatch centered primarily on the secondary involvement with the dead.

Guests from near and far were invited formally to attend a potlatch; the Tlingit word for potlatch means "to invite." Representatives of the hosts traveled to other villages, where they called out the ceremonial names of the guests before their houses. When the guests arrived, the hosts and guests performed songs and dances of greeting and also staged mock battles. The guests were taken to the hosts' houses, where they remained for about a month, although most potlatches spanned only four days. The formalities began as the hosts cried and sang sad or "heavy" songs belonging to their clan; this represented the final mourning of the hosts for the deceased. The guests in turn offered speeches of condolence, which were accepted by the hosts, who then replied with speeches of gratitude. Afterward the mood of the potlatch changed as participants became less somber. The hosts displayed their ceremonial wealth and sang songs that the modern Tlingit call "national songs"; these described ancestral crests. Guests were feasted repeatedly, and food was put into the fire for the dead of the host clan, who were considered present. To coax the hosts back to a normal state, the guests joked, and lighter songs were exchanged. The potlatch climaxed when the hosts transferred the titles and ceremonial objects of the deceased to his or her successor and others of the matrilineal group. In addition, individual hosts contributed wealth for particular guests. At this time of gift giving, the hosts first named the members of their group. Then, as a particular host offered a gift, he or she could in song or speech convey his or her kin ties to the deceased and thank the guests for their aid. He or she then named the deceased members of his or her lineage or clan before naming the receiver of the gift. The number of gifts that a guest received and their quality became status markers for the rank of that person. The hosts burned some gifts for their lineage ancestors, who supposedly received the noncorporeal essence of these artifacts. As the potlatch drew to a close, the guests prepared to leave with their gifts and with the excess food, thanking their hosts for their kindness in songs and dances of gratitude.

By the end of a potlatch the bones and ghost of the honored dead were thought to be at home in the village cemetery, and the person's spirit had traveled to a distant "village of the dead." Another noncorporeal entity was believed to return to the living to be reincarnated in matrilineal descendants of the deceased, while names, ceremonial titles, and lineage or clan artifacts went to his or her immediate successor. Kan (1986, 198) writes, "The rebirth of the deceased and the death's failure to interrupt the continuity of the matrilineal group were dramatically expressed by addressing the new owner of the title or the regalia as if he were the deceased himself."

The potlatch was foremost a memorial ceremony that allowed a group of hosts to honor all of their recently deceased relatives and individuals, but it also was to honor their particular ancestors. Thus, it provided continuity between the living and the dead of a matrilineal group and gave mourners the opportunity for a profound expression of sorrow. It was during a potlatch, too, that the successor validated his or her claim to a particular rank and status by assuming specific titles or the management of ceremonial equipment. In analyzing Northwest Coast Indian potlatches, ethnographers often have placed the greatest emphasis on competitive aspects, both within the host group and between the hosts and their guests, as individuals or groups vied for rank, status, and prestige. Competition seems to have been most keen among host lineages of nearly equal rank in their efforts to "grab" a high-ranking name, rather than between hosts and guests. Although this element clearly was important, Kan emphasizes that among hosts and guests there also was a major stress on group or individual "love and respect" for ancestors. Finally, reciprocity in different forms was a pervasive aspect of potlatch traditions. Reciprocity between the living and the dead of a lineage or clan and reciprocity between hosts and guests were especially prominent. In sum, a potlatch fostered both competition, to separate, and cooperation, to unite the participants.

Historic Changes in Tlingit Life

Aboriginal Tlingit life inevitably changed as a result of Russian and American influences. The material culture changed with trade, religion changed with the arrival of Christian missionaries, and patterns of settlement, social life, and subsistence changed as the Tlingit adapted to the white economy.

TRADE AND GOVERNMENT   From the time the Russians reestablished themselves at Sitka in 1804 until 1867, Sitka was virtually the only Russian center in southeastern Alaska. During the early period of contact the trade item most desired by the Tlingit was iron. They were keen traders always ready to accumulate material wealth at the expense of someone else. Russians and shipborne European or Anglo-American traders found them cunning and dangerous hagglers. Traders who ventured to deal with the Tlingit were most eager to obtain sea otter pelts. As trading intensified the Indians were increasingly selective. They wanted woolen blankets because they were trading away their animal pelt clothing; they also desired firearms and obtained them from non-Russian sources. Standard early trade items included tobacco; vessels of tin, iron, or copper; axes; glassware; and clothing, especially gaudy uniforms. During the span of Russian contact, the Russians never had any effective political control over the Tlingit. The Indians governed themselves, and the Russians did their best to keep violence to a minimum in the vicinity of Sitka.

In 1867 the formal transfer of Alaska from Russian to American ownership took place at Sitka. The Tlingit were not permitted in Sitka for the ceremonies, but they watched from canoes in the harbor. With occupancy by the United States, fortune seekers of almost every variety arrived, and to the Indians this influx must have been shocking. Russian inhabitants had the option of returning to Russia within three years or becoming United States citizens; nearly all of them left within a few weeks of the transfer. For ten years civil government did not exist, and the U.S. military garrisons stationed at Sitka, Tongass, and Wrangell were a primary source of trouble rather than a means to establish order. The Tlingit clashed repeatedly with the military over Indian deaths that went uncompensated, which led to murders and the destruction or threatened destruction of Tlingit settlements. The most serious difficulties were the failure of the military to understand Indian mores, the wholesale smuggling of intoxicants, and the prevalence of stills among the Indians. After the troops departed, only the U.S. Revenue-Cutter Service vessels and the collector of customs represented legal authority. In 1878 the customs officer at Wrangell stated that within the space of a month he had a thousand complaints from Indians but had no way to deal with them. The difficulty became acute with the influx of miners who wintered that year at Wrangell. In 1880 gold was discovered near the present city of Juneau, which brought more miners and confusion; still, it was not until 1884 that a civil government began to function in the more populous areas of Alaska.

CHRISTIAN INFLUENCE   Russian efforts to Christianize the Tlingit never were very successful because of the strong aboriginal religious system, the restricted area of Russian penetration, and the scarcity of clergy. A Russian priest made an unsuccesful attempt to vaccinate the people of Sitka against smallpox in 1834. In 1835 a smallpox epidemic struck. No Russian died, but half of the Tlingit are estimated to have perished. When the Indians realized their shamans could not cure the disease, they lost faith in these curers and turned to the Russian medical doctor for vaccinations. Europeans introduced syphilis to the area, but according to reports in 1843, it was relatively uncommon.

The Presbyterian Sheldon Jackson was successful in establishing a mission at Sitka in 1878, and a lasting school was founded in 1880. The missionaries found that Tlingit women were more amenable than the men to the strictures of Christianity. Since women were influential in this matrilineal society, working through them became an important avenue of cultural change. Girls also attended school more regularly than boys and became interpreters more often than men, which gave them increased standing and influence. Certain biblical messages the missionaries considered important could be accepted readily by the Tlingit. For example, the sacrifice of Jesus Christ for the sins of mankind was fully comprehensible in terms of compensation. A Tlingit also considered it much better to give than to receive, which again was a Christian ideal but with a different meaning. The people then came to expect gifts as rewards for becoming Christians. When asked to attend church, an old Tlingit was likely to respond, "How much you pay me?" Compensation also was expected by parents when they permitted their children to attend school. The schools were the most important institution for the introduction of systematic change among the Tlingit, and it was through the schools that the missionaries were most successful in winning converts.

One of the diverse problems of concern to the missionaries was the condition of Tlingit slaves. Except in rare instances, slaves were not freed when Alaska was purchased by the United States, because there was no effective governmental representative to force emancipation. The missionaries also took a firm stand against cremation, shamans, the potlatch system, polygyny, and intoxicants.

CHANGES IN SOCIAL LIFE, SETTLEMENTS, AND SUBSISTENCE   By the early 1880s most changes in Tlingit life were material ones. Women had stopped wearing the labrets that had begun going out of fashion fifty years before. Bracelets and finger rings made from silver coins were popular. Skin garments were being replaced by cloth clothing, and woolen blankets were worn as capes. The people raised vegetables, especially potatoes, introduced by the Russians, and

Figure 9-9. | A funeral picture at Yakutat before the Thunderbird House screen of the Wolf clan. The house was built in about 1919. (Photograph by Fhoki Kayomori, courtesy of the Alaska Historical Library.)

women were the gardeners. Intoxicants, unknown in aboriginal times, had become an important trade item. A discharged American soldier taught the people how to distill their own alcohol, and this drink, called hoochinoo, became extremely popular.

Apparently, settlements had begun to consolidate in late prehistoric times, and this pattern became intensified. Early in the twentieth century the forces leading to population concentrations included decline in Tlingit numbers due to war and disease; depletion of fish and game in some areas by whites; the availability of better boats, which provided mobility from a consolidated settlement; the efforts of traders, missionaries, and federal officials to have fewer and larger settlements for more efficient trade, Christianization, and administration; the desire of the Indians to live in larger communities; and the economic advantages of settling near white communities. During the same era, frame dwellings built to house nuclear families became more popular, but at some villages, such as Hoonah, clan houses were occupied until quite recently. (See Figure 9-9.) In 1944 almost all of Hoonah was destroyed by fire, and only after this time were nuclear family residence units constructed.

As mentioned earlier, the house group was the most functionally integrated social unit in aboriginal Tlingit society. It was likewise the most important economic and ceremonial unit within a clan. In aboriginal times, however, each man in a house group supplied pelts for his own nuclear family. In historic times when trapping became a primary means of livelihood, individual trappers built cabins on clan lands and claimed local areas for their exclusive exploitation. The economic focus shifted from the house group to the individual, and the cohesion of the house group began to decline. This was one factor leading to the construction of nuclear family dwellings.

The economy continued to center on fishing and the sea, but new skills associated with fishing were beginning to emerge. The halibut hooks of old were replaced by modern metal hooks. Individuals of both sexes began to work in canneries, and some men were attracted to jobs in the gold mines. A few men hunted sea otter until 1911 when laws were introduced to protect these animals clearly headed for extinction. The skills of the men as woodcarvers and metalworkers led them to manufacture craft items for the tourist trade, and women wove robes and baskets for the same market. Knowing the independent nature of the Tlingit, it is understandable that they were not reliable employees. To be ordered about was to be insulted, and as domestic servants or laborers they usually did not satisfy their white employers.

The potlatch system continued to function, and it retained much of the pageantry and drama known in aboriginal times. The predilection for borrowing and imitating the songs, dances, and costumes of foreigners continued. For example, some shipwrecked Japanese arrived at Dry Bay in 1908; in performances in 1909 a memorable imitation of Japanese clothing and hairstyles was presented by the women. Changes also took place in the form of potlatch gifts. Blankets from traders came to be more important than Chilkat robes; silver dollars were a favorite gift item, followed closely by store-bought food. Totem poles were still erected occasionally. (See Figure 9-10.)

Figure 9-10. | The totem pole erected at the town of Kake in 1971 is 136 feet high, reportedly the tallest pole ever raised. (Courtesy of the Alaska Division of Tourism.)

| Becoming Modern: The Role of Church Brotherhoods

Perhaps the best means of tracing Tlingit entry into the modern world is with a discussion of church-centered voluntary associations. As noted earlier, Christian influence was brought to bear among the Tlingit by both the Russian Orthodox and Presbyterian churches. Missionaries from both churches emphasized eliminating traditional aspects of Tlingit life, and met with resistance because of this. Still, the pressures to convert were great, and most Tlingit did convert sooner or later. The Orthodox church was the first to establish brotherhoods among the converts to help them live a Christian life; the Presbyterian church soon followed suit. In the long run, the Alaska Native Brotherhood was the most successful at promoting Indian assimilation into the white way of life.

RUSSIAN ORTHODOX BROTHERHOODS   As previously mentioned, the earliest effort to Christianize the Tlingit began in 1834, but it made no headway until after the terrible smallpox epidemic from 1835 to 1837. The inability of Tlingit shamans to cope with the disease compared unfavorably with the vaccine used by the Russians and the apparent power of their holy water, and this led to a more favorable attitude toward Orthodoxy. By the end of the Russian era in 1867 over four hundred Tlingit had become at least tacit members of the Russian Orthodox church. Orthodox success was modest in part because the Tlingit had retained their political independence, were able to maintain their religious and social systems, and had limited contacts with priests. Following the purchase of Alaska by the United States, Tlingit participation in Orthodoxy declined, especially after most Russians departed.

In the late 1800s an increase in Orthodox membership was brought about by the Presbyterian missionary efforts mentioned previously. In the 1880s and 1890s especially, the Presbyterians became identified with the civil government centered at Sitka in southeastern Alaska. Its agents were largely anti-native, and at least some of them considered the Orthodox foreign and suspect. The Presbyterians and their allies in government were less sympathetic to traditional Tlingit life than were the Orthodox priests, who increased their missionary efforts in the 1880s. In brief, since the pressures to convert were great, most Tlingit decided it was in their best interest to convert to Orthodoxy, and by the early 1900s most of those who lived in Sitka had become members of this church.

One of the most active Orthodox priests was Anatolii Kamenskii, who felt that the traditional culture of the Tlingit and the excessive consumption of alcoholic beverages by many of them were great barriers to their living a Christian life. His approach was to establish for these people church brotherhoods devoted to both temperance and mutual aid. The idea was not new locally because persons of Russian descent previously had maintained such organizations in the area. The first seventeen members of the initial Orthodox brotherhood for the Tlingit at Sitka were sworn in in 1896; among them were three leaders, one from each of the most notable local clans. Most Tlingit apparently refused to join because of Kamenskii's emphasis on eliminating traditional aspects of Tlingit life. Internal competition led to a second brotherhood at Sitka in 1904, and the competition led to increased membership in both brotherhoods. Despite growth of the brotherhoods, the priests remained unsuccessful in their attempts to stifle traditional Tlingit ceremonial life. (See Figure 9-11.)

Somewhat later, high-ranking Tlingit joined the first brotherhood because they realized the potential for influencing village life in new ways through this organization. Although the Russian church workers were pleased to receive them, their membership meant that compromises were required with respect to brotherhood goals; for example, these aristocrats could not be expected to abandon potlatches. Quite obviously, brotherhood membership was viewed differently by the Tlingit members and Orthodox organizers. High-ranking Tlingit membership conferred legitimacy on brotherhoods in the eyes of other members, and the aristocrats came to be considered in the manner of lineage and clan heads. As Kan notes (1985, 206), "They were expected to be generous, modest, dignified, honest, and careful, but eloquent, in their speech." Most important,

Figure 9-11. | In a Russian Orthodox Church, traditional Tlingit artifacts were placed with the corpse of a high-ranking Sitka Tlingit, circa 1900. (Photograph by Elbridge W. Merrill, courtesy of the Sheldon Jackson College Library, Sitka, Alaska.)

the brotherhoods soon spread from Sitka to other major Tlingit communities. However, following the Russian Revolution in 1917 most Orthodox priests left Alaska, and as a result formal church services became rare. As an alternative, the Tlingit-led brotherhood meetings in villages came to focus the religious lives of Orthodox members. Through the 1950s local Indian leaders of the brotherhoods sustained their view of Orthodoxy with its particularly Tlingit aspects. A net result has been that the process of Americanization was thwarted and varied dimensions of Tlingit culture have thrived into the present.

THE ALASKA NATIVE BROTHERHOOD   The Alaska Native Brotherhood (ANB) was founded in 1912 by ten men, nine Tlingit and one Tsimshian, who all were established Presbyterian leaders strongly committed to integration into white society. An important concept of the ANB, which was intensively studied by Philip Drucker (1958), was its regional focus. Chapters, or camps as they are termed, were organized initially at Sitka, Juneau, and Douglas. By the 1920s chapters had been established in most southeastern Alaskan Indian villages. Within a few years of its organization, a parallel group, the Alaska Native Sisterhood, was formed for women and was made up mostly of local women's church groups. These organizations held a joint annual convention attended by three delegates from each local chapter in addition to the officers and past presidents of the central organization. Decisions were made at other times by an executive committee.

The brotherhood colors were red for salmon and yellow for gold; these were displayed on ceremonial sashes. The official song was "Onward, Christian Soldiers." The primary goal of the organization was stated clearly in the first article of its constitution: "The purpose of this organization shall be to assist and encourage the Native in his advancement from his native state to his place among the cultivated races of the world, to oppose, discourage, and overcome the narrow injustice of race prejudice, and to aid in the development of the Territory of Alaska, and in making it worthy of a place among the States of North America" (Drucker 1958, 165). The aim of the brotherhood clearly was the rapid assimilation of the Tlingit into white society in southeastern Alaska. The Indian's ties with the past had to be broken, and the brotherhood attempted to do this in two different ways. First, it strongly encouraged the use of English; in fact, eligibility for membership was restricted in Article II to "English speaking members of the Native residents of the Territory of Alaska," and the constitution was printed in English. Second, the brotherhood aimed to destroy the potlatch system that represented the aboriginal past in the minds of both the missionaries and the Indians.

Brotherhood policy concentrated on gaining rights for Indians equal to those of whites. The Russo-American treaty of sale stated that the uncivilized tribes, which included most Tlingit and other aboriginal Alaskans, were to be subject to such laws as the United States might pass. With the purchase, no attempt was made to negotiate treaties nor to establish Indian reservations, and therefore the citizenship status of aboriginal Alaskans remained unclear. They were not "wards of the government" in the sense of reservation or treaty Indians. They came to consider themselves as citizens, but the whites in Alaska usually regarded them in the same light as Indians in the rest of the United States. Until they were declared citizens, the Tlingit could not file on mining claims, and this was a cause of resentment. Under the terms of the Dawes Act of 1887 or the Territorial Act of 1915 they could become citizens by demonstrating that they were following a civilized way of life, but few persons sought citizenship under these laws. The issue of citizenship was forced in 1922 by a Tlingit lawyer, William L. Paul, who was extremely active in brotherhood affairs. The case in question involved a Tlingit who had voted previously but whose vote was challenged in a primary election. Through court action by Paul he was cleared of illegal voting. As a result of Paul's efforts, Alaskan Indians, in theory, had full voting rights before the federal government passed the Citizenship Act of 1924 granting full citizenship to all Indians who were not previously citizens. In 1924 William Paul was the first Indian elected to the territorial legislature.

Through the years the ANB actively fought for Indian rights. By 1929 the segregated white-Indian school system in Alaska had been successfully challenged in the courts. About 1929, Indians openly objected to "For Natives Only" signs in the balconies of motion-picture houses, and an effective boycott brought an end to the practice. Not until 1946 did the territorial legislature pass an antidiscrimination law, however. In 1939 the brotherhood organized fishermen's unions under the Wagner Act and soon became affiliated with the American Federation of Labor, although the brotherhood retained its power as the bargaining agent. The ANB attempted to recruit Athapaskan and Eskimo members beginning about 1962, but the Alaska Federation of Natives formed in 1966 became the most active cover organization working for the causes of Alaskan Aleuts, Eskimos, and Indians.

The original brotherhood goal of doing away with aboriginal customs had only partly been reached by mid-century. The principal target for attack, the potlatch, was regarded as heathen and most deplored; however, as Drucker points out, it actually was primarily a social, not a religious, rite. Certain potlatch customs became incorporated into the brotherhood structure; these included addressing persons of the opposite moiety in a ceremonial fashion; fining individuals for infractions; making gifts to the organization; and gift giving by the family of a deceased person for burial services provided by the opposite moiety through the brotherhood. In one sense the ANB served as a new institution through which the moieties reciprocated. Furthermore, although the ideal of speaking English continued, the business meetings of local chapters were sometimes conducted in Tlingit, particularly since the most active members normally were older and were not likely to speak English with ease.

| Land Claims Settlement and the Sealaska Corporation

With land and property rights paramount in aboriginal Tlingit life, it is not surprising that the seizure of their lands by whites without compensation has been a lasting source of contention. Until recently, white settlement in southeastern Alaska was more widespread and intensive than elsewhere in the state, and it seldom had clear legal justification. In 1935, under pressure from the ANB, the U.S. Congress passed legislation permitting the Tlingit and Alaska Haida to sue the United States for land losses. Much of southeastern Alaska had been set aside as the Tongass National Forest, Glacier Bay National Monument, and a reservation on Annette Island for Tsimshian Indians immigrating from Canada. The Tlingit and Alaska Haida sued for $80 million, but the Court of Claims decided that they were entitled to only $7.5 million as compensation for the sixteen million acres of land involved.

The Alaska Native Claims Settlement Act of 1971, described at the close of Chapter 4, included Tlingit claims not settled by earlier court decisions. Under the terms of the act, the Tlingit and Alaska Haida formed one of the original twelve regional corporations, the Sealaska Corporation. (See Figure 9-12.) The largest of the regional corporations, Sealaska has about sixteen thousand stockholders, the vast majority of them Tlingit. Company assets were about $420 million in 1984, and revenues that year were $230 million. These statistics might suggest that the shareholders are economically secure, if not wealthy, yet this is not the case. Most revenues have been reinvested in property or business being promoted by the corporation or consumed by administrative costs, leaving individual members hoping for profits far more often than realizing them.

As far as the typical Tlingit is concerned, the Sealaska Corporation has

Figure 9-12. | The office building built by the Sealaska Corporation in downtown Juneau. (Photograph by the author.)

failed. Mismanagement to varying degrees by Tlingit and whites has caused substantial financial losses, which has led stockholders to develop a negative impression. The well-paid managers are not only a significant drain on corporation finances, but their life-styles have alienated stockholders. One of the major investments, begun in 1980, has been in establishing an outlet for forest products from corporation land. Soon after the project began, however, timber prices fell, and they have remained low. A major subsidiary of Sealaska, Ocean Beauty Seafoods, obtains and processes fish and shellfish, but it too is stagnating, in this case because of declining catches and foreign competition. Furthermore, in 1982 botulism was found in a can of salmon produced by Ocean Beauty. This led to a costly recall and a subsequent lack of confidence in its products. The number of Tlingit employed by the corporation is a focus for stockholder dissatisfaction. The corporation employed about twenty-one hundred of its members in the summer of 1984 and about one thousand in the winter, yet this was only an eighth of the employee total. Thus, "local hire" has been a major issue. The managers are sympathetic but point out that the Tlingit often lack the skills needed for many of the jobs. Also, some companies that have been purchased already had reliable and skilled employees, which is one reason that they could be successful from the start.

Although Sealaska has disappointed shareholders, it has not been able to change its structure or management in significant ways, and thus the future does not appear bright, despite current assets and revenues. Shareholders worry especially because as the Alaska Native Claims Settlement Act now stands, shares can be sold to the public beginning in 1991; non-natives then can acquire Sea-laska assets and land. (Surveys have shown that as many as 40 percent of stock-holders in the corporation might sell their stock in a time of economic stress.) With this in mind, native Alaskans joined in 1983 to form the United Tribes of Alaska. Its primary goal is to strip the corporations of their land-holding rights and place the land under the direct control of individual villages or groups of settlements. By 1985, of the nearly 250 villages under the settlement act, 80 had joined the new organization.

| Comparisons with Other Indians

The Tlingit and Yurok placed far more stress on wealth than did any of the other peoples discussed. They shared a sharp social distinction between rich and poor persons, and they carefully defined the contexts in which wealth changed hands. Salmon fishing was the basis for the livelihoods of both groups, and neither were subjected to starvation. How do we explain their different atti-tudes toward wealth in ecological, social, and political contexts?

The Crow and Tlingit shared matrilineal descent systems, which invites comparison. Special attention should be given to the rights and duties in the matrilineages and matriclans. At the same time, neither of these peoples were strictly matrilineal in all aspects of their social lives, which leads to further com-parisons. One may also strive to explain why the Tlingit, as opposed to the Crow, did not organize at the supraclan or tribal levels.

Note that the Cahuilla, Mesquakie, and Tlingit each had moieties and the Crow had phratries. What were the similarities and differences in moiety and phratry structure or form and in their function or purpose?

This is an appropriate point at which to examine the culture area concept with special reference to three peoples described. The Kuskowagamiut are in the Eskimo culture area, while the Tlingit and Yurok are in the Northwest Coast culture area. Yet, all three populations depended heavily on salmon for food, a parallel suggesting that other aspects of their lives might have been significantly similar. It is profitable to compare the Kuskowagamiut with the Yurok, and more especially with the Tlingit, and to ask whether the Kuskokwim Eskimo life-style might not fit in the Northwest Coast culture area. What important economic, so-cial, political, and religious characteristics did these Eskimos share with both the Tlingit and Yurok, and what did they share only with the Tlingit? After making these comparisons, the reader will be more fully aware of the limitations and the problems inherent in the culture area concept.

| Additional Readings

An overview of Tlingit ethnography for the late historic period is only available in the account published in German by Aurel Krause (1885), translated into English by Erna Gunther (1956). The only comprehensive ethnographic reconstruction for one geographical segment of the Tlingit population is the three-part study of Yakutat area people by Frederica de Laguna (1972). Tlingit social life as it existed at Klukwan is brilliantly described in a book by Kalervo Oberg (1973). The best study of totem poles that has special reference to the Tlingit is by Edward Keithahn (1963), and the best general work to date is the two-volume monograph titled *Totem Poles* by Marius Barbeau (National Museums of Canada, 1950; reprinted in 1964). *Northwest Coast Indian Art* (Seattle, 1965), by Bill Holm, is the most insightful book-length discussion of the subject. The best comparative study of Northwest Coast Indians is *Cultures of the North Pacific Coast* (San Francisco, 1965), by Philip Drucker.

Some recent article-length studies about the Tlingit deserve special recommendation. Sergei Kan (1983, 1985, 1986), whose articles are cited in the text, sets a new standard in his interpretation of symbolism in Tlingit culture. Steve Langdon (*Ethnology* 18: 101–19, 1979) explores Tlingit and Haida adaptations to different environmental settings with particular insight. Kenneth D. Tollefson (*Ethnology* 18:229–47, 1984) proposes a highly useful model for examining Tlingit social change as a process in ethnohistorical contexts.

| Bibliography

Bancroft, Hubert H. 1886. *History of Alaska, 1730–1885. The works of Hubert Howe Bancroft,* vol. 33. San Francisco.

de Laguna, Frederica. 1952. Some dynamic forces in Tlingit society. *Southwestern Journal of Anthropology* 8:1–12.

———. 1960. *The story of a Tlingit community.* Bureau of American Ethnology Bulletin no. 172. Washington, DC. Based on archaeological and ethnographic fieldwork in 1949 and 1950, this report concentrates on the Angoon area and its people. The archaeological data are supplemented by historical records and ethnographic field information.

———. 1972. *Under Mount Saint Elias.* Smithsonian Contributions to Anthropology, vol. 7. This three-part ethnohistory and ethnographic reconstruction, based on fieldwork in the early 1950s, is the most thorough presentation for any segment of the Tlingit population. It is especially strong where Krause is weak, in dealing with the individual in a cultural context.

———. 1983. "Aboriginal Tlingit sociopolitical organization. In *The development of political organization in native North America,* 1979 Proceedings of the American Ethnological Society, Elisabeth Tooker, ed., 71–85. Washington, DC.

Drucker, Philip. 1950. *Culture element distributions: XXVI. Northwest Coast.* Anthropological Records, vol. 9, no. 3.

———. 1955. Sources of Northwest Coast culture. In *New interpretations of aboriginal American culture history,* Clifford Evans and Betty Meggers, eds., 59–81. Anthropological Society of Washington, DC.

———. 1958. *The native brotherhoods.* Bureau of American Ethnology Bulletin no. 168. Washington, DC. The Alaska Native Brotherhood, which has been a Tlingit-dominated organization since its founding in 1912, is the subject matter for half of this study. The second half of the volume is devoted to a similar organization in British Columbia. Drucker's largely historical study is a highly significant contribution since it is devoted to one of the organized efforts by the Tlingit to promote assimilation into white Alaskan society.

Federal Field Committee for Development Planning in Alaska. 1968. *Alaska natives and the land.* Washington, DC.

Fraser, Douglas. 1962. *Primitive art.* Garden City.

Goldschmidt, Walter R., and Theodore H. Haas. 1946. *Possessory rights of the natives of southeastern Alaska.* Report to the commissioner of Indian affairs. Mimeo.

Jackson, Sheldon. 1880. *Alaska.* New York.

Jonaitis, Aldona. 1986. *Art of the Northern Tlingit.* Seattle.

Jones, Livingston F. 1914. *A study of the Thlingets of Alaska.* New York.

Kamenskii, Anatolii. 1985. *Tlingit Indians of Alaska.* Sergei Kan, trans. Fairbanks.

Kan, Sergei. 1983. Words that heal the soul. *Arctic Anthropology* 20(2):47–59.

———. 1985. Russian Orthodox brotherhoods among the Tlingit. *Ethnohistory* 32: 196–222.

———. 1986. The 19th-century Tlingit potlatch. *American Ethnologist* 13:191–212.

Kashavaroff, Andrew P. 1927. How the white men came to Lituya and what happened to Yeahlth-kan who visited them. *Alaska Magazine* 1:151–53.

Keithahn, Edward L. 1963. *Monuments in cedar* (rev. ed.). Seattle. This study is particularly useful in any attempt to trace the origins, antiquity, and development of various forms of totem poles.

Krause, Aurel. 1885. *The Tlingit Indians.* 2 vols. Jena. Translated edition, Erna Gunther, trans., American Ethnological Society, 1956. The 1881–82 field study by Aurel and Arthur Krause, written by the former, is the standard Tlingit source. The breadth and balance of the study make it the first to be consulted in any serious study of the Tlingit.

Lisianskii, Urey F. 1814. *A voyage round the world.* London.

McClellan, Catharine. 1954. The interrelations of social structure with northern Tlingit ceremonialism. *Southwestern Journal of Anthropology* 10:75–96.

Malaspina, D. Alejandro, and Don Jose de Bustamante y Guerra. 1885. *Political-scientific trip around the world* (translated title). Madrid.

Niblack, Albert P. 1890. The Coast Indians of southern Alaska and northern British Columbia. *Annual Report of the Smithsonian Institution, 1887–88,* 225–386. Washington, DC.

Oberg, Kalervo. 1973. *The social economy of the Tlingit Indians.* Seattle. This book is based on fieldwork at Klukwan in 1931–32 and stands beside the studies of Krause and de Laguna in terms of merit. Oberg's discussions of the social system and economy are outstanding for their clarity and breadth.

Olson, Ronald L. 1967. *Social structure and social life of the Tlingit Indians of Alaska.* University of California Anthropological Papers, no. 26.

Porter, Robert P. 1893. *Report on population and resources of Alaska at the Eleventh Census: 1890.* Washington, DC.

Romanowsky, S., and E. Frankenhauser. 1849. Five years of medical observations in the colonies of the Russian-American Company. *Medical Newspaper of Russia* 6:153–61. St. Petersburg. (Translated from German and reprinted in *Alaska Medicine* 4:33–37, 62–64, 1962.)

Swanton, John R. 1908. Social condition, beliefs, and linguistic relationship of the Tlingit

Indians. *Bureau of American Ethnology, 26th Annual Report,* 391–512. Washington, DC. This study based on fieldwork in 1904 at Sitka and Wrangell is not a balanced ethnography, nor does it purport to be, but it does serve as a good supplement to the works of Krause and Oberg.

Veniaminov, Ivan. 1984. *Notes on the islands of the Unalaska district.* Lydia T. Black and R. H. Geoghegan, trans.; Richard A. Price, ed. Kingston, Ontario.

Wardwell, Allen, compiler. 1964. *Yakutat south.* Chicago.

Willard, Mrs. Eugene S. 1884. *Life in Alaska.* Philadelphia.

Yarrow, Andrew L. 1985, Mar. 17. Alaska's natives try a taste of civilization. *New York Times Magazine.*

Young, Samuel H. 1927. *Hall Young of Alaska.* Chicago.

10 The Hopi: Farmers of the Desert

Your beautiful rays,
may they color our faces;
being dyed in them,
somewhere at an old age
we shall fall asleep old women.

Woman's prayer to the sun, for a newborn girl
Hopi*

ALTHOUGH Plains Indian warriors seem to some people to have the most romantic appeal of any Indians, they shone only briefly in their bellicose glory. Indians
who farmed in the Southwest and lived in pueblos probably better typify American Indian life, or at least have been more lasting than most Indian groups and
provide a better basis for a stereotype of Indians. Massive pueblos, painted pottery, colorful ceremonies, and kachina dolls characterize these people to most
outsiders. While Plains warriors have faded into memory, Pueblo peoples, such
as the Hopi of northeastern Arizona, continue to live in their desert setting, and
some of them have clung tenaciously to their identity as Indians. Their culture
does not survive in all its past vitality, but it is remarkable that they have endured
as a people at all given the centuries of forces bent on their destruction. As an
example of the persistence of their ways, Christian missionaries began working
among the Hopi in 1629, but by the 1950s fewer than 2 percent of the Hopi were
practicing Christians.

I have singled out the Hopi for attention for additional reasons. Nowhere
else are Indians so intimately associated with one locality. Nowhere else among
Indians do the past and present blend into such a consistent whole. Furthermore, a wealth of information exists about the Hopi. They long have attracted
the attention of ethnographers, resulting in detailed studies of their lifeways. The
best American Indian ethnography, in my opinion, is the Hopi study *Old Oraibi*
by Mischa Titiev (1944).

People, Population, Language, and Habitat

Hopi, the term that these people applied to themselves, means "good" or
"peaceful," the ideal for all individuals in this society. The Hopi language is of the
Aztec-Tanoan phylum and the Uto-Aztecan family. The aboriginal population of
the Hopi numbered approximately twenty-eight hundred. After dropping to two
thousand in 1907, it has now reached about seven thousand. Their Arizona
homeland is one of deserts and plateaus with sporadic and unpredictable rain-
fall. (See Figure 10-1.) The only reason the Hopi and their ancestors have been
able to farm in this arid area is that there are seepages. Rainwater from the upland sandstone region seeps down to a layer of shale and emerges at the ends of
mesas in moist areas and springs. At higher elevations on the mesas, juniper and
scattered pinyon grow. This flora is replaced by grassland nearer the valley
floors, and in the lower sections desert vegetation, including saltbrush, grease-
wood, and sagebrush, dominates. In damp localities or along irregularly flowing
streams, cottonwoods and willows grow.

Early Contacts with the Spanish

In July of 1540 the Hopi saw the first Spanish. A small group under Pedro
de Tovar came from the pueblo of Zuni, where Francisco Coronado, the expedition leader, rested. When de Tovar arrived at one of the eastern Hopi settle-

---

*A prayer recited at the edge of a village with the offering of a meal five days after birth.

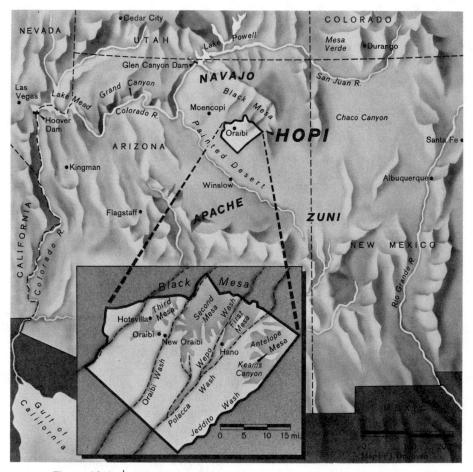

Figure 10-1. | Homeland of the Hopi Indians.

ments, he was met with hostility; he attacked the village and defeated the Indians. De Tovar then peacefully visited the six other Hopi communities, and later a party of the same expedition traveling to the Grand Canyon passed through Hopi country without meeting any resistance. The Spanish search for gold led Antonio de Espejo to enter the region in 1583, and he was welcomed by the people in the five villages. More lasting contact was made by Juan de Onate in 1598 when the Hopi peacefully submitted to the authority of the Spanish king. The Spanish hoped to make these people Christians, but Franciscan missionaries did not settle among them until 1629. Churches were built at three settlements, and two more missionaries joined the first three. The Franciscans reported great progress, but the poisoning of one of the priests in 1633 suggests that not all Hopi were contented charges. Vigorous Franciscan efforts to destroy the old Hopi religion led to cruel punishments for backsliding Indians. In 1655 a missionary caught a Hopi performing an "act of idolatry." The man was beaten severely in public and again beaten inside the church; turpentine was applied to his body and ignited, and he died. The missionary was relieved of his post, but no punitive action was taken against him.

In 1650 the Hopi refused to join the other Pueblo peoples in a revolt against the Spanish, but they supported fully the Pueblo Revolt in 1680. Their major contribution was to kill the four missionaries stationed among them. The Hopi indirectly aided the insurrection by permitting Indian refugees from the Rio Grande pueblos to live among them when the Spanish struck back; two communities were constructed for these friendly allies. The Hopi feared Spanish reprisals, and three villages were relocated on mesa tops that could be better defended than their valley bottom settings. The Spanish returned in 1692, and when the Indians willingly swore to support the Spanish king, peace was established. By 1699 the Spanish were in firm control of the Rio Grande pueblos, and this led a Hopi faction that favored Catholicism to request missionaries from the authorities at Santa Fe. A missionary visited, but after he left, the community was summarily destroyed by the anti-Catholic Hopi faction. The men who resisted were killed; their wives and children were scattered among the remaining settlements. The pagan Hopi under the leadership of a man from Oraibi went to Santa Fe and told the Spanish governor that the Hopi would make peace if they were permitted to continue their old religion. This, however, was unacceptable to the Spanish. In retaliation for the murder of Christian Hopi the Spanish in 1701 attempted to defeat the Hopi in battle, but the smallness of the Spanish force and the adequate defensive positions of the Hopi led the attackers to withdraw. The Hopi retained their freedom not so much by their military skill and determination as by the distance that separated them from Santa Fe and the difficulties the Spanish were having with other Indians. Throughout the 1740s and early 1750s the Hopi thwarted all Spanish efforts to bring them under effective control.

Beginning in 1755 the course of Hopi history gravitated increasingly toward accepting the Spanish. When a sequence of dry years exhausted their reserve of food, they were faced with hunger. By 1779 many of them had abandoned their homeland and moved among the Zuni to survive. The next year most Hopi were so scattered that the local population was reduced to about eight hundred persons. In the midst of this struggle came the smallpox epidemic in 1781. In this same year, however, rain was plentiful, and the bountiful crops made it possible for the population to reconsolidate. Pressures by marauding Navajos forced the Hopi to request aid from the Spanish in 1818, but the Spanish, who were faced with their own survival problems, were unable to help. The most striking characteristic of Hopi historical contacts with the Spanish was the ability of these Indians to withstand Spanish pressures toward acculturation, particularly in the religious sphere. Hopi resistance against the Spanish evidently was not unanimous, but the pro-Spanish faction seems to have been of minor importance.

| Aboriginal Life of the Hopi

Unlike the peoples discussed in earlier chapters, the Hopi are sedentary farmers whose lives center in small, stable villages. They, more than any other Pueblo people, display an appealing continuity with the past. Their ancestors settled in northern Arizona at least a thousand years ago, and the Hopi village of Oraibi is one of the oldest continuously occupied settlements north of Mexico.

ORIGIN MYTH   In primeval times, according to a myth recorded at Oraibi, there was no light or living thing on earth, only a being called Death. Three caves beneath the earth's surface likewise were engulfed in darkness. In the lowest cave people existed in crowded and filthy conditions. Two brothers, The Two, lamented the plight of the people and pierced the cave roof; they grew one plant after another trying to reach the second world. After a particular type of cane grew tall enough, the people and animals climbed it to the second cave world. This level finally was filled with people, and they ascended to the third cave. Some climbers fell back to the second world, as had also happened in the ascent from the first cave. In the third cave the darkness was dispelled by fire found by the brothers. The people built houses and kivas and traveled from one place to another. Great turmoil developed here when women neglected their duties as wives and mothers, preferring instead to dance in the kivas. Finally the people, along with Coyote, Locust, Spider, Swallow, and Vulture, emerged at the fourth level, which was the earth. They wandered about with only torches to light their way. Together the people and the creatures with them attempted to create light. Spider spun a white cotton blanket that gave off some light. The people then processed a white deerskin and painted it turquoise. This skin was so bright that it lighted the entire world. The painted deerskin became the sun, and the blanket was the moon. Stars were released from a jar by Coyote.

Once the earth was lighted, the creatures realized that the land area was limited by surrounding water. The Vulture fanned the water with its wings, and as the waters flowed away, mountains appeared. The Two made channels for the waters through the mountains, and canyons and valleys were formed. The people saw the tracks of Death, Masau'u, and followed them to the east. They caught up with Masau'u, and a girl conspired with him to cause the death of a girl she envied. This was the first death among people, the conspirator was the first witch, and her descendants became the witches of the world. The dead girl was seen living in the cave world below the earth, which had become an idyllic place. The witch caused conflicts with people who had emerged on earth before the Hopi, particularly the Navajo and Mexicans. Another deity helped people by making their maize and other seeds ripen in a single day. Of the two brothers who led the people from the underworld, the younger brother was the ancestor of the Oraibi people. The older brother went east but promised to return when the Hopi needed him. After many generations and in accord with this promise the older brother's descendants, the Bahana, were to return when the Hopi were poor and in need. The Bahana would be rich and would bring food and clothing for the Hopi. The Hopi would reject the Bahana, but the Bahana would treat them kindly.

APPEARANCE AND CLOTHING   A Hopi girl wore her hair long until she passed through a puberty ceremony; it then was put up in two disk-shaped bundles, one over each ear. After she married, her hair was parted in the middle and worn long again. A woman's clothing consisted of a wraparound cotton blanket that passed under her left arm and was fastened together over the right shoulder. This garment extended a short distance below her knees, and she wore leggings as well as moccasins. Men wore headbands to control their hair, which might be relatively short or long and knotted behind the neck. Everyday male clothing included a breechclout of deerskin or cotton cloth and a cotton cloth kilt, belted at the waist. A man also might wear deerskin leggings and moccasins or sandals.

SETTLEMENTS AND MANUFACTURES   At the south end of Black Mesa are three tongues of land, and on the westernmost, called Third Mesa, the village of Oraibi is located. (See Figure 10-2.) This is the community where Mischa Titiev worked, and whenever possible the descriptions will focus there. The pueblo is laid out in a series of eight nearly parallel streets with scattered kivas (ceremonial structures) and a plaza between two streets. In aboriginal times the square houses were made from stones dressed and set in place for the floor and walls by the men. The roof beams were placed on the uppermost course of stones, and the women for whom a house was being built prepared and applied a mud plaster to the inner walls. A woman and her friends completed the roof by adding brushwood, grass, and finally mud. The dwellings were owned by women, and a new one usually was built next to the residence of the woman's mother or another close female relative. Houses were windowless, and no doors opened on the street. They often were multistory with access through an opening in the ceiling, beneath which was placed a notched log ladder. On one side of a room were bin metates or milling stones of different degrees of coarseness for grinding maize (see Figure 10-3), and fireplaces completed the furnishings. Rooms without any outside opening often were used for storing food and material goods. A kiva or ceremonial structure was a rectangular subterranean room entered by descending a ladder from an opening in the roof. The section of the floor where observers sat was slight raised, and the remaining portion included a fire pit and sipapu, a hole in the floor through which spirits were thought to enter. Along most walls were stone compartments that held sacred objects. At Oraibi there were about fifteen kivas, each owned by a matriclan.

The most elaborate manufactures of the Hopi were textiles, usually woven by men. They carded and spun cotton into thread and then wove textiles on looms in their homes or in kivas. The fiber often was dyed black, green, orange, red, or yellow. On a vertical loom suspended between the ceiling and the floor they made square and rectangular cloth for blankets. Belts were made on a waist

Figure 10-2. | The village of Oraibi with melons and peaches drying on the roof in the foreground. (Courtesy of the Southwest Museum, Los Angeles, CA.)

loom attached to a beam at one end and to the weaver's waist at the other, being held taut with his body. Women wove only rabbit-skin blankets on vertical looms. The most important textiles woven by men for women were for wedding robes, belts, dresses, and shawls. For themselves, men wove kilts and sashes for ceremonies, and blankets, kilts, and shirts for daily use.

The pottery made by women was either undecorated ware for cooking and storage or polished and decorated forms for other uses. Clay was collected from nearby deposits, soaked, and kneaded into a paste, with ground sandstone added to the paste of utility wares. Long coils were added to a flat clay bottom, and each seam was pinched to join the preceding piece and then obliterated by hand-smoothing. The completed containers were dried, and utility ware was fired without further processing. A pot to be decorated was smoothed and thinned with a piece of sandstone after it had dried. The vessel then was moistened and polished with a stone, later to be painted. Pottery was painted black, orange, red, white, and yellow, and the prevalent designs were quite similar to those used in early historic times, when old designs were revived after falling out of use. In 1895 an archaeologist excavated an abandoned Hopi pueblo, and one of his Indian workmen was the husband of a woman who was widely recognized as one of the best Pueblo potters, Nampeyo. She found the beautifully executed, painted pottery unearthed at the site fascinating and studied the sherds to

Figure 10-3. | A Hopi woman grinding grain in a bin metate. (Courtesy of the Southwest Museum, Los Angeles, CA.)

become familiar with the patterns. She developed a style based on these originals, and it became very popular.

SUBSISTENCE ACTIVITIES   The Hopi economic year began when crops were planted. The time to sow was established by a Sun Watcher, who based his determination on the occurrence of the sunrise at a particular spot on the horizon. At the stipulated time, the men of a matriclan planted as a group, and this work unit continued through the harvest. A married man planted the clan land allotted to his wife and her immediate family. Men owned crops until the harvest was taken into a wife's house; afterward it was her property. Farmland at the foot of Black Mesa was watered by ground seepage or from stream overflow (floodwater farming). A plot was prepared by trampling the weeds or cutting them with a broad-bladed implement and breaking up the soil with a pointed stick. Maize, the most important crop by far, was planted in holes made with a digging stick. Ten to twenty seeds were dropped into a single foot-deep hole, and if a planting did not sprout in about ten days, it might be reseeded. As plants grew they were weeded, and the soil was loosened about the roots. Fields, which were about one acre in extent, were not rotated nor was the maize hilled. Beans sometimes were planted among the maize stalks but more often were raised in separate plots. Squash and cotton too appear to have been raised in separate acreage. During planting and harvesting, someone impersonating Masau'u, the God of Death, was usually present, but there were no specific planting and harvest rituals. Most other Hopi subsistence activities also were group endeavors, organized by individuals or societies to embrace some or all community members. One cooperative, communal task was to clear sand and debris from village springs that were owned by the village chief but used by everyone.

About forty types of plants were cultivated in the 1930s. Of this number, only five species were aboriginal (kidney and tepary beans, maize, cotton, and squash); four others may have existed prior to Spanish times but more likely were postcontact domestics (Aztec and lima beans, gourds, and sunflowers). Five species were introduced during the Spanish period (chili peppers, onions, peaches, watermelons, and wheat); all others were introduced by Mormon farmers or other Anglo-Americans. Ten species of wild plants were cared for by the Hopi, but the seeds apparently were not sown regularly. Seeds from two different species of wild tobacco were sown when necessary to provide sufficient leaves for ceremonial uses. Likewise, wild dock root was used for dye, and the seeds sometimes were planted. Fifty-four different wild plants were eaten, fifty were used to make or decorate artifacts, sixty-five were used medicinally, and forty had ceremonial or magical purposes. Although there is some overlap in these listings, the Hopi obviously used a wide variety of plant species. About two hundred wild flowering plants grew locally, of which half commonly were used.

The primary staple, maize, was the symbol of life to the Hopi, and they grew three varieties. In early historic times the flint variety was important since the hull of each grain was hard and not easily destroyed by weevils in storage. The flint variety was so difficult to grind, however, that it declined in importance. The most popular variety of maize in recent times has been the flour type, which is grown by every farmer. Sweet corn was raised in small quantities, with only two different named strains.

A wide variety of dishes were prepared from maize. The harvested product usually was stored on the cob and shelled as needed. Ground maize was made into gruel, dumplings, soups, and bread. Hominy was prepared by soaking shelled maize in a mixture of juniper wood ash and water, then boiling the grains and washing them to remove the hulls. Maize also was roasted on the ear, parched, or baked in pits. One important food made of maize, *piki,* was used as bread. It was made from a finely ground cornmeal mixed with water, using ashes as leavening, and was cooked on a special stone slab over a fire. The stone was heated and greased, and the bluish-gray liquid was poured onto it. After cooking, the piki was folded or rolled into "loaves" for later consumption. It often was eaten by dipping one end into liquid food and biting off the moistened portion.

Compared with farming rituals, the ceremonial preparations for a hunt were elaborate. The most important species hunted were antelope, cottontails, and jackrabbits. Rabbits often were hunted in the late summer, when crops did not require attention. A man organizing a hunt could be from any clan so long as he made prayer offerings to the God of the Hunt. Details of the time for the hunt were announced by a crier, and the next day the organizer performed further rituals. In the hunt, men formed a surround and moved in until they could kill the encircled animals with throwing sticks (boomerangs, rabbit-killing sticks) or with hurled clubs. The surround was formed repeatedly, and the game continued to be taken until the leader called an end to the hunt. When they returned to the village, each man gave his kill to his mother, sister, wife, or father's sister. The recipient made a ritual offering to the dead animal to restore the game to the God of the Hunt.

Before hunting antelope, deer, and mountain sheep, the organizer as well as all the others in the party made prayer offerings, and there was ritual smoking. The surround method was used to capture these animals in aboriginal times. The pattern seems to have been to run down and suffocate an antelope. A deer apparently was shot with arrows or clubbed to death but not stabbed. Once again, a ritual propitiation of the deceased animal occurred. Coyote hunts were conducted by kiva members collectively, and as usual the surround technique was employed. After a hunt each coyote was taken to the kiva and given a lighted corn husk cigarette and spoken to as a child before the owner took the animal home.

DESCENT, KINSHIP, AND MARRIAGE   As already indicated, the Hopi traced descent through females (matrilineal), and grooms always joined the households of their brides (matrilocal). Matrilineages were very important in social terms, and matriclans were overwhelmingly important ceremonial units.

A male individual termed his mother the same as his mother's sister and did not distinguish between them in normal conversation. Father and father's brother were termed alike, but mother's brother was termed differently. The designations for females in the first ascending generation paralleled those for males, because father's sister was distinguished from mother and mother's sister (bifurcate merging terminology). This usage is reasonable since mother and mother's sister were of the same clan, and father was in the same clan as father's brother. In the cousin terminology, parallel cousins were termed as siblings, whereas mother's brother's children were termed as one's own children, and a father's sister's daughter was called the same as father's sister. Finally, a father's sister's son was termed father (Crow type cousins). (See Figure 10-4.) The most distinguishing characteristic of the cousin term is the ignoring of certain generational distinctions. The kinship terminology provided the framework for lifelong responsibilities, with particular forms of behavior expected in each set of relationships. One of the most bitter overt displays of anger against a relative was to renounce kinship ties.

SOCIAL DIMENSIONS   The Hopi knew of no term for household, yet this social unit dominated and guided the life of each individual. A child was born into this unit and retained a strong emotional identity with it throughout life. The household consisted of a core of women—grandmother, daughters, and

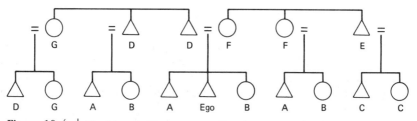

Figure 10-4. | The historic Hopi system of kinship terminology.

daughters' daughters—plus unmarried sons and in-marrying husbands. All except the husbands belonged to the same matriclan; also members of the lineage were those males born into the unit but now married and living in the houses of their wives. When the members of a household outgrew its space, a room was added on to accommodate the newer members. This adjacent household retained its ties with the parent matrilineage, held farmland in common, and worshipped a common fetish (sacred bundle). The lineage fetish was in the custody of the oldest female lineage head, and the associated ceremonies were conducted largely by the old woman's brother or son. These ritual obligations were passed down the most direct maternal line. Common lineage problems were discussed at the original lineage residence, and it remained the heart of the matrilineage, sometimes even after it was abandoned as a residence. From a leading matrilineage, with the greatest rights and duties, subordinate (daughter) lineages developed. As a daughter lineage grew, it might become socially removed from the original group and lose the underlying ties. The distant lineages would become separate clans if they created new bundles and acquired distinct names. Members of a named group who traced their ties through the same bundle formed a matriclan even though they could not trace connecting genealogical ties.

By 1906, about thirty named matriclans existed at Oraibi, a number that represented splits as well as the possible settlement there of new clans. The names, including Bear, Bow, Butterfly, and Lizard, were linked with happenings in mythological times or referred to clan ancestors. These ancestors were termed *wuya* and might or might not be tangibly represented by a clan bundle. A bundle sometimes included more than one wuya; this led to alternative names for the clan and probably represented the consolidation of two clans. Clans formed nine larger groups (phratries) that were associated with the mythological past but not named; possibly, clans of the same phratry stemmed ultimately from the same lineage base. Members of the same phratry shared common ceremonial and land-holding interests, and they could not marry within the group (phratry exogamy).

POLITICAL LIFE   Overall village control was in the hands of the village chief and the war chief. The village chief was from the Bear clan, and a sacred stone in his possession verified his authority. The stone reportedly was brought from the underworld by the legendary village founder. The stone was engraved with motifs, including human figures, and their interpretation was the basis for a division of lands among the clans. The stone was inspected as a part of each Soyal Ceremony that the village chief headed. The village chief had not only the greatest sacred responsibilities at Oraibi but important secular duties as well. He settled land disputes, the most important differences between villagers. His sacred duties, in addition to those dealing with the Soyal Ceremony, included offering prayers for village welfare. It was the village chief who remained up late each night smoking and musing about pueblo conditions after most people had gone to sleep. For any critical community matter, his advice was sought, although he could not compel the actions of others. The office of the village chief was passed to a brother or to a sister's son after a long period of training. The village chief wore no badge of office, but he had a distinctive style of body painting for certain ceremonies and a sacred stick or cane of authority.

The only person at Oraibi with permanent power was the war chief, who attained his position by being the most outstanding warrior. He had the right to inflict either verbal or physical punishment for nonconformity. On occasion, when parties of men were organized for a community project, certain kachinas, as friends of the gods, assembled the workmen and directed their activities. A lazy man might be reprimanded or even in extreme instances beaten by a kachina. The authority and power of the overt leaders never extended beyond the village. No means existed for uniting the Hopi as a tribe; in fact, the only time they clearly joined in a common cause was during the Pueblo Revolt of 1680.

The Hopi prided themselves on being peaceful people who disliked shedding the blood even of animals, and yet they were organized for armed conflict. They fought to defend their pueblo, and the role of a warrior was recognized as dangerous, important, and necessary. In primeval times, when the Hopi supposedly emerged from the underworld, the Kokop and Spider clans introduced a warrior society. Every man was a member, but not all were of the same rank. Members were divided into ordinary warriors and stick-swallowers. Boys were trained for warfare with a rigorous program of cold baths, races, archery practice, and rising early. The Warrior Society held a ceremony each year during the late fall, using the sacred equipment held by the Spider and Kokop clans. The two days of rituals involved making prayer objects, ritual smoking, offering prayers, and building altars. A war medicine was prepared and drunk, after which were exhibitions of stick-swallowing by one branch of the membership. For the real warriors, those who acknowledged killing and scalping an enemy, a special initiation that involved fasting and secret rituals took place.

Warfare was said always to have been defensive. Men went into battle clad in ordinary clothing but with the addition of caps made from mountain lion skin to which eagle feathers were attached. A warrior fought with a bow and arrows, stone club, spear, and throwing stick. Before a battle the men prayed to Masau'u and to long-dead warriors, and they also sang songs to make themselves brave. Armed only with a stone club, the war chief led them into conflict. A slain enemy was scalped to the accompaniment of a scalping song, and scalps were carried into the pueblo on poles. A Navajo scalp was considered worthless, but one from an Apache or Ute was valued. The permanent resting place for a scalp was in the home of its taker. A scalp was washed with yucca suds and intermittently "fed" by its owner.

RELIGIOUS SYSTEM   The Hopi religious system was precise, the ceremonial round was exacting, and the kachinas played a vital ceremonial role. To maintain the balance in nature and to sustain human relationship with the gods, each individual was obligated to contribute to the best of her or his ability. Through this contribution an individual expressed a desire to be *hopi* or good, but being hopi involved more than goodness alone. A Hopi ideally was cooperative, self-effacing, and nonaggressive, and the particulars of such behavior were spelled out in detail. A Hopi had moral and physical strength, good health, and accepted collective responsibilities while concentrating on good thoughts. Conversely, an evil or bad person was *kahopi*, with personality traits opposite those of the ideals.

Central Concepts   The association of people with the gods was built around the concept of continuity between life and death. An integrated relationship was maintained between the living and the dead, with the spirits of the dead supposedly becoming clouds that brought rain to the living. The activities of kachinas on earth and in the underworld were thought to benefit the living. To the Hopi there was a duality in being human. People possessed a physical body and a "breath-body," spirit or soul. When an individual died, preparations for burial were in many ways the same as for the newborn; the corpse was sprinkled with cornmeal, bathed, and given a new name. The breath-body was believed to journey to the underworld, where its existence was like that of the Hopi on earth, except that when the dead consumed food they took only of its essence. Because of their weightlessness, the dead supposedly could rise into the sky and become clouds. By bringing rain, the deceased aided the living in a very meaningful manner. The God of Death, Masau'u, logically was a god of fertility since the rain led to fertility and growth. The sun, also a god of fertility, was thought to have an intimate association with the dead. The sun supposedly spent half of its time in the underworld, the land of the dead, and half of its time on earth. It was by prayers and offerings to the dead and to the sun that blessings were realized on earth.

Dual concepts integrated Hopi society still further. An individual was born to this earth; in death she or he was believed to be born to the underworld, only again to "die" in the underworld and become reborn on earth. Even in death, breath-bodies were thought to be capable of returning to earth. As there was an earthly life cycle for an individual, there was a daily and yearly cycle for the sun. Each morning the sun left its eastern home and at sunset entered its western home; thus, it furnished light equally to the earth and the underworld. On a yearly basis, winter began with the summer solstice and ended with the winter solstice, while summer began about mid-December and lasted until about mid-June. The winter solstice on earth was thought to be a summer solstice in the underworld, and the reverse also was considered true. When a major ceremony was being held on earth, a minor one was supposedly celebrated in the underworld by the kachinas. As would be expected, death in theory held no fears, for the living and the dead were believed to be one.

Ceremonies   The Hopi religious system required a series of annual and biannual ceremonies to be held by particular religious associations or societies. Every important ceremony was controlled by a particular organization that was linked to a different matriclan. Each of these societies was headed by a male elder of the leading lineage in the clan; this lineage also owned a bundle called the "mother" or "heart" of the clan, which consisted of an ear of maize, feathers, and coverings, as well as other sacred objects. Ceremonies were held in a kiva associated with the clan and at times established by phases of the moon, the location of the sun when it rose, or the number of days since a previous ritual had ended. The pattern for all major ceremonies was similar. The rituals spanned nine days, during which kiva members were not permitted to eat fatty foods, meat, and salt. Sexual activities were restricted before as well as during these celebrations. The specifics of the ceremonies included the use of altars and associated wooden, stone, or clay tablets painted with motifs symbolic of animals, clouds, maize, and rain. Sand paintings and certain fluids with a water base likewise wcrc important, and prayer offerings were left at the proper shrines. (See Figures 10-5 and 10-6.)

The performance of each major ceremony was the responsibility of a secret society, and it was essential for each Hopi to participate actively in the affairs of one or more of these societies. At about nine years of age, boys and girls were initiated into either the Kachina Society or the Powamu Society, the latter being more restricted in membership. Within the next few years, girls also joined one of several women's societies, and boys joined those for men. Occasionally, a woman joined a man's society and vice versa to fulfill a particular role, but by and large the ceremonial societies were divided along sexual lines. The organization of women's societies was similar to that of males: they were controlled by a lineage in a particular clan, possessed bundles, carried out secret rituals in a kiva, and performed certain ceremonies in public.

The ritual calendar may arbitrarily be considered to begin with the winter solstice or Soyal Ceremony. The Soyal was conceived around that mysterious moment each year when, in Hopi thinking, the sun rises at the same place for four days, and the days are shortest. The principal purpose of the Soyal Ceremony, which was conducted by those males who had completed the Tribal Initiation, was to induce the sun to begin the trip back to its summer home so that it would bring warmth enough for the crops to be planted. The ceremony had the complementary purposes of inducing fertility in both women and plants, and participation was villagewide. The typical smoking and prayers were accompanied by the manufacture of a large number of prayer offerings of corn husks, feathers, and prayer sticks. The kachinas performed, and select men and women danced.

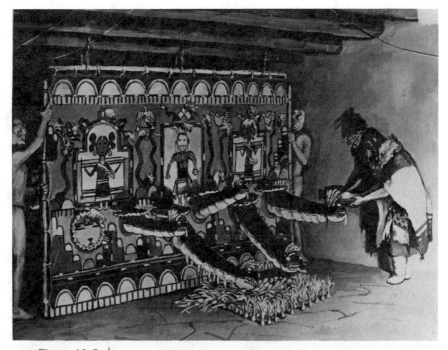

Figure 10-5. | A 1900 illustration of water serpents in a kiva being manipulated behind a screen in a symbolic harvest of small maize plants. (Courtesy of the Smithsonian Institution, National Anthropological Archives, neg. no. 1813-B.)

The Powamu Ceremony, which began when the February new moon first was seen, centered on the forced growth of beans in the kiva of the Powamu Society. When the beans sprouted, they were cut and bundled to be presented by kachinas to the grower's uninitiated offspring, his ceremonial children, and favored relatives. If a child was to be initiated into the Powamu Society, he or she was allowed to see the sacred rituals for the first time on the fifth day. This new knowledge was not to be revealed, under threat of punishment by the kachinas. The initiated children became members of the Powamu Society and later were permitted to impersonate kachinas, to participate in kachina rituals, and to become kachina fathers or ceremonial sponsors. Not all children were inducted into the Powamu Society; the children who were not were inducted into the Kachina Society on the sixth day of the Powamu Ceremony.

Another high point in the ceremonial round was reached in August, when the Antelope and Snake societies combined for a major ceremony every other year. On alternate years the Blue and Gray Flute societies held a ceremony. The two societies manufactured prayer offerings jointly, then went to their respective kivas, where they performed secret rituals. Snake Society members collected snakes to be part of the dance of a Snake man, who used his lips or teeth to hold the snake's head in his mouth as he danced around the plaza several times. (See

Figure 10-6. | Sand mosaic in the Antelope kiva. (Courtesy of the Field Museum of Natural History, Chicago.)

Figure 10-7.) During this time another man brushed the dancer's shoulders with a "snake whip," a short stick with eagle feathers attached. Each snake was danced with and then released on the ground at the plaza. The snakes then were gathered together in a circle and sprinkled with cornmeal by females of the Snake clan. Finally, younger men of the Snake Society picked up as many snakes as they could handle and took them to shrines in each of the four cardinal directions.

The public performances of Snake Society members have attracted more popular interest among whites than any other American Indian ritual. The reason is that the snake dancers carried prairie rattlers in their mouths as often as they carried harmless species such as the bull snake. Snake Society members handled poisonous and harmless snakes with equal ease. Although prairie rattler bites occasionally are fatal, illness or death from snakebite among the dancers was not reported. Various explanations have been offered concerning the Indians' ability to handle poisonous snakes. No evidence suggests that the members had an immunity to snake venom or that the snakes were charmed or drugged. Furthermore, the Hopi did not have an effective antidote for venom, which was proven by laboratory tests of their snake medicine. Historically, there appear to have been two different reasons for Hopi success in handling rattlesnakes. In 1883 a herpetologist visited a kiva where rattlesnakes were being kept for a dance; he inspected the fangs of one rattler and found them intact. After the dance he sent two of the rattlesnakes that had been used to the U.S. National Museum, and the venom glands were found to contain poison. Thus, it would seem almost certain that the fangs were milked before the public ceremony. The next snake was captured by a herpetologist who recovered it from a shrine following a snake dance in 1932. The snake's fangs had been cut away rather skillfully. Similar evidence that the fangs were being cut out in recent times was obtained in 1951 when another rattlesnake recovered after a ceremony was found to have had its fangs removed. Thus, the limited evidence indicates that the Hopi in aboriginal times and into historic times milked the poison from the fangs of rattlesnakes, but that between 1883 and 1932 they shifted to cutting away the fangs. The logical conclusion is that as the Hopi came to understand white attitudes toward rattlesnake bites, they eliminated the risk by an operation on the dangerous snakes.

The final ceremony of major importance was the Tribal Initiation. Controlled by the Agaves Society, it was held only when this society had at least one candidate for initiation. During this ceremony, adolescent males were initiated

Figure 10-7. | A Snake Dance at Old Oraibi. (Courtesy of the Southwest Museum, Los Angeles, CA.)

into one of four secret societies; the Agaves, Horns, Singers, or Wuwutcim. It should be recalled that a male could not be a fully participating adult in Hopi society until he had passed through this initiation. The Tribal Initiation was the most complex of the ceremonies and a cornerstone of Hopi religion. It took place in November at a time established by the Sun Watcher. A new fire was made in the Agaves kiva by the kiva chief, and some embers were carried to the other participating kivas. An idol called Dawn Woman was brought from her shrine and exhibited on top of the kivas until the fifth day of the ceremony, when she was returned to her shrine after "delivering" her offspring. All candidates slept in their kivas, and the dances performed on the third and fifth days were clearly associated with fertility, with phallic symbols and simulated pregnancies presented. These events, and many others, symbolized the ritual rebirth of male children into manhood and reaffirmed the integration between the living and the dead.

The Kachina Cult   Once long ago, according to Tawaqwaptiwa, the late village chief of Oraibi, after the Hopi had departed from the uppermost level of the underworld, they wandered on earth with their gods, the kachinas. They were attacked by Mexicans, and all the gods were killed. The dead returned to the underworld, and the Hopi divided their ceremonial paraphernalia to impersonate them. From then on, impersonations of kachinas formed the core of Hopi rituals.

When a man wore the sacred costume of a kachina, he became a friend of the gods, and his basketry or leather mask was the most sacred item of his costume. As masks wore out, became soiled, or broke, they were replaced or repaired, but this did not detract from their sacredness. The chief kachina masks were the only ones not replaced or duplicated. It was possible also to vary a new kachina mask from the original without impairing its supernatural associations.

Participation as a kachina was open to all village men under the general sanction of the village chief, and the activities of the kachinas were under the control of the Badger and Kachina clans. Kachinas were present at Oraibi from the winter solstice until the summer solstice, and then they were supposedly in the underworld except for Masau'u Kachina, representing the God of Death, who was about the earth all year long. While a Hopi adult did not believe that an impersonator was a god but rather a friend of the gods, small children were told that these were actual gods.

Kachina "dolls" have attracted widespread attention from whites and have been collected avidly for many years. These carvings are stylized renditions of the disguises worn by the men who portrayed kachinas. They are small painted and adorned wooden images usually made by men prior to kachina performances. The figures were presented to children by kachinas and were considered by them as gifts from the gods. These kachina images were hung from the rafters of the homes to familiarize the children with the many different forms. Although kachina figures frequently are called dolls, this is a misnomer. They were not toys but served mainly to instruct uninitiated children about one as-

Figure 10-8. | Kachina figures. (Courtesy of the UCLA Museum of Cultural History.)

pect of the religious system. Over 240 different forms were made by the Hopi; they fit into six groups, including chief kachinas, clowns, and runners. A figure was carved from cottonwood tree roots, shaped, and then smoothed before appendages such as ears or horns were pegged in place. A thin layer of white clay was applied, and the clay was painted in vivid colors, the same ones used for the body paintings of real kachinas. Finally, feather adornments often were added to complete the figure. (See Figure 10-8.)

Sorcery   To the Hopi, communitywide prosperity indicated that each individual had contributed his or her utmost, and the ideals of the Hopi Way thus were achieved. But what about failures? Why was it that during some years rain did not fall, winds dried the ground and blew seeds away, and the streams did not flow with water? Obviously, it was essential to be able to explain why nature sometimes did not respond to the complex ceremonies. The burden of failure was said to rest with individuals, persons who were kahopi, thinking evil and doing evil; these persons were witches.

The origin of witchcraft was traced to Spider Woman, who caused the first human death. Hopi have reported that they believed a typical village included more witches than ordinary people. Witches might be male or female and from any clan; no one was considered to be incapable of witchcraft. A village chief or ceremonial leader might be suspect simply because he held an important office. Any self-assertive person was open to the accusation of being a witch because such behavior was not hopi. One could become a witch either by voluntarily practicing sorcery or by unknowingly being inducted into a society of witches as a child. In the latter instance, existing witches reportedly carried off a related child while it slept and inducted it into a secret society that followed the pattern of other Hopi secret societies. The initiate was taught the witches' art of assuming the shape of an animal to pursue their nefarious craft by night. The power of a witch was derived from association with an animal familiar, such as a coyote, owl, wolf, or small black ant, from whom the greatest forces of evil emanated; quite logically, sorcerers supposedly possessed "two hearts," their own and that of their animal familiar. Sorcerers reportedly worked evil by sending pestilence to the fields, by causing land erosion, or by driving off rain clouds and replacing them with a conjured windstorm. A witch was not content with destroying crops but killed people as well. Murder probably was the most important activity of a sorcerer because it was believed that he or she extended his or her own life by killing one relative each year. In Hopi belief, a relative was killed or caused to be ill when a sorcerer shot stiff deer hairs, ants, a bit of bone, or some other object into his or her body without breaking the skin.

Ordinary people believed they could best protect themselves against a witch, who was most likely a near relative, by wearing stone arrow points regarded as the ends of lightning flashes associated with the clouds. The Hopi did not attempt to interfere with the activities of witches because they believed that they would die prematurely or encounter misfortune. A witch's spirit supposedly thirsted and hungered for the underworld and approached it by one step a year. The sanctions against a witch were not in this world but in the underworld; when his or her spirit arrived there, it was supposedly burned in an oven and became a beetle.

Shamans   Some persons harmed and killed people by supernatural means, but others, shamans, cured people through their special abilities. A society of Hopi curers existed in early historic times, but it became extinct before being reported adequately. In any event, in the more recent past there were curing specialists who relied on pharmacopoeia and massaging techniques. Some shamans were secular healers; they set broken bones and prepared herbs for patients. Their rather complex body of knowledge required specialized training, and a secular shaman was likely to pass his information on to a sister's son. In another category were the shamans who performed supernatural cures. These "two-hearted" individuals were supposed to employ their powers only for curing illness caused by witches. Obviously, such a person would be suspect in a sorcery case and considered a dangerous individual in any event. He would chew jimsonweed root or some other plant to induce a vision that aided in diagnosing the source of a malady.

LIFE CYCLE As might be anticipated, the Hopi stress on fertility led to certain forms of behavior thought conducive to pregnancy. A woman was supposed to pray to the sun at each dawn, and she was believed to be most likely to conceive if she had sexual intercourse while menstruating. Pregnancy was recognized by failure to menstruate, and if a woman suspected that she was carrying twins, she sought a shaman's aid to make the twins one. To bear twins was considered difficult, and it was thought that if both lived one parent would die. A pregnant woman prayed to the sun and sprinkled cornmeal while she prayed to ease the labor of childbirth. She was active during her pregnancy, and she as well as her husband observed diverse taboos.

A woman bore her offspring in the house of her mother, often the same dwelling in which she had been born. She was unaided and gave birth while squatting over a layer of sand. The blood, afterbirth, and sand were covered with cornmeal and hidden in a special crevice. Immediately after delivery, the grandmother entered the room, severed the umbilical cord, and took charge. In a short time the father's closest female relative, his mother or sister, arrived to wash the head of the neonate and to direct the activities of the next twenty days, which culminated in a naming ceremony and a feast. Later in life the child developed warm social ties with his father's close female relatives. The father was nowhere to be seen during the birth, and usually for forty days thereafter he withdrew to his kiva away from the bustle and confusion in the house of his wife.

An infant was nursed whenever it cried and was not weaned for two to four years or even longer. To quiet an unhappy child a mentor might rub her or his sexual organ, and a small child might masturbate without reproof. When children were able to walk, they were encouraged to urinate and defecate outside the house; if they should defecate inside, they might be scolded or slapped on the head. Matters pertaining to sex were accepted among the Hopi with casual regard. Since a child slept in the same small room with his or her parents, their sexual activities were easily observable. Children were not instructed about sexual matters but came to understand them through observation. It was not unusual for men and sometimes women to urinate before persons of the opposite sex. Furthermore, jokes that we would consider obscene were taught to small boys to be used when they performed as ceremonial clowns. Yet, shyness was characteristic of young girls, and a licentious person sometimes was called crazy.

When kachinas were abroad, children were warned that when they misbehaved something out of the ordinary would happen; girls were told to prepare ground cornmeal and boys to trap small mammals for the giants who were coming, or else the giants would take them away. A few days later awesome giant kachinas arrived, wearing frightening masks and carrying weapons and a basket in which to take away children. Having been previously instructed by parents, the kachinas cited particular transgressions of children and threatened to seize them. Parents defended them, and girls offered the kachinas baked cornmeal, which was accepted, although the small animals proffered by the boys were rejected. Finally, the kachinas left, but only after they had received gifts of meat

Figure 10-9. | Young children being introduced into the ceremonial round in a Flute Dance. (Courtesy of the Field Museum of Natural History.)

from the parents. Children were also exposed to kachinas and other ritualistic figures during their initiation into the ceremonial round. (See Figure 10-9.)

The onset of puberty was not given ceremonial recognition for either boys or girls, but it was customary for boys in their early teens to begin sleeping in a kiva rather than at home. A girl was, however, expected to pass through a ceremony before she married. Each year girls between the ages of sixteen and twenty assembled at the house of a paternal aunt of one girl. The event usually was directed by a female who recently had passed through the rituals, and she was aided by two boys. For most of four days the girls ground maize in a darkened room; they observed food taboos and drank liquids only at midday. The boys organized a rabbit hunt on the third day, and the girls spent most of their time baking piki. Afterward, the girls appeared for the first time with new coiffures termed "butterfly wings" or "squash blossoms." A girl continued to wear her hair in this manner until she married. She was most likely to marry someone from within the community (village endogamy) soon after passing through this ceremony.

Fornication between teenagers was expected and was formalized in the *dumaiya*. As a boy began sleeping in a kiva, he was free to roam the pueblo at night and did so wrapped in a blanket so that he could not be easily identified. As the members of his amourette's household slept, he crept in carefully to the side of the girl, who in a whisper asked who it was. The boy answered, "It is I," and from the sound of his voice, the girl identified her caller. If she were willing, which usually was the case since the boy went only where he thought he would be received, he passed the night with the girl, leaving just before daylight. A dumaiya supposedly was secret, but it could not remain so in a small community like Oraibi. The girl's parents did not interfere if they regarded the boy as an acceptable husband for their daughter. A girl was not likely to have only a single lover, and before long she might become pregnant. If this happened, the girl named the boy she liked best as the father, and the formalities of arranging a marriage were begun. It also was possible for a girl to propose directly to a boy during certain festive or ceremonial occasions. A couple did not court unless they stood in a proper social relationship with one another. A person could not marry another in the same clan or phratry and was not supposed to marry someone from his father's clan or phratry, but the latter rule was not observed with care.

After the relatives of a couple approved a match, the girl ground maize for three days at the groom's house to demonstrate her abilities as a homemaker. There was no comparable trial for the groom. While the girl was in the boy's home, his paternal aunts attacked the boy's mother and and her sisters with mud and water for permitting the girl to "steal" their "sweetheart." An atmosphere of jovial hostility surrounded the fight. On the fourth morning the couples' hair was washed in one container by their respective mothers and female relatives. A mingling of their hair symbolized the marital union. Once again the paternal aunts of the boy attempted halfheartedly to disrupt the ritual. After their hair had dried, the couple stood at the mesa edge to pray to the sun and later returned to the groom's home for a wedding breakfast. They were now man and wife, but they continued to live in the groom's house until the bride's wedding costume was completed by his male relatives and any other men who offered to help. The men prepared the cotton and wove two sets of wedding garments, a small robe, and a white-fringed belt; in addition they prepared skins and sewed white moccasins and leggings. During the manufacture of these items the groom's family feasted the workers. After a month or more, the garments were completed; wearing one set and carrying the second in a reed container, the bride returned home. Her husband informally and unobtrusively took up residence in her household. The wedding garments were very important because they were supposedly required for entering the underworld after death.

All Hopi women appear to have married, but such was not the case for men. Indirect pressure was put on a girl by her brothers and her mother's brothers to bring another male into their economic unit. A boy's parents did not encourage him to marry because they then lost him as a productive family member. Any form of plural marriage was prohibited, but many unions were transient. It appears that over 35 percent of the people had from one to eight divorces. The most common grounds for divorce was adultery, followed by what probably would be termed incompatibility in our society. Divorce was a simple matter since it was only necessary for a man to rejoin his natal household or for a woman to order her husband from her household. The primary pressures against a divorce came from a girl's family since they did not relish losing an economically productive male. The mother and her small children continued to reside in their old abode; an older offspring might join either parent.

The social core of a household consisted of a line of females. Within this setting the closest bonds were between a mother and her daughters. Daughters were destined to spend their lives in their mother's home or in an adjacent residence, and eventually they assumed their mother's role. From her mother a girl learned domestic skills and the norms of proper behavior. A mother guided the most important decisions in the ceremonial life of a girl and was likely to have a voice in the selection of her mate. As a girl's menarche arrived, she was instructed by her mother about caring for herself. The girl was not isolated at this time, nor at any other menstrual period; neither was she restricted from participating in ceremonies while menstruating. Were a mother to die, the mother's sister, who was called mother, replaced the biological mother in the girl's affection. Between a mother and her son the social bonds were not as close. A mother indulged an offspring of either sex, but a son in his early teens soon found his identity with a kiva group. A man's natal home remained the residence with which he felt most identified, however. He returned there if divorced and was a frequent caller in his mother's house. Like a girl, a man identified closely with his mother's sister, especially if the mother had died. A father was not overtly important in the upbringing of his children. He was, however, interested in having his daughter find a good husband, who by his farming activities could lighten the father's economic labors. A father took comparatively little active interest in a son until the latter's tribal initiation. Then the father selected the boy's ceremonial sponsor, which was an important decision. As a boy grew older, his father assumed a major role as his teacher. He imparted farming and ceremonial skills as well as advice about being hopi. (See Figure 10-10.)

The maternal uncle of a young boy was the only male of his parents' generation who was of the same lineage and clan as himself. If such an uncle were a ceremonial leader, a boy might follow him in office, which called for systematic training of the youth. A mother's brother was likely to be the most important figure of authority associated with the boy's home, and he did not hesitate to apply discipline. A mother's brother was not all sternness toward his sister's children, however. He often told them myths or tales about their clan and occasionally presented them with gifts. One very warm relationship was between a man's sister and his son. As a small child, a boy soon learned that he was always a welcome guest in this woman's home. Here he received favored foods and frequent demonstrations of love and affection. As he grew older, he took game to his paternal aunt and exhibited his warm feeling toward her. Sexual relations with this aunt and her daughters were possible, and Titiev suspects that in the recent past a youth may have been expected to marry a father's sister's daughter.

Figure 10-10. | An old man and a child. (Courtesy of the Southwest Museum.)

As death approached it was said that a person's body became swollen. Youths as well as most adults left the house because they feared being present at the time of a death. The body and hair of a deceased person were washed, and then he or she was reclothed. After a man was wrapped in a deerskin or a woman in her wedding blankets, the corpse was flexed into a sitting position. Prayer offerings were fashioned by the father of the deceased or another male in his clan. A prayer feather was placed beneath each foot and in each hand, as well as over the navel, the supposed location of a person's spirit. The face was covered with cotton, symbolic of the time the dead become clouds, while food and water were placed with the body as sustenance on the journey to the underworld. The body was carried to the cemetery by men from the house of the deceased; here a hole had been dug just large enough to receive the bundled corpse. It was faced west, and soil was spread hastily on top. Men who attended the dead purified themselves afterward by washing in a boiled juniper preparation, and there was a ritual in the household of the deceased to protect members against spirits. The next day the man who had manufactured the prayer offerings took cornmeal and five prayer sticks to the grave. The prayer sticks were supposed to help the person on his or her travels to the land of the dead, and the food was to feed the spirit. A prayer was offered, and the spirit was told not to return for anyone else in the community. Later, household residents washed their hair and smoked themselves over hot coals on which pinyon gum had been placed. All possessions of the deceased were thrown away. A separate cemetery was provided for the stillborn, infants, and children. It was believed that the spirit of an infant did not travel to the underworld but lingered above the house, to be reborn again as a person of the opposite sex. The death of an adult was surrounded with misgivings and fear despite the fact that in Hopi belief most dead were to be reborn into a peaceful world that was an intimate part of the Hopi Way.

Recent Historic Changes in Hopi Life

After early contacts and hostilities with the Spanish, the next serious problem faced by the Hopi was how to deal with another group of non-Indians who began to enter their country as early as 1826. Among the earliest Hopi and Anglo-American contacts was a conflict that took place in 1834; white trappers raided Hopi gardens and killed about fifteen people. In 1850 the Hopi asked Anglo-American authorities in Santa Fe for help in controlling Navajo intrusions on their grazing lands, but the authorities took no action until later. Most Hopi took a cautious approach toward these whites. Everyone knew the origin myth in which an elder brother of the Hopi, a Bahana, departed and promised to return when the Hopi were in need. They reasoned that perhaps Anglo-Americans were the Bahanas, or White Gods, but no one knew for certain how to identify them. In the long run, contact with these whites did not aid the Hopi but set the stage for a serious rupture in Hopi society as well as conflicts over land.

ESTABLISHMENT OF THE RESERVATION   The Hopi were recognized by the federal government in 1870 when the Moqui Pueblo Agency was established, and a school supervised by missionaries was founded in 1874. The Moqui Pueblo Reservation (later changed to Hopi Indian Reservation) was created by an executive order in 1882, but the land set aside was for Indian, not exclusively Hopi, use. Passage of the Dawes Act in 1887 resulted in federal pressures on the Hopi to shift from family and community landholdings to individual allotments. The BIA attempted to force the allotment program in 1907 but did not succeed. Conflicts with the Navajo over grazing lands intensified since there had been no boundary survey when the Hopi Reservation was established, and Navajo encroachment on Hopi lands has continued. Through a series of executive orders the Navajo Reservation came to surround the Hopi, and about 1937 the BIA reduced the area officially designated as Hopi land to about one-fourth its original size, or one thousand square miles.

CHANGES IN THE SUBSISTENCE CYCLE By the beginning of the present century, the Hopi subsistence cycle had undergone major changes. The primary reliance on maize, beans, and squash had remained, but new crops and animals had become increasingly important. Probably the most important new animal was the sheep, and virtually every man had at least a small flock by 1900. Each animal was owned by an individual, but they were herded cooperatively by men. Most often a man tended a combined flock for a few days, and then his brother, with whom he was a herding partner, took charge. Sheep were held as wealth and were butchered only for ceremonial feasts. Any unconsumed meat was dried as jerky or dried, pounded, and mixed with fat as pemmican. Cattle were less popular because of their initial cost and because the pattern of allowing them to graze freely led to the destruction of crops, with ensuing disputes over crop damage. Horses, which were broken to the saddle, were difficult to maintain, due to the nuisance of rounding them up each day for pasturing, usually at a considerable distance from the community. Like the sheep, they were individually owned but often were tended jointly by men.

THE RUPTURE AT ORAIBI Events that occurred in the late nineteenth and early twentieth century had a profound effect on later Hopi life, especially in the village of Oraibi, so it is important to detail them here. In the earliest contacts with Anglo-Americans it appears that the chiefs at Oraibi were unfriendly. In 1871 the Moqui Pueblo special agent was well received everywhere except at Oraibi, and the Oraibi people were angry when neighboring villagers accepted whites. For a number of years the Oraibi chief had been a man serving only until one of his two eligible sons was old enough to assume the position. The younger son, Lololoma, became the village chief some time prior to 1880, and he continued his father's antiwhite policies. Soon after assuming office, Lololoma traveled to Washington, D.C., with a party of Hopi to appeal to the federal government to contain Navajo encroachments on their land. After the trip, Lololoma reversed his attitude toward Anglo-Americans and became the leader of the progressive, friendly, or pro-Anglo faction. The anti-Anglo faction, called conservatives or hostiles, was led by a male called Uncle Joe by Anglos but actually named Lomahongyoma. He was a leader in the Soyal Society, head of the Blue Flute kiva, and from the same phratry as Lololoma; this made his challenge to the latter's leadership legitimate. The progressives and conservatives grouped behind their able leaders, and the great drama at Oraibi began.

Because a critical issue in the dispute was the precise identity of the Anglo-

Americans, each faction drew on sacred myths to validate its stand. Were these Anglos the Bahanas? The hostile faction said no, for a real Bahana would be able to speak the Hopi language and could produce a stone matching the one held by the village chief at Oraibi. Obviously, these Anglos were not Bahanas, and if the progressives accepted them as gods, they were likely to arouse the anger of a supernatural who would send a flood to end the world. The progressives traced Hopi difficulties not to Anglo-Americans but to the underworld and witchcraft. The sides chosen by particular individuals were influenced by a number of factors, among which were their clan and phratry ties as well as the nature of their close kin ties with the outstanding personalities in the conflict.

The conservatives categorically rejected American ways. When they refused to send their children to school at Keams Canyon in 1887, Lololoma identified them to government agents, and some were arrested. Those who remained then confined Lololoma to a kiva, from which he was rescued by U.S. Army soldiers. The year 1887 also was critical because it marked the passage by Congress of the Dawes Act, which as noted before was designed primarily to divide tribal lands into individual allotments. When soldiers arrived at Oraibi in 1891 to survey village lands preparatory to making allotments, the hostiles disrupted them. The soldiers then tried to unseat the leader, but they were surrounded. When the hostiles made a ceremonial declaration of war, the soldiers prudently withdrew. A larger U.S. military force sent to Oraibi shortly afterward arrested some hostile and progressive leaders and took them to an army fort for temporary imprisonment.

By 1891 the differences between the progressive and hostile factions were beyond reconciliation. The hostiles were more numerous, and their leader Lomahongyoma declared himself village chief. Neither side would cooperate with the other in holding the sacred ceremonies, nor would the factions lend ceremonial equipment to one another. In 1894, U.S. soldiers made another effort to survey Oraibi lands preparatory to the division of clan landholdings into individual allotments. The hostiles again resisted, their leader Lomahongyoma and others were imprisoned briefly at Alcatraz (see Figure 10-11), and the lands were not allotted. By 1897 each faction was holding its own Soyal Ceremony, and there was no more interference from the other.

What happened at Oraibi affected the entire tribe because the village contained twelve hundred of the twenty-two hundred Hopi listed on the official census of 1890. Laura Thompson (1950) has pointed out that behind the rupture at Oraibi was the problem of land. Not only were there Navajo encroachments, but disputes also had arisen between clans over the lands of an abandoned pueblo. Successful farming in the past had been based on community recognition of clan holdings and clan cooperation in farming, but federal pressures were great to have the Indians accept individual family land allotments between 1892 and 1911.

About 1901 there was a change in the leadership of the progressives. Lololoma died, and a younger sister's son replaced him. This young, aggressive man, Tawaqwaptiwa, was selected over his older brother because of his more forceful qualities. In September of 1906 open conflict developed. After some scuffling

Figure 10-11. | The original caption on this picture reads: "Mosqui Indians Chief Lo-Ma-Hung-Yo-Ma, arrested at Oraibi, November 25th and 26th 1894, for seditious conduct and confined at Alcatraz Island, California, since January 3rd 1895." (Courtesy of the Southwest Museum, Los Angeles, CA.)

the conservative leader Lomahongyoma, by then back from Alcatraz, drew a line on the ground, and a push-of-war was held. Before the pushing began it was decided that the losers would leave the pueblo. Lomahongyoma was the object to be pushed, with people pushing him from behind or in front. The conservatives lost the struggle, and that same evening about three hundred of them took their belongings and abandoned the settlement. They founded the new village of Hotevilla, about seven miles to the north of Oraibi. The nature of the split clearly illustrates that the sociopolitical structure of the community could not resolve conflicts of this nature.

BIA authorities came on the scene soon after the rupture. They sent the conservative leaders to jail and relieved Tawaqwaptiwa temporarily as chief. He was sent to the Indian school at Riverside, California, to learn to speak English and practice American ways. When he returned to Oraibi in 1910, he was extremely anti-American; Titiev (1944, 94) records accounts that describe him as "quarrelsome, stubborn, vindictive, and unusually licentious." Over the next twenty years, Tawaqwaptiwa managed to alienate most of the remaining residents of Oraibi. By 1933 only 109 Hopi remained in Oraibi. Some had moved to New Oraibi, on the valley floor beneath Oraibi, and others had settled some forty miles to the northwest at Moencopi on the Navajo Reservation. As Thompson

(1950) has pointed out, the disintegration of Oraibi relieved the local pressures for land, but social cohesion did not develop in the offshoot communities. The most conservative community by the 1940s was Hotevilla. The people had had a nearly complete ceremonial cycle when they left Oraibi that September night in 1906. Through the years their resistance against whites had become almost an end in itself, and for good reason: after the split, most of the Hotevilla men had been impounded by the federal government, and the women and children had found it difficult to survive until their return. Then, too, children had been forced by soldiers to attend school, and the people had been forcefully dunked in sheep-dip during a 1912 epidemic. These people scorned outside interference and wanted to be left alone.

After 1906 a complete ceremonial round could no longer be held at Oraibi because some clans were no longer represented, but Chief Tawaqwaptiwa faced the situation calmly as he aged. He maintained that the time would soon come when everyone would abandon him, and he alone would carry on the Soyal. Then there would be a great famine, and following it, all of the old ceremonies would be reinstituted at Oraibi. Again the village would thrive in all of its colorful glory. Tawaqwaptiwa waited and waited, and died still waiting.

| Emergence of Modern Hopi

By the 1940s about four thousand Hopi lived in fourteen settlements, including Moencopi, on land set aside for them adjacent to the Little Colorado River. The critical problems facing the people were increasing land erosion and a population increase on a land base made smaller by Navajo encroachments. The erosion apparently resulted from a dry climatic phase and overgrazing by livestock. For many years the federal government had encouraged herding, and sheep had become essential in the Hopi economy. To remedy the erosion problem, federal efforts centered on a program of livestock reduction. The people of the Third Mesa area were required to reduce their holdings by nearly 45 percent, while reductions on the other two mesas were to be about 20 percent. This meant that residents of the Oraibi area were hardest hit by the program. They attempted to resist the reductions but were unsuccessful. Along with the reduction, the federal government introduced better stock management practices and organized cooperatives. Farming practices were not changed dramatically at this time; however, the plow was replacing the digging stick. As in the past, fields either were watered from stream flooding or were dry land plots. An effort was made to irrigate Hopi lands, but it was not especially successful and at best could have affected only four hundred acres. Most men raised a wide variety of crops but with limited harvests. The essentially meatless diet consisted mainly of maize (see Figure 10-12), white flour, beans, potatoes, sugar, and coffee. The nutritive value of the diet was below normal standards for children and barely sufficient for adults.

The most profound changes to affect the Hopi world during the emergence of the modern period occurred at Oraibi. Here all aspects of life under-

Figure 10-12. | Hopi women cleaning corn. (Courtesy of the Field Museum of Natural History, Chicago.)

went tremendous readjustments following the 1906 rupture. When the full ceremonial cycle no longer could be held, the kiva-centered life of males was destroyed, and the significance of the nuclear family increased proportionally. This lessened the position of males and strengthened that of females. The net result was the fostering of a previously unheard-of male individualism. Since the Oraibi land base was not adaptable to the accumulation of farmlands or to male control of such lands, ambitious males moved toward wage labor. Another avenue open to individual males was political leadership, but in this role an individual encountered the disapproval of personal achievement that was still prevalent among the Hopi.

No modern ethnographer has devoted more attention to the Hopi than Mischa Titiev. In addition to his fieldwork in 1932–34, he spent ten summers at Oraibi between 1937 and 1966. As a result of these studies, Titiev proposed that abandonment of traditional Hopi life grew in intensity following the construction of paved highways linking Black Mesa with cities and towns in northern Arizona and New Mexico. No longer isolated physically, the Hopi turned outward toward the white world. Many people bought automobiles or trucks, ending travel by wagon or on the backs of burros and horses. Men began commuting daily to jobs in nearby towns or weekly to more distant cities, returning to the village on weekends. Some of these men continued to farm clan lands but only on the weekends. Surplus crops now could be transported over highways to be sold at distant markets, and in times of local food scarcity, a staple such as maize could be imported. Good roads also brought large numbers of tourists, especially during ceremonies such as the Snake-Antelope Dance.

In its physical aspects, Oraibi had undergone less profound but equally far-reaching changes. The number of occupied houses was about the same as in the early 1930s, but larger houses were being built. Cinder block and cement were replacing local stone and adobe as building materials. As in the past, women performed lighter house-building tasks such as plastering. Outhouses became common, and most people owned store-bought furniture and appliances. The matrilocal marriage residence pattern and clan ownership of houses continued, but in recent years no woman has shared a household with her mother. When a woman married, she wanted an official American civil or religious ceremony to document the event, because experience had taught that documents were required in any legal dealings with whites. Each bride, even if she married elsewhere, still received traditional wedding garments from relatives.

The population of Oraibi was 112 in 1933 and had increased to about 130 in the mid-1960s. The emigration of young adults was more than counteracted by a decline in infant mortality attributable to Western medical practices. The young who remained at Oraibi were indifferent to the orthodoxy of the Hopi Way beyond participating in an occasional kachina dance. Gods of old had come to be displaced by technological forms; to obtain water had become a secular, not a sacred, process.

Not so very long ago the consumption of alcohol was shunned by the Hopi. But some veterans returning from World War II were heavy drinkers, and intoxicants became increasingly popular, with accompanying drunkenness. Social life changed in yet another respect because numerous clans died out and some others were represented only by males. They, too, will become extinct unless outsiders who are members marry into Oraibi. Political life assumed an unprecedented turn when a woman became the village chief because the people could not agree on a male successor. Hopi religion has disintegrated, and the Soyal Ceremony is no longer performed. By 1955 at Oraibi the only remnant of this ceremonial event was that two men stayed up all night making prayer sticks for the sun.

Contemporary Issues

The present-day Hopi face a number of issues that have deep and complex historical roots. In these issues, nothing less than Hopi lands and identity is at stake. Though they are presented separately here, these issues are actually intricately interwoven.

TRADITIONALISTS VERSUS PROGRESSIVES The differences between the two major Hopi factions clearly did not diminish following the push-of-war at Oraibi; on the contrary, they have intensified. The separation became institutionalized as an indirect result of the Indian Reorganization Act of 1934. Under this act, tribes were encouraged to form their own local governments along guidelines suggested by the BIA. With federal encouragement the Hopi held an election, and the Hopi Tribal Council was formed. The conservatives or traditionalists largely boycotted the election, and as a result the progressives formed the tribal government. In all likelihood the election was invalid because the voter participation rate probably was lower than the 30 percent required by federal regulations. However, the tribal council was recognized by the BIA. This election and the administrative decision that it was valid led to a bitterness that was to grow among the traditionalists.

Soon after the council was formed, the federal government unilaterally reduced the size of the original Hopi Reservation, and this reduction of their land base, which never had been considered adequate by the Hopi, led many progressives to abandon their previous support of the BIA. As a result the council could not obtain a quorum to hold meetings. The ineffectiveness of the council continued until the Indian Claims Commission Act was passed in 1946. The progressives then pressured the BIA to revitalize the council in order to press a land claim against the federal government, and the bureau cooperated. The Hopi claim was pressed by a rump council, which was recognized by the federal government. The same type of council, illegitimate in the view of traditionalists, leased a thirty-thousand-acre area to the Peabody Coal Company for a strip mine in 1966. Traditionalists, who were dumbfounded by the land claims case and coal lease, sued in federal court to stop the mining operation, but the court ruled that the Hopi Tribal Council was a legal governing body and had the right to negotiate the lease.

In 1976 the Indian Claims Commission agreed to compensate the Hopi with a $5 million settlement for more than two million acres of land that they had lost. The progressives were anxious to accept the money, but traditionalists felt that to give up any claim to Hopi land was sacrilegious because it would betray their sacred trust with their ancestors. Before the claims commission award could be pressed further, it had to be accepted by the tribe. Only 5 percent of the Hopi attended the meeting held to discuss and vote on the settlement. The majority of those present voted for acceptance, which was considered sufficient evidence for approval by the federal government. Again the traditionalists "lost" by refusing to participate in the decision making. The final step, to hold public hearings about dispersing the money, has not been held. Apparently the BIA and council are unwilling to have another confrontation with traditionalists on the issue.

MINING OF BLACK MESA COAL   A recent Hopi-white problem has posed an added threat to the Indians. To meet the ever-increasing demands for electrical power in southern California, the Las Vegas area of Nevada, and sectors of Arizona, the Western Energy Supply and Transmission Associates (WEST) was formed by municipal, state, and federal power companies. The Mohave plant in eastern Nevada began operations in 1970 and is powered by coal that is strip-mined at Black Mesa in Hopi and Navajo country about 270 miles to the east. Pulverized coal and water are pumped as slurry through a pipeline to the Mohave power plant. The transport system requires up to twenty-seven hundred gallons of water a minute, drawn from deep wells. Aside from the serious air pollution created by the mining operation, there is the danger that if the deep well casings crack or break, the water of shallow wells and springs on which the Hopi depend would be drawn deep into the ground. If this happened, they could no longer live in the area. Another problem is a lowering of the water table; by 1980 it had dropped about ten feet. An additional hazard is posed by the runoff from the ridges of overburden (spoil banks) left by the strip-mining operation. It generally is acknowledged that following surface mining in the arid West, the landscape can be rehabilitated but not restored to its original condition. Reclamation efforts by the Peabody Coal Company have been less than successful. Finally, despite the ruling of a federal judge in 1974 that the people of Black Mesa must be justly compensated for the loss of grazing land, destruction of homes, and capital improvements, this has not happened.

THE HOPI-NAVAJO LAND DISPUTE Another long-festering problem involves Hopi land rights and the Navajo. When the Hopi Reservation was created by executive order in 1882, the order did not specify that the land was for exclusive Hopi use. The Navajo who lived nearby grew rapidly in population and gradually came to occupy much of the land on the Hopi Reservation that traditionally had belonged to the Hopi. In the 1930s about 1.8 million acres of Hopi land, from a total of 2.4 million acres, were made part of the Navajo Reservation. In 1962 the Supreme Court ruled that the land detached from the Hopi had in fact been set aside for both tribes; however, the Navajo continued their effective control. In 1974 a congressional act designated that one sector of this detached land was to belong to the Navajo and another sector was to be for the exclusive use of the Hopi. As a result, Hopi who were living on Navajo land and Navajo living on Hopi land were to be relocated by July 6, 1986. Before this date was reached, all the Hopi had left the land assigned to the Navajo, and 1,000 of the 1,240 Navajo families on Hopi land had been relocated. Navajo relocation has been underfunded, poorly managed, and stoutly resisted by a small number of families involved. Although some Navajo had not yet moved when the final date arrived, it appears that within a few years the Hopi will have this land again for their exclusive use.

The major immediate Hopi concerns, especially for the traditionalists, are the desecration of land by the Peabody Coal Company and the pending cash settlement for lands lost. A Hopi prophecy states that Indian lands will be seized or spoiled, that those of the Hopi will be the last to go, and that if the Hopi and their friends cannot prevent this loss, the world will end by turning over.

Comparisons with Other Indians

The peoples described up to this point have either focused their food-getting energies on hunting and fishing or farming and hunting. Differences in subsistence patterns invite comparison in terms of supernatural involvements. We may seek to establish whether the key edibles were or were not enmeshed in rituals and ceremonies. The mythological origins of foods do not seem nearly as important as ongoing supernatural associations represented in ceremonies designed to perpetuate species, rituals related to preharvest and harvest activities, or supernatural involvements in handling foods after they were obtained. Great differences separate the peoples in these respects. Comparisons might well take into consideration species characteristics, the settings in which the edibles matured, and whether one or more persons harvested a particular food.

The Hopi appear to have had more permanent settlements than any of the other peoples, although the Yurok and Tlingit have occupied the same sites for generations. The relative degree of sedentation for the members of one society as opposed to another has important cultural implications. For example, fully sedentary people can build substantial houses and accumulate far more material goods than those who move about often. Further comparisons based on differences in settlement stability invite the identification of potential social, political, and religious correlates.

Additional Readings

The monograph by Ernest and Pearl Beaglehole (1935) provides a good introduction to the Hopi, as does the Hopi section in the 1934 book by Cyril D. Forde. The best works about a particular village are Mischa Titiev's studies made at Old Oraibi. Alexander M. Stephen's (1936) diary offers a wealth of information about most aspects of Hopi life, but it is difficult to use. The best biography of a Hopi man was edited by Leo Simmons (1942). *No Turning Back* (Albuquerque, 1964), the story of Polingaysi Qoyawayma (Elizabeth Q. White), as told to Vada F. Carlson, concerns a woman and her adjustments to the American and Hopi life-styles. The best ethnohistory is included in a book by Edward H. Spicer (1962), and Laura Thompson's (1950) work is a superior source of information about the emergence of the Hopi into modern times. One (19) of the two *Southwest* volumes of the *Handbook of North American Indians,* William C. Sturtevant, general editor (Washington, DC, 1979), includes a wealth of information about the Hopi and other Pueblo Indians in prehistoric, ethnographic, and historical contexts.

Bibliography

Beaglehole, Ernest and Pearl. 1935. *Hopi of the Second Mesa.* American Anthropological Association Memoir no. 44.

Blundell, William E. 1971, April 18. Ecological shootout at Black Mesa. *Wall Street Journal.*

Bunzel, Ruth L. 1929. *The Pueblo potter.* New York. The discussion of Hopi and other Pueblo Indian pottery is one of the finest studies of aboriginal ceramics. The text is particularly noteworthy when dealing with the ways in which designs were conceived and executed.

Colton, Harold S. 1949. *Hopi kachina dolls.* Albuquerque.

Colton, Mary-Russel F. 1938. The arts and crafts of the Hopi Indians. *Museum Notes, Museum of Northern Arizona* 11:3–24.

Cushing, Frank H. 1923. Origin myth from Oraibi. *Journal of American Folklore* 36: 163–70.

Forde, Cyril D. 1934. *Habitat, economy and society.* London.

Harris, David. 1980, Mar. 16. Last stand for an ancient Indian way. *New York Times Magazine.*

Hurbert, Virgil. 1937. An introduction to Hopi pottery design. *Museum Notes, Museum of Northern Arizona* 10:1–4.

Josephy, Alvin M. 1971, July. The murder of the Southwest. *Audubon,* 52–67.

Jones, Volney H. 1950. The establishment of the Hopi Reservation, and some later developments concerning Hopi lands. *Plateau* 23:17–25.

Oliver, James A. 1958. *Snakes in fact and fiction.* New York.

Simmons, Leo W., ed. 1942. *Sun Chief.* New Haven. This Hopi autobiography is an extremely valuable document, for it offers great insight into the life of one individual.

Spicer, Edward H. 1962. *Cycles of conquest.* Tucson.

Stephen, Alexander M. 1936. *Hopi journal.* Columbia University Contributions to Anthropology, vol. 23, 2 pts.

Sullivan, Cheryl. 1986, June 30. Navajo Indians resist U.S. law forcing them to yield land to Hopis. *Christian Science Monitor.*

Thompson, Laura, and Alice Joseph. 1944. *The Hopi Way.* Chicago.

Thompson, Laura. 1950. *Culture in crisis.* New York. The ethnographic background to Hopi life is provided in summary form, with the addition of the 1942–44 findings of Thompson and her co-workers and assistants. The volume is devoted in part to Hopi administration by the Bureau of Indian Affairs, but also provides diverse information about Hopi acculturation.

Titiev, Mischa. 1943. Notes on Hopi witchcraft. *Papers of the Michigan Academy of Science, Arts, and Letters* 28:549–57.

———. 1944. *Old Oraibi.* Papers of the Peabody Museum of American Archaeology and Ethnology, vol. 22, no. 1. The classic study of a Hopi community through time—a key source.

———. 1972. *The Hopi Indians of Old Oraibi.* Ann Arbor.

Whiting, Alfred F. 1950. *Ethnobotany of the Hopi.* Museum of Northern Arizona Bulletin no. 15.

11 The Iroquois: Warriors and Farmers of the Eastern Woodlands

Great Spirit, who dwellest alone, listen now to the words of thy people here assembled. The smoke of our offering arises. Give kind attention to our words, as they arise to thee in the smoke. We think of thee for this return of the planting season. Give to us a good season, that our crops may be plentiful.

A portion of the Planting Ceremony speech of the Seneca that is typical of ceremonial prayers. (Morgan, 1954, vol. 1, 188)

ANTHROPOLOGISTS LONG HAVE HAD a special fondness for the Iroquois, and not without good reason. The first essentially modern account of an aboriginal people was written about them by the Jesuit missionary Father Joseph F. Lafitau and published in 1724. But because this work appeared in French, it did not make an immediate impact on Americans or Europeans. Then in 1851 Lewis Henry Morgan published a book about the Iroquois that became a model for ethnographic reports. Furthermore, the Iroquois played a decisive role in shaping the North American colonial empires of the British and French and continued in importance during the American Revolution. From colonial times to the present, the names of outstanding Iroquois leaders have been known to many Americans. During the colonial period, Hendrick was an outstanding Iroquois warrior and military leader, Joseph Brant was an Iroquois warrior and politician, while Red Jacket was a great orator. Kateri Tekakwitha, an Iroquois born about 1656, was canonized as a saint by the Roman Catholic church in 1980. General Ely S. Parker, an Iroquois who served as secretary to General Ulysses S. Grant, drafted the terms of peace at Appomattox to end the Civil War. Finally, there is the Iroquois Jay Silverheels, better known as Tonto of "Lone Ranger" fame. The Iroquois, famous in war and politics and representative of the Eastern Woodlands culture area, have retained their identity with a rare resilience, but now their battles most often are fought in courtrooms.

| People, Population, and Language

The Iroquois commonly are considered a tribe, but they are more properly termed a nation. The five original tribes were joined by a closely related one in historic times, and unrelated tribes were also absorbed through adoption. Individuals in such tribes were considered secondary members of the Iroquois community.

The Iroquois confederation known as the Five Nations or Iroquois League originally included the Cayuga, Mohawk, Oneida, Onondaga, and Seneca tribes. The word *Iroquois* is based on an Algonkian word, translated "real adder," with a French suffix. The aboriginal Iroquois lived from Lake Champlain and Lake George in the east to the Genesee River drainage and Lake Ontario in the west. The northern boundary was the St. Lawrence River, and Iroquois domain extended south to the upper Susquehanna River. (See Figure 11-1.) Each nation occupied an oblong strip of country, and it is estimated that collectively at the time of early historic contact they numbered ten thousand.

The Iroquois spoke a language of the Macro-Siouan phylum and the Iroquoian family. Each of the five original Iroquois League tribes had its own dialect. The Cherokee dialect, which is of the same family as the Iroquois language, separated from Iroquois about 100 B.C. Separations of the member dialects within Iroquois took place about A.D. 700.

At some unknown time in prehistory, the Tuscarora split from what was later to become the League and settled along the Roanoke and nearby rivers in North Carolina and Virginia. Hostilities with white settlers erupted in the Tusca-

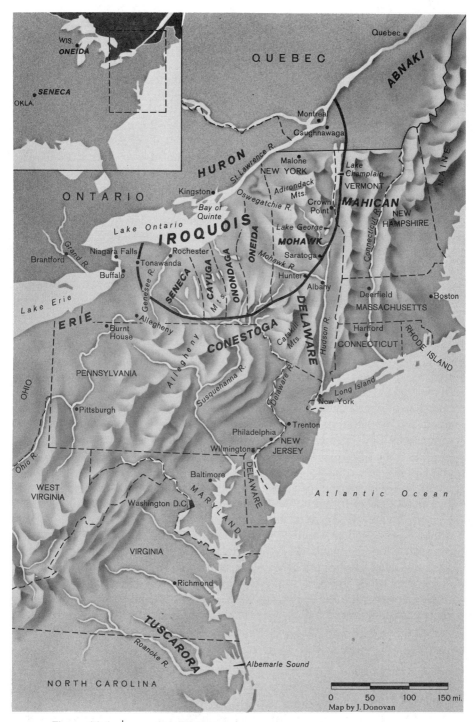

Figure 11-1. | Area of early historic Iroquois occupation.

rora wars of 1711 and 1712–13. The second war ended with some Tuscarora moving north to join the League members. They were adopted formally by the Oneida in 1722 as members of the League, and the Iroquois then became the Six Nations. By 1904 the Six Nations numbered at least sixteen thousand, and the modern Iroquois population is estimated to be about twenty thousand.

Origin Myth

The Iroquois origin myth asserts that in the beginning there were six men who were carried about by the winds since there was no land. They learned of a woman in the heavens and decided that one of them should go there since they felt that they would perish without women. The man chosen was named Wolf, and he was carried high on the backs of birds to a tree near a spring where the woman went for water. When she appeared they talked, and Wolf gave her bear fat to eat. He soon seduced her, and the master of the heavens cast her out for this act. She fell onto the back of a turtle in a sea of water where otter and fish were digging up clay from the bottom to form land. The land grew little by little to its present configuration. All people are descended from this woman who gave rise to people identified with the wolf, turtle, and other species.

Early Iroquois Involvements with Whites

The French entered the St. Lawrence River system in 1534 with the explorations of Jacques Cartier, and they soon established contact with the Algonkian, Huron, and Montagnais Indians. By the time the imaginative and aggressive French explorer Samuel de Champlain turned his attention to the south, he had allied himself with the Algonkians against their enemies, the Iroquois League tribes. Little did Champlain realize what a powerful adversary he was to confront. As Francis Parkman (1901, 9) wrote, the League was "foremost in war, foremost in eloquence, [and] foremost in their savage arts of policy. . . ." In 1609 Champlain, with a group of Algonkians, canoed to the lake that bears his name and met a party of Iroquois. The Iroquois attacked with confidence, only to be defeated by the white men in strange garb who used exotic weapons. (See Figure 11-2.) Although they initially were defeated in battle, the Iroquois had political genius and a strategic location, so Europeans colonizing in the Northeast were obligated to work out agreements satisfactory to these Indians. The goals of member tribes sometimes differed from those of the League itself, and this required further European accommodations, especially in the seventeenth and eighteenth centuries.

THE FUR TRADE   Early Iroquois relations with the French, Dutch, and English focused primarily on the fur trade. These Indians were drawn into the fur trade because they wanted European manufactures, especially the firearms that could help them advance their political interests. The Mohawk, as the easternmost Iroquois tribe, became middlemen in the fur trade, meaning that they ob-

Figure 11-2. | The defeat of the Iroquois by Samuel de Champlain and Algon-kians at Lake Champlain in 1609. (By permission of the Champlain Society.)

tained furs from other Indians and exchanged them with Europeans for goods that they then traded back to the other Indians for monetary profit and political advantage. In this way the Mohawk increased their influence over other tribes of the League as well as over non-Iroquois. Yet, the Mohawk were not powerful enough to conquer the other Iroquois, and they depended on them to obtain furs from more distant Indians. For example, the Seneca, the most numerous tribe of the League and the westernmost one, partially controlled Mohawk access to furs. Among Europeans involved in fur trading, the French dominated to the north along the St. Lawrence River drainages; the Dutch, followed by the English, came to control the Hudson River sector and regions to the south. This distri-bution of European colonials forced the Iroquois to contend with the intense rivalry between the French and English.

QUEEN ANNE'S WAR AND KING GEORGE'S WAR As colonial Europeans be-gan dealing with one League tribe after another, the tribes debated within the League about whom to choose as allies. These decisions usually led to raids and counter-raids by both the Europeans and their Indian allies. During Queen Anne's War (the War of the Spanish Succession) between the English and French, beginning in 1702, the Iroquois as a whole remained neutral because their inter-ests were divided. However, in 1704 those Mohawk who had been induced by French Jesuits to settle at St. Louis or Caughnawaga, near Montreal, accompanied a French-led party to Deerfield, Massachusetts, where about 110 English were taken prisoner and about 50 others were killed.

When Queen Anne's War ended in 1713, English control over much of eastern North America was consolidated, and members of the League were recognized as British subjects. For the Iroquois the most important implication was that the Mohawk valley was opened to white settlers. Queen's Fort (later Fort Hunter) had been founded in 1711, and a Church of England missionary began working with the Indians there but with little success. Indian children soon wearied of attending school, and the general conditions among adults were not what the missionary desired. One of his principal complaints was the traffic in intoxicants from Dutch traders to the Indians. The Iroquois passion for alcohol is well documented, and the missionary unsuccessfully attempted to stem its flow. In 1719 he abandoned the mission. Incidentally, it was in 1712 that the Jesuit Father Lafitau arrived in New France and began his six-year stay at Caughnawaga, working among the Mohawk there.

In the 1710s, colonial British traders from Pennsylvania began to expand into Ohio, using their Iroquois allies to protect them from the Indians living there. Soon thereafter the League expanded its membership to include the Tuscarora, who began leaving North Carolina as white settlers moved into their homeland. The Pennsylvania traders continued to move westward from 1740 to 1748 during King George's War (the War of the Austrian Succession) between the French and the English. At that time the Iroquois attempted to remain neutral, although some Mohawk fought the French. When the war had ended, an English missionary who went to Albany and Fort Hunter found cause for both joy and anxiety. The Mohawk received him in friendly fashion and obviously had retained at least some of what they had been taught by his predecessors. One Indian had even taken it on himself to spend most of his time preaching and instructing others. The distressing aspects of the scene were that intoxicants had become popular and highly disruptive in Indian domestic life and that the Roman Catholic priests at Fort Frontenac (Kingston, Ontario) had been successful in inducing more Mohawk to move to Canada.

THE FRENCH AND INDIAN WAR   About 1750 the French sought to dominate the Lake Erie and Lake Ontario regions as well as to establish closer contacts with the Cayuga, Onondaga, and Seneca by building a mission at the junction of the Oswegatchie and St. Lawrence rivers. A major in the militia, George Washington, unsuccessfully attempted to induce the French to abandon one post they had seized. He later fought the French to dislodge them from the upper Ohio River area but was defeated; this greatly strengthened the position of the French with local Indians. In 1756 a formal war, the French and Indian War (Seven Years' War), was declared between England and France. The English were defeated soundly until they took Fort Frontenac, which soon forced the French to withdraw from Fort Duquesne, later called Fort Pitt and then Pittsburgh. In 1759 the English began a two-pronged attack against the French that led to an end of French colonial power in Canada. At the famous battle for Quebec on the Plains of Abraham the English line met the charging French and did not fire until the advancing army was thirty-five paces away. The French force nearly was destroyed, and a French effort to retake Quebec ended in failure. In the spring of 1760 the English formulated a plan to take Montreal with converging armies. The plan succeeded, and by the end of the year the French had been forced to surrender their principal holdings in North America.

At the opening of the French and Indian War, the Iroquois sought neutrality, but this proved impossible. It was in the best interest of some Mohawk to support the English, whereas the Seneca aided the French. With an English victory the political power of the Iroquois diminished because the English no longer needed them as a buffer against the French. As a result, English colonists now became able to settle Indian lands to the west without serious Iroquois intervention.

The British government acted in 1763 to license traders to Indians and to prohibit the alienation of Indian lands except with the approval of the governor-in-council. These were two extremely important precedents in guiding Indian policies in Canada and the United States.

THE AMERICAN REVOLUTION AND JOSEPH BRANT The final drama in which the Iroquois were to play a significant role in American history began in 1775. The Iroquois were as a whole loyal to the British, and at best the colonial rebels could hope only to neutralize them. The loyal subjects of the Crown in turn did their utmost to induce the Iroquois to support the British cause actively. The second Continental Congress created an Indian Department with northern, middle, and southern divisions, and charged the commissioner of each with rendering the Indians neutral. The northern commissioner met with the Iroquois and made a systematic effort to insure their neutrality. Joseph Brant, an Iroquois who was loyal to the British, visited England in 1775 to clarify the position of Iroquois whom he represented. While there he was made a captain in His Majesty's Army and pledged Iroquois support. On his return Brant led a force of Mohawk against the American rebels. With the Declaration of Independence in 1776, the political break between rebel colonists and the British was complete, and war began. The policy of unanimity among the League tribes broke down as a result of the conflict. The Mohawk and Onondaga were divided internally, some supporting each side; the Cayuga and Seneca supported the loyalists; the Oneida and Tuscarora were in theory neutral but in fact gave the rebels aid.

After the successful attack of forces under Joseph Brant and Walter Butler to the south of the Mohawk River, the Americans organized an army against these Iroquois. In 1779 the troops of General John Sullivan succeeded in destroying Iroquois communities, crops, and grain caches. Iroquois effectiveness was ended, and many fled to Canada, abandoning their traditional lands forever. In Canada the Mohawk settled temporarily near Montreal, where they were given lands. When the treaty of peace was signed in 1783, no mention was made of the Indians and their future status. In recognition of Mohawk aid, the British granted these Indians land along the northern shore of Lake Ontario and along Grand River, which flows into Lake Erie. About sixteen hundred Iroquois began moving to the Grand River drainage in 1784. A separate treaty was made between the Six Nations and the United States, in which the Oneida and Tuscarora, who had remained relatively neutral in the conflict, were permitted to retain most of their land, but the other League nations, who had fought for the British, were forced to relinquish claim to most of their land.

THE WAR OF 1812   The last time the Six Nations asserted political power in an international dispute was in the War of 1812. The Americans were quick to assure the Six Nations members that invading forces would not disturb their interests, but the Iroquois were unimpressed. Yet, they were unwilling to commit themselves wholeheartedly to the British cause for good historical reasons; an initial call to arms for the British brought forth fewer than fifty Iroquois. Later victories by the Canadians induced some five hundred Six Nations warriors to fight with distinction, but before the end of the war any effective Iroquois cooperation had ceased.

Early Historic Iroquois Life

One difficulty in assembling Iroquois sources is in separating information about the Iroquois in general from that pertaining to a single member tribe. The problem cannot be resolved successfully because we do not have parallel information for all the League tribes. The descriptions to follow represent a composite view stressing the Mohawk and Seneca. A second difficulty is in obtaining comprehensive accounts of early historic conditions; thus, the sketch to follow represents a reconstruction of Iroquois life from diverse historic sources.

CLOTHING   Iroquois garments were made principally from deerskins sewn with deer-bone awls and sinew threads. Women wore underskirts that hung from the waist to just above the ankles, with designs in porcupine quills along the lower border. Over this garment they wore long dresses with fringed sleeves and fringe along the bottom. From their knees to their moccasins they wore short leggings, and in cold weather they wore a skin cape about the shoulders. Men wore kilts that reached their knees, were belted at the waist, and were fringed at the bottom and decorated with dyed quills sewn on to form designs. Men also wore fringed shirts and long, fringed leggings; on their feet they wore quill-decorated moccasins.

SETTLEMENTS AND MANUFACTURES   The Iroquois customarily built villages on hilltops and usually occupied a particular community for about ten years. After this period accessible farmland was relatively unproductive, firewood scarce, and dwellings decaying. About twelve Iroquois villages, each with three to six hundred residents, are reported to have existed before the turn of the eighteenth century. The Mohawk had three communities, and a series of major and minor trails connected these with the other settlements of the League. Villages were not dispersed widely but clustered along an east-west line. Spe-

Figure 11-3. | Model of an Iroquois village with a longhouse under construction. (From the collections of the Rochester Museum and Science Center, Rochester, NY.)

cially trained runners could carry messages throughout the League in about three days.

A typical village was surrounded by a ditch and up to three rows of wooden palisades. Beyond the enclosure were many acres of cultivated fields. Dwellings, which were of the well-known longhouse type, were from 50 to 130 feet long and about 16 feet wide. A house was built of seasoned posts, poles, and bark. Bark was stripped from trees in sheets, and these were stacked to flatten as they dried. Four stout posts with forked tops, one at each corner, formed the outline of the structure. Smaller forked poles were spaced between the main posts, and in the crotches of the forks poles were strung; other poles were placed at right angles to form the rafters. The arched roof was made with bent poles, and an entire frame was covered with overlapping sections of bark lashed into place and held firm with retaining poles. (See Figure 11-3.)

A house interior was partitioned into two main sections, each about twelve feet long; between these main sections were compartments for storing maize and other provisions. Along the center of a longhouse were fireplaces, with each family occupying an apartment opposite a fire. Smoke from the fires drifted through an oblong roof opening that also admitted light. In windy or rainy weather bark slabs covered this opening. Each family had an apartment with two platforms, and there might be as many as twenty apartments in a house. (See Figure 11-4.) An upper platform, some five feet above the ground and six feet from front to back, was covered with bark, reed mats, and skins. The lower platform was of similar dimensions and was about two feet above the ground. On these platforms family members lounged or napped during the day and slept at night. At each end of a longhouse was a doorway leading into the storage rooms that opened to the outside. The outer doors were of bark and were hinged at the top. In the winter a skin covering was added to the door.

For a small family or as a temporary residence, a less permanent dwelling was built. It was triangular in outline, with poles at each corner converging at the top, and was covered with overlapping bark slabs. An opening in one side served as the doorway, and one at the top was for smoke from the interior fireplace.

Maize was stored in houses as well as in underground caches. These excavated pits were lined with bark, and the grain was placed inside. Bark slabs were added as waterproof roofing, and the cache was covered with soil. Similar underground caches were lined with deerskins to hold dry meat.

The relatively permanent nature of their settlements made it possible for the Iroquois to accumulate a wide range of material objects. Surprisingly, few manufactures were of stone although it was widely available as a raw material. Arrow points and ax blades were fashioned from chipped stone, while mortars and adz blades were produced by grinding and polishing. Bark was an important raw material from which diverse forms were made. Among these were barrel-shaped storage containers, trays for mixing cornmeal, deep troughlike receptacles for maple sap, and ladles. Deep-bowled wooden ladles were used to eat soup or hominy. Grit-tempered pottery vessels of up to six-quart capacity were used for cooking and storage. Basketry was limited, but containers made from animal skins commonly were used to store household items. A skin bag hung from the waist of a hunter or warrior contained most of the artifacts he required while traveling.

CONVEYANCES Summer travelers used overland trails, waterways, or a combination of the two. To carry a load, a tumpline was passed over the forehead and attached to a basket, cradleboard, or pack frame. A pack frame, made from sections of hickory, was fitted to the back and might be supported by a chest strap, a tumpline, or both. A canoe was covered with the bark of red elm or hickory since both trees were small in this area and the bark could be pried off in one piece. Canoes were from twelve to forty feet long. The rounded ribs and the gunwales were made from ash, and both ends had a slight upturn. They were propelled with single-bladed paddles. For winter travel, snowshoes were made of hickory frames laced with babiche. They were relatively short and broad and well adapted to walking through timbered areas. Reportedly, a person could travel as many as fifty miles a day on snowshoes.

Figure 11-4. | Model of one portion of a Seneca longhouse. (From the collections of the Rochester Museum and Science Center, Rochester, NY.)

SUBSISTENCE ACTIVITIES   Most food was cultivated, and the right to use a plot belonged to the persons who cleared and planted it. Farming was a primary activity of women, who appear to have cleared the land, sowed the seeds, cut the weeds, and harvested the crops. The most important plant raised was maize, and at least fifteen varieties were identified. The women also planted varieties of beans and squash. The most important farming tools were the digging stick and a hoe made with a scapula blade. Tobacco was also raised for smoking in elbow pipes made from fired clay. Once planted, tobacco seeded itself and from year to year required only thinning. The leaves were picked in the fall after a frost and were dried before use. Tobacco was used only in pipes and often was kept in a weasel-skin pouch attached to a man's belt. Women collected wild plant foods, including over thirty different wild fruits and about fifty plant products ranging from roots to leaves. These were added to the maize-bean-squash diet and were important if crops failed.

Beyond the farmlands of a settlement were hunting, fishing, and collecting areas belonging to the community. From harvest time until midwinter, people abandoned their villages and scattered to hunt; again in the early spring they left their villages to collect maple sap, fish, and hunt pigeons. Deer were hunted communally by driving them between converging lines of brush with bowmen concealed at the end. The most effective means for taking a single deer was to set a spring-pole snare in the animal's trail. When the snare peg was tripped, the spring pole righted itself, and the deer was lifted into the air by its hind legs.

Snares were set for bears on their trails, and as an animal became entangled, a heavy pole fell on its back to pin it down. Bears also were chased for long distances until they tired and could be shot with arrows. When a large animal was killed in the winter near the home of a hunter, he brought it in on a toboggan improvised from bark. At other times the prey was butchered at the kill site; the meat was removed from the bones, dried before a fire, and placed in bark containers for transport.

In the late spring as women planted crops near the villages, men fished and harvested birds. A common fishing technique was to use cone-shaped traps about three feet long made from converging splints of black ash bound together with fiber cords. Such a trap was placed beneath the water facing a rapid or ripples, and the fisherman used a stick to guide fish downstream into it. Birds were snared with elm-bark nooses, and some species, especially quail and pigeons, were taken in nets made from shredded bark. After completing their spring subsistence activities, men spent most of the summer engaged in ceremonies, council meetings, and war.

The only scheduled meal was in the morning, and at this time men ate before the women and children. At other times people ate when they were hungry, but a woman always offered food to visitors and to her husband when he returned from working. Foods prepared from maize dominated, with hominy, cornmeal "bread," succotash, roasted corn, and boiled corn probably eaten most often. Of these the most important food was hominy gruel called *sagamite,* which is an Algonkian term. To prepare bread the kernels were taken from the ear, boiled in water with wood ashes to remove the hulls, ground in a tree trunk mortar with a wooden pestle, passed through a sieve, and shaped into loaves that were boiled in water. For roasting, the ears were placed in a line next to a fire. After roasting, some ears were shelled and the grains dried further in the sun and stored. To store maize on the cob, the husks were stripped back and braided into bundles of twenty ears each. To the maize diet, meats and soups might be added as well as wild vegetable products.

DESCENT, KINSHIP, AND MARRIAGE A longhouse was occupied by women of a matrilineage, their in-marrying husbands, and their children (matrilineal and matrilocal). The matrilineages were joined into fifteen named matriclans; among these were the Bear, Beaver, Deer, Hawk, Turtle, and Wolf clans. The clans of the Cayuga, Onondaga, Seneca, and Tuscarora were divided into moieties, but the Mohawk and Oneida had no moiety divisions and had only the Bear, Turtle, and Wolf clans. The matriclans cut across national lines so that members of the Wolf clan, for example, were found in each nation, in different villages within a nation, and in one or more households within a settlement. Where the moiety division existed, it once was said to have formed the exogamous unit; any combination of marriages between persons of opposite moieties was permitted. By Lewis Henry Morgan's time only clan exogamy and matrilineal descent prevailed. Inheritances were bequeathed by a man to his brothers, his sister's children, or some other person in his matriclan. The importance of the clan cannot

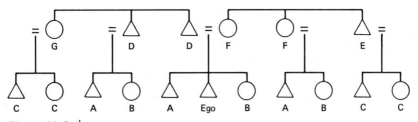

Figure 11-5. | The early historic Iroquois system of kinship terminology.

be overestimated in Iroquois society; not only was it the property-holding unit, but it was empowered to invest, and renew if necessary, political leaders. Members cooperated in economic and political life and judged disputes with other clans. Furthermore, each clan had a common burial ground, held religious ceremonies, and could adopt outsiders.

In the kinship terminology, a person referred to her or his father and father's brother by the same word, and called the mother the same as mother's sister. There were separate and different words for father's sister and mother's brother (bifurcate merging terms). The words for parallel cousins (father's brother's or mother's sister's children) were the same as for biological brothers and sisters, but cross-cousins (father's sister's or mother's brother's children) were called cousins. This, then, is the Iroquois type of cousin terminology. (See Figure 11-5.) By extension, all individuals of one's matriclan, irrespective of their tribal affiliations, were drawn into the system as blood relatives. The basis of Iroquois political life was an extension of household and community kinship ties at the national and league levels.

SOCIAL DIMENSIONS The Iroquois often have been characterized, especially in older writings, as one of the best examples of a matriarchy, but this is an unfortunate label. It does not appear that they were overtly controlled by women. Because the Iroquois were matrilineal and matrilocal and because women were a very powerful political force, it certainly is appropriate to label the Iroquois as a matricentered or matrifocal society. The position of Iroquois women in the early seventeenth century, and probably for many earlier years, was well summarized by Lafitau (1974, 69): "In them [women] resides all the real authority: the lands, fields and all their harvest belong to them; they are the soul of the councils, the arbiters of peace and war; they hold the taxes and the public treasure; it is to them that the slaves are entrusted; they arrange the marriages; the children are under their authority; and the order of succession is founded on their blood."

The Iroquois clearly distinguished between the activities of men and women, and no close bonds other than family ties joined members of the opposite sex. Men sought the company of men, and women preferred to associate with other women. The primary duties of women were to care for children; to plant, cultivate, and harvest crops; to collect wild food products, and to prepare meals. Men concentrated their energies on hunting, politics, and warfare. The behavioral ideals for each sex were set forth in their oral traditions, and children were taught these values by their parents. Each person was identified with the totemic group of his or her mother but also had a personal totem, or perhaps more aptly, a guardian spirit comparable to the Algonkian manitou. A guardian spirit, or *oki,* was acquired in a dream or vision; represented by an object in a personal medicine bundle, its purpose was to aid the possessor.

When a woman died, her farmland, along with her domestic property, usually was inherited by her children, although she might will them to other persons. A man's property normally was passed to his matrilineage, whose members disposed of his separate dwelling or apartment in a longhouse as well as his other material goods. The members might keep some items by which to remember the deceased. A man too could will his property to his wife or children if he made his desires known before a witness. (See Figure 11-6.)

An analysis of historical references to Tuscarora personality characteristics by Anthony F. C. Wallace (1958) provides what possibly are general traits of aboriginal Iroquois. Their "demandingness," which Wallace thought masked their extreme dependency, was best exhibited in their expectations of others; they never ceased, it seems, to expect goods and services. The same attitude was reflected in their use of intoxicants; their desire apparently knew no limits in early historic times. They blamed the difficulties resulting from intoxication on the white traders or on the rum itself but not on the person drinking it. Another striking characteristic of the Tuscarora and apparently of other Iroquois was the absence of fear of heights. They were observed to walk over creeks on small poles without hesitancy and could stride along the peak of a gabled roof casually and without any fear.

DREAMS Wallace (1958) has studied early historic records about Iroquois dreams and found that the meanings they attached to dreams were in some respects similar to ideas developed by Sigmund Freud. The Iroquois in general believed that dreams expressed inner and symbolic unconscious desires, which if frustrated could cause psychosomatic illness. An individual could not always interpret his dreams properly, in which case he consulted a shaman versed in such matters. The dreamers most often mentioned in the literature were adolescent boys who embarked on vision quests, warriors who feared torture, and the ill who feared death. The young boys had dreams of the visitation form, according to the twofold Iroquois dream classification of Wallace. In these, the supernatural communicated with the dreamer, bestowing power such as good fortune in hunting or war or some other inordinate ability. One of the most important powers given was a capacity to predict the future. Symptomatic dreams told one of the desires of his soul. Wallace (1958, 244) wrote that "the only way of forestalling realization of an evil-fated wish was to fulfill it symbolically. Others were curative of existing disorders, and prophylactic only in the sense of preventing ultimate death if the wish were too long frustrated. The acting out patterns can also be classified according to whether the action required

Figure 11-6. | A 1724 illustration of an Iroquois burial. (From Lafitau 1724.)

is mundane or sacred and ceremonial." It was under the compulsion of fulfilling a symptomatic dream that men were tortured by their friends, sought some material object even if it meant great hardships, held traditional but special ceremonies, or introduced a new ritual.

In summary, Wallace's (1958, 247) concluding paragraph is best quoted. "The culture of dreams may be regarded as a useful escape-valve in Iroquois life. In their daily affairs, Iroquois men were brave, active, self-reliant, and autonomous; they cringed to no one and begged for nothing. But no man can balance forever on such a pinnacle of masculinity, where asking and being given are unknown. Iroquois men dreamt; and, without shame, they received the fruits of their dreams and their souls were satisfied."

ENTERTAINMENT Diversion in the form of games of chance and skill played an important part in Iroquois religious and social life. The contests were between individuals or teams organized within a community or beyond it, even including different tribes. The teams generally seem to have been divided along clan lines. These people were avid gamblers, and betting on the outcome of a game was intense: a man might gamble all of his property on the outcome of a game. The favorite game was lacrosse, played on a field about 450 yards long. Each of the six to eight players on a team carried a crook that had netting strung from the curved end to about halfway up the stick; the ball could be moved only with this racket. The object was to drive a deerskin ball from midfield through the opposing team's goal, which consisted of two poles near each other at one end of the field. The rules allowed a variation from five to seven in the number of goals necessary to win a game. Another game was to throw a javelin through a rolling hoop or to throw it farther than an opponent could.

The snow snake game was played mainly by children. The snow snake was a thin, smoothed hickory shaft some six feet in length, with the forward end increased in diameter and slightly upturned. There were up to six players, with three to a side, and each hurled his snow snake across a snow surface. The game was scored according to the distance achieved until the specified number of points had been reached by one side. The snow boat game was based on the snow snake principle. A snow boat, constructed from a solid piece of beech wood, looked like a round-bottomed vessel with an upturned bow. The boat had small feathers at the top of the stern and an oblong central opening in which was placed an arched piece of wood hung with rattles. On a hillside each player trampled a runway in the snow, iced the depression, and propelled two or three boats down the chute and as far as possible across the snow below.

POLITICAL LIFE: THE LEAGUE OF THE IROQUOIS The League of Hodenosaunee or Iroquois was originated to bring peace among warring Iroquois tribes. The League was structured to handle civil affairs only; most military activities were pursued outside its framework. The date of the League's founding is open to dispute. Some authorities place it as early as A.D. 1400 and others as late as 1600; the latter date seems more likely.

The original League included fifty permanent offices that were filled with persons from each of the five member tribes. The Onondaga contributed fourteen; Cayuga, ten; Mohawk and Oneida, nine each; and the Seneca, eight. These representatives have been called sachems in the literature. This title is derived from a word used by diverse Algonkian language speakers in the eastern United States to refer to the holders of hereditary offices. Among the Iroquois a sachem was called Counselor of the People. Sachems were always men and were drawn from the matriclans of the tribes; for example, three Mohawk sachems were chosen from each of the three matriclans. The sachems collectively formed the Council of the League, which had legislative, executive, and judicial authority over the combined tribes. Historically, the first annual League meetings were held at Onondaga to invest new sachems. In theory, and seemingly in fact, each member tribe had an equal voice. The unequal distribution of sachemships among the tribes was not a key to power because decisions made in the name of the League were unanimous. When the Tuscarora were adopted by the Oneida in 1722, they too became members of the League.

The stated purpose of the League was to avoid the kind of constant wars that had occurred before its foundation. League meetings were called to deal with internal and external affairs, to invest new sachems as well as mourn the ones replaced, or to carry out religious obligations. The influence of any particular sachem depended on his abilities as a speaker. Occasionally, conflict arose between different members of the same clan in different tribes. An individual's allegiance was strongest toward his own household, less important toward the clan in general, and least important beyond his tribe. Feuds sometimes erupted between clans of different League tribes, but no doubt these quickly were brought before the League Council for settlement.

Sachems did not seek nor gain distinction as individuals but acted collectively, and their achievements were reflected only in group judgments. At a League Council meeting, sachems could not decide an issue according to their personal feelings, but were obligated to reflect their constituency. The frequency of interaction among member tribes and the close kinship bonds created a feeling of League unity even when the organization was not in session. Member tribes frequently joined to hunt, fight, and participate in religious ceremonies. If a group of individuals, such as a band of warriors, chiefs, or women, thought a particular matter was important, they met to discuss the issue and appointed an orator to convey their views to a sachem. If the sachem considered the subject significant, he would introduce it at the next meeting. If an alien tribe desired to submit a question to the League, the foreign ambassador first went to the Seneca, who decided whether a question of foreign origin was important enough for a League meeting. If so, they sent runners to the Cayuga with a wampum belt into which had been "read" the time, place, and purpose of the meeting. Each member tribe in turn notified the one to the east. When the topic for consideration was of widespread interest, people came from all over the League territory. A meeting opened with prayers, and the matter at hand was put forth by the envoy, who then withdrew from the meeting. Discussions were held, and orators spoke about the issue. When the time to reach a decision arrived, groups of sachems debated among themselves until they agreed. The next step was for one from each group to act as a spokesman in consultations with other sachems who were similarly selected. Finally, the varying conclusions were offered. If unanimity could not be reached, the matter was set aside. When a unanimous decision was achieved, an orator summarized the proceedings and gave the decision to the envoy. Only once, it appears, was the principle of unanimity set aside; this was when the Oneida sachems refused to agree with the others to side against the colonists during the American Revolution. The conclusion then was to permit each member tribe to determine its own position.

In the original League were the sachems Daganoweda and Hiawatha, the legendary founders of the League. Their offices were not filled on their deaths. Although in theory each sachem had the same power as any other, certain sachem-ships were more honored than others. The most notable example was the Onon-daga sachem position titled Tododaho; this man had two other sachems as his assistants. The Seneca sachem Donehogaweh was the Keeper of the Door in the council house, and the Onondaga sachem Honowenato was the Keeper of the Wampum for the League. Certain obligations were attached permanently to a particular tribe of the League. The Onondaga, since they were centrally located in the League, were in charge of the council hearth and wampum. In ordinary session the Council of the League met each fall among the Onondaga. Special sessions, however, might be convened among any member tribe. The Seneca were the Keepers of the Door because they faced the hostile tribes to the west. The Mohawk, the easternmost Iroquois, were given the right to receive tribute, suggesting that the Indians to the east were subject peoples.

Any important decision was recorded through the medium of wampum. In treaties with whites as well as with other Indians, wampum belts were exchanged to bind the contract. The decision or agreement was "talked into" the beads, and the Keeper of the Wampum taught the texts to his successor. The wampum beads were spiral-shaped freshwater shells strung together or made into belts. The word *wampum* is derived from Algonkian and means "a string of white beads." In general, the Iroquois used white beads in a religious context and purple ones as a mnemonic device to recall the details of political decisions.

At the death, or removal from office, of a sachem, his successor was "raised-up" at a council meeting. His former name, the one acquired as an infant, was dropped, and his new name designated the office he was to hold. The meeting was held at the council headquarters or capital of the tribe involved in the re-placement, and the tribe of the sachem to be elevated served as hosts to the League. There were prayers, a mourning rite for the sachem to be replaced, reci-tations of ancient traditions by reading the wampums, and finally the investiture of the new sachem. The religious ceremonies were punctuated with feasting, games, and social dances that relieved the solemnity of the occasion. Sachemships were passed along matrilineal lines, with an office normally passing to a brother or to a sister's son. The abilities of logical successors were considered, and the person thought most fitted for the office was invested. If no such individual existed within a matrilineage, which was rare, the selection was made from another closely related matrilineage. The most influential person in selecting a sachem was the oldest woman in the matrilineage through which the clan title passed. In the event that it was necessary to displace a sachem before his death, this action could be taken only by the clan council of the nation to which the sachem belonged.

Each nation handled its own domestic problems through its sachems. Thus, the nine Mohawk sachems were the final authorities on Mohawk internal affairs, and they functioned in the same manner as did the League Council as a whole. Furthermore, if a sachem from one tribe visited another in the League, he was accorded the same status that he enjoyed at home.

After the League had been functioning for an unknown length of time, a nonhereditary office, that of chief, was created. Such a person was called Pine Tree Chief, An Elevated Name, or Brace in the Long House. Chiefs were elected by the clans of a nation for the lifetime of the individual. There was no set number of chiefs, and they were selected on the basis of such qualifications as oratorical skills or deeds in warfare. The chiefs first served as local leaders and as advisers to the sachems. Later they sat in the League Council and rivaled the sachems in authority; at this time they were invested by the sachems. According to tradition, the creation of the office of chief was the only innovation in League structure after it was founded. In general, the League was bound to follow as closely as possible the organization and purposes established at its founding.

WARFARE   The League was structured to handle only civil affairs, and most military activity was pursued outside its framework. If a sachem planned to participate in warfare, he first was obligated to resign his office temporarily. When the League as a whole declared war against an enemy tribe, hostilities were coordinated by the sachem war chiefs, although these men did not necessarily play a part in the direct conflict.

The principal weapon used by the Iroquois was a wood stave or self bow with a slight outward curve at the ends; a bow was so rigid that it could be strung only with practice. The arrows were feather-vaned and tipped with antler or flint arrowpoints. About fifteen arrows were carried in a skin quiver that hung on a man's back. One club used in close combat was made from a two-foot length of ironwood with a large knot at the end. Another form of club had a slightly curved wooden handle, and set into the convex surface was a sharp, curved antler point. The famous tomahawk apparently was not an aboriginal Iroquois weapon, but it was known among the eastern Algonkians, from whom the word was derived. The blade was hafted in the manner of a modern hatchet; tomahawks soon were manufactured from metal in Europe for the Indian trade and sometimes had a pipe bowl at the head. (See Figure 11-7.)

Near the center of each settlement was a war post, and a chief who sought

Figure 11-7. | An aquatint of an Iroquois warrior in 1787. (Courtesy of the Library of Congress.)

to organize a fighting party whooped about the village, stuck a red tomahawk adorned with red feathers into the war post, and danced around it. Any man willing to join the party participated in the dance. After a band of warriors had been organized, women began preparing food for the venture. The standard fare was very dry, pulverized maize mixed with maple sugar and placed in a bearskin bag. A Pine Tree Chief customarily led a raiding party, and each was organized as a small contingent that might join one or more similar units. The units had no overall commander; each party leader was responsible for his group. Participants were free to act according to their personal feelings, and proper behavior could not be dictated. Just before they left, they peeled the bark from a large tree and with red paint depicted on the tree the number of raiders. They painted an animal symbol on the bow of the canoes to represent the enemy they were setting out to conquer. At their camps each night, the attackers marked trees with symbols indicating the size of their party and its destination. When the party returned, they painted the marked tree, or one nearby, with a pictorial account of the venture. In the painting, the canoe paddlers faced the settlement, scalps were symbolized in black paint, and the number of prisoners was indicated by bindings used to fetter captives. When a party returned from a raid or war, the authority of the temporary leader ended. Since warfare focused the lives of men and brought them glory and prestige, the organizer of a war party could recruit a following easily. The Iroquois considered themselves at war with all Indians with whom they had no alliance; thus, there always were potential victims.

When a returning war party passed through a League village, its captives were forced to run the gauntlet naked, and according to Cadwallader Colden (1755, vol. 1, 9), "the Women are much more cruel than the Men." As the warriors approached their home village, they sounded a war whoop and danced as they led their captives. At the war post they were welcomed and praised by an elder. In reply, warriors narrated their exploits and performed the War Dance. Captives were repatriated only under extenuating circumstances. A man either was adopted into the tribe or was tortured to death. The one exception was to free an extremely brave enemy warrior. If the warriors had lost one of their number to an enemy, the Iroquois widow could adopt any male prisoner to take the place of her husband. First, however, he was obliged to run a gauntlet to his new home. The women and children lined up with whips, and the potential adoptee ran between the lines. If he stumbled and fell, he was considered an unworthy person and was killed; if he ran the lines successfully, he became a member of the tribe.

The fact that widows had first choice concerning the fate of captives has been cited as evidence that women were important in decision making. In addition, there are records of women inducing men to go on war parties or restraining them under certain circumstances. Evidence such as this has led to the generalization that Iroquois society was dominated by women. In a review of ethnohistorical writings about the status of Iroquois women, Cara B. Richards (1957) has concluded that they gained dominance in relatively recent times. She notes that early reports state that the fate of captives was determined by the captor and the council. If a woman disagreed with their decision, she could not take effective counteraction until after the captor and council released the prisoner. Later in time the release of a prisoner by the council became an unimportant formality, indicating increased female authority. One factor leading to the expanding importance of women in decision making may have been the instability in village life after the introduction of firearms and the subsequent increase in mortality among warriors.

The general League pattern was to assimilate distantly related defeated tribes. Thus, after the Erie, Huron, and Neutral were conquered, they were brought into the League, but not with a voice equal to that of the original Five Nations.

The League tribes are famous not only for their complex political structure and its successful implementation, but for their treatment of prisoners. The tortures conceived were diverse and diabolical. A summary of their methods prepared by Nathanial Knowles (1940, 188) gives a good idea of the variations. Among the techniques were: "applying brands, embers, and hot metal to various parts of body; putting hot sand and embers on scalped head; hanging hot hatchets about neck; tearing out hair and beard; firing cords bound around body; mutilating ears, nose, lips, eyes, tongue, and various parts of the body; searing mutilated parts of the body, biting or tearing out nails; twisting fingers off; driving skewers in finger stumps; pulling sinews out of arms; etc." Only the Onondaga tortured young and old, male and female; the other tribes reserved their tortures for men. The usual practice, except for a person slated for possible adoption, was to begin abusing a captive soon after he was taken, and to begin his systematic torture when he arrived in the settlement of the captor. The prisoner was forced to run around inside a longhouse as young men burned him, primarily on the legs, until he fainted. As he was slowly being tortured, he was expected to sing about his lack of fear. After a captive fainted, he was revived and the tortures repeated. Care was taken to see that he did not die from the tortures because he was to mount a platform at dawn. Here he was bound so that he could move about and was tortured more before the entire community. When the captive was very near the point of dying, he was stabbed to death or his head was smashed. Normally the body of a tortured person was cooked and eaten.

RELIGION   For the Iroquois, the world was occupied by a host of invisible spirits. The most powerful deity was the Great Spirit, who created people, other animals, plants, and forces for good in nature. The Great Spirit indirectly guided human affairs but could not be appealed to directly. He was capable of countering the Evil Spirit by applying his energies, and people passed through life between these competing fraternal deities. Among the lesser supernatural controlling forces for good was the Thunderer, who was capable of bringing rain or exacting vengeance, especially against witches. Associations of the Thunderer with productivity are reflected in prayers offered to him when crops were planted and the thanks expressed after a harvest. The Spirit of the Winds commanded the winds and therefore could be helpful or harm people. The Three Sisters, the spirits of maize, beans, and squash, were conceived as lovely women and collectively called Our Life. Everything that aided people, including particular plants, fire, and water, had its spiritual associations. Some spirits assumed human form and were assigned specific obligations, and all bore the general name, the Invisible Aids. It was possible to communicate with the lesser spirits for good by burning tobacco, since it was thought that through this medium prayers and special needs could be made known to the gods. Gratitude was expressed in thanksgiving statements.

The Evil Spirit controlled a host of lesser spirit beings who brought pestilence to people and to crops, but few of these forces were systematized in the thinking of the Iroquois. One organized group of evil supernaturals was the False Faces, who were able to send death and destruction. They existed as contorted and evil-appearing faces and lived in out-of-the-way places; it was thought that anyone who chanced to see them would become paralyzed.

The most dreaded antisocial actions were believed to be performed by witches in league with the Evil Spirit. Anyone could conceivably assume the form of an animal, bird, or reptile in his or her desire to do evil. Witches were supposedly difficult to detect because they transformed themselves into inanimate objects at will. Witches were thought to have a society with regular initiations; to become a member an initiate supposedly had to kill his closest friend by supernatural means. Anyone who saw a witch practicing was free to kill him or her, and the normal punishment for unconfessed witches was death. It was possible to establish at a council meeting whether someone was a witch; if the accused confessed and promised to reform, he or she was freed.

Religious specialists, or Keepers of the Faith, were chosen by female and male elders of the matriclans and were expected to serve when requested. Both sexes were represented in nearly equal numbers, and all members held equal rank. Each was invested by being given a new name announced at the next general meeting of the nation. Their primary duty was to arrange and conduct the main religious ceremonies; sachems and chiefs were ex officio Keepers of the Faith. Among their other duties was the censuring of antisocial behavior; the strongest form of censure was to report serious transgressions to the tribal council. A person could choose to relinquish the obligations of Keeper of the Faith by assuming his or her old name.

Major Ceremonies   The Iroquois held six major religious ceremonies; in sequence of occurrence they were the Maple, Planting, Strawberry, Green Maize, Harvest, and New Year's (Midwinter) ceremonies. The first five were similar in many respects, as in sharing the common feature of public confessions prior to group observances. During these confessions, confessors held a string of white wampum as a symbol of sincerity. The audience did not pass judgment on transgressions, but it was expected that future behavior would reflect renewed purpose and intent. On the day of any ceremony, sacred rituals were held in the morning. The religious aspects included speeches by the Keepers of the Faith about the precedent and purpose of the ceremony, offerings of burnt tobacco,

prayers, and thanksgiving speeches. In the afternoon and evening, social festivities included dances and feasting. One of the most popular dances was the
Feather Dance, which included not only a dance but accompanying songs of
thanksgiving.

The seven-day New Year's Ceremony usually was held in early February.
Before the rituals began, people who had dreamed went from house to house
asking the residents to guess the nature of their dreams. Dreams were regarded
as important supernatural signs and were treated seriously. When someone suggested a reasonable text and meaning for a dream, the dreamer ceased his or
her quest for an interpretation. If the accepted text and its meaning included
statements about the future behavior of the dreamer, she or he was obligated to
behave as directed. Jesuit missionaries who witnessed the dream procedure in
1656 recorded it as a violent affair, with the dreamer threatening and actually
destroying a great deal of household property until he or she was satisfied with
an interpretation.

The New Year's events were initiated by two Keepers of the Faith disguised
in skin robes and corn husks that hung from their heads, over their bodies, and
from their wrists and ankles. Their skins were painted, and they carried pestles
for pounding maize as they visited every household during the morning. In each
dwelling they made a formal statement concerning the ceremony and sang a
song of thanksgiving. In the afternoon they returned to recite a second speech
and sing another song. The day's activities included strangling one or two white
dogs that symbolized purity. The body of a sacrificed dog was spotted with red
paint and adorned with feathers; white wampum was hung from its neck, and it
was suspended from a branch or a pole erected for this purpose. On the following day, in the morning, again at noon, and in the evening the Keepers of the
Faith returned to the houses. Dressed as warriors, they stirred the ashes in the
fireplace with a shovel, sprinkled ashes over the hearth, and offered a prayer,
followed by a thanksgiving song. The people dressed in their best clothing and
visited each house twice during the day. The next two days, the third and fourth,
were allotted to dancing and additional visits. At this time, too, groups of boys,
accompanied by an old woman carrying a large basket, visited each house. The
boys danced for the family, and if they were given presents, they went to the next
dwelling. If they received nothing, they attempted to steal whatever they could
before they moved on; if caught in the theft, they gave the item back without
hesitation. After they had visited the houses, they feasted on their take. On the
fifth day the white dog or dogs were taken from the poles and placed on a platform in the council house. A speech was made by a Keeper of the Faith about the
meaning of the sacrifice and expressing thanks to the Great Spirit. A song was
sung, and the dog's body was carried out to be burned in a fire built by the Keepers of the Faith. This ritual was to purge any evil and transfer it to the sacrificed
animal, who carried the message of contrition to the Great Spirit. The offering
also reflected the thanks of the people for the year's rewards. As the dog burned,
a Keeper of the Faith recited an invocation three times to gain the attention of the
Great Spirit. The most important event of the sixth day was the Thanksgiving

Dance, and the final day was devoted to gambling. Some evidence suggests that the white dog sacrifice was not associated with the New Year's Ceremony in aboriginal times.

False Face Society   A group organized to counteract the Evil Spirit and his emissaries was the famous False Face Society. A male became a participant by dreaming that he was a member and left the society by dreaming that he was no longer active. The only woman member was the Keeper of the False Faces, who not only kept the ceremonial paraphernalia but was supposed to be the only one who knew the identity of all the members. A False Face Society probably was represented in each village; its duties included curing illness and keeping evil spirits at bay. If someone was ill with a disease often treated by the society, and if he or she dreamed of false faces, it was a sign that the person could be cured by the False Face Society. The society was most noted for its ability to cure eye inflammations, nosebleeds, swellings, and toothaches. The Keeper of the False Faces was notified when someone hoped to be cured, and she assembled the members, each of whom covered himself with a face mask and blanket and carried a turtle-shell rattle. The members sprinkled the patient with hot ashes, per-

Figure 11-8. | Seneca False Face Society mask. (Courtesy of the UCLA Museum of Cultural History.)

formed a dance, and then withdrew. Another function of the False Face Society was to clear disease from a village at regular intervals.

The False Face Society masks were inspired by mythological beings and creatures seen during dreams. A mask was carved from a living basswood tree and portrayed one of about a dozen facial types. As the most distinguishing feature some had crooked mouths, others a smile, some a protruding tongue, and so on. They might be painted black, brown, red, or white. (See Figure 11-8.) Another type of mask was made from braided and sewn corn husks. These represented important farming and hunting deities. Corn-husk masks also could be differentiated according to facial features.

Later Historic Changes in Iroquois Life

The preceding chapters about specific peoples all have included sections about the life cycle, but comparable information is largely unavailable for the Iroquois. Thus, our attention now shifts to historic changes in Iroquois life, and especially in their belief system since it is so well documented.

THE NEW RELIGION The unity underlying Iroquois political power declined precipitously with the French and Indian War, and the American Revolution provided a final blow. The Seneca were torn in two directions. Some favored neutrality, but most supported the British cause. Among the Seneca leaders was Cornplanter, who received a British commission as captain. To persuade other Iroquois to remain neutral, the Americans laid waste to their villages and farmlands in 1779; and about 1780 Cornplanter and his followers moved to the upper Allegheny River drainage.

Shortly afterward the Americans were searching for an Indian group to counteract the influence of Joseph Brant and his pro-British Mohawk, and they selected Cornplanter. He accepted the responsibility, apparently willing to change his pro-British stance because he perceived the Americans as more powerful, and actively sought supporters for the Americans. In the course of his official travels he went to Philadelphia on a number of occasions and became acquainted with the Quakers. In 1796 the Commonwealth of Pennsylvania granted Cornplanter a fee patent title to three separate plots of land, each about a mile square, very near the New York state line on the Allegheny River. One plot was called Burnt House, and here Cornplanter had soon gathered about him some four hundred persons in thirty dwellings. One of the persons living in the home of Cornplanter was his half-brother, Handsome Lake or Ganiodayo. (See Figure 11-9.) Quaker missionaries went to Burnt House in 1798, and one of them, Henry Simmons, stayed at the settlement. In his study of what happened at Burnt House at this time, Merle H. Deardorff (1951) has included information from the Simmons diary, an ethnographic gem, and other Quaker writings. We learn that Simmons was asked by Cornplanter about his beliefs and that Simmons offered answers cautiously. As Deardorff (1951, 90) writes:

Questions about theology and morals had been referred to Simmons, and answered in the Quaker way: Look inside. You have a Light in there that will show you what is good and what is bad. When you know you have done wrong, repent and resolve to do better. Outward forms and books and guides are good; but they are made by men. The Great Spirit himself puts the Inner Light in every man. Look to it. Learn to read and write so that you may discover for yourself whether or not the white man's Book is true. Learn to distinguish good from evil so that you may avoid the pricks of conscience in this world and prosper; and that you may avoid punishment in the next.

The missionary, however, did note many forms of behavior that were not compatible with his beliefs. He particularly was annoyed at the preparations for a "Dancing Frolick," and the council decided to stop them, in part as a result of

Simmons's objections. Furthermore, the Iroquois men returned from Pittsburgh with intoxicants that they had received in trade for furs, and consumption of these led to a community binge of several weeks' duration. This brought reproval from the Quaker, and the contrite Indians resolved that two chiefs would be appointed to curb drinking. The killing of a witch and dances held for the dead were other distressing events that Simmons witnessed.

At the house of Cornplanter, his half-brother Handsome Lake appeared to be near death in June 1799. On the fifteenth of the month Handsome Lake had a vision, the details of which were recorded by Simmons. In summary, Handsome Lake had seen three men carrying different types of bushes with berries attached. The men had asked him to eat some of the berries, for by doing so he would live to see berries ripen in the summer. The men had told him that the Great Spirit was unhappy about the drunkenness of the people, and had said that if Handsome Lake recovered he was not to drink intoxicants. The three men had said further that a fourth man would visit him later. When Handsome Lake regained consciousness, he asked Cornplanter to assemble the council, repeat what had occurred in the vision, and have each person eat a dried berry; these instructions were followed. Handsome Lake still was very ill, and within a short time he had a vision in which the fourth man, assumed to be the Great Spirit, came to take Handsome Lake because he pitied him in his suffering. When Handsome Lake awoke, he sent for Cornplanter and after talking with him fell into a trance for seven hours. Simmons (Deardorff 1951, 91) wrote, "His legs and arms were cold, his body warm but breathless." Handsome Lake revealed later that he had been led by a guide clothed in a "clear sky colour" and carrying a bow and a single arrow. Soon he had met his dead son and Cornplanter's recently dead daughter. The girl had told of her unhappiness because her father and brother argued, while the son of Handsome Lake had revealed that he was sorry that he had not cared for his father better. The guide then had stated that sons should treat their fathers well, that Handsome Lake must not drink intoxicants, and that he must give up all dances save the Green Maize Ceremony. The guide had pointed toward a river where canoes were loaded with barrels of whiskey, and where an evil man in charge of the cargo was (Deardorff 1951, 91) "going about very busy doing and making all the noise and mischief he could amongst the people." Furthermore, Handsome Lake had been told that if all the people agreed, it would be proper to accept whites as teachers. Finally, the guide had said that Handsome Lake was to return among the living and he would see no more of these things until he died; in death he would return to this setting if he behaved properly.

When Handsome Lake recovered, he began preaching his doctrine, which came to include the rejection of schools and a return to a subsistence-based economy. In 1802 his cause received American support when Handsome Lake went to Washington, D.C., with other Iroquois and President Thomas Jefferson condoned his teachings. Partly because of this official sanction, Handsome Lake became an acknowledged prophet. From the time of his recovery until his death, Handsome Lake visited Seneca communities to influence the behavior of others.

By 1807 his fame as a prophet had spread widely among the Iroquois and to other eastern tribes as well. When the War of 1812 began, the Iroquois had learned their lesson, and most of them did not participate. Handsome Lake in particular preached neutrality because of his continuing close ties with the Quakers. In 1815 the prophet moved to Onondaga, and it was here that he died the same year.

As Deardorff has noted, the Handsome Lake revelations or Gaiwiio (Good Message), came to be joined by a body of teachings that included biographical material, prophecy, law, parable, and anecdote. Believers called the entire system the New Religion. The Good Message was not the only basis for the New Religion; some of the more important changes proposed in the revelation had been initiated before Handsome Lake's trances. If the text of the revelations had been the only document to survive, Handsome Lake might have been assumed to be a great innovator, but from the diaries of the Quaker missionaries it is obvious that the revelations were in step with what were recognized and pressing problems at Burnt House. Although much of the Handsome Lake doctrine was influenced by Quaker and earlier Jesuit missionaries and some aspects were novel, these teachings also had deep roots in Iroquois religious life of old. The emphasis on confession, the continuity in honoring traditional gods, and the prominence of the annual ceremonial round are examples. Furthermore, the Iroquois had long placed considerable emphasis on prophetic dreams, and this too was a critical element in the Handsome Lake revelations. Like all successful prophets, Handsome Lake is remembered because he was the right man at the right moment in history. Most important, and unlike many other Indian prophets, he was willing to adapt his basic ideas to accommodate Quaker beliefs and even certain material aspects of white culture such as agricultural methods. This flexibility contributed to the improvement of Iroquois life in his time and unquestionably aided in the long-term survival of the Good Message. Soon after Handsome Lake's death, other Christian missionaries proselytized among the Seneca, and the Indians labored in council to establish a uniform approach to religion. The time-honored pattern of unanimity, however, could not be reached, and by 1820 the New Religion had become separate from other Iroquois religious patterns.

The Good Message was not recorded systematically until 1845, and no single text has become standard. By 1949 the New Religion was being taught in ten ceremonial structures, each termed a longhouse, on the meeting circuit of the Six Nations. Most of the preachers required four days to relate the Good Message. The Tonawanda Longhouse was called symbolically the Central Fire, and here were kept the most sacred strings of wampum that had belonged to Handsome Lake.

The New Religion includes the following tenets: the prohibition of intoxicants; obedience of children toward their parents and care of aged parents; faithfulness of married couples; reproval of gossiping or boasting; killing of witches; awareness of a hell for sinners and heaven for persons who have lived good lives or repented of having lived evil lives; and the acceptance of the ways of whites save for schools. As has been noted by Edmund Wilson (1960, 87), the New Religion "has a scope and a coherence which have made it endure as has the teaching of no other Indian prophet, and it is accepted at the present time by at least half the Iroquois world as a source of moral guidance and religious inspiration."

OTHER CHANGES The course toward modern Iroquois life was set in the early nineteenth century. Many of those Iroquois who sympathized with the British had moved to Canada, and the ones in the United States had settled on small reservations. Each of these two major groups had its own chiefs, councils, and wampum, and each became increasingly involved in reservation politics and relationships with the respective governments. In the early 1800s the Iroquois in both countries continued to hunt over broad areas that reached beyond reservation boundaries and to plant traditional crops in old ways. However, as increasing numbers of white settlers occupied nearby land, Iroquois life began to change in basic ways.

The ability of the Indians to hunt profitably declined as the supply of game diminished; furthermore, they no longer could move from one area to another as the productivity of their farmland declined. Consequently, they turned increasingly to plow agriculture, farming in the manner of whites. In New York State, the Iroquois depended heavily on annuities derived from the sale of land to obtain items of material culture such as blankets, guns, and farming equipment. Annuity payments unquestionably eased their transition to a more sedentary life-style. The greatest threat to their security was continued encroachment of whites on their lands; another concern was the conflict arising from the pull of traditional Iroquois culture and the attractions of white culture. This inevitably caused factions to develop on the reservations, and these have continued into the present.

Modern Life: The Six Nations Reserve

A modern stronghold of the Iroquois is in western Ontario along the Grand River. As compensation for lands lost in New York State following the American Revolution, the Mohawk war chief Joseph Brant received the original tract of 675,000 acres from the British. In 1784–85 about 1,450 League members began to settle along Grand River; they were accompanied by nearly 400 persons from other tribes who had lived among the Iroquois before the American Revolution. Although the Mohawk were the majority, the fact that other League tribes were represented exemplified the ideal structure of the League.

Brant claimed that the land grant showed British recognition of Iroquois national sovereignty, and he felt free to do as he wished with the land. Soon he had sold about half of the acreage to whites. He felt that white farmers in their midst would encourage Indian men to farm. The Mohawk, Oneida, and Tuscarora lived largely along upper Grand River and became known as the Upper Tribes. Many had been Christianized before migrating to the reserve, and they were as a group reasonably responsive to becoming more like white Canadians. Down the river were the Lower Tribes, the Cayuga, Onondaga, and Seneca, who retained a far more traditional way of life and were receptive to the Good Message of Handsome Lake.

People in the Six Nations Reserve lived on scattered homesteads by the 1950s, and individual holdings were inherited by members. The stress placed by Canadians on paternal inheritance had confused the traditional matrilineal system. Inheritance rights, like individual rights to band membership, were calculated patrilineally according to the Canadian authorities but matrilineally by the Iroquois. Another difference was that Canadians considered the nuclear family an important social unit, and their emphasis on it robbed the clans of important functions. A newly married couple on reserve land now lived either with the husband's or wife's relatives only until they could establish an independent household (neolocal residence). The exogamous nature of the matriclans continued to be observed by some people, but others felt it was acceptable to marry anyone to whom close genealogical ties could not be established. The matrilineages remained important in selecting sachems and chiefs of the clan, but disputes arose over which were the leading lineages with the vested rights. Members of the leading lineages of a clan most often made an effort to retain their clan ties so that they would not lose their political and religious authority. A real difficulty, however, stemmed from the fact that even some conservative families no longer could trace their clan affiliations.

By 1956 the reserve population, most of whom were Mohawk and Cayuga, numbered about sixty-five hundred. In the 1950s Annemarie A. Shimony studied reserve Indians who had adopted some white ways but had categorically rejected assimilation into greater-Canadian culture. No attempt is made here to summarize her wealth of information; instead, the focus is first on the New Religion and then on political developments since a critical year, 1924.

THE NEW RELIGION ON THE RESERVE The New Religion had four local congregations, each symbolized by a type of fire and centered at a different longhouse. The Central Fire was the Tonawanda Longhouse in New York State. Here preachers on the longhouse circuit were invested, but the Central Fire had no jurisdiction over the Home Fires. The rituals of the four longhouses were essentially the same. Each longhouse had wampum to validate its legitimacy, and the particular one to which a person belonged was determined by matrilineage ties and by its proximity. Longhouses were the traditional rectangular wooden buildings, usually with doors and wood-burning stoves at each end and with benches along the walls.

Longhouse leaders were Keepers of the Faith or deacons, as they more commonly were called. Each longhouse had a leading male and female Keeper of the Faith, chosen on the basis of merit. They guided all longhouse functions. With a breakdown of the clan structure, Keepers of the Faith as a group had an increased voice in community affairs. A second longhouse functionary, the Keeper of the Fire, was the guardian of the longhouse wampum. His moiety and clan affinities were unimportant, but he had to be a staunch believer in the New Religion. The wampum was symbolic of the longhouse traditions, and the people believed that Canadian officials sought to destroy the wampum and thereby eliminate the longhouses. The final longhouse leader was the Speaker, who presented traditional and extemporaneous speeches to the congregation. Such persons did not hold a formal office, nor were they usually preachers on the longhouse circuit. A Speaker was required to have a talent for public speaking and knowledge of traditional speeches.

A longhouse served many functions in the members' efforts to resist becoming like other Canadians. The organization fulfilled social, medical, economic, and political needs. Social gatherings included softball or lacrosse games, raffles, and dances. Organized social activities sponsored outside the longhouse usually were closed to longhouse members by their own dogma. The longhouse ceremonial round was rich in detail; it was based on the Handsome Lake revelations plus the aboriginal planting and harvest ceremonies, and the old and new means for curing. An important aspect of almost any longhouse function was the recitation of a formal address of thanks to the Great Spirit for the continued life of the persons attending and thanks to the participants for attending. In all longhouse activities the ritual and social language was Iroquois; speaking English was disapproved of in any context. To the members, participation in longhouse events gave real purpose to life and at the same time offered a systematic philosophy for living. People were encouraged to remember the teachings of Handsome Lake and to live good lives. At times the younger members were told not to imitate such fashion extremes of whites as high-heeled shoes and low-cut dresses for girls. Neither should one listen to the radio, watch television, or drink intoxicants, for such behavior was not in keeping with the New Religion. Behind it all was the real fear that the longhouse members would become carbon copies of their white Canadian neighbors. The conflict of values seems often to have led to trauma at the time of death for those individuals who had at some time followed forbidden white ways.

For members of the New Religion and other Iroquois as well, there was a deeply rooted focus on death. Death supposedly could be caused by failure to accept a time-honored view about the spirit world, by showing a lack of respect for plants or animals, or by failing to hold rituals as directed. Furthermore, the dead had great power over the living, and to neglect them was an invitation to disease and death. In general, it was thought that souls resided in a pleasant upperworld or else suffered punishment. Souls bent on evil could assume animal forms, but ordinarily they were nonmaterial or a light vapor. All of this concern with death and the dead necessitated the proper performance of obligations to the dead. To avert death and illness for the community or the individual, the Ceremony for the Dead was held at least once and preferably twice each year.

POLITICAL DEVELOPMENTS SINCE 1924 The sachems, who were either Christians or members of the New Religion, represented traditional authority and formed the official political body of the Six Nations Reserve until 1924. The longhouse sachems considered that their Christian counterparts were not legitimate officeholders unless they had been invested at a longhouse ceremony, which was comparable to raising up a sachem in the old League. With respect to Canadian officials, the sachems were divided over whether or not they favored closer rapport. In 1924 some World War I veterans, especially those from the Upper Tribes, formed a group known as the Progressive Warriors and sought Canadian recognition of an elected council. In an ensuing investigation of Six Nations Reserve affairs, the sachems would not present their case to Canadian representatives; thus, the government heard from only the acculturated faction, which supported elected chiefs. The Canadians favored elected leaders since they received little cooperation from the sachems, who represented the traditional confederacy council. An elected council was installed in 1924; the New Religion sachems were locked out of the council house, and Royal Canadian Mounted Police officers enforced the government's decision. The supporters of the confederacy were bitter against the Canadians as well as against their factional opposites, and the bitterness continues to the present. In an ethnohistorical account about the recent past on the reserve, Sally M. Weaver (1972) has noted that the confederacy council refused to disband after the elected council was instituted and continued to hold regular meetings in the hope of being reinstated as the only legitimate authority.

POPULATION DISPERSAL AND DIVISIONS   Life became difficult on the Six Nations Reserve during the Great Depression (1929–39); some families left to find seasonal work, while others returned because on the reserve they could at least raise their own food. Again during World War II, the population dispersed as many people left the reserve to find factory jobs or enlist in the services. Following this exodus came another change during the 1950s as increasing numbers of residents worked in nearby cities and the reserve itself became steadily more suburban.

At present, Six Nations Reserve residents remain deeply divided, as some support a Christian life-style and others adhere to the longhouse traditions. The groups are socially distinct and basically antagonistic; they are brought together primarily in organized sporting events. Those faithful to the longhouse are proud of being Iroquois, adhere to the New Religion, and participate in the annual round of what have become traditional ceremonies. They speak at least one Indian language, follow the matrilineal descent system, and support the confederacy, whose chiefs usually are longhouse members. Those residents who belong to the Christian group may identify themselves as Iroquois, yet their behaviors and beliefs appear to be much the same as those of white Canadians. Most residents, whether Christian or longhouse supporters, are preoccupied with local politics, and particular issues have varied combinations of supporters. Confederacy members in general resent the power of the band council, which began expanding its dominance in the 1960s. They likewise object to accepting social benefits, such as aid to the aged and unmarried mothers, provided by the Canadian government, because to do so is to acknowledge federal control. However, they do accept this and other aid despite their philosophical objections.

As effective formal education and urbanization have impinged increasingly on reserve residents, the importance of farming has declined rather abruptly. Most residents hold unskilled or semiskilled jobs to which they commute daily. Very few families rely on welfare aid. Life on the reserve in general has been less attractive in recent years, and only about half of the band members live there. Another change is apparent in marriage patterns; by the early 1970s at least 40 percent of the marriages were between an Indian and a white. An overall view of the reserve at present would seem to indicate that the vitality of the confederacy is diminishing steadily.

Modern Life: The Caughnawaga Reservation

Recall that some of the Mohawk were attracted to Canada by Jesuit missionaries in the late seventeenth century. Known as the Praying Indians, they made three moves before settling in 1719 on mission land that was to become the Caughnawaga Reservation in 1830. Plots were allotted to families, and other land was held for future generations. The holdings could be leased to anyone but were sold or given only to other members of the reservation. The reservation extends for about eight miles along the St. Lawrence River and is up to four miles wide. In the 1940s the reservation population was nearly 3,000 persons. Some 2,700 were Roman Catholics, 250 were Protestants, and fewer than 100 belonged to the New Religion. The Roman Catholics have been losing ground since the 1920s. Some persons have become Protestants, and since World War I small numbers have been attracted to the doctrines of Handsome Lake.

ECONOMIC ADJUSTMENTS   Following the move to Caughnawaga in the early 1700s, the economy of the migrants underwent a series of major adjustments. At first the Jesuit priests attempted to teach the men to farm, but because this was regarded as women's work, men continued to hunt or fight enemies at every opportunity. Before long, increasing numbers of men were attracted to the fur trade and worked as canoemen or voyageurs for French trading parties, sometimes fighting as they moved through hostile country. After the British controlled the area, the Mohawk continued working in the fur trade until its decline about 1800. Following this stage some of the men were employed by the logging industry to raft timber through rapids and along fast water; this work was as dangerous as being a canoeman or warrior. At about this time some men finally turned to farming, and others became the first medicine show Indians, traveling about New England by horse and buggy selling Indian medicinal preparations. Others seem to have performed with circuses during summer months and returned to the reservation for the winter. Another group became obsessed by alcohol; although they found temporary employment in Montreal, much of their time was spent drinking excessively.

In 1886 the Dominion Bridge Company began construction of a cantilever bridge across the St. Lawrence River, using reservation land for a bridge abutment. In obtaining permission to use the land the company agreed to hire reservation Indians, but only for unskilled labor jobs. The Mohawk were unhappy with this arrangement and could not be kept off the bridge as the span was being built. Soon it became apparent that they not only were unafraid of heights but were pleased with the new experience. The din of riveting did not faze them in the least. After pestering the crew foreman, a few men finally were hired, and they turned out to be excellent workers. It appears that three crews were trained on this bridge. In the erection of a bridge of this type, precut and drilled beams and girders are hoisted into place with a crane or derrick, temporarily bolted and plumbed, then riveted. The Iroquois were to become members of riveting crews, the most dangerous as well as the most lucrative work.

The Caughnawaga Mohawk continued to work on bridges and systematically trained riveting crews. By 1907 there were over seventy skilled workers, about half of whom were employed on the Quebec Bridge, which spans the St. Lawrence River near Quebec City. On August 29, 1907, disaster occurred; the span fell, and ninety-six men, including thirty-five Caughnawaga, were killed. Bridge work now took on a new meaning; obviously dangerous, it became a more attractive form of employment than either timber rafting or performing in circuses. The reservation women had a somewhat different attitude; one of their first moves was to force the gangs to work on many different projects so that a similar disaster could not affect so many families. Since there were relatively few bridge jobs in Canada, some men found employment on other high steel projects. The women also demonstrated that their Christian faith had not been shaken by purchasing a large crucifix of St. Francis Xavier for the church.

THE BROOKLYN MOHAWK About 1926 three or four high steel crews from the reservation went to New York City to work, and three more gangs arrived in 1928. With the construction of Rockefeller Center in the 1930s, more gangs arrived in the city. They became members of the Brooklyn local of the International Association of Bridge, Structural, and Ornamental Iron Workers and roomed nearby in the North Gowanus area. By the late 1940s, the North Gowanus locality was occupied by about 125 Mohawk steelworkers and their families. While their families lived in Brooklyn, the men traveled across the country, working on various jobs. The reason offered for moving about was the overtime pay at distant jobs, but this simply was a rationalization for their desire to wander. They would hear of a new job, and they soon would leave for it with little or no warning.

North Gowanus consisted mainly of tenements and some factories. The Mohawk lived within ten blocks of each other in the best houses. Households were composed of related families and their families who occupied one or adjacent apartment buildings. The residences were furnished in the manner typical for local whites with the addition of Mohawk artifacts on a wall or mantel. In these homes, where the men frequently were away, many women spent their free time making what have come to be regarded as typically Indian craft items. These were sold at fairs in the New York State area by the most Indian-looking men of the group. Other members of a household were single girls from the reservation. They worked in nearby factories, not infrequently married non-

Indians, and were lost to the Iroquois community. The boys raised in these households adjusted well to school life, but they dropped out after fulfilling the minimum state requirements to become workers in high steel. Since very little training was necessary, it was not long before a boy could work as an adult in one of the gangs and earn about $150 a week (circa 1955).

Social life of the Brooklyn Mohawk centered at a particular bar in the North Gowanus neighborhood. The high steel men dropped by at the end of the work day; on weekends and in the evening they brought their wives. On the walls of the bar were a reproduction of *Custer's Last Stand,* drawings of Iroquois warriors, and steelworkers' helmets. According to Morris Freilich (1958, 479), "Periodically, the Indians tear the place apart; they feel it their right, since it is their home. If outsiders give any sign of attempting to make it their clubroom too, blood flows fast and furious." The combative nature of the individual Mohawk existed still, and examples of bloody fights were not uncommon. They nurtured the element of daring in their jobs and in dealings with others, and their continued use of intoxicants led to other forms of recklessness. Again to quote from Freilich (1958, 478), "Some examples from my field work include driving 90 miles per hour on a winding road at night in the mountains of New York State in an old car while inebriated; accepting a dare to go faster than the speedometer could register and two men having sexual intercourse with a girl while her fiance was asleep beside her."

Ties with Caughnawaga were maintained by the Brooklyn residents. Reservation members came to work in Brooklyn, and relatives arrived to visit, especially in any time of crisis. A man might take his family to the reservation for the summer, but he remained with them for only a short time. When a steelworker retired, he was likely to return to the reservation, but his adjustment to the uneventful and sedentary life was difficult. One response was to return to Indian ways to the point of not speaking English and to become deeply involved in reservation politics and social life.

In a search for the reasons behind the striking success of the Mohawk in high steel work, Freilich has made some noteworthy observations. First, he felt that they were behaving in the pattern of warriors, exhibiting no fear of heights as a warrior would in theory not fear the enemy or death. From listening to a conversation about heights among moderately intoxicated Mohawk, he learned that they did in fact fear heights. They concealed their fear to prove their courage and to maintain their reputation as being unafraid. Surprisingly, work in high steel was highly compatible with many essential features of the old Mohawk way of life. The men left home to work for extended periods as they had left to hunt and fight in aboriginal times. There was danger and possible death in what they did, just as there had been of old. When a man returned, he could boast of the tall buildings on which he had worked, just as he once had boasted of his skills in combat. The modern steelworker was subject to little authority, and if he was displeased he could quit his job just as he formerly had been able to drop out of a war party. These and other parallels lent support to the traditional status of the male in a nontraditional setting.

ATTITUDES: IROQUOIS AND WHITE   Iroquois and white American attitudes were in so many ways fundamentally different that it is little wonder each
group failed to understand the other. Whites were in general thrifty, coveting
wealth to accumulate more wealth; the Iroquois were generous and wasteful
with money and material things. Whites were orderly in keeping house, and
their dwellings, which were built by contractors, followed standard plans. Indian
houses were untidy, jerry-built, and often left unfinished. Whites were time-
oriented and considered promptness a great virtue, but "Indian time" meant
being late or not appearing at all. The old Tuscarora demandingness ran wild in
their dealings with the State of New York. The state supplied schools, school
buses, welfare, road maintenance, and other services. The Indians not only accepted these but expected more. Their dependency, to their thinking, was based
on obligations of the federal and state authorities stemming from old injustices
that were both real and imagined.

Iroquois Nationalism

In recent years the Iroquois have attempted to assert their nationalism by
means of diverse protests. For example, most of the United States Iroquois have
refused to vote, although they all have had the right to do so since the Citizenship Act of 1924. By not voting they have indicated that they do not recognize
United States political domination over them and in the process have reinforced
their own identity. During World War I they separately declared war on Germany.
In World War II when subject to selective service as a result of the Citizenship
Act, some went to jail or in other ways evaded the draft. The Iroquois in New
York State have resisted strongly all efforts by state officials to intervene in their
affairs. Justification for the Indian position has been that treaties with the federal
government implied equality in national standing between the Six Nations and
the United States. Predictably, the Iroquois have resisted both state and federal
income taxes and have fought efforts to use reserved lands for the St. Lawrence
Seaway, needs of the Power Authority of New York State, and the relocation of
highways. These disputes usually have been complicated by the fact that elected
chiefs cooperate with the whites, but hereditary chiefs do not.

In 1958 the very dynamic nationalistic Iroquois leader Mad Bear accepted
an invitation to visit Cuba, where he met with Fidel Castro. Mad Bear and his
followers hoped that they could be admitted to the United Nations under Cuban
sponsorship. The emergence of highly nationalistic governments in various
parts of the world has given the Iroquois hope, strengthened their position, and
contributed to the consolidation of their own nationalism.

In trying to maintain ownership of their land, the Iroquois have become
deeply involved with New York State and federal government agencies in recent
years. The St. Lawrence Seaway and the Power Authority of New York State have
nibbled away at Iroquois lands, but a more bitter dispute involved the federal
government and the Seneca. To control flooding of the Ohio River, a series of
dams were to be built on the Allegheny River. The Seneca opposed the one that

was to be built at Kinzua, Pennsylvania, because the reservoir would flood ten thousand acres of their best land in the Allegheny Reservation in New York State and would require the relocation of 130 families. The Seneca involved sought to have an alternate plan accepted that would not involve their lands, but the U.S. Army Corps of Engineers objected because of its greater cost. The Indians attempted to block the project through the courts, but each of the 1957–59 decisions supported the right of the federal government to condemn the land involved. The Seneca persistently maintained that a Six Nations treaty assured their lasting right to the land and that the federal government had no right to abrogate it. The treaty, signed in 1794, stated the following about these and other Iroquois lands: "Now the United States acknowledges all the land within the aforementioned boundaries to be the property of the Seneka nation; and the United States will never claim the same, nor disturb the Seneka nation. . . ." However, the dam was eventually built. After a long and complicated court battle, the Seneca, with the aid of Quakers, received $15 million in direct damages and rehabilitation monies for the land and homes they lost.

Yet, times are changing! In 1976 the Seneca of the Allegheny Reservation signed an agreement with the State of New York as equals. This was the first time since the early 1800s that the state had recognized the sovereign or national status of the Seneca. To build a highway through the reservation, the state attempted to exercise its power of eminent domain, but the courts, including the U.S. Supreme Court, held that the state had no right to condemn reservation lands for the highway. As a result, the state negotiated with the Seneca and received an easement of, but not title to, 795 acres of land. In return the state agreed to pay $2 million, give the Indians *title* to 795 acres of land from the adjoining Allegheny State Park, and provide other benefits.

The Iroquois long have been adamant in asserting that the governments of Canada and the United States must acknowledge their distinct national identity and deal with them as a sovereign nation on the basis of negotiated treaties. In the recent past, the federal government of the United States had refused to entertain the concept of "nations within a nation," but as indicated in the previous paragraph, the federal courts began to be far more sympathetic to sovereignty cases in the mid-1970s. The Iroquois have been among those Indians most persistent in pressing claims for lands illegally taken from them over the years. The Mohawk and Cayuga of New York State, who are pressing claims, are willing to accept monetary settlements, but other Iroquois want land plus damages. One of the difficulties in many of these cases is the split among the Indians themselves; traditionalists, represented largely by longhouse supporters, often are unwilling to compromise as much as progressives, who live on the same reservations. Yet, both sides seek the day when the League of the Iroquois or Hodenosaunee again will guide the destiny of its people.

| Comparisons with Other Indians

The unique structure of the League and its effectiveness in dealing with other Indians and colonial Europeans invite "what if" questions. What if the Hopi had achieved a political institution comparable to the League; what internal changes in their political life might have produced a league structure, or was the possibility unrealistic? What if the Iroquois had been patrilineal and patrilocal; what forms of kinship terminology could have emerged? What if aboriginal Iroquois men had been farmers; what accompanying sociocultural differences might be anticipated? Exercises such as these lead to speculations about and greater insight into peoples' identities in historical, functional, and ecological terms.

The bellicose quality of the Iroquois invites comparison with other peoples described, especially the Crow. What characteristics did they share in terms of recruitment for warfare, organization, methods, and constraints placed on warriors? It also is worthwhile to identify other clear adjustments that peoples made to support the war complex.

| Additional Readings

The book by Lewis H. Morgan (1851) remains the standard Iroquois source; one of the most comprehensive more recent studies of these people is by Annemarie A. Shimony (1961). The best overview about particular Iroquois tribes is in the *Northeast* volume (15) of the *Handbook of North American Indians,* William C. Sturtevant, general editor (Washington, DC, 1978). Included in this volume are noteworthy ethnohistorical articles by Elisabeth Tooker. Ethnographers have retained their particular fondness for the Iroquois and have published many books about them in recent years. *The Death and Rebirth of the Seneca,* by Anthony F. C. Wallace (New York, 1970), may be the finest ethnohistory by an Americanist. *The Iroquois Struggle for Survival* (Syracuse, 1986) and *The Iroquois and the New Deal* (Syracuse, 1981), both by Lawrence M. Hauptman, examine aspects of recent political life in perceptive detail. Another volume of particular interest is *The Reservation* (Syracuse, 1978), by Ted C. Williams. The author is an anthropologist and the son of a Tuscarora sachem; the text concerns life on the Tuscarora Reservation in the 1930s and 1940s.

| Bibliography

Beauchamp, William M. 1926. The principal founders of the Iroquois League and its probable date. *Proceedings of the New York State Historical Association* 24:27–36.

Biggar, H. P., ed. 1925. *The Works of Samuel de Champlain,* vol. 2. Toronto.

Colden, Cadwallader. 1755. *The history of the Five Indian Nations of Canada.* 2 vols. London.

Deardorff, Merle H. 1951. The religion of Handsome Lake: Its origin and development. Bureau of American Ethnology Bulletin no. 149, 79–107. Washington, DC.

Fenton, William N. 1940. Problems arising from the historic northeastern position of the Iroquois. *Essays in Historical Anthropology of North America.* Smithsonian Miscellaneous Collections, vol. 100, 159–251. An excellent study of the Iroquoian tribes from the time of early historic contact until the modern period.

———. 1941. Tonawanda longhouse ceremonies: Ninety years after Lewis Henry Morgan. Bureau of American Ethnology Bulletin no. 128, 140–66. Included is a detailed summary outline of the Tonawanda Seneca ceremonial calendar that provides comparable detail for each event.

———. 1951a. Locality as a basic factor in the development of Iroquois social structure. Bureau of American Ethnology Bulletin no. 149, 35–54.

———. 1951b. The concept of locality and the program of Iroquois research. Bureau of American Ethnology Bulletin no. 149, 1–12.

———. 1951c. Iroquois studies at the mid-century. *Proceedings of the American Philosophical Society* 95:296–310.

Fenton, William N. 1957. Long-term trends of change among the Iroquois. In *Cultural stability and cultural change,* 30–35. American Ethnological Society.

Freilich, Morris. 1958. Cultural persistence among the modern Iroquois. *Anthropos* 53: 473–83.

Gridley, Marion E., ed. 1960. *Indians of today,* 3d ed. Chicago.

Hewitt, John N. 1892. Legend of the founding of the Iroquois League. *American Anthropologist* 5:131–48.

Indians of Quebec and the Maritime Provinces. N.d. Department of Citizenship and Immigration, Indian Affairs Branch. Ottawa.

Johnston, Charles M. 1964. *The valley of the Six Nations.* Toronto.

Kinzua Dam (Seneca Indian Relocation). 1964. Hearings before the Subcommittee on Indian Affairs of the Committee on Interior and Insular Affairs, House of Representatives, 88th Congress, 1st session. Washington, DC.

Knowles, Nathaniel. 1940. The torture of captives by the Indians of eastern North America. *Proceedings of the American Philosophical Society* 82:151–225.

Lafitau, Joseph François. 1974. *Customs of the American Indians compared with the customs of primitive times,* William N. Fenton and Elizabeth L. Moore, eds. and trans., vol. 1. Toronto. (Vol. 2, Toronto, 1977.) This was the first systematic study of the Iroquois and often is stated to be a classic in ethnographic writings.

Lydekker, John W. 1938. *The faithful Mohawks.* Cambridge.

McKenney, Thomas L., and James Hall. 1933. *The Indian tribes of North America,* vol. 1. Edinburgh.

Morgan, Lewis H. 1851. *League of the Ho-De-No-Sau-Nee or Iroquois.* 2 vols. New York. (Editions published in 1901 and 1904 were edited and footnoted by Herbert M. Lloyd and were reproduced in 1954 by the Human Relations Area Files.) The standard Iroquois ethnography and a key Iroquois source; more precisely, a detailed description of one group of Seneca living between 1841 and 1850 and capable of recalling the past.

Mitchell, Joseph. (*See* Wilson, Edmund.)

Parkman, Francis. 1892. *A half-century of conflict.* 2 vols. Boston.

———. 1901, 1902. *The conspiracy of Pontiac and the Indian war after the conquest of Canada.* 2 vols. Boston.

Richards, Cara B. 1957. Matriarchy or mistake: The role of Iroquois women through time. In *Cultural stability and cultural change,* 36–45. American Ethnological Society.

Schoolcraft, Henry R. 1846. *Notes on the Iroquois.* New York.

Shimony, Annemarie A. 1961. *Conservatism among the Iroquois at the Six Nations Reserve.* Yale University Publications in Anthropology, no. 65. New Haven. The best comprehensive study of the Iroquois since Morgan's ethnography, the second key Iroquois source, and one of the finest studies of North American Indians.

Speck, Frank G. 1955. *The Iroquois.* Cranbrook Institute of Science Bulletin no. 23.

Stone, William L. 1838. *Life of Joseph Brant-Thayendanegea.* 2 vols. New York.

Thwaites, Reuben G. 1898. *Travels and explorations of the Jesuit missionaries in New France,* vol. 13. Cleveland, OH.

Voget, Fred. 1951. Acculturation at Caughnawaga: A note on the native-modified group. *American Anthropologist* 53:220–31.

Wallace, Anthony F. C. 1951. Some psychological determinants of culture change in an Iroquoian community. Bureau of American Ethnology Bulletin no. 149, 55–76.

———. 1958. Dreams and the wishes of the soul: A type of psychoanalytic theory among the seventeenth century Iroquois. *American Anthropologist* 60:234–48.

Weaver, Sally M. 1972. *Medicine and politics among the Grand River Iroquois.* National Museum of Man Publications in Ethnology, no. 4.

———. 1978. Six Nations of the Grand River, Ontario. In *Handbook of North American Indians,* William C. Sturtevant, gen. ed., vol. 15, 525–36. Washington, DC.

Wilson, Edmund. 1960. *Apologies to the Iroquois.* (Includes a reprinting of "The Mohawks in High Steel," by Joseph Mitchell.) New York. The study by Mitchell is the most complete discussion of the history of Iroquois work in high steel and should be consulted in conjunction with the study of the same subject by Morris Freilich. The balance of Wilson's book is a sensitive analysis of the modern scene in New York State and in Ontario, Canada.

Wintemberg, William J. 1931. Distinguishing characteristics of Algonkian and Iroquoian cultures. *Annual Report, 1929, National Museum of Canada,* 65–125.

12 The Eastern Cherokee: Farmers of the Southeast

My companions, men of renown, in council, who now sleep in the dust, spoke the same language [anti-removal] and I now stand on the verge of the grave to bear witness to their love of country. My sun of existence is fast approaching to its sitting and my aged bones will soon be laid in the bosom of this earth we have received from our fathers who had it from the Great Being above. When I sleep in forgetfulness, I hope my bones will not be deserted by you.

Woman Killer, a man reportedly over eighty years of age in 1830, argues against selling Cherokee land at the time of their pending removal from North Carolina. (Strickland, 1977, 379)

IN THE EARLY history of the Southeast, four tribes were larger and more influential than any others: the Cherokee, Chickasaw, Choctaw, and Creek. Along with the Seminole, who arose as a distinct entity in historic times, they have been called the Five Civilized Tribes. The largest aboriginal nation in the southeastern United States was the Cherokee; the one with the greatest political influence early in its history was the Creek. The Choctaw soon were divided internally, which dissipated their political effectiveness, while Chickasaw strength declined early in the historic period. Each nation owned land that white settlers coveted, and with the federal Removal Bill of 1830 these Indians were moved west of the Mississippi River. They often were driven from their homes and their property seized illegally; thousands died from the calculated cruelties and gross negligence of white oppressors. Some Cherokee who lived in the southern Appalachian Mountains refused to leave. They hid in the mountains, and when it was safe, they reestablished themselves in North Carolina, where they have continued to live. This chapter describes these people because they successfully resisted removal and because they are the largest aboriginal tribe remaining in the Southeast culture area. Furthermore, they exhibit a vitality that is refreshing, and the numerous scholarly studies about them make it possible to plot the changes in their way of life with considerable precision.

| People, Population, and Language

Many theories, most of them fanciful, have been offered to account for the presence of the Cherokee in the Southeast. The archaeological record is sufficient for Joffre L. Coe (1961) to suggest that ancestors of the Cherokee occupied the southeastern area for thousands of years. At the time of historic contact their number was estimated at twenty-two thousand, but this may be an exaggerated figure. Cherokee is a corruption of Tsalagi, the term they used for themselves. Their language belongs to the Iroquoian family and to the Macro-Siouan phylum; thus, their closest linguistic relatives are the Iroquois. When first encountered they lived in what is now eastern Tennessee and western North Carolina and spread into Kentucky on the north and Georgia to the south. (See Figure 12-1.) They occupied the Great Smoky Mountains, and in part because of the rugged nature of the terrain, they lived in four regional groups that had a certain degree of mutual isolation reflected in dialectic differences. The people discussed in this chapter are designated as the Eastern Cherokee to distinguish them from the Cherokee of Oklahoma. The Eastern Cherokee own about fifty-seven thousand acres in western North Carolina, and in 1980 they numbered about forty-eight hundred.

| Early Contacts and Conflicts with Whites

The expedition led by Hernando de Soto possibly passed through a Cherokee community in 1540, but not until the late 1600s were white intrusions relatively common. Firearms and other trade goods became available about 1700,

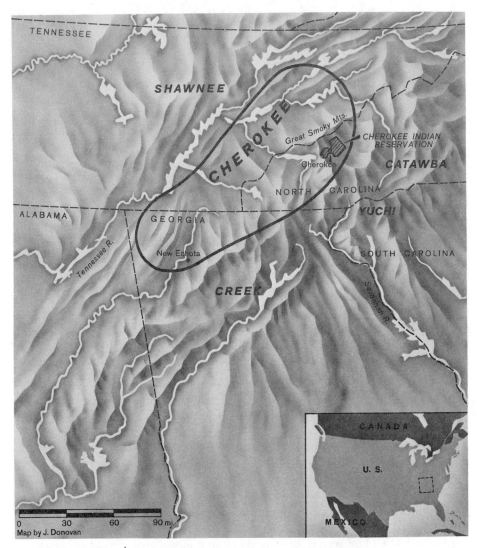

Figure 12-1. | Aboriginal range of the Eastern Cherokee Indians.

and shortly thereafter traders settled among them. It was not long before the Cherokee were embroiled in hostilities with white colonists from the eastern seaboard, and old rivalries with other Indians became intensified. In a series of conflicts with English colonists in 1759–61, many settlements were destroyed and the Cherokee were defeated. Soon thereafter intrusions by white settlers became increasingly common, and the Cherokee were forced to give up large sectors of land. In the American Revolution, they understandably fought on the side of the British, an alliance that led to the repeated destruction of their settlements. Peace was made in 1794, and some Cherokee decided to settle west of the Mississippi River because they felt that whites would never be satisfied in their desire for more land. Most Cherokee remained, however, and became prosperous farmers, even organizing a government modeled after that of the United States. Yet, pressures by whites for land never ceased, and by 1839 all the Cherokee had been forced from their homes. About one thousand escaped to live in the mountains as fugitives; the descendants of these persons are the Eastern Cherokee who now live in the North Carolina mountains.

| Early Historic Cherokee Life

The Cherokee were not described in reasonable detail until the mid-1700s, and since their ties with traders and other whites were well established by then, an aboriginal baseline ethnography was never assembled. The description that follows therefore focuses on their early historic life.

SETTLEMENTS AND MANUFACTURES   In reasonably early historic times, the Cherokee lived in scattered settlements because relatively level plots of ground suitable for cultivation were scarce. They built communities near streams and rivers to have access to fish and the game attracted to water, and also for religious reasons. A large settlement might encompass 450 acres, but a typical community covered a much smaller area. A large village or a number of smaller ones formed a political aggregate, or band, of from 350 to 600 persons. As a group approached the larger number, the tendency was for a portion to separate and organize as a new unit. In the early 1700s some sixty settlements were represented by about thirty-five bands.

People lived in rectangular houses built by setting poles vertically, weaving twigs between them, and coating the walls inside and out with a mixture of moist clay and grass. These gable-roofed houses sometimes had two stories and often were divided into rooms. In one room was a fireplace, and above it a hole in the roof let the smoke out. The most prominent furnishings were raised beds made of poles with wooden crosspieces covered with mats and skins. A cone-shaped building, termed a hot house, appears to have been used as a bathhouse for purification or as sleeping quarters on cold nights. The most imposing structure was the council house, used for religious or social functions as well as political ones; some of these buildings accommodated five hundred people. A council house was seven-sided, framed with logs, and had a roof supported by concentric circles of interior posts. The entire structure was covered with earth except for a narrow doorway and a smokehole at the center of the roof. Inside were benches and a central fireplace.

Among Cherokee domestic artifacts were a wide variety of well-made large and small baskets woven from split canes. These probably served as dishes, storage containers, carrying baskets, sifters, and winnowing trays. The Cherokee also made superior pottery containers for use in cooking food and for storage. Also outstanding were their pipes made with long wooden stems and platform bowls of stone with sculpted figures of animals or persons.

CLOTHING AND APPEARANCE   As was true for other Indians in the Southeast, the Cherokee made most clothing of deerskins sewn with sinew thread. A man's basic garment was a breechclout, and women wore knee-length skirts. Their moccasins were of deerskin, and they wore bison-skin robes during cold weather. Summer capes were made of feathers attached to a fiber base. Buckskin shirts and cloth boots were added in early historic times. The most distinctive personal adornment was the ear decoration of males. A section of the outer border of each ear was cut free, stretched, and wound with wire to hold it in an expanded arc. (See Figure 12-2.) This aboriginal practice declined in popularity when silver jewelry became popular in the late 1700s. Wealthy persons wore collarlike bands of clam-shell beads around their necks. Youthful warriors were tattooed by pricking the skin with a needle and rubbing bluish coloring in the openings. Designs of animals, flowers, and geometric forms were tattooed on the chest or muscular parts of the body. All the hair was plucked from a man's

Figure 12-2. | Three Cherokee men during a visit to England in 1762. (Courtesy of the British Museum.)

head except for a scalp lock at the back; it was decorated with beads or feathers. The hair of women appears to have been drawn back into a very long bundle held with ribbons.

SUBSISTENCE ACTIVITIES AND CONVEYANCES

The most important crops in aboriginal times appear to have been maize, beans, pumpkins, and tobacco, but the Cherokee began to raise cultigens of European origin even before whites appeared in their area. In early historic times, and presumably before, the maize harvest was critical for economic welfare. Gardens were planted, tended, and harvested by women, who were helped by men. When the maize crop failed, families dispersed to hunt and collect plant products. Even in ordinary times, wild plants were important in the diet; included were berries, grapes, persimmons, plums, nuts, and wild roots.

The most important meat animals were bison, deer, and game birds. Large game and birds were killed with self bows strung with bear sinew. The reed arrows were headed with points made from bone, fish scales, or metal. Small game was taken with darts shot from blowguns; a nine-foot blowgun fashioned from a reed had an effective range of sixty feet. Fish were harvested with hooks, leisters, or traps, and any discovered in shallow water were driven into baskets. Dogs were the only aboriginal domestic animal, but in later times hogs, horses, and other species of European derivation were raised.

The only important conveyance was the dugout canoe. Made from a log up to forty feet long, the canoe was hollowed by building a fire along one side and chipping out the charred wood. A vessel was about two feet wide, straight-sided, flat-bottomed, and capable of carrying twenty persons. Canoes made of wood frames covered with bark were known but were not important.

DESCENT, KINSHIP, AND MARRIAGE

Descent was traced through females (matrilineal), and a person was prohibited from marrying a member of his or her own matriclan (clan exogamy) or father's clan. A man's preferred mate was from his father's father's or mother's father's clan. After a man married and moved to another settlement, he still was regarded as a member of the clan of his birth. The members of a localized clan segment made certain that a spouse was mourned properly and that men fulfilled familial obligations. Violations led to public whippings by the women of the clan involved. A widow was expected to marry her deceased husband's brother (levirate), and a widower was supposed to take his deceased wife's sister as a spouse (sororate).

The aboriginal Cherokee kinship terminology reportedly was of the Crow system, meaning that the cousin terms were of the Crow type and descent was matrilineal. In this cousin terminology, a father's sister's daughter and mother's brother's daughter were termed differently from each other and from sisters or parallel cousins (mother's sister's and father's brother's daughters). However, a father's sister's daughter was classed with father's sister. The kinship terminology made it possible to distinguish precisely the four matrilineages that were most

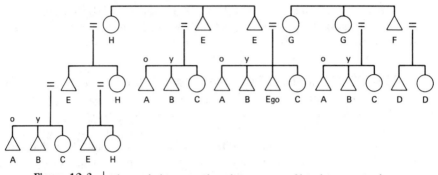

Figure 12-3. | The early historic Cherokee system of kinship terminology.

important to an individual: those of mother, father, mother's father, and father's father. (See Figure 12-3.)

SOCIAL DIMENSIONS   Eighteenth-century Cherokee households usually consisted of a number of nuclear families related through females (matrilineal extended family). Ideally, the household included an elderly couple, their daughters, the daughters' husbands (matrilocal residence), unmarried males born into the household, and the daughters' daughters. The mutual obligations of household members and their relationship with the members of other such units were defined with precision. A father taught his son to hunt, but a mother's brother, who lived in another household, was a child's disciplinarian. An in-marrying male was respectful toward his in-laws but was expected to joke with his wife's brothers and brothers-in-law; through the jokes of others, one became aware of his erring ways. In-marrying males retained close ties with their natal households and the clans of their birth, yet a household's members formed the most closely cooperating economic unit in the society.

In social and political terms, matrilineages were less important than matriclans. Members of the same clan in a band acted collectively. Apparently, seven named clans were represented in each village, and members of a clan cooperated closely at the village level. The seven clans in a settlement allotted farmlands to member households and regulated marriage. Another important obligation of a clan was to settle disputes with the members of another clan. The most serious crime was murder. If someone killed a person in another clan, all local members of the murderer's clan were held responsible, and all males of the dead person's clan were obligated to seek revenge. Preferably the offender himself was killed in revenge, although one of his clan mates might be substituted.

Eighteenth-century Cherokee ideals about adult behavior emerge with clarity from an analysis of myths and ethnographic accounts. A good person interacted congenially with others to maintain harmonious interpersonal relations. As Fred Gearing (1962, 31) has noted, a guiding principle behind behavior was embodied in the statement "thou shalt not create disharmony." In their ethos a person studiously avoided face-to-face conflict, he or she was cautious in dealings with others, and if overt conflict did arise she or he withdrew emotionally and physically if at all possible. Conflict was expressed at a distance through gossip and backbiting or more seriously in the use of magic to cast a spell over an adversary. An important means for eliminating personal animosities was a yearly ceremony to expose and purge ill feelings against other villagers.

The obligations of women tended to be much the same throughout the year. They cooked and prepared foods for storage, cared for children and the ill, and fashioned artifacts for domestic use. Farming activities introduced the greatest change from this routine. As Gearing has described the tempo of eighteenth-century Cherokee life, the routine of the males varied seasonally. In the summer after helping women plant the crops, young men played stickball, sometimes hunted, and constructed or repaired buildings. In the late summer they helped harvest the crops and then devoted three weeks to a series of ceremonies. In the fall and winter the young men hunted, fought, and held ceremonies.

Among the Cherokee and other Indians in the Southeast, stickball, the generic game from which lacrosse is derived, was a popular sport. Every player carried a stick that had a small loop and a pocket attached at the end. The object of the game was to carry a small ball across the goal of the opposite team. The ball could be carried in one hand, in the mouth, or in the mesh pocket of the stick. Any means, including the use of the stick, could be employed to obtain the ball; injuries, both purposeful and unintended, were difficult to prevent. The playing of stickball was a social event with many ceremonial aspects. For example, a man was not to have sexual intercourse with his wife for at least seven days before participating in a game, and if she was pregnant, he could not play. Several shamans were active for each side and a rite was performed at running water. On the night before the game a dance was held, magic was invoked against opponents, and other rituals took place. During a game itself, each side tried to disable the best players on the other team.

POLITICAL LIFE Early in their history, the Cherokee had a well-organized political life, although it was localized and did not unite the nation as a whole. This political organization changed as it was affected by both British influences and inclusion of warriors.

Early Organization Each Cherokee village, with an average of about 325 residents, was politically autonomous. Control was in the hands of a council of elders, the heads of clans, and representatives of two organizations, called the Whites and Reds, that stood in opposition to one another. The Whites symbolized peace, and members were traditionally old, passive, and mild-mannered. White chiefs achieved their goals through diplomacy and reached decisions by consensus. The Reds, by contrast, symbolized war; members were expected to be young, active, and impetuous. Reds generally were young males who had married into a village and thus occupied a marginal position within the social system. As Reds aged, they became associated with the Whites and gradually found themselves integrated into community life.

In the fall, at a time between the Harvest Ceremony and the rekindling of a sacred fire, a white flag was raised above the council house to indicate that the Whites now were assuming control of a settlement, and the people assembled in the council house. A small number of elderly men sat near the center of the building, and other men and women sat on benches in separate clusters by clan. Older men spoke at length, younger males made their opinions known, but women seldom expressed themselves at these times. A village council considered relations with other Indians or Europeans, decided questions of war or peace, and determined trading arrangements. The general council of elderly men, called Beloved Men, was led by a chief priest, three other priests, and a secular officer, all of whom lived near the council house. An inner council consisted of seven Beloved Men, one from each clan. Questions before the council were stated repeatedly until a consensus of support or opposition was reached. Deliberations might span days or even weeks until unanimous decisions were reached. The priests could not coerce or compel others to act in a particular manner; instead, they were arbitrators who reconciled differences. It appears that the members of each clan discussed particular problems among themselves before a council meeting and attempted to reach a unified position. The seven clan representatives met with the priests, expressed their feelings, and reported back to their constituents to discuss the matter; they then reassembled as a body to deliberate. If a clan had maneuvered as much as possible and still could not support an emerging consensus, it withdrew from the deliberations to avoid an open conflict.

A village council served one large settlement or a cluster of smaller communities, but no larger political structure united the bands or the nation. Each village was an independent political entity that sought to live in harmonious relations with other such units. Gearing (1962, 83) has reasoned that prior to 1730 the Cherokee comprised a "jural community," meaning that they were united by cultural and social ties. The members of one village might cooperate with those in another, and they appear never to have fought each other, although they often were at war with adjacent tribes. Some villages were more important than others because of their strategic location, the learning of their priests, or the importance of a secular leader, but no village appears to have been dominant for very long. Conflict between Cherokee villages most likely developed if a man killed someone from another village. This was a matter to be resolved by the members of the clans involved, and since each clan was represented by fictive brothers in every other village, these ties, and the ideals of proper behavior in times of disputes, were enough to avert open conflict.

British Influences   In 1730 the village council still functioned at the local level as it had in the past, but British colonial administrators began viewing the Cherokee as a single political unit rather than as an aggregate of independent villages. Thus, when a raiding party attacked a frontier settlement or interfered with the activities of a white trader, all of the Cherokee were held responsible. To avoid unexpected reprisals, a tribal political network began to develop among the Cherokee. The first person to emerge with political authority beyond the village level was Moytoy, a man from the Tennessee River drainage group (Overhill Cherokee) who presumably was a war chief. He was crowned "Emperor" of the Cherokee in 1730 by the British representative Alexander Cuming, who was largely responsible for originating the office. The Overhill settlements long had been influential, and they became more important as the military effectiveness of the Chickasaw declined. This placed the Overhill communities on the French frontier and led to their strategic importance to the British and Cherokee alike. The influence of Moytoy was not acknowledged among all Cherokee, but his political office was widely recognized as legitimate. A smallpox epidemic in 1738–39 appears to have killed about half of the people, and as a result the curers, who probably were the war party doctors, lost their position of respect, so much so that they destroyed their ritual equipment. This resulted in even more power shifting to political leaders. With the death of Moytoy in 1741, his son Amouskositte became the leader. Presumably, it was he who threatened to destroy a Cherokee village and kill all the inhabitants if they did not kill a man who had murdered a trader. The pressure to take action against the murderer had come originally from the governor of South Carolina, who threatened to cut off trade to the Cherokee. Without arms and ammunition they would have been unable to defend themselves against the French and their Indian allies. Thus, the actions of any one village began to be subordinated to tribal interests.

In this and other episodes, particular individuals emerged as spokesmen for the Cherokee but only in dealing with alien powers. By 1753 a priest state was beginning to emerge, roughly paralleling the village-level organization. The capital settlement was the residence of the most notable leader and the chief priest. Other leaders from representative villages met there to deliberate. The major problem was how to prevent warriors from launching raids. The tribal council could punish raiders after the fact but had no institutionalized network to prevent raids. The inability of Amouskositte's successor to prevent raids against frontier settlements led to a war with the English that lasted from 1759 to 1761. The destruction of numerous villages forced the Cherokee to sue for peace. Raids continued to be a problem, however, and as white settlers boldly began farming Cherokee land, retaliatory raids increased.

Influence of Warriors   By 1768 the Cherokee had decided to include outstanding warriors among the decision makers at the tribal council meetings. Heretofore warriors had played an integral part in council decisions only during preparations for conflict and when actually at war. Although the tribal council in theory remained opposed to reprisal raids, integrating the warriors into the tribal political organization meant that any activities they undertook would be legitimate. The American Revolution and the opening of Kentucky to white settlers split the Cherokee into two factions. Most young warriors sided with the British and were armed by them; the old men only sought peace. Raids by warriors led American military forces to destroy nearly all Cherokee settlements, but the people were not destroyed. When their villages were burned, they fled to the mountains, and after the conflict they returned to reestablish farming communities. Although they repeatedly were forced to give up land, in 1800 they still held title to about forty-three thousand square miles, about half of it in Tennessee and the remainder in adjacent sectors of Alabama, Georgia, and North Carolina.

WARFARE In the 1700s much of Cherokee energy was focused on raids and war as a direct and indirect result of white contact. When a council decided to make war, a red flag was raised over the council house, and the Reds began their preparations. Rituals by priests, fasting and dances by warriors, narrations of heroic deeds, and ritual bathing all were involved. An oration by the war speaker preceded the formal departure of a war party. When venturing forth, the warriors were elaborately painted red and black. The war club, with a projection at one end, was either hand-held or thrown. Warriors also used bows and arrows and spears when fighting. In early historic times, the metal tomahawk of European manufacture was popular, but these and earlier weapons were replaced by imported firearms and knives as they became available. (See Figure 12-4.)

In enemy country, a war party erected a small post bearing carved symbols that indicated their past exploits; such a post appears to have been a declaration of war. If the raiders succeeded in an attack, they might carve symbols on a nearby tree to record their victory. Two categories of men, warriors and chiefs, appear to have fought, and some women were famous for their abilities in battle. The leader of a war party had only nominal control over his following, and apparently a warrior could leave at any time except during actual combat. A war party attacked stealthily, attempting to kill and scalp as many persons as they could before withdrawing with captives if at all possible. Before returning home, the raiders painted the scalps they had taken red and tied them to a pole that was carried ahead of the line of warriors as they entered their village. Captives might be adopted, but more often they were tortured to death slowly by males and females, young and old. Women whose relatives had been killed by members of the victim's tribe were the most persistent torturers.

RELIGION Many Cherokee activities in the 1700s were linked to a round of religious observances. In the fall, the first of three important ritual sets was the Harvest Ceremony. Held in late September after the maize crop had matured, this celebration included processions in which green boughs were carried and also four days of dancing. Religous dances were held in the council house, and social dances in which women participated were also held. Soon after these festivities and when the moon was new, the council house became the center for ritual offerings to a sacred fire. Later a priest led the villagers to a river, where each person bathed seven times, and then they all feasted. About ten days after the completion of this ceremony, rituals were held to negate any ill

Figure 12-4. | Pencil drawings by George Catlin of Cherokee men. (Courtesy of the New York Historical Society, New York City.)

feelings that a person might harbor against others. The purpose was for each individual to become ritually pure. Then the sacred fire in the council house was extinguished and rekindled. The members of each household lit new fires in their homes from embers of the new sacred fire. The people bathed in a river, permitted their old clothing to drift away, and put on new garments when they emerged. During the time between these ceremonies the most important political conferences of the year were held.

| Later Historic Changes in Cherokee Life

When George Washington initiated a policy of Indian assimilation in 1789, he expected the process to be completed within fifty years for all Indians east of the Mississippi River. Assimilation was to be achieved by teaching English to Indians, introducing the farming methods of whites, and imposing the concept of private land ownership. In 1794 the Cherokee signed a treaty of peace with white Americans. This was meant to end the bitter conflict that for twenty years had destroyed the aboriginal basis of Cherokee culture and had sapped the energies of the surviving Indians. Many of them concluded that the selective adoption of white ways was not only desirable but also essential for survival. However, the process of Indian assimilation was hampered by the anti-Indian attitude of many whites along the frontier.

Missionaries were to play a key role in Christianizing and civilizing the Cherokee, and the first series of Protestant ones arrived among them in 1799. As the historian William G. McLoughlin (1984) noted in his seminal study of early missionary activities among the Cherokee, their resistance to becoming Christian was far greater than the missionaries had anticipated. Before long these Indians tried to revive their religion of old, but with little success. In the early 1800s the Cherokee were still attempting to adopt white ways on a selective basis and at their own pace, but the launching of the Jacksonian era in 1828 brought changes in federal policies toward Indians that doomed these efforts.

ADOPTION OF WHITE WAYS   The Cherokee Nation founded in 1820 was modeled after the government of the United States, with executive, judicial, and legislative branches. A capital with buildings in the Euro-American architectural style was constructed at New Echota, Georgia, in 1825. Soon after the nation was founded, Sequoya (George Gist), who was of Cherokee and white ancestry, presented to the leaders a proposal for writing their language. In 1809 Sequoya had become impressed with the importance of writing, and he had originated a system whereby symbols represented syllables in the Cherokee language. (See Figure 12-5.) Within a few months after the syllabary was adopted in 1821, thousands of Cherokee had learned to read and write their own language. A print shop was established at New Echota, and the first issue of a newspaper, the *Cherokee Phoenix*, appeared in 1828. By this time the Cherokee were numbered among the Civilized Tribes. Their population was about 13,500 in addition to nearly 150 white men who had married Cherokee women and about 75 white women who had Cherokee husbands. At this time, too, they owned nearly 1,300 Negro slaves, which indicates that some members of the nation were succeeding in the Southern economic system.

REMOVAL   The rich farmlands of the more southern Cherokee, their ever-increasing affluence, and the discovery of gold in northern Georgia were too much for covetous whites. With the 1830 federal policy to remove all eastern Indians to land west of the Mississippi River, the new Cherokee Nation was doomed. Some members of the tribe signed an agreement with federal agents to move to Oklahoma and give up their land for $5 million. Despite the fact that the agreement was not made by the leaders of the nation, the federal government considered it binding on all Cherokee. In 1838 a white military force began dislodging people from their lands and making certain that they migrated west. The most inaccessible and conservative groups in the north, those with less-desirable lands, were not pressured as much, and many were able to hide in the mountains.

Figure 12-5. | Sequoya (circa 1760–1843) originated the Cherokee syllabary adopted by the Cherokee Nation in 1821. (From McKenney and Hall 1933.)

The southernmost groups, those who had most successfully adapted to the Southern farming economy and to white governmental procedures, were the ones forced to migrate to Indian Territory.

FORMATION OF THE EASTERN BAND OF CHEROKEE   About a thousand conservative Cherokee escaped to the mountains of North Carolina to hide until 1842. As an indication of their traditional nature, it was recorded a few years later that only a few mixed-blooded and no full-blooded Indians spoke English. William H. Thomas, a white trader and the adopted son of a chief, emerged as influential with this group. He spoke Cherokee, became the Indian agent, and eventually established the right of the Cherokee to remain in the locality. With the money paid to compensate for the illegal seizure of their property, Thomas and other sympathetic whites began buying parcels of land for the Indians, because Indians could not legally own land under the state constitution. The plots were held by Thomas in his name; when he became ill and in debt following the Civil War, his creditors claimed all this land. However, Congress sued the creditors to preserve the land for these Indians, and the matter was settled in favor of the Cherokee in 1874. To protect them in the future, the commissioner of Indian affairs was made their trustee, and a deed for their holdings was obtained in 1876. The Cherokee refugees who had reestablished themselves in North Carolina became relatively prosperous farmers. Yet, they still spoke Cherokee, maintained their clan organization, and kept many traditions of old intact. During the Civil War those who fought did so for the Confederacy, although a few later joined the Union Army. Unfortunately, a returning Union soldier carried smallpox, and more than one hundred of the two thousand Indians died of the disease. By and large, the Cherokee lived throughout this period as self-sufficient farmers on scattered homesteads where they grew maize as their most important crop and raised livestock. (See Figure 12-6.)

During the time that their right to the land was in question, the Cherokee drafted a constitution providing for a chief and one representative for each settlement. In 1870 this body began to function as the Eastern Band of Cherokee, but it was not incorporated formally until 1889. The 1887 passage of the Dawes Act and separate efforts to allot Oklahoma Indian lands led to rumors that Eastern Cherokee land was to be allotted. A long-standing complaint, and one that would recur, was that some whites used devious means to become tribal members in the hope of obtaining land. Some whites reportedly became "five-dollar Indians" by paying this amount as a bribe to be entered on the roll. The enrollment of these whites, in addition to the children of white-Indian marriages, has, over the years, meant that there are a significant number of "white Indians."

SCHOOLS　Schools for Cherokee children were launched by missionaries in the early 1800s with modest success, but they were discontinued with Cherokee removal. In 1881 the Society of Friends opened a school on a contractual basis with the federal government, an arrangement that lasted until 1892. The Quakers succeeded in upsetting the pattern of Indian life, but not nearly as much as did their educational successors in the BIA. The pattern of formal education under the BIA was for a child to attend a day school through the fourth grade and then attend a local boarding school through the ninth grade; his or her education was completed at a distant boarding school such as the one for Indians in Carlisle, Pennsylvania. The goal of compulsory education was to destroy Indian life; children were punished for speaking Cherokee, chained to their beds if they repeatedly ran away, and forced to learn white ways.

POLITICAL, SOCIAL, AND ECONOMIC UNITS　When William H. Gilbert studied the Eastern Cherokee in 1932, the political units created after removal were continuing to function. The six towns had locally elected officers, and an elected band council regulated land usage. The State of North Carolina controlled taxation and law, and the federal government had jurisdiction over education and welfare. The towns were not only political units but also served important economic and social functions.

An organization called the free labor company or *gadugi* existed in most Eastern Cherokee villages. A typical gadugi had about a dozen members who annually elected officers, including one person who served as director. Although small, these companies were a source of pride among local residents,

Figure 12-6. | A North Carolina Cherokee home in 1888. (Courtesy of the Smithsonian Institution, National Anthropological Archives, neg. no. 1000-B.)

and they provided significant services to their membership. Participants contracted their labor as a unit and helped each other in farming and other activities; a number of women cooked for the workers. Members also could borrow money from the collective treasury. The gadugi was an important cooperative enterprise historically and apparently had an aboriginal base, but as it developed, the membership became limited to conservative Indians. As the free labor companies began hiring themselves out to whites with increasing frequency, around 1910, they were judged taxable by the State of North Carolina, which led to their decline.

The aboriginal Cherokee had performed a wide variety of dances, and by the early 1930s most of these were still remembered. Of the large number still performed, one of the best known was the Booger Dance. The word *booger* had the same root as the English word *bogey* meaning goblin, but in its Cherokee context it closely approximated the idea of a ghost. Masks worn during the dance were designed as caricatures of aliens. (See Figure 12-7.) Originally the dance may have been performed to induce warriors to join war parties and to dilute the harmful effects of the spirits of foreigners. By the 1930s, however, the dance was almost free from religious associations. The masks at that time portrayed enemies: Negroes; Chinese, who were identified with an old Cherokee myth; and whites. The dances were performed by a small number of men and sometimes by a few women, all of whom were disguised. The performers danced in a circle, frightened children, and joked with adults who stood in a proper joking relationship to them.

The gadugi, the dances, the importance of clans in regulating marriage,

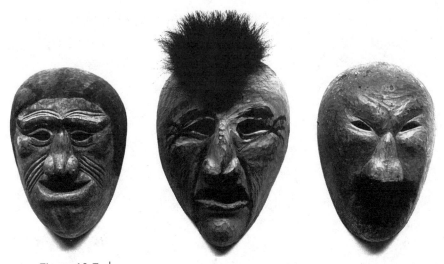

Figure 12-7. | Booger Dance masks. (Courtesy of the UCLA Museum of Cultural History.)

and much of the additional substance of traditional life were waning in importance by the late 1950s. Furthermore, as the Cherokee entered the modern era, earlier decisions about the qualifications of an Indian contributed to a reformation of what it meant to be an Eastern Cherokee.

| Becoming Modern

As long as the Eastern Cherokee remained relatively isolated subsistence farmers, the federal government was only moderately interested in them, and they could, and did, maintain a traditionally oriented lifeway. However, as the network of roads expanded and as the people were drawn more firmly into the national economy, their capacity to resist external pressures declined. As a result, many Eastern Cherokee found their sense of being Indian increasingly challenged.

ECONOMIC BASE The Eastern Cherokee lands consist of nearly fifty-seven thousand acres in western North Carolina adjacent to the Great Smoky Mountains National Park. The Qualla Boundary area with some forty-four thousand acres is the largest reservation. Eighty percent of it consists of mountain slopes, and the balance is bottomland, although not the rich bottomland of nearby areas. Until the turn of the century these holdings were adequate for the subsistence-based agriculture of the Cherokee. They also raised cattle and hogs, but stock-fencing laws and then the chestnut blight, which depleted the prime source of food for hogs, had ended these enterprises by the late 1920s. By this time, too, the population had increased, and all possible land had been brought under cultivation. This combination of factors brought a crisis in the economy. Eastern Cherokee isolation was broken by an ever-expanding network of roads, and the Indians were drawn into a cash economy. Most persons maintained gardens for produce, but they also needed wage employment. Since comparatively few jobs were available, the standard of living became increasingly depressed. The tourist trade began to emerge around the turn of the present century, but it was not sizeable until after World War II. Tourists then began to arrive in greater and greater numbers, and by the late 1950s over two million automobiles were passing through the town of Cherokee, North Carolina, each summer.

The community of Cherokee was no ordinary reservation because the Eastern Band of Cherokee Indians, a legal corporate entity, owned the land. Some Cherokee family lines had occupied a particular acreage for generations, but they did not own land as individuals. The tribal council dealt with land allotments and reallocations as well as leases of land to non-Indians; these were controlled with particular care and on a short-term basis. Leases to business establishments provided about 80 percent of the money received by the council. One function of the council was to settle disputes over land; these were made more difficult by the fact that some boundaries were ill-defined.

During the late 1950s a majority of the approximately seven hundred households depended on subsistence farming for most of their food, and intermittent wage labor in the summer was the major source of cash. Some families relied on welfare payments during at least part of the winter; this also was characteristic of non-Indian farmers in the region. Very few individuals had full-time jobs that provided their sole income, and conservative families had the most difficulty in making the transition from subsistence farming to a cash economy. In spite of the depressed standard of living for most persons, very few Eastern Cherokee were willing to move away permanently. Most of those who moved away temporarily did so after World War II for reasons including residence at boarding schools, time spent in the armed service, or temporary jobs elsewhere.

In 1972 the Eastern Cherokee met in a general council for the first time since 1838. They gathered to decide whether they should accept nearly $2 million from the federal government for twenty-five million acres of land lost to whites. They agreed to receive the settlement and divide the money; each person received less than $300. This finally resolved an old grievance, and other factors were beginning to favor them as well. The tourist industry continued to expand broadly, and two-thirds of the nearly 175 enterprises, although not the most lucrative, were Cherokee-owned. Light industries were being introduced, there was a surge in construction jobs, and tribal assets had increased significantly. However, as a group their average income was still only 60 percent of the national average.

EDUCATION The New Deal for Indians that began in 1934 was a concerted effort to accept the diversity in cultural and historical background of the different tribes under federal control. It was a humanistic endeavor to respect the integrity of Indian cultural traditions and to encourage their ongoing vitality.

An effort was made to teach the Cherokee syllabary in federal schools, but the program was abandoned because of a lack of local interest. Some local programs did succeed, however. Attempts to do away with boarding schools were not successful until 1954 because of the distance separating some homes and school facilities. A study by Sharlotte Neely Williams of Eastern Cherokee education, which is the key source for information about schooling, indicates that in 1954 some high school students began attending county schools. With reference to the previous pattern, Williams (1971, 44) has written, "The students were boarded at schools so that their association with Anglo-American cultural phenomena would outweigh their exposure to Cherokee culture in their homes." Further changes included the consolidation of four grade schools as the Cherokee Elementary School in 1962 and the end of the last Indian day school in 1965.

In the 1950s the educational stress continued to be on vocational training with an emphasis on farming skills; academic courses were similar to those in other sectors of rural North Carolina. Since wage labor employment was difficult to obtain and the farms were declining in value, it was hard for high school students trained in this way to succeed locally. As the tourist business increased and some industries began to move into the area, employment opportunities expanded, but because the Indians tended to be noncompetitive in terms of white values, they were at a distinct disadvantage in the job market.

In the early 1970s a new direction for Eastern Cherokee education seemed to be emerging through the Headstart and Follow Through programs. The small classes, well-trained teachers, predominantly Cherokee teacher aids, and communitywide interest suggested an intensity of concern over education that was far greater than in the recent past. Over 90 percent of the children spoke English at home, and thus they did not have to learn a "school" language. Furthermore, there were physical reminders of their Cherokee heritage such as paintings of Indians along the halls and Indian as well as white dolls with which to play. Classroom instruction included Cherokee culture when appropriate, and instruction in the aboriginal language was initiated in the Follow Through program.

VOLUNTARY ASSOCIATIONS   The game of stickball remained a popular sport, and each township fielded a stickball team until they were done away with in the 1930s at the insistence of the BIA. Two reasons appear to have accounted for the repression. One was that the games were played as battles, which resulted in many injuries, and the other was that spectators were so unruly that serious disturbances sometimes resulted. Softball games replaced the stickball contests but did not serve as a direct substitute. The teams were organized by township and attendance was good, but the rivalry and spectator participation was subdued. In 1959 the Chamber of Commerce began sponsoring weekly stickball games played by teams representing all the townships. The frequency of the encounters led to increased competitiveness, which resulted in some serious injuries to players, and spectator involvement recalled the problems of the 1930s.

In 1914 the Cherokee Indian Fair began to be held on an annual basis in the fall and was attended by all Cherokee. Later, rides and games of chance were provided by a traveling carnival company. The most important dimension of the fair, however, was that fostered by the Fair Association, whose president was the tribal chief. The association's goal was to show progress in farming and business enterprises, and diverse exhibits for which there were competitive prizes became important. The fair also featured a stickball game with twelve players, apparently drawn from the conservative population, on a team. Some teams still observed rituals before a game, as in aboriginal times.

LANGUAGE   All Cherokee spoke English in the late 1950s, but some older persons rarely conversed in it, and although their aboriginal culture had long since disappeared, a large percentage of the population, especially those identified as conservative, spoke Cherokee as well. In one sector, about 40 percent of the households spoke Cherokee by preference. Households in which the aboriginal language was used most often were composed of full-blooded Indians or those who had only a quarter of non-Indian blood. John Gulick (1960) has reasoned that the prevalence of spoken Cherokee has been, and will continue to be, sustained as long as such persons marry one another. The persons who had retained their language of old appeared to have done so because it symbolized their Indian identity. The syllabary developed by Sequoyah was still in use, and the Bible printed in it continued to be available. Some of the free labor companies recorded their minutes in the syllabary, but its most important use appears to have been to record the formulas of shamans.

KINSHIP AND FAMILIES   The old kinship terminology was only known to some of the most elderly Eastern Cherokee in the late 1950s. The majority of persons familiar with the Cherokee terms used them in a way comparable to English usage. In other words, the terminology that had made it possible to distinguish relatives according to lineage and clan lines had been modified for bilateral usage.

It appears that these people preferred nuclear family household units, and most houses were so occupied. A significant number of households contained a number of related nuclear families—that is, small extended families. These extended families often included the nuclear families of siblings, or a nuclear family plus grandchildren. The larger living units tended to occur more often among conservative families, and one reason might have been because they placed a high value on hospitality. These people also tended to be poor and lived together out of necessity. Then, too, daughters with nonlegitimate children often lived in their parents' households. Yet, no clear evidence suggests that large households represented continuity with former residence patterns.

The matriclans that had regulated marriage in aboriginal and early historic times had declined. In the early 1950s older people still were familiar with the clan system, and about 80 percent of the marriages were in accord with it. By the mid-1950s the percentage had dropped to 20, and it was not certain that all of these marriages had in fact taken clan regulations into conscious consideration.

Common law marriages seemingly were typical, and nonlegitimate offspring were not stigmatized. Notably, those young adults with a minimum percentage of Indian blood tended to marry persons with a greater proportion in order to insure Eastern Cherokee rights for their children.

DIVERGING VALUE SYSTEMS　In the 1950s when persons identified as Eastern Cherokee considered their Indianness in abstract terms, they expressed a clear dichotomy between "full bloods" and "white Indians." A "full blood" was genetically Indian or nearly so, spoke Cherokee, belonged to a free labor company, and subscribed to the traditional Cherokee value system. "White Indians" had the attitudes and values of whites, spoke English, and had comparatively little Indian blood. This dichotomy was neat, but it did not always appear valid even to the Cherokee themselves. A person might be judged an Indian in one context and white in another; clearly, there were gradations of Indianness and context was an important consideration.

This led Robert K. Thomas to define four value systems among these people (cited in Gulick 1960). The conservatives, who possibly numbered about one-fourth of the population, were "true Indians" in blood, language, and behavior. "Generalized Indians" thought of themselves as Indian, but unlike conservatives, attempted to accommodate the white world. They accepted important values of conservatives and whites alike. "Rural-white Indians" did not look like Indians, had a minimal amount of Indian inheritance, and patterned their general attitudes after those of whites in the rural South. Such persons seldom were active in purely Cherokee institutions but were likely to be members of such white organizations as the 4-H Club. These individuals might interact with "generalized Indians" but did not usually function well with conservatives. Finally, the "middle-class Indians," the smallest group in numerical terms, were involved in nonfarming businesses or were office workers. They tended to socialize with non-Indians holding similar jobs.

The behavioral system of the conservative segment was analyzed by John Gulick and his associates (1960) and found to be not an odd assortment of "survivals," but an integrated configuration, which Gulick termed the Harmony Ethic. A critical component was the minimization of overt and direct aggression in face-to-face situations; the aggression that did occur was expressed indirectly as gossip and sorcery. A high positive value was placed on being generous with other people in terms of rendering personal services and providing food. Conservatives did not assert themselves; they withdrew in the face of potential conflict and made a point of minding their own business. Given these attitudes, no well-defined leaders held sway even in situations where they might be expected. For example, the officers in a free labor company worked together as a group rather than in a hierarchical decision-making structure, and tended to render decisions that reflected common consent. Because the concept of disagreement ran contrary to this value system, conservatives tended to cast an affirmative vote or to not vote at all.

The Contemporary Cherokee Scene

Unquestionably, the factor having the greatest external impact on contemporary Eastern Cherokee life is tourism; its scope and importance cannot be overestimated. In 1985, over nine million people visited Great Smoky Mountain National Park, which borders on Cherokee landholdings. This was nearly three times as many visitors as for any other national park. One reason for the popularity of the Smoky Mountain park is that the area is within a two-day drive for two-thirds of the people in the United States.

While at the park many tourists visit the town of Cherokee. One major attraction is a play, *Unto These Hills* by Kermit Hunter, that focuses on Cherokee Indian history. It is billed as the most popular outdoor drama in the United States; over four million people have paid to see it since the play opened in 1950. Additional attractions include the Museum of the Cherokee Indian, the Qualla Arts and Crafts Center, the Oconaluftee Indian Village, the Cyclorama Wax Museum, Santa's Land, and Cherokee Bingo. In and near Cherokee are about fifty motels, twenty-five campgrounds, and seventy souvenir stores. Numerous tourist-oriented shops have an official greeter dressed as an Indian who can be photographed next to a totem pole, tepee, or tourist for a fee. (See Figure 12-8.)

Figure 12-8. | Millions of families visit Cherokee, North Carolina, each year, and having a picture of one's children taken with an Indian is popular. (Photograph by the author.)

One long-standing objection of the Cherokee to the tourist-oriented businesses is that they employ Indians at relatively low-paying service jobs while the white businesspersons who own them reap substantial profits. At the same time, the tribe as a whole does profit from leases of land to whites for businesses. The people have retained control themselves over one important business, Cherokee Bingo, which has benefited the Indian economy both directly and indirectly. Drawn by the promise of fifty-thousand-dollar and even one-million-dollar jackpots, avid bingo players arrive by chartered buses from many cities in the eastern and central United States and Canada. The bingo hall holds four thousand people and employs about two hundred persons. The Cherokee receive 6 percent of the gross income, and in their 1986 contract they were guaranteed $400,000 a year. Bingo revenues in the recent past suggest that they will earn considerably more than that figure in the immediate future. Bingo also attracts travelers to tourist-oriented establishments such as motels and restaurants, thus stimulating the local economy to the benefit of the Indians.

The Cherokee Historical Association is largely responsible for major tourist promotions in the town of Cherokee, including the presentation of *Unto These Hills* and the establishment and maintenance of the Museum of the Cherokee Indian. Contrary to what might be expected, the association is not owned and operated by the Cherokee Indians but by white businesspersons. The Eastern Cherokee accuse the Cherokee Historical Association of unjustly implying that its enterprises are owned by the Indians. Some Indians also are distressed by the manner in which Cherokee history is presented in *Unto These Hills*. The play presents them as simple savages until their Great White Father, William H. Thomas, and white missionaries save them and their land at the time their removal is threatened. In brief, the drama suggests that the status of the Cherokee currently is dependent on whites, a concept not considered accurate by many living Cherokee.

Although the Eastern Cherokee economy has been linked closely to the tourist industry, a recent development may lead to a more rewarding economic alternative. Congress passed the Indian Tribal Government Tax Status Act in 1982, which enables tribes to issue tax-exempt bonds in the manner of local governments. As a result, the Eastern Band of Cherokee was able to buy the Carolina Mirror Company of North Wilkesboro, North Carolina, in 1986. The band paid $28.8 million in a leveraged buy-out involving $1.5 million and $32 million worth of high-yield securities (junk bonds) that they sold to investors. The mirror company agreed to employ some Cherokee in a small plant to be built on the reserve, but this is not nearly as important as the entry of the band into the innovative investment bond market.

| The Outlook for Cherokee Identity

One of the most overworked and least satisfying words used by anthropologists with reference to historic changes in Indian life is *acculturation*. It often is employed with the presumption that total assimilation is the logical end product, yet there is no justification for this assumption in the definition of the word. In general, acculturation is used to indicate the ways in which Indians are becoming more like white Americans; it might be more correct to use the word *accommodation*. With this in mind we may consider the Eastern Cherokee further as they have been described by Harriet J. Kupferer and Williams.

The aboriginal Cherokee first accommodated white traders and soon became dependent on them in economic terms. This in part led to their political involvements with the eighteenth-century colonists. Both before and after removal, marriages with whites not only introduced white blood but also affected Eastern Cherokee accommodation because the outsiders moved into their homes. Before 1880 the general pattern was for persons of mixed blood to identify with the Cherokee, not with whites. When the missionary-teachers and later teachers alone entered the scene, they emphasized Anglo-American rather than Cherokee ways in an effort to absorb these Indians into the dominant cultural system. Kupferer (1966) has reasoned that the conservative-modern dichotomy became crystallized as a result of the emphasis formal education gave to white ways and its competition with the Cherokee lifeway. The Harmony Ethic emerged in competition with the Protestant ethic.

In the decade following 1934, the federal government's efforts to revitalize Eastern Cherokee culture failed, possibly because absorption had come to be accepted as the only possible goal by most persons. The great influx of tourists after World War II brought an increasing awareness of what it was to be an Indian; in practical terms, one of the immediate effects was a market for craft items. Williams (1978) feels that these people have an expanding interest in reestablishing their clear identity as Indians and that this is best reflected in the Follow Through program and aided by instruction in the Cherokee language. Similarly, pride is growing in business enterprises that focus on Indian productions. If efforts to revitalize Cherokee culture continue to expand, the differences between conservative and modern Eastern Cherokee should decline, and their lasting identity as a people will become more assured.

| Comparisons with Other Indians

The value system or ethos of a people is essentially the total of their behavioral principles, and we find that these were well defined for peoples described in recent chapters. The "Protestant ethic" of the Yurok, the Hopi Way, the New Religion of the Iroquois, and the Harmony Ethic of the Eastern Cherokee are examples. After identifying each, comparisons are worthwhile in terms of how people actually behaved relative to their ethical systems, the historic pressures to change them, their responses, and what they do and did to counter nonconformity.

Eastern Cherokee and Mesquakie comparisons are especially pertinent. In neither case is a baseline ethnography available, which makes clear background data unavailable. However, we do know that both peoples were battered by colonial powers seeking farmland and yet retained their identity even though surrounded by whites. They were not put under the same form of federal control as most Indians. Further comparisons might focus on their changing political and economic lives to generalize about the process, not the specific traits, of their sociocultural change and adaptation. If we assume that the continuity of Indianness is a desirable and attainable goal, what might the members of each society do to achieve this end most effectively?

Additional Readings

Historical information about the Cherokee in a 1900 report by James Mooney has been republished as *Historical Sketch of the Cherokee* (Chicago, 1975); another recent reprint is that of the 1887 publication *The Cherokee Nation of Indians,* by Charles C. Royce (Chicago, 1975). A more recent study is by John R. Finger, *The Eastern Band of Cherokee, 1819–1900* (Knoxville, 1984). William O. Steele, in *The Cherokee Crown of Tanaassy* (Winston-Salem, NC, 1977), examines the exploits of Alexander Cuming in early English-Cherokee relations. Fred Gearing's (1962) analysis of historic Cherokee political developments is worthy of careful study, as is the presentation of the early historic legal system titled *A Law of Blood* (New York, 1970), by John P. Reid.

William G. McLoughlin describes early acculturation by missionaries in *Cherokees and Missionaries 1789–1839* (New Haven, CT, 1983). The most insightful studies of more recent culture change are by Harriet J. Kupferer (1966) and John Gulick (1960). The 1973 edition of Gulick's book (Chapel Hill) provides an update in the Epilogue by Sharlotte Neely Williams. The book *Southeastern Indians Since the Removal Era* (Athens, GA, 1978), edited by Walter L. Williams, provides a further update. *The Journal of Cherokee Studies,* which began publication in 1977, is a valuable source for varied articles about the Cherokee.

Bibliography

Bloom, Leonard. 1942. The acculturation of the Eastern Cherokee: Historical aspects. *North Carolina Historical Review* 19:323–58.

Coe, Joffre L. 1961. *Cherokee archaeology.* Bureau of American Ethnology Bulletin, vol. 180, no. 7. Washington, DC.

Cotterill, R. S. 1954. *The southern Indians.* Norman.

Fogelson, Raymond D. 1971. The Cherokee ballgame cycle. *Ethnomusicology* 15:327–38.

Fogelson, Raymond D., and Paul Kutsche. 1961. *Cherokee economic cooperatives: The gadugi.* Bureau of American Ethnology Bulletin, vol. 180, no. 11. Washington, DC.

French, Laurence. 1977. Tourism and Indian exploitation. *The Indian Historian* 10 (4): 19–24.

Gearing, Fred. 1962. *Priests and warriors.* American Anthropological Association Memoir no. 93. This is the major ethnohistorical study about eighteenth-century Cherokee political organization. Gearing carefully plots the major changes in political structure and explains why shifts occurred.

Gilbert, William H. 1943. *The Eastern Cherokee.* Bureau of American Ethnology Bulletin no. 133, 169–413. Washington, DC. In 1932 Gilbert made a field study among these people that focused on an analysis of the kinship terminology, but he also considers diverse aspects of life at that time, and presents a brief review of ethnohistorical sources that is very useful.

―――. 1965. Eastern Cherokee social organization. In *Social anthropology of North American tribes,* Fred Eggan, ed., 283–338. Chicago.

Gulick, John. 1960. *Cherokees at the crossroads.* Chapel Hill. Based on 1956–58 field studies by Gulick and his students, this is the most comprehensive and thoughtful presentation of changing Cherokee life in recent times.

Kupferer, Harriet J. 1966. *The "Principal People," 1960.* Bureau of American Ethnology Bulletin, vol. 196, no. 78. Washington, DC. In 1959–60 the author studied the Eastern Cherokee and focused especially on degrees of acculturation as reflected in educational attitudes and health concepts.

―――. 1968. The isolated Eastern Cherokee. In *The American Indian today,* Stuart Levine and Nancy O. Lurie, eds., 143–59.

McKenney, Thomas L., and James Hall. 1933. *The Indian tribes of North America,* vol. 1. Edinburgh.

McLoughlin, William G. 1984. *Cherokees and missionaries, 1789–1839.* New Haven.

Mooney, James. 1900. Myths of the Cherokee. *Bureau of American Ethnology, 19th Annual Report,* pt. 1.

Speck, Frank G., and Leonard Broom. 1951. *Cherokee dance and drama.* Berkeley and Los Angeles.

Strickland, William. 1977. Cherokee rhetoric. *Journal of Cherokee Studies* 2:375–83.

Swanton, John R. 1946. *The Indians of the southeastern United States.* Bureau of American Ethnology Bulletin no. 137. Washington, DC.

Williams, Sharlotte Neely. 1971. *The role of formal education among the Eastern Cherokee Indians, 1880–1971.* MA thesis, University of North Carolina at Chapel Hill.

―――. 1975. The Quaker era of Cherokee Indian education. *Appalachian Journal* 2:314–22.

―――. 1978. Acculturation and persistence among North Carolina's Eastern Band of Cherokee Indians. In *Southeastern Indians since the removal era,* Walter L. Williams, ed. Athens, GA.

13 The Natchez: Sophisticated Farmers of the Deep South

A great number of years ago there appeared among us a man and his wife, who came down from the sun. Not that we believe that the sun had a wife who bore him children, or that these were the descendants of the sun; but when they first appeared among us they were so bright and luminous that we had no difficulty to believe that they came down from the sun.

A priest described the origin of the Great Sun and his lineage. (Le Page du Pratz, 1947, 312)

ALONG THE EASTERN bank of the lower Mississippi River emerged the most elaborate American Indian cultures reported north of Mexico. Nowhere else were similar heights of complexity reached, and the group that best represents this climax of achievements is the Natchez. They maintained a highly developed class system, possessed luxuries of rare elaboration, and paid homage to a god-king. The Natchez are included here because of their social differentiation and because they were better described early in their history than any other Indians of the Southeastern culture area at a similar level of achievement. Also, in their relationship with the French they passed through stages that were well defined and often paralleled the developments between Europeans and other North American Indians.

People, Language, and Population

The word *Natchez* apparently is derived from a French interpretation of the name of their settlement called Naches, but these people called themselves the Theloel. The language of the Natchez is classed in the Macro-Algonkian phylum and the Algonkian family, but it is distinct and has no close ties to any other. It is interesting to note that while the women spoke the same language as the men, women were said to "soften and smooth their words, whereas the speech of the men is more grave and serious" (Le Page du Pratz 1774, 312). Since the French learned the language from women, their pronunciation was feminine and was ridiculed by both Natchez men and women. At the end of the seventeenth century, the Natchez numbered about thirty-five hundred, and in 1720 they could assemble twelve hundred warriors, including refugees they had absorbed and the Tiou, who were a dependent people. By 1731 only three hundred warriors could be mustered, and by a few years later they had become a remnant people, although a few survived into the present century. (See Figure 13-1 for their aboriginal range.)

History of Natchez-French Relations

The Natchez attacked the Spanish expedition under the original command of Hernando de Soto as it descended the Mississippi River in 1543. The next known contact was with the French explorer Sieur de La Salle in 1682. In an important study of the course of French-Natchez relations, Andrew C. Albrecht (1946) labeled this as a first phase, one of visiting explorers. The Natchez were gracious hosts to the La Salle party. They provided the French with food and smoked the peace calumet with them, but these Indians were not overawed by the Europeans. La Salle was respectful toward them since he was well aware that they were the most powerful tribe in the region. Friendly relations were disrupted temporarily when two Frenchmen were killed in 1690, but in 1698 four missionaries sent from French Canada to the lower Mississippi remained briefly among the Natchez. In 1700 one baptized 185 children. In the same year Pierre de Iberville established friendly relations between the Natchez and the French

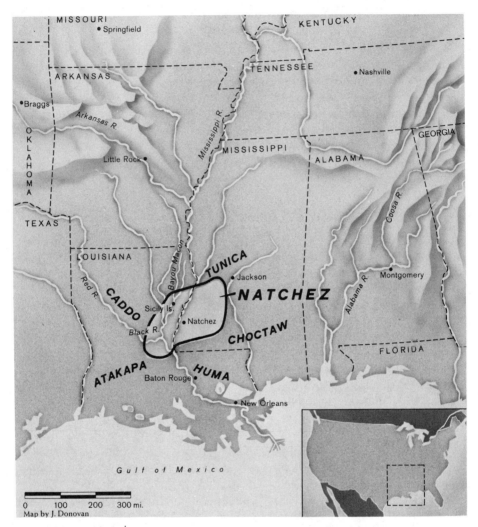

Figure 13-1. | Aboriginal range of the Natchez Indians.

who were penetrating from the lower Mississippi River. De Iberville attempted to wrest political control from the French in Canada to establish an independent colony.

With the arrival of missionaries and fur traders from Canada, a second phase of contact began, but neither the traders nor the Roman Catholic missionaries were very successful. As will be understood later, the religious system of the Natchez was so highly integrated with social and political life that the task of making Christians of these people was nearly impossible. In addition, the great distance between the lower Mississippi River and eastern Canada made these trading and mission ties tenuous. The French administration that was established by de Iberville independent of Canada became the most influential force in the lives of the Natchez. During the early 1700s English traders operating from the Carolinas were successful in winning the support of a leading Natchez called Bearded Chief, who apparently dominated the communities of White Apple, Hickory, and Grigras. The settlements of Grand Village, the home of the Great Sun who was the reigning ruler, and Flour were loyal to the French.

The third phase of Natchez-French relations emerged in 1713 with the establishment of a French trading post in the midst of the Natchez. Antoine Crozat was granted a monopoly on all the trade in Louisiana, with the stipulation that he was to bring slaves from Africa and settlers from France. The post built by Crozat possibly was at Grand Village, but it did not succeed. Intrigue by English traders and Bearded Chief apparently led to its being plundered in 1715. The French now found themselves in a tenuous position; the obvious solution was to subjugate the Natchez and establish military control over the area.

The fourth phase, military control, began in 1716 when Jean de Bienville, with a force of no more than fifty men, tricked the Indians so that he was able to seize and kill those who had plundered the trading post and had killed some Frenchmen. The Natchez agreed to peace with the French and aided in the construction of the stockaded Fort Rosalie, which was built to the west of their villages and overlooked the Mississippi River. For the moment, relations temporarily became stabilized, with the Natchez controlling their settlements and the small French garrison representing the outpost of an empire. In 1717 Crozat terminated his monopoly, and soon afterward the Western Company of John Law assumed the responsibility for trading and colonizing. It obtained the right to grant lands to private individuals and proceeded to do so. The company attempted to settle the country with a French landed nobility who would bring with them tenants, skilled craftsmen, and slaves.

In 1718 the fifth phase began when concession holders began arriving, and two years later French immigrants were well established. The French farmers prepared the land for raising tobacco, and Indian-French relationships were quite congenial. In 1718 the colonist to whom we are most indebted for our knowledge of the Natchez settled in the area. He was Antoine S. Le Page du Pratz, a Dutchman by birth, who remained in Louisiana until 1734. The French were provided land and food by the Indians, who in turn were offered guns, powder, lead, intoxicants, and cloth; this was highly satisfactory to both parties. Then in 1723 at Fort Rosalie an old Natchez warrior was killed needlessly by a soldier, and his murderer went unpunished by the French commander of the fort. In retaliation the Natchez killed some French settlers. Peace was reestablished within a few days, but a course toward further hostilities had been set. After the peace the French attacked White Apple, demanding and receiving the head of a leader who had been hostile to them. The Natchez could not understand this deception by the French and subsequently avoided contacts with them.

At this crucial point in Natchez-French relations two deaths occurred among the Natchez that quite possibly led to temporary Indian disorganization. In 1725 the younger brother of the Great Sun, Tattooed Serpent, died, and three years later the Great Sun himself died. Thus, in 1728 a young and inexperienced Great Sun was in power. In the next year, 1729, a new commander of the Fort Rosalie garrison decided quite arbitrarily that he required the land of White Apple for settlement. When he told the Natchez leader of the community to forfeit the village, the noble refused, and the commander became furious. The Natchez parleyed to decide what course of action should be taken. They decided that because the French were becoming more numerous, were corrupting the Natchez youth, and were breaking their promises, the French should be destroyed. Thus began the sixth and final phase, the Natchez revolt. The Great Sun agreed, and the Natchez sought the aid of neighboring tribes. In spite of an attempt by the leaders to keep their decision from the women, one noblewoman, Tattooed Arm, the mother of the Great Sun, prodded her son into revealing the general plan. She warned the French, but the commander would not take this and other warnings seriously. Finally the Natchez fell upon the French and killed more than two hundred persons who were at or near the fort. As an aside, it is perhaps noteworthy that the Natchez warriors had such great contempt for the French commander that he was not killed until late in the massacre and then was beaten to death by a commoner with a wooden war club.

The Yazoos, allies and neighbors of the Natchez to the north, killed the small number of French among them but not until after the massacre by the Natchez. Apparently Tattooed Arm, the woman who had warned the French, altered the time of the attack and made the Natchez uprising premature, which angered their allies. The Choctaw were to have aided the Natchez but could not do so because of the time change. They were angry, too, because the Natchez did not share the spoils with them, and so the Choctaw subsequently aided the French against the Natchez. In late January 1730 a French and Choctaw force, estimated at between seven hundred and sixteen hundred, attacked the Natchez at two forts they had constructed. A larger French force arrived in mid-February and bombarded the Natchez with cannon fire. Before long, however, the French began to run low on ammunition, and their Choctaw allies talked of withdrawing. By mutual agreement the Natchez released the captives they still held, and the French withdrew to the Mississippi River. Then the Natchez with their loot slipped across the Mississippi River and escaped. They ascended the Red River to the Black River and built a fort at Sicily Island. In 1731 another French and Indian force was sent against the Natchez, and about four hundred, including the Great Sun, were forced to surrender. Some of these Natchez were sold into slavery in the West Indies, while what happened to the others is not known.

Aboriginal Life of the Natchez

The Natchez stand clearly apart from all the Indians described in earlier chapters. Natchez social conventions, political organization, and religious institutions not only were of a different nature, but in many ways were more highly developed. It is assumed, and with good reason, that Natchez culture had its roots far to the south and that it was introduced into the Southeast in prehistoric times by migrants from Mexico. Fortunately, one careful observer, Le Page du Pratz, lived among the Natchez at the time their culture was flowering, and his writings from the early 1700s are the material on which the following account is based.

ORIGIN MYTH   The mythological beginnings of the Natchez offer special insight into the form of sociopolitical structure that they developed. According to tradition, a man and his wife entered an already established community to the southwest of historic Natchez country. The newcomers were so bright in appearance that they seemed to have come from the sun. The man said he had noted that the people did not have effective means for governing themselves and that he had come from the sky in order to instruct them. He told the people about the Great Spirit and what they must do to please him. Among the rules of behavior were a series of prohibitions: do not kill except in self-defense; do not have sexual intercourse with a woman not one's wife; do not steal, nor lie, nor become intoxicated. Finally, he said that the people should give freely of what they had to those in need. After hearing these rules of conduct, the people agreed to their wisdom and asked the man to be their leader. He said he would do so only under certain conditions. Among these were that the people must obey him but no other and they must move to another country to which he would lead them; finally, he set forth the rules for selecting his successor. He said too that they should build a temple in which the leaders could communicate with the Great Spirit. In the temple would be an eternal fire that he would bring from the sun. The people agreed to these and other conditions, and the sacred fire was brought from the sun. This man then became the first Great Sun.

SETTLEMENTS AND MANUFACTURES   The main area of Natchez settlement was along the eastern bank of the Mississippi River near the present city of Natchez, but the Natchez also seem to have controlled adjacent land on the western bank of the river. During the French period, the main settlement area was a rolling plain of black soil covered with grasses, hickory forests, cane thickets in the draws, and pine or hardwood forests nearby. Nine communities may have existed in the early historic period, but five usually are mentioned by later sources. Grand Village, the principal settlement and the one that may have been termed Naches, was the residence of the Great Sun, and the other villages were nearby. These included Grigras, a community of refugees among the Natchez; Hickory, sometimes termed Walnut; Flour, and White Apple, which has also apparently been called White Earth. That there were five distinct villages is by no means certain; the designations simply may have been references to neighborhoods around Grand Village. The only site identified with reasonable certainty is Grand Village, which has been partially excavated. It is difficult to reconstruct the configuration of a typical settlement, and the text to follow is a composite of reported characteristics.

In the center of Grand Village was an open plaza measuring 250 by 300 paces with a flat-topped mound at each end. On top of one mound was a temple, and on the other was the home of the Great Sun. The temple mound was about eight feet high, relatively steep on three sides, and sloped gently to form a ramp on the side toward the open plaza. The temple on top probably was about thirty feet long and somewhat narrower. This structure was built of thick logs ten feet in height and plastered on the outside with mud. The roof was ridged, and three large wooden figures of birds adorned the peak. Entered through a rectangular doorway, the temple was divided into two rooms. In the larger outer room was a perpetual fire, and on a nearby platform was a cane coffin containing the bones of the most recently deceased Great Sun. In the inner room were two special boards with unidentified items attached. The wooden box that contained the stone statue of the first Great Sun probably was kept here. Reportedly, he turned himself into stone because he feared that his remains would be tainted if placed in the ground. The bones of other persons probably were stored in this room.

The home of the Great Sun was on an earthen mound some eight feet high, and the house itself was twenty-five feet wide and forty-five feet long. All other houses were at ground level, but the eight homes nearby were larger than the other houses. At the death of a Great Sun his house was burned, and the same mound probably was increased in size and used as a foundation for the home of his successor. The houses in general appear to have been square, rectangular, or, less often, round. Their straight walls were not less than fifteen feet high, and they had rectangular doorways but no windows. Hickory trees were embedded in the ground at the four corners; they were bent over at the tops and tied to form a dome. Along the sidewalls similar poles were embedded in the earth, bent, and tied to the primary dome branches. Poles forming the inner walls were tied in place, and the inner as well as outer walls were spread with a clay and moss plaster and covered with split cane mats. The roof was covered with a mixture of sod and grass and topped with cane mats. Houses were occupied for about twenty years. In the winter a fire was built for warmth, and the smoke filtered out the entrance. It appears that the houses may have been scattered widely. Somewhere near a village were raised platforms on which the bodies of deceased persons were placed. Covering a body was a woven mat smeared with mud; the head of the individual was left uncovered so that food offerings might be placed beside it. After the flesh had decayed, the bones were moved to the temple.

A number of household artifacts were reported among the Natchez, and others were excavated from a historic site. Within the cane-walled dwellings were household goods not usually reported north of Mexico. The most prominent furnishings were beds made from poles and cane with bearskins over the frame, a bison skin cover, and log pillow. When relaxing during the day, the people sat either on the beds or on short-legged wooden stools. In common use were pottery vessels, including some with shallow bowls decorated with incised scrolls or meanders. Some large pots for bear oil held up to forty pints. A wide variety of cane basketry included sieves of various grades for sifting maize, containers for small items of adornment, and hampers for maize. Knives were made from split sections of hard cane, and stone-bladed axes served for heavy woodworking.

APPEARANCE AND CLOTHING The Natchez were striking in appearance, according to the French. Their proud air and noble bearing became the American Indian stereotype among Europeans. Le Page du Pratz (1758) described them as five and a half feet or more in height, lean, sinewy, with rectangular features, coarse black hair, and black eyes. To him they were "naturals," but to other French observers they were "savages." As infants their foreheads were flattened by the straps that held them in cradleboards. A woman wore short bangs in front and bound her long hair in a mulberry thread net with tassels at the ends. Her ears were pierced, and from each large hole hung an elongated shell ornament. Around her neck she might wear strings of small stones or perforated shell disks. Around a man's head was a band of short hair. A few hairs were allowed to grow long at the crown, and white feathers were worn in these scalp locks. Often the young Natchez dandies painted themselves red and wore bracelets made of steamed deer ribs bent in circles and then polished to a high luster. They might carry fans of turkey tail feathers, and they wore necklaces of stone beads like those of the women. The people plucked their axillary hair, and the men plucked their whiskers.

The tattoos of these people were impressive in their diversity and complexity. Youthful males and females were tattooed with lines on the face. Persons of the nobility and warriors were elaborately tattooed on the body, head, and limbs. The patterns were of serpents, suns, and other undescribed forms. Warriors who had slain an enemy were permitted to tattoo themselves as evidence of their kills, and for a brave deed a man had the right to tattoo a war club on his shoulder with a sign beneath symbolizing the people involved in his conquest. The tattooing method was to prick the skin until blood flowed freely and then rub charcoal, red pigment, or blue pigment into the openings. Warriors pierced their earlobes and expanded the holes until they would hold decorative plugs about an inch in diameter.

Males younger than twelve years and girls younger than nine went without clothing. An older girl's primary garment consisted of a short fringed skirt made from the threads of mulberry inner bark. An adult woman wore a deerskin that was fitted about the waist and reached the knees. Some upper-class women wore cloaks of netting made on a loom from mulberry inner bark. The netting was covered with overlapping rows of bird feathers. In cold weather a woman wore a cape, probably of skins, that passed under her right armpit and fastened over the left shoulder. Ordinary men wore skin breechclouts that were belted and colored white; breechclouts of nobles were black. The leggings of men reached from their thighs to their ankles, but they wore skin moccasins only when traveling. In cold weather a man wore a poncholike shirt of deerskin that was sleeved and reached below the knees. In severe weather a bison-skin robe with the hair intact and facing inward was worn. Deerskin garments were sewn with sinew after an awl was used to pierce the skins. Class distinctions in dress and adornment included elaborate tattoos for the nobility, feather-covered mantles for noblewomen, and black breechclouts for the chiefs or nobles. Infants of the nobility wore two or three pearls about their necks. These ornaments were taken from the temple and were returned when a child was about ten years old.

SUBSISTENCE ACTIVITIES AND CONVEYANCES   Cultivated crops were the most important source of food; hunting and fishing clearly were secondary. A plot to be farmed was cleared of cane, which was dried and burned, and the ground was broken up with an L-shaped mattock of hickory. Maize was planted by making holes in the ground with a digging stick and dropping a few grains of corn into each hole. The Natchez probably cultivated their crops with a hoe made by hafting a bison scapula blade at right angles to a wooden handle. The principal cultigen was maize, and from two varieties some forty named dishes were prepared in the Natchez area. Maize was mixed with beans, smoke-dried, ground into meal, prepared as hominy, or parched. Ground meal was made into cakes that were roasted in ashes, baked, or boiled in water. Additional crops included pumpkins and beans, while two species of wild grass were cultivated along riverbanks. The Natchez made bread from walnuts and consumed chestnuts as well as acorns, but these were not important dietary items. There were no set mealtimes except for feasts. When an ordinary meal was served, the males, including those who were very young, ate before the females.

One of the primary reasons the French established plantations in the Natchez region was for the cultivation of tobacco. The Indians had raised tobacco in aboriginal times, and the people were described as avid smokers. They smoked pipes of unknown form and inhaled the smoke. Smoking was not merely a pleasant activity; pipes and smoking played an important part in events surrounding war and peace.

Hunting was most important in the fall, and deer sometimes were pursued by about a hundred men at a time as a sport. Once a deer was located and surrounded, men forced the animal to run back and forth until it was exhausted. It was taken alive to the Great Sun or his representative, who killed it and divided the meat among the leaders of the hunt. In ordinary hunting a man wore a deer disguise when animals were cautious, and imitated the deer's call to attract an animal closer. Hunters used self bows of locust wood strung with plant fiber or twisted sinew. Arrows of cane or wood had feather vanes and heads made from splinters of bone, garfish scales, stone, or a fire-hardened shaft tip. Cane-shafted spears were tipped with flint points and used when hunting large game such as bear, bison, or deer. Bison were taken in winter on grasslands away from the river. They were approached by wearing a disguise or else stalked against the wind. When a kill was made near a settlement, the hunter returned with the choice parts and sent his wife to retrieve the remainder of the animal. Meat was either cooked or smoke-dried for future use. Bear meat was eaten only if lean, but bears were killed when they were fat to obtain the oil. These animals were smoked out of their holes in trees, and if a cub was found, it was sometimes taken alive to the village and tamed. The only domestic animal of the Natchez was the dog. It was used to tree turkeys so that they could be killed with arrows. Fishing was a less important means of obtaining food than either farming or hunting. Among the fishing devices were gill nets made from organic fibers and fish arrows that had pointed bone tips and wooden floats attached by a cord to the shaft. Hooks likewise were used, and the species most often taken were suckers and catfish.

For water transportation, both rafts and canoes were used. Rafts were used to carry relatively light loads and were made from bundles of cane lashed together. For transporting heavy loads, large canoes were made from hollowed-out cypress or poplar logs. The interior of the log was removed by controlled burning, followed by chipping away the charred wood. These dugout canoes were some forty feet long, had three-foot beams, and could carry up to twelve tons.

SOCIAL DIMENSIONS   Natchez social life was structured primarily around the people's relationship to the Great Sun. This leader held absolute control over his subjects and was served by the tribe as a whole but especially by personal retainers and slaves. He was spoken to at a distance of four steps; he was thanked and bowed to no matter what he said, and when leaving his presence a person walked backward. He was saluted whenever seen by ordinary persons, and he could have a person killed by saying to a retainer, "Go and rid me of that dog." The administrative offices delegated by the Great Sun included two war chiefs, two leading priests at the temple, two men who dealt with the external affairs of war and peace, one in charge of public works, and four who arranged public feasts. The decisions of the Great Sun were tempered by the amount of influence brought to bear upon him by near relatives, particularly his brother and mother. He also consulted a council of elders, the leaders of the various villages, and outstanding old warriors.

More printer's ink has been spilled over the Natchez social system than over that of any other people. Studies of their marriage and descent pattern have suggested that it was unique and difficult, if not impossible, to explain in terms of existing sources. A thoughtful reevaluation of the original sources by Carol Mason (1964) appears to have resolved what sometimes has been termed the Natchez riddle or paradox, and conclusions similar to Mason's were reached by Elisabeth Tooker (1963). Since the previous debate now seems to have had a spurious basis, no purpose is served by presenting it. As Mason reconstructed the system, the Great Sun was at the apex of the social hierarchy, and nearly as important were his siblings, his mother, and other near relatives through females (matrilineage) who, like himself, were members of the Sun matrilineage. All such persons were required to marry persons from other lineages (matrilineage exogamy). Children of a Sun man belonged to their mother's lineage because of the matrilineal descent system, but since they were indirect issue of the Sun lineage, they were accorded the title of "noble"; they were "honored persons" if their relationship was more distant. The titles of "noble" and "honored person" were ascribed for these persons, but they also could be achieved by commoners. An ordinary person could become titled by performing heroic deeds in warfare or by sacrificing his infant at the death of a Sun.

Summarily, the Sun matrilineage was the ranking social group and was exogamous. According to the Natchez, the Great Spirit sent the first Great Sun among the people and established the line of Suns as persons to rule and guide the Natchez population. Of the Great Sun's eldest daughter's children, the eldest son became the next Great Sun, and the eldest daughter's eldest son succeeded him. Thus, the leadership passed along a matrilineage from one oldest son to another one in the next generation.

POLITICAL LIFE AND WARFARE From early French attitudes toward the Natchez, it is apparent that they were considered successful warriors under able leaders. Although the Great Sun headed the nation, a Great War Chief appointed by him was in charge of warfare. At one period this position was held by Tattooed Serpent, the brother of the Great Sun and a very powerful individual in his own right. There were lesser war chiefs, probably leaders of different villages, and warriors of three grades: apprentice, ordinary, and true warriors. Most, if not all, men belonged to one of these three categories or were numbered among the old warriors. When hostilities were contemplated, a pole was raised at the entrance of the house where a decisive meeting was to be held. Attached to the pole was the war calumet, a pipe adorned with red feathers, tufted and tasseled in black, with the black skin from the neck of a buzzard surrounding the pipe itself. The meeting was attended by old warriors, the Great War Chief, lesser war chiefs, and the Great Sun. The grievance against the potential enemy was presented vividly by the Great War Chief. The rationale for aggressive action was real or fabricated; it might be that another people had hunted on Natchez lands, for example. The offense was discussed, but the opinions of the old warriors were decisive. A delegation of warriors led by an old warrior went to the offenders carrying a peace calumet but without gifts so that they could not be considered appeasers. Arriving under these circumstances, they generally were received well and were sent home with gifts as an admission of the wrong done to them. Open conflict seldom erupted if this approach to an offense was taken.

When an attack was anticipated, the Natchez usually decided in council to defend themselves rather than appease the aggressors. They warned outlying families to join the main group and posted guards at the approaches to their settlements. Another defensive move was to build palisaded fortifications. Forts were rather complex structures built around a tall tree that served as a watchtower. The trunks of trees were stripped of branches and were set in the ground to reach a height of about ten feet. The palisades were arranged in a roughly circular form with an overlap at the ends. Inside were structures to protect the women and children from arrows. The entrance was protected by towers, and in the passage to the outside were placed brambles and thorns. When an attack was imminent, emissaries carrying a peace calumet were sent to enlist the aid of friendly peoples. In the meantime the Great War Chief cited in council the reasons for defending themselves. He sought the support of warriors by reminding the older ones of their honor and pointing out the vengeance they could obtain, and holding out for youths the hope of glory.

If the council decided to fight another people, the warriors hunted and returned with their kills to the home of the Great War Chief. For the three-day celebration that followed, the warriors painted their bodies different colors and wore only breechclouts held in place by belts decorated with rattles. A war club was stuck in a man's belt, and he carried a round bison-skin shield in one hand and his bow in the other. At a clearing, a pole that represented the enemy was erected; it was carved to look like a man, painted red, and had a war calumet attached to it. At the base of the pole was placed a large dog roasted for the occasion, and nearby were placed different foods. One dish contained coarse cornmeal cooked in fat; the coarseness of the meal was a reminder that warriors did not require dainty foods. They also were served deer meat to make them swift as a deer. Before the meal the oldest warrior, who was no longer active, recounted his deeds of bravery and instructed the party how to begin a battle and to fight. The old man then lit the war calumet, and the Great War Chief smoked it first. The others smoked in rank order, and the old warrior drew on the pipe last before returning it to the pole. The Great War Chief ate a piece of dog meat, and the others followed in succession. By partaking of the dog a warrior demonstrated his willingness to participate in the pending hostilities. Later the war drink, a powerful emetic, was brought forth, and each person who drank it vomited violently. The retching could be heard at a great distance, according to one observer. Each man ran up to the war pole, uttered a death cry as he struck it, and told of his past deeds of valor. After seasoned warriors had recounted their achievements, each apprentice warrior told what he hoped to accomplish, and then a war dance was performed. During the three days of ceremony, dances were held before the temple, along with recitations of personal accomplishments and the singing of death songs. The women prepared food for the men to take on their expedition, and old men refurbished war clubs and incised graphic symbols on a bark tablet. A symbol of the sun, representing the Natchez, was set above the figure of a naked man with a war club. An arrow was shown as though about to strike a fleeing woman, near whom was the sign of the enemy nation. Another set of symbols recorded the forthcoming month and the day when an attack would take place in force, if this was included in the planning.

A raiding party of twenty to three hundred warriors traveled only at night as they neared an enemy, and sent scouts to reconnoiter. The party's long pole with fetishes attached was leaned toward the enemy each time the warriors camped. If any sign was interpreted as an ill omen for the venture, the men returned to their villages in spite of their elaborate preparations. Likewise, when raiding parties encountered each other unexpectedly they withdrew. An attack was made at daybreak, and the persons to be killed were dispatched as quickly as possible. Women and children were taken alive, as was at least one man if at all possible. The raiders withdrew as quietly as they had arrived, taking their prisoners and leaving behind the inscribed bark, two red-painted arrows crossed and stuck in the ground, and the scalped dead. If the raid had been anticipated and the enemy had prepared themselves in a palisaded fortification, the Natchez searched for hunting parties to kill. If one of the raiders was killed, his comrades attempted to scalp him, to prevent the enemy from obtaining a Natchez scalp; on their return the Great War Chief would compensate the dead man's family for its loss. The party returned home in honor if they had captured a living enemy man.

Back in their own village they planted two poles in the ground if a male

Figure 13-2. | The plan of a fort and illustration of methods of torture. (From Le Page du Pratz 1758, vol. 2.)

captive had been taken; on them a crosspiece was lashed near the ground and another somewhat higher than a man's head. The captive was stunned with a blow at the base of the skull and was scalped by his captor. The victim's naked body was tied in spread-eagle fashion on the pole frame. (See Figure 13-2.) The young persons in the assembled throng gathered canes and lighted them; the first flaming cane was applied to the captive by his captor. The torturer was free to apply the cane anywhere he chose, and it was most likely to be on the arm with which the victim had best defended himself. The victim was then burned by the others as he sang his song of death. Some sacrificial victims were reported to have sung for seventy-two hours without pause before dying. However, not all captive males were dealt with in this manner; if a young woman whose husband had been killed claimed the captive, he was given to her as a husband. Captive women and children had their hair cut short and became the servants of their captors.

Warriors who had distinguished themselves were given new names by the Great War Chief. These denoted particular levels of achievement in warfare. For example, the name Great Man Slayer could be claimed by a warrior after he had taken twenty scalps or ten prisoners. A warrior also might tattoo his body to commemorate an achievement or might be elevated in social class.

RELIGIOUS SYSTEM The Natchez religious system was a formalized network of beliefs, ceremonies, and dogma maintained by specialists who devoted all their time to supernatural matters. These persons, who were priests in a generic sense, served as guardians of the major temple. One of these men explained Natchez religion to Le Page du Pratz. The latter recorded that they believed in an all-powerful Great Spirit who created all things good and was surrounded by lesser spirits that did his bidding. A particularly malignant spirit led the spirits of evil, but because it was tied up forever by the Great Spirit, it could do no great harm. The Great Spirit reportedly molded the first man from clay, and the figure grew to the proportions of a normal man. It was believed that woman probably was created in the same manner, but since man was created first, he was stronger and more courageous.

The reigning Great Sun, the highest authority on earth, combined the qualities of a god and a king. His power and authority over things religious were paramount, and his decisions were very important in secular matters. In this theocratic state, all religious, social, and political control was, in theory, in the hands of this individual. The Great Sun was surrounded by warriors and retainers wherever he went. When he traveled about, he was carried on a litter by eight warriors (see Figure 13-3); in his dwelling he sat on a small wooden throne. The Great Sun was distinguished in his dress from others; for example, his normal headdress was a net covered with black feathers and bordered in red decorated with white seeds; hanging from the top of the headdress were long white feathers in front and shorter ones behind. Lesser suns appear to have worn similar headpieces.

The core of religious life was a sacred temple fire tended by eight elders; two of them cared for the fire continually and were killed if they permitted the fire to go out. When ordinary persons walked in front of a temple, they put down any load that they might be carrying and extended their arms toward the temple as they wailed loudly. The same type of behavior was followed when they passed before the Great Sun. The Great Sun visited the temple daily to make certain that the fire still burned, and each morning at sunrise he faced the east, bowed to the ground, and wailed three times. With a special calumet he blew smoke first toward the rising sun and then in each of the other cardinal directions. Thus, the Great Sun venerated the sun and was in turn venerated by all other persons in the tribe. What we see is a direct line of continuity from the past functionally linked to the Great Spirit, the Great Suns, and an eternal fire.

Ceremonies   The heads of families took their first harvest of any food to the temple; the guardians received it and conveyed it to the Great Sun, who could distribute it as he chose. Seeds to be sown were blessed at the temple before they were planted. The thirteen months of the calendar were named for the most important food of the prior month, and the beginning of each month was celebrated by a feast where either the Great Sun or a lesser sun presided. The feast of the first month, corresponding roughly to March, was called Deer, and marked the beginning of a new year. Each year during the month of Deer a celebration was held to commemorate the liberation of a former Great Sun who had been captured by enemies. After ceremonies and ritual acts, gifts were presented to the Great Sun as he sat on his throne.

The seventh or Great Corn month was ushered in by the most important yearly ceremony, the one that celebrated the first harvest of maize. The corn

Figure 13-3. | The Great Sun being carried on a litter. (From Le Page du Pratz 1758, vol. 2.)

used in the ceremony was from virgin ground and had been sown and tended by warriors. When the crop was harvested and stored in a granary of cane, the Great Sun was notified. All the villagers assembled at the cache to receive the Great Sun, who arrived on his litter with a canopy of flowers. After a fire was kindled by rubbing sticks together, maize was presented to the female Suns and then to all other women. The maize was cooked and eaten during a feast that was followed by speeches and dancing throughout the night to the accompaniment of a drum and gourd rattles. When dancing, the women moved in one direction and the men in the opposite direction (see Figure 13-4), and as a person tired he or she was replaced by someone from the audience. The next day a ball game was held. The warriors were divided into two teams, one led by the Great Sun and the other by the Great War Chief. In the hair of the Great Sun's men were white feathers, and the other team wore red feathers. The object of the game was to force a ball to one end of the plaza. The winning team was presented with gifts by the captain of the losing team, and the winners were permitted to wear their feather headdresses until the game was played again. After the ball game, a war dance was performed by the warriors. The festivities were not over until all of the harvested maize had been consumed. The celebrations just described were at the capital settlement, but similar festivities were led by local Suns at other settlements.

Religion embraced more than the temple cult, for there were thought to be a host of spirits that probably were lesser agents of the Great Spirit. Power existed in the honey locust tree, and under one such tree near the temple the wood was kept for the sacred fire. Any tree struck by lightning was burned completely by the Indians, and snakes were regarded with terror. The Great Sun and people of all classes fasted to bring rain. When commoners fasted on certain days, they smeared black paint on their faces and did not eat until the sun had set.

Shamans   The position of Natchez shamans is obscure, but they appear to have functioned outside the Sun-centered theocracy. An individual aspiring to become a shaman went into isolation for nine days and consumed nothing but water until a spirit appeared. During this time he or she reportedly learned certain skills such as how to change the weather or cure illness. Spirit aids were kept in a small basket and included such tangible objects as owl heads, animal teeth, small stones, and hair from a deer. Shamans had very real obligations to those they served. Were a patient to die, the shaman might be killed, but success brought material gain. Among the techniques for curing and for changing weather were fasting, smoking, singing, and dancing. One cure included making an incision at the locus of an illness and sucking blood from the wound. When the shaman spit the blood into a container, not only blood was seen but also a for-

Figure 13-4. | A dance scene. (From Le Page du Pratz 1947.)

eign object such as a piece of wood, straw, or leather; the illness was attributed to this item.

LIFE CYCLE   Soon after babies were born, they were tied to a cradleboard, and strips of deerskin were bound over their foreheads to flatten them. The cradleboard was placed in a bed beside the baby's mother. Infants were smeared with bear oil to keep flies from biting them and to make them supple. When nearly a year old, infants were encouraged to walk; they were nursed until they weaned themselves or until the mother again became pregnant. As children grew they came under the influence of an elder male in their extended family; this man counseled all the nuclear families within his group. A child termed this man father, but he might be a great-grandfather or even a great-great-grandfather. Children were discouraged from fighting with the threat that they would be sent away from the Natchez. Boys were encouraged to exercise and gradually acquire adult skills from about the age of twelve, and the sexual division of labor was instilled at this time. Hunting, fishing, fighting, some farming, and the manufacturing of most artifacts were male activities. Carrying home game or fish, most of the farming, preparing food, and manufacturing clothing, baskets, or pottery were female responsibilities, along with the raising of children.

Following puberty, youths were free to have sexual intercourse, and girls apparently did not bestow sexual favors without material gain. A potential husband was proud of the amount of property his bride-to-be might accumulate in this manner. Males did not marry until they were about twenty-five, but females appear to have been somewhat younger. Once the couple decided to marry, the man went before the heads of their respective families to be questioned. If no close blood ties existed and if the pair loved each other, the elders sanctioned the marriage. On the wedding day the woman was led by the elder of her family, and followed by the remainder of her family, to the home of the man. Here they were greeted and invited into the house where, after a pause, the elders of both families asked the couple whether they loved each other and were willing to be husband and wife. The ideals of domestic harmony were set forth, the couple exchanged vows, and a gift was made to the bride's father. The bride's mother handed her a laurel branch to hold in one hand and an ear of corn to hold in the other hand. She gave the corn to her husband, and he said, "I am your husband," to which she answered, "I am your wife." Finally the husband told his wife, "There is our bed, keep it tight," which was an injunction against committing adultery. After a special meal the couple and their guests danced from early evening through the night. This description of a marriage by Le Page du Pratz does not specify whether or not these customs were observed by everyone. The need for such clarification is evident since other descriptions of Natchez marriages differ from this form.

Plural marriages were known, with sororal polygyny being the most common form, although nonsororal polygyny was also practiced. Plural marriages were more common among the nobility than among commoners. A noble with many wives retained only one or two in his house; the others lived at their natal homes where they were visited by him. In polygynous households, the wife who bore the first offspring supervised the other wives. Divorce was extremely rare for most persons, but an upper-class woman married to a common man was free to take other husbands. Furthermore, such a woman could have her husband put to death if he committed adultery. This is an unusual form of the double standard of morality. Berdaches (transvestites) were reported, but their position in the society is not clear.

The writings of Le Page du Pratz and a few others convey the essence of the ideals that guided adult life. Tribal unity did not prevail during the brief historical era, and there is good evidence of a power struggle among leading upper-class persons that influenced intervillage affairs. Some communities were friendly to the French while others were hostile, suggesting that the Great Sun could not, or did not, effectively control all the members of his lineage. Yet, it appears that villagewide harmony existed and the upper class did not abuse its power. The people in general were honorable in their dealings with each other and with the French. Recall that in the myth about the acceptance of the first Great Sun, certain specific rules of behavior were stated; they were maintained insofar as possible by the priests and the upper class in general.

One of the most vivid descriptions by Le Page du Pratz was of the funeral for the Great War Chief, Tattooed Serpent, who was the brother of the Great Sun and nearly as powerful. When he died everyone was greatly distressed because each brother had vowed to kill himself at the death of the other. The temple guardians urged Le Page du Pratz, who was influential among the Natchez and a friend of the Great Sun, to avert the leader's potential suicide. Le Page du Pratz and other whites went to the home of the Great Sun and talked with him. The Great Sun was grieved deeply over the death but was successfully restrained from committing suicide.

At the house of Tattooed Serpent his corpse lay on the bed he had occupied while alive. His face was painted red, and he was clothed in his finest garments, including a feather headdress. Beside the bed were his weapons and the peace calumets he had received during his life. From a pole stuck into the ground hung forty-six linked sections of red-painted cane representing the number of enemies he had killed. Gathered around the body were his "chancellor," physician, chief domestic, pipe bearer, two wives, some old women, and a volunteer from among the noblewomen, all of whom were to be killed as a part of the funeral ceremony. The next day included a Dance of Death and two rehearsals for the deaths of persons to be killed. At about this time, the commoner parents of a child strangled their offspring out of respect for Tattooed Serpent; by doing so they were raised to noble standing and would not be killed when the Great Sun died. Some warriors also had apprehended a common man who had been married to a Sun woman but had fled at her death to avoid being killed. His capture once again slated him for death, but three old women related to him offered themselves to be killed in his place. The man in turn was elevated to the upper class by the women's sacrifice.

On the day of the funeral, the "master of ceremonies" was painted red

Figure 13-5. | The burial of Tattooed Serpent, brother of the Great Sun. (From Le Page du Pratz 1947.)

above the waist and wore a garment about his waist with a red and white feather fringe. On his head was a crown of red feathers, and he carried a red staff with black feathers hanging from the upper part and a crosspiece near the top. When this impressively arrayed individual approached the house of the deceased, he was greeted with "hoo" and by wailing indicating death. A procession formed behind the master of ceremonies; he was followed by the oldest warrior carrying the staff from which hung the red cane rings and a war pipe that reflected the honor of the dead man. These men were in turn followed by six temple guardians who carried the body on a litter (see Figure 13-5); then came those who were to be killed, each accompanied by eight relatives who served as executioners. Each of these relatives was subsequently freed from the probability of being killed at the death of the Great Sun and seemingly was raised to the class of noble. The procession circled the house of the deceased three times, and then the litter bearers walked in intersecting circles to the temple. The dead child was thrown repeatedly in the path of the bearers and retrieved by its parents. After the body of Tattooed Serpent was placed in the temple, the sacrificial victims, their hair covered with red paint, were drugged with tobacco and strangled. Within the temple the two wives of Tattooed Serpent and two men were buried in the grave with him. The other victims were buried elsewhere, and the funeral ended by burning the home of Tattooed Serpent.

With a great man's death, pomp, pageantry, and human sacrifice unrolled; the death of a Sun was a tragic highlight to life. The number of persons killed at the funeral of Tattooed Serpent unquestionably was fewer than would have been considered fitting before the French arrived. For other people to die was of lesser moment, and yet any death was surrounded with further deaths. When an outstanding female Sun died, her husband, a commoner, was strangled by their eldest son. Then the eldest surviving daughter ordered twelve small children killed and placed around the bodies of the deceased couple. In the plaza fourteen platforms were erected, and on each was a man who was to die during the funeral. These men danced before the house of the deceased every fifteen minutes and then returned to their platforms. It was said that after four days the March of the Bodies ritual took place. The dead children previously had been placed outside the dead woman's home, and with them were the live victims. The woman was carried out on a litter, and the small bodies were dropped repeatedly before the procession so that by the time the litter reached the temple the corpses of the children were in pieces. After the woman's body was inside the temple, the fourteen victims were strangled, but not before they had received water and wads of tobacco that drugged them into unconsciousness. The living mourned for an important deceased person by weeping for four days. In general, mourners cut their hair but did not paint their faces, and they avoided public gatherings. The temporary grave was on a raised platform. A shelter of branches formed a vault over the body, and there was an opening at the end near the head where food was placed. The mourners grieved at the grave each day at dawn and at sunset for a month. After the flesh had decayed, the bones were placed in a basket in a temple.

The custom of executing persons at the death of the Suns and other upper-class individuals may seem barbaric and senseless, but it had very real advantages to the individuals involved. In their belief system, one's spirit under such circumstances would accompany the deceased upper-class person to the world of the dead and serve him or her there in perennial happiness. The same future awaited all others who observed the rules of the society during their lifetimes. It was thought that a person who had broken the rules of the people would go to a place covered with water; naked, she or he would be bitten by mosquitoes and have only undesirable foods to eat.

| Tattooed Serpent's Oration

Only a few short years following the dramatic burial ceremonies for Tattooed Serpent, the Natchez nearly were extinct. It seems fitting to record a speech that Tattooed Serpent made to Le Page du Pratz (1774, 40–41) after a war with the French and shortly before the Natchez were destroyed.

I did not approve, as you know, the war our people made upon the French to avenge the death of their relation, seeing I made them carry the *pipe of peace* to the French. This you well know, as you first smoked in the pipe yourself. Have the French two hearts, a good one to-day, and to-morrow a bad one? As for my brother and me, we have but one heart and one word. Tell me then, if thou art, as thou sayest, my true friend, what thou thinkest of all this, and shut thy mouth to everything else. We know not what to think of the French, who, after having begun the war, granted a peace, and offered it of themselves; and then at the time we were quiet, believing ourselves to be at peace, people come to kill us, without saying a word.

Why . . . did the French come into our country? We did not go to seek them: they asked for land of us, because their country was too little for all the men that were in it. We told them they might take land where they pleased, there was enough for them and for us; that it was good the same sun should enlighten us both, and that we would walk as friends in the same path; and that we would give them of our provisions, assist them to build, and to labour in their fields. We have done so; is not this true? What occasion then had we for Frenchmen? Before they came, did we not live better than we do, seeing we deprive ourselves of a part of our corn, our game, and fish, to give a part to them? In what respect, then, had we occasion for them? Was it for their guns? The bows and arrows which we used, were sufficient to make us live well. Was it for their white, blue, and red blankets? We can do well enough with buffalo skins which are warmer; our women wrought feather-blankets for the winter, and mulberry-mantles for the summer; which indeed were not so beautiful; but our women were more laborious and less vain than they are now. In fine, before the arrival of the French, we lived like men who can be satisfied with what they have; whereas at this day we are like slaves, who are not suffered to do as they please.

The Demise of the Natchez

John R. Swanton (1946), whose study of Natchez sources is monumental, has stressed that these people were not destroyed by the two French campaigns against them; in fact, the French efforts were quite clumsy. What did destroy the Natchez were frequent skirmishing with other Indians and the illness and death caused by physical exposure in the swamps where they took refuge. Those who escaped or were not at the fort at Sicily Island when the French made their 1731 attack, some 180 warriors, eventually joined the Chickasaw, against whom the French turned for having received these refugees. Some of the Natchez did not remain with or join the Chickasaw after their defeat, but lived with the Creek. This group probably included the largest number of survivors. They came to occupy a town near the Coosa River in Alabama, and in 1764 they had about 150 warriors. In 1832 the Natchez and the Creek were displaced to Indian Territory as a result of the federal removal policy. To complicate the matter further, some of the Natchez who joined the Catawba after their wars with the French later left them and lived with the Cherokee. In 1907 Swanton located some Natchez near Braggs, Oklahoma, in the southwestern part of the Cherokee nation; five of the individuals he found still knew some of the language. In 1934 when Mary R. Haas worked among the Natchez living near Braggs, she found that only two Natchez speakers had survived.

| Comparisons with Other Indians

The scope of available information about the Natchez makes most comparisons difficult except in terms of social and political life. The Natchez political structure was far more developed than that reported for the other peoples in this book. One might seek to identify its most salient characteristics and compare these with the historic "priest state" of the Cherokee and with the League of the Iroquois. Special attention should be given to ascribed as opposed to achieved status differences among leaders, contrasts in clothing and adornments between ordinary people and their leaders, the recruitment of leaders, their extraordinary rights and duties, and their number of retainers. Broader comparisons with the political networks of peoples presented throughout the book are ir.·ited. Note how unorganized, largely individualistic responses to external stress among the Chipewyan give way to more unified but still largely unstructured responses by the Kuskokwim Eskimos compared with the far more developed organization of the Mesquakie, and so on.

Natchez social structure placed inordinate stress on birth order and sex within a leading lineage. How does this compare with the Iroquois and Hopi? What key traits are shared by all, and how can we explain the similarities and differences?

| Additional Readings

The most worthwhile source is by Le Page du Pratz (1774); this was the primary source consulted for this chapter. For additional details and a comparative view of the Natchez and other Indians in the Southeast, the best source is the 1946 publication by John R. Swanton.

| Bibliography

Albrecht, Andrew C. 1944. The location of the historic Natchez villages. *Journal of Mississippi History* 6:67–88.

———. 1946. Indian-French relations at Natchez. *American Anthropologist* 48:321–54.

———. 1948. Ethical precepts among the Natchez Indians. *Louisiana Historical Quarterly* 31:569–97.

Caldwell, Joseph R. 1958. *Trend and tradition in the prehistory of the eastern United States.* American Anthropological Association Memoir no. 88.

Ford, James A., and Clarence H. Webb. 1956. *Poverty Point, a Late Archaic site in Louisiana.* Anthropological Papers of the American Museum of Natural History, vol. 46, pt. 1. New York.

Griffin, James B., ed. 1952. *Archaeology of eastern United States.* Chicago.

Haag, William G. 1961. The Archaic of the lower Mississippi Valley. *American Antiquity* 26:317–23.

Haas, Mary R. 1939. Natchez and Chitimacha clans and kinship terminology. *American Anthropologist* 41:597–610.

Le Page du Pratz, Antoine S. 1774. *The history of Louisiana.* Paris. (Published in London, 1758; reprinted at New Orleans, 1947.) Between the years 1718 and 1734 the author lived most of the time near the Natchez, where he owned a plantation. The observations by Le Page du Pratz concerning these Indians are the most systematic of all the firsthand accounts. The book is very enjoyable to read and is at the same time highly informative.

Mason, Carol. 1964. Natchez class structure. *Ethnohistory* 11:120–33.

Neitzel, Robert S. 1965. *Archaeology of the Fatherland site.* Anthropological Papers of the American Museum of Natural History, vol. 51, pt. 2. New York. This volume is a detailed report about excavations on the Fatherland Plantation, where Grand Village is located.

Quimby, George I., Jr. 1942. The Natchezan culture type. *American Antiquity* 7:255–75.

Swanton, John R. 1911. *Indian tribes of lower Mississippi Valley and adjacent coast of the Gulf of Mexico.* Bureau of American Ethnology Bulletin no. 43. Washington, DC.

———. 1928. Social organization and social usages of the Indians of the Creek Confederacy. *Bureau of American Ethnology, 42nd Annual Report.*

———. 1946. *The Indians of the southeastern United States.* Bureau of American Ethnology Bulletin no. 137. Washington, DC. Virtually all that is known about Natchez ethnography is in this volume. It is a monumental regional culture history and a key secondary source on the Natchez.

———. 1953. *The Indian tribes of North America.* Bureau of American Ethnology Bulletin no. 145. Washington, DC.

Tooker, Elisabeth. 1963. Natchez social organization: Fact or anthropological fancy? *Ethnohistory* 10:358–72.

Name Index

Subject Index

461

SIBERIAN ESKIMO

BERING SEA ESKIMO

KUSKOWAGAMIUT

ALEUT

PACIFIC ESKIMO

KOYUKON

NORTH ALASKAN ESKIMO

INGALIK TANANA

TANAINA

EYAK

AHTENA

NABESNA

HAN

MACKENZIE ESKIMO COP

KUTCHIN

HARE

ESKI

TLINGIT

TUTCHONE

MOUNTAIN

SATUDENE

DOGRIB

TAHLTAN

KASKA

SLAVE

TSETSAUT

HAIDA

TSIMSHIAN

SEKANI

BEAVER

SARSI

C

CARRIER

BELLABELLA
BELLACOOLA

KWAKIUTL

1

SHUSWAP

LAKE

KUTENAI

BLACKFOOT

NOOTKA

2
3

6 4
5
7

8

9
10

11   12   13

14

17

18

GROS
VENTRE

15   16

20   21   22   23

19

FLATHEAD

NEZ
PERCE

C

1 CHILCOTIN
2 COMOX
3 LILLOOET
4 NICOLA
5 COWICHAN
6 THOMPSON
7 OKANAGON
8 KLALLAM
9 QUILEUTE
10 QUINAULT
11 TWANA
12 COLUMBIA
13 SANPOIL
14 KALISPEL
15 KLIKITAT
16 YAKIMA
17 SPOKAN
18 COEUR D'ALENE
19 WALLAWALLA
20 WISHRAM
21 TENINO
22 UMATILLA
23 CAYUSE

(after Murdock, 1960) Map by J. Donovan